Seventh Edition

Ethics and the
Conduct of Business

Seventh Edition

Ethics and the Conduct of Business

John R. Boatright
Loyola University Chicago

PEARSON

Boston   Columbus   Indianapolis   New York   San Francisco   Upper Saddle River
Amsterdam   Cape Town   Dubai   London   Madrid   Milan   Munich   Paris   Montreal   Toronto
Delhi   Mexico City   Sao Paulo   Sydney   Hong Kong   Seoul   Singapore   Taipei   Tokyo

Editorial Director: Craig Campanella
Editor in Chief: Dickson Musslewhite
Executive Editor: Ashley Dodge
Editorial Project Manager: Kate Fernandes
Director of Marketing: Brandy Dawson
Senior Marketing Manager: Laura Lee Manley
Marketing Assistant: Lisa Kirlick
Production Manager: Fran Russello
Art Director: Jayne Conte
Cover Designer: Bruce Kenselaar
Manager, Rights and Permissions: Charles Morris
Full-Service Project Management: Mogana Sundaramurthy/Integra Software Services, Ltd.
Printer/Binder: Edwards Brothers Malloy
Cover Printer: Lehigh-Phoenix Color/Hagerstown

Credits and acknowledgments borrowed from other sources and reproduced, with permission, in this textbook appear on appropriate page within text (or on page xi).

Many of the designations by manufacturers and seller to distinguish their products are claimed as trademarks. Where those designations appear in this book, and the publisher was aware of a trademark claim, the designations have been printed in initial caps or all caps.

Library of Congress Cataloging-in-Publication Data
Boatright, John Raymond
  Ethics and the conduct of business / John R. Boatright. —7th ed.
    p. cm.
  Includes index.
  ISBN-13: 978-0-205-05313-1 (alk. paper)
  ISBN-10: 0-205-05313-0 (alk. paper)
  1. Business ethics. 2. Social responsibility of business. I. Title.
  HF5387.B6 2012
  174'.4—dc23
                                        2011027194

10 9 8 7 6 5 4 3

Student Edition
  ISBN-10:   0-205-05313-0
  ISBN-13: 978-0-205-05313-1

A la Carte Edition
  ISBN 10:   0-205-21447-9
  ISBN 13: 978-0-205-21447-1

CONTENTS

PREFACE

The field of business ethics has grown in recent decades into an interdisciplinary area of study that has found a secure niche in both liberal arts and business education. Credit for this development belongs to many individuals—both philosophers and business scholars—who have succeeded in relating ethical theory to the various problems of ethics that arise in business. They have shown not only that business is a fruitful subject for philosophical exploration but also that practicing managers in the world of business can benefit from the results.

Ethics and the Conduct of Business, seventh edition, is a comprehensive and up-to-date discussion of the most prominent issues in the field of business ethics and the major positions and arguments on these issues. It is intended to be used as a text in business ethics courses on either the undergraduate or M.B.A. level. The substantial number of cases included provides ample opportunity for a case-study approach or a combined lecture–discussion format. There has been no attempt to develop a distinctive ethical system or to argue for specific conclusions. The field of business ethics is marked by reasonable disagreement that should be reflected in any good textbook.

The focus of *Ethics and the Conduct of Business* is primarily on ethical issues that corporate decision makers face in developing policies about employees, customers, and the general public. The positions on these issues and the arguments for them are taken from a wide variety of sources, including economics and the law. The study of ethical issues in business is not confined to a single academic discipline or to the academic world. The issues selected for discussion are widely debated by legislators, judges, government regulators, business leaders, journalists, and, indeed, virtually everyone with an interest in business.

An underlying assumption of this book is that ethical theory is essential for a full understanding of the positions and arguments offered on the main issues in business ethics. Fortunately, the amount of theory needed is relatively small, and much of the discussion of these issues can be understood apart from the theoretical foundation provided here. The book also contains a substantial amount of legal material, not only because the law addresses many ethical issues but also because management decision making must take account of the relevant law. Many examples are used throughout the book in order to explain points and show the relevance of the discussion to real-life business practice.

Preparation of the seventh edition of *Ethics and the Conduct of Business* has provided an opportunity to incorporate new developments and increase its value in the classroom. The major changes from the previous edition are as follows:

- A revision of Chapters 1 and 2 which identifies the ethics of market transactions and the ethics of roles, relationships, and firms and provides the ethical principles that guide each kind of ethics.
- New material in Chapter 2 on psychological approaches to ethical reasoning in addition to the previous discussion of a philosophical approach, and a new useful framework for ethical reasoning built around seven principles of commonsense morality.
- A revised Chapter 3 that now contains all the material on ethical theory in a compact, easily understood form.
- A revised Chapter 14 on international business, which has been substantially rewritten and expanded and includes a new section on doing business in ethically challenging environments of pervasive human rights abuses.
- Seven new cases, which bring the total number of cases to 50 for a net addition of three cases.
- New cases on Merck's development of Vioxx, Hewlett-Packard's insertion of a smart chip in printers, Bankers Trust's handling of derivative sales to Procter & Gamble, lead paint on

Mattel toys made in China, the bribery scandal at Siemens, the use of the federal False Claims Act by a whistle-blower, and the fiduciary duty of corporate directors.

I am grateful for the support of Loyola University Chicago, especially the School of Business Administration and deans Abol Jalilvand and Kathleen A. Getz. I have benefited from the resources of the Raymond C. Baumhart, S.J., Chair in Business Ethics, which was created to honor a former president of Loyola University Chicago, who was also a pioneer in the field of business ethics. To Ray Baumhart I owe a special debt of gratitude. Finally, my deepest expression of appreciation goes to my wife Claudia, whose affection, patience, and support have been essential for the preparation of the seventh edition, as they were for the ones previous.

John R. Boatright

ACKNOWLEDGMENTS

I would like to express my gratitude for permission to use material from the following sources:

John R. Boatright, *Ethics in Finance*, 2nd ed. (Malden, MA: Blackwell Publishers, 2008). Copyright © 1999, 2008 by John R. Boatright.

John R. Boatright, "The Shareholder Model of Corporate Governance," in Robert W. Kolb, ed., *Encyclopedia of Business Ethics and Society* (Thousand Oaks, CA: Sage Publications, 2008). Reprinted by permission of Sage Publications.

SUPPORT FOR INSTRUCTORS AND STUDENTS

MyThinkingLab is an online resource that offers a wealth of tools to help student learning and comprehension, including practice quizzes, videos, primary source readings, and more. MyThinkingLab also includes a rich array of interactive tools enhanced with audio and video to engage students in learning. Please see your Pearson representative for more information or visit www.MyThinkingLab.com.

Instructor's Manual with Tests (0-205-05340-8): For each chapter in the text, this valuable resource provides a detailed outline, list of objectives, and discussion questions. In addition, test questions in multiple-choice, true/false, fill-in-the-blank, and short answer formats are available for each chapter; the answers are page referenced to the text. For easy access, this manual is available at www.pearsonhighered.com/irc.

PowerPoint Presentation Slides for Ethics and the Conduct of Business (0-205-05339-4): These PowerPoint slides help instructors convey ethical principles in a clear and engaging way. For easy access, they are available at www.pearsonhighered.com/irc.

MyTest Test Generator (0-205-05342-4): This computerized software allows instructors to create their own personalized exams, edit any or all of the existing test questions, and add new questions. Other special features of the program include random generation of test questions, creation of alternate versions of the same test, scrambling question sequence, and test preview before printing. For easy access, this software is available at www.pearsonhighered.com/irc.

1

Ethics in the World of Business

((•─Listen to the **Chapter Audio** on **mythinkinglab.com**

CASE 1.1 ✳─Explore the Concept on **mythinkinglab.com**

Merck and the Marketing of Vioxx

On September 30, 2004, Merck & Co. announced the withdrawal of Vioxx, its highly profitable pain reliever for arthritis sufferers, from the market.[1] This announcement came only seven days after company researchers found in a clinical trial that subjects who used Vioxx more than 18 months had a substantially higher incidence of heart attacks. Merck chairman and CEO Raymond V. Gilmartin described the action as "the responsible thing to do." He explained, "It's built into the principles of the company to think in this fashion. That's why the management team came to such an easy conclusion."[2] In the lawsuits that followed, however, damaging documents emerged casting doubt on Merck's claim that it had acted responsibly by taking appropriate precautions in the development and marketing of the drug.

For decades, Merck's stellar reputation rested on the company's emphasis on science-driven research and development. Merck employed some of the world's most talented and best-paid researchers and led other pharmaceutical firms in the publication of scientific articles and the discovery of new medicines for the treatment of serious conditions that lacked a satisfactory treatment. For seven consecutive years in the 1980s, Merck was ranked by *Fortune* magazine as America's most respected company. Merck received widespread accolades in particular for the decision, made in 1978, to proceed with research on a drug for preventing river blindness (onchocerciasis), which is a debilitating parasite infection that afflicts many in Africa, even though the drug was unlikely to pay for itself. Eventually, Merck decided to give away the drug, called Mectizan, for as long as necessary at a cost of tens of millions of dollars per year. This kind of principled decision making was inspired by the words of George W. Merck, the son of the company's founder: "We try never to forget that medicine is for the people. It is not for the profits. The profits follow, and if we have remembered that, they have never failed to appear. The better we have remembered it, the larger they have been."

Vioxx is an example of Merck's innovative research. Developed as a treatment for the pain of arthritis, the drug acts as an anti-inflammant by suppressing an enzyme responsible for arthritis pain. Other drugs in the class of nonsteroidal anti-inflammatory drugs (NSAIDs) inhibit the production of two enzymes COX-1 and COX-2. However, COX-1 is important for protecting the stomach lining, and so ulcers and stomach bleeding are potential side effects of these drugs. The distinctive benefit of Vioxx over other NSAID pain relievers, such as ibuprofen (Advil) and naproxen (Aleve), is that it inhibits the production of only the COX-2 enzyme, and not COX-1. After approval by the Food and Drug Administration (FDA) in May 1999, Vioxx quickly became a popular best seller. More than 20 million people took Vioxx between 1999 and 2004, and at the time of the withdrawal, with 2 million users, Merck was earning $2.5 billion annually or 11 percent of the company's total revenues from the sale of the drug.

The success of Vioxx came at a critical time for Merck. Not only were the patents on several profitable drugs due to expire, opening the way for generic competition, but also the competitive environment of the entire pharmaceutical industry was undergoing rapid change. Competition from generic drugs increased dramatically due to federal legislation and also due to the rise of large, powerful managed care organizations, which sought to cut the cost of drug treatments through the use of formularies that restricted the drugs doctors could prescribe. The development of new drugs was increasingly shifting to small entrepreneurial research companies focused on specific technologies, which reduced the competitive advantage of the traditional large pharmaceutical firms. Merck's competitors responded to changes in the competitive environment by acquiring small companies, developing new products that duplicated ones already on the market (so-called "me-too" drugs), entering the generics market, seeking extensions of patents after making only slight improvements, and engaging in aggressive marketing, including the use of controversial direct-to-consumer (DTC) advertising.

The first four strategies—growth by acquisition, the development of "me-too" drugs, the production of generics, and making improvements merely to extend patents—conflicted with Merck's culture and values. However, under the previous CEO, Roy Vagelos (who guided Merck through the development of Mectizan for river blindness), the company greatly increased its emphasis on marketing. This emphasis was considered necessary given the short time available to sell a drug before the patent expired. In particular, evidence was needed not only to prove a product's safety and effectiveness in order to gain FDA approval but also to persuade physicians to prescribe it instead of the competitors' medications. Since much of the information that could persuade doctors was part of a drug's label, marketers needed to be involved in the development of a product from the earliest research stages in order to prepare a persuasive label. The label could be improved further by conducting tests which were not scientifically necessary but which generated clinically proven results that could be useful in persuading physicians. Under Gilmartin, the company's formally stated strategy became: "Turning cutting-edge science into novel medicines that are true advances in patient care with proven clinical outcomes."

In announcing the withdrawal of Vioxx, Gilmartin described the evidence of increased risk of heart attacks as "unexpected." In the first lawsuits against Merck that came to trial, evidence was presented to show that company scientists had considered the potential heart problems with Vioxx as early as 1997. The first hint of trouble came in that year as Merck scientists noticed that Vioxx appeared to suppress the production of a substance in the body that acted naturally to reduce the incidence of heart attacks. Although the significance of this discovery was recognized, no follow-up investigations were undertaken.

More significant evidence that Vioxx might contribute to heart attacks was produced by a study concluded in 2000 that was designed to compare the gastrointestinal effects of Vioxx and naproxen in order to improve the label of the Merck product by proving that Vioxx was less harmful to the stomach lining. Although the study, called VIGOR (for Vioxx Gastrointestinal Outcomes Research), showed that Vioxx users had heart attacks at a rate four to five times that of the naproxen group, researchers were uncertain whether the difference was due to an adverse effect of Vioxx in causing heart attacks or a beneficial effect of naproxen in preventing them. The heart attacks in the trial occurred mainly in the Vioxx subjects already at greatest risk of heart attacks, and all subjects were prohibited from taking aspirin (which is known to prevent heart attacks) in order to gain reliable results from the study since aspirin affects the stomach. When the results of the VIGOR study were published in November 2000 in the prestigious *New England Journal of Medicine*, the beneficial effects of naproxen were emphasized in a way that implied that Vioxx was safe for people without the risk factors for heart attacks. After initially resisting pressure by the FDA to include a warning on the Vioxx label, Merck finally agreed in April 2002 to add the evidence of an increased incidence of heart attacks. However, the language on the label emphasized, again, the uncertainty of the cause and recommended that people at risk of heart attacks continue to use an anti-inflammant for protection.

In the meantime, Merck continued its aggressive marketing campaign. Between 1999 and 2004, Merck spent more than $500 million on DTC television and print advertising. This expenditure was intended to keep pace with the heavy spending by Pfizer for its competing COX-2 inhibiter Celebrex. Merck also maintained a 3000-person sales force to meet with doctors for face-to-face conversations about Vioxx. To support this effort, Merck developed materials that provided salespeople with responses to questions from skeptical physicians.[3] One document, called an "obstacle handling guide," advised that questions about the risk of heart attacks be answered with the evasive explanations that Vioxx "would not be expected to demonstrate reductions" in heart attacks and was "not a substitute for aspirin." Another document titled "Dodge Ball Vioxx" concluded with four pages that were blank except for the word "DODGE!" in capital letters on each page. Company documents also describe an effort to "neutralize" skeptical doctors by enlisting their support or at least defusing their opposition by offers of research support or engagements as consultants.[4]

The study that conclusively established that Vioxx increased the risk of heart attacks was called APPROVe (Adenomatous Polyp Prevention on Vioxx), which, according to critics, had only a marketing and not a legitimate scientific purpose.[5] Although the company could have delayed the withdrawal until ordered to do so by the FDA, Merck acted voluntarily. Gilmartin said that the company "was really putting patient safety first."[6] However, one critic replied, "If Merck were truly acting in the interest of the public, of course, they should have done more studies on Vioxx's safety when doubts about it first surfaced."[7] Another critic observed that such studies could have been conducted for a fraction of the cost of the $500 million spent on advertising.[8] An editorial in the *New York Times* declared that "companies must jump at the first hint of risk and warn patients and doctors of any dangers as clearly and quickly as possible. They should not be stonewalling regulators, soft-pedaling risk to doctors or promoting drugs to millions of people who don't need them."[9] A 179-page report commissioned by the Merck board concluded, by contrast, that executives and researchers acted with integrity in addressing incomplete and conflicting evidence and that "their conclusions were reached in good faith and were reasonable under the circumstances."[10] The report closed with the observation that the quick response after the APPROVe study "is not consistent with the view that Merck's corporate culture put profits over patient safety."[11]

INTRODUCTION

The Vioxx crisis was an unusually difficult and damaging experience for Merck, which has both a history of responsible conduct and a commitment to the highest standards of ethics. Although Merck's culture is built on strong values, these were not enough to prevent a series of decisions that, right or wrong, seriously damaged the company's carefully built reputation. Merck executives appear to have considered carefully the possible health risk posed by Vioxx, and yet the push for profits may have led them to conclude too easily that Vioxx was not the cause of the heart attacks suffered by test subjects and that further studies were not necessary. The increased role of marketing, including heavy consumer advertising, in a traditionally science-driven culture was probably a factor in whatever mistakes were made, as was the change in strategy to seek evidence of the products' superiority as part of a marketing campaign to influence physicians. However, Merck's strategy could not avoid some adjustment given the changed competitive environment that was created by forces outside the company's control.

All business organizations face the daunting challenge of adhering to the highest standards of ethics while, at the same time, remaining competitive and providing the products and services that the public demands. The task of managers in these organizations is to make sound business decisions that enable a company to achieve its mission. Some of these decisions involve complex ethical issues that may not be readily apparent, and success in making sound business decisions may depend on understanding these ethical issues and resolving them effectively. This book is about the ethical issues that arise for managers—and, indeed, for all people, including employees, consumers, and members of the public. Corporate activities affect us all, and so the ethical conduct of business is a matter of concern for everyone. The ethical issues examined in this book are those considered by managers in the ordinary course of their work, but they are also matters that are discussed in the pages of the business press, debated in the halls of Congress, and scrutinized by the courts. This is because ethical issues in business are closely tied to important matters of public policy and to the legislative and judicial processes of government. They are often only part of a complex set of challenges facing the whole of society.

BUSINESS DECISION MAKING

Although ethical issues in business are very diverse, the following examples provide a useful starting point.

1. *The Sales Rep.* A sales representative for a struggling computer supply firm has a chance to close a multimillion-dollar deal for an office system to be installed over a two-year period. The machines for the first delivery are in the company's warehouse, but the remainder would have to be ordered from the manufacturer. Because the manufacturer is having difficulty meeting the heavy demand for the popular model, the sales representative is not sure that subsequent deliveries can be made on time. Any delay in converting to the new system would be costly to the customer; however, the blame could be placed on the manufacturer. Should the sales representative close the deal without advising the customer of the problem?

2. *The Research Director.* The director of research in a large aerospace firm recently promoted a woman to head an engineering team charged with designing a critical component for a new plane. She was tapped for the job because of her superior knowledge of the engineering aspects of the project, but the men under her direction have been expressing resentment at working for a woman by subtly sabotaging the work of the team. The director believes that it is unfair to deprive the woman of advancement merely because of the prejudice of her male colleagues, but quick completion of the designs and the building of a prototype are vital to the success of the company. Should he remove the woman as head of the engineering team?

3. *The Marketing Director.* The vice president of marketing for a major brewing company is aware that college students account for a large proportion of beer sales and that people in this age-group form lifelong loyalties to particular brands of beer. The executive is personally uncomfortable with the tasteless gimmicks used by her competitors in the industry to encourage drinking on campuses, including beach parties and beer-drinking contests. She worries about the company's contribution to underage drinking and alcohol abuse among college students. Should she go along with the competition?

4. *The CEO.* The CEO of a midsize producer of a popular line of kitchen appliances is approached about merging with a larger company. The terms offered by the suitor are very advantageous to the CEO, who would receive a large severance package. The shareholders of the firm would also benefit, because the offer for their stock is substantially above the current market price. The CEO learns, however, that plans call for closing a plant that is the major employer in a small town. The firm has always taken its social responsibility seriously, but the CEO is now unsure of how to balance the welfare of the employees who would be thrown out of work and the community where the plant is located against the interests of the shareholders. He is also not sure how much to take his own interests into account. Should he support a merger that harms the community but benefits the shareholders and himself?

These four examples give some idea of the ethical issues that arise at all levels of business. The individuals in these cases are faced with questions about ethics in their relations with customers, employees, and members of the larger society. Frequently, the ethically correct course of action is clear, and people in business act accordingly. Exceptions occur, however, when there is uncertainty about ethical obligations in particular situations or when considerations of ethics come into conflict with the practical demands of business. The sales representative might not be sure, for example, about the extent to which he is obligated to provide information about possible delays in delivery. And the director of research, although convinced that discrimination is wrong, might still feel that he has no choice but to remove the woman as head of the team in order to get the job done.

In deciding on an ethical course of action, we can rely to some extent on the rules of right conduct that we employ in everyday life. Deception is wrong, for example, whether we deceive a friend or a customer. And corporations no less than persons have an obligation not to discriminate or cause harm. However, business activity also has some features that limit the applicability of our ordinary ethical views. In business settings, we encounter situations that are significantly different from those of everyday life, and business roles place their own obligations on us. For example, the CEO, by virtue of his position, has responsibilities to several different constituencies, and his problem in part is to find the proper balance.

Two Distinguishing Features

One distinguishing feature of business is its *economic* character. In the world of business, we interact with each other not as family members, friends, or neighbors, but as buyers and sellers, employers and employees, and the like. Trading, for example, is often accompanied by hard bargaining, in which both sides conceal their full hand and perhaps engage in some bluffing. And a skilled salesperson is well versed in the art of arousing a customer's attention (sometimes by a bit of puffery) to clinch the sale. Still, there is an "ethics of trading" that prohibits the use of false or deceptive claims and tricks such as "bait-and-switch" advertising.

Employment is also recognized as a special relationship, with its own standards of right and wrong. Employers are generally entitled to hire and promote whomever they wish and to lay off or terminate workers without regard for the consequences for the people affected. (This right is being increasingly challenged, however, by those who hold that employers ought to fire only for cause and to follow rules of due process in termination decisions.) Employees also have some protections, such as a right not to be discriminated against or to be exposed to workplace hazards. There are many controversies about the employment relationship, such as the rights of employers and employees with regard to privacy and freedom of speech, for example.

The ethics of business, then, is at least in part the ethics of economic or market activity, such as the conduct of buyers and sellers and employers and employees. So we need to ask, what are the ethical rules or standards that ought to govern these kinds of activities? And how do these rules and standards differ from those that apply in other spheres of life?

A second distinguishing feature of business is that it typically takes place in *organizations.* An organization, according to organizational theory, is a hierarchical system of functionally defined positions designed to achieve some goal or set of goals. Consequently, the members of a business organization, in assuming a particular position, take on new obligations to pursue the goals of the firm. Because business involves economic transactions and relationships that take place in markets and also in organizations, it raises ethical issues for which the ethics of everyday life has not prepared us. Although the familiar ethical rules about honesty, fairness, promise keeping, and the like are applicable to business, it is necessary in many cases to rethink how they apply in business situations. This is not to say that the ethics of business is different from ethics in everyday life, but only that business is a different context, and it presents us with new situations that require us to think through the ethical issues.

Levels of Decision Making

Decision making occurs on several distinct levels: the level of the *individual,* the level of the *organization*, and the level of the *business system.* Situations that confront individuals in the workplace and require them to make a decision about their own response are on the level of individual decision making. An employee with an unreasonably demanding boss, for example, or with a boss who is discovered padding his expense account faces the question: "What do *I* do?" Whether to live with the difficult boss or to blow the whistle on the padding is a question to be answered by the individual and acted on accordingly.

Many ethical problems occur at the level of the organization in the sense that the individual decision maker is acting on behalf of the organization in bringing about some organizational change. Sexual harassment, for example, is an individual matter for the person suffering the abuse, but a manager in an office where sexual harassment is happening must take steps not only to rectify the situation but also to ensure that it does not occur again. The decision in this case may be a disciplinary action, which involves a manager acting within his or her organizational role. The manager may also institute training to prevent sexual harassment and possibly develop a sexual harassment policy, which not only prohibits certain behavior but also creates procedures for handling complaints. Responding to harassment as a manager, as opposed to dealing with harassment as a victim, involves decisions on the organizational level rather than the individual level. The question here is, "What do *we as an organization* do?"

Problems that result from accepted business practices or from features of the economic system cannot be effectively addressed by any single organization, much less a lone individual. Sales practices within an industry, for example, are difficult for one company to change single-handedly, because the company is constrained by competition with possibly less-ethical competitors. The most effective solution is likely to be an industry-wide code of ethics, agreed to by all. Similarly, the lower pay for women's work results from structural features of the labor market, which no one company or even industry can alter. A single employer cannot adopt a policy of comparable worth, for example, because the problem is systemic, and consequently any substantial change must be on the level of the system. Systemic problems are best solved by some form of regulation or economic reform. On the systemic level, the relevant question is, "What do *we as a society* do?"

Identification of the appropriate level for a decision is important, because an ethical problem may have no solution on the level at which it is approached. The beer marketer described earlier may have little choice but to follow the competition in using tasteless gimmicks because the problem has no real solution on the individual or organizational level. An effective response requires that she place the problem on the systemic level and seek a solution appropriate to that level. Richard T. DeGeorge has described such a move as "ethical displacement," which consists of addressing a problem on a level other than the one on which the problem appears.[12] The fact that some problems can be solved only by displacing them to a higher level is a source of great distress for individuals in difficult situations, because they still must find some less-than-perfect response on a lower level.

CASE 1.2   ✳️ ⎣Explore the Concept on mythinkinglab.com

The Ethics of Hardball

Toys "R" Us: Fair or Foul?

Hardball tactics are often applauded in business, but when Child World was the victim, the toy retailer cried foul.[13] Its complaint was directed against a major competitor, Toys "R" Us, whose employees allegedly bought Child World inventory off the shelves during a promotion in which customers received $25 gift certificates for buying merchandise worth $100. The employees of Toys "R" Us were accused of selecting products that Child World sold close to cost, such as diapers, baby food, and infant formula. These items could be resold by Toys "R" Us at a profit, because the purchase price at Child World was barely above what a wholesaler would charge, and then Toys "R" Us could redeem the certificates for additional free merchandise, which could be resold at an even higher profit. Child World claimed that its competitor bought up to $1.5 million worth of merchandise in this undercover manner and received as much as $375,000 worth of gift certificates. The practice is apparently legal, although Child World stated that the promotion excluded dealers, wholesalers, and retailers. Executives at Toys "R" Us did not deny the accusation and contended that the practice is common in the industry. Child World may have left itself open to such a hardball tactic by slashing prices and offering the certificates in an effort to increase market share against its larger rival.

Home Depot: Good Ethics or Shrewd Business?

When weather forecasters predicted that Hurricane Andrew would strike the Miami area with full force, customers rushed to stock up on plywood and other building materials.[14] That weekend the 19 Home Depot stores in southern Florida sold more 4-foot-by-8-foot sheets of exterior plywood than they usually sell in two weeks. On August 24, 1992, the hurricane struck, destroying or damaging more than 75,000 homes, and in the wake of the devastation, individual price gougers were able to sell basics like water and food as well as building materials at wildly inflated prices. But not Home Depot. The chain's stores initially kept prices on plywood at pre-hurricane levels, and when wholesale prices rose on average 28 percent, the company announced that it would sell plywood, roofing materials, and plastic sheeting at cost and take no profit on the sales. It did limit quantities, however, to prevent price gougers from reselling the goods at higher prices. In addition, Home Depot successfully negotiated with its suppliers of plywood, including Georgia-Pacific, the nation's largest plywood producer, to roll back prices to pre-hurricane levels. Georgia-Pacific, like Home Depot, has a large presence in Florida; the company runs 16 mills and distribution centers in the state and owns 500,000 acres of timberland. Although prices increased early in anticipation of Hurricane Andrew, Home Depot was still able, with the cooperation of suppliers, to sell half-inch plywood sheets for $10.15 after the hurricane, compared with a price of $8.65 before, thereby limiting the increase to less than 18 percent. Home Depot executives explained their decision as an act of good ethics by not profiting from human misery. Others contend, however, that the company made a shrewd business decision.

ETHICS, ECONOMICS, AND LAW

Businesses are economic organizations that operate within a framework of law and regulation. They are organized primarily to provide goods and services, as well as jobs, and their success depends on operating efficiently and competitively. In a capitalist system, firms must compete effectively in an open market by providing goods and services that customers want and by doing so at a low price, which is possible only when the desired goods and services are produced efficiently. Profit is not the end or purpose of business, as is commonly asserted, but is merely the return on the investment in a business that is possible only when the business is competitive. Business has often been described as a game, in which the aim is to make as much profit as possible while staying within the rules of the game, which are set mainly by government through laws and regulations.[15] On this view, profit is a measure and the reward of success, but it cannot be gained without also aiming to be competitive. Moreover, it is necessary, in pursuing profits, to observe certain ethical standards, as well as laws and regulation, as a means to the end of profit making.

Both economics and law are critical to business decision making, but the view that they are the only relevant considerations and that ethics does not apply is plainly false. Even hard-fought games like football have a code of sportsmanship in addition to a rule book, and business, too, is governed by more than the legal rules. In addition, a competitive business system, in which everyone pursues his or her self-interest, depends for its existence on ethical behavior and is itself justified on ethical grounds. However, the relationships of business ethics to economics and the law are very complicated and not easily summarized. The following discussion is intended to clarify these relationships.

The Relationship of Ethics and Economics

According to economic theory, firms in a free market utilize scarce resources or factors of production (labor, raw materials, and capital) in order to produce an output (goods and services). The demand for this output is determined by the preferences of individual consumers who select from among the available goods and services so as to maximize the satisfaction of their preferences, which is called "utility." Firms also seek to maximize their preferences or utility by increasing their output up to the point where the amount received from the sale of goods and services equals the amount spent for labor, raw materials, and capital—that is, where marginal revenues equal marginal costs. Under fully competitive conditions, the result is economic efficiency, which means the production of the maximum output for the least amount of input.

Economics thus provides an explanatory account of the choices of economic actors, whether they be individuals or firms. On this account, the sole reason for any choice is to maximize utility. However, ethics considers many other kinds of reasons, including rights and justice and other noneconomic values. To make a choice on the basis of ethics—that is, to use ethical reasons in making a decision—appears at first glance to be incompatible with economic choice. To make decisions on economic grounds and on ethical grounds is to employ two different kinds of reasoning. This apparent incompatibility dissolves on closer inspection. If the economists' account of economic reasoning is intended to be merely an explanation, then it tells us how we *do* reason in making economic choices but not how we *ought* to reason. Economics as a science need do no more than offer explanations, but economists generally hold that economic reasoning is also justified. That is, economic actors *ought* to make utility-maximizing choices, which is an ethical, and not merely an economic, judgment.

JUSTIFICATION OF THE MARKET SYSTEM.   The argument for this position, that economic actors ought to make utility-maximizing choices, is the classical defense of the market system, which is discussed more fully in Chapter 2. In *The Wealth of Nations*, Adam Smith, the "father" of modern economics, justified the pursuit of self-interest in exchange on the grounds that by making trades for our own advantage, we promote the interests of others. The justification for a free-market capitalist system is, in part, that by pursuing profit, business firms promote the welfare of the whole society. Commentators on Adam Smith have observed that this argument assumes a well-ordered civil society with a high level of honesty and trust and an abundance of other moral virtues. Smith's argument would not apply well to a chaotic society marked by pervasive corruption and mistrust. Furthermore, in his defense of the free market in *The Wealth of Nations*, Smith was speaking about *exchange*, whereas economics also includes *production* and *distribution*.[16] The distribution of goods, for example, is heavily influenced by different initial endowments, access to natural resources, and the vagaries of fortune, among other factors. Whether the vast disparities in wealth in the world are justified is a question of distribution, not exchange, and is not addressed by Smith's argument.

Moreover, certain conditions must be satisfied in order for business activity to benefit society. These include the observance of minimal moral restraints to prevent theft, fraud, and the like. Markets must be fully competitive, with easy entry and exit, and everyone must possess all relevant information. In addition, all costs of production should be reflected in the prices that firms and consumers pay. For example, unintended consequences of business activity, such as job-related accidents, injuries from defective products, and pollution, are costs of production that are often not covered or internalized by the manufacturer but passed to others as spillover effects or *externalities*. Many business ethics problems arise when these conditions for the operation of a free market are not satisfied.

SOME CONDITIONS FOR FREE MARKETS.   A common view is that ensuring the conditions for free markets and correcting for their absence is a job for government. It is government's role, in other words, to create the rules of the game that allow managers to make decisions solely on economic grounds. However, the task of maintaining the marketplace cannot be handled by government alone, and the failure of government to do its job may create an obligation for business to help. Although government does enact and enforce laws against theft and fraud, including such specialized forms as the theft of trade secrets and fraud in securities transactions, there are many gray areas in which self-regulation and restraint should be exercised. Hardball tactics like those allegedly employed by Toys "R" Us (Case 1.2) are apparently legal, but many companies would consider such deliberate sabotage of a competitor to be an unacceptable business practice that is incompatible with the market system.

Recent work in economics has revealed the influence of ethics on people's economic behavior. Economists have shown how a reputation for honesty and trustworthiness, for example, attracts customers and potential business partners, thus creating economic opportunities that would not be available otherwise. Similarly, people and firms with an unsavory reputation are punished in the market. People are also motivated in their market behavior by considerations of fairness. This is illustrated by the "ultimatum bargaining game," in which two people are given a certain amount of money (say $10) on the condition that one person proposes how the money is to be divided (e.g., $5 to each) and the second person accepts or rejects the proposed division. The first person can make only one proposal, and if the proposal is rejected by the second person, the money is taken away and each person receives nothing. Economic theory suggests that the second person would accept any proposal, no matter how small the share, if the alternative is no money at all. Hence, the first person could offer to share as little as $1 or less. But many people who play the game will refuse a proposal in which they receive a share that is considered too small and hence unfair.[17] They would rather have nothing than be treated unfairly.

Economists explain the behavior of companies like Home Depot (Case 1.2) by the fact that considerations of fairness force firms to limit profit-seeking behavior. Consumers remember price gouging and other practices that they consider unfair and will punish the wrongdoers by ceasing to do business with them or even by engaging in boycotts. One study found that people do not believe that scarcity is an acceptable reason for raising prices (despite what economists teach about supply and demand),[18] and so Home Depot and Georgia-Pacific, which are there for the long haul, have more to lose than gain by taking advantage of a natural disaster. Evidence also indicates that people in a natural disaster feel that everyone ought to make some sacrifice, so that profit seeking by a few is perceived as shirking a fair share of the burden.[19]

Finally, when economics is used in practice to support matters of public policy, it must be guided by noneconomic values. Economic analysis can be applied to the market for cocaine as easily as to the soybean market, but it cannot tell us whether we should allow both markets. That is a decision for public-policy makers on the basis of other considerations. A tax system, for example, depends on sound economic analysis, but the U.S. tax code attempts to achieve many aims simultaneously and to be accepted as fair. In drafting a new tax code, a demonstration that a particular system is the most efficient from a purely economic perspective would not necessarily be persuasive to a legislator who may also be concerned about considerations of fairness.

The Relationship of Ethics and the Law

Business activity takes place within an extensive framework of law, and some people hold that law is the only set of rules that applies to business activity. Law, not ethics, is the only relevant guide. The reasons that lead people to hold this view are varied, but two predominate.[20]

TWO SCHOOLS OF THOUGHT.   One school of thought is that law and ethics govern two different realms. Law prevails in public life, whereas ethics is a private matter. The law is a clearly defined set of enforceable rules that applies to everyone, whereas ethics is a matter of personal opinion that reflects how we choose to lead our own lives. Consequently, it would be a mistake to apply ethical rules in business, just as it would be a mistake to apply the rules of poker to tennis. A variant of this position is that the law represents a minimal level of expected conduct that everyone should observe. Ethics, on the other hand, is a higher, optional level. It's "nice" to be ethical, but our conduct has to be legal.

Both versions of this school of thought are mistaken. Although ethics does guide us in our private lives, it is also applicable to matters in the public realm. We can identify business practices as ethical or unethical, as, for example, when we say that discrimination or consumer fraud is wrong. Moral judgments are also made about economic systems. Thus, most people believe that capitalism is morally justified, although it has many critics who raise moral objections.

The other school of thought is that the law embodies the ethics of business. There are ethical rules that apply to business, according to this position, and they have been enacted by legislators into laws, which are enforceable by judges in a court. As a form of social control, law has many advantages over ethics. Law provides more precise and detailed rules than ethics, and the courts not only enforce these rules with state power but also are available to interpret them when the wording is unclear. A common set of rules known to all also provides a level playing field. Imagine the chaos if competing teams each decided for themselves what the rules of a game ought to be. For these reasons, some people hold that it is morally sufficient in business merely to observe the law. Their motto is, "If it's legal, then it's morally okay."[21]

In countries with well-developed legal systems, the law is a relatively complete guide for business conduct. In the United States, much of what is unethical is also illegal. However, many other countries of the world have undeveloped legal systems so that ethics, not law, provides the main source of guidance. The relative lack of international law leaves ethics as an important guide for global business. Moreover, no legal system can embrace the whole of morality. Ethics is needed not only to address situations not covered by law but also to guide the creation of new law. The 1964 Civil Rights Act, for example, was passed by Congress in response to the recognition that discrimination, which was legally practiced at the time, is morally wrong.

WHY THE LAW IS NOT ENOUGH.   Despite their differences, these two schools of thought have the same practical implication: Managers need to consider only the law in making decisions. This implication is not only false but also highly dangerous. Regardless of the view that a practicing manager takes on the relationship of law and ethics, reliance on the law alone is a prescription for disaster, as many individuals and firms have discovered. Approval from a company's legal department does not always assure a successful legal resolution, and companies have prevailed in court only to suffer adverse consequences in the marketplace. As a practical matter, then, managers need to consider both the ethical and legal aspects of a situation in making a decision for many reasons, including the following.

First, the law is inappropriate for regulating certain aspects of business activity. Not everything that is immoral is illegal. Some ethical issues in business concern interpersonal relations at work or relations between competitors, which would be difficult to regulate by law. Taking credit for someone else's work, making unreasonable demands on subordinates, and unjustly reprimanding an employee are all ethically objectionable practices, but they are best left outside the law. Some hardball tactics against competitors may also be legal but ethically objectionable. Whether the effort of Toys "R" Us to sabotage a promotion by its competitor is acceptable behavior (see Case 1.2) is open to dispute, but not every legal competitive maneuver is ethical. Generally, legislatures and the courts are reluctant to intervene in ordinary business decisions unless significant rights or interests are at stake. They rightly feel that outsiders should not second-guess the business judgment of people closer to a problem and impose broad rules for problems that require a more flexible approach. Companies also prefer to handle many problems without outside interference. Still, just because it is not illegal to do certain things does not mean that they are morally okay.

Second, the law is often slow to develop in new areas of concern. Christopher D. Stone points out that the law is primarily reactive, responding to problems that people in the business world can anticipate and deal with long before they come to public attention.[22] The legislative and judicial processes themselves take a long time, and meanwhile much damage can be done. This is true not only for newly emergent problems but also for long-recognized problems where the law has lagged behind public awareness. For example, sexual harassment was not recognized as a legal wrong by the courts until 1977, and it took successive court decisions over two more decades for the legal prohibition on sexual harassment to fully develop. At the present time, legal protections for employees who blow the whistle and those who are unjustly dismissed are just beginning to develop. Employers should not wait until they are forced by law to act on such matters of growing concern.

Third, the law itself often employs moral concepts that are not precisely defined, so it is impossible in some instances to understand the law without considering matters of morality. The requirement of *good faith*, for example, is ubiquitous in law. The National Labor Relations Act requires employers and the representatives of employees to bargain "in good faith." One defense against a charge of price discrimination is that a lower price was offered in a good-faith attempt to meet the price of a competitor. Yet the notion of good faith is not precisely defined in either instance. Abiding by the law, therefore, requires decision makers to have an understanding of this key moral concept. Other imprecisely defined legal concepts are "fair dealing," "best effort," and "due care."

A fourth argument, closely related to the preceding one, is that the law itself is often unsettled, so that whether some course of action is legal must be decided by the courts. And in making a decision, the courts are often guided by moral considerations. Many people have thought that their actions, although perhaps immoral, were still legal, only to discover otherwise. The courts often refuse to interpret the law literally when doing so gives legal sanction to blatant immorality. Judges have some leeway or discretion in making decisions. In exercising this discretion, judges are not necessarily substituting morality for law but rather expressing a morality that is embodied in the law. Where there is doubt about what the law is, morality is a good predictor of how the courts will decide.

Fifth, a pragmatic argument is that the law is a rather inefficient instrument, and an exclusive reliance on law alone invites legislation and litigation where they are not necessary. Many landmark enactments, such as the Civil Rights Act of 1964, the National Environment Policy Act of 1969, the Occupational Safety and Health Act of 1970, and the Consumer Protection Act of 1972, were passed by Congress in response to public outrage over the well-documented failure of American businesses to act responsibly. Although business leaders lament the explosion of product-liability suits by consumers injured by defective products, for example, consumers are left with little choice but to use the legal system when manufacturers themselves hide behind "If it's legal, it's morally okay." Adopting this motto, then, is often shortsighted, and businesses may often advance their self-interest more effectively by engaging in greater self-regulation that observes ethical standards.

ETHICS AND MANAGEMENT

Most managers think of themselves as ethical persons, but some still question whether ethics is relevant to their role as a manager. It is important for people in business to be ethical, they might say, but being ethical in business is no different than being ethical in private life. The implication is that a manager need only be an ethical person. There is no need, in other words, to have specialized knowledge or skills in ethics.

Nothing could be further from the truth. Although there is no separate ethics of business, situations arise in business that are not easily addressed by ordinary ethical rules. We have already observed that the obligation to tell the truth is difficult to apply to the dilemma faced by the sales rep. In addition, the manager of a sales force might face the task of determining the rules of acceptable sales practices for the whole organization and ensuring that the rules are followed. More broadly, high-level managers have a responsibility for creating and maintaining an ethical corporate climate that protects the organization against unethical and illegal conduct by its members. Furthermore, a well-defined value system serves to guide organizations in uncertain situations and to gain acceptance of painful but necessary change.

Ethical Management and the Management of Ethics

A useful distinction can be made between *ethical management* and the *management of ethics.* Business ethics is often conceived as acting ethically as a manager by doing the right thing. This is ethical management. Acting ethically is important for both individual success and organizational effectiveness. Ethical misconduct has ended more than a few promising careers, and some business firms have been severely harmed and even destroyed by the actions of a few individuals. Major scandals in the news attract our attention, but people in business face less momentous ethical dilemmas in the ordinary course of their work. These dilemmas sometimes result from misconduct by others, as when a subordinate is ordered to commit an unethical or illegal act, but they are also inherent in typical business situations.

The management of ethics is acting effectively in situations that have an ethical aspect. These situations occur in both the internal and external environments of a business firm. Internally, organizations bind members together through myriad rules, procedures, policies, and values that must be carefully managed. Some of these, such as a policy on conflict of interest or the values expressed by a company's mission statement, explicitly involve ethics. Effective organizational functioning also depends on gaining the acceptance of the rules, policies, and other guides, and this acceptance requires a perception of fairness and commitment. For example, an organization that does not "walk the talk" when it professes to value diversity is unlikely to gain the full cooperation of its employees. With respect to the external environment, corporations must successfully manage the demands for ethical conduct from groups concerned with racial justice, human rights, the environment, and other matters.

In order to practice both ethical management and the management of ethics, it is necessary for managers to possess some specialized *knowledge.* Many ethical issues have a factual background that must be understood. In dealing with a whistle-blower or developing a whistle-blowing policy, for example, the managers of a company should be aware of the motivation of whistle-blowers, the measures that other companies have found effective, and, not least, the relevant law. Some of this background is provided in Chapter 4 on whistle-blowing. In addition, many ethical issues involve competing theoretical perspectives that need to be understood by a manager. Whether it is ethical to use confidential information about a competitor or personal information about an employee depends on theories about intellectual property rights and the right to privacy that are debated by philosophers and legal theorists. Although a manager need not be equipped to participate in these debates, some familiarity with the theoretical considerations is helpful in dealing with practical situations.

To make sound ethical decisions and to implement them in a corporate environment are *skills* that come with experience and training. Some managers make mistakes because they fail to see the ethical dimensions of a situation. Other managers are unable to give proper weight to competing ethical factors or to see other people's perspectives. Thus, a manager may settle a controversial question to his or her satisfaction, only to discover that others still disagree. Moral imagination is often needed to arrive at creative solutions to problems. Finally, the resolution of a problem usually involves persuading others of the rightness of a position, and so the ability to explain one's reasoning is a valuable skill.

The need for specialized knowledge and skills is especially acute when business is conducted abroad.[23] In global business, there is a lack of consensus on acceptable standards of conduct, and practices that work well at home may fare badly elsewhere. This is especially true in less-developed countries with lower standards and weak institutions. How should a manager proceed, for example, in a country with exploitive labor conditions, lax environmental regulations, and pervasive corruption? Even the most ethical manager must rethink his or her beliefs about how business ought to be conducted in other parts of the world.

Ethics and the Role of Managers

Every person in business occupies a role. A role is a structured set of relationships with accompanying rights and obligations. Thus, to be a purchasing agent or a personnel director or an internal auditor is to occupy a role. In occupying a role, a person assumes certain rights that are not held by everyone as well as certain role-specific obligations. Thus, a purchasing agent is empowered to make purchases on behalf of an organization and has a responsibility to make purchasing decisions that are best for the organization. To be a "good" purchasing agent is to do the job of a purchasing agent well.

The obligations of a particular role are sometimes added to those of ordinary morality. That is, a person who occupies a role generally assumes obligations over and above those of everyday life. Sometimes, however, role obligations come into conflict with our other obligations. In selecting people for promotion, a personnel director, for example, is obligated to set aside any considerations of friendship and to be wholly impartial. A person in this position may also be forced to terminate an employee for the good of the organization, without regard for the impact on the employee's life. A personnel director may even be required to implement a decision that he or she believes to be morally wrong, such as terminating an employee for inadequate cause. In such situations, the obligations of a role appear to be in conflict with the obligations of ordinary morality.

Various justifications have been offered for role obligations. One justification is simply that people in certain positions have responsibilities to many different groups and hence must consider a wide range of interests. The decisions of a personnel director have an impact on everyone connected with a business organization, and so denying a friend a promotion or terminating an employee may be the right thing to do, all things considered. A more sophisticated justification is that roles are created in order to serve society better as a whole. A well-designed system of roles, with accompanying rights and obligations, enables a society to achieve more and thereby benefits everyone. A system of roles thus constitutes a kind of division of labor. As in Adam Smith's pin factory, in which workers who perform specific operations can be more productive than individuals working alone, so, too, a business organization with a multiplicity of roles can be more productive and better serve society.

We cannot understand the role obligations of managers without knowing more about their specific role. Managers serve at all levels of an organization—top, middle, and lower—and fulfill a variety of roles. Usually, these are defined by a job description, such as the role of a purchasing agent or a personnel director. Uncertainty arises mainly when we ask about the role of top managers, that is, high-level corporate executives who make key decisions about policy and strategy. The higher one goes in a business organization, the more roles one occupies. Many of the ethical dilemmas for top managers are due to conflicts between three main roles.

1. *Managers as Economic Actors.* One inescapable requirement of the manager's role is to make sound economic or business decisions that enable a firm to succeed in a competitive market. As economic actors, managers are expected to consider primarily economic factors in making decisions, and the main measure of success is profitability. This is the goal of managers who serve as economic actors even if they operate a sole proprietorship, a partnership, or any other kind of business enterprise. However, as previously noted, ethical issues are intertwined with business considerations in decision making, and the soundness of business decisions often depends on the recognition of these ethical issues and their appropriate resolution.

2. *Managers as Company Leaders.* As leaders of business organizations, managers are entrusted with enormous assets and given a charge to manage these assets prudently. Employees, suppliers, customers, investors, and other so-called stakeholders have a stake in the success of a firm, and managers are expected to meet all of their legitimate expectations and to balance any conflicting interests. Corporations are also human communities in which individuals find not only the means to support themselves but also personal satisfaction and meaning. Top managers, in particular, serve these roles by building and maintaining a company's culture, developing a shared purpose and strategic vision, and, most importantly, meeting challenges and creating a strong, enduring organization.

3. *Managers as Community Leaders.* Top managers of companies exert enormous power both inside and outside their organizations. Although they are not elected in a democratic process, they nevertheless have many attributes of government officials, such as the power to make decisions that profoundly impact society. The CEO or chairman of a large corporation also serves as an ambassador, representing the company in its relations with its myriad constituencies. In any political system, such great power must be legitimized by showing how it serves some generally accepted societal goals, and managerial power is no exception. So, top managers are expected to demonstrate corporate leadership that serves the interests of society as a whole.

Many of the ethical dilemmas facing managers involve not merely a conflict between one's personal morality and the morality of a role but also a conflict between the moral demands of different roles. For example, a manager may have to balance fairness to employees or a benefit to the community against an obligation to act in the best interest of the company. Or a CEO may find that he or she cannot easily serve both as a company leader and a community leader when a decision must be made about a merger that would close a local plant. Some of the hardest dilemmas in business ethics result from such role conflicts.

ETHICS IN ORGANIZATIONS

The manager who seeks to act ethically and to ensure the ethical conduct of others—which have been identified in this chapter as "ethical management" and "the management of ethics"—must have the ability not only to understand ethical issues and resolve them effectively but also to appreciate the challenges of ethical decision making and ethical conduct in an organizational setting. The fact that much business activity takes place in organizations has profound consequences for the manager's role responsibilities for several reasons.

First, much decision making in business is a collaborative endeavor in which each individual may play only a small role. Many organizational decisions get made without any one person coming to a decision or being responsible for it. Second, this collaborative decision-making process is subject to dynamic forces that may not be recognized or understood by any of the participants. As a result, decisions get made that have consequences no one intended or expected. Third, many organizational acts are not the result of any one person's actions but are collective actions that result from a multiplicity of individual actions. Many corporate acts are thus "deeds without doers."[24] Fourth, organizations themselves create an environment that may lead otherwise ethical people to engage in unethical conduct. Organizational life, according to sociologist Robert Jackall, poses a series of "moral mazes" which people must navigate at their own peril.[25]

Consequently, the typical case of wrongdoing in organizations involves missteps that are due more to inadequate thought than deliberate malice, where people get tripped up in a moral maze. The following two sections discuss the findings, mainly of psychologists and sociologists, about how ethical mistakes result from flaws in individual decision making and from organizational forces.

Individual Decision Making

Wrongdoing is often attributed to the proverbial "bad apple," the individual who knows that an action is wrong but deliberately does it anyway. Such persons can be condemned for having a bad character, and the lesson for others is to develop a good character. This is misleading both as an analysis of the causes of bad conduct and as a prescription for ensuring good conduct. Of course, there are bad apples, and they should not be hired or, if hired, should be let go once their rottenness is known. This "bad apples" explanation is not very convincing, however, when wrongdoing is committed by people we would identify as good employees or managers. Moreover, when misconduct is widespread in an organization, as is often the case in major scandals, it is not plausible to believe that dozens if not hundreds of people are all "bad apples." Some other explanations are needed, and fortunately psychologists and sociologists have offered many.

First, many individuals work in environments in which they lack strong guidance and receive conflicting signals.[26] Often there is strong pressure to follow orders and get the job done. Barbara Toffler, who chronicled the last days of Arthur Andersen in a book, relates the tale of an undergraduate who interned at a major accounting firm where he was ordered to make an accounting entry that appeared to be irregular. When he told his superior, "This doesn't look right to me. Why am I doing it?" the reply was, "You're doing it because I told you to do it."[27] Employees who are told, "Just do it!" without more explicit instructions and without adequate resources may perceive these words as an implicit order to do whatever it takes to get a job done. Employees are also urged to be "team players" and go along with whatever is being done. Senior managers, in giving orders, often prefer not to give detailed guidance, in part to avoid operational responsibility ("Just do it, and don't tell me how you got it done"). They also sometimes lack an appreciation of the operational difficulties of a job and thus leave to subordinates the task of solving problems their own ways.

Second, individuals are prone to rationalization and can often effectively persuade themselves that a course of action is morally right or, at least, is not wrong under the circumstances. Saul Gellerman in the article "Why 'Good' Managers Make Bad Ethical Choices" identifies four dangerous rationalizations.[28]

- A belief that the activity is within reasonable ethical and legal limits—that is, that it is not "really" illegal or immoral.
- A belief that the activity is in the individual's or the corporation's best interest—that the individual would somehow be expected to undertake the activity.
- A belief that the activity is "safe" because it will never be found out or publicized; the classic crime-and-punishment issue of discovery.
- A belief that because the activity helps the company, the company will condone it and even protect the person who engages in it.

A particularly common rationalization in business is "everybody's doing it." This retort may even justify some actions when refraining would put a company at a competitive disadvantage (when competitors engage in deceptive advertising, for example) or when business cannot be conducted without so acting (e.g., engaging in foreign bribery).[29] Other rationalizations include "No real harm is done" or "No harm no foul"; "I deserve this" or "They owe this to me" (sometimes used to justify pilfering); "It's for a good cause" (the ends justify the means); and "If I don't do this, someone else will" (restraint is futile; the consequences will happen anyway).

Sociologists who have studied crime, including the kind of white-collar crime that occurs in business, have described a process of rationalization they call "neutralization" that enables lawbreakers to deny the criminality of their behavior.[30] Among the techniques of neutralization are claims that one is not really responsible ("I was out of my mind"), that any real harm was done ("No one will miss that amount of money"), that the victim deserved the harm ("I was only paying him back"), that one's accusers are being unfair ("I'm being singled out for blame"), and that one was following some higher duty or loyalty ("I had to protect my friends"). All the rationalizations detailed here show the immense capacity of people to engage in self-deception.

Third, psychologists have identified a number of features of human decision making that produce errors of judgment.[31] Two of these researchers contend that "unethical business practices may stem not from the traditionally assumed trade-off between ethics and profits or from a callous disregard of other people's interest or welfare, but from psychological tendencies that foster poor decision making, both from an ethical and a rational perspective."[32] Some of these "psychological tendencies" are *biases* that shift our decisions in one direction or another, while others are *heuristics* or rule-of-thumb methods that we employ in reasoning.

Among the biases discovered by psychologists are the following:

- *Loss Aversion Bias.* People tend to weigh losses more heavily than gains and thus take greater risks to avoid losing something they have than to gain something that they do not have.
- *Framing Effect.* People's decisions depend on how the choices are presented or framed. Thus, the loss aversion bias leads people to choose alternatives that are framed in terms of losses rather than gains.
- *Confirmation Bias.* This is the tendency of people to seek and process information that confirms existing attitudes and beliefs instead of seeking and processing information that poses challenges to their attitudes and beliefs.
- *Cognitive Dissonance.* Related to the confirmation bias, cognitive dissonance is the tendency of people to dismiss information that would disrupt their existing attitudes and beliefs.
- *Commitment and Sunk Costs.* Once commitments are made and resources expended, people tend to persist in a course of action, even in the face of information that should lead them to reconsider their initial decision.
- *Hindsight Bias.* People tend to believe that events are more predictable than they are, and consequently they blame themselves for not anticipating events that occur.
- *Causation Bias and Illusion of Control.* People often find causal patterns in random events, which leads to the belief that they have a greater ability to control events than is warranted.
- *Overoptimism and Overcofindence Bias.* People are unduly confident of their own knowledge and abilities and thus overestimate the likelihood of success.
- *Self-interest Bias.* People tend to make judgments, especially about fairness, that favor themselves.
- *Risk Perception Bias.* People make poor judgments about risk, overestimating some risk and discounting others, often ignoring low-probability events and favoring certain over uncertain outcomes.

The main heuristics people employ are as follows:

- *Anchoring and Adjustment Heuristic.* People tend to form an initial choice ("anchor") early in the decision-making process and then adjust the choice in response to additional information. Thus, the final decision is heavily influenced by the initial choice, especially given that people often fail to make adequate adjustments.
- *Representativeness Heuristic.* This is the tendency of people to utilize recent and vivid examples rather than objective statistical data. For example, a person purchasing an automobile may rely on a friend's experience with one model instead of reading test reports.

• *Availability Heuristic.* People tend to make decisions based on the available information at hand rather than seeking out new sources of information. Information may be "available," for example, because it is more recent or vivid or because it is easier or more comfortable to remember.

These biases and heuristics have developed in the process of evolution to enable human beings to decide and act quickly, especially in dangerous situations with too much information to process fully. Generally, they serve us well but can lead to mistakes. They can cause us, for example, to fail to consider important consequences or what could go wrong, to discount the possibility of random events, to misidentify causes, to be overoptimistic or overconfident, and to favor people like ourselves. Psychologists have also noted that biases and heuristics prevent us from foreseeing disasters that we should have seen coming[33] and lead us to overlook the unethical conduct of others.[34] Instances of defective products, accounting fraud, and industrial accidents have been closely studied to reveal the psychological factors that explain how such bad decisions could have been made by decent, diligent, well-intentioned individuals.

Organizational Decision Making

When a company produces a defective product (e.g., Merck's Vioxx or Toyota's accelerator mechanism) or collapses from massive accounting fraud (as did Enron and WorldCom) or experiences a major industrial accident (e.g., the Bhopal disaster), the fault generally lies with a series of decisions that can be understood only by examining organizational factors. With the benefit of hindsight, some mistaken decisions can often be found, but sometimes all of the decisions involved seemed reasonable at the time. In such cases, the causes of major scandals and disasters must be sought in the decision-making processes.

Decision making in organizations is marked by four features that contribute to mistakes, big and small. First, major decisions are not made all at once with all their consequences and ramifications understood; rather they are made over time in a series of small steps, no one of which may raise any particular concerns. Second, as they are made over time, these multiple decisions develop a commitment to a course of action that is usually difficult to stop. Once a project is underway, there may be considerable sunk costs that cannot be recovered, and anyone who proposes a halt to a project bears a burden of proof to justify it, whereas little justification is needed to proceed with a project underway. Stopping a project also means that mistakes were made, which it may be difficult for managers to admit since someone must bear the blame. With commitment to a course of action also comes a psychological tendency to interpret evidence in ways that support one's beliefs and interests. This factor probably goes far toward explaining why Merck executives misinterpreted the results of the VIGOR study and concluded that they were due to the heart-protection benefit of naproxen and not to any harmful effect from Vioxx (see Case 1.1).

The third and fourth factors are the most important: These are the diffusion of information and the fragmentation of responsibility that occur in organizational decision making.[35] The information that would show that a product has a defect, for example, may exist within an organization in an unassembled form in which different facts are known to different individuals. However, unless this information is assembled and made known to at least one person, there may be no reason for anyone in the organization to conclude that a product is defective. Furthermore, information is distributed in organizations on a need-to-know basis, and each decision maker may have sufficient information for the decisions that that person makes. So unless one individual is specifically charged with discovering defects, no decision maker would typically have a reason to have access to all the information that would be necessary to reveal a defect.

With diffusion of information comes fragmentation of responsibility. Each decision in a series may be made by different individuals or groups, all of whom are discharging their specific responsibility and doing so well based on the information available to them. Thus, a researcher testing a drug for its efficacy in treating a certain condition may assume that other researchers have already proven its safety, so safety is not *that* researcher's responsibility. And the salespeople who pitch the drug to doctors assume that the researchers have done their job to test its safety and efficacy; that is not *their* responsibility. In the end, when a drug is recalled, it may be that no one is responsible since no one has failed in discharging his or her responsibility. It is often said that "the buck stops at the top," that the CEO or some other senior executive has a responsibility to ensure, in this example, that a drug is safe, but that person is hostage to a host of decisions made by others that he or she cannot fully assess. In such cases, only the organization as a whole can be blamed or held responsible, and the only remedy to prevent a recurrence is to improve the decision-making process within the organization.

Conclusion

Business ethics, as presented in this book, is concerned with identifying and understanding the ethical issues that arise in business and with developing the knowledge and skills needed by a practicing manager to address these issues and to make sound business decisions—that is, decisions that are sound from both an ethical and a business perspective. Ethical issues are an inevitable element of business decision making and are deeply intertwined with managerial practice and economic activity generally. Business ethics is important for managers because the ethical issues examined in this book are involved in many business decisions upon which the success of individual managers, business organizations, and, indeed, the whole economic system depend. Both economics and law are important guides for business decision making, but, as this chapter has shown, they are not complete. Nor is business ethics understood merely as the treatment of ethical issues from a philosophical perspective. As the work of psychologists and sociologists on organizational misconduct show, it is not enough merely to determine a right course of action. Misconduct in organizations is also the result of flaws in individual and organizational decision making that can be corrected only by changes in decision-making processes. Although this book deals mainly with the treatment of ethical issues in business, practicing managers must also address the larger challenge of preventing misconduct within organizations.

CASE 1.3   ✳ Explore the Concept on mythinkinglab.com
Beech-Nut's Bogus Apple Juice

When Lars Hoyvald joined Beech-Nut in 1981, the company was in financial trouble.[36] In the competitive baby food industry, the company was a distant second behind Gerber, with 15 percent of the market. After faltering under a succession of owners, Beech-Nut was bought in 1979 by Nestlé, the Swiss food giant, which hoped to restore the luster of the brand name. Although he was new to Beech-Nut, Hoyvald had wide experience in the food industry, and his aim, as stated on his résumé, was "aggressively marketing top quality products."

In June 1982, Hoyvald was faced with strong evidence that Beech-Nut apple juice for babies was made from concentrate that included no apples. Since 1977, the company had been purchasing low-cost apple concentrate from a Bronx-based supplier, Universal Juice Company. The price alone should have raised questions, and John Lavery, the vice president in charge of operations, brushed aside tests that showed the presence of corn syrup. Two employees who investigated Universal's "blending facility" found merely a warehouse. Their report was also dismissed by Lavery. A turning point occurred when a private investigator working for the Processed Apple Institute discovered that the Universal plant was producing only sugared water. After following a truck to the Beech-Nut facility, the investigator informed Lavery and other executives of his findings and invited Beech-Nut to join a suit against Universal.

Although some executives urged Hoyvald to switch suppliers and recall all apple juice on the market, the president was hesitant. Even if the juice was bogus, there was no evidence that it was harmful. It tasted like apple juice, and it surely provided some nutrition. Besides, he had promised his Nestlé superior that he would return a profit of $7 million for the year. Switching suppliers would mean paying about $750,000 more each year for juice and admitting that the company had sold an adulterated product. A recall would cost about $3.5 million. Asked later why he had not acted more decisively, Hoyvald said, "I could have called up Switzerland and told them I had just closed the company down. Because that is what would have been the result of it."

Fearful that state and federal investigators might seize stocks of Beech-Nut apple juice, Hoyvald launched an aggressive foreign sales campaign. On September 1, the company unloaded thousands of cases on its distributors in Puerto Rico. Another 23,000 cases were shipped to the Dominican Republic to be sold at half price. By the time that state and federal authorities had forced a recall, the plan was largely complete. In November, Hoyvald reported to his superior at Nestlé, "The recall has now been completed, and due to our many delays, we were only faced with having to destroy approximately 20,000 cases." Beech-Nut continued to sell bogus apple juice until March 1983.

CASE 1.4 ✳ Explore the Concept on mythinkinglab.com
KPMG's Tax Shelter Business

In the 1990s, KPMG, one of the "big four" accounting firms, began offering tax shelters to corporations and wealthy investors. In addition to standard audit and consulting services, KPMG aggressively developed and marketed a number of innovative ways for clients to avoid taxes. Not only did individuals and businesses reduce taxes on billions of dollars of gains, but also KPMG partners pocketed many millions for their assistance.

Acting like any business developing a new product, KPMG established a "Tax Innovation Center" to generate ideas and to research the accounting, financial, and legal issues.[37] Previously, tax shelters had been individualized for particular clients, but the new ones were intended to be generic, mass-marketed products. Once a strategy was approved, it was energetically promoted to likely clients by the firm's sales force. KPMG tax professionals were turned into salespeople. They were given revenue targets and urged to use telemarketing and the firm's own confidential records to locate clients. The strategies—which bore such acronyms as OPIS, BLIPS, FLIP, and SOS—generally involved complicated investments with cooperating foreign and offshore banks that generated phantom losses that could be used to offset capital gains or income from other investments. The shelters were accompanied by opinion letters from law firms that assessed their legality. The gain to KPMG and their clients and the loss to the U.S. Treasury were significant. The four main tax shelters marketed by the firm generated over $11 billion in tax deductions for clients, which yielded at least $115 million in fees for KPMG and cost the government $2.5 billion in lost tax revenue.[38]

During the period in which the KPMG tax shelters were sold, no court or Internal Revenue Service (IRS) ruling had declared them illegal. However, KPMG had failed to register the shelters with the IRS as required by law. Registration alerts the tax authorities to the use of the shelters and permits them to investigate their legality. One KPMG partner attributed this failure to a lack of specific guidance by the IRS on the rules for registration and the agency's lack of interest in enforcing the registration requirement.[39] Furthermore, this partner calculated that for OPIS, the firm would pay a penalty of only $31,000 if the failure to register were discovered. This amount was more than outweighed by the fees of $360,000 for each shelter sold.[40]

Until the courts or Congress explicitly outlaw a tax shelter, the line between legal and illegal tax strategies is often difficult to draw. The IRS typically employs the "economic substance" test: Do the transactions involved in a tax shelter serve a legitimate investment objective or is their only effect to reduce taxes? A tax shelter that offers no return beyond a tax saving is abusive in the view of the IRS. However, an IRS ruling is not legally binding until it is upheld by the courts, and the courts have occasionally held some shelters to be legal even if they do not involve any risk or potential return. One reason for such decisions is that tax shelters typically involve legitimate transactions combined in unusual ways. As one observer notes, "Most abusive shelters are based on legal tax-planning techniques—but carried to extremes. That makes it hard to draw sharp lines between legitimate tax planning and illicit shelters."[41] Even when a shelter like those sold by KPMG is found to be legal, a tax savings is almost always the only outcome. According to an IRS commissioner, "The only purpose of these abusive deals was to further enrich the already wealthy and to line the pockets of KPMG partners."[42]

When a tax shelter is found by the court to be abusive, the usual outcome is simply a loss of the tax advantage so that the client pays what would be owed otherwise plus any penalties. The issuer is seldom sanctioned. KPMG and other marketers of tax shelters generally protect themselves, first, by having the client sign a statement affirming that he or she understands the structure of the transaction and believes that it serves a legitimate business purpose. This makes it more difficult for the client to sue the firm. KPMG also sent all related documents to its lawyers in order to protect them from disclosure by claiming lawyer–client privilege.

Although some partners at KPMG thought that the tax shelters were illegal and raised objections, others argued for their legality—and, in any event, their shelters were an immensely profitable part of the firm's business. Aside from the huge fees, the motivation to market the shelters came from the KPMG culture, which *New York Times* business reporter Floyd Norris characterized as that of a "proud old lion." He writes, "Of all the major accounting firms, it was the one with the strongest sense that it alone should determine . . . the rules it would follow. Proud and confident, it brooked no criticism from regulators."[43]

Notes

1. Much of the information for this case comes from "Report of the Honorable John R. Martin, Jr. to the Special Committee of the Board of Directors of Merck & Co., Inc. Concerning the Conduct of Senior Management in the Development and Marketing of Vioxx," 5 September 2006, henceforth cited as "Martin Report."
2. Quoted in John Simons, "Will Merck Survive Vioxx?" *Fortune*, 1 November 2004.
3. Anna Wilde Mathews and Barbara Martinez, "E-Mails Suggest Merck Knew Vioxx's Dangers at an Early Stage," *Wall Street Journal*, 1 November 2004.
4. Barry Meier and Stephanie Saul, "Marketing of Vioxx: How Merck Played Game of Catch-Up," *New York Times*, 11 February 2005.
5. Alex Berenson, "Evidence in Vioxx Suits Shows Intervention by Merck Officials," *New York Times*, 24 April 2005.
6. Mathews and Martinez, "E-Mails Suggest Merck Knew Vioxx's Dangers at an Early Stage."
7. Simons, "Will Merck Survive Vioxx?"
8. Ibid.
9. "Punishment for Merck," *New York Times*, 23 August 2005.
10. Martin Report, p. 177.
11. Ibid, p. 179.
12. Richard T. DeGeorge, *Competing with Integrity in International Business* (New York: Oxford University Press, 1993), 97–99.
13. This case is adapted from Suzanne Alexander, "Child World Says Rival Cheats; Toys 'R' Us Answers: 'Grow Up,' " *Wall Street Journal*, 19 September 1991, B1.
14. This case is adapted from Steve Lohr, "Lessons from a Hurricane: It Pays Not to Gouge," *New York Times*, 22 September 1992, D1.
15. Albert Z. Carr, "Is Business Bluffing Ethical?" *Harvard Business Review*, 46 (January–February 1968), 148.
16. Amartya Sen, "Does Business Ethics Make Economic Sense?" *Business Ethics Quarterly*, 3 (1993), 45–54.
17. The results of experiments with the ultimatum bargaining game are presented in Robert H. Frank, *Passions within Reason: The Strategic Role of the Emotions* (New York: W. W. Norton, 1988), 170–74. For a discussion of the implications for business ethics, see Norman E. Bowie, "Challenging the Egoistic Paradigm," *Business Ethics Quarterly*, 1 (1991), 1–21.
18. Daniel Kahneman, Jack L. Knetch, and Richard Thaler, "Fairness as a Constraint of Profit-Seeking: Entitlements in the Market," *American Economic Review*, 76 (1986), 728–41.
19. Douglas C. Dacy and Howard Kunreuther, *The Economics of Natural Disasters* (New York: Free Press, 1969), 115–16.

20. Lynn Sharp Paine, "Law, Ethics, and Managerial Judgment," *Journal of Legal Studies Education*, 12 (1994), 153–69.

21. This phrase is taken from Norman E. Bowie, "Fair Markets," *Journal of Business Ethics*, 7 (1988), 89–98.

22. Christopher D. Stone, *Where the Law Ends: The Social Control of Corporate Behavior* (New York: Harper & Row, 1975), 94.

23. See Thomas Donaldson, "Values in Tension: Ethics Away from Home," *Harvard Business Review*, 4 (September–October 1996), 48–62.

24. David Luban, Alan Strudler, and David Wasserman, "Moral Responsibility in the Age of Bureaucracy," *University of Michigan Law Review*, 90 (1991–92), 2366.

25. Robert Jackall, *Moral Mazes: The World of Corporate Managers* (New York: Oxford University Press, 1988).

26. For a discussion of these problems, see Joseph L. Badaracco, Jr., and Allen P. Webb, "Business Ethics: A View from the Trenches," *California Management Review*, 37 (1995), 8–28.

27. Barbara Toffler, *Final Accounting: Ambition, Greed, and the Fall of Arthur Andersen* ((New York: Broadway Books, 2004), 257.

28. Saul W. Gellerman, "Why 'Good' Managers Make Bad Ethical Choices," *Harvard Business Review* (July–August 1986), 85.

29. For a discussion of the conditions under which this rationalization might have justificatory force, see Ronald M. Green, "When Is 'Everyone's Doing It' a Moral Justification?" *Business Ethics Quarterly*, 1 (1991), 75–93.

30. Gresham M. Sykes and David Matza, "Techniques of Neutralization: A Theory of Delinquency," *American Sociological Review*, 22 (1957), 664–70. For an application of the criminology literature to business ethics, see Joseph Heath, "Business Ethics and Moral Motivation: A Criminological Perspective," *Journal of Business Ethics*, 83 (2008), 595–614.

31. The seminal work in this area was done by Daniel Kahneman and Adam Tversky, for which Kahneman was awarded the Nobel Prize in economics in 2002 (Tversky had died earlier).

32. David M. Messick and Max H. Bazerman, "Ethical Leadership and the Psychology of Decision Making," *Sloan Management Review* (Winter 1996), 9–22.

33. Max H. Bazerman and Michael D. Watkins, *Predictable Surprises: The Disasters You Should Have Seen Coming, and How to Prevent Them* (Boston, MA: Harvard Business School Press, 2004).

34. Gino Francesca, Don A. Moore, and Max H. Bazerman, "See No Evil: Why We Overlook Other People's Unethical Behavior," in *Social Decision Making: Social Dilemmas, Social Values, and Ethical Judgments*, ed. Roderick M. Kramer, Ann E. Tenbrunsel, and Max H. Bazerman (New York: Routledge, 2009) 241–63.

35. These factors are described in John Darley, "How Organizations Socialize Individuals into Evildoing," in *Codes of Conduct: Behavioral Research into Business Ethics*, ed. David M. Messick and Ann E. Tenbrunsel (New York: Russell Sage Foundation, 1996), 13–43.

36. Much of the information for this case is taken from James Traub, "Into the Mouth of Babes," *New York Times Magazine*, 24 July 1988.

37. The process of developing and marketing tax-shelter products is described in detail in *The Role of Professional Firms in the U.S. Tax Shelter Industry*, Report Prepared by the Permanent Subcommittee on Investigations of the Committee on Homeland Security and Governmental Affairs, United States Senate, 13 April 2005.

38. U.S. Department of Justice, Press Release and Statement of Facts, 29 August 2005.

39. Cassell Bryan-Low, "KPMG Didn't Register Strategy: Former Partner's Memo Says Fees Reaped from Sales of Tax Shelter Far Outweigh Potential Penalties," *Wall Street Journal*, 17 November 2003, C1.

40. Ibid.

41. Howard Gleckman, Amy Borrus, and Mike McNamee, "Inside the KPMG Mess: Why Eight Partners May Be Facing Jail Time—and What the Justice Dept.'s Suit Could Mean for the Tax-Shelter Business," *Business Week*, 5 September 2005, 46–47.

42. Jonathan D. Glater, "8 Former Partners of KPMG Are Indicted," *New York Times*, 30 August, 2005, C5.

43. Floyd Norris, "KPMG, a Proud Lion, Brought to Heel," *The New York Times*, 30 August 2005, C1.

2

Ethical Decision Making

((•—[**Listen** to the **Chapter Audio** on **mythinkinglab.com**

CASE 2.1 ✳—[**Explore** the **Concept** on **mythinkinglab.com**

HP and the Smart Chip

As a leading innovator in the highly competitive computer printer business, Hewlett-Packard has promoted its "SureSupply" campaign, which tracks and manages users' toner and ink levels, provides alerts when the cartridge needs to be replaced, and directs users to the HP online store.[1] HP literature boasts, "With a couple of clicks of a button, customers can access cartridge information, pricing and purchasing options that best meet their needs from the reseller of their choice." The key to SureSupply is a "smart chip," which is embedded in a cartridge and communicates with the computer to provide information and send messages and alerts. Originally used only with more expensive, high-end printers, HP subsequently extended its smart chip technology across its line of products.

Despite HP's claim to be providing a "free user-friendly tool," some customers took a different view of the smart chip. Users of HP ink-jet printers complained that the smart chip was programmed to send a premature low-on-ink (LOI) message, while substantial ink remained in the cartridge. They also contended that the smart chip would render a cartridge inoperable after a predetermined shutdown date that is not disclosed to users. This date was usually the earlier of 30 months after the initial installation or 30 months after the "install-by" date. In some instances, a cartridge could shut down even before it had been installed. Although HP cartridges carry a warranty, the warranty does not apply, among other conditions, for "products receiving a printer generated expiration message." The smart chip also guides users to HP's own Web store, where they may order a new cartridge. Once the smart chip had shut down a cartridge, it could not easily be refilled, thus requiring replacement with a new one. (The European Union has prohibited manufacturers from installing smart chips in cartridges in an effort to promote recycling. Indeed, the European Parliament uses only recycled cartridges.) The HP promotional materials, users' manuals, and packaging reveal little about the features of the smart chip. The box containing a cartridge generally lists the date of the warranty expiration but not any shutdown date. In an issue unrelated to the smart chip, some users were disconcerted to learn that certain color ink-jet printers used colored ink when printing in black and white in a process known as "underprinting" or "under color addition," which resulted in more rapid depletion of colored ink. This feature, too, was not commonly disclosed.

When several separate suits were filed between 2005 and 2008 (the courts denied requests for class-action status), HP vigorously defended its practices, denying that it had done anything wrong or improper. The company contended that, overall, the smart chip provided a helpful service to users and ensured a better printing experience. The smart chip was necessary, the company explained, to enable users to monitor ink levels and be prepared when a replacement was needed. In any event, the monetary loss to customers was minor compared with the convenience. The smart chip was also beneficial to HP since replacement cartridges provided approximately half of the revenues of the Imaging and Printing Group, and "consumables" of all kinds generated approximately 10 percent of HP's total revenue. Typically, printers, like razor holders, are sold at very low cost since the profits lie mainly in the products that go with them. The profit margin on HP's ink and toner cartridges ranged between 50 and 60 percent.

Despite the denials of any wrong or improper conduct, HP agreed in 2010 to settle the suits, which were consolidated into one. In the settlement, HP agreed to state in all on-screen messages, manuals, and other information that the ink-level information is an estimate only, that actual ink levels may vary, and that the customers need not replace a cartridge until the print quality is no longer acceptable. HP also agreed to explain on its website and in manuals the use of expiration dates and underprinting and also to explain how underprinting may be minimized or eliminated. Finally, HP agreed to set aside $5 million to provide e-credits to customers who had purchased certain printers and cartridges. These e-credits, which ranged in amounts from $2 to $6 depending on the printer in question, could be applied only in the HP online store. The settlement did not address the use of the smart chip, and it continues to be used by HP and many other manufacturers.

INTRODUCTION

Did HP do anything wrong? The company and its customers have different interests that may lead them to different answers. Taking the moral point of view, which is explained in the previous chapter, requires us to be impartial and to seek out the best reasons. These reasons may not be easy to identify, however, or to apply. As a business, HP may rightly seek to develop its products and market them with a view to profits within certain limits. The smart chip, in the company's view, serves not only to sell more cartridges but also to benefit its customers, which is a win-win situation. Customers may complain not only that they pay more than is necessary for products but that they have been misled or deceived. Yet, how much information is HP obligated to provide? Perhaps we should not consider only a business and its customers since others are affected, as well. A potential business in recycled cartridges is thwarted by the smart chip, and the social problem of waste is exacerbated, as witness the different response of the European Union. Should these matters also be taken into account in our ethical reasoning?

In order to identify what makes acts right and wrong and to determine what we ought to do or what our duties and responsibilities are in particular cases, it is necessary to understand the elements of ethical decision making. What rules or principles apply to business practice? This chapter answers this question by dividing business ethics into two parts. The first part considers the ethics of the marketplace in which two parties, a buyer and a seller, come together to trade or make an exchange. Although simple in concept, such market transactions are governed by a host of rules or principles that constitute a market ethics. As prominent as market transactions are to business, much business activity also involves roles and relationships, such as the role of an employee and the employer–employee relationship, which are more than mere market transactions. The second part of business ethics involves roles and relationships in business, including firms, which are governed by yet other rules and principles. Finally, this chapter offers a framework for ethical decision making that consists of seven basic principles that are widely accepted in business practice.

MARKET ETHICS

The ethics of business is, in large part, the ethics of conduct in a market. In a market, individuals and business firms engage in economic exchanges or transactions in which they relate to each other mainly or entirely as buyers and sellers. Each market participant offers up something in trade in return for something that is valued more, and, in theory, each party leaves the market better off than before, or at least no worse off. Of course, business is more than buyer–seller exchanges, but a useful place to start an examination of ethical decision making in business is with an understanding of the ethics of market transactions.

What duties or obligations do market participants have to each other in making trades or exchanges? Do market actors have any rights that can be violated in market transactions? Are any market transactions unfair or unjust or otherwise morally objectionable? These questions can be addressed in the context of simple market exchanges without introducing the complications that come from considering business as conducted in firms, which is considered following a discussion of ethics in markets transactions.

The Market System

In a capitalist economy, major decisions about what goods and services to produce, in what volume to produce them, how to manufacture and market them, and so on are made primarily through a market. Decisions in a market are made on the basis of prices, which in turn result largely from supply and demand. The principal aim of business firms in a market system is to maximize the return on investment or, in other words, to make a profit. Individuals, as well, are assumed in economic theory to be market actors who trade with each other or else buy products from or sell their labor or other goods to a firm. Individuals, too, make decisions in a market on the basis of prices and seek to maximize their own welfare to the limits of their assets. Individuals make a "profit" for themselves to the extent that what they gain in trade exceeds what they give up.

The market system is characterized by three main features: (1) *private ownership* of resources and the goods and services produced in an economy; (2) *voluntary exchange*, in which individuals and firms are free to enter into mutually advantageous trades; and (3) the *profit motive*, whereby economic actors engage in trading solely to advance their own interests or well-being.

Private ownership in the form of property rights is necessary for a market system because this is what is transferred in market exchanges. In the sale of a house, for example, the seller, who owns it, transfers the right to that property to the buyer, who becomes the new owner. A sale differs from theft or confiscation, moreover, by being voluntary. Whenever a trade takes place voluntarily, we can be sure that both parties believe themselves to be better off (or, at least, no worse off), because, by assumption, no one willingly consents to being made worse off. Finally, it is assumed that each market participant trades solely with a view to his or her own advantage. If two people want the same thing, then a trade might not be possible. But if each person has what the other wants more, then a trade is to the advantage of both. Therefore, trading in a market is an instance of mutually advantageous cooperation.

The main justification of a market system over other forms of economic organization is its promotion of efficiency and hence welfare.[2] The simplest definition of efficiency is obtaining the greatest output for the least input. That is, given any volume of our limited resources—which include raw materials, labor, land, and capital—we want to achieve the greatest volume of goods and services possible. Efficiency is generally considered to be desirable because these goods and services increase our overall welfare, and the more of them that we can get, the greater our level of welfare.

For example, if Alice sells a book to Bart for $10, she apparently values having $10 more than the possession of the book, hence her willingness to sell; and similarly Bart would apparently rather have the book than the $10 he currently possesses, hence his willingness to buy. Before the transaction, there was an opportunity to increase the overall level of welfare, and the exchange that takes place turns this opportunity into a reality. Every economic exchange can thus be seen as a welfare-increasing event, and the more trades that take place, the greater the level of welfare. Similarly, when firms engage in production, they see an opportunity to purchase inputs, such as raw materials, machinery, and labor, which can be combined to yield a product that can be sold to consumers. Like Alice, the sellers of the raw materials, machinery, and labor would rather have the money they receive for selling their various assets, and, like Bart, the consumers would rather have the product than the money they give up in payment. In the end, everyone is better off.

What is true of individual market actors, whether people or firms, is also true of an economy as a whole. In an economy built on markets, laborers, in search of the highest possible wages, put their efforts and skill to the most productive use. Buyers seeking to purchase needed goods and services at the lowest possible price force sellers to compete with one another by making the most efficient use of the available resources and keeping prices at the lowest possible level. The resulting benefit to society as a whole is due not to any concern with the well-being of others, but solely to the pursuit of self-interest. By seeking only personal gain, each individual is, according to a famous passage in Adam Smith's *The Wealth of Nations*, "led by an invisible hand to promote an end which was no part of his intention." Smith continued, "Nor is it always the worse for the society that it was no part of it. By pursuing his own interest he frequently promotes that of the society more effectually than when he really intends to promote it."

In addition to welfare enhancement, the market system is morally desirable because it promotes freedom or liberty. The opportunity to make trades is an exercise of liberty by which individuals are able to advance their interests in society, thus promoting democracy. A market is an instance of what Friedrich von Hayek calls a *spontaneous order*, which contrasts with the *planned order* of a state-owned, socialist economy, in which a central authority sets goals and organizes people's activities to achieve them.[3] In a spontaneous order, the only goals are those that individuals set for themselves, and the only coordination is that provided by the rules for people's interaction, which permit them to enlist the cooperation of others, each in the pursuit of his or her own goals. The advantages of spontaneous order are, first, that it protects and expands the basic rights to liberty and property. Second, a spontaneous order will generate a much greater complexity than could be produced by deliberate design. A planned order is limited by the vision and skill of a few people, but a spontaneous order allows everyone to participate in an economy and make a contribution.

A stronger argument for the market system and perhaps the decisive reason for the failure of socialism is the ability of markets to utilize information. A central planner faces the formidable task of gathering all available information about such matters as people's preferences for products, the supply of raw materials, the capacity and condition of machines and workers, the state of distribution facilities, and many other factors. Not only is the amount of information required for economic decision making immense, but also the details are constantly changing. Put simply, the information-gathering and processing requirements of central planning outstrip the capabilities of any one person or group of people. Markets solve this problem by enabling individuals to utilize the information that they possess in ways that can be known by others. This is done mainly through the price system. The prices of all manner of goods and services reflect the available information, and these prices may fluctuate as new information becomes available. Thus, the market system may be justified on the multiple grounds of enhancing welfare, securing rights and liberty, and utilizing all available information.

Ethics in Markets

If a market transaction is wholly voluntary, then how can one market actor wrong another? In a free market, every participant seeks his or her own benefit and has no obligation to protect or promote or otherwise consider the interest of the other party. Exclusive self-interest is an accepted and justified motive for trading. However, in a market people are able to get what they want only with the cooperation and voluntary consent of others; acquisition without consent is a kind of theft. Consequently, everyone's gains in a market are by mutual agreement or consent, in which case no moral wrongs are possible. Indeed, the philosopher David Gauthier has characterized perfectly competitive markets as morally free zones, where there is no place for moral evaluation.[4] A world where all activity took place in a perfectly competitive market would have no need of morality.

The idea that a market is a morally free zone such that no wrong can occur from each participant pursuing his or her own advantage with the voluntary consent of others presupposes, as Gauthier makes explicit, the ideal of a perfectly competitive, properly functioning market. In such a market, it is assumed, first, that everyone completes an exchange by fulfilling the terms of all agreements. Every market transaction can be viewed as a kind of contract, and so one moral requirement of a market system is that each participant observe all contracts made. In law, a failure to do this would be called a *breach of contract*, which is a legal and moral wrong.

Second, a voluntary exchange precludes *force* or *fraud*. Any transfer by force is not a market transaction but an instance of theft or expropriation, which is an obvious legal and moral wrong. By contrast, fraud is a more subtle wrong that is not an uncommon occurrence in market transactions and that, like force, is also prohibited by law. Indeed, fraud, which is discussed in the next section, is a major concern in business ethics.

Third, market transactions can result in harm to persons that constitute a *wrongful harm* when the harm results from some wrongful act. For example, the harm done to the buyer of a defective product is a *wrongful* harm if the seller has a duty to ensure the safety of the product when properly used. Similarly, an employer has a duty not to discriminate, and so the refusal to hire or promote a person on the basis of race or sex is also an instance of a wrongful harm. Such wrongful harms are the subject of the law of torts, which is often the basis of suits for injury or loss of some kind.

Fourth, perfect markets require a number of conditions, and when these fail to obtain, the personal and social benefits that result from mutually advantageous cooperation, as described in Adam Smith's invisible hand argument, may not occur. The absence of these conditions leads to a number of commonly recognized situations known as *market failures*, which are discussed later in this chapter.

Consequently, wrongs can occur in actual, as opposed to ideal or perfect markets, and market ethics may be characterized as the ethical rules that apply in imperfect market exchanges or transactions to address recognized market failures. Because market failures are also addressed by much government regulation, there is an extensive overlap between business ethics and the moral rationale or justification for this regulation. Market ethics, which is to say the ethics that applies when the conditions for perfect markets do not obtain, can be categorized under the four headings of (1) observing agreements or contracts, (2) avoiding force and fraud, (3) not inflicting wrongful harms, and (4) acting responsibly in cases of market failures. Since much of business ethics consists of this market ethics, a further examination of the four headings follows.

Breaches and Fraud

Breach of contract and fraud, which are two wrongs that can occur in market transactions, are not only major concerns of law but also of common morality. Indeed, they are violations of two basic moral values: promise keeping and honesty. Every market trade or exchange is a kind of promise, and so a failure to honor what is agreed to in a transaction is the breaking of a promise. And inasmuch as fraud necessarily involves a knowing or intentional falsehood, it is a form of dishonesty. Much of business ethics can be reduced to two rules: keep your promises and be honest!

BREACHES OF CONTRACT. A market actor who fails to perform—by not delivering promised goods or refusing to pay, for example—is obviously breaching an agreement or contract, and such cases of nonperformance are obviously wrong and require little explanation. However, actual contracts are often vague, ambiguous, incomplete, or otherwise problematic so that reasonable people may be uncertain or disagree about whether a contract's terms have been fulfilled. Disputes of this kind, which are not uncommon, are often taken to court. In actual business practice, three main ethical problems with contracts arise.

First, many contracts in business are not explicitly formulated but are left implicit because of a desire or a need to avoid excessive legalism and to keep some flexibility. Business is sometimes better conducted with a handshake than a written contract. Thus, employee contracts may contain explicit terms about pay and job description, but leave implicit any promises of specific job responsibilities, advancement opportunities, or guarantes of job security. Such matters may be better left to the unstated understandings of implicit contracts rather than to the legally enforceable language of explicit contracts. However, implicit contracts are subject to disagreements, and since they are generally not legally enforceable, they may be violated with impunity. For example, a laid-off employee may believe that he had been guaranteed greater job security than was the case, or a company may change its policy to offer less job security, which may be legally permissible in the absence of an explicit contract.

Second, a perfect contract in which every detail and contingency are addressed may be impossible to formulate because the transaction is too complex and uncertain to plan fully. Even if a fully explicit contract is sought, it may be impossible to draft it in complete detail. For example, in hiring a chief executive officer (CEO), neither the CEO nor the board of a company can anticipate all the situations that might arise and agree upon detailed instructions for acting in each one. Indeed, the CEO is being hired precisely for an ability to manage complexity and to handle unanticipated events successfully. The best that can be done is typically to require the CEO to exert his or her best effort, to set and reward certain goals, and to impose a fiduciary duty to act in the shareholders' interest. The CEO's contract with a firm is necessarily an incomplete contract.

Third, the contracts that occur in market exchanges often consider only the duties or obligations of each party to the other and fail to specify the remedies in cases of breach. What ought to be done in cases where one party is unable or unwilling to fulfill a contract? Such situations are often the subject of ethical and legal disputes. While remedies for breaches can usually be made explicit, there is evidence that firms often prefer to leave this matter implicit, in which case courts are called upon to determine a just outcome.[5] One problematic area of justice in breaches occurs when a party does not observe a contract in which the cost of observance would exceed the penalty for breach. A question of ethics arises, for example, when homeowners who owe more on a mortgage than a house is worth walk away and return the house to the bank. On the one hand, the homeowner has signed a loan agreement to repay the full amount of the loan, and, on the other, the contract signed provides only for repossession as the penalty for nonpayment.

These three features of contracts—being implicit and incomplete and lacking remedies—give rise to many situations in which the ethical course of action is unclear and disputable. One possible guide in such cases is to try to determine what more explicit and complete contracts the parties might have agreed to before the situation arose. To use this guide is to ask what is the fairest resolution for both parties.

FRAUD.   Fraud is one of the most common violations of business ethics, and the many fraud statutes on the books provide a powerful arsenal of legal tools to prosecute people for a wide variety of misdeeds. Consequently, it is essential for business people to understand what actions constitute fraud. A few incautious remarks have led to costly legal judgments and fines and even to years of imprisonment for not a few executives, and some companies have been seriously damaged and even bankrupted by fraudulent schemes.

Fraud is commonly defined as *a material misrepresentation that is made with an intent to deceive and that causes harm to a party who reasonably relies on it.* This definition contains five elements: (1) the making of a false statement or the *misrepresentation* of some fact; (2) *materiality*, which means that the fact in question has some important bearing on the business decision at hand; (3) an *intent to deceive*, which is a state of mind in which the speaker knows that the statement is false and desires that the hearer believe it and act accordingly; (4) *reliance*, by which the hearer believes the statement and relies on it in making a decision; and (5) *harm*, which is to say that the decision made by the hearer on the basis of the misrepresentation leads to some loss for that person. The first three conditions bear on whether the speaker has acted wrongly, while the last two are relevant to whether the hearer has been wronged and deserves some compensation.

The simplicity of this definition is deceptive because each of the five elements hides a host of subtle pitfalls for the unwary. For starters, a misrepresentation need not be spoken or written but may be implied by word or deed, as when, for example, a used car dealer resets an odometer, which is a clear case of consumer fraud. Partial statements and omissions may constitute fraud when they are misleading within the context provided. Thus, the used car dealer who fails to disclose certain faults or presents them in a way that minimizes their seriousness may be guilty of fraud. Saying nothing, which avoids the risk that a partial statement is misleading, may still constitute fraud if one has a duty to disclose. Such a duty may be the result of one's position or the nature of the facts. Thus, a real estate agent has a duty, as an agent, to inform a buyer of certain facts about a home sale, and the seller generally has a duty to disclose certain hidden faults, such as termite damage.

Generally, opinions, predictions, and negotiating positions do not constitute facts that can be misrepresented. It is not usually considered material in negotiation to conceal or even lie about the amount one is willing to accept or pay, which is known as one's reservation price. Certain amounts of bluffing and exaggeration in negotiation are usually permissible, also on the grounds that the harm is not material. However, one's intentions—such as making a promise that might not be kept—are commonly regarded as facts about a speaker's state of mind so that the misrepresentation of such matters may constitute fraud.

Although intent, being a mental state, is difficult to ascertain, the fact that a person knows the true state of affairs is usually sufficient to establish it. More difficult are cases of willful ignorance, where a seller of a house, for example, declines to engage a termite inspector to check suspicious deposits of sawdust in the basement, so he can truthfully tell a buyer, "I don't know," when asked about any termites. Finally, it is often difficult to know whether a party to a transaction actually relied on a misrepresentation in making a decision or did so reasonably. Thus, a seller's deceptive claim to be ignorant of termite damage may have played no role in the buyer's decision. And even if it did, should the buyer have engaged his or her own termite inspector instead of relying (perhaps unreasonably) on the seller's vague denial? Generally, in negotiation, it is unwise to act solely on the other party's words, and market participants have some obligation to determine the facts themselves.

Wrongful Harms

Although buyers and sellers in market exchanges have no duty to consider the other party's interest, they still have the obligations of basic morality toward each other and deserve compensation when they suffer some loss when the other party acts in violation of some obligation. For example, a manufacturer has an obligation beyond any warranty extended (which is a kind of contract) to exercise due care and avoid negligence in producing goods, so that a buyer of the product who is injured has some claim for compensation. In law, this claim is based not on contract law but on tort law, which is the law of wrongful harms. Although wrongful harms can occur in the course of a market transaction—buying the product, in this case—they occur in many instances that do not involve markets at all. Thus, a company might be sued for a defective product not only by the injured buyer but also by anyone who suffers an injury from a defective product. The ethics involved in wrongful harms overlaps with but is much more extensive than merely market ethics.

Market participants give their voluntary consent to a transaction, and in general, consent is an excusing condition when harm is inflicted. That is, the buyer of a stock that declines in value may lose in a transaction, but he or she believed at the time of the purchase that the stock was a good value and was aware of the possibility of loss. Such a person has only himself or herself to blame for the loss. The seller can say, "I am not to blame; it's your own fault." On the other hand, the buyer of a defective product consents to the purchase but not to the possibility of injury. Similarly, the victims of a stock fraud, such as the Ponzi scheme perpetrated by Bernard Madoff, cannot be said to have consented to their losses. The ethical transgressions in both cases do not lie in the market transactions themselves but in the wrongs that accompany them, namely, the negligence of the manufacturer and the fraud of Mr. Madoff.

The wrongs in wrongful harms are many and varied and constitute much of business ethics and the whole of tort law. On the side of the violators, these wrongs involve a failure to fulfill a duty, often the duty of *due care*, or involve its opposite, the commission of *negligence*. That is, manufacturers have a duty to exercise due care and not be negligent in the products they market to consumers, in the working conditions they provide for employees, in their environmental impacts they have on communities, and so on. Generally, due care and negligence apply to unintentional harms, but companies also have a duty to avoid intentional harms that result not from negligence but from deliberate or purposeful actions. On the side of victims, wrongful harms typically involve a violation of *rights*. Thus, consumers have a right to safe products; employees have a right to a safe and healthy workplace; everyone has privacy rights, property rights, a right not to be discriminated against, and so on. The violations of these rights—whether they are due to negligence or intentional actions, or are committed in markets transactions or not—are wrongful harms.

Market Failures

The virtues of the market system, including its efficiency and Adam Smith's "invisible hand" argument, occur only under certain ideal conditions and not necessarily in the real world where we live. Some departures from these ideal conditions are serious enough to be described by economists as market failures. Indeed, much of business ethics involves questions about how to respond to such failures.[6]

CAUSES OF MARKET FAILURES. Markets fail for four main kinds of reasons, which may be grouped under the headings of perfect competition, perfect rationality, externalities, and collective choice.

First, the argument that free markets are efficient presupposes *perfect competition*. This condition is satisfied when there are many buyers and sellers who are free to enter or leave the market at will and a large supply of relatively homogeneous products that buyers will readily substitute one for another. In addition, each buyer and seller must have full knowledge of the goods and services available, including prices. In a market with these features, no firm is able to charge more than its competitors, because customers will purchase the competitors' products instead. Also, in the long run, the profit in one industry can be no higher than that in any other, because newcomers will enter the field and offer products at lower prices until the rate of profit is reduced to a common level.

Competition in actual markets is always imperfect to some degree. One reason is the existence of monopolies and oligopolies, in which one or a few firms dominate a market and exert an undue influence on prices. Competition is also reduced when there are barriers to market entry (as in pharmaceuticals that require costly research), when products are strongly differentiated (think of the iPhone, which many people strongly prefer despite similar alternatives), when some firms have information that others lack (about new manufacturing processes, for example), and when consumers lack important information. Competition is also reduced by *transaction costs*, that is, the expense required for buyers and sellers to find each other and come to an agreement.

Second, the argument that free markets are efficient makes certain assumptions about human behavior. It assumes, in particular, that the individuals who engage in economic activity are fully rational and act to maximize their own utility.[7] This construct, commonly called *Homo economicus* or *economic man*, is faulty for at least two reasons. One is that people often lack the ability to gather and process the necessary information to act effectively in their own interests. Economic actors have what is described as *bounded rationality*. The other reason is that human motivation is much more complex than the simple view of economic theory. People often give money to the poor or return a lost wallet, for example, with no expectation of gain. Altruism and moral commitment play a prominent role in our economic life, along with self-interest, and yet economic theory gives them scant regard.[8]

Also, firms do not always act in the ways predicted by economic theory. To compensate for people's bounded rationality, business organizations develop rules and procedures for decision making that substitute for the direct pursuit of profit. Firms also do not necessarily seek optimal outcomes, as economists assume, but, in the view of some organizational theorists, they settle for merely adequate solutions to pressing problems through a process known as *satisficing*. The immediate aim of firms, according to these theorists, is to achieve an *internal* efficiency, which is to say, the well-being of the firm, rather than *external* efficiency in the marketplace.[9]

Third, the efficiency argument assumes that there are no spillover effects or *externalities*, which is to say that all costs of production are reflected in the prices of goods and services and are not passed on to others. An externality is present when the manufacturer of a product is permitted to pollute a stream, for example, thereby imposing a cost on businesses downstream. Other examples of externalities in present-day markets include inefficient use of natural resources (automobile drivers do not pay the full cost of the gasoline they use and hence overconsume it), occupational injuries (which may result when employers underinvest in safety when not they but their employees bear the cost), and accidents from defective products (where consumers, like injured employees, bear the preponderance of the cost).

The task of dealing with externalities falls mainly to governments, which have many means at their disposal.[10] Polluters can be forced to internalize the costs of production, for example, by regulations that prohibit certain polluting activities (the use of soft coal, for example), set standards for pollution emissions, create tax incentives for installing pollution-control devices, and so on. Some free-market theorists have proposed solutions to the problem of externalities that make use of market mechanisms. Allowing firms that pollute less than the law allows to "sell" the difference to others as a "right to pollute" is one example.

The fourth objection to the efficiency argument concerns the problem of *collective choice*.[11] In a market system, choices that must be made for a whole society—a transportation policy, for example—are made by aggregating a large number of individual choices. Instead of leaving to a central planner a decision about whether to build more roads or more airports, we allow individuals to decide for themselves whether to drive a car or to take an airplane to their destination, and through a multitude of such individual decisions, we arrive at a collective choice. The underlying assumption is that if each individual makes rational choices—that is, choices that maximize his or her own welfare—then the collective choice that results will also be rational and maximize the welfare of society as a whole.

PUBLIC GOODS AND THE PRISONER'S DILEMMA.   The validity of the assumption about collective choice is open to question, most notably, in the case of *public goods*. A market economy has a well-known bias in favor of private over public consumption, that is, the production of goods that can be owned and used by one person as opposed to goods that can be enjoyed by all. Automobiles are an example of a private good. Roads, by contrast, are a public good in that their use by one person does not exclude their use by others. As a result of this bias in favor of private consumption, people spend large sums on their own cars but little to build and maintain a system of roads. Public parks, a free education system, public health programs, and police and fire protection are all examples of public goods that are relatively underfunded in an otherwise affluent society.[12]

The reason for this bias is simple: There is little profit in public goods. Because they cannot be packaged and sold like toothpaste, there is no easy way to charge for them. And although some people are willing to pay for the pleasure of a public park, for example, others, who cannot be excluded from enjoying the park as well, will be *free riders*; that is, they will take advantage of the opportunity to use a public good without paying for it. Indeed, if we assume a world of rational economic agents who always act in their own interest, then everyone would be a free

Prisoner B

		Confess	Not Confess
Prisoner A	Confess	A: 5 Years B: 5 Years	A: 0 Years B: 20 Years
	Not Confess	A: 20 Years B: 0 Years	A: 1 Year B: 1 Year

FIGURE 2.1 Prisoner's Dilemma

rider, given the chance. To act otherwise would be irrational.[13] Consequently, public goods are ignored by the market and are typically left for governments to provide, if they are provided at all.

The assumption that rational individual choices always result in rational collective choices is also brought into question by the *prisoner's dilemma*.[14] Suppose that two guilty suspects have been apprehended by the police and placed in separate cells where they cannot communicate. Unfortunately, the police have only enough evidence to convict them both on a minor charge. If neither one confesses, therefore, they will receive a light sentence of one year each. The police offer each prisoner the opportunity of going free if he confesses and the other does not. The evidence provided by the suspect who confesses will then enable the police to convict the other suspect of a charge carrying a sentence of 20 years. If they both confess, however, they will each receive a sentence of five years. A matrix of the four possible outcomes is represented in Figure 2.1.

Obviously, the best possible outcome—one year for each prisoner—is obtained when both do not confess. Neither one can afford to seek this outcome by not confessing, however, because one faces a 20-year sentence if the other does not act in the same way. Confessing, with the prospect of five years in prison or going scot-free, is clearly the preferable alternative. The rational choice for both prisoners, therefore, is to confess. But by doing so, they end up with the second-best outcome and are unable to reach the optimal solution to their problem.

The dilemma in this case would not be solved merely by allowing the prisoners to communicate, because the rational strategy for each prisoner in that case would be to agree not to confess and then turn around and break the agreement by confessing. The prisoner's dilemma is thus like the free-rider problem discussed earlier. If each prisoner has the opportunity to take advantage of the other's cooperation without paying a price, then it is rational to do so.[15] The true lesson of the prisoner's dilemma is that to reach the best possible outcome, each must be assured of the other's cooperation. The prisoner's dilemma is thus an assurance problem.[16] It shows that a rational collective choice can be made under certain circumstances only if each person in a system of cooperative behavior can be convinced that others will act in the same way.

The prisoner's dilemma is not an idle intellectual puzzle. Many real-life situations involve elements of this problem.[17] Consider the following example. The factories located around a lake are polluting the water at such a rate that within a few years none of them will be able to use the water and they will all be forced to shut down or relocate. The optimal solution would be for each factory to install a water-purification system or take other steps to reduce the amount of pollution. It would not be rational for any one factory or even a few to make the investment required, however, because the improvement in the quality of the water would be minimal and their investment wasted. Without assurance that all will bear the expense of limiting the amount of pollution, each factory will continue to pollute the lake and everyone will lose in the end. The most rational decision for each factory individually will thus result in a disastrous collective decision.

The usual solution to prisoner's dilemma cases—along with those involving externalities and public goods—is government action. By ordering all the factories around the lake to reduce the amount of pollution and backing up that order with force, a government can assure each factory owner that the others will bear their share of the burden. As a result, they could achieve an end that they all desire but could not seek without this assurance. Regulation of this kind is not necessarily incompatible with the operation of a free market. Thomas C. Schelling points out that voluntarism versus coercion is a false dichotomy because coercion can enable firms to do what they want to do but could not do voluntarily.[18] Firms are not always averse to internalizing costs and providing public goods, Schelling observes, as long as they are not penalized more than their competitors.[19] This condition can also be secured by government regulation. Another solution for prisoner's dilemma cases is the availability of trustworthy partners and an ability to identify them. If the prisoners in the dilemma situation were trustworthy and their trustworthiness known to each other, then they could confidently not confess and reach the optimal solution. Similarly, the factory owners around the lake could dispense with government regulation if they were all known for their trustworthy character.

Market Outcomes

Although markets operate, in theory, to make each participant better off and thereby to increase the welfare of all, they also result in distributions of income and wealth that may be criticized on moral grounds. In particular, market transactions function as a means for distributing goods and services, and in so doing, they may produce much greater gains for some parties than for others, so as to increase inequality in society. Thus, a skillful trader, such as Warren Buffett, may parlay a string of successful trades into great wealth, while another trader, through misjudgment or misfortune, may lose everything. How people fare in markets may depend not only on skill or luck but also their inborn abilities and circumstances of birth, over which they have no control. Market returns are also a function of the amount of risk taken. Thus, an entrepreneur like Bill Gates who bets everything on a single idea stands to reap a fortune or endure failure. Some moral philosophers, such as Robert Nozick (who is considered in the next chapter), argue that market outcomes are just, no matter how unequal they may be, merely because they result from voluntary transactions. Others, such as John Rawls (who is also discussed in Chapter 3), hold that market outcomes may need to be altered when they lead to unjust levels of inequality. In any event, the moral justification of markets must address the question of the justness of market outcomes.

Summary

This section shows that much of business ethics is market ethics. This is true not only because much of business is conducted in markets but also because of the importance of imperfect markets and market outcomes for business ethics. In perfect markets there is little if any need for ethics or morality; we would conduct our affairs harmoniously by voluntary, mutually advantageous cooperation. Much of ethics in business is necessary, therefore, to address problems in *im*perfect markets. These problems include instances of not abiding by agreements (breaches), making false statements (fraud), failures to observe duties and violations of rights (torts), market failures, and market outcomes. In law, the problems breach of contract, fraud, and torts are addressed by contract law and the law of fraud and torts, respectively, and market failures and market outcomes are appropriate subjects for government regulation and legislation, including antitrust law, consumer law, employment law, securities law, environmental law, taxation, and the like.

ROLES, RELATIONSHIPS, AND FIRMS

Insofar as business activity takes place in a market, it involves mainly discrete *transactions*, in which each person pursues his or her own self-interest and is bound only by the ethics of the marketplace. However, business is more than market activity or transactions; it also consists of *roles* that people assume and *relationships* that they build. These roles and relationship evolve out of markets in that people agree *in market transactions* to assume certain roles and enter into certain relationships. Once these roles and relationships are created, though, they give rise to certain moral duties or obligations and to certain rights that are also a part of business ethics. Like the market ethics of transactions, the ethics of roles and relationships are voluntarily entered into for mutual advantage, but many of these roles and relationships preclude us from acting solely in our own interest. Indeed, many of them explicitly commit us to acting in the interests of others, thereby forgoing or subordinating our own interests.

The moral importance of roles and relationships is well recognized in the professional ethics of, say, physicians and attorneys, who, before assuming these roles, are bound only by market ethics and the common morality of our society. In particular, they have no duty or obligation to serve other people's interests. Once they assume these roles and build relationships, though, by accepting others as patients or clients, they are pledged to forgo their self-interest and act solely in the interest of these other persons. They enter into these roles and relationships voluntarily, of course, and they are compensated for doing so. However, they now occupy a different moral space: Their actions are now bound by the professional ethics of physicians and attorneys, respectively. Some business people are also professionals—these include accountants, engineers, and others with specialized training—and they, too, are committed to the ethics of their professions. The two most important roles and relationships in business, however, are those of *agent* and *fiduciary.* Like professional roles and relationships, these are entered into voluntarily in market transactions, but by agreeing to become an agent or a fiduciary, a person takes himself or herself out of a market and enters a new moral space in which one is pledged to serve the interests of others and to be bound by the ethics of that role or relationship.

Agents and Principals

An *agent* is a party who has been engaged to act on behalf of another, called the *principal,* and the relationship between the two is called an *agency relationship*. Agency relationships are ubiquitous in business and everyday life because of the need to engage other people's skills and knowledge and to allow them exercise judgment and discretion on our behalf.

To illustrate: In some instances, such as plumbing repairs, we simply hire a worker to perform a specified job, just as a firm engages contractors or suppliers in a market. In other situations, though, it is necessary for a service provider to employ skills and knowledge and to exercise judgment and discretion in acting on our behalf. We cannot ask a physician or an attorney, for example, to perform a particular job at our direction like a plumber; we must ask them to use their skills and knowledge on our behalf without close direction and to act as we would ourselves if only we had their expertise. Another example of an agency relationship occurs in real estate where selling a house requires considerable knowledge and skill, as well as time. Consequently, a seller may engage a real estate agent to act on the seller's behalf, doing what the seller (who is now a principal) would do if that person had the real-estate agent's knowledge and skills. An agent thus becomes an extension of the principal, acting in the principal's place, with a duty to use his or her abilities and expertise solely for the principal's benefit.

Business firms have need of many specialized services and thus engage numerous outside service providers as agents. Among such agents are law and accounting firms, banks and investment advisers, insurance agencies, advertising and public relations agencies, management consulting firms, human resource and compensation specialists, safety experts, and the like. The employees of these outside firms have agency duties to their clients. Inside a firm, employees are a major group of agents, especially those employees whose job is not merely to perform a specific task, like assembly line workers, but to exercise judgment and discretion over matters where they know, perhaps better than their employer-principal, how a job is to be performed. Employees are also agents in matters where they can legally bind their employer or can expose the employer to legal liability. Thus, a purchasing agent who can sign a contract that legally commits a company to a purchase or a truck driver whose accidents can lead to lawsuits for injuries are considered agents of their employer.

The main duties of agents are to work as directed, perform tasks with competence and care, and act in all matters within the sphere of their role in the interest of the principal. More specifically, an agent has a duty to act only within the scope of his or her authority and not to exceed it; to avoid conflicts of interest that interfere with an ability to act in the employer's interest; and to preserve the confidentiality of information. Both conflict of interest and confidentiality are important areas of business ethics that are considered at length in Chapter 5.

Fiduciaries and Professionals

In law, all agents are fiduciaries, though not all fiduciaries are agents who are pledged to serve the interest of a principal and empowered to act on that party's behalf. The defining characteristics of a fiduciary are thus different from those of an agent. Although agency relations in business are ubiquitous, nonagent fiduciaries are less common but still very important roles in business. Being a professional is also a carefully defined role that applies to only a few but important business occupations.

FIDUCIARIES.   A *fiduciary* is a person who has been entrusted with the care of another's property or assets and who has a responsibility to exercise discretionary judgment in this capacity solely in this other person's interest. Common examples of fiduciaries are trustees, guardians, executors, and, in business, officers and directors of corporations, who have a fiduciary duty to the corporation and its shareholders. Partners in a business venture are fiduciaries for each other, and banks and investment firms are fiduciaries for their depositors and clients. Fiduciaries provide a valuable service for individuals who are unable for some reason to manage their own property or assets. A fiduciary is one part of a *fiduciary relationship*, in which the other party is the beneficiary of the fiduciary's service.

A *fiduciary duty* may be defined as the duty of a person in a position of trust to act solely in the interest of the beneficiary, without gaining any material benefit except with the knowledge and consent of this person. A fiduciary relationship has two elements: *trust* and *confidence*. Something is entrusted to the care of a person with the confidence that proper care will be taken. Broadly, the duty of a fiduciary is to act in the interest of the beneficiary. This duty, which requires the subordination of self-interest, contrasts with market conduct, in which everyone is assumed to act out of self-interest. As Justice Benjamin Cardozo famously observed, "Many forms of conduct permissible in a workaday world for those acting at arm's length, are forbidden to those bound by fiduciary ties. A trustee is held to something stricter than the morals of the market place. Not honesty alone, but the punctilio of an honor the most sensitive, is the standard of behavior."[20]

The main elements of fiduciary duty are candor, care, and loyalty.

1. *Candor.* A fiduciary has a duty of candor to disclose all information that the beneficiary would consider relevant to the relationship. Thus, it would be a violation of a fiduciary duty for an attorney or an investment banker to conceal important information from a client. Similarly, the director of a company would fail in a fiduciary duty by remaining silent about matters that are critical to a decision under discussion.

2. *Care.* When property or assets are entrusted to a fiduciary—the trustee of a trust, for example—that person should manage what is entrusted with due care, which is the care that a reasonable, prudent person would exercise. It might be a breach of fiduciary duty, for example, for a trustee to invest trust assets in high-risk securities.

3. *Loyalty.* A duty of loyalty requires a fiduciary to act in the interest of the beneficiary and to avoid taking any personal advantage of the relationship. In general, acting in the interest of a beneficiary is acting as the beneficiary would if that person had the knowledge and skills of the fiduciary. Taking personal advantage, by contrast, is deriving any benefit from the relationship without the knowledge and consent of the beneficiary.

PROFESSIONALS.   The conduct of physicians, lawyers, engineers, and other professionals is governed by special professional ethics. Which occupations are professions is subject to dispute, but the three commonly accepted defining features of a profession are as follows:

1. A specialized body of knowledge. Professionals do not merely have valuable skills, like those of a plumber, but possess a highly developed, technical body of knowledge that requires years of training to acquire.

2. A high degree of organization and self-regulation. Professionals have considerable control over their own work, and, largely through professional organizations, they are able to set standards for practice and to discipline members who violate them.

3. A commitment to public service. The knowledge possessed by professionals serves some important social need, and professionals are committed to using their knowledge for the benefit of all.

These three features are closely related and mutually reinforcing. It is because professionals possess a specialized body of knowledge that they are given a high degree of control over their work. For the same reason, we leave it to professionals to determine what persons need to know to enter a profession and whether they know it. There is a danger in giving so much independence and power to professionals, but we have little choice if we are to enjoy the benefit of their valuable specialized knowledge. Consequently, professionals enter into an implicit agreement with society: In return for being granted a high degree of control over their work and the opportunity to organize as a profession, they pledge that they will use their knowledge for the benefit of all. Without this guarantee, society would not long tolerate a group with such independent power.

The standards of a profession include both technical standards of competence and ethical standards. Ethical standards are generally presented in a code of professional ethics, which is not only a mechanism for the self-regulation of a profession but also a visible sign of the profession's commitment to public service. A code of ethics is not an option for a professional but something that is required by the nature of professionalism itself. Developing a code of ethics is often the first step taken by an occupational group that is seeking recognition as a profession.

Firms

Business is conducted not only in markets but also in firms. Thus, markets and firms—or business organizations or corporations—are two basic spheres of business activity to which ethics applies. The focus of this chapter so far has been on markets, although firms have also been considered as market actors. The question arises, therefore, whether firms should be understood merely as market actors for which market ethics is sufficient or whether there is also an ethics for firms and their activities. In brief, what attention must business ethics give to the fact that much business activity takes place in firms, as well as in markets?

THE ECONOMIC VIEW. Standard economic theory has viewed the firm as a market actor like an individual, making decisions with a view to seeking maximum profits. The firm itself has traditionally been considered to be a "black box," whose internal workings are irrelevant to economics. The result has been a neglect of any moral issues that arise from the existence of firms as distinct entities. Individuals may act rightly or wrongly, virtuously or not, but the firm itself is merely a market actor that raises no ethical issues beyond those of individuals acting in a market. This view has been replaced in recent decades, however, with an understanding of the firm as a combination of markets and relationships.

The starting point of this new economic view is a 1937 article by the Nobel Prize–winning economist Ronald Coase, "The Nature of the Firm," in which he asked why all economic activity does not takes place in a market?[21] That is, why do firms exist at all? His answer was that some economic activity is more efficiently organized in hierarchical relationships rather than in markets. Thus, according to Coase, there are two fundamental ways of organizing economic production: in markets and in firms, using transactions and relationships, respectively. In a market, all activity is conducted by voluntary, mutually advantageous transactions. In a hierarchical firm, people submit to authority relationships and agree to work in cooperation with or at the direction of others.

Much of the activity of a firm with outside parties—both individuals and other firms—is conducted in arm's-length market transactions, which fall in the domain of market ethics. These other parties include suppliers in commodities markets, consumers in products markets, workers in labor markets, investors in financial markets, and so on. Indeed, much of a firm's activities consist of market transactions or contracts, and the inside of a firm has many elements of a market system. For example, employees may be aware of their other employment opportunities and may leave if another employer offers higher pay. However, employees also become agents of the employer and assume the duties of an agent while they are employed. Some members of a firm, including the chief officers and board directors, are also fiduciaries with the standard fiduciary duties. To the extent that employees or other individuals or groups enter into these relationships, they take themselves out of a market and become organized in systems of roles and relationships.

The outcome of the economic view of the firm, then, is that business ethics consists of both the ethics of transactions in a market and the ethics of roles and relationships in a firm. And these two ethics apply to both individuals and firms. Like individuals, firms in markets have the market ethics obligations to observe all agreements or contracts, avoid force and fraud, not inflict wrongful harms, and act responsibly in cases of market failures. Business firms can also be agents and fiduciaries, and in these roles and relationships, they have duties similar to individuals.

THE SOCIOLOGICAL VIEW. Whereas economists speak of *firms*, sociologists prefer the term *organization* as the unit of analysis. This term stresses the similarity of business corporations with other, nonbusiness organizations in which human beings associate for some end. All organizations are characterized by a common purpose or goal, a structure of roles and relationships, and some decision-making processes. Viewed as an organization, the firm is a kind of community with all the needs for morality that arise in such organized human groups.

This expanded view of the business firm incorporates most of the economic view and adds other elements. Chief among these elements is the existence of distinctive *organizational ethical climates*, which embody certain values, beliefs, assumptions, perceptions, and expectations.[22] The ethical climate of an organization can profoundly influence how members identify moral issues, make moral judgments, arrive at decisions, and ultimately act. Organizations with a good ethical climate can foster exemplary moral conduct, while organizations that lack one can socialize otherwise good people into wrongdoers.[23] A task for the leaders of organizations is to determine the desired ethical climate and to create and sustain it. Members of an organization must understand the organizational ethical climates that they encounter, including the climates' positive and possibly negative impacts.

A second element introduced by the sociological view is *organizational justice*. In organizations, decisions are made that impact individuals and groups in different ways, benefiting some and harming others, and it is critical for smooth organizational functioning that these decisions be accepted as just.[24] People in organizations have a strong sense of fair treatment, of "how things should be," and they react quickly when they believe they are being treated unfairly. Much of the concern with organizational justice revolves around the rules and policies of organization, both written and unwritten. Managers must ensure, therefore, that an organization's rules and policies are perceived as just, in both their formulation and implementation.

Organizational harms constitute a third element that raises ethical issues on the sociological view. Many of the wrongs that are committed by business are attributable to the whole organization rather than the actions of a few identifiable individuals. They often result from a sequence of decisions that may be made without a full understanding of their consequences. Indeed, it is often difficult to identify any specific individuals who caused a company to produce, say, a defective product or an industrial accident. As one writer observes, "[T]he harm may seem to be an organizational product that bears no clear stamp of any individual actor."[25] It is not sufficient, therefore, for individuals in organizations to attend only to their own ethics and strive to be ethical themselves; it is necessary, as well, to appreciate the powerful forces that cause individuals to participate in organizational wrongdoing and to develop procedures and systems that prevent organizational harms.

Summary

Business ethics, understood as the ethical rules and principles that apply to business conduct, may be divided into two ethics: the ethics of the market and the ethics of roles and relationships. In the absence of any roles or relationships, including those in firms, individuals and firms relate to each other as market actors who are bound only by the ethics governing market transactions. Although this market ethics is extensive, it does not include a requirement that market actors consider any interests but their own. The justification for this market ethics is due primarily to the fact that the two parties in a market transaction reach a mutually beneficial agreement and give their consent to it. Much of the need for ethics in markets, as well as for regulation, occurs when markets are imperfect because of market failures or when market outcomes are unfair.

Although market actors typically have no obligation to consider the interests of others, such an obligation may nevertheless arise through the market itself when individuals and firms agree to assume certain roles or to enter into certain relationships. Such roles and relationships are ubiquitous in business, and the obligations that attend these roles and relationships, including activity conducted in firms, constitute much of business ethics. The exact content of these role and relationship obligations are determined by the agreements or contracts that create them. For example, employers and employees are free to contract on various terms, so the obligations that each has toward the other depend, in part, on the specifics of the contracts themselves (although some obligations in the employer–employee relationship, such as to provide a safe and healthy workplace, are due to market ethics). Thus, an employer may have no obligation to offer a pension plan, but when one is offered, the employer (voluntarily) assumes, by contract, the obligations of a fiduciary. The justification for these role and relationship obligations and their specific terms derives, like the justification of market transactions, from the voluntary consent that creates them.

Finally, business firms are constituted by myriad roles and relationships that involve a complex set of obligations. Many of these obligations are those of market ethics, while others arise from specific roles and relationships. Because firms are community-like organizations to which people devote much of their life and on which their livelihood depends, managers must attend to the organizational ethical climate, to justice within the organization, and to the possible organizational harms that could be produced.

ETHICAL REASONING

Understanding business ethics as the ethics of market transactions and the ethics of roles and relationships provides some useful guidance for decision makers. For starters, anyone in business should begin by asking whether one is dealing with other parties purely as market actors or whether one is in a particular role or relationship. Many of the rules and principles of market ethics and of the ethics of roles and relationships are clearly defined: One should keep all agreements and avoid fraud, for example, and employees should be loyal agents for their employer. In many situations, however, the precise contours of one's duties or obligations are far from clear and require moral reflection. For example, one may be uncertain whether the failure to disclose certain information constitutes fraud or whether a certain disclosure is a violation of an agent's duty. The duty of an agent to preserve confidentiality might have an exception for whistle-blowing to protect others, or this duty might be outweighed by a more stringent duty to blow the whistle. Such moral uncertainty requires business people to engage in ethical reasoning to determine what ought to be done or what is the right thing to do.

Ethical reasoning varies in level from the ordinary moral deliberation that everyone engages in before acting to the very sophisticated moral arguments that draw heavily on ethical theory. Complex moral controversies over such ethical issues as privacy, discrimination, worker health and safety, and international labor standards require a deep understanding of the relevant facts in addition to the relevant ethical principles. Examples of ethical reasoning are provided by the extensive studies that governmental and nongovernmental bodies engage in before making recommendations on important matters. Any recommendations made by such bodies are only as strong as the arguments supporting them. Some of the most difficult moral controversies are those in which competing or conflicting ethical considerations are involved. For example, affirmative action designed to correct past discrimination is alleged by its opponents to be itself a form of discrimination. And foreign sweatshops may involve exploitation of workers but are, at the same time, a significant resource for development. Finally, ethical reasoning must be reconciled with powerful business imperatives. If the ethical course of action involves significant costs that reduce profits, for example, then the arguments for it need to be very compelling.

What Is Ethical Reasoning?

Ethical reasoning can be understood both as an intellectual procedure for justifying ethical judgments and as a psychological process whereby people actually form ethical judgments. For an account of the former concept of ethical reasoning we need to turn to philosophy; for the latter, psychology provides an explanation.

A PHILOSOPHICAL ACCOUNT OF ETHICAL REASONING.   What does it mean for a person to engage in ethical reasoning? One philosophical account is that engaging in ethical reasoning means taking the *moral point of view*. This point of view has two important features.[26] First is a willingness to *seek out and act on reasons*. The best action, according to one writer, is "the course of action which is supported by the best reasons."[27] This does not get us very far without some account of what are the best reasons (which is the task of ethical theory), but it indicates a commitment to use reason in deliberating about what to do and to construct moral arguments that are persuasive to ourselves and others. Moral rules should not be accepted merely because they are a part of the prevailing morality. Rather, we should attempt to justify the rules we act on by means of the most general and comprehensive kinds of reasons available. These reasons are typically abstract ethical principles that employ such concepts as rights, justice, and ultimate goods.

Second, the moral point of view requires us to be *impartial*. We must regard the interests of everyone, including ourselves, as equally worthy of consideration and give all interests equal weight in deciding what to do. The moral point of view is the opposite of being purely self-interested. The idea of a personal morality—that is, a morality to be followed only by ourselves—is absurd. Morality by its very nature is public, in the sense that it involves a shared set of rules that can be observed by everyone.[28] A good test of the moral point of view is whether we would feel comfortable if our colleagues, friends, and family were to know about a decision we had made. Would we be willing to have an article on it appear on the front page of the local newspaper, for example? A decision made from the moral point of view can withstand and even invites this kind of openness and scrutiny.

A PSYCHOLOGICAL ACCOUNT OF ETHICAL REASONING.   The psychologist Lawrence Kohlberg has proposed the theory that people develop the cognitive ability to engage in moral reasoning through a series of stages from infancy to adulthood.[29] At each stage, an individual is motivated to be moral and perceives morality in distinct ways, as represented in Exhibit 2.1. At the lowest or "pre-conventional" level, which occurs in infancy, individuals are concerned only with the avoidance of punishment (stage 1) and the pursuit of their own welfare (stage 2). At the second level of "conventional morality," children seek to conform to the expectation of others (stage 3) and understand the importance of rules and laws in enabling a stable social order (stage 4). Only on the highest level of "post-conventional" morality do fully formed adults develop the cognitive ability to understand morality as a social contract that facilitates cooperation (stage 5) and to engage in principled ethical reasoning in which abstract, universal moral principles, such as rights and justice, are recognized as the basis of morality (stage 6).

On Kohlberg's psychological account, the aim of cognitive development should be to advance to successively higher levels, which also represent morally superior modes of ethical reasoning.[30]

Level 1	**Stage 1: Obedience and Punishment Orientation**
Pre-Conventional	Motivation: What's going to happen to me?
Morality	Perspective: Recognizes only self and own interests.
	Stage 2: Self-Interest Orientation
	Motivation: What's in it for me?
	Perspective: Sees that others have interests that can be manipulated for own benefit.
Level 2	**Stage 3: Good Interpersonal Relations**
Conventional Morality	Motivation: Conformity to the expectations of others.
	Perspective: Respects the interests of others.
	Stage 4: Authority and Social Order Orientation
	Motivation: Conformity to requirements of living in society.
	Perspective: Recognizes importance of system for social order.
Level 3	**Stage 5: Social Contract and Individual Rights Orientation**
Post-Conventional Morality	Motivation: To satisfy self-interest by cooperating with others.
	Perspective: Recognizes that people have different interests that can be reconciled by mutually advantageous cooperation.
	Stage 6: Universal Principle Orientation
	Motivation: To live in a just society of free and equal persons.
	Perspective: Respects all people as free and equal, and recognizes abstract general moral principles as binding on all people.

EXHIBIT 2.1   Kohlberg's Six Stages of Moral Development

Indeed, level 3, which consists of stages 5 and 6, looks very much like the philosophers' account of the moral point of view. At this level, individuals engage in ethical reasoning that reflects an understanding of the ethical theories that are described in the next chapter. Although Kohlberg's stages are invariant in the sense that one must pass through them in the order outlined, there is no guarantee that everyone will continue to progress to the highest level. Indeed, Kohlberg claimed that most adults are at the conventional level and that fewer than 20 percent of adults develop to the level of principled ethical reasoning.

A Framework for Ethical Reasoning

No framework can be comprehensive enough to capture the full complexity and diversity of ethical reasoning. However, it is possible to formulate a few basic ethical principles that are commonly recognized by business people and are expressed in corporate codes of conduct.

Of course, a framework is of no use unless a person recognizes that a situation presents an ethical issue which requires some moral reflection. So an awareness of the ethical dimensions of a situation is a necessary precondition for the application of any framework. One factor that might make one aware of an ethical issue is a consideration of any *harm* that is done. What makes moral wrongdoing of any significance is that someone is usually made worse off. Not every action that harms another is wrong, but any harm should be investigated for possible wrongdoing. That is, anytime a person is harmed, we should stop to consider whether a moral wrong has occurred. Hence, a careful consideration of the consequences of any action helps increase moral awareness. For example, illegal copying of software might seem like a victimless crime, but a thorough search for consequences would reveal the harm done to software developers and legitimate users. The whole of society would be worse off without respect for intellectual property rights. Another factor that increases moral awareness is the language used to describe actions. Thus, to speak of *stealing* software or of software *piracy* makes us aware of the moral issues at stake.

Once we are aware that there may be a moral issue in a situation, the next task is to identify that issue. This task is facilitated by gathering and understanding all the relevant facts, including the full range of consequences. Following this step, the major task of ethical reasoning is to identify the relevant ethical concepts or principles. These may be grouped under seven headings.

1. *Welfare.* We often use the overall impact on people's welfare—"The greatest good for the greatest number"—as a justification for making social improvements, and we consider the alleviation of suffering (after a natural disaster, for example) to be a moral imperative. Although the promotion of welfare is a good, a person may have no duty or obligation to promote it in any given instance, and some harm may result without anyone being responsible for it. In general, inflicting harm becomes a moral matter only when some wrong is committed, which was described previously as a *wrongful harm*. Still, welfare is an important value in ethical reasoning: Welfare should be promoted, and any infliction of harm requires some moral justification. In business, the welfare principle requires that a manager take into account the impact that personnel decisions and policies have on employees, that products and services have on consumers, and that corporate activities have on communities. Although layoffs, for example, are sometimes unavoidable, they should be done in ways that minimize the human cost and enable employees to seek other employment. Manufacturers have an obligation to ensure that their products are reasonably free of defects that can cause serious injury or death. When companies engage in activities that harm communities—as when banks were charged with refusing loans in poor areas, a now-illegal practice known as "redlining"—they commit a moral wrong.

2. *Duty.* A duty or an obligation is a moral requirement to act in a certain way, something that we *ought* to do. Such a requirement may be one imposed on all persons, such as a duty to tell the truth or to keep promises. Many duties in business arise from agreements or contracts, which are kinds of promises, and from the assumption of specific roles and relationships, as is done by agents and fiduciaries (who have an agency and a fiduciary duty, respectively). Duties are especially associated with professionalism since professionals explicitly assume certain responsibilities that they have a duty to fulfill. A person who has a duty is expected to fulfill it without regard for his or her own interest, which means that a person with a duty, say a fiduciary, is expected to be diligent, to exercise care and loyalty, to not engage in self-dealing, and to avoid conflicts of interest that would interfere with the performance of a duty.

3. *Rights.* A right is an entitlement whereby a person is due certain treatment from others. Rights are often said to be correlated with duties such that if one person has a right, then another person has a duty to treat others in a certain way. In business, certain rights are generally recognized for employees, including the right to privacy, a right not be discriminated against, and a right to a safe and healthy workplace. Other rights are commonly accorded to consumers (consumer rights) and investors (the rights of bondholders and shareholders). One of the most important rights in business is property rights, which are basic to markets (since a transaction is a transfer of property rights) and important for profitability (without patent rights, for example, innovation would be discouraged). Rights are also closely related to the welfare principle inasmuch as many wrongful harms are wrong precisely because they involve the violation of some right. For example, a person may be harmed when refused a job, but a refusal to hire itself may not be a wrongful harm unless it involves a violation of a right, such as the right not to be discriminated against.

4. *Fairness.* Fairness or justice—which means, very roughly, equal treatment or different treatment according to some justified differences—is applied to a wide range of activities and practices in business. We speak of fairness in market exchanges (with regard to committing fraud, for example, taking unfair advantage of another or setting a fair price); of fair competition (which rules out monopolies, anticompetitive sales practices, and price-fixing); of fair labor practices (treating employees fairly in hiring and promotion, offering fair wages, allowing collective bargaining); of the fair sharing of burdens (not being a freeloader or a free-rider); and of fairness to creditors and investors (treating them fairly in bankruptcy, for example, or in matters of corporate governance). Fairness or justice is also closely related to rights inasmuch as unfair or unjust treatment often involves violating someone's rights. Thus, discrimination is unfair, but it is also a violation of rights. In this case, applications of the concepts of fairness and rights may be merely different ways of describing the same moral wrong.

5. *Honesty.* Although honesty may be regarded as a duty—a duty to tell the truth—it is important enough in business to be considered a basic ethical principle. As previously noted, markets require a certain amount of information, and fraud, which involves the misrepresentation of a material fact, is a prominent violation of market ethics. Furthermore, the business system requires an abundance of accurate and reliable information. This is especially true of financial information, which companies are required to disclose and which is subject to certified audits. Accounting fraud is a particularly serious breach of honesty that causes a great deal of harm. Honesty is a value that is lost when bribes are paid to public officials since such corrupting payments deprive countries of the honest services of their officials. Honesty is also an important element in developing the kind of trust, with employees, customers, and the public, that success in business requires. It is integral to a company's reputation.

6. *Dignity.* The concept of dignity expresses the fundamental ethical principle that all people deserve respect as human beings. All moral systems regard persons as autonomous moral agents who should be free to make their own decisions and pursue their aims in life. This view is expressed in Immanuel Kant's idea that everyone should be treated as ends in themselves and not as a means to be used solely for the benefit of others. Human dignity is denied when people are subject to violence, coercion, manipulation, degradation, or the risk of serious injury or death. Often, people's dignity is denied when their rights—especially fundamental human rights—are violated. The principle of dignity is most commonly employed in business in operations in less-developed countries where standards of acceptable business conduct may be lower or ineffectively enforced. In particular, environmental damage from mining and oil production and working conditions in garment factories have been criticized as violating a principle of dignity or respect for persons.

7. *Integrity.* Integrity is an elastic term that denotes a person of character or virtue who holds the right values and has the courage of his or her convictions.[31] According to Robert Solomon, "Integrity is not so much a virtue itself as it is a complex of virtues, the virtues working together to form a coherent character, an identifiable and trustworthy personality."[32] The concept is also widely adopted in business codes of conduct not only to describe an ideal for employees but also to characterize the company itself. Motorola, for example, has adopted the slogan "Uncompromising Integrity" as its guide for conduct worldwide. Lynn Paine also uses the term "integrity strategy" to describe a value-based form of internal control, which she calls "moral self-governance."[33] A person or an organization with integrity would be one that adheres to the other six ethical principles described here.

These seven principles of accepted business conduct express virtually the whole of business ethics. Their usefulness as a guide, though, is limited by the problem of interpretation or application. How one uses this framework in practice is critical. The main value of these principles lies in posing a set of questions that a person should ask when making a decision in a situation that raises ethical issues: Who is affected by any proposed course of action? Is anyone harmed, and if so, can the harm be justified? What is my duty in this situation? In particular, are there any special duties that belong to any role or relationship that I am in? Are anyone's rights being violated, and if so, can the violation be justified? Is any proposed course of action fair to all affected parties? Am I being entirely honest in my decision? Am I showing respect for all persons involved? Finally, is the decision one that would be made by a person of integrity?

In addition to these questions, there are others that can guide one in making the right decision by testing whether one has applied the seven principles correctly. Since the results of ethical reasoning must be defensible to others and not merely acceptable to oneself, a person might consider how the decision would appear to other parties, especially any ones adversely affected. This can be tested by how confident one feels that any decision could be defended in a public forum (the "sunshine test"), or by how willing one would be for a full account of one's actions to appear in a newspaper (the "newspaper test"), or by how one feels looking in a mirror (the "mirror test"), or by how one would like to be remembered (the "legacy test") and what one would want engraved on a tombstone (the "tombstone test").

CONCLUSION

Ethical decision making in business is often difficult and complex. Some situations are easily handled because what one ought to do or what is right and wrong are evident. Those situations that give us pause or produce moral anguish require careful thought and ultimately an ability to engage in ethical reasoning. This chapter contributes to an understanding of ethical decision making by offering a division of business ethics into two parts: an ethics of the market and an ethics of roles and relationships, including firms. In business, we deal with some parties purely as market actors who are on the other side of a market transaction or exchange. For such market activity, certain moral rules or standards apply. Much of business, however, involves roles and relationships and takes place in firms or organizations. These roles, relationships, and firms arise in a market, but, by mutual agreement in a market, we take ourselves out of the market and govern our actions by a different "ethics," the ethics of these roles and relationships.

When we attempt to think through the ethical issues that arise in business, we are engaging in ethical reasoning, which may be conducted on different levels. Ethical theories, which are presented in the next chapter, can guide ethical reasoning on the highest level by providing the most comprehensive and fundamental grounds for our moral beliefs and judgments. Fortunately, substantial moral arguments can be constructed that do not require an understanding of these theories. Most of our everyday ethical reasoning employs familiar ethical concepts and principles that can be readily understood and applied. Accordingly, this chapter provides a framework of seven basic ethical principles that are sufficient for most business decision making. For those who seek more, though, the next chapter provides a survey of the main philosophical theories of ethics.

CASE 2.2 ✳ Explore the Concept on mythinkinglab.com

Lavish Pay at Harvard

In 2004, Jack R. Meyer, the head of Harvard University's $20-billion endowment fund, was under pressure to change the compensation plan for the fund's top investment managers. The previous year, the top five managers of Harvard Management Company, who were university employees, received a total of $107.5 million. The two most successful managers earned more than $34 million each, while Mr. Meyer's own paycheck was $6.9 million.[34]

A few Harvard alumni protested. Seven members of the class of 1969 wrote a letter to the university president calling the bonuses "unwarranted, inappropriate and contrary to the values of the university." One signer of the letter explained, "Our collective concern is that we think the amounts of money being paid to these folks are by almost any measure obscene."[35] They added, "Harvard should use its endowment for the benefit of students, not for the benefit of people who manage the endowment."[36] The alumni suggested that the millions of dollars paid to fund managers should be used instead to reduce tuition. Angry threats were made to withhold gifts to the university unless the compensation was reduced. The letter said, "Unless the University limits payments to financial managers to appropriate levels . . . we see no reason why alumni should be asked for gifts."[37]

The compensation of the endowment fund managers far exceeded the salaries of Harvard faculty members and administrators, including the president, who made around half a million dollars. The 5-percent hike in tuition for Harvard students in 2004 was equal to the $70 million paid to the two highest earners. One critic noted, "The managers of the endowment took home enough money last year to send more than 4,000 students to Harvard for a year."[38]

Although Harvard has the largest university endowment, the salaries and bonuses paid to the managers greatly exceeded the compensation paid at any other school. The head of Yale's third-place endowment was slightly over $1 million in 2003.[39] However, Yale, like most universities, does not manage its investment fund in-house. When management of an endowment is outsourced, the managers are not university employees, and the fees paid to them, which may be as high or even higher than those at Harvard, do not need to be reported.

Mr. Meyer and his team of managers have produced consistently superior returns for the Harvard endowment. Over a period of 14 years, he increased the endowment from $4.7 billion to $22.6 billion. Over the previous 10 years, the Harvard fund had an average return of 16.1 percent, which is far above the 12.5 percent return of the 25 largest endowments.[40] If the fund had produced average returns during this period, the endowment would have been one-half of what it was in 2004, which is a difference of almost $9 billion. One person observed, "With results like that the alumni should be raising dough to put a statue of Jack Meyer in Harvard Yard, not taking potshots at him."[41] Mr. Meyer observed, "The letter [from members of the class of 1969] fails to recognize that there is a direct connection between bonuses and value added to Harvard. If you don't pay the $17.5 million bonus, you don't get the approximately $175 million in value added—so their math is a little perverse."[42] Moreover, the school's large endowment is used in ways that benefit students. Endowment income covers 72 percent of undergraduate financial aid,[43] and the university charges no tuition to students from families earning less than $60,000.[44] Harvard's immense endowment also enables the school to increase the faculty in growing areas and to expand its facilities.

In the end, Harvard decided to cap the compensation of fund managers. The result was that Jack Meyer and his team of managers left to start their own investment companies, at which many could earn 10 times their Harvard salary. Harvard Management Company also placed large amounts of endowment assets with these new firms. In so doing, it reduced the percentage of assets managed in-house and incurred the higher fees of outside managers, though they did not have to be reported. The university administration declined to defend its previous pay policy, which produced such stellar returns but drew considerable moral outrage. Business writer Michael Lewis speculates that Harvard's leaders were afraid to say what they thought. He observes, "We have arrived at a point in the money-management game where the going rate for the people who play it well is indefensible even to the people who understand it. No one wants to be seen thinking it is normal for someone to make US$25-million a year."[45]

CASE 2.3 ❋ Explore the Concept on mythinkinglab.com

Fraud at WorldCom

When WorldCom filed for bankruptcy on July 22, 2002, its stock, which was once worth more than $180 billion, became virtually worthless.[46] Although the company reported $107 billion in assets, it had accumulated more than $41 billion in debt in the course of a buying spree that had fueled its rapid growth. The downfall of WorldCom was sealed in late June, when the company revealed that more than $3.8 billion had been improperly booked as revenue, a figure that eventually rose to $11 billion. The revelation of improper accounting forced WorldCom to write down more than 75 percent of its reported assets. WorldCom set new world records for the largest company ever to go bankrupt, surpassing Enron, and for the largest accounting fraud.

WorldCom started as a small long-distance carrier founded in Clinton, Mississippi, in 1984, by nine investors. One of the founders was Bernard J. (Bernie) Ebbers, who was a former milkman, bartender, high school basketball coach, and, at the time, owner of 13 budget hotels. After Mr. Ebbers was asked to take the helm of the struggling company, it began to expand through aggressive acquisitions. Between 1991 and 1997, 65 regional and national telephone companies were bought, culminating in 1997 with the purchase of MCI, then the nation's second-largest long-distance carrier. In 1995, the emerging conglomerate assumed the name WorldCom. The acquisitions enabled WorldCom's stock to become a darling of Wall Street through creative accounting devised by the company's whiz-kid CFO, Scott Sullivan.

Mr. Sullivan utilized several accounting treatments that served to steadily increase WorldCom's earnings, along with its stock price.[47] In each acquisition, the value of the assets was reduced by charging future expenses against them. The result was lower earnings initially but a guarantee of higher earnings over time. The value of the assets was further reduced by transferring funds to "cookie-jar" reserves that could be tapped when needed to meet analysts' earnings expectations. In addition, some of the book value of the assets acquired was shifted from tangible or hard assets, which had to be charged against earnings over a short period, to intangible assets, such as brand name and good will, which could be amortized over longer periods of time. As a result, a smaller amount due to the acquisitions had to be charged against earnings as the company was growing. The overall effect of these accounting treatments was to give a picture of a growing company with a reliable, steadily rising income. This effect was critical for WorldCom's growth since acquisitions were financed with WorldCom stock, and the rising price of the stock enabled the company to make more acquisitions.

This rosy financial picture did not match the company's operations. Bernie Ebbers was known as a hands-off manager with little concern for the integration of the companies he acquired. The employees and customers of the acquired companies remained segmented, and departments of the company, including the critical legal staff, were located in different cities. Each office had its own policies and managerial style. More importantly, the telephone routing equipment, that handled calls and the customer and maintenance services were not combined into a seamless system. Complaints from disgruntled users flooded the company. The company culture that was developing encouraged "a systemic attitude conveyed from the top down that employees should not question their superiors, but simply do what they were told."[48] In a report issued after WorldCom's collapse, Mr. Ebbers was recalled as saying that the project to write a code of ethics was "a colossal waste of time," and the writers of the report observed, "While we have heard numerous accounts of Ebbers' demand for results—on occasion emotional, insulting, and with express reference to the personal financial harm he faced if the stock price declined—we have heard none in which he demanded or rewarded ethical business practices."[49]

Despite its dysfunctional operations, WorldCom was able to continue its accounting-aided financial success as long as new acquisitions were found. This strategy by acquisitions came to a halt when the company's ambitious bid to acquire Sprint was scuttled by the U.S. Department of Justice in July 2000. Suddenly the revenues to meet analysts' expectations had to be found elsewhere. It was reported that at this point, "Ebbers appeared to lack a strategic sense of direction, and the Company began drifting."[50] Scott Sullivan had a plan, though. In October 2000, he ordered the controller David F. Myers and the accounting director Buford Yates, Jr., to divert funds that had been set aside, as required by accounting rules, to pay for line expenses. WorldCom's telephone system required the lease of telephone lines from other companies to complete calls, and the cost of these leases constituted a major expense, approximately 42 percent of total revenues. Because the revenues to pay for line expenses were collected several months before the payments were due, generally accepted accounting principles (GAAP) required that funds be set aside as an accounting accrual so that the receipts and expenditures matched. If the cost of the line leases was less than the amount set aside, the difference could be added to revenue as an accrual release, but not before the expenses were paid.

The task of making the accounting entry that would release the accruals fell to Betty Vinson, a diligent, hardworking, loyal employee, who, it was said by a colleague, would "do anything you told her to do."[51] Ms. Vinson said that she was "shocked" when she was told to transfer $828 million from the reserved accruals to current revenues, and she expressed her view that the accounting entry was improper.[52] She made the entry reluctantly, and on October 26, 2000, she and another colleague announced their plans to resign. When he heard this news, Mr. Ebbers assured Mr. Myers that the accountants would never be asked to do this again. Scott Sullivan also attempted to placate the distraught accountants. He is reported to have said, "Think of it as an aircraft carrier. We have planes in the air. Let's get the planes landed. Once they are landed, if you still want to leave, then leave. But not while planes are in the air."[53] Mr. Sullivan assured them that the transfer was not illegal and that he would assume full responsibility. The two accountants agreed to stay.

At the end of the first quarter of 2001, it became evident that WorldCom would not meet its expected earnings target without a boost from accounting. Increased competition in the telephone industry, overcapacity of telephone lines, and a decreased demand for telephone services combined to reduce the revenues of all companies. This time, there were not enough accruals for line leases left to cover the expected shortfall, and so Mr. Sullivan developed another plan. Ms. Vinson was ordered to record $771 million of line expenses as capital investment. In its bid to grow, WorldCom had entered into expensive long-term leases of telephone lines that were being underutilized, and the excess expense was a drain on the company's bottom line. Mr. Sullivan's rationale for recording a portion of the line lease payments as capital investment was that the unused capacity was a resource that would enable the company to grow. On the books, a capital investment shows up as an asset rather than as an expense, and its cost can be spread over a longer period of time. Although she put together a résumé and began looking for another job, she made the accounting entry, backdating it to February. For the remainder of 2001, Ms. Vinson was asked to repeat the accounting procedure, improperly recording $560 million in the second quarter, $743 million in the third quarter, and $941 million in the fourth, each time hoping the entry would be the last.[54] After realizing that the transfers would have to continue through 2002 if WorldCom were to meet analysts' expectations, she and another colleague announced to Mr. Myers that they would no longer make these improper entries into the company's books.

Further entries proved unnecessary. In March, investigators from the Securities and Exchange Commission (SEC) began asking for documents, and Cynthia Cooper, WorldCom's head of internal audit, also initiated inquiries. Betty Vinson and Buford Yates hired an attorney and agreed to talk with federal investigators in the hopes of avoiding indictments. On April 26, 2002, Mr. Ebbers was dismissed by the board of directors for a lack of strategic vision and also because of difficulties from his outside business interests and his inability to repay loans made by the company. On June 20, Ms. Cooper and her internal audit staff presented their findings to the board of directors, which demanded the resignations of Sullivan and Yates. On June 26, the SEC brought civil charges of fraud against WorldCom and began criminal proceedings against Bernie Ebbers, Scott Sullivan, David Myers, Buford Yates, and Betty Vinson. All were found guilty. Ebbers was sentenced to 25 years in prison, and Sullivan, to five. Myers and Yates each got one year, and Betty Vinson received a sentence of five months in prison and five months of home detention. Although Ms. Vinson played a small role and was put into a difficult situation by her superiors, the U.S. attorney who prosecuted the case said that "just following orders" is not an excuse for breaking the law.[55]

CASE 2.4 ✴ ⸢Explore the Concept on mythinkinglab.com

Broken Trust at Bankers Trust

Bankers Trust (now part of Deutsche Bank) was a leading seller of complex derivatives, which include futures, options, swaps, and other financial instruments whose value is based on (or derived from, hence the name "derivatives") other securities.[56] One Bankers Trust client was the consumer products giant Procter & Gamble (P&G), which used derivatives extensively. One type of derivative frequently used by P&G is an interest rate swap, in which the holder of, say, fixed interest bonds can exchange the payment of a fixed rate of interest with another party and pay, in effect, a variable rate. The other party pays the fixed rate to the bondholder and accepts from the swapholder a variable rate. Such an agreement is beneficial to a company with bond obligations that carry a high fixed interest rate if it believes that interest rates will remain low or even fall, because it will pay less interest at a variable rate. However, the other side of the swap is betting that interest rates will rise, because, otherwise, it would lose money by paying a fixed rate in return for accepting a variable rate. An interest rate swap is a pure bet on the direction of interest rates.

In 1993, which was a time of low interest rates, P&G had a debt load of approximately $5 billion. Of that debt, $200 million of fixed interest bonds had been covered with an interest rate swap that was expiring, and P&G asked Bankers Trust for help in creating a new swap. After some negotiation, P&G accepted an offer from the bank to enter into a complicated swap in which the variable interest rate that P&G would pay would set in six months according to a complex formula (which Bankers Trust refused to reveal, claiming that it was proprietary) based on the difference or "spread" between five-year and 30-year treasury bonds.[57] The formula "leveraged" the bet on interest rates since each percentage point rise in interest rates would result in a disproportionately large increase in the amount of variable interest paid by P&G. In two transactions, one on November 2, 1993, and the other on February 14, 2004, P&G entered into the swaps with Bankers Trust. Trouble developed almost immediately when the Federal Reserve began raising interest rates. Although the six-month lock-in of interest rates had not yet occurred, the cost to P&G of getting out of the swaps had soared so that P&G's borrowing costs would be increasing to more than 14 percent over the standard interest rate, costing the company approximately $130 million in additional interest.

In a swap option, any loss to one party is a gain in the same amount to the other side of the bet. So a large loss at P&G would result in a bonanza for Bankers Trust. Unlike several other Bankers Trust clients who claimed that they had been misled about the risks they were taking, P&G admitted that it knowingly took a great risk if interest were to rise—as they did. Edwin L. Artz, the chairman of P&G, said, "The issue here is Bankers Trust's selling practices." He continued, "There's a notion that end users of derivatives must be held accountable for what they buy. We agree completely, but only if the terms and risks are fully and accurately disclosed."[58] Specifically, P&G felt it had been misled by assurances from Bankers Trust that it could get out of the swaps with little loss before the variable rate set in six months. Bankers Trust maintained that it had assured P&G that it would buy back the company's swap position only at the current market rate as calculated by the bank. Every derivative has a current market value, and as a dealer in derivatives Bankers Trust stood ready to buy back any derivative it sold—but at the current market price, which might involve a considerable loss to the selling party. The bank denied that it had ever promised that it could limit P&G's losses, which in any event would be impossible since the extent of any losses cannot be known in advance. Anyone dealing in options knows that no such assurance could be given. In the end, P&G was able to get out of the swaps but at a price of paying an interest rate of nearly 20 percent for four years.

The position of Bankers Trust was that it was merely a seller of a product that P&G wanted and that all appropriate disclosures had been made. In particular, the bank insisted that it was not a fiduciary with any obligation to protect P&G's interest. P&G was a sophisticated investor which could understand the risks it was taking and determine its risk tolerance. Bankers Trust was not a trusted adviser in this instance but merely a trader. This position was compromised, however, by audio tapes that recorded conversations of Bankers Trust employees involved in the P&G transactions. (Most banks routinely record conversations in order to settle disputes over trades.) In discussing the swaps sold to P&G, one employee was recorded as saying, "They would never know. They would never know how much money was taken out of that." To this, a colleague who agreed replied, "That's the beauty of Bankers Trust." Other comments include these: "This could be a massive huge future gravy train," and "It's like Russian roulette, and I keep putting another bullet in the revolver every time I do one of these." A video of a training session recorded an instructor saying, "[W]hat Bankers Trust can do for [clients] is get in the middle and rip them off—take a little money." It was alleged that employees at Bankers Trust used the acronym ROF for "rip-off factor" in their conversations and messages.

Bankers Trust denied that these taped conversations were representative of the culture at the bank, and a spokesperson said that "these stupid and crude comments . . . were the basis of disciplinary actions against these individuals last year."

Notes

1. Information for this case is taken mainly from *In re: HP Inkjet Printer Litigation,* Master File No. C053580 JF, Second Consolidated and Amended Class Action Complaint, United States District Court, Northern District of California; and *In re: HP Inkjet Printer* Litigation, Master File No. C05-3580 JF, Stipulation of Settlement, United States District Court, Northern District of California.

2. For discussion of the ethical justification market system, see Allen Buchanan, *Ethics, Efficiency, and the Market* (Totowa, NJ: Rowman and Littlefield, 1988); Gerald Dworkin, Gordon Bermant, and Peter G. Brown, eds., *Markets and Morals* (Washington, DC: Hemisphere, 1977); Virginia Held, ed., *Property, Profits, and Economic Justice* (Belmont, CA: Wadsworth, 1980); Allan Gibbard, "What's Morally Special about Free Exchange?" in Ellen Paul, Fred Miller, Jr. and Jeffrey Paul, eds., *Ethics and Economics* (Oxford: Blackwell, 1985); and Amartya Sen, *On Ethics and Economics* (Oxford: Blackwell, 1987).

3. Friedrich A. von Hayek, *The Constitution of Liberty* (Chicago, IL: University of Chicago Press, 1960); and *Law, Legislation, and Liberty*, 3 vols. (Chicago, IL: University of Chicago Press, 1973, 1976, 1979). For Hayek's critique of socialist planned economies, see *The Road to Serfdom* (Chicago, IL: University of Chicago Press, 1944).

4. David Gauthier, *Morals by Agreement* (Oxford: Oxford University Press, 1986), ch. 4. For criticism, see Daniel M. Hausman, "Are Markets Morally Free Zones?" *Philosophy and Public Affairs*, 18 (1989), 317–33.

5. Stewart Macaulay, "Non-contractual Relations in Business: A Preliminary Study," *American Sociological Review*, 28 (1963), 55–67.

6. For an insightful account of the relation between business ethics and market failures, see Joseph Heath, "Business Ethics Without Stakeholders," *Business Ethics Quarterly*, 16 (2006), 533–57.

7. For a brief discussion of this assumption, see Sen, *On Ethics and Economics*, 10–28.

8. Some economists and behavioral scientists recognize altruism and moral commitment and attempt to incorporate them into economic theory. See, for example, Edmund S. Phelps, ed., *Altruism, Morality, and Economic Theory* (New York: Russell Sage Foundation, 1975); Harvey Leibenstein, *Beyond Economic Man* (Cambridge, MA: Harvard University Press, 1976); David Collard, *Altruism and Economy: A Study in Non-Selfish Economics* (New York: Oxford University Press, 1978); Howard Margolis, *Selfishness, Altruism, and Rationality: A Theory of Social Choice* (Cambridge: Cambridge University Press, 1982); Amitai Etzioni, *The Moral Dimension: Towards a New Economics* (New York: Free Press, 1988); and Robert H. Frank, *Passions Within Reason: The Strategic Role of the Emotions* (New York: W. W. Norton, 1988).

9. On the concepts of bounded rationality and satisficing, see Herbert A. Simon, *Administrative Behavior: A Study of Decision Making Processes in Administrative Organization*, 3rd ed. (New York: Free Press, 1976), originally published in 1947; James G. March and Herbert A. Simon, *Organizations* (New York: John Wiley, 1958); and Richard M. Cyert and James G. March, *A Behavioral Theory of the Firm* (Upper Saddle River, NJ: Prentice Hall, 1963).

10. See Buchanan, *Ethics, Efficiency, and the Market*, 24–25.

11. For an insightful study of this problem, see Amartya Sen, *Collective Choice and Social Welfare* (San Francisco,

CA: Holden Day, 1970). Also, Kenneth Arrow, *Social Choice and Individual Values*, 2nd ed. (New York: John Wiley, 1963).

12. The disparity between private and public consumption in the United States is the major theme in John Kenneth Galbraith, *The Affluent Society* (Boston, MA: Houghton Mifflin, 1958).

13. If everyone attempts to be a free rider, however, then certain kinds of collective choices are impossible unless people are coerced in some way. See Mancur Olson, *The Logic of Collective Action* (Cambridge, MA: Harvard University Press, 1965), 44.

14. For discussion of the prisoner's dilemma, see any book on game theory, such as R. Duncan Luce and Howard Raiffa, *Games and Decisions* (New York: John Wiley & Sons, 1957).

15. This point is made by Russell Hardin, "Collective Action as an Agreeable n-Person Prisoners' Dilemma," *Behavioral Science*, 16 (1971), 472–79.

16. C. Ford Runge, "Institutions and the Free Rider: The Assurance Problem in Collective Action," *Journal of Politics*, 46 (1984), 154–81.

17. For the empirical significance of the prisoner's dilemma, see Anatol Rapoport and Albert M. Chammah, *The Prisoner's Dilemma* (Ann Arbor, MI: University of Michigan Press, 1965); and Robert Axelrod, *The Evolution of Cooperation* (New York: Basic Books, 1984).

18. Thomas C. Schelling, "Command and Control," in *Social Responsibility and the Business Predicament*, ed. James W. McKie (Washington, DC: The Brookings Institution, 1974), 103–05.

19. Ibid., 103.

20. *Meinhard* v. *Salmon*, 164 N.E. 545 (1928).

21. Ronald M. Coase, "The Nature of the Firm," *Economica*, N.S., 4 (1937), 386–405.

22. Bart Victor and John B. Cullen, "The Organizational Bases of Ethical Work Climates," *Administrative Science Quarterly*, 33 (1988), 101–25; Deborah V. Cohen, "Creating Ethical Work Climates: A Socio-Economic Perspective," *Journal of Socio-Economics*, 24(2) (1995), 317–43; James E. Wimbush and Jon M. Shepard, "Toward an Understanding of Ethical Climate: Its Relationship to Ethical Behavior and Supervisory Influence," *Journal of Business Ethics*, 13(8) (1994), 637–48.

23. See, for example, John M. Darley, "How Organizations Socialize Individuals into Evildoing," in *Codes of Conduct: Behavioral Research into Business Ethics*, eds., David M. Messick and Ann E. Tenbrunsel (New York: Russell Sage Foundation, 1996), 13–43.

24. For an introduction to the large literature on organizational justice, see Blair H. Sheppard, Roy J. Lewicki, and John W. Minton, *Organizational Justice: The Search for Fairness in the Workplace* (New York: Lexington Books, 1992).

25. Darley, "How Organizations Socialize Individuals into Evildoing," 13.

26. The concept of the moral point of view is developed in Kurt Baier, *The Moral Point of View: A Rational Basis of Ethics* (Ithaca, NY: Cornell University Press, 1958). A similar account is offered in James Rachels, *The Elements of Moral Philosophy*, 4th ed. (New York: McGraw-Hill, 2002), chap. 1.

27. Baier, *Moral Point of View*, 88.

28. Ibid., 195–96.

29. Lawrence Kohlberg, *The Psychology of Moral Development: The Nature and Validity of Moral Stages* (San Francisco, CA: Harper & Row, 1984).

30. Lawrence Kohlberg, "The Claim to Moral Adequacy of a Highest Stage of Moral Judgment," *Journal of Philosophy*, 70 (1973), 630–46.

31. For a discussion of the concept of integrity in business ethics, see Robert Audi and Patrick E. Murphy, "The Many Faces of Integrity," *Business Ethics Quarterly*, 16(1) (2006), 3–21.

32. Robert C. Solomon, *Ethics and Excellence: Cooperation and Integrity in Business* (New York: Oxford University Press, 1992), 168.

33. Lynn Sharp Paine, "Managing for Organizational Integrity," *Harvard Business Review* (March/April 1994), 106–17.

34. Stephanie Strom, "Harvard Managers' Pay Criticized," *New York Times*, 4 June 2004, A18.

35. Ibid.

36. Charles Stein, "Harvard Pays 2 Top Money Managers $25 M: Endowment's Salaries Down from Last Year; Critics Call System Lavish," *Boston Globe*, 23 November 2004, D1.

37. Stephen M. Marks, "Alums Decry University Investor Salaries," *Harvard Crimson*, 12 December 2003.

38. Strom, "Harvard Managers' Pay Criticized."

39. Ibid.

40. Charles Stein, "Harvard Will Keep Disputed Pay Policy Under New Chief," *Boston Globe*, 15 October 2005, B7.

41. Steve Bailey, "Harvard's PR Problem," *Boston Globe*, 10 September 2004, D1.

42. Marks, "Alums Decry University Investor Salaries."

43. William C. Symonds, "Leaving Harvard Greener: Investment Superstar Jack Meyer's Legacy Is Worth Every Penny He Was Paid," *BusinessWeek*, 24 January 2005, 44.

44. Sara Rimer and Alan Finder, "Harvard to Aid Students High in Middle Class," *New York Times*, 11 December 2007, A1.

45. Michael Lewis, "Harvard Fund Managers Deserve Better: Meyer's Team Shamed Out by 'High' Salaries that Weren't," *Financial Post Investing*, 21 January 2005, IN1.

46. Information on this case, unless indicated otherwise, is taken from Dennis R. Beresford, Nicholas deB. Katzenbach, and C. B. Rogers, Jr., "Report of Investigation by the Special Investigative Committee of the Board of Directors of WorldCom, Inc.," 31 March 2003, hereafter "Report of Investigation."

47. For details, see Kurt Eichenwald, "For WorldCom, Acquisitions Were Behind Its Rise," *New York Times*, 8 August 2002, A1.

48. Beresford, Katzenbach, and Rogers, "Report of Investigation," 21.

49. Ibid., 19.

50. Ibid., 49.

51. Susan Pulliam, "Over the Line: A Staffer Ordered to Commit Fraud, Balked, Then Caved," *Wall Street Journal*, 23 June 2003, A1.
52. Ibid.
53. Ibid.
54. Ibid.
55. Ibid.
56. Information on the case is taken mainly from Saul Hansell, "P&G Sues Bankers Trust Over Swap Deal," *New York Times*, 28 October 1994; Saul Hansell, "Bankers Trust Settles Suit with P&G," *New York Times*, 10 May 1996; Floyd Norris, Procter's Tale: Gambling in Ignorance," *New York Times*, 30 October 1994; and Kelley Holland and Linda Himelstein, "The Bankers Trust Tapes," *BusinessWeek*, 16 October 1995.
57. This spread is a useful indicator of expected interest rates since long-term bonds are more reflective of expectations that short-term ones.
58. Hansell, "P&G Sues Bankers Trust Over Swap Deal."

3

Ethical Theories

((•—Listen to the **Chapter Audio** on **mythinkinglab.com**

CASE 3.1   ❋—Explore the Concept on **mythinkinglab.com**

Big Brother at Procter & Gamble

In early August 1991, a former employee of Procter & Gamble telephoned *Wall Street Journal* reporter Alecia Swasy at her Pittsburgh office to report some disturbing news.[1] "The cops want to know what I told you about P&G," he said. This 20-year veteran of the company had just been grilled for an hour by an investigator for the Cincinnati fraud squad. The investigator, Gary Armstrong, who also happened to work part-time as a security officer for P&G, had records of the ex-manager's recent long-distance calls, including some to Swasy.

Alecia Swasy had apparently angered CEO Edward Artz with two news stories about troubles at P&G that the company was not ready to reveal. An article in the *Wall Street Journal* on Monday, June 10, 1991, reported that B. Jurgen Hintz, executive vice president and heir apparent as CEO, had been forced to resign over difficulties in the food and beverage division. The next day, on Tuesday, June 11, a long article on the division's woes quoted "current and former P&G managers" as saying that the company might sell certain product lines, including Citrus Hill orange juice, Crisco shortening, and Fisher nuts. Swasy believed that Artz had deliberately lied to her when she tried to confirm the story of Hintz's departure in a telephone conversation on Saturday, and that he tried to sabotage the *Journal* by allowing the news to be released to the rival *New York Times* and the Cincinnati newspapers in time for the Sunday editions while the public relations department continued to deny the story to Swasy.

Immediately after the two articles appeared in the *Wall Street Journal*, Artz ordered a search of P&G's own phone records to determine the source of the leaks to the press. When this investigation failed to uncover any culprits, the company filed a complaint with the Hamilton County prosecutor's office, which promptly opened a grand jury investigation. The grand jury then issued several subpoenas calling for Cincinnati Bell to search its records for all calls in the 513 and 606 area codes, which cover southern Ohio and northern Kentucky, and to identify all telephone calls to Alecia Swasy's home or office and all fax transmissions to the newspaper's Pittsburgh office between

March 1 and June 15. The search combed the records of 803,849 home and business telephone lines from which users had placed more than 40 million long-distance calls.

P&G contended that it filed the complaint because of "significant and ongoing leaks of our confidential business data, plans and strategies," which included not only leaks to the news media but also leaks to competitors as well. The legal basis for the grand jury probe was provided by a 1967 Ohio law that makes it a crime to give away "articles representing trade secrets," and a 1974 Ohio law that prohibits employees from disclosing "confidential information" without the permission of the employer. However, reporters are generally protected by the First Amendment right of freedom of the press, and Ohio, Pennsylvania, and 24 other states have so-called "shield laws" that protect the identities of reporters' confidential sources.

Information about an executive's forced departure is scarcely a trade secret on a par with the formula for Crest toothpaste, and the use of the phrase "articles representing trade secrets" has been interpreted in the Ohio courts to mean documents such as photographs and blueprints, not word-of-mouth news. Any law that limits First Amendment rights must define the kind of speech prohibited and demonstrate a compelling need, but the 1974 law does not specify what constitutes confidential information or the conditions under which it is protected. Thus, some legal experts doubt the law's constitutionality. P&G denied that any reporter's First Amendment rights were being violated: "No news media outlet is being asked to turn over any names or any information. The investigation is focused on individuals who may be violating the law."

The response to P&G's role in the investigation was quick and angry. The Cincinnati chapter of the Society of Professional Journalists wrote, in a letter to CEO Artz: "The misguided action Procter & Gamble is taking threatens to trample the First Amendment and obviously reflects more concern in identifying a possible leak within the company rather than protecting any trade secrets. . . . Your complaint has prompted a prosecutorial and police fishing expedition that amounts to censorship before the fact and could lead to further abuse of the First Amendment by other companies also disgruntled by news media coverage." An editorial in the *Wall Street Journal* asked, "What possessed P&G?" and questioned the legality by saying, "We understand that P&G swings a big stick in Cincinnati, of course, and maybe the local law can, like Pampers, be stretched to cover the leak. It is not funny, though, to the folks being hassled by the cops."

The sharpest criticism came from William Safire, the *New York Times* columnist, who objected to Edward Artz's contention that P&G's mistakes are not "an issue of ethics." Safire concluded a column entitled "At P&G: It Sinks" with the words: "It's not enough to say, 'our leak hunt backfired, so excuse us'; the maker of Tide and Ivory can only come clean by showing its publics, and tomorrow's business leaders, that it understands that abuse of power and invasion of privacy are no mere errors of judgment—regrettably inappropriate—but are unethical, bad, improper, wrong."

In the end, no charges were filed against any individual, and the company continued to deny any wrongdoing. A spokesperson for P&G asserted that the press "has the right to pursue information, but we have the right to protect proprietary information." Fraud squad investigator Gary Armstrong later went to work for Procter & Gamble full-time.

INTRODUCTION

Procter & Gamble's heavy-handed investigation was undeniably a violation of accepted business ethics. Using the framework for ethical reasoning presented in Chapter 2, one can easily fault P&G for violating several of the seven principles listed. However, the critics of P&G did not cite any harmful consequences of the investigation beyond the chilling effect it might have had on employees and members of the press. They complained instead about the abuse of power and invasion of privacy. In particular, P&G was charged with violating certain rights—the right of reporters to search out newsworthy information and the right of ordinary citizens not to have their telephone records searched. Less certain is whether an employee has the right to disclose information to a reporter. Consequences aside, however, there is something objectionable about a company snooping on its own employees and using law enforcement officials for company purposes. Although P&G's conduct appears questionable, it is not easy to specify exactly the moral wrongs. Moreover, reasonable people might disagree about what is wrong in this case and on the more general issues involved. The framework in Chapter 2 cannot settle all controversies that might arise from this and other cases.

Controversial issues in business ethics are difficult precisely because they are not easily settled by our ordinary moral beliefs and the simple rules and principles of morality. When reasonable persons disagree about these matters, we need to go beyond our conflicting positions and seek common ground in ethical theory. Put simply, the really hard questions of ethics require that we think deeply and search out the best reasons available. For a deeper understanding of ethical reasoning than that provided by the framework presented in Chapter 2, we may turn to the ethical theories that have been developed over the centuries by major moral philosophers. These theories are not only a valuable resource for enabling us to think through ethical issues in business but also the foundation for the ethics of business. The arguments that are presented in subsequent chapters about a wide range of business ethics issues all draw upon these various ethical theories. Some familiarity with these theories, then, will greatly improve the moral compass that we use to navigate the treacherous ethical terrain of the business world.

UTILITARIANISM

It is customary to divide ethical theories into two groups, usually called teleological and deontological. The most prominent historical examples of a teleological and a deontological theory are utilitarianism and the ethical theory of Immanuel Kant, respectively. Teleological theories hold that the rightness of actions is determined solely by the amount of good consequences they produce. (The word "teleological" is derived from the Greek word "telos," which means an end.) Actions are justified on teleological theories by virtue of the end they achieve, rather than some feature of the actions themselves. Deontological theories, by contrast, deny that consequences are relevant to determining what we ought to do. Deontologists typically hold that we have a duty to perform certain acts not because of some benefit to ourselves or others, but because of the nature of these actions or the rules from which they follow. (The word "deontological" is derived from "deon," the Greek word for duty.) Thus, lying is wrong, a deontologist would say, by its very nature, regardless of the consequences. Other examples of nonconsequentialist reasoning in ethics include arguments based on principles such as the Golden Rule and those that appeal to basic notions of rights, human dignity, and respect for other persons.

Different parts of the utilitarian doctrine were advanced by philosophers as far back as the ancient Greeks, but it remained for two English reformers in the nineteenth century to fashion them into a single coherent whole. The creators of classical utilitarianism were Jeremy Bentham (1748–1832) and John Stuart Mill (1806–1873). In their hands, utilitarianism was not an ivory-tower philosophy but a powerful instrument for social, political, economic, and legal change. Bentham and Mill used the principle of utility as a practical guide in the English reform movement.

The Principle of Utility

Classical utilitarianism can be stated formally as follows:

> *AN ACTION IS RIGHT IF AND ONLY IF IT PRODUCES THE GREATEST BALANCE OF PLEASURE OVER PAIN FOR EVERYONE.*

So stated, the utilitarian principle involves four distinct theses:

1. *Consequentialism.* The principle holds that the rightness of actions is determined solely by their consequences. It is by virtue of this thesis that utilitarianism is a teleological theory.

2. *Hedonism.* Utility in this statement of the theory is identified with pleasure and the absence of pain. Hedonism is the thesis that pleasure and only pleasure is ultimately good.

3. *Maximalism.* A right action is one that has not merely some good consequences but also the greatest amount of good consequences possible when the bad consequences are also taken into consideration.

4. *Universalism.* The consequences to be considered are those of everyone.

Consequentialism requires that the results or consequences of an act be measured in some way so that the good and bad consequences for different individuals can be added together and the results of different courses of action compared. According to hedonism, the good and bad consequences to be considered are the pleasure and pain produced by an act. Virtually every act produces both pleasure and pain, and the principle of utility does not require that only pleasure and no pain result from a right action. An action may produce a great amount of pain and still be right on the utilitarian view as long as the amount of pleasure produced is, on balance, greater than the amount of pleasure produced by any other action. Utilitarianism assumes that the amount of pain produced by an action can be subtracted from the amount of pleasure to yield the net amount of pleasure— in the same way that an accountant subtracts debts from assets to determine net worth.

The thesis of universalism requires us to consider the pleasure and pain of *everyone alike.* Thus, we are not following the principle of utility by considering the consequences only for ourselves, for our family and friends, or for an organization of which we are a part. Utilitarianism does not require us to ignore our own interest, but we are permitted to place it no higher and no lower than the interest of anyone else. The utilitarian principle does not insist that the interest of everyone be *promoted*, though. In deciding whether to close a polluting plant, for example, we need to consider the impact on everyone. No matter what decision is made, the interests of some people will be harmed. Utilitarian reasoning obligates us only to include the interests of everyone in our calculations, not to act in a way that advances every individual interest.

ACT AND RULE UTILITARIANISM.   In classical utilitarianism, an action is judged to be right by virtue of the consequences of performing *that action*. As a result, telling a lie or breaking a promise is right if it has better consequences than any alternative course of action. Utilitarian morality thus seems to place no value on observing rules, such as "Tell the truth" or "Keep your promises," except perhaps as "rules of thumb," that is, as distillations of past experience about the tendencies of actions that eliminate the need to calculate consequences in every case. This result can be avoided if we consider the consequences of performing not just particular actions but also *actions of a certain kind*. Although some instances of lying have consequences that are better than telling the truth, lying in general does not. As a kind of action, then, truth-telling is right by virtue of the consequences of performing actions of that kind, and any instance of truth-telling is right because actions of that kind are right.

This suggestion leads to a distinction between two versions of utilitarianism, one in which we calculate the consequences of each act and another in which we consider the consequences of following the relevant rule. These two versions are called act-utilitarianism (AU) and rule-utilitarianism (RU), respectively. They may now be expressed formally in the following way:

(AU) An action is right if and only if it produces the greatest balance of pleasure over pain for everyone.

(RU) An action is right if and only if it conforms to a set of rules the general acceptance of which would produce the greatest balance of pleasure over pain for everyone.[2]

Both act-utilitarianism and rule-utilitarianism have their merits, and there is no consensus among philosophers about which is correct.[3] Act-utilitarianism is a simpler theory and provides an easily understood decision procedure. Rule-utilitarianism seems to give firmer ground, however, to the rules of morality, which are problems for all teleological theories.

PROBLEMS WITH CALCULATING UTILITY.   There is little difficulty in calculating that some actions produce more pleasure for us than others. A decision to spend an evening at a concert is usually the result of a judgment that listening to music will give us more pleasure at that time than any available alternative. Confronted with a range of alternatives, we can usually rank them in order from the most pleasant to the least pleasant. A problem arises, however, when we attempt to determine exactly how *much* pleasure each course of action will produce, because pleasure cannot be measured precisely in terms of quantity, much less quality. Moreover, utilitarianism requires that we calculate utility not only for ourselves but for all persons affected by an action.

Some critics contend that this requirement imposes an information burden on utilitarian decision makers that is difficult to meet. In order to buy a gift for a friend that will produce the greatest amount of pleasure, for example, we need to know something about that person's desires and tastes. Consider, for example, the task faced by a utilitarian legislator who must decide whether to permit logging in a public park. This person must identify all the people affected, determine the amount of pleasure and pain for each one, and then compare the pleasure that hiking brings to nature lovers versus the pain that would be caused to loggers if they lost their jobs. The abilities of ordinary human beings are inadequate, critics complain, to acquire and process the vast amount of relevant information in such a case. The response of utilitarians to these problems is that we manage in practice to make educated guesses by relying on past experience and limiting our attention to a few aspects of a situation.

Comparing the pleasure and pain of different people raises a further problem about the *interpersonal comparison of utility.* Imagine two people who each insists after attending a concert that he or she enjoyed it more. There seems to be no way in principle to settle this dispute. Some philosophers and economists consider this problem to be insoluble and a reason for rejecting utilitarianism both as an ethical theory and as a basis for economics.[4] Others argue for the possibility of interpersonal comparisons on the basis that regardless of whether we can make such comparisons precisely, we do make them in everyday life with reasonable confidence.[5] We may give away an extra ticket to a concert, for example, to the friend we believe will enjoy it the most based on past experience. The problem of the interpersonal comparison of utility is not insuperable, therefore, as long as rough comparisons are sufficient for utilitarian calculations.

Cost–Benefit Analysis

The utilitarian ideal of a precise quantitative method for decision making is most fully realized in *cost–benefit analysis.* This method differs from classical utilitarianism, with its measure of pleasure and pain, primarily in the use of monetary units to express the consequences of various alternatives. Any project in which the dollar amount of the benefits exceeds the dollar amount of the damages is worth pursuing, according to cost–benefit analysis, and from among different projects, the one that promises the greatest net benefit, as measured in dollars, ought to be chosen.[6]

The chief advantage of cost–benefit analysis is that the prices of many goods are set by the market, so that the need to have knowledge of people's pleasures or preference rankings is largely eliminated. The value of different goods is easily totaled to produce a figure that reflects the costs and benefits of different courses of action for all concerned. Money also provides a common denominator for allocating resources among projects that cannot easily be compared otherwise. Would scarce resources be better spent on preschool education, for example, or on the development of new sources of energy? In cost–benefit analysis, decision makers have an analytic framework that enables them to decide among such disparate projects in a rational, objective manner.

PROBLEMS WITH ASSIGNING MONETARY VALUES.   Cost–benefit analysis is criticized for problems with assigning monetary values to costs and benefits. First, not all costs and benefits have an easily determined monetary value. The value of the jobs that are provided by logging on public land can be expressed precisely in dollars, as can the value of the lumber produced. But because the opportunity for hikers to enjoy unspoiled vistas and fresh-smelling air is not something that is commonly bought and sold, it has no discernible market price. Experts in cost–benefit analysis attempt to overcome the problem of assigning a dollar figure to nonmarket goods with a technique known as *shadow pricing.* This consists of determining the value reflected by people's market and nonmarket behavior. For example, by comparing the prices of houses near airports, busy highways, and the like with the prices of similar houses in less noisy areas, it is possible to infer the value that people place on peace and quiet. The value of life and limb can be similarly estimated by considering the amount of extra pay that is needed to get workers to accept risky jobs.

There are some pitfalls in using the technique of shadow pricing, especially when human life is involved. Many people buy houses in noisy areas or accept risky jobs because they are unable to afford decent housing anywhere else or to secure safer employment. Some home buyers and job seekers may not fully consider or appreciate the risks they face, especially when the hazards are unseen or speculative. Also, the people who buy homes near airports or accept work as steeplejacks are possibly less concerned with noise or danger than is the general population. We certainly do not want to assume, however, that workplace safety is of little value simply because a few people are so heedless of danger that they accept jobs that more cautious people avoid.[7]

Second, some applications of cost–benefit analysis require that a value be placed on human life. Although this may seem heartless, it is necessary if cost–benefit analysis is to be used to determine how much to spend on prenatal care to improve the rate of infant mortality, for example, or on reducing the amount of cancer-causing emissions from factories. Reducing infant mortality or the death rate from cancer justifies the expenditure of some funds, but how much? Would further investment be justified if it reduced the amount available for education or the arts? No matter where the line is drawn, some trade-off must be made between saving lives and securing other goods. The purpose of assigning a monetary value to life in a cost–benefit analysis is not to indicate how much a life is actually worth but to enable us to compare alternatives where life is at stake.

Several methods exist, in fact, for calculating the value of human life for purposes of cost–benefit analysis.[8] Among these are the discounted value of a person's future earnings over a normal lifetime, the value that existing social and political arrangements place on the life of individuals, and the value that is revealed by the amount that individuals are willing to pay to avoid the risk of injury and death. When people choose through their elected representatives or by their own consumer behavior not to spend additional amounts to improve automobile safety, for example, they implicitly indicate the value of the lives that would otherwise be saved. Using such indicators, economists calculate that middle-income Americans value their lives between $3 million and $5 million.[9] Experts in risk assessment calculate that the "break-even" point where the amount expended to save a life is worth the cost is about $10 million.[10]

Third, people's individual and collective decisions are not always rational. People who drive without seat belts are probably aware of their benefit *for other people* but are convinced that nothing will happen *to them* because they are such good drivers.[11] As a result, they (irrationally) expose themselves to risks that do not accurately reflect the value they place on their own lives. Mark Sagoff observes that the choices we make as consumers do not always correspond to those we make as citizens. He cites as examples the fact that he buys beverages in disposable containers but urges his state legislators to require returnable bottles and that he has a car with an "Ecology Now" sticker that leaks oil everywhere it is parked.[12]

Should All Things Be Assigned a Monetary Value?

A further criticism of cost–benefit analysis is that even if all the problems with assigning monetary values could be solved, there are still good reasons for not assigning a monetary value to some things. Steven Kelman argues that placing a dollar value on some goods reduces their perceived value, because they are valued precisely because they cannot be bought and sold in a market. Friendship and love are obvious examples. "Imagine the reaction," Kelman observes, "if a practitioner of cost–benefit analysis computed the benefits of sex based on the price of prostitute service."[13] In *The Gift Relationship: From Human Blood to Social Policy*, Richard M. Titmuss compares the American system of blood collection with that of the British. In the United States, about half of all blood is purchased from donors and sold to people who need transfusions.[14] The British system, by contrast, is purely voluntary. No one is paid for donating blood, and it is provided without charge to anyone in need. As a result, the giving of blood and the receipt of blood have an entirely different significance. If blood has a price, then giving blood merely saves someone else an expense, but blood that cannot be bought and sold becomes a special gift that we make to others.[15]

Although some things are cheapened in people's eyes if they are made into commodities and traded in a market, this does not happen if goods are assigned a value merely for purposes of comparison. It is the actual buying and selling of blood that changes its perceived value, not performing a cost–benefit analysis. Moreover, Titmuss himself argues in favor of the British system on the grounds that the system in the United States is (1) highly wasteful of blood, resulting in chronic acute shortages; (2) administratively inefficient because of the large bureaucracy that it requires; (3) more expensive (the price of blood is five to fifteen times higher); and (4) more dangerous, because there is a greater risk of disease and death from contaminated blood.[16] In short, a cost–benefit analysis shows that it is better not to have a market for blood.

KANTIAN ETHICS

Immanuel Kant (1724–1804) wrote his famous ethical treatise *Foundations of the Metaphysics of Morals* (1785) before the rise of English utilitarianism, but he was well acquainted with the idea of founding morality on the feelings of pleasure and pain, rather than on reason. Accordingly, Kant set out to restore reason to what he regarded as its rightful place in our moral life. Specifically, he attempted to show that there are some things that we ought to do and others that we ought not to do merely by virtue of being rational. Moral obligation thus has nothing to do with consequences, in Kant's view, but arises solely from a moral law that is binding on all rational beings. Although Kant's own expression of his theory is difficult to understand, the main thrust can be formulated in two intuitive principles: universalizability and respect for persons.

The Universalizability Principle

The universalizability principle can be illustrated by one of Kant's own examples:

> [A] man finds himself forced by need to borrow money. He well knows that he will not be able to repay it, but he also sees that nothing will be loaned him if he does not firmly promise to repay it at a certain time. He desires to make such a promise, but he has enough conscience to ask himself whether it is not improper and opposed to duty to relieve his distress in such a way.

What (morally) ought this man to do? A teleological theory would have us answer this question by determining the consequences of each alternative course of action, but Kant regarded all such appeals to consequences as morally irrelevant. As a deontologist, he held that the duty to tell the truth when making promises arises from a rule that ought to be followed without regard for consequences. Even if the man could do more good by borrowing money under false pretenses— by using it to pay for an operation that would save a person's life, for example—the action would still be wrong.

Kant addressed the problem of making a lying promise with a principle that he called the *categorical imperative*. His own cryptic statement of the categorical imperative is as follows:

ACT ONLY ACCORDING TO THAT MAXIM BY WHICH YOU CAN AT THE SAME TIME WILL THAT IT SHOULD BECOME A UNIVERSAL LAW.

Rendered into more comprehensible English, Kant's principle is, act only on rules (or maxims) that you would be willing to have everyone follow. The categorical imperative suggests a rather remarkable "thought experiment" to be performed whenever we deliberate about what to do. Suppose, for example, that every time we accept a rule for our own conduct, that very same rule would be imposed, by some miracle, on everyone. We would become, in other words, a universal rule maker. Under such conditions, are there some rules that we, as rational beings, simply could not accept (i.e., will to become universal law)?

Applying this to Kant's example, if the man were to obtain the loan under false pretenses, the rule on which he would be acting might be formulated: Whenever you need a loan, make a promise to repay the money, even if you know that you cannot do so. Although such a rule could easily be acted on by one person, the effect of its being made a rule for everyone—that is, of becoming a universal law—would be, in Kant's view, self-defeating. No one would believe anyone else, and the result would be that the phrase "I promise to do such-and-such" would lose its meaning. To Kant's own way of thinking, the objection to the rule just stated is not that every-one's following it would lead to undesirable consequences—that would be utilitarianism—but that everyone's following it describes an impossible state of affairs. Willing that everyone act on this rule is analogous to a person making plans to vacation in two places, say Acapulco and Aspen, *at the same time*. A person could will to go to either place, but willing the metaphysical impossi-bility of being in two places at once is not something that a rational person could will to do.

Regardless of whether Kant is successful in his attempt to show that immoral conduct is somehow irrational, many philosophers still find a kernel of truth in Kant's principle of the categorical imperative, which they express as the claim that all moral judgments must be *universalizable*. That is, if we say that an act is right for one person, then we are committed to saying, as a matter of logical consistency, that it is right for all other relevantly similar persons in relevantly similar circumstances. By the same token, if an act is wrong for other people, then it is wrong for any one person unless there is some difference that justifies making an exception. This *principle of universalizability* expresses the simple point that, as a matter of logic, we must be consistent in the judgments we make.

The principle of universalizability has immense implications for moral reasoning. First, it counters the natural temptation to make exceptions for ourselves or to apply a double standard. Consider a job applicant who exaggerates a bit on a résumé but is incensed to discover, after being hired, that the company misrepresented the opportunity for advancement. The person is being inconsistent to hold that it is all right for him to lie to others but wrong for anyone else to lie to him. An effective move in a moral argument is to challenge people who hold such positions to cite some morally relevant difference. Why is lying right in the one case and wrong in the other? If they can offer no answer, then they are forced by the laws of logic to give up one of the inconsistent judgments.

Second, the universalizability principle can be viewed as underlying the common question, "What if everyone did that?"[17] The consequences of a few people cheating on their taxes, for example, are negligible. If everyone were to cheat, however, the results would be disastrous. The force of "What if everyone did that?" is to get people to see that because it would be undesirable for everyone to cheat, no one ought to do so. This pattern of ethical reasoning involves an appeal to consequences, but it differs from standard forms of utilitarianism in that the consequences are hypothetical rather than actual. That is, whether anyone else actually cheats is irrelevant to the question, "What if everyone did that?" The fact that the results would be disastrous *if everyone did* is sufficient to entail the conclusion that cheating is wrong.

Respect for Persons

Kant offered a second formulation of the categorical imperative, which he expressed as follows:

ACT SO THAT YOU TREAT HUMANITY, WHETHER IN YOUR OWN PERSON OR THAT OF ANOTHER, ALWAYS AS AN END AND NEVER AS A MEANS ONLY.

These words are usually interpreted to mean that we should respect other people (and ourselves!) as human beings. The kind of respect that Kant had in mind is compatible with achieving our ends by enlisting the aid of other people. We use shop clerks and taxi drivers, for example, as a means for achieving our ends, and the owners of a business use employees as a means for achieving their ends. What is ruled out by Kant's principle, however, is treating people *only* as a means, so that they are no different, in our view, from mere "things."

In Kant's view, what is distinctive about human beings, which makes them different from "things" or inanimate objects, is the possession of reason, and by reason Kant means the ability to posit ends and to act purposefully to achieve them. In acting to achieve ends, human beings also have free will that enables them to create rules to govern their own conduct. This idea of acting on self-devised rules is conveyed by the term *autonomy*, which is derived from two Greek words meaning "self" and "law." To be autonomous is quite literally to be a lawgiver to oneself, or self-governing. A rational being, therefore, is a being who is autonomous. To respect other people, then, is to respect their capacity for acting freely, that is, their autonomy.

Kant's ethical theory thus yields at least two important results: the principles of universalizability and respect for persons, which are important elements of ethical reasoning that serve as valuable additions to the utilitarian approach.

VIRTUE ETHICS

Despite their differences, utilitarianism and Kantian ethics both address the question, What actions are right? Virtue ethics asks instead, what kind of person should we be? Moral character rather than right action is fundamental in this ethical tradition, which originated with the ancient Greeks and received its fullest expression in Aristotle's *Nicomachean Ethics*. The role of ethics according to Aristotle is to enable us to lead successful, rewarding lives—the kinds of lives that we would call "the good life." The good life in Aristotle's sense is possible only for virtuous persons—that is, persons who develop the traits of character that we call "the virtues." Aristotle not only made the case for the necessity of virtue for good living but also described particular virtues in illuminating detail.

What Is a Virtue?

Defining virtue has proven to be difficult, and philosophers are by no means in agreement.[18] Aristotle described virtue as a character trait that manifests itself in habitual action. Honesty, for example, cannot consist in telling the truth once; it is rather the trait of a person who tells the truth as a general practice. Only after observing people over a period of time can we determine whether they are honest. Mere feelings, like hunger, are not virtues, according to Aristotle, in part because virtues are *acquired* traits. A person must *become* honest through proper upbringing. A virtue is also something that we actually *practice*. Honesty is not simply a matter of knowing how to tell the truth but involves habitually telling the truth. For these reasons, Aristotle classified virtue as a *state* of character, which is different from a feeling or a skill. Finally, a virtue is something that we *admire* in a person; a virtue is an excellence of some kind that is worth having for its own sake. A skill like carpentry is useful for building a house, for example, but not everyone need be a carpenter. Honesty, by contrast, is a trait that everyone needs for a good life.

A complete definition of virtue must be even more encompassing, because a compassionate person, for example, must have certain kinds of feelings at the distress of others and also the capacity for sound, reasoned judgments in coming to their aid. Virtue, for Aristotle, is integrally related to what he calls *practical wisdom*, which may be described roughly as the whole of what a person needs in order to live well. Being wise about how to live involves more than having certain character traits, but being practically wise and being of good moral character are ultimately inseparable. Although the problems of defining virtue are important in a complete theory of virtue ethics, the idea of virtue as a trait of character that is essential for leading a successful life is sufficient for our purposes.

Most lists of the virtues contain few surprises. Such traits as benevolence, compassion, courage, courtesy, dependability, friendliness, honesty, loyalty, moderation, self-control, and toleration are most often mentioned. Aristotle also considered both pride and shame to be virtues on the grounds that we should be proud of our genuine accomplishments (but not arrogant) and properly shamed by our failings. More significantly, Aristotle lists justice among the virtues. A virtuous person not only has a sense of fair treatment but can also determine what constitutes fairness.

Defending the Virtues

Defending any list of the virtues requires consideration of the contribution that each character trait makes to a good life. In particular, the virtues are those traits that everyone needs for the good life irrespective of his or her specific situation. Thus, courage is a good thing for anyone to have, because perseverance in the face of dangers will improve our chances of getting whatever it is we want. Similarly, Aristotle's defense of moderation as a virtue hinges on the insight that a person given to excess will be incapable of effective action toward any end. Honesty, too, is a trait that serves everyone well because it creates trust, without which we could not work cooperatively with others.

In defending a list of virtues, we cannot consider merely their contribution to some end, however; we must also inquire into the end itself. If our conception of a successful life is amassing great power and wealth, for example, then would not ruthlessness be a virtue? A successful life of crime or lechery requires the character of a Fagin or a Don Juan, but we scarcely consider their traits to be virtues—or Fagin and Don Juan to be virtuous characters. The end of life—that at which we all aim, according to Aristotle—is *happiness*, and Aristotle would claim that no despot or criminal or lecher can be happy, no matter how successful such a person may be in these pursuits. Defending any list of virtues requires, therefore, that some content be given to the idea of a good life. What is the good life, the end for which the virtues are needed?

The virtues, moreover, are not merely means to happiness but are themselves constituents of it. That is, happiness does not consist solely of what we get in life but also includes who we are. A mother or a father, for example, cannot get the joy that comes from being a parent without actually having the traits that make one a good parent. Similarly, Aristotle would agree with Plato that anyone who became the kind of person who could be a successful despot, for example, would thereby become incapable of being happy because that person's personality would be disordered in the process.

To summarize, defending a list of the virtues requires both that we determine the character traits that are essential to a good life and that we give some content to the idea of a good life itself. Virtue ethics necessarily presupposes a view about human nature and the purpose of life. This point is worth stressing because the possibility of applying virtue ethics to business depends on a context that includes some conception of the nature and purpose of business.

Virtue in Business

Virtue ethics could be applied to business directly by holding that the virtues of a good businessperson are the same as those of a good person (period). Insofar as business is a part of life, why should the virtues of successful living not apply to this realm as well? However, business-people face situations that are peculiar to business, and so they may need certain business-related character traits. Some virtues of everyday life, moreover, are not wholly applicable to business. Any manager should be caring, for example, but a concern for employee welfare can go only so far when a layoff is unavoidable. Honesty, too, is a virtue in business, but a certain amount of bluffing or concealment is accepted and perhaps required in negotiations. Regardless of whether the ethics of business is different from that of everyday life, we need to show that virtue ethics is relevant to business by determining the character traits that make for a good businessperson.

Applying virtue ethics to business would require us, first, to determine the end at which business activity aims. If the purpose of business is merely to create as much wealth as possible, then we get one set of virtues. Robert C. Solomon, who develops a virtue ethics–based view of business in his book *Ethics and Excellence*, argues that mere wealth creation is not the purpose of business. Rather, a virtue approach, according to Solomon, considers business as an essential part of the good life.[19]

Solomon contends that individuals are embedded in communities and that business is essentially a communal activity, in which people work together for a common good. For individuals this means achieving a good life that includes rewarding, fulfilling work; and excellence for a corporation consists of making the good life possible for everyone in society. Whether any given character trait is a virtue in business, then, is to be determined by the purpose of business and by the extent to which that trait contributes to that purpose.

RIGHTS AND JUSTICE

Rights play an important role in business ethics and, indeed, in many ethical issues in society. Both employers and employees are commonly regarded as having certain rights. Employers have the right to conduct business as they see fit, to make decisions about hiring and promotion, and to be protected against unfair forms of competition. Employees have the right to organize and engage in collective bargaining and to be protected against discrimination and hazardous working conditions. Consumers and the general public also have rights in such matters as marketing and advertising, product safety, and the protection of the environment. Some American manufacturers have been accused of violating the rights of workers in developing countries by offering low wages and substandard working conditions.

The introduction of rights into the discussion of ethical issues is often confusing. First, the term *rights* is used in many different ways, so that the concept of a right and the various kinds of rights must be carefully distinguished. Second, many rights come into conflict. The right of an employee to leave his or her employer and join a competitor conflicts with the legitimate right of employers to protect trade secrets, for example, so that some balancing is required. Third, because of the moral significance that we attach to rights, there is a tendency to stretch the concept in ways that dilute its meaning. For example, the rights to receive adequate food, clothing, and medical care, mentioned in the Universal Declaration of Human Rights, are perhaps better described as political goals rather than rights. Fourth, there can be disagreement over the very existence of a right. Whether employees have a right to due process in discharge decisions, for example, is a subject of dispute. For all these reasons, the claim of a right is frequently the beginning of an ethical debate rather than the end.

The Nature and Value of Rights

The concept of a right can be explained by imagining a company that treats employees fairly but does not recognize due process as a right.[20] In this company, employees are dismissed only for good reasons after a thorough and impartial hearing, but there is no contract, statute, or other provision establishing a right of due process for all employees. Something is still missing, because the fair treatment that the employees enjoy results solely from the company's voluntary acceptance of certain personnel policies. If the company were ever to change these policies, then employees dismissed without due process would have no recourse. Contrast this with a company in which due process is established as a right. Employees in this company have something that was lacking in the previous company. They have an independent basis for challenging a decision by the company to dismiss them. They have something to stand on, namely, their rights.

Rights can be understood, therefore, as *entitlements*.[21] To have rights is to be entitled to act on our own or to be treated by others in certain ways without asking permission of anyone or being dependent on other people's goodwill. Rights entitle us to make claims on other people either to refrain from interfering in what we do or to contribute actively to our well-being—not as beggars, who can only entreat others to be generous, but as creditors, who can demand what is owed to them. This explanation of rights in terms of entitlements runs the risk of circularity (after all, what is an entitlement but something we have a right to?), but it is sufficiently illuminating to serve as a beginning of our examination.

Several different kinds of rights have been distinguished.

1. *Legal and Moral Rights. Legal rights* are rights that are recognized and enforced as part of a legal system. In the United States, these consist primarily of the rights set forth in the Constitution, including the Bill of Rights, and those created by acts of Congress and state legislatures. *Moral rights*, by contrast, are rights that do not depend on the existence of a legal system. They are rights that we (morally) *ought* to have, regardless of whether they are explicitly recognized by law. Moral rights derive their force not from being part of a legal system but from more general ethical rules and principles.

2. *Specific and General Rights.* Some rights are *specific* in that they involve identifiable individuals. A major source of specific rights is contracts, because these ubiquitous instruments create a set of mutual rights as well as duties for the individuals who are parties to them. Other rights are *general* rights, because they involve claims against everyone, or humanity in general. Thus, the right of free speech belongs to everyone, and the obligation to enforce this right rests with the whole community.

3. *Negative and Positive Rights.* Generally, *negative* rights are correlated with obligations on the part of others to refrain from acting in certain ways that interfere with our own freedom of action. *Positive* rights, by contrast, impose obligations on other people to provide us with some good or service and thereby to act positively on our behalf.[22] The right to property, for example, is largely a negative right, because no one else is obligated to provide us with property, but everyone has an obligation not to use or take our property without permission. The right to adequate healthcare, for example, is a positive right insofar as its implementation requires others to provide the necessary resources.

Natural Rights

Among the moral rights that are commonly recognized, one particular kind that is prominent in historical documents is *natural rights*, which are thought to belong to all persons purely by virtue of their being human.[23] Natural rights are characterized by two main features: *universality* and *unconditionality.* Universality means that they are possessed by all persons, without regard for race, sex, nationality, or any specific circumstances of birth or present condition. Unconditionality means that natural or human rights do not depend on any particular practices or institutions in society. The unconditionality of rights also means that there is nothing we can do to relinquish them or to deprive ourselves or others of them. This feature of natural, or human, rights is what is usually meant by the phrase *inalienable rights*, which is used in the American *Declaration of Independence.*[24]

The most prominent natural rights theory is that presented by John Locke (1633–1704) in his famous *Second Treatise of Government* (1690).[25] Locke began with the supposition of a state of nature, which is the condition of human beings in the absence of any government. The idea is to imagine what life would be like if there were no government and then to justify the establishment of a political state to remedy the defects of the state of nature. Locke held that human beings have rights, even in the state of nature, and that the justification for uniting into a state is to protect these rights. The most important natural right for Locke is the right to property. Although the bounty of the earth is provided by God for the benefit of all, no one can make use of it without taking some portion as one's own. This is done by means of labor, which is also a form of property. "Every man has property in his own person," according to Locke, and so "[t]he labor of his body and the work of his hands . . . are properly his."

Justice

Justice, like rights, is an important moral concept with a wide range of applications. We use it to evaluate not only the actions of individuals but also social, legal, political, and economic practices and institutions. Questions of *justice* or *fairness* (the two terms are used here interchangeably) often arise when there is something to distribute. If there is a shortage of organ donors, for example, we ask, what is a just or fair way of deciding who gets a transplant? If there is a burden, such as taxes, we want to make sure that everyone bears a fair share. Justice is also concerned with the righting of wrongs. It requires, for example, that a criminal be punished for a crime and that the punishment fit the crime by being neither too lenient nor too severe. To treat people justly is to give them what they deserve, which is sometimes the opposite of generosity and compassion. Indeed, we often speak of tempering justice with mercy.

The concept of justice is relevant to business ethics primarily in the distribution of benefits and burdens. Economic transformations often involve an overall improvement of welfare that is unevenly distributed, so that some groups pay a price while others reap the rewards. Is the resulting distribution just, and if not, is there anything that is owed to the losers? Justice also requires that something be done to compensate the victims of discrimination or defective products or industrial accidents. Because justice is also an important concept in evaluating various forms of social organization, we can also ask about the justice of the economic system in which business activity takes place.

The Nature and Value of Justice

The ancient Greek philosopher Aristotle distinguished three kinds of justice.

1. *Distributive justice,* which deals with the distribution of benefits and burdens.
2. *Compensatory justice*, which is a matter of compensating persons for wrongs done to them.
3. *Retributive justice,* which involves the punishment of wrongdoers.

Both compensatory and retributive justice are concerned with correcting wrongs. Generally, compensating the victims is the just way of correcting wrongs in private dealings, such as losses resulting from accidents and the failure to fulfill contracts, whereas retribution—that is, punishment—is the just response to criminal acts, such as assault or theft.[26]

Questions about distributive justice arise mostly in the evaluation of our social, political, and economic institutions, where the benefits and burdens of engaging in cooperative activities must be spread over a group. In some instances, a just distribution is one in which each person shares equally, but in others, unequal sharing is just if the inequality is in accord with some principle of distribution. Thus, in a graduated income tax system, ability to pay and not equal shares is the principle for distributing the burden. Generally, distributive justice is *comparative,* in that it considers not the absolute amount of benefits and burdens of each person but each person's amount relative to that of others.[27] Whether income is justly distributed, for example, cannot be determined by looking only at the income of one person but requires us, in addition, to compare the income of all people in a society.

The rationale of compensatory justice is that an accident caused by negligence, for example, upsets an initial moral equilibrium by making a person worse off in some way. By paying compensation, however, the condition of the victim can be returned to what it was before the accident, thereby restoring the moral equilibrium. Similarly, a person who commits a crime upsets a moral equilibrium by making someone else worse off. The restoration of the moral equilibrium in cases of this kind is achieved by a punishment that "fits the crime." Both compensatory justice and retributive justice are *noncomparative.* The amount of compensation owed to the victim of an accident or the punishment due to a criminal is determined by the features of each case and not by a comparison with other cases.

A useful distinction not discussed by Aristotle is that between just *procedures* and just *outcomes.*[28] In cases of distributive justice, we can distinguish between the procedures used to distribute goods and the outcome of those procedures, that is, the actual distribution achieved. A similar distinction can be made between the procedures for conducting trials, for example, and the outcomes of trials. If we know what outcomes are just in certain kinds of situations, then just procedures are those that produce or are likely to produce just outcomes. Thus, an effective method for dividing a cake among a group consists of allowing one person to cut it into the appropriate number of slices with the stipulation that that person take the last piece. Assuming that an equal division of the cake is just, a just distribution will be achieved, because cutting the cake into equal slices is the only way the person with the knife is assured of getting at least as much cake as anyone else. Similarly, just outcomes in criminal trials are those in which the guilty are convicted and the innocent are set free. The complex rules and procedures for trials are those that generally serve to produce those results.

Aristotle's Principle of Distributive Justice

Aristotle described justice as a kind of equality, but this is not very helpful since equality is subject to varying interpretations.[29] The extreme egalitarian position that everyone should be treated exactly alike has found few advocates, and most who call themselves egalitarians are concerned only to deny that certain differences ought to be taken into account. A more moderate egalitarianism contends that we ought to treat like cases alike. That is, any difference in the treatment of like cases requires a moral justification.

Aristotle expressed the idea of treating like cases alike in an arithmetical equation that represents justice as an equality of ratios.[30] Let us suppose that two people, A and B, each receive some share of a good, P. Any difference in their relative shares must be justified by some relevant difference, Q. Thus, a difference in pay, P, is justified if there is a difference in some other factor, Q, that justifies the difference in P—such as the fact that one person worked more hours or was more productive. Aristotle added the further condition that the difference in each person's share of the good must be *proportional* to the difference in his or her share of the relevant difference. If one person worked twice as many hours as another, then the pay should be exactly twice as much—no more and no less. Aristotle's principle of distributive justice can be stated in the following manner.[31]

$$\frac{\text{A'S SHARE OF P}}{\text{B'S SHARE OF P}} = \frac{\text{A'S SHARE OF Q}}{\text{B'S SHARE OF Q}}$$

This account of Aristotle's principle of distributive justice is obviously not complete until the content of both P and Q are fully specified. What are the goods in question? What features justify different shares of these goods? Among the goods distributed in any society are material goods such as food, clothing, housing, income, and wealth, which enable people to purchase material goods. There are many nonmaterial goods, including economic power, participation in the political process, and access to the courts, which are also distributed in some manner. Finally, Aristotle counted honor as a good, thereby recognizing that society distributes status and other intangibles.

Among the many different justifying features that have been proposed are ability, effort, accomplishment, contribution, and need.[32] In setting wages, for example, an employer might award higher pay to workers who have greater training and experience or greater talent (ability); to workers who apply themselves more diligently, perhaps overcoming obstacles or making great sacrifices (effort); to workers who have produced more or performed notable feats (accomplishment) or who provide more valued services (contribution); or, finally, to workers who have large families to support or who, for other reasons, have greater need.

Rawls's Egalitarian Theory

In *A Theory of Justice* (1971), the contemporary American philosopher John Rawls (1921–2002) offers two principles that he thinks express our considered views about justice. Rawls begins by asking us to imagine a situation in which rational, free, and equal persons, concerned to advance their own interests, attempt to arrive at unanimous agreement on principles that will serve as the basis for constructing the major institutions of society. Rawls stipulates further that these individuals are asked to agree on the principles of justice behind a *veil of ignorance* which prevents them from knowing many facts about themselves and their situation. Behind this veil, the bargainers are forced to be impartial and to view proposed principles from the perspective of all persons at once. Without any knowledge of their race or sex, for example, they are unlikely to advocate or support discriminatory principles, because they could be among the victims of discrimination.

Now, what principles would rational, self-interested persons freely agree to in a position of equality behind a veil of ignorance? Rawls thinks that there are two, which he states as follows:

1. Each person is to have an equal right to the most extensive total system of basic liberties compatible with a similar system of liberty for all.
2. Social and economic inequalities are to be arranged so that they are both
   a. to the greatest benefit of the least advantaged, and
   b. attached to offices and positions open to all under conditions of fair equality of opportunity.[33]

The reasoning behind the first principle is that an equal share of whatever goods are available is the most that any person could reasonably expect, given the requirement of unanimous agreement. Like the person who cuts the cake knowing that he will get the last piece, persons in the original position would opt for equal shares. The first principle is a rational rule to follow, Rawls says, when your place will be determined by your worst enemy. The second principle recognizes, however, that there are two conditions under which rational, self-interested persons would make an exception to the first principle and accept less than an equal share of some goods. According to principle 2a, called the *difference principle*, an unequal distribution is justified if everyone would be better off with the inequality than without it. If it is possible to increase the total amount of income, for example, but not possible to distribute it equally, then the resulting distribution is still just, according to Rawls, as long as the extra income is distributed in such a way that everyone benefits from the inequality. Principle 2b, the *principle of equal opportunity*, is similar to the view that careers should be open to all on the basis of talent. Whether a person gets a certain job, for example, ought to be determined by competence in that line of work and not by skin color, family connections, or any other irrelevant characteristic.

Nozick's Entitlement Theory

Robert Nozick (1938–2002) offers a theory of justice, called the entitlement theory, which stands alongside Rawls's egalitarianism as a major contemporary account of justice. The principles of justice in Nozick's theory differ from Rawls's theory in two major respects. First, they are *historical* principles as opposed to *nonhistorical* or *end-state* principles.[34] Historical principles, Nozick explains, take into account the process by which a distribution came about, whereas end-state principles evaluate a distribution with regard to certain structural features at a given time. Second, the principles of justice in both Aristotle's and Rawls's theories are *patterned*.[35] A principle is patterned if it specifies some feature in a particular distribution and evaluates the distribution according to the presence or absence of that feature. Any principle of the form "Distribute according to _____," such as "Distribute according to IQ scores," is a patterned principle, as is the socialist formula, "From each according to his abilities, to each according to his needs."

Nozick thinks that any acceptable principle of justice must be nonpatterned because any particular pattern of distribution can be achieved and maintained only by violating the right to liberty. Upholding the right to liberty, in turn, upsets any particular pattern of justice. He argues for this point by asking us to consider a case in which there is a perfectly just distribution, as judged by some desired pattern, and also perfect freedom. Now suppose that a famous athlete—Nozick suggests Wilt Chamberlain—will play only if he is paid an additional 25 cents for each ticket sold and that many people are so excited to see Wilt Chamberlain play that they will cheerfully pay the extra 25 cents for the privilege. Both Wilt Chamberlain and the fans are within their rights to act as they do, but at the end of the season, if one million people pay to see him play, then Wilt Chamberlain will have an additional income of $250,000, which is presumably more than he would be entitled to on a patterned principle of justice. By exercising their right to liberty, though, Wilt Chamberlain and the fans have upset the just distribution that formerly prevailed. In order to maintain the patterned distribution, it would be necessary to restrict the freedom of Wilt Chamberlain or the fans in some way, such as prohibiting the extra payment or taxing away the excess.

NOZICK'S THREE PRINCIPLES.   The entitlement theory can be stated very simply. A distribution is just, Nozick says, "if everyone is entitled to the holdings they possess."[36] Whether we are entitled to certain holdings is determined by tracing their history. Most of what we possess comes from others through transfers, such as purchases and gifts. Thus, we might own a piece of land because we bought it from someone, who in turn bought it from someone else, and so on. Proceeding backward in this fashion, we ultimately reach the original settler who did not acquire it through a transfer but by clearing the land and tilling it. As long as each transfer was just and the original acquisition was just, our present holding is just. "Whatever arises from a just situation by just steps is itself just," Nozick writes.[37] In his theory, then, particular distributions are just not because they conform to some pattern (equality or social utility, for example) but solely because of antecedent events.

Nozick's theory requires at least two principles: a principle of just transfer and a principle of just original acquisition. Because holdings can be unjustly appropriated by force or fraud, a third principle, a principle of rectification, is also necessary in order to correct injustices by restoring holdings to the rightful owners. If we rightfully possess some holding—a piece of land, for example, by either transfer or original acquisition—then we are free to use or dispose of it as we wish. We have a right, in other words, to sell it to whomever we please at whatever price that person is willing to pay, or we can choose to give it away. As long as the exchange is purely voluntary, with no force or fraud, the resulting redistribution is just. Any attempt to prevent people from engaging in voluntary exchanges in order to secure a particular distribution is a violation of liberty, according to the entitlement theory.

A world consisting only of just acquisitions and just transfers would be just, according to Nozick, no matter what the pattern of distribution. Some people, through hard work, shrewd trades, or plain good luck, would most likely amass great wealth, whereas others, through indolence, misjudgment, or bad luck, would probably end up in poverty. However, the rich in such a world would have no obligation to aid the poor,[38] nor would it be just to coerce them into doing so. Each person's share would be determined largely through his or her choices and those of others. Nozick suggests that the entitlement theory can be expressed simply as "From each as they choose, to each as they are chosen."

The entitlement theory supports a market system with only the absolute minimum of government intervention, as long as the principles of just acquisition and just transfer are satisfied. The reason is that a system in which we have complete freedom to acquire property and engage in mutually advantageous trades (without violating the rights of another person, of course) is one in which our own rights are most fully protected. To critics who fear that unregulated markets would lead to great disparities between rich and poor and a lowering of the overall welfare of society, Nozick has a reply. The point of justice is not to promote human well-being or to achieve a state of equality; it is to protect our rights. Because a market system does this better than any other form of economic organization, it is just.

Conclusion

This chapter presents the main concepts and theories of ethics that have been developed over centuries by major moral philosophers. The value of any theory for business ethics is its usefulness in evaluating business practices, institutional arrangements, and economic systems. In general, all of these theories justify most prevailing business practices, the institution of the modern corporation, and capitalism or the market system, but they also provide the basis for some criticism and improvement. In the subsequent chapters, this theoretical foundation is used to explore a wide range of practical business ethics topics.

CASE 3.2   ✴ Explore the Concept on mythinkinglab.com

Exporting Pollution

As an assistant to the vice president of environmental affairs at Americhem, Rebecca Wright relishes the opportunity to apply her training in public-policy analysis to the complex and emotion-laden issues that her company faces.[39] Rebecca is convinced that cost–benefit analysis, her specialty, provides a rational decision-making tool that cuts through personal feelings and lays bare the hard economic realities. Still, she was startled by the draft of a memo that her boss, Jim Donnelly, shared with her. The logic of Jim's argument seems impeccable, but the conclusions are troubling—and Rebecca is sure that the document would create a furor if it were ever made public. Jim is preparing the memo for an upcoming decision on the location for a new chemical plant. The main problem is that atmospheric pollutants from the plant, although mostly harmless, would produce a persistent haze; and one of the particles that would be released into the atmosphere is also known to cause liver cancer in a very small portion of the people exposed. Sitting down at her desk to write a response, Rebecca reads again the section of the memo that she had circled with her pen.

From an environmental point of view, the case for locating the new plant in a Third World country is overwhelming. These reasons are especially compelling in my estimation:

1. The harm of pollution, and hence its cost, increases in proportion to the amount of already existing pollution. Adding pollutants to a highly polluted environment does more harm than the same amount added to a relatively unpolluted environment. For this reason, much of the Third World is not efficiently utilized as a depository of industrial wastes, and only the high cost of transporting wastes prevents a more efficient utilization of this resource.

2. The cost of health-impairing pollution is a function of the forgone earnings of those who are disabled or who die as a result. The cost of pollution will be least, therefore, in the country with the lowest wages. Any transfer of pollution from a high-wage, First World country to a low-wage, Third World country will produce a net benefit.

3. The risk of liver cancer from this plant's emissions has been estimated at one-in-a-million in the United States, and the resulting cancer deaths would occur mostly among the elderly. The risk posed by the new plant will obviously be much less in a country where people die young from other causes and where few will live long enough to incur liver cancer from any source. Overall, the people of any Third World country might prefer the jobs that our plant will provide if the only drawback is a form of cancer that they are very unlikely to incur.

4. The cost of visibility-impairing pollution will be greater in a country where people are willing to spend more for good visibility. The demand for clear skies—which affects the aesthetics of the environment and not people's health—has very high-income elasticity, and so the wealthy will pay more than the poor to live away from factory smoke, for example. Because the cost of anything is determined by how much people are willing to pay in a market, the cost of visibility-impairing pollution in a First World country will be higher than the same amount of pollution in a Third World country. Thus, people in the United States might prefer clear skies over the benefits of our plant, but people elsewhere might choose differently.

CASE 3.3   ✴ Explore the Concept on mythinkinglab.com

Clean Hands in a Dirty Business

Even with her newly minted M.B.A., Janet Moore was having no luck finding that dream job in the marketing department of a spirited, on-the-move company. Now, almost any job looked attractive, but so far no one had called her back for a second interview. Employers were all looking for people with experience, but that requires getting a job first. Just as she began to lose hope, Janet bumped into Karen, who had been two years ahead of her in college. Karen, too, was looking for a job, but in the meantime she was employed by a firm that was planning to add another marketing specialist. Janet was familiar with Karen's employer from a case study that she had researched for an M.B.A. marketing course, but what she had learned appalled her.

The company, Union Tobacco, Inc., is the major U.S. manufacturer of snuff, and her case study examined how this once staid company had managed to attract new customers to a product that had long ago saturated its traditional market.[40] Before 1970, almost all users of snuff—a form of tobacco that is sucked rather than chewed—were older men. The usual form of snuff is unattractive to nonusers because of the rough tobacco taste, the unpleasant feel of loose tobacco particles in the mouth, and the high nicotine content, which makes many first-time users ill. Snuff, to put it mildly, is a hard sell.

The company devised a product development and marketing campaign that a federal government report labeled a "graduation strategy." Two new lines were developed, a low-nicotine snuff in a tea-bag-like pouch with a mint flavor that has proved to be popular with young boys, and a step-up product with slightly more nicotine, a cherry flavor, and a coarse cut that avoids the unpleasantness of tobacco floating in the mouth. Both products are advertised heavily in youth-oriented magazines with the slogan "Easy to use, anywhere, anytime," and free samples are liberally distributed at fairs, rodeos, and car races around the country.

The strategy has worked to perfection. Youngsters who start on the low-nicotine mint- and cherry-flavored products soon graduate to the company's two stronger, best-selling brands. Within two decades, the market for snuff tripled to about 7 million users, of which 1 million to 2 million are between the ages of 12 and 17. The average age of first use is now estimated to be $9^1/_2$ years old. Janet also reported in her case study that snuff users are more than four times more likely to develop cancers of the mouth generally and 50 times more likely to develop specific cancers of the gum and inner-cheek lining. Several suits had been filed by the parents of teenagers who had developed mouth cancers, and tooth loss and gum lesions have also been widely reported, even in relatively new users.

Karen admitted that she was aware of all this but encouraged Janet to join her anyway. "You wouldn't believe some of the truly awful marketing ploys that I have been able to scuttle," she said. "Unless people like you and me get involved, these products will be marketed by people who don't care one bit about the little kids who are getting hooked on snuff. Believe me, it's disgusting work. I don't like to tell people what I do, and I sometimes look at myself in the mirror and ask what has become of the idealism I had starting out. But there will always be someone to do this job, and I feel that I have made a difference. If you join me, the two of us together can slow things down and avoid the worst excesses, and maybe we'll even save a few lives. Plus, you can get some experience and be in a better position to move on."

Janet admitted to herself that Karen had a strong argument. Maybe she was being too squeamish and self-centered, just trying to keep her own hands clean. Maybe she could do others some good and help herself at the same time by taking the job. But then again. . . .

CASE 3.4 ✳ Explore the Concept on mythinkinglab.com

A Sticky Situation

Kent Graham is still on the telephone, receiving the good news that he has just secured his largest order as an account manager for Dura-Stick Label Products.[41] His joy is tinged with uncertainty, however.

Dura-Stick is a leader in label converting for the durable-products marketplace. Label converting consists of converting log rolls of various substrates (paper, polyester, vinyl) into die-cut, printed labels. The company specializes in high-performance labels for the automotive, lawn and garden, and appliance industries. Dura-Stick has a well-deserved reputation for quality, technical knowledge, and service that enables the company to command a premium price for its products in a very competitive market.

Kent Graham has been with Dura-Stick for two years. Because he came to the company with 10 years in the label industry, he was able to negotiate a very good salary and compensation plan, but his accomplishments since joining Dura-Stick have been mediocre at best. Kent fears that his time with Dura-Stick might be limited unless he starts closing some big accounts. Furthermore, with a wife and two children to support, losing his job would be disastrous. Kent was on a mission to land a big account.

Kent called on Jack Olson at Spray-On Inc., a manufacturer of industrial spraying systems for the automotive painting industry. Dura-Stick has been providing Spray-On with various warning and instructional labels for about 20 years. Jack has been very pleased with Dura-Stick's performance, especially the quality of its manufacturing department under the direction of Tim Davis. After giving Kent another excellent vendor evaluation report, Jack began to describe a new project at Spray-On, a paint sprayer for household consumer use that needs a seven-color label with very precise graphics. This label is different from the industrial two-color labels that Dura-Stick currently supplies to Spray-On.

Jack explained that this was the biggest project that Spray-On has undertaken in recent years and that it would generate a very large order for some label company. Jack then asked Kent, "Does Dura-Stick produce these multicolor, consumer-type labels?" Kent thought for a moment. He knew that a "yes" would give him a better shot at the business, and Dura-Stick might be able to handle the job, even though the company's experience to date was only with two-color labels. Almost without thinking, he replied, "Sure we can handle it, Jack, that's right up our alley!" "That's great news," Jack shot back. "Now take this sample and give me your proposal by Monday. Oh, and by the way, I hope your proposal looks good, because I would really feel confident if this important project were in the hands of your production people!"

Kent gave the sample to Marty Klein, who is responsible for coordinating the costs and price quotes for new opportunities. Marty took one look at the sample and said emphatically, "We'll have to farm this one out." Kent's heart sank down to his shoes. He knew that Jack would want to work with Dura-Stick only if the labels were produced at Dura-Stick's facility. Yet, he still allowed Marty to put the numbers together for the proposal. Kent presented the proposal to Jack at Spray-On. "Gee, Kent, these prices are pretty high, about 20 percent higher than your competition. That's pretty hard to swallow."

Kent knew that the price would be high because it included the cost of another company producing the labels plus Dura-Stick's usual profit margin, but he countered cheerily, "You know the quality that we provide and how important this project is to your company. Isn't it worth the extra 20 percent for the peace of mind that you will have?"

"Let me think about it," Jack replied.

The next day, Kent got a phone call from Jack.

"Congratulations, Kent, Dura-Stick has been awarded the business. It was a tough sell to my people, but I convinced them that the extra money would be well spent because of the excellent production department that you have. If it wasn't for the fact that Tim Davis will personally oversee production, you guys probably would not have gotten this business."

Kent had to bite his tongue. He knew that Tim would not be involved because the labels would be produced in Kansas City by Labeltec, which would then send the finished labels to Dura-Stick for shipment to Spray-On's facility. Kent also knew that Jack would be completely satisfied with the quality of the labels. Besides, this order was crucial to his job security, not to mention the well-being of his company.

While Jack continued to explain Spray-On's decision, Kent pondered how he should close this conversation.

CASE 3.5 ✳ Explore the Concept on mythinkinglab.com

An Auditor's Dilemma

Sorting through a stack of invoices, Alison Lloyd's attention was drawn to one from Ace Glass Company. Her responsibility as the new internal auditor for Gem Packing was to verify all expenditures, and she knew that Ace had already been paid for the June delivery of the jars that are used for Gem's jams and jellies. On closer inspection, she noticed that the invoice was for deliveries in July and August that had not yet been made. Today was only June 10. Alison recalled approving several other invoices lately that seemed to be misdated, but the amounts were small compared with the $130,000 that Gem spends each month for glass jars. "I had better check this out with purchasing," she thought.

Over lunch, Greg Berg, the head of purchasing, explained the system to her. The jam and jelly division operates under an incentive plan whereby the division manager and the heads of the four main units—sales, production, distribution, and purchasing—receive substantial bonuses for meeting their quota in pretax profits for the fiscal year, which ends on June 30. The bonuses are about one-half of annual salary and constitute one-third of the managers' total compensation. In addition, meeting quota is weighted heavily in evaluations, and missing even once is considered to be a deathblow to the career of an aspiring executive at Gem. So the pressure on these managers is intense. On the other hand, there is nothing to be gained from exceeding a quota. An exceptionally good year is likely to be rewarded with an even higher quota the next year, because quotas are generally set at corporate headquarters by adding 5 percent to the previous year's results.

Greg continued to explain that several years ago, after the quota had been safely met, the jam and jelly division began prepaying as many expenses as possible—not only for glass jars but also for advertising costs, trucking charges, and some commodities, such as sugar. The practice has continued to grow, and sales also helps out by delaying orders until the next fiscal year or by falsifying delivery dates when a shipment has already gone out. "Regular suppliers like Ace Glass know how we work," Greg said, "and they sent the invoices for July and August at my request." He predicts that Alison will begin seeing more irregular invoices as the fiscal year winds down. "Making quota gets easier each year," Greg observed, "because the division gets an ever-increasing head start, but the problem of finding ways to avoid going too far over quota has become a real nightmare." Greg is not sure, but he thinks that other divisions are doing the same thing. "I don't think corporate has caught on yet," he said, "but they created the system, and they've been happy with the results so far. If they're too dumb to figure out how we're achieving them, that's their problem."

Alison recalled that upon becoming a member of the Institute of Internal Auditors, she agreed to abide by the IIA code of ethics. This code requires members to exercise "honesty, objectivity, and diligence" in the performance of their duties but also to be loyal to the employer. However, loyalty does not include being a party to any "illegal or improper activity." As an internal auditor, she is also responsible for evaluating the adequacy and effectiveness of the company's system of financial control. But what is the harm of shuffling a little paper around? she thinks. Nobody is getting hurt, and it all works out in the end.

Notes

1. The information in this case is taken from Alecia Swasy, *Soap Opera: The Inside Story of Procter & Gamble* (New York: Touchstone, 1994); James S. Hirsch, "Procter & Gamble Calls in the Law to Track News Leak," *Wall Street Journal*, 12 August 1991, A1; James S. Hirsch and Milo Gegelin, "P&G Says Inquiry on Leak to Journal Was Done Properly," *Wall Street Journal*, 13 August 1991, A3; James S. Hirsch and Milo Gegelin, "What Possessed P&G," *Wall Street Journal*, 13 August 1991, A16; James S. Hirsch, "No Charges Are Expected in P&G Affair," *Wall Street Journal*, 14 August 1991, A3; Mark Fitzgerald, "Cops Investigate News Leak," *Editor & Publisher*, 17 August 1991, 9, 39; James S. Hirsch, "P&G Won't Bring Criminal Charges as a Result of Probe," *Wall Street Journal*,

19 August 1991, A3, A5; William Safire, "At P&G: It Sinks," *New York Times*, 5 September 1991, A25; "P&G Looks for a News Leak," *ABA Journal* (November 1991), 32; "Biggest Business Goofs of 1991," *Fortune*, 13 January 1992, 80–83.

2. This formulation of RU follows that given by David Lyons for what he calls "ideal rule-utilitarianism." David Lyons, *Forms and Limits of Utilitarianism* (Oxford: Oxford University Press, 1965), 140.

3. Some philosophers hold that there is no difference between the two formulations. See Lyons, *Forms and Limits of Utilitarianism*, chap. 3. Also, R. M. Hare, *Freedom and Reason* (Oxford: Oxford University Press, 1963), 130–36; and Alan F. Gibbard, "Rule-Utilitarianism: Merely an Illusory Alternative?" *Australasian Journal of Philosophy*, 43 (1965), 211–20.

4. See, for example, Lionel Robbins, *An Essay on the Nature and Significance of Economic Science* (London: Macmillan, 1932), 140; and Kenneth Arrow, *Social Choice and Individual Values*, 2nd ed. (New York: John Wiley, 1963), 9.

5. A defense of interpersonal comparisons of utility by a prominent economist is I. M. D. Little, *A Critique of Welfare Economics*, 2nd ed. (Oxford: Oxford University Press, 1957), chap. 4.

6. For an authoritative exposition, see E. J. Mishan, *Cost-Benefit Analysis* (New York: Praeger, 1976).

7. These points are made by Steven Kelman, "Cost-Benefit Analysis: An Ethical Critique," *Regulation* (January–February 1981), 33–40.

8. See M. W. Jones-Lee, *The Value of Life: An Economic Analysis* (Chicago, IL: University of Chicago Press, 1976). Also, Michael D. Bayles, "The Price of Life," *Ethics*, 89 (1978), 20–34. For trenchant criticism of these methods, see Steven E. Rhoads, "How Much Should We Spend to Save a Life?" in *Valuing Life: Public Policy Dilemmas*, ed. Steven Rhoads (Boulder, CO: Westview Press, 1980), 285–311.

9. Peter Passell, "How Much for a Life? Try $3 to $5 Million," *New York Times*, 29 January 1995, D3.

10. Ibid.

11. Rosemary Tong, *Ethics in Public Policy Analysis* (Upper Saddle River, NJ: Prentice Hall, 1986), 20.

12. Mark Sagoff, "At the Shrine of Our Lady of Fatima, or Why Political Questions Are Not All Economic," *Arizona Law Review*, 23 (1981), 1283–98.

13. Kelman, "Cost-Benefit Analysis: An Ethical Critique," 39.

14. Richard M. Titmuss, *The Gift Relationship: From Human Blood to Social Policy* (London: Allen & Unwin, 1971).

15. Peter Singer, "Rights and the Market," in *Justice and Economic Distribution*, ed. John Arthur and William H. Shaw (Upper Saddle River, NJ: Prentice Hall, 1978), 213.

16. Titmuss, *Gift Relationship*, 246.

17. For a discussion of the logical force of this question, see Colin Strang, "What if Everyone Did That?" *Durham University Journal*, 53 (1960), 5–10.

18. For analyses of the virtues, see Philippa Foot, *Virtues and Vices and Other Essays in Moral Philosophy* (Berkeley, CA: University of California Press, 1978); Peter T. Geach, *The Virtues* (Cambridge: Cambridge University Press, 1977); Gregory E. Pence, "Recent Work on the Virtues," *American Philosophical Quarterly*, 21 (1984), 281–97; James D. Wallace, *Virtues and Vices* (Ithaca, NY: Cornell University Press, 1978); G. H. von Wright, *The Varieties of Goodness* (London: Routledge & Kegan Paul, 1963).

19. Robert C. Solomon, *Ethics and Excellence: Cooperation and Integrity in Business* (New York: Oxford University Press, 1992), 104.

20. This method of explaining rights is derived from Joel Feinberg, "The Nature and Value of Rights," *The Journal of Value Inquiry*, 4 (1970), 243–57. Reprinted in Joel Feinberg, *Rights, Justice, and the Bounds of Liberty* (Princeton, NJ: Princeton University Press, 1980), 143–55; and in David Lyons, ed., *Rights* (Belmont, CA: Wadsworth, 1979), 78–91.

21. This term is used in H. J. McCloskey, "Rights," *The Philosophical Quarterly*, 15 (1965), 115–27; and also in Richard A. Wasserstrom, "Rights, Human Rights, and Racial Discrimination," *The Journal of Philosophy*, 61 (1964), 628–41. For a useful survey of different accounts, see Rex Martin and James W. Nickel, "Recent Work on the Concept of Rights," *American Philosophical Quarterly*, 17 (1980), 165–80.

22. Closely related is a distinction between negative and positive liberty. A poor man is free (in a negative sense) to buy a loaf of bread, for example, as long as no one stands in his way, but he is not free (in a positive sense) unless he has the means to buy the bread. Compare these two senses in the case of "fee for service" medical care, which secures free *choice*, and socialized medicine, which provides free *access*. Which system of medical care is more "free"? The classic discussion of this distinction is Isaiah Berlin, "Two Concepts of Liberty," in *Four Essays on Liberty* (Oxford: Oxford University Press, 1969), 118–72.

23. Among the many works describing natural or human rights are Maurice Cranston, *What Are Human Rights?* (New York: Basic Books, 1963); B. Mayo, "What Are Human Rights?" in *Political Theory and the Rights of Man*, ed. D. D. Raphael (Bloomington: Indiana University Press, 1967), 68–80; D. D. Raphael, "Human Rights, Old and New," in *Political Theory and the Rights of Man*, 54–67; Maurice Cranston, "Human Rights, Real and Supposed," in Raphael, *Political Theory and the Rights of Man*, 43–53; and A. I. Melden, *Rights and Persons* (Berkeley and Los Angeles: University of California Press, 1977), 166–69.

24. See Stuart M. Brown, Jr., "Inalienable Rights," *The Philosophical Review*, 64 (1955), 192–211; and B. A. Richards, "Inalienable Rights: Recent Criticism and Old Doctrine," *Philosophy and Phenomenological Research*, 29 (1969), 391–404.

25. Locke's theory of natural rights is the subject of great controversy. Two articles that provide a good introduction are W. Von Leyden, "John Locke and Natural Law," *Philosophy*, 31 (1956), 23–35; and William J. Wainwright, "Natural Rights," *American Philosophical Quarterly*, 4 (1967), 79–84.

26. Aristotle makes the distinction between compensatory and retributive justice in terms of voluntary and involuntary

relations. A contract is a voluntary arrangement between two people, whereas the victim of an assault enters into the relation involuntarily. Many commentators have found this a rather awkward way of making the distinction.

27. The distinction between comparative and noncomparative justice is discussed in Joel Feinberg, "Comparative Justice," *The Philosophical Review*, 83 (1974), 297–338, reprinted in Joel Feinberg, *Rights, Justice, and the Bounds of Liberty* (Princeton, NJ: Princeton University Press, 1980), 265–306.

28. The distinction is discussed in Brian Barry, *Political Argument* (London: Routledge & Kegan Paul, 1965), 97–100.

29. For a discussion of the connection, see Gregory Vlastos, "Justice and Equality," in *Social Justice*, ed. Richard B. Brandt (Upper Saddle River, NJ: Prentice Hall, 1962), 31–72.

30. For a discussion of Aristotle's principle, see Hans Kelsen, "Aristotle's Doctrine of Justice," in *What Is Justice* (Berkeley and Los Angeles: University of California Press, 1957), 117–36; and Renford Bambrough, "Aristotle on Justice," in *New Essays on Plato and Aristotle*, ed. Renford Bambrough (London: Routledge & Kegan Paul, 1965), 159–74.

31. Taken from William K. Frankena, "Some Beliefs about Justice," in *Freedom and Morality*, ed. John Bricke (Lawrence, KS: University Press of Kansas, 1976), 56.

32. For a discussion of this list, see Nicholas Rescher, *Distributive Justice* (Indianapolis, IN: Bobbs-Merrill, 1966), chap. 4.

33. Rawls, *A Theory of Justice*, 302.

34. Robert Nozick, *Anarchy, State and Utopia* (New York: Basic Books, 1974), 153–55.

35. Ibid., 155–60.

36. Ibid., 151.

37. Ibid.

38. Individuals could voluntarily agree with others to contribute to the relief of poverty, in which case an obligation would exist. See ibid., 265–68.

39. This case is based on a memo written by Lawrence Summers, then chief economist at the World Bank. See "Let Them Eat Pollution," *The Economist*, 8 February 1992, 66.

40. Material for this case is taken from Alix M. Freedman, "How a Tobacco Giant Doctors Snuff Brands to Boost Their 'Kick,'" *Wall Street Journal*, 26 October 1994, A1, A6; and Philip J. Hilts, "Snuff Makers Are Accused of a Scheme to Lure Young," *New York Times*, 27 April 1995, A13.

41. This case was prepared by Kerry Winans under the supervision of Professor John R. Boatright. Copyright 1995 by John R. Boatright.

4

Whistle-Blowing

((•⊸ **Listen** to the **Chapter Audio** on **mythinkinglab.com**

CASE 4.1 ⁕⊸**Explore** the **Concept** on **mythinkinglab.com**

Time's Persons of the Year

In a year of momentous events, *Time* magazine honored three whistle-blowers as "persons of the year" for 2002.[1] With the collapse of Enron and WorldCom and the aftermath of 9/11 still reverberating, this annual cover story brought recognition to three women who played important roles in these calamities.

Sherron Watkins wrote a lengthy memo to Ken Lay, her top boss at Enron, warning of the financial time bomb hidden in the company's questionable off-balance-sheet partnerships.[2] "I am incredibly nervous," she wrote, "that we will implode in a wave of accounting scandals." Cynthia Cooper, the head of internal auditing at WorldCom, unraveled the accounting irregularities that enabled CEO Bernie Ebbers and CFO Scott Sullivan to hide almost $4 billion in losses (a figure that eventually totaled more than $9 billion).[3] And Coleen Rowley, a career FBI agent in Minneapolis, sent a confidential 13-page memo to the agency's director, Robert Mueller, contradicting his claim that there was no evidence that terrorists were planning the 9/11 attacks.[4] She complained that the head office in Washington, DC, had ignored pleas from the Minneapolis branch to investigate Zacarias Moussaoui, the alleged missing twentieth highjacker, who had been eager to learn how to fly a Boeing 747, and had also overlooked reports from an agent in Phoenix about Middle-Eastern students seeking to enroll in flying schools there.

In each case, these "persons of the year," all women who occupied relatively high positions, had exhibited extraordinary courage and determination to establish the truth and make it known to those in charge. None of them sought public acclaim or even thought of themselves as whistle-blowers. They submitted their memos confidentially to the appropriate parties. Watkins responded to an open invitation by Lay, the chairman of the board, for Enron employees to air their concerns after the sudden departure of CEO Jeffrey Skilling. She explained to Lay that Skilling probably saw the coming collapse and wanted to avoid involvement. Cooper reported her findings to the audit committee of WorldCom's board because Ebbers and Sullivan, her superiors, were deeply implicated. Only Rowley went outside the usual chain of command by writing directly to the FBI director. Their memos became public when they were leaked during preparations for congressional hearings. Watkins and Rowley were eventually called to testify before Congress, but Cooper was excused to avoid interfering with a Justice Department investigation of WorldCom.

Their motivation, in each case, was to save the organization and, for Watkins and Rowley, the top leaders from serious mistakes. Watkins apparently thought that Lay was unaware of the danger facing the company and that, once informed, he would take corrective action. (She would discover later that Lay's immediate response was to seek an opinion from a company lawyer on whether she could be terminated.) Rowley sought to apprise FBI director Mueller of the truth so that he could correct his public statements and avoid the political damage that might result from any revelations about the bungled Moussaoui investigation. She also urged Mueller to undertake reforms that she thought would strengthen the agency. Only Cooper seemed to be aware that her revelations could cause great problems for her superiors, Ebbers and Sullivan in this case, but she recognized that the board of directors rightly controls the corporation and has ultimate responsibility for protecting it. She no doubt thought that the audit committee of the board, which has the task of ensuring proper accounting, would take appropriate action, as indeed it did.

A further similarity is that each woman did not voice vague, unfounded concerns but assembled a carefully documented list of possible wrongdoings. The charges in their memos were made more credible by the women's expertise and insider's knowledge. Watkins obtained a master's degree in accounting and had risen in the ranks at Arthur Andersen, where she worked on the Enron account before being recruited by the company in 1993. At Enron, she held four high-level finance positions in seven years, eventually becoming vice president of corporate development. In her memo, she explained in detail the problems with two off-the-books partnerships, the Condor and the Raptor deals, and urged that they be reviewed by independent law and accounting firms. Cooper and her staff worked many weeks, often after hours, untangling WorldCom's irregular accounting practices, and in a meeting with the audit committee in Washington, DC, she was able to explain how CFO Sullivan and the company's controller had systematically recorded expenses as capital investments, a clear violation of accounting rules. In keeping with Rowley's sole purpose "to provide the facts within my purview so that an accurate assessment can be obtained," she provided an exhaustive account with footnotes of the Minneapolis agents' investigation of Moussaoui and the obstacles thrown up by the Washington head office.[5]

Much has been made of the fact that all three of these whistle-blowers are women, a feature they share with two other prominent whistle-blowers, whose stories were made into popular movies, namely, Karen Silkwood and Erin Brockovich.[6] However, research suggests that women are less likely than men to blow the whistle.[7] Several other common factors, though, may explain why these women became whistle-blowers. They had benefited from the breaks in the glass ceiling that allowed them to assume high positions, which in turn enabled them to witness wrongdoing and to have credibility reporting it. At the same time, they were still outsiders in a clubby male culture and did not share the values of their male colleagues or their sense of belonging. Anita Hill, who herself gained national attention by raising charges of sexual harassment in the confirmation process for Supreme Court justice Clarence Thomas, calls these women "insiders with outsider values."[8] Hill suggests that women's sensitivity to their own mistreatment in the workplace may make them more sensitive to other kinds of wrongdoing and more willing to speak out against them. As one journalist observed, these whistle-blowers prove that "there are women talented enough to break through the glass ceiling who are even more willing to break more glass to make the climb to the top worth it."[9]

Questions have also been raised about whether these women *were* even whistle-blowers. Although each wrote an explosive memo, it was sent confidentially to a person at the top of the organization with the aim of protecting the organization. No one went outside the chain of command. Only Coleen Rowley's memo to the audit committee of the board produced decisive, corrective action. After Watkins met personally with Lay, he turned the memo over to the same law firm that had approved many Enron transactions, and, unsurprisingly, this firm found no substance to the charges she raised. The memos by Watkins and Rowley provided top leaders with an opportunity to protect themselves before any bad news reached the public. And all three memos came to light only because of congressional hearings.

Watkins's action, in particular, has been criticized. Her memo advises Lay to develop a "clean up plan" that consists in the best case to clean up "quietly if possible," and in the worst case to develop public relations, investor relations, and customer assurance plans, legal actions, dismissals, and disclosure. By assuming that Lay was uninformed about Enron's financial problems, some charge that Watkins bolstered his legal defense strategy of ignorance. One expert on whistle-blowing said, "She spoke up, but I don't see any evidence that she resisted or went beyond in some way to demand a remedy."[10] Dan Ackman of *Forbes* magazine was more critical: A whistle-blower, literally speaking, is someone who spots a criminal robbing a bank and blows the whistle alerting police. That's not Sherron Watkins. What the Enron vice president did was write a memo to the bank robber, suggesting he stop robbing the bank and offering ways to avoid getting caught. Then she met with the robber, who said he didn't believe he was robbing the bank, but said he'd investigate to find out for sure. Then, for all we know, Watkins did nothing, and her memo was not made public until congressional investigators released it six weeks after Enron filed for bankruptcy.[11]

Whether Watkins, Cooper, and Rowley are whistle-blowers in a precise sense, most people would probably agree with *Time* magazine that "They were people who did right just by doing their jobs rightly—which means ferociously, with eyes wide open and with the bravery the rest of us always hope we have and may never know if we do." In an interview, Watkins recalled a quotation from Martin Luther King, Jr., that was handed out to all Enron employees: "Our lives begin to end the day we become silent about things that matter." Could Enron's collapse have occurred if more employees had taken these words to heart?

INTRODUCTION

There have always been informers, or snitches, who reveal information to enrich themselves or to get back at others. However, whistle-blowers like *Time* magazine's "persons of the year" are generally conscientious people who expose some wrongdoing, often at great personal risk. The term "whistle-blower" was first applied to government employees who "go public" with complaints of corruption or mismanagement in federal agencies. It is now used in connection with similar activities in the private sector.[12]

Whistle-blowers often pay a high price for their acts of dissent. Watkins, Cooper, and Rowley emerged from their experience relatively unscathed, but most whistle-blowers are not so fortunate. Retaliation is common and can take many forms—from poor evaluations and demotion to outright dismissal. Some employers seek to blacklist whistle-blowers so that they cannot obtain jobs in the same industry. Many whistle-blowers suffer career disruption and financial hardship resulting from the job dislocation and legal expenses, and there is severe emotional strain on them and their families as coworkers, friends, and neighbors turn against them.

Given the high price that whistle-blowers sometimes pay, should people really be encouraged to blow the whistle? Is the exposure of corruption and mismanagement in government and industry the best way to correct these faults? Or are there more effective ways to deal with them without requiring individuals to make heroic personal sacrifices? Should whistle-blowers be protected, and if so, how can this best be done?

In addition to these practical questions, there are more philosophical issues about the ethical justification of whistle-blowing. Do employees have a right to blow the whistle? Although they usually act with the laudable aim of protecting the public by drawing attention to wrongdoing on the part of their organization, whistle-blowers also run the risk of violating genuine obligations that employees owe to employers. Employees have an obligation to do the work that they are assigned, to be loyal to their employer, and generally to work for the interest of the company, not against it. In addition, employees have an obligation to preserve the confidentiality of information acquired in the course of their work, and whistle-blowing sometimes involves the release of this kind of information. Cases of whistle-blowing are so wrenching precisely because they involve very strong conflicting obligations. It is vitally important, therefore, to understand when it is morally permissible to blow the whistle and when whistle-blowing is, perhaps, not justified. Our first task, though, is to develop a definition of whistle-blowing.

WHAT IS WHISTLE-BLOWING?

As a first approximation, whistle-blowing can be defined as the release of information by a member or former member of an organization that is evidence of illegal and/or immoral conduct in the organization or conduct in the organization that is not in the public interest. There are several points to observe in this definition.

First, blowing the whistle is something that can be done only by a member of an organization. It is not whistle-blowing when a witness to a crime notifies the police and testifies in court. It is also not whistle-blowing for a reporter who uncovers some illegal practice in a corporation to expose it in print. Both the witness and the reporter have incriminating information, but they are under no obligation that prevents them from making it public. The situation is different for employees who become aware of illegal or immoral conduct in their own organization because they have an obligation to their employer that would be violated by public disclosure. Whistle-blowing, therefore, is an action that takes place within an organization.

The difference is due to the fact that an employee is expected to work only as directed, to go through channels, and, more generally, to act in all matters for the well-being of the organization. Also, the information involved is typically obtained by an employee in the course of his or her employment as a part of the job. Such information is usually regarded as confidential so that an employee has an obligation not to reveal it, especially to the detriment of the employer. To "go public" with information that is damaging to the organization is generally viewed as violating a number of obligations that an employee has as a member of the organization.

Second, there must be information. Merely to dissent publicly with an employer is not in itself blowing the whistle; whistle-blowing necessarily involves the release of *nonpublic information*. According to Sissela Bok, "The whistleblower assumes that his message will alert listeners to something they do not know, or whose significance they have not grasped because it has been kept secret."[13] A distinction can be made between *blowing the whistle* and *sounding the alarm*. Instead of revealing new facts, as whistle-blowers do, dissenters who take a public stand in opposition to an organization to which they belong can be viewed as trying to arouse public concern, to get people alarmed about facts that are already known rather than to tell them something they do not know.

Third, the information is generally evidence of some significant kind of misconduct on the part of an organization or some of its members. The term "whistle-blowing" is usually reserved for matters of substantial importance. Certainly, information about the lack of preparedness by the FBI to protect American citizens against terrorist acts like those on 9/11 would justify the memo that Coleen Rowley sent to the director of her agency. Some whistle-blowing reveals violations of law, such as the accounting fraud at WorldCom that Cynthia Cooper uncovered, but an employee could also be said to blow the whistle about activities that are legal but contrary to the public interest, such as waste and mismanagement in government procurement or threats to the environment. Information of this kind could alert the public and possibly lead to new legislation or regulation. However, merely exposing incompetent or self-serving management or leaking information to influence the course of events is not commonly counted as whistle-blowing. Lacking in these kinds of cases is a serious wrong that could be averted or rectified by whistle-blowing.

Fourth, the information must be released outside normal channels of communication. In most organizations, employees are instructed to report instances of illegal or improper conduct to their immediate superiors, and other means often exist for employees to register their concerns. Some corporations have an announced policy of encouraging employees to submit any suspicions of misconduct in writing to the CEO, with an assurance of confidentiality. Others have a designated official, often called an *ombudsman*, for handling employee complaints. Whistle-blowing does not necessarily involve "going public" and revealing information outside the organization. There can be *internal* as well as *external* whistle-blowing. However, an employee who follows established procedures for reporting wrongdoing is not a whistle-blower. Thus, Watkins, Cooper, and Rowley are probably not whistle-blowers in a precise sense.

A definition of whistle-blowing also needs to take into account *to whom* the whistle is blown. In both internal and external whistle-blowing, the information must be revealed in ways that can reasonably be expected to bring about a desired change. Merely passing on information about wrongdoing to a higher-up or a third party does not necessarily constitute whistle-blowing. Going to the press is often effective because the information ultimately reaches the appropriate authorities. Reporting to a credit-rating agency that a person faces bankruptcy, by contrast, would not usually be an instance of whistle-blowing but of ordinary snitching because the receiving party in this case is not an appropriate authority.

Fifth, the release of information must be something that is done voluntarily, as opposed to being legally required, although the distinction is not always clear. Watkins and Rowley were called to testify before congressional committees. Although such testimony may be legally required, the call to testify may come only after witnesses volunteer that they have incriminating evidence. However, in a state supreme court case, *Petermann* v. *International Brotherhood of Teamsters*, a treasurer for a union had no desire to be a whistle-blower, but he refused to perjure himself before a California state legislative body as he had been ordered to do by his employer.[14] Although Petermann acted with considerable courage, it is not clear whether he should be called a whistle-blower because he had little choice under the circumstances. His testimony was legally compelled.

A sixth point is that whistle-blowing must be undertaken as a moral protest; that is, the motive must be to correct some wrong and not to seek revenge or personal advancement. This is not to deny that a person with incriminating evidence could conceivably be justified in coming forth, whatever the motive. People "go public" for all sorts of reasons—a common one being fear of their own legal liability—and by doing so, they often benefit society. Still, it is useful to draw a line between the genuine whistle-blower and corporate malcontents and intriguers. Because the motives of whistle-blowers are often misperceived in the organization, employees considering the act must carefully examine their own motivation.

Putting all these points together, a more adequate (but unfortunately long-winded) definition of whistle-blowing is as follows: Whistle-blowing is the voluntary release of nonpublic information, as a moral protest, by a member or former member of an organization outside the normal channels of communication to an appropriate audience about illegal and/or immoral conduct in the organization or conduct in the organization that is opposed in some significant way to the public interest.

THE JUSTIFICATION OF WHISTLE-BLOWING

The ethical justification of whistle-blowing might seem to be obvious in view of the laudable public service that whistle-blowers provide—often at great personal risk. However, whistle-blowing has the potential to do great harm to both individuals and organizations.

The negative case against whistle-blowing is given vigorous expression in a widely cited passage from a 1971 speech by James M. Roche, who was chairman of the board of General Motors Corporation at the time. He writes, "Some critics are now busy eroding another support of free enterprise—the loyalty of a management team, with its unifying values of cooperative work. . . . However this is labelled—industrial espionage, whistle blowing, or professional responsibility—it is another tactic for spreading disunity and creating conflict."[15]

In the same vein, Sissela Bok observes that "the whistleblower hopes to stop the game, but since he is neither referee or coach, and since he blows the whistle on his own team, his act is seen as a violation of loyalty."[16]

As these remarks indicate, the main stumbling block in justifying whistle-blowing is the duty of loyalty that employees have to the organization of which they are a part. The public service that whistle-blowers provide has to be weighed against the disruptive effect that the disclosure of information has on bonds of loyalty. Does a person in a position to blow the whistle have a greater obligation to the public or to the organization? Where does the greater loyalty lie?

That we have an obligation to the public is relatively unproblematic; it is the obligation to prevent serious harm to others whenever this is within our power. An obligation of loyalty to an organization is more complex, involving, as it does, questions about the basis of such an obligation and the concept of loyalty itself. What does an employee owe an employer, and, more to the point, does the employment relation deprive an employee of a right to reveal information about wrong-doing in the organization? In order to answer these questions, let us begin with a commonly used argument against the right of an employee to blow the whistle.

The Loyal Agent Argument

According to one argument, an employee is an *agent* of an employer.[17] An agent is a person who is engaged to act in the interests of another person (called a *principal*) and is authorized to act on that person's behalf. This relationship is typical of professionals, such as lawyers and accountants, who are called upon to use their skills in the service of a client. Employees are also considered to be agents of an employer in that they are hired to work for the benefit of the employer. Specifically, an employee, as an agent, has an obligation to work as directed, to protect confidential information, and, above all, to be loyal. All these are seemingly violated when an employee blows the whistle.

The loyal agent argument receives considerable support from the law, where the concept of agency and the obligations of agents are well developed. Although our concern is with the *moral* status of employees, the law of agency is a rich source of relevant insights about the employment relation.[18] According to one standard book on the subject, "an agent is a person who is authorized to act for a principal and has agreed so to act, and who has power to affect the legal relations of his principal with a third party."[19] Agents are employed to carry out tasks that principals are not willing or able to carry out for themselves. Thus, we hire a lawyer to represent us in legal matters where we lack the expertise to do the job properly.

The main obligation of an agent is to act in the interest of the principal. We expect a lawyer, for example, to act as we would ourselves, if we had the same ability. This obligation is expressed in the *Second Restatement of Agency* as follows: "an agent is subject to a duty to his principal to act solely for the benefit of the principal in all matters connected with his agency."[20] The ethical basis of the duty of agents is a contractual obligation or an understood agreement to act in the interests of another person. Lawyers agree for a fee to represent clients, and employees are similarly hired with the understanding that they will work for the benefit of an employer.

Are Whistle-Blowers Disloyal Agents?

At first glance, a whistle-blower is a disloyal agent who backs out of an agreement that is an essential part of the employer–employee relationship. A whistle-blowing employee, according to the loyal agent argument, is like a lawyer who sells out a client—clearly a violation of the legal profession's code of ethics. Closer examination reveals that the argument is not as strong as it appears. Although employees have an obligation of loyalty that is not shared by a person outside the organization, the obligation is not without its limits. Whistle-blowing is not something to be done without adequate justification, but at the same time, it is not something that can never be justified.

First, the law of agency does not impose an absolute obligation on employees to do whatever they are told. Rather, an agent has an obligation, in the words of the *Second Restatement*, to obey all *reasonable* directives of the principal. This is interpreted to exclude illegal or immoral acts; that is, employees are not obligated as agents to do anything illegal or immoral—even if specifically instructed by a superior to do so. Questions can arise, of course, about the legal and moral status of specific acts. Is an agent free to disobey an order to do something that is suspect but not clearly illegal or immoral, for example? Borderline cases are unavoidable, but in situations where a crime is being committed or people are exposed to the risk of serious injury and even death, the law of agency is clear: An employee has no obligation to obey.

The law of agency further excludes an obligation to keep confidential any information about the commission of a crime. Section 395 of the *Second Restatement of Agency* reads in part: "An agent is privileged to reveal information confidentially acquired . . . in the protection of a superior interest of himself or a third person." The *Restatement* does not define what is meant by a "superior interest" except to note that there is no duty of confidentiality when the information is about the commission of a crime. "[I]f the confidential information is to the effect that the principal is committing or is about to commit a crime, the agent is under no duty not to reveal it."[21] Protecting oneself from legal liability can reasonably be held to be a "superior interest," as can preventing some serious harm to others.

Second, the obligations of an agent are confined to the needs of the relationship. In order for a lawyer to represent a client adequately, it is necessary to impose a strong obligation of loyalty, but the obligation of loyalty required for employees to do their job adequately is less stringent. The obligation of agents to follow orders exactly stems, in part, from the fact that they may be binding the principal to a contract or exposing the principal to tort liability. The duty of confidentiality is justified by the legitimate right of an employer to maintain the secrecy of certain vital information. Thus, Coleen Rowley is legally barred, for good reason, from divulging information about an investigation. She could not have "gone public" with her information without violating her duty as an FBI agent.

Employees are hired for limited purposes, however. As Alex Michalos points out, a person who has agreed to sell life insurance policies on commission is committed to performing *that* activity as a loyal agent. "It would be ludicrous," he continues, "to assume that the agent has also committed himself to painting houses, washing dogs, or doing anything else that happened to give his principal pleasure."[22] Similarly, a quality control inspector is not hired to overlook defects, falsify records, or do anything else that would permit a danger to exist. Information about irregularities in safety matters is also not the kind that the employer has a right to keep confidential, because it is not necessary to the normal operation of a business.

To conclude, the loyal agent argument does not serve to show that whistle-blowing can never be justified. The obligations that employees have as agents of an organization are of great moral importance, but they do have limits. Specifically, the agency relation does not require employees to engage in illegal or immoral activities or to give over their whole life to an employer.

The Meaning of Loyalty

The concept of loyalty itself raises some questions. One is whether whistle-blowing is always an act of disloyalty or whether it can sometimes be done out of loyalty to the organization. The answer depends, in part, on what we mean by the term "loyalty." If loyalty means merely following orders and not "rocking the boat," then whistle-blowers are disloyal employees. But loyalty can also be defined as a commitment to the true interests or goals of the organization, in which case whistle-blowers are often very loyal employees. Thus, whistle-blowing is not necessarily incompatible with loyalty, and, indeed, in some circumstances, loyalty may require employees to blow the whistle on wrongdoing in their own organization.

All too often, the mistake of the whistle-blower lies not in being disloyal to the organization as such but in breaking a relation of trust with a few key members of an organization or with associates and immediate superiors. Insofar as an employee has a duty of loyalty, though, it cannot be merely to follow orders or to go along with others. Loyalty means serving the interests and goals of an organization, which can sometimes lead to divided loyalties and uncertainties about what is best for an organization.

THE SOCIOLOGICAL EVIDENCE.   Some evidence for the claim that whistle-blowers are often loyal—perhaps even too loyal—to the organizations they serve is provided by Myron Glazer, a sociologist who interviewed 55 whistle-blowers in depth. One of his findings is that

> Virtually all of the ethical resisters . . . had long histories of successful employ-ment. They were not alienated or politically active members of movements advocating major changes in society. On the contrary, they began as firm believers in their organizations, convinced that if they took a grievance to superiors, there would be an appropriate response. This naiveté led them into a series of damaging traps. They found that their earlier service and dedication provided them with little protection against charges of undermining organizational morale and effectiveness.[23]

The irony of this finding is that whistle-blowers are often loyal employees who take the first steps toward whistle-blowing in the belief that they are doing their job and acting in the best interests of the company.

EXIT, VOICE, AND LOYALTY.   As further evidence that the relationship between whistle-blowing and loyalty is far more complex than it first appears, the economist Albert O. Hirschman argues, in a book entitled *Exit, Voice, and Loyalty*, that members of organizations and people who deal with organizations, such as customers of a firm, can respond to dissatisfaction either by leaving the organization and having no further dealings with it (exit) or by speaking up and making the dissatisfaction known in the hope of bringing about change (voice). Loyalty is a factor that keeps people from exiting an organization; but, at the same time, it activates the voice option. According to Hirschman, those who exercise the voice option are often the most loyal and are convinced that by speaking up they can get the organization back on the right track.[24]

On Hirschman's analysis, exit is a more extreme form of dissent than voice, but business firms do not usually regard an employee's departure as a form of disloyalty. In fact, whistle-blowers are often treated in ways designed to get them to leave voluntarily. It may benefit an organization in the short run to get rid of troublemakers, but Hirschman argues that in the long run, encouraging employees to use the exit option will harm the organization by depriving it of those people who can bring about healthy change. As a result of loyalty, these potentially most influential customers and members will stay on longer than they would ordinarily, in the hope or reasoned expectation that improvement or reform can be achieved from within. Thus, loyalty, far from being irrational, can serve the socially useful purpose of preventing deterioration from becoming cumulative, as it so often does when there is no barrier to exit.[25]

A further complication is the fact that employees typically have a number of loyalties, both inside and outside an organization, which can come into conflict. Although employee loyalty is morally required, a company is not a single entity to which the employee owes loyalty but is, rather, a complex of individuals, groups, projects, and missions. Loyalty to one aspect of a company may require disloyalty to another. An employee may not be able to be loyal to an immediate superior whose order conflicts with loyalty to a company's mission to provide quality service, for example. Employees are also citizens who may have a duty of loyalty to obey the law or pursue some public good. To whom should an employee be loyal when asked, for example, to discharge pollutants into a stream? Merely appealing to a general duty of loyalty does not resolve these kinds of conflicts.[26]

Even if we limit loyalty to a specific employer, questions about what loyalty means still arise. *The Code of Ethics for Government Service*, for example, contains the following instruction for federal employees: "Put loyalty to the highest moral principles and to country above loyalty to persons, party, or government department." This lofty statement is a prescription for confusion when employees of an administration or an agency are called upon to be team players.

Conditions for Justified Whistle-Blowing

The following are some questions that should be considered in deciding whether to blow the whistle in a specific case.[27]

1. *Is the situation of sufficient moral importance to justify whistle-blowing?* A cover-up of lethal side effects in a newly marketed drug, for example, is an appropriate situation for disclosure because people's lives are at stake. But situations are not always this clear. Is whistle-blowing warranted if the side effects are not lethal or debilitating but capable of causing temporary discomfort or pain? What if the drug is the most effective treatment for a serious medical problem, so that the harm of the side effect is outweighed by the benefit of using the drug? In such a case, we need to ask how serious is the potential harm compared with the benefit of the drug and the trouble that would be caused by blowing the whistle. The less serious the harm, the less appropriate it is to blow the whistle. In addition to the moral importance of the situation, consideration should also be given to the extent to which harm is a direct and predictable result of the activity that the whistle-blower is protesting. For example, a toy that might be hazardous under unusual circumstances warrants whistle-blowing less than one that poses a risk under all conditions. Sissela Bok contends that the harm should also be imminent. According to her, an alarm can be sounded about defects in a rapid-transit system that is already in operation or is about to go into operation, but an alarm should not be sounded about defects in a system that is still on the drawing boards and is far from being operational.[28]

2. *Do you have all the facts and have you properly understood their significance?* Whistle-blowing usually involves very serious charges that can cause irreparable harm if they turn out to be unfounded or misinterpreted. A potential whistle-blower, therefore, has a strong obligation to the people who are charged with wrongdoing to make sure that the charges are well founded. The whistle-blower should also have as much documentation and other corroboration as possible. A whistle-blower's case is stronger when the evidence consists of verifiable facts and not merely hunches or rumors. Because whistle-blowing cases often end up in court, the proof should also be strong enough to stand up under scrutiny. The support for the charges need not be overwhelming, but it should meet the ordinary legal standard of a preponderance of the evidence. Employees often have access to only some of the facts of a case and are liable, as a result, to form false or misleading impressions. Would-be whistle-blowers must be careful, therefore, not to jump to conclusions about matters that higher-level managers, with a fuller knowledge of the situation, are in a better position to judge. Typically, employees have only one kind of expertise, so they are not able to make an accurate judgment when different kinds of knowledge are needed.

3. *Have all internal channels and steps short of whistle-blowing been exhausted?* Whistle-blowing should be a last rather than a first resort. It is justified only when there are no morally preferable alternatives. The alternatives available to employees depend to a great extent on the provisions an organization makes for dissent, but virtually every organization requires employees to take up any matter of concern with an immediate superior before proceeding further—unless that person is part of the problem. Courts will generally not consider a complaint unless all possible appeals within an organization have been exhausted. Some progressive corporations have recognized the value of dissent in bringing problems to light and have set up procedures that allow employees to express their concern through internal channels. Steps of this kind reduce the need for whistle-blowing and the risks that external whistle-blowers take. It is possible to justify not using internal channels, however, when the whole organization is so mired in the wrongdoing that there is little chance that using them would succeed. Another justification for "going public" before exhausting internal channels is the need for a quick response when internal whistle-blowing would be too slow and uncertain. Two engineers at Morton Thiokol expressed concern to their superiors about the effects of low temperature on the O-rings on the booster rockets for the *Challenger* spacecraft, but their warning never reached the officials at NASA who were responsible for making the decision to go ahead with the launch. The engineers spoke out after the *Challenger* explosion— for which they were disciplined by Morton Thiokol—but their whistle-blowing was too late to avert the disaster. To be effective, they would have had to blow the whistle before the decision was made to launch the spacecraft. This would have required them to go outside the company and contact the officials at NASA directly.

4. *What is the best way to blow the whistle?* Once a decision is made to "go public," a host of other questions have to be answered. To whom should the information be revealed? How much information should be revealed? Should the information be revealed anonymously or accompanied by the identity of the whistle-blower? Often an anonymous complaint to a regulatory body, such as the Environmental Protection Agency or the Securities and Exchange Commission, is sufficient to spark an investigation. The situation might also be handled by contacting the FBI or a local prosecuting attorney or by leaking information to the local press. The less information that is revealed, the less likely an employee is to violate any duty of confidentiality. Employees can also reduce conflicts by waiting until they leave an organization to blow the whistle. Whistle-blowing is also more likely to be effective when an employee presents the charge in an objective and responsible manner. It is especially important that a whistle-blower stick to the important issues and refrain from conducting crusades or making personal attacks on the persons involved. Organizations often seek to discredit whistle-blowers by picturing them as disgruntled misfits or crazy radicals; intemperate, wide-ranging attacks undermine the whistle-blower's own credibility. Many whistle-blowers recommend developing a clear plan of action. Do not blow the whistle impulsively, they advise, but think out each step and anticipate the possible consequences.[29]

5. *What is my responsibility in view of my role in the organization?* The justification for blowing the whistle depends not only on the wrongdoing of others but also on the particular role that a whistle-blower occupies in an organization. Thus, an employee is more justified in blowing the whistle—and may even have an obligation to do so—when the wrongdoing concerns matters over which the employee has direct responsibility. When an employee is a professional, the question of whether to blow the whistle must be considered in the context of professional ethics. Professionals, such as lawyers, accountants, and engineers, have a greater obligation to blow the whistle under some circumstances and are restricted or prohibited from whistle-blowing under others.

6. *What are the chances for success?* Insofar as whistle-blowing is justified because of some good to the public, it is important to blow the whistle only when there is a reasonable chance of achieving that good. Whistle-blowing may be unsuccessful for many reasons. Sometimes the fault lies with the whistle-blower who fails to make a case that attracts widespread concern or to devise an effective plan of action; other times it is simply that the organization is too powerful or the public not sufficiently responsive.

IS THERE A RIGHT TO BLOW THE WHISTLE?

Even though whistle-blowing can be justified in some situations, the sad fact remains that courageous employees who perform a valuable public service are often subjected to harsh retaliation. Our reaction when this occurs is, "There ought to be a law!" and, indeed, many have been proposed in Congress and various state legislatures.[30] Few have passed, however, and there are some strong arguments against providing legal protection for whistle-blowers. In this section, we will examine the debate over the moral justification of laws to protect whistle-blowers against retaliation. It will be useful, first, to survey the existing legal protection.

Existing Legal Protection

Retaliation against federal employees who report instances of waste and corruption in government is prohibited by the Civil Service Reform Act of 1978, which also set up the Merit System Protection Board (MSPB) to receive and act on complaints of retaliation.[31] The provisions of this act were strengthened by the Whistleblower Protection Act of 1989, which allows the Office of Special Counsel to represent federal employees before the MSPB and provides numerous procedural safeguards. Still, the act has many loopholes that Congress has been reluctant to close despite widespread dissatisfaction among federal employees.

Some protection for whistle-blowers in both the public and private sectors exists in the antiretaliation provisions of various pieces of federal legislation. The National Labor Relations Act of 1935 (NLRA) forbids employers to retaliate against any employee who files a charge with the National Labor Relations Board (NLRB). Title VII of the 1964 Civil Rights Act protects employees who file a charge of discrimination, participate in an investigation or proceeding connected with a charge, or oppose an activity of a company that the employee believes is discriminatory. The Occupational Safety and Health Act of 1970 also prohibits retaliation against any employee who files a complaint with the Occupational Safety and Health Administration or testifies in a proceeding. Other federal acts with antiretaliatory provisions are the Surface Mining Act, the Railway Safety Act, the Surface Transportation Safety Act, the Safe Drinking Water Act, the Toxic Substance Control Act, the Clean Air Act, the Water Pollution Control Act, the Energy Reorganization Act, and the Solid Waste Disposal Act.

The Sarbanes-Oxley Act of 2002 (SOX) creates for the first time whistle-blower protection for private-sector employees.[32] Passed by Congress in response to massive fraud at Enron, WorldCom, and other companies, this act prohibits retaliation against any employee "for providing to a law enforcement officer any truthful information relating to the commission or possible commission of any Federal offense." In addition to requiring that every publicly traded company establish an independent audit committee of the board with responsibility for detecting fraud, the act supports internal whistle-blowing by mandating that all companies, whether publicly traded or not, have procedures for employees to make confidential allegations about suspected fraudulent activity. Employees who avail themselves of SOX protection are entitled to be made whole by such means as reinstatement, back pay, and reimbursement for legal expenses, and also to receive "special damages" for such noneconomic losses as emotional distress. Under SOX, an employer who retaliates against a whistle-blower may be subject to a fine or imprisonment or both.

Perhaps the most effective federal statute for protecting whistle-blowers is the once-moribund federal False Claims Act of 1863 (amended 1986). This act was originally passed by Congress to curb fraud during the post–Civil War reconstruction period by allowing private citizens who blow the whistle on fraud against the government in federal procurement (e.g., defense contracting) or federal benefits programs (e.g., Social Security and Medicare) to share in the financial recovery. The False Claims Act has been updated to encourage individuals to report any fraud against the government that they observe by entitling whistle-blowers to receive between 10 percent and 30 percent of the funds recovered in any suit.[33] In many instances, the government will investigate and prosecute on the basis of the evidence provided by the whistle-blower, but if the government declines to prosecute, the whistle-blower can pursue legal action alone, acting on behalf of the government in a so-called *qui tam* action. If successful in the *qui tam* suit, the individual may be entitled not only to an award but also to the recovery of legal expenses. The largest award to date was made to a former quality assurance manager for GlaxoSmithKline, Cheryl Eckard. She received approximately $96 million from the $750 million in penalties that the company paid to the government for selling substandard drugs to Medicare and Medicaid, and she is entitled to millions more from states that had been defrauded.[34]

The 2010 Wall Street Reform and Consumer Protection Act (the Dodd-Frank Bill) strengthens existing whistle-blower antiretaliation protection in other federal legislation and introduces some new provisions for the securities markets and other areas not covered by prior legislation. The act includes provisions for awards to whistle-blowers similar to the federal False Claims Act and protection for employees who make disclosures to the newly created Consumer Financial Protection Bureau. In addition, it directs the Securities and Exchange Commission to create a special whistle-blower office to oversee enforcement of the whistle-blower provisions of the act.

More than two-thirds of the states have passed laws designed to protect whistle-blowers. Most of these apply only to government employees, but a few—Michigan's Whistle Blowers Protection Act, for example—extend more widely. Most of these state statutes specify the procedures that a whistle-blower must follow to receive protection and place requirements on the persons to whom the information is disclosed and on the kind of information that the whistle-blower discloses.

Another source of protection for whistle-blowers is state court decisions limiting the traditional right of employers to fire at will. These decisions protect workers against retaliation for many reasons besides whistle-blowing, but they also leave some whistle-blowers unprotected. A further discussion of the issues in this kind of protection is in Chapter 8.

The Arguments against Whistle-Blower Protection

There are many problems with drafting legislation for protecting whistle-blowers. First, a law recognizing whistle-blowing as a right is open to abuse. Whistle-blowing might be used by disgruntled employees to protest company decisions or to get back at their employers. Employees might also find an excuse to blow the whistle in order to cover up their own incompetence or inadequate performance. Alan F. Westin notes, "Forbidding an employer to dismiss or discipline an employee who protests against illegal or improper conduct by management invites employees to take out 'antidismissal insurance' by lodging a whistle-blowing complaint."[35]

Second, legislation to protect whistle-blowers would encroach on the traditional right of employers to conduct business as they see fit and would add another layer of regulation to the existing legal restraints on business, thereby making it more difficult for managers to run a company efficiently. The courts would be called upon to review and possibly reverse a great many personnel decisions. The likely increase in employee litigation could also, according to Westin, "create an informer ethos at work that would threaten the spirit of cooperation and trust on which sound working relationships depend."[36]

Third, if whistle-blowing were protected by law, what should be the legal remedy for employees who are unjustly dismissed? Reinstatement in the workplace, which is the usual remedy in union contract grievance procedures, may not be feasible in the case of employees who are perceived as being disloyal. As an alternative to reinstatement, though, whistle-blowers could be offered a monetary settlement to compensate them for the losses suffered by being wrongly dismissed. An award could be arrived at by negotiation or arbitration, or it could result by allowing dismissed employees to sue for tort damages.

The Arguments for Whistle-Blower Protection

The main argument in defense of a law to protect whistle-blowers is a utilitarian one that rests on the contribution whistle-blowers make to society. There is a direct benefit in having instances of illegal corporate conduct, gross waste and mismanagement, and dangers to the public brought to light. This benefit can be achieved, the argument goes, only if whistle-blowers are encouraged to come forward and make their information known. Ralph Nader makes the further point that because employees are often the first to know about hazards, allowing them greater freedom to speak out makes it easier to enforce existing laws and to bring about desirable changes in corporate behavior.[37]

These benefits must be balanced against the undeniable harm that a greater incidence of whistle-blowing would have on business firms. Insofar as companies are less efficient—either because of the greater regulation or the loss of loyalty within organizations—a right to blow the whistle is not justified on utilitarian grounds.

A second argument for providing legal protection for whistle-blowers appeals to the First Amendment right of freedom of speech. A distinction needs to be made, though, between the appeal to freedom of speech as a legal argument and as a moral argument. Our rights under the Constitution protect us for the most part only against acts of government and not against those of private employers. Consequently, the freedom of speech that we have as a matter of legal right does not necessarily prevent corporations from retaliating against whistle-blowers, although it does confer some protection on government employees who speak out as citizens.

Although the First Amendment right of free speech cannot be used as a *legal* argument for holding that whistle-blowing is a protected activity in the private sector, it can still be maintained that there is a *moral* right to freedom of speech and that (morally) there ought to be a law extending this right to whistle-blowers.[38] At least one writer has urged that we recognize a right that is broader than merely freedom of speech, namely, a right to follow one's own conscience. Whistle-blowers are often led to speak out not by a desire to serve the public good but to do what they feel is morally required of them. "Thus," this writer concludes, "the interests that weigh in favor of providing legal protection to the external whistleblower are not those embodied in an employee's obligation to society, but rather those embodied in his interest as an individual to act in accordance with the dictates of conscience."[39]

DEVELOPING A WHISTLE-BLOWING POLICY

Companies have many incentives to develop a whistle-blowing policy.[40] No company is immune from wrongdoing, and an effective policy on whistle-blowing enables a company to deal with misconduct internally, thereby preventing embarrassing public disclosure. For a policy to be effective, however, employees must be assured that their reports will be taken seriously—which means that an investigation will be conducted and appropriate action taken. More importantly, employees must feel confident that they will not suffer any retaliation.

Benefits and Dangers of a Policy

Although companies might prefer to ignore some wrongdoing and to continue profitable but questionable practices, they can also benefit from learning about problems early and taking corrective action before the problems become public. The lack of a policy will not prevent whistle-blowing by a company's employees, and the increasing public acceptance of whistle-blowing combined with expanded legal protection makes whistle-blowing all the more likely. The aftermath of a whistle-blowing incident also creates problems that are best avoided. In particular, dismissing whistle-blowers with legitimate complaints sends the wrong signal to other employees, and yet allowing whistle-blowers to remain in the workplace may cause tension and strife. These equally undesirable alternatives can be avoided by eliminating the need for any employee to go outside of the normal channels of communication. An effective whistle-blowing policy can have the added benefit of affirming a company's commitment to good ethics and creating an ethical corporate climate.

Whistle-blowing policies also benefit employees by providing them with a channel of communication for responding to perceived wrongdoing in the organization. Employees are likely to welcome an opportunity to express their legitimate concerns without the risk of going public with damaging information. Whistle-blowing policies involve some dangers, however. Encouraging employees to report on each other can create an environment of mistrust and intimidation, especially if people feel vulnerable to the possibility of false accusations.

Components of a Whistle-Blowing Policy

A well-designed whistle-blowing policy should include the following components.

1. *An Effectively Communicated Statement of Responsibility.* Employees should understand that they have a responsibility to report all concerns about serious unethical or illegal conduct through the appropriate internal channels.

2. *A Clearly Defined Procedure for Reporting.* A procedure should be established that allows employees to report their concerns in a confidential manner. The procedure should specify the persons to whom reports are to be made and the proper form, and employees should be made aware of the procedure. Some companies use an ethics "hot line" that allows employees to make a report by calling an 800 number; other companies insist that reports be made to a person's immediate superior unless that person is involved in the suspected wrongdoing. Multiple means of reporting concerns and the choice of anonymous reporting are available in some companies with whistle-blowing policies.

3. *Well-Trained Personnel to Receive and Investigate Reports.* The success of a whistle-blowing policy depends heavily on the skill of the personnel who receive and investigate the reports from employees. Especially critical is the ability to maintain confidentiality and to conduct a fair and thorough investigation. For these reasons, the personnel should be well-trained and have sufficient authority within the organization, and the program should be evaluated periodically for effectiveness.

4. *A Commitment to Take Appropriate Action.* Employees must be assured that their reports of suspected wrongdoing will not be ignored or misused. Not only should the purposes of a whistle-blowing policy be effectively communicated to all employees, but the company must also assure employees by both word and deed that their reports will be used only for these purposes. The best policies also stipulate that reporting employees will be informed about the outcome of an investigation and the action taken.

5. *A Guarantee Against Retaliation.* By far, the most critical component in any whistle-blowing policy is the assurance that employees will not suffer retaliation for making reports in good faith. Retaliation can be prevented, however, only if the importance of the policy is effectively communicated to everyone in the organization and there is a credible commitment to the policy's success by top management. Companies must be on guard, of course, for employees who might abuse an ethics hot line or other reporting mechanisms for personal ends, but a fair and thorough investigation should reveal the facts of the case apart from the reporting employee's motives.

A whistle-blowing policy by itself will neither protect an organization from wrongdoing nor prevent whistle-blowing outside of prescribed channels. A poorly designed or implemented policy also runs the risk of doing more harm than good. Still, a policy with regard to whistle-blowing is worth considering by any company that is committed to ethical conduct.

CONCLUSION

Whether or not to blow the whistle on misconduct in an organization is the most difficult decision that some people ever have to make. The decision is wrenching personally because the stakes are so high. Yet many whistle-blowers say that they could not have lived with themselves if they had stayed silent. The decision is also difficult ethically, because whistle-blowing involves a conflict between two competing duties: to protect the public and to be loyal to an organization. Although loyalty is not always overriding, as the loyal agent argument holds, neither is it inconsequential. Deciding between these duties often requires that an employee exercise very careful judgment.

The one certain conclusion of this chapter is that whistle-blowing is ethically permissible under certain carefully specified conditions. (Whether it can ever be ethically required is a different question that seldom arises. Everyone has an obligation not to be a part of illegal and immoral activity, but exposing it at great risk to oneself is usually regarded as beyond what duty requires.) Blowing the whistle is only one response that an employee can make to corporate misconduct, however, and the act of whistle-blowing itself can take many different forms. So in addition to *whether* to become a whistle-blower, employees are faced with the further question of *how* to blow the whistle in a justified manner.

Finally, it is evident that employees who are justified in blowing the whistle ought not to suffer retaliation. What ought to be done to protect whistle-blowers from this fate is less clear. A plausible case can be made for legislation in this area, but the difficulty is drafting laws that achieve the desired result without interfering unduly in the legitimate conduct of business.

CASE 4.2 ✳ Explore the Concept on mythinkinglab.com
A Whistle-Blower Accepts a "Deal"

As the head of corporate audit for a major pharmaceutical company, I was involved in the lengthy approval process that the Food and Drug Administration requires before a new drug can be brought to market.[41] The reviewer for the FDA was asking some tough questions about the data supporting our application to market a new drug. Although I managed to answer the reviewer's questions to his apparent satisfaction, doubts were beginning to form in my own mind about the reliability of the data I was defending, so I instructed my staff to get photocopies of the original research reports for me as soon as possible.

The photocopies provided evidence of "double books." The raw data in the original reports were entirely different from the data in our FDA application and showed the new drug failing every required test. I had heard rumors of other questionable conduct by the project director, and I suspected that he was implicated in the falsification of the data, although I had no proof for any accusations. I rejected the idea of blowing the whistle on the company by telling everything to the FDA and decided instead to follow the procedure outlined in the company's own whistle-blowing policy. Accordingly, I prepared a report stating only the facts that I could document, and I sent it to the next highest level above the person involved, which in this situation was the legal department of the corporation.

My internal whistle-blowing prompted a quick response. I was summoned to meet with the board of directors which had a team of lawyers from an outside firm present. The original research reports had apparently been destroyed, but there was no question about the authenticity of the photocopies that I still retained because the raw data were accompanied by the researchers' signatures and the dates of entry. After friendly but close questioning, the board of directors offered me a "deal." They would give me all of the resources that I needed to get the drug approved by the FDA, but they promised that the drug would never be marketed. The board intended to correct the problems within the company (and the project director soon resigned), but it wanted to avoid the embarrassment of public exposure. The board's plan was to request that approval of the drug be withdrawn afterward by telling the FDA that mistakes had been made in the marketing projections. I accepted the deal and succeeded in getting the drug approved. The board kept its word, and 10 years later the drug is still not on the market.

After my "deal" with the board, other changes were made. Corporate policy was revised so that I no longer had ready access to company records. The FDA has the authority to conduct "surprise" audits at any time, and the policy had been to allow my office to mimic FDA audits, so that the company would always be "FDA-ready." Under the new policy, audits must be prearranged with the department involved, and the department can stop an audit and reschedule it at any point. Finally, the department is allowed to review the audit report before it is submitted. To my knowledge, there has been no repetition of the events of 10 years ago, but my ability to uncover such misconduct has been severely limited. Oftentimes I wonder whether I should have accepted that "deal."

CASE 4.3   ✳ Explore the Concept on mythinkinglab.com

A Whistle-Blower's Quandary

As a vice-president for Pharmacia (which was acquired by Pfizer in 2003), Dr. Peter Rost was in charge of worldwide marketing for the drug Genotropin, which is a synthetic human growth hormone that is used to treat a limited range of hormonal deficiencies in children and the elderly.[42] Beginning in 1997 and continuing to 2003, Pharmacia aggressively promoted Genotropin for conditions beyond those for which the drug had received approval from the Food and Drug Administration (FDA). Physicians may legally prescribe an FDA-approved drug for such "off-label" use, but pharmaceutical companies are strictly prohibited from any promotional activities designed to encourage physicians to prescribe a drug for any but approved uses. However, Pharmacia attempted to persuade physicians to prescribe Genotropin for short children without any hormonal deficiency as well as for elderly patients as an antiaging therapy. Among the means used to increase prescriptions were kickbacks to physicians in the form of all-expense-paid company-sponsored conferences, paid participation in drug studies, and lucrative consulting positions. These efforts produced results. During the period 1997 to 2003, approximately 25percent of all prescriptions for children and 60 percent of prescriptions for adults were for off-label use.

Dr. Rost became aware of the illegal promotional activities in his role as head of marketing for Genotropin, and he immediately protested to his superiors. After an investigation by Pharmacia, the off-label promotion activities, including the kickbacks to physicians, were curtailed but not eliminated. Soon after Pfizer's acquisition of Pharmacia, which occurred on April 16, 2003, Dr. Rost presented evidence to his new superiors of the illegal off-label marketing of Genotropin. Without Dr. Rost's knowledge, Pfizer conducted its own investigation, and exactly one month after the acquisition, on May 16, 2003, Pfizer voluntarily notified the FDA and the other relevant government agencies of the illegal off-label promotion activities and within a few days provided them with extensive documentation of the kickbacks, as well as information about the corrective actions that were being taken.

Unaware of his employer's disclosures to the federal government, Dr. Rost decided to file a complaint under the federal False Claims Act (FCA), which he did on June 5. The FCA allows private individuals to aid the federal government in investigating and prosecuting fraud in federal procurement and benefit programs, including Medicare and Medicaid. In return for the service that such whistle-blowers provide in combating fraud—which the federal government cannot practically do on its own—a complainant can receive a percentage of the amount recovered. This percentage varies greatly, depending on circumstances, but can range from roughly 10 percent to 30 percent. The FCA requires that any individual receiving an award must present information that he or she possesses from personal experience that has never been publicly disclosed. That is, a complainant must be the "original" source of the information and have "direct and independent" knowledge. These conditions are necessary in order to prevent an opportunistic use of the law to collect an award based on publicly available information.

Although the promotion of off-label use of a drug is illegal, it is not itself a violation of the FCA. Separately, Pfizer paid $35 million to settle charges of bribery and improper promotion in connection with Genotropin. In a complaint under the FCA, it is necessary to show that the illegal promotional activity caused the submission of a false claim to the government. Evidence that a false claim was submitted must be more specific than arguing that the illegal promotional activity was likely to cause the submission of false claims. The evidence provided by Dr. Rost focused mainly on one physician, Dr. Pamela Clark, who practiced in Louisville, Kentucky. Dr. Clark, who attended several Pharmacia-sponsored conferences in exotic locales and received some compensation for various services rendered to Pharmacia, allegedly wrote Genotropin prescriptions for eight Medicaid patients to treat growth hormone deficiency (GHD), for which Genotropin is an FDA-approved use. However, Dr. Rost maintained that this use is permitted "on-label" only if the diagnosis is based on at least two tests for GHD, and Dr. Clark performed only one test for each patient. Dr. Rost presented no evidence to show that Pharmacia had encouraged doctors to perform only one test for a diagnosis of GHD. As further evidence that false claims were submitted, Dr. Rost cited eight physicians in Indiana who prescribed Genotropin for an off-label treatment of 10 patients for whom Medicaid paid 122 claims, but he could offer no evidence that any of these physicians had ever been targeted by Pharmacia promotional activities.

The FCA further requires that a claim submitted to the federal government contain some falsehood. The Medicaid claims in question were filed by the pharmacies which processed the physicians' prescriptions. Federal law requires that any kickback in the prescription of a drug be disclosed, and so any party who does not disclose receiving a kickback is in violation of the antikickback law. However, the pharmacies in these cases did not receive a kickback; the physicians did, and the pharmacies in submitting the claims were certifying only that *they* had not received a kickback. A claim that Medicaid receives for reimbursement for a drug that has been improperly prescribed as the result of a kickback fails to make a required disclosure—and is in that respect false—but the fault lies with the dishonest physicians and not with the pharmacies. Pharmacia, by their illegal promotion of off-label use directed toward physicians, did not cause any pharmacy to submit a false claim.

Faced with many questions, Dr. Rost had to decide whether to proceed with filing an FCA complaint. He had acted as a whistle-blower within the organization, and in so doing he had initiated a chain of events that led Pfizer to voluntarily investigate itself and report the findings to the FDA. In the end, Pfizer ceased the illegal off-label promotional activities and settled with the government at considerable cost. Although a federal investigation continued, the Department of Justice eventually decided, after two and one-half years of consideration, not to take further action. Dr. Rost had performed a valuable service as a courageous employee, for which he suffered some on-the-job retribution[43] and was eventually fired.[44] But should he also be rewarded with millions of dollars as a complainant under the federal False Claims Act?

Notes

1. Richard Lacayo and Amanda Ripley, "Persons of the Year," *Time*, 30 December 2002, 30.

2. Information on Watkins is taken from Amanda Ripley and Maggie Singer, "The Special Agent," *Time*, 30 December 2002, 34; Mimi Schwartz and Sherron Watkins, *Power Failure: The Inside Story of the Collapse of Enron* (New York: Doubleday, 2003).

3. Information on Cooper is taken from Amanda Ripley, "The Night Detective," *Time*, 30 December 2002, 44; Kurt Eichenwald and Simon Romero, "Inquiry Finds Effort at Delay at WorldCom," *New York Times*, 4 July 2002, C1.

4. Information on Rowley is taken from Amanda Ripley and Maggie Singer, "The Special Agent," *Time*, 30 December 2002, 34; James Risen and David Johnston, "Traces of Terror: The Intelligence Reports," *New York Times*, 24 May 2004, A1; Jim Yardley, "Traces of Terror: The Agent," *New York Times*, 25 May 2004, A10; Neil A. Lewis, "Traces of Terror: The Overview," *New York Times*, 29 May 2004, A1; Philip Shenon, "Traces of Terror: The Intelligence Reports," *New York Times*, 31 May 2004, A20; Neil A. Lewis and Don Van Natta, Jr., "Traces of Terror: The Hearings," *New York Times*, 6 June 2004, A28; David Johnston and Neil A. Lewis, "Traces of Terror: The Congressional Hearings," *New York Times*, 7 June 2004, A1; Robin Toner, "Traces of Terror: The Whistle-Blower," *New York Times*, 7 June 2004, A23.

5. "Coleen Rowley's Memo to FBI Director Robert Mueller: An Edited Version of the Agent's 13-Page Letter," 21 May 2002, http://time.com/time/covers/1101020603/memo.html, last accessed 9 December 2004.

6. Paul Fahri, "A Whistle that Can Pierce the Glass Ceiling: Are Women More Likely to Warn of Problems?" *Washington Post*, 6 July 2002.

7. Marcia P. Miceli, Janelle B. Dozier, and Janet P. Near, "Blowing the Whistle on Data-fudging: A Controlled Field Experiment," *Journal of Applied Social Psychology*, 21 (1991), 301–25; and Randi Sims and John P. Keenan, "Predictors of External Whistleblowing: Organizational and Intrapersonal Variables," *Journal of Business Ethics*, 17 (1998), 411–21.

8. Anita F. Hill, "Insider Women with Outsider Values," *New York Times*, 6 June 2002, A31.

9. Helen Thomas, "Women Whistle-blowers Did Right Thing," *Houston Chronicle*, 15 June 2002, A40.

10. Myron Peretz Glazer, quoted in Caroline E. Mayer and Amy Joyce, "Blowing the Whistle," *Washington Post*, 10 February 2002, H1.

11. Dan Ackman, "Sherron Watkins Had Whistle, but Blew It," http://www.forbes.com/2002/ 02/14/ 0214watkins.html, last accessed 9 December 2004.

12. For a discussion of the etymology of the word, see William Safire, *Safire's Political Dictionary*, 3rd ed. (New York: Random House, 1978), 790.

13. Sissela Bok, "Whistleblowing and Professional Responsibility," *New York Education Quarterly*, 11 (1980), 7–10.

14. *Petermann* v. *International Brotherhood of Teamsters*, 174 Cal. App. 2d 184, 344, P. 2d 25 (1959). This case is discussed further in Chapter 8 in the section on unjust dismissal because Petermann was fired for testifying.

15. James M. Roche, "The Competitive System to Work, to Preserve, and to Protect," *Vital Speeches of the Day* (May 1971), 445.

16. Bok, "Whistleblowing and Professional Responsibility," 330.

17. One form of this argument is examined in Alex C. Michalos, *A Pragmatic Approach to Business Ethics* (Thousand Oaks, CA: Sage Publications, 1995), 44–53.

18. The concept of agency is not confined to law but occurs in economics (especially the theory of the firm) and organizational theory. For a useful collection of articles exploring the ethical relevance of agency theory, see Norman E. Bowie and R. Edward Freeman, eds., *Ethics and Agency Theory* (New York: Oxford University Press, 1992).

19. Raphael Powell, *The Law of Agency* (London: Pitman and Sons, 1965), 7.

20. *Second Restatement of Agency*, Sec. 387. A Restatement is not a statute passed by a legislature but a summary of the law in a given area, written by legal scholars, which is often cited in court opinions. Other important Restatements are those on contracts and torts.

21. *Second Restatement of Agency*, Sec. 358, Comment f.

22. Michalos, *A Pragmatic Approach to Business Ethics*, 51.

23. Myron Peretz Glazer and Penina Migdal Glazer, "Whistleblowing," *Psychology Today* (August 1986), 39. See also Myron Peretz Glazer and Penina Migdal Glazer, *The Whistle-Blowers: Exposing Corruption in Government and Industry* (New York: Basic Books, 1989).

24. Albert O. Hirschman, *Exit, Voice, and Loyalty* (Cambridge, MA: Harvard University Press, 1970), 77.

25. Ibid., 79.

26. Charles Peters and Taylor Branch, *Blowing the Whistle: Dissent in the Public Interest* (New York: Praeger, 1972), 269.

27. For similar lists, see Richard T. DeGeorge, *Business Ethics*, 6th ed. (Upper Saddle River, NJ: Prentice Hall, 2006), 307–15; Gene G. James, "Whistle Blowing: Its Moral Justification," in *Business Ethics: Readings and Cases in Corporate Morality*, 4th ed., ed. W. Michael Hoffman, Robert E. Frederick, and Mark S. Schwartz (New York: McGraw-Hill, 2001), 294.

28. Bok, "Whistleblowing and Professional Responsibility," 307.

29. For a more thorough discussion of the practical aspects of whistle-blowing, see Peter Raven-Hansen, "Dos and Don'ts for Whistleblowers: Planning for Trouble," *Technology Review*, 83 (May 1980), 34–44.

30. See Martin H. Malin, "Protecting the Whistle-blower from Retaliatory Discharge," *Journal of Law Reform*, 16 (Winter 1983), 277–318; Douglas Massengill and Donald J. Petersen, "Whistleblowing: Protected Activity or Not?" *Employee Relations Law Journal*, 15 (Summer 1989), 49–56; and Elleta Sangrey Callahan and Terry Morehead Dworkin, "Internal Whistleblowing: Protecting the Interests of the Employee, the Organization, and Society," *American Business Law Journal*, 37 (1991), 267–308.

31. Two studies of the MSPB in 1980 and 1983 showed that it had done little to encourage employees to report waste and corruption or to prevent retaliation against those who did. See Rosemary Chalk, "Making the World Safe for Whistleblowers," *Technology Review*, 91 (January 1988), 55.

32. Public Company Accounting Reform and Investor Protection (Sarbanes-Oxley) Act, Pub. L. No. 107–204, 116 Stat. 745.

33. See Elleta Sangrey Callahan and Terry Morehead Dworkin, "Do Good and Get Rich: Financial Incentives for Whistleblowing under the False Claims Act," *Villanova Law Review*, 37 (1992), 273–336.

34. Gardiner Harris and Duff Wilson, "Glaxo to Pay $750 Million for Sale of Bad Products," *New York Times*, 26 October 2010. The award was a percentage of the amount received by the federal government, which was $436.4 million, so the whistle-blower's share was 22 percent.

35. Westin, *Whistle Blowing!* 134.

36. Ibid., 136. The points in this paragraph are made by Westin.

37. Ralph Nader, Peter J. Petakas, and Kate Blackwell, eds., *Whistle Blowing: The Report of the Conference on Professional Responsibility* (New York: Grossman, 1972), 4.

38. This is advocated by Patricia H. Werhane, "Individual Rights in Business," in *Just Business: New Introductory Essays in Business Ethics*, ed. Tom Regan (New York: Random House, 1984), 114–18.

39. Malin, "Protecting the Whistle-blower from Retaliatory Discharge," 309.

40. For discussions of whistle-blowing policies, see Tim Barnett, "Why *Your* Company Should Have a Whistleblowing Policy," *SAM Advanced Management Journal*, 57 (1992), 37–42; and Marcia P. Miceli and Janet P. Near, *Blowing the Whistle: The Organizational and Legal Implications for Companies and Employees* (New York: Lexington Books, 1992), chap. 7.

41. This case is based on an experience reported to Professor John T. Delaney, University of Iowa. Some details have been changed. Used with the permission of Professor Delaney.

42. Information for this case is taken mainly from *United States of America ex rel. Dr. Peter Rost v. Pfizer Inc. and Pharmacia Corporation*, Civil Action No. 03-11084-JLT, United States District Court, District of Massachusetts, 30 August 2006; and *United States of America ex rel. Peter Rost v. Pfizer, Inc. and Pharmacia Corporation*, Civil Action No. 03-11084-PBS, United States District Court, District of Massachusetts, 14 September 2010.

43. Alex Berenson, "At Pfizer, the Isolation Increases for a Whistle-Blower," *New York Times*, 8 June 2005.

44. Alex Berenson, "Pfizer Fires a Vice President Who Criticized the Company's Sales Practices," *New York Times*, 2 December 2005.

5

Trade Secrets and Conflict of Interest

(((•—[**Listen** to the **Chapter Audio** on **mythinkinglab.com**

CASE 5.1   ☀—[**Explore** the **Concept** on **mythinkinglab.com**

The Aggressive Ad Agency

Rob Lebow was used to aggressive advertising agencies. As director of corporate communications for Microsoft Corporation, the giant computer software producer located in Redmond, Washington, Lebow helped to administer the company's $10 million advertising budget. So when it was announced in the fall of 1987 that Microsoft was conducting an agency review, putting its business up for grabs, he was prepared for a flood of calls and letters. One particular piece of mail that caught his eye was a specially prepared flier from a small agency in Boston named Rossin Greenberg Seronick & Hill (RGS&H).

Under the leadership of its president, Neal Hill, this five-year-old advertising agency had accounts totaling $26 million and a growth rate of 65 percent for the past year. Although its business was concentrated in New England, RGS&H was attempting to become a national force by going after high-tech industries. As part of this strategy, the agency recruited two talented people who had worked on an account for the Lotus Corporation at another firm. Jamie Mambro and Jay Williams, who were creative supervisors at Leonard Monahan Saabye in Providence, Rhode Island, joined RGS&H on November 2.

A few days later, Neal Hill read a news story in a trade publication about the agency review by the Lotus rival. Because Microsoft's new spreadsheet program, Excel, was competing directly against Lotus 1-2-3, the industry leader, this seemed to be an ideal opportunity for RGS&H.

The flier was sent by Neal Hill on November 20, after two previous letters and several telephone calls elicited no response from Microsoft. Included in the flier was a round-trip airline ticket from Seattle to Boston and an invitation that read in part:

You probably haven't thought about talking to an agency in Boston . . . But, since we know your competition's plans, isn't it worth taking a flier? . . . You see, the reason we know so much about Lotus is that some of our newest employees just spent the past year and a half working on the Lotus business at another agency. So they are intimately acquainted with Lotus' thoughts about Microsoft—and their plans to deal with the introduction of Excel.

In order to do an effective job for a client, advertising agencies must be provided with a certain amount of confidential information that would be of value to competitors. Many companies include a confidentiality clause in their contracts with advertising agencies, and Lotus had such an agreement with its agency, Leonard Monahan Saabye. Even in the absence of a confidentiality clause, however, advertising agencies generally recognize an obligation to preserve the confidentiality of sensitive information.

On the other hand, offering the experience of employees who have handled similar accounts is an accepted practice in the advertising industry. As the president of one firm observed, "There's a thin line between experience and firsthand recent knowledge." But, he continued, "I can't imagine a new-business presentation in which the agency didn't introduce people who worked on the prospect's kind of business."[1]

Rob Lebow was left to wonder: Was Neal Hill at RGS&H offering Microsoft the experience of two employees who had worked on the Lotus account, or was he offering to sell confidential information? In either event, what should Lebow do?

If the new employees at RGS&H had information about Lotus's advertising strategy for countering the introduction of Excel, this could be of considerable value to Microsoft. Anticipating the moves of rivals is often critical to the success of a campaign. However, moving even a part of Microsoft's business to another agency—especially to a small, untested agency like RGS&H—would surely attract the attention of Lotus. In the rumor-filled world of advertising, the presence of two employees who had formerly worked on a Lotus account would not go unnoticed. Therefore, any information that RGS&H had might be "too hot to touch."

Rob Lebow recognized that he could decline the offer in different ways. He could merely ignore the flier, or he could return it with the reply "Thanks but no thanks." Another possibility was to forward the flier to Lotus. Even the rumor that Microsoft had communicated with RGS&H could be damaging to the company, and so being open with Lotus would provide some protection. However, Lotus has a reputation within the industry of being quick to sue, and considerable harm could be done to RGS&H—and to the two new employees, Jamie Mambro and Jay Williams, who might be unaware of the offer made in the flier.

Thus, any decision that Rob Lebow made was bound to have significant ethical, legal, and practical implications.

INTRODUCTION

It is not surprising that corporations such as Microsoft and Lotus attempt to protect themselves against the loss of trade secrets and to utilize what they can learn about their competitors. Information is a valuable business asset that generally provides companies with a significant advantage over competitors who lack it. We need to ask, however, what rights do companies have in maintaining the secrecy of valuable information? And what corresponding obligations do employees have not to disclose company trade secrets to outsiders or use them for their own advantage? Because companies also seek to learn about each other through competitor intelligence gathering, the ethics of such activities is also a critical issue.

There is considerable justification for holding that companies have some rights with respect to trade secrets and other intellectual property, such as patents, copyrights, and trademarks. In general, employees have an obligation of confidentiality not to disclose or use information acquired during their employment. On the other hand, employees have the right to change jobs or to start up a business of their own using some of the skill and knowledge they have acquired while working for a former employer. Furthermore, companies have a right to use their own employees' skill and knowledge that have been legitimately acquired elsewhere and to gather legitimate competitor intelligence. The challenge for individuals and companies, as well as the law, is to balance all of these competing rights and obligations.

TRADE SECRET PROTECTION

Trade secrets pose a complex set of problems about the rights and obligations of companies possessing valuable information, as well as the rights and obligations of employees and competitors. The courts have long struggled with these problems without much success. Even what information constitutes a trade secret is a source of contention. A rough definition of a trade secret is that it is information used in the conduct of a business and is not commonly known by others. Section 757 of the *Restatement of Torts* defines a trade secret as follows:

> A trade secret may consist of any formula, pattern, device or compilation of information which is used in one's business, and which gives him an opportunity to obtain an advantage over competitors who do not know or use it.

Examples of trade secrets include the ingredients or chemical composition of a product, the design of a machine, the details of a manufacturing process, methods of quality control, results of marketing surveys, financial projections, and lists of customers and suppliers.

A distinction is made in the *Restatement* between trade secrets and confidential business information. The latter is information concerning specific matters, such as the salary of an employee, which is kept secret but not actually used to manufacture anything or provide a service. The amount of a specific bid is also not a trade secret, but the procedure of a company for calculating bids might be. A former employee who is knowledgeable about the bidding procedure of a company, for example, might be able to use that information to enter lower bids.

The *Restatement* admits that an exact definition is not possible, but it lists six factors that can be used to determine what information is protectable as a trade secret. These are

> (1) the extent to which the information is known outside his business; (2) the extent to which it is known by employees and others involved in his business; (3) the extent of measures taken by him to guard the secrecy of the information; (4) the value of the information to him and his competitors; (5) the amount of effort or money expended by him in developing the information; (6) the ease or difficulty with which the information could be properly acquired or duplicated by others.

Prior to 1996, trade secrets were protected only by state laws, except where government information was involved. Subsequently, Congress made the theft of trade secrets a federal offense by passing the Economic Espionage Act of 1996 (EEA). This act is intended to prevent the theft of trade secrets for the benefit of foreign governments, which has been estimated to cost U.S. firms tens of billions of dollars annually. The penalties for individuals convicted of foreign economic espionage include prison sentences of up to 15 years and fines up to $500,000. The EEA also applies to domestic espionage, such as a theft of trade secrets involving two American firms. The fines for individuals convicted of domestic economic espionage range up to $250,000 and sentences up to 10 years.

Although the EEA is aimed primarily at foreign espionage, some observers consider the domestic provisions of the act to have a greater impact.[2] The EEA defines theft very broadly as the knowing misappropriation of a trade secret without the owner's consent. The act also defines a trade secret broadly as "All forms and types of financial, business, scientific, technical economic, or engineering information . . . if (a) the owner thereof has taken reasonable measures to keep such information secret; and (b) the information derives independent economic value, actual or potential, from not being generally known to, and to being readily ascertainable through proper means by the public." Because of these definitions, many trade secret disputes between companies could be subject to criminal prosecution, and every company needs to be more careful in the acquisition of a competitor's information.

There are three major arguments for trade secret protection. One argument views trade secrets as a kind of property and attempts to apply common-law principles of *property* rights to them. In the second argument, cases involving trade secrets are considered in terms of the right to compete and the principles of *fair competition*. The third argument holds that employees who disclose trade secrets to others or who use them for their own gain violate an obligation of *confidentiality* that is part of the employer–employee relationship.

Trade Secrets as Property

Imagine a lone inventor who, after years of hard work, develops an improved process for manufacturing a common product and builds a factory to turn out the product using the new process. Even if the innovations are not sufficiently original to be patentable, we can accept that he owns the results of his creative efforts, at least to the extent that it would be wrong for a worker in the factory to disclose the details of the manufacturing process to a competitor, especially if the employee had been sworn to secrecy.[3]

Trade secrets, along with patents, copyrights, and trademarks, are commonly regarded in the law as intellectual property that can be said to belong to an owner. Patents, copyrights, and trademarks, in particular, are like tangible property in that the owner has a right of exclusive use and the right to sell, license, or otherwise assign ownership to others. This right does not depend on keeping the information secret. Ownership of a trade secret, by contrast, does not confer a right of exclusive use but only a right not to have the secret misappropriated or wrongfully acquired by others. Once the information is widely known, it ceases to be a protectable trade secret. All forms of intellectual property are unlike tangible property, however, in that they are not inherently exclusive; that is, their use by one person does not preclude their use by another.

The question of who owns what becomes more complicated if the inventor is himself employed by a manufacturer of the product in question. As long as he gets his ideas while performing unrelated work for his employer, however, and conducts the experiments on his own time using his own materials and facilities, it seems only right that he be recognized as the sole owner of the improved manufacturing process and be permitted—perhaps after leaving his present employer—to sell the secrets of the process to another manufacturer or to go into business for himself. If, on the other hand, he is hired as an inventor to develop improved methods of manufacture or if he does his creative work on his employer's time with the resources of his employer, then some or all the rights of ownership could reasonably be claimed to belong to the employer.

THE WEXLER CASE.   The case of *Wexler* v. *Greenberg* is instructive in this regard. Alvin Greenberg was employed as chief chemist for the Buckingham Wax Company, which manufactured floor cleaners, polishes, and other maintenance materials. One of his tasks as chief chemist was to analyze the products of competitors and to use the results to develop new formulas. After eight years with the company, Greenberg left to join Brite Products, which had previously purchased exclusively from Buckingham. With the formulas that Greenberg had developed while working for Buckingham, Brite was able to dispense with Buckingham as a supplier and become a manufacturer itself, whereupon Buckingham sued to prevent Greenberg and his new employer from using the formulas on the grounds that they were trade secrets which Greenberg had misappropriated.

According to the decision in this landmark case, an employer has the burden of showing two things: "(1) a legally protectable trade secret; and (2) a legal basis, either a covenant or a confidential relationship, upon which to predicate relief."[4] Information is protectable as a trade secret, in other words, only as long as it meets certain conditions, one of which is that it is genuinely a secret. Furthermore, the owner of a trade secret is protected against the use of this information by others only when it is disclosed by an employee in violation of an obligation of confidentiality, for example, or when a competitor obtains it by theft, bribery, industrial espionage, or some other impermissible means.

In overturning a lower court ruling that held that Greenberg had an obligation of confidentiality not to disclose the formulas, the Supreme Court of Pennsylvania ruled in favor of Greenberg citing the fact that the supposed trade secrets had not been disclosed to Greenberg by his employer but had been developed by Greenberg himself. The court explained,

> The usual situation involving misappropriation of trade secrets in violation of a confidential relationship is one in which an employer *discloses to his employee* a pre-existing trade secret (one already developed or formulated) so that the employee may duly perform his work. . . . It is then that a pledge of secrecy is impliedly extracted from the employee, a pledge which he carries with him even beyond the ties of his employment relationship. Since it is conceptually impossible, however, to elicit an implied pledge of secrecy from the sole act of an employee turning over to his employer a trade secret which he, the employee, has developed, as occurred in the present case, the appellees must show a different manner in which the present circumstances support the permanent cloak of confidence cast upon Greenberg.

The formulas, moreover, were not significant discoveries on Greenberg's part but were merely the result of routine applications of Greenberg's skill as a chemist. As such, they were, in the court's view, the kinds of technical knowledge that any employee acquires by virtue of being employed. Even though the formulas are trade secrets, which the Buckingham Wax Company is permitted to use, they properly belong to Greenberg, who has a right to use them in his work for a new employer. Society also makes an investment in the development of information; it is not the exclusive property of an individual or a firm. Because patentable ideas and other innovations are generally built on foundations that have been laid by others, even companies that have spent a great deal for research cannot claim sole right of ownership.

THE BASIS FOR PROPERTY RIGHTS.   One source for the argument that patentable ideas, trade secrets, and the like are a form of property is the Lockean view that we own the results of our own labor.[5] Patent and copyright laws are based in part on the premise that inventors and writers who work with their minds and turn out such products as blueprints and novels should have the same right of ownership that is accorded to creators of more tangible objects. Insofar as intellectual property is created by individuals who have been hired by a company for that purpose and paid for their labor, it follows, in the Lockean view, that the company is the rightful owner. Just as the products made on an assembly line belong to the company and not to the workers who make them, so too do inventions made by people who are hired to invent. The company has paid them for their efforts and provided them with the wherewithal to do their work.

In addition, there are good utilitarian reasons for holding that companies have property rights to certain kinds of information. First, society generally benefits from the willingness of companies to innovate, but without the legal protection provided by patent and trade secret laws, companies would have less incentive to make the costly investments in research and development that innovation requires. Second, patent and copyright laws encourage a free flow of information, which leads to additional benefits. Patent holders are granted a period of 17 years in which to capitalize on their discoveries, but even during the period of the patent, others can use the information in their research and perhaps make new discoveries.

The existence of legal protection for trade secrets, patents, and other forms of intellectual property also has its drawbacks. A patent confers a legal monopoly for a fixed number of years, which raises the price that the public pays for the products of patent holders during that time. Trade secrets permit a monopoly to exist as long as a company succeeds in keeping key information out of the hands of competitors. Because there is no requirement that patents be used, a company could conceivably patent a large number of processes and products that rival its own and thereby prevent competitors from using them.[6] The owner of copyrighted material can prevent the wide dissemination of important information either by denying permission to print it or by charging an exorbitant price.

These drawbacks can be minimized by the optimal trade-off between the advantages and disadvantages of providing legal protection for patents, trade secrets, and the like. This trade-off is achieved, in part, by the limits on what can be patented or copyrighted or protected as a trade secret. Other means for achieving the optimal trade-off include placing expiration dates on patents and copyrights and defining what constitutes infringements of patents and copyrights. Thus, the Copyright Act of 1976 includes a provision for "fair use" that permits short quotations in reviews, criticism, and news reports.

CLARIFYING THE OWNERSHIP OF IDEAS.   Many companies attempt to clarify the ownership of patentable ideas by requiring employees to sign an agreement turning over all patent rights to the employer. Such agreements are morally objectionable, however, when they give companies a claim on discoveries that are outside the scope of an employee's responsibilities and make no use of the employer's facilities and resources.[7] Courts in the United States have often invalidated agreements that force employees to give up the rights to inventions that properly belong to them. The laws in most of the other industrialized countries of the world provide for sharing the rights to employee inventions or giving additional compensation to employees, especially for highly profitable discoveries.[8]

The ownership of ideas is a difficult area, precisely because the contributions of employers and employees are so difficult to disentangle. Arguably, the law in the United States has tended to favor the more powerful party, namely, employers. Contracts or other agreements that spell out in detail the rights of employers and employees are clearly preferable to ambiguous divisions that often land in the courts. These arrangements must be fair to all concerned, however, and granting employees a greater share of the rewards might be a more just solution—and also one that benefits corporations in the long run by motivating and retaining talented researchers.

Fair Competition

The second argument for trade secret protection holds that companies are put at an unfair competitive disadvantage when information they have expended resources in developing or gathering can be used without cost by their competitors. Even when the information is not easily classifiable as property and there is no contract barring disclosure or use of the information, it may still be protected on grounds of fairness in trade.

In *Wexler* v. *Greenberg*, the court considered not only who owns the formulas that Greenberg developed for the Buckingham Wax Company but also whether placing restrictions on Greenberg's use of the formulas in his work for another company unfairly deprived him of a right to compete with his former employer. According to the decision in *Wexler*,

> any form of post-employment restraint reduces the economic mobility of employees and limits their personal freedom to pursue a preferred course of livelihood. The employee's bargaining position is weakened because he is potentially shackled by the acquisition of alleged trade secrets; and thus, paradoxically, he is restrained because of his increased expertise, from advancing further in the industry in which he is most productive. Moreover . . . society suffers because competition is diminished by slackening the dissemination of ideas, processes and methods.

The problem of trade secrets, in the view of the court, is one of accommodating the rights of both parties: "the right of a businessman to be protected against unfair competition stemming from the usurpation of his trade secrets and the right of an individual to the unhampered pursuit of the occupations and livelihoods for which he is best suited."

THE ASSOCIATED PRESS CASE.   A good illustration of the fair competition argument is provided by a 1918 case, in which the Associated Press complained that a news service was rewriting its stories and selling them to newspapers in competition with the Associated Press.[9] The defendant, International News Service, argued in reply that although the specific wording of a news story can be regarded as a form of property, like a literary work, which belongs to the writer, the content itself cannot belong to anyone. Further, there is no contract between the parties that International News Service had breached. In the words of Justice Louis D. Brandeis:

> An essential element of individual property is the legal right to exclude others from enjoying it. . . . But the fact that a product of the mind has cost its producer money and labor, and has a value for which others are willing to pay, is not sufficient to insure to it this legal attribute of property. The general rule of law is, that the noblest of human productions—knowledge, truths ascertained, conceptions, and ideas—become, after voluntary communication to others, free as the air to common use.

In this view, information that cannot be patented or copyrighted has the same legal status as trade secrets, so that a plaintiff must show that there is a breach of contract or some other wrongful means of acquisition. Accordingly, Brandeis continued,

> The means by which the International News Service obtains news gathered by the Associated Press is . . . clearly unobjectionable. It is taken from papers bought in the open market or from bulletins publicly posted. No breach of contract, or of trust and neither fraud nor force, are involved. The manner of use is likewise unobjectionable. No reference is made by word or act to the Associated Press. . . . Neither the International News Service nor its subscribers is gaining or seeking to gain in its business a benefit from the reputation of the Associated Press. They are merely using its product without making compensation. That, they have a legal right to do; because the product is not property, and they do not stand in any relation to the Associated Press, either of contract or trust, which otherwise precludes such use.

A majority of the justices of the Supreme Court sided with the Associated Press, however, arguing that the case should be decided not on grounds of property rights or breach of contract but on considerations of fair competition. Although the public may make unrestricted use of the information contained in news stories, the two parties were direct competitors in a business in which the major stock in trade is news, a product that requires the resources and efforts of a news-gathering organization. In selling news stories based on dispatches from the Associated Press, the International News Service was, in the words of the majority opinion, "endeavouring to reap where it has not sown, and . . . appropriating to itself the harvest of those who have sown." The opinion further held:

> We need spend no time, however, upon the general question of property in news matter at common law, or the application of the Copyright Act, since it seems to us the case must turn upon the question of unfair competition in business. . . . The underlying principle is much the same as that which lies at the base of the equitable theory of consideration in the law of trusts—that he who has fairly paid the price should have the beneficial use of the property. It is no answer to say that complainant spends its money for that which is too fugitive or evanescent to be the subject of property. That might . . . furnish an answer in a common-law controversy. But in a court of equity, where the question is one of unfair competition, if that which complainant has acquired fairly at substantial cost may be sold fairly at substantial profit, a competitor who is misappropriating it for the purpose of disposing of it to his own profit and to the disadvantage of complainant cannot be heard to say that it is too fugitive and evanescent to be regarded as property. It has all the attributes of property necessary for determining that a misappropriation of it by a competitor is unfair competition because contrary to good conscience.

NONCOMPETITION AGREEMENTS.   Because of the difficulty of imposing legal restraints on employees after they leave, many companies require employees to sign a noncompetition agreement when they are hired. These agreements typically restrict an employee from working for a competitor for a certain period of time or within a given geographical territory after leaving a company. Agreements not to compete are a common feature of the sale of a business, and the courts have generally not hesitated to enforce them.

But there is little justification for restricting employees in this way. Noncompetition agreements are almost entirely for the benefit of the employer and inflict a burden on employees that is out of proportion to any gain. At least 12 states consider them so unfair that they are prohibited entirely.[10] Where noncompetition agreements are permitted by law, the courts have generally imposed a number of tests to determine whether they are justified.[11] These tests are that the restrictions contained in an agreement (1) must serve to protect legitimate business interests; (2) must not be greater than that which is required for the protection of these legitimate interests; (3) must not impose an undue hardship on the ability of an employee to secure gainful employment; and (4) must not be injurious to the public. Legitimate business interests include the protection of proprietary information or customer relations, but the purpose of an agreement cannot be merely to protect an employer against competition.

In determining whether restrictions are greater than those required to protect the legitimate interests of an employer, three factors are important. These are the time period specified, the geographical area, and the kind of work that is excluded. The value of trade secrets is reduced over time, so that a noncompetition agreement designed to protect trade secrets can justifiably restrain an employee only during the time that they have value. Without a time limit on an agreement, an employee could be prevented from working for a competitor even after formerly proprietary information becomes common knowledge. Similarly, an employer with a legitimate interest in protecting the customers it serves in New York City, for example, might be justified in preventing a sales representative from working for a competitor in that area but not elsewhere.

Noncompetition agreements that specify the kind of work too broadly also run the risk of hampering an employee unduly. In one case, a woman in Georgia signed a contract with an employment agency in which she agreed not to work in any capacity for a period of one year for any competitor within a 25-mile radius. The Supreme Court of Georgia ruled that the time period and the area were reasonable but that the phrase "in any capacity" was unreasonably broad, because it would bar her from doing any work for a competitor and not merely the work that she had done for her former employer.[12] Generally, agreements prohibiting employees from working on a particular project or soliciting specific clients, for example, are less likely to be objectionable than vague restrictions such as writing computer programs or selling insurance.

The Confidentiality Argument

The third argument for trade secret protection is that employees who disclose trade secrets to others or use them themselves are guilty of violating an obligation of confidentiality. This argument is based on the view that employees agree as a condition of employment to become agents of an employer and be bound by the duty that agents have to preserve the confidentiality of certain information.[13] Section 395 of the *Restatement of Agency* states that an agent has an obligation

> not to use or to communicate information confidentially given him by the principal or acquired by him during the course of or on account of his agency . . . to the injury of the principal, on his own account or on behalf of another . . . unless the information is a matter of general knowledge.

The obligation of confidentiality does not end with the employment relation but continues to exist after an employee leaves one job for another. Employees who sign an explicit confidentiality agreement may be bound by more stringent contractual obligations than those contained in the agency relation.

Companies can also have an obligation of confidentiality that prohibits them from misappropriating trade secrets. A company that inveigles trade secrets from another company under the guise of negotiating a license agreement or a merger, for example, might be charged with a violation of trade secret law, because the process of negotiation creates a relation of confidentiality. (It might also be charged with failing to negotiate in good faith.) It is also not uncommon for companies to reject ideas brought to them by outsiders, only to adopt them later as their own. The courts have ruled in many such instances that inventors and others have a right to expect that their ideas will be received in confidence and not misappropriated.

The argument for an obligation of confidentiality provides strong support for the right of employers to trade secret protection, but it too has a number of shortcomings. It assumes, for example, that the information was received from the employer and was not, as in the case of Alvin Greenberg, developed by the employee. The obligation of confidentiality is also limited by the right of employees to use their skill and knowledge in the pursuit of a trade or occupation.

CONFIDENTIALITY AGREEMENTS.   Many employees sign a confidentiality agreement which creates an explicit contractual obligation that is often more stringent than the obligation of confidentiality that employees ordinarily have as agents. Although confidentiality agreements have some advantages for both employers and employees, they are open to the same objections as agreements to assign patent rights to employers and to refrain from postemployment competition. Because they are usually required as a condition of employment, employees are effectively coerced into giving up rights to which they might otherwise be entitled.

By relying on an enforceable obligation of confidentiality, companies often place unnecessary restraints on employee mobility and career prospects. Michael S. Baram contends that litigation rarely preserves either the secrecy of company information or the liberty of employees, and that both of these are better served by more sophisticated management.[14] Among the policies he suggests are improving security procedures in the workplace; securing the legal protection of patents, copyrights, and trademarks whenever possible; segmenting information so that fewer people know the full scope of a trade secret; limiting information to those with a need to know; and using increased pensions and postemployment consulting contracts to keep employees from taking competitive employment.

In addition, the incentive for employees to leave with valuable trade secrets can be reduced by greater recognition of employees for their contributions. Not infrequently, employees go to a competitor or set up a business of their own because of a feeling that they have not been fairly treated. Baram concludes that the key to protecting trade secrets lies in improved employee relations, in which both employers and employees respect the rights of the other and take their obligations seriously. And a key element in improving employee relations is an ethical climate of fair play. Employers might find that treating employees fairly provides more protection for trade secrets than relying on the law.

COMPETITOR INTELLIGENCE GATHERING

Not all use of a company's trade secrets and other confidential business information is unethical or illegal. The systematic collection and analysis of competitor intelligence has become an accepted practice in the corporate world, and companies that do not avail themselves of this valuable tool may find themselves at a disadvantage. This is especially true in a global environment where some of America's competitors have long-established and highly efficient intelligence units.

Computers have greatly facilitated competitor intelligence gathering, first, by making immense volumes of information available in open-access databases and, second, by enabling companies to store and sort through the information they have compiled. Much of the information used for intelligence purposes is publicly available from news sources, trade publications, court records, regulatory filings, and presentations at industry meetings, and some is also obtained from employees' own contacts with customers, suppliers, and even competitors themselves. The challenge is to piece the information together so that conclusions can be drawn.

Although competitor intelligence gathering has shed its unsavory cloak-and-dagger image, it still has ethical and legal limits that companies ignore at their peril. Unethical collection practices often lead to costly litigation and possibly to criminal prosecution under the Economic Espionage Act of 1996. The outcome of any legal action is uncertain because of confusion in the law. A lack of ethics in competitor intelligence gathering also creates a climate of mistrust that hampers normal business activity and forces companies to adopt costly defensive measures. Most importantly, companies that routinely cross ethical boundaries in gaining competitor intelligence can scarcely expect others to respect their own trade secrets and confidential business information.

The ethical and legal limits on competitor intelligence gathering are generally concerned with the *methods* used to acquire the information.[15] The importance of the method of acquisition is due to the point that trade secrets are protected, according to the *Wexler* decision, only if there is a legal basis "upon which to predicate relief," which means that some *duty* has been breached. The duties in question are most often breached by using improper methods to acquire information from a competitor. Thus, a company that carelessly allows a trade secret to become known has no right to prevent competitors from using it. Companies do have a right, however, to prevent the use of a trade secret that is sold by an employee, for example, or stolen by a competitor, because theft is present in both cases and there is a duty not to steal. The unethical methods for gathering competitor intelligence can be grouped under four headings, each of which involves a breach of a particular duty.

1. *Theft and Receipt of Unsolicited Information.* Theft of information, either by an employee or an outsider, is obviously an improper method for acquiring information because it involves a violation of *property rights*. Examples of employee theft include freely offering information to competitors to take revenge, selling it for monetary reasons, and taking it to a new job in order to advance one's career. Companies that receive the information, for whatever reason it is offered, are receiving, in effect, stolen property. More controversial, however, are cases in which an employee inadvertently leaves a document where it can be seen or taken by a competitor or carelessly discloses information in casual conversation. Suppose that a competitor's bid on an important project is accidentally enclosed along with the specifications that are sent by the customer. Would it be ethical to use that knowledge in preparing one's own bid? Or does the information still belong to the competitor?

2. *Misrepresentation.* To gain information under false pretenses is a form of deception that violates the duty to be *honest* in all dealings. Posing as a customer to obtain information from a competitor, for example, is an act of dishonesty. Other devious practices include asking consulting firms to solicit information from competitors under the guise of doing a study of the industry and getting friendly customers to make phony requests for bids from competitors, which might contain confidential technical information about the bidder's products. Because useful bits of information are sometimes picked up during job interviews with a competitor's employees, some companies have advertised and conducted interviews for positions that do not exist, in the hope that some applicants would inadvertently reveal trade secrets of their present employer.[16]

3. *Improper Influence.* The employment relation is built on *trust*, and to induce an employee to reveal information through bribery or some other means is to exert an improper influence that undermines that trust. An employee who accepts a bribe and turns over a company's secrets has broken a bond with the employer, but the company that offers the bribe has obtained those secrets by inducing that break. Improper influence can be exerted not only by bribery but also by promising or holding out the possibility of a job or some other opportunity. Offering to purchase from a supplier in return for a competitor's price list would be an example of improper influence. More direct would be plying a competitor's employee with drinks in order to make that person less discrete.

4. *Covert Surveillance.* Some methods for obtaining information intrude in ways that companies have not anticipated and taken steps to prevent. These can be said to violate a company's right to privacy. Employees who talk about confidential matters in a public place, for example, can have no expectation of privacy, but planting hidden microphones in a competitor's place of business is a form of espionage that intrudes into an area that is regarded as private. Virtually all of the high-tech gadgetry that government intelligence agencies use to spy on enemies abroad is available for competitor intelligence gathering at home. Whether corporations have a right to privacy is controversial, but if covert surveillance were to become an accepted practice, companies would be forced to take costly defensive measures. Respecting a company's reasonable expectations of privacy, then, is in everyone's best interests.

The importance of ethics in competitor intelligence gathering has led some companies to adopt policies that give employees firm guidelines on acceptable practices and also set the tone for practices within their industries. Not only can a well-designed policy protect a company from the consequences of unethical or illegal intelligence gathering, but it can also enable a company to gain the maximum benefit from competitor intelligence by making the ethical and legal limits known to all employees. Companies can protect themselves from prosecution under the Economic Espionage Act by showing that any illegal conduct by an employee was in violation of an effective EEA-compliance program.

CONFLICT OF INTEREST

Among the many ethical problems in the collapse of Enron Corporation, conflict of interest looms large. A report of the Enron board of directors assigns much of the blame to a host of partnerships set up by Andrew S. Fastow, the company's former chief financial officer (CFO). These partnerships—which included LJM1, LJM2, Chewco, JEDI, Southhampton, and four Raptor partnerships—had the effect of removing from Enron's books unwanted assets and liabilities. They also greatly enriched Mr. Fastow along with other top Enron executives and favored investors. These supposedly independent entities contributed to Enron's demise because they created liabilities for the company should the price of Enron stock fall, as it did.

The conflict of interest for Mr. Fastow arose when he negotiated the terms of the deals on behalf of the partners with a company that he had a duty to serve. He was in effect bargaining with himself (or his subordinates) over matters in which he stood to gain. In some negotiations involving Enron payments to the partnerships, he reportedly did not reveal his stake or seek approval of transactions as the company's code of ethics required. In two instances, the board waived the conflict-of-interest clause in the ethics code to permit the CFO's dual role, but the waivers themselves raise ethical concerns. Richard C. Breeden, a former chairman of the Securities and Exchange Commission, observed, "The very notion that the chief financial officer of a major corporation would have divided loyalties to this degree of magnitude is something I wouldn't have believed any board of directors would allow—or that any C.F.O. would accept." He added, "The C.F.O. is the financial conscience of the company, the guardian of the numbers. If he has a conflict, how can the system work?"[17]

Enron's public auditing firm, Arthur Andersen, has also been accused of conflict of interest. Although Andersen auditors were troubled by the partnerships—especially whether they were truly independent entities or merely accounting fictions—they apparently did not bring their concerns to the board, as would be expected. One possible reason for this failure is that Andersen also provided consulting services that were far more lucrative than auditing. When an accounting firm occupies such a double role, it has an incentive to ignore accounting irregularities in order to keep a consulting client. Moreover, Andersen auditors performed some of the company's internal bookkeeping, thus blurring the line between conducting an independent audit and managing a company's own financial operations. Auditors who make money keeping a client's books are scarcely independent judges of the integrity of the information they contain.

In creating the partnerships, Enron engaged several major investment banks, which also encountered conflicts of interest. The conflicts here arise when a firm's analysts feel pressure to maintain "buy" recommendations in order to keep Enron's lucrative deal-structuring business. As a result, many investors maintained confidence in Enron even as the company's troubles were becoming known to its investment advisers. Ironically, the Chinese walls that investment banks build between their analysis and advisory services in order to prevent conflict of interest may have prevented analysts from knowing about Enron's deteriorating condition.

Enron's law firm, Vinson & Elkins, was also accused of a conflict of interest when it was engaged to give a legal opinion after concerns were raised about certain deals in an anonymous letter to the chairman Kenneth Lay. The writer of that letter, Sherron S. Watkins (a whistle-blower who is profiled in Case 4.1), wrote, "Can't use V&E due to conflict—they provided some true sale opinions on some of the deals." Vinson & Elkins was engaged, and the firm gave a clean bill of health to deals they helped develop. In addition, Enron's board of directors was accused of conflict of interest because the company contributed heavily to charities and institutions with which the members were involved and, in one instance, to the political campaign of a member's husband. The suspicion is that the board members' independence was undermined by the generosity of these gifts.

Companies and their employees have an obligation to avoid *conflicts of interest* of the kinds illustrated by the Enron case. Virtually all corporate codes of ethics address conflict of interest because it interferes with the ability of employees to act in the best interests of a firm. Accepting gifts or lavish entertainment from suppliers, for example, is generally prohibited or strictly limited for the simple reason that the judgment of employees is apt to be compromised. Company codes usually contain guidelines on investing in customers, suppliers, and competitors of an employee's firm for the same reason.

Prohibitions on conflict of interest cannot be so extensive, however, as to prevent employees from pursuing unrelated business opportunities, taking part in community and political affairs, and generally acting as they see fit in matters outside the scope of their employment. One problem with conflict of interest is in drawing a line between legitimate and illegitimate activities of employees in the pursuit of their personal interests. A further problem is the large gray area that surrounds conflict-of-interest situations. Perhaps no other ethical concept in business is so elusive and subject to dispute. Many people charged with conflict of interest see nothing wrong with their behavior. It is important, therefore, to define the concept clearly and to understand the different kinds of conflicts of interest.

What Is Conflict of Interest?

The Enron case features numerous individuals and firms with interests that conflict. It would be inaccurate, however, to define a conflict of interest as merely a clash between conflicting or competing interests because these are present in virtually every business relationship. In the relation between buyer and seller, for example, each party strives to advance his or her own interest at the expense of the other, but neither party faces a conflict of interest as the term is commonly understood.

The conflict in a conflict of interest is not merely a conflict between conflicting interests, although conflicting interests are involved. The conflict occurs when a personal interest comes into conflict with an obligation to serve the interests of another. More precisely, we can say that a conflict of interest is a conflict that occurs when a personal interest interferes with a person's acting so as to promote the interests of another *when the person has an obligation to act in that other person's interest*. This obligation is stronger than the obligation merely to avoid harming a person and can arise only when the two persons are in a special relationship, such as employer and employee.

Specifically, the kind of obligation described in this definition is that which character-izes an agency relation in which one person (an agent) agrees to act on behalf of another (the principal) and to be subject to that person's control. This fact explains why conflict of interest is most often encountered by professionals—lawyers, doctors, and accountants, for example—and among fiduciaries, such as executors and trustees. Employees of business firms are also in an agency relation in that they have a general obligation to serve the interests of an employer.

An important feature of an agency relation is its open-endedness. An agent is obligated to perform not merely this or that act but, in the words of the *Second Restatement of Agency*, "to act solely for the benefit of the principal *in all matters concerned with his agency*."[18] The duties of an agent are not determined solely by a list of moral rules but by the nature of the interests to be served. This open-ended character of the agency relation explains why it is a conflict of interest for an agent to acquire *any* interest that is contrary to that of a principal, because the kinds of situations in which an agent might be called upon to act in the interest of another are not easily anticipated.

To complete the definition of conflict of interest, some account should also be given of a personal interest. Roughly, a person has an interest in something when the person stands to gain a benefit or an advantage from that thing. "Having an interest" is not the same as "taking an interest." A person can take an interest in someone else's interest, especially when that person is a family member or a close associate. In that case, however, the benefit or advantage accrues to someone else. Furthermore, the benefit or advantage is usually restricted to a financial gain of some kind. Merely satisfying a desire, for example, would not seem to be enough, for otherwise a lawyer who secretly hopes that the client will be convicted would face a conflict of interest, as would a lawyer who prefers to play golf instead of spending the time adequately representing a client. The benefit or advantage would also have to be substantial enough to interfere significantly with a person's performance of an obligation.

Some Relevant Distinctions

All instances of conflict of interest are morally suspect, but some are more serious than others. In their rules on conflict of interest, company codes of ethics and codes for professionals, such as lawyers and accountants, contain a number of relevant distinctions that can aid us in understanding the concept of conflict of interest.

ACTUAL AND POTENTIAL CONFLICT OF INTEREST. There is a distinction between *actual* and *potential* conflicts of interest.[19] A conflict is actual when a personal interest leads a person to act against the interests of an employer or another person whose interests the person is obligated to serve. A situation constitutes a potential conflict of interest when there is the possibility that a person will fail to fulfill an obligation to act in the interests of another, even though the person has not yet done so.[20]

Andrew S. Fastow was apparently in an actual conflict-of-interest situation by virtue of having a duty to serve the interests of Enron at the same time that he stood to gain from negotiating favorable terms for the partnerships in which he had a stake. If another person at Enron were bargaining on behalf of the company, then he might have been free to serve the interests of himself and the other partners. However, it appears that he was attempting to serve both interests simultaneously.

Obviously, the categories of actual and potential conflict of interest involve subjective elements. A person of integrity might be able to have a strong personal interest in some matter and yet still serve the interests of another. Merely having a competing interest creates a potential conflict of interest, but determining whether an actual conflict of interest exists would require us to make a judgment about that person's objectivity. Similarly, whether an interest creates a potential conflict depends on the strength of the influence it exerts on a person. Owning a small amount of stock in a company, for example, is unlikely to influence anyone's conduct, and so most employers do not impose an absolute prohibition on investments. More often they place a dollar limit on outside financial interests, or else they require a disclosure of stock ownership so that the potential for conflict of interest can be evaluated in each case.

PERSONAL AND IMPERSONAL CONFLICT OF INTEREST.   A second distinction can be made between *personal* and *impersonal* conflicts of interest. The definition developed in the preceding section is phrased in terms of a personal interest that comes into conflict with the interests of another. A conflict can also arise when a person is obligated to act in the interests of two different persons or organizations whose interests conflict. Thus, a lawyer who represents two clients with conflicting interests may not stand to gain personally from favoring one or the other, and yet, according to Rule 1.7(a) of the American Bar Association's *Model Rules of Professional Conduct*, such an arrangement constitutes a conflict of interest.[21] A lawyer who has a personal interest that conflicts with the interests of a client has a personal conflict of interest, whereas a lawyer who represents two clients with conflicting interests faces an impersonal conflict of interest.

Insofar as Andrew Fastow stood to gain financially from the partnerships he headed, he faced a personal conflict of interest. However, even if he had no personal stake, there would still be an impersonal conflict of interest if he took an active role in the management of the partnerships. His role as the CFO of Enron commits him to acting in the best interests of the shareholders in all matters, and this duty cannot be fulfilled if he is also committed to serving the interests of the members of the partnerships. For example, deciding whether an unusually profitable investment opportunity should be allocated to Enron or to a partnership would require him to favor one set of interests over the other. This is an instance of the biblical injunction that a person cannot serve two masters.

INDIVIDUAL AND ORGANIZATIONAL CONFLICT OF INTEREST.   Third, conflicts of interest can be either *individual* or *organizational*. In the agency relation, the agent is typically a person acting in the interests of a principal, which may be another person or an organization. However, organizations can be agents as well and hence parties to conflicts of interest. For example, many large accounting firms, like Arthur Andersen, provide management services to companies they also audit, and there is great concern in the profession that this dual function endangers the independence and objectivity of accountants.[22] Advertising agencies whose clients have competing products face a similar kind of conflict of interest. Investment banking houses have also been accused of conflict of interest for financing takeovers of companies with which they have had long-standing relations. Further, large law firms face the possibility of conflict of interest when they have clients with competing interests—even when the work is done by different lawyers in the firm.

For an accountant to provide management services to a company that he or she also audits—or for an individual ad person, banker, or lawyer to accept clients with conflicting interests—is a clear conflict of interest. But why should it be a conflict when these functions are performed by different persons in different departments of a firm? The answer is that an accounting firm, for example, also has an interest that is shared by every member of the organization, and the interests of the firm can affect decisions about individual clients. Thus, when management services are more lucrative than auditing, firms may have an incentive to concentrate on them to the detriment of other functions. They may also be tempted to conduct audits in ways that favor the clients to whom they provide management services.

Similarly, the creative work for competing advertising accounts is generally done by independent groups, but there is an incentive to commit greater resources and talent to more valuable accounts. In addition, when an organization such as an advertising agency takes on a client, there is an organizational commitment of loyalty that goes beyond merely delivering agreed-upon services. For an organization to work for and against a client at the same time is incompatible with this kind of organizational commitment. In addition, advertising campaigns involve sensitive information about product development and marketing strategies that is not easily kept confidential. Investment banks and large law firms encounter similar challenges to their ability to serve the interests of all clients to the fullest.

The Kinds of Conflicts of Interest

The concept of conflict of interest is complex in that it covers several distinct moral failings that often run together. It is important to separate them, though, in order to have a full understanding both of the definition of conflict of interest and of the reasons that it is morally wrong for a person to be in a conflict-of-interest situation. Briefly, there are four kinds of conflicts of interest: (1) exercising biased judgment, (2) engaging in direct competition, (3) misusing a position, and (4) violating confidentiality. Each of these calls for some explanation.

BIASED JUDGMENT. The exercise of judgment is characteristic of professionals, such as lawyers, accountants, and engineers, whose stock in trade is a body of specialized knowledge that is used in the service of clients. Not only are professionals paid for using this knowledge to make judgments for the benefit of others but also part of the value of their services lies in the confidence that can be placed in a professional's judgment. Accountants do not merely examine a company's financial statements, for example; they also attest to the accuracy of those statements and to their compliance with generally accepted accounting principles, or GAAP. The National Society of Professional Engineers' *Code of Ethics for Engineers* stipulates that engineers shall not submit plans or specifications that are unsafe or not in conformity with accepted engineering standards.[23] So an engineer's signature on a blueprint is also a warrant of its quality.

Judgment is not exclusively a feature of professional work. Most employees are called upon to exercise some judgment in the performance of their jobs. Purchasing agents, for example, often have considerable latitude in choosing among various suppliers of a given product. The judgment of purchasing agents in all matters, however, should be used to make decisions that are in the best interests of the employing firm. For a purchasing agent to accept a bribe or kickback in return for placing an order constitutes a clear conflict of interest. The reason is simple. Bribes and kickbacks are usually intended to induce an employee to grant some favor for a supplier at the expense of the employer. Other factors that could influence the judgment of an employee include outside business interests, such as an investment in a competitor or a supplier, or dealings with businesses owned by family members.

Whether it is a potential conflict of interest for a purchasing agent to accept a gift from a supplier who expects favorable treatment in the future is less clear. An answer to this question depends largely on the value of the gift, the circumstances under which it is offered, the practice within the industry, and whether the gift violates any law. The code of ethics of a large bank, for example, states that employees should not accept gifts where the purpose is "to exert influence in connection with a transaction either before or after that transaction is discussed or consummated. Gifts, for any other purpose, should be limited to those of nominal value." "Gifts of nominal value," the code continues, "generally should be limited to standard advertising items displaying a supplier's logo." A maximum value of $25 is suggested as a guideline.

DIRECT COMPETITION. For an employee to engage in direct competition with his or her employer is a conflict of interest. One reason, of course, is that an employee's judgment is apt to be impaired by having another interest. In addition, the quality of the employee's work might be reduced by the time and effort devoted to other activities. Unlike other kinds of outside business interests, however, direct competition is generally prohibited by companies even when it is disclosed and there is no danger of impaired judgment or diminished work performance. Consider this case, which is taken from a policy statement issued by the Xerox Corporation:

> The wife of a Xerox tech rep inherits money. They decide it would be profitable to open a copy shop with her money and in her name in a suburban city. The territory they choose is different from his. However, there are several other copy shops and an XRC [Xerox Resource Center] in the vicinity. She leases equipment and supplies from Xerox on standard terms. After working hours, he helps his wife reduce costs by maintaining her equipment himself without pay. He also helps out occasionally on weekends. His job performance at Xerox remains as satisfactory as before. One of the

nearby competitive shops, also a lessee of Xerox equipment, writes to his manager complaining that the employee's wife is getting free Xerox service and assistance.

The conflict of interest in this case consists mainly in the fact that the employee's investment and work outside of his employment at Xerox place him in direct competition with the company. The territory is different from his own, and so he would never have to make decisions on the job that could be influenced by his wife's business. The outside interest also has no effect on the quality of his work for Xerox. Still, on the assumption that the husband benefits from his wife's business venture, he is competing directly with his employer, because Xerox operates an XRC in the area.

In addition, by maintaining the equipment in his wife's shop himself, the employee harms the company by depriving it of the potential for additional business. It would be a conflict of interest for the tech rep to do service for any copy shop using equipment of any make, as long as he is employed by Xerox. His skill as a technician, which is in part the result of company training, belongs in a sense to the company, and he would be free to exercise these skills only upon leaving the employment of Xerox. Finally, the employee is indirectly harming the interests of Xerox by upsetting the relations between the company and other lessees of Xerox equipment.

MISUSE OF POSITION.   Misuse of position constitutes a third kind of conflict of interest. In April 1984, a reporter for the *Wall Street Journal* was fired for violating the newspaper's policy on conflict of interest. The firing occurred after R. Foster Winans, a contributor to the influential stock market column "Heard on the Street," admitted to his employer and investigators from the Securities and Exchange Commission that he conspired over a four-month period, beginning in October 1983, with two stockbrokers at Kidder, Peabody & Company to trade on the basis of advance information about the content of the column. One of the charges against R. Foster Winans was that he misused his position as a *Wall Street Journal* reporter to enrich himself in violation of a provision in the newspaper's code of ethics that reads as follows:

> It is not enough to be incorruptible and act with honest motives. It is equally important to use good judgment and conduct one's outside activities so that no one—management, our editors, an SEC investigator with power of subpoena, or a political critic of the company—has any grounds for even raising the suspicion that an employee misused a position with the company.[24]

Consider the hypothetical case of a bank manager who, in the course of arranging home improvement loans, makes it a point to ask customers whether they have lined up a contractor. She casually drops the name of her brother who operates a general contracting business and mentions that a number of bank customers have been very satisfied with the work of his company. The bank manager's mention of her brother is clearly improper if she misuses her power to grant or deny a loan to induce customers to use him as a contractor. A conflict of interest is still present, though, even if she does not allow her personal interest to have any effect on the decisions she makes on behalf of her employer. There is no conflict between the interests of the manager and those of the bank, and the bank is not harmed in any significant way. Still, the manager has taken the opportunity to advance her personal interests while acting in her capacity as an official of the bank. Holding a position with a company or other organization gives a person powers and opportunities that would not be available otherwise, and an employee has an obligation not to use these powers and opportunities for personal gain.

Extortion also constitutes a misuse of position. Unlike bribery, with which it is often confused, extortion does not involve the use of a payment of some kind to influence the judgment of an employee. Rather, extortion in a business setting occurs when a person with decision-making power for a company demands a payment from another party as a condition for making a decision favorable to that party. For example, a purchasing agent who threatens a supplier with a loss of business unless the supplier agrees to give a kickback to the purchasing agent is engaging in extortion. Extorting money from a supplier in this way is a conflict of interest, even if the company is not directly harmed, because the purchasing agent is violating an obligation to act in the position solely for the interests of the employer.

VIOLATION OF CONFIDENTIALITY. Finally, violating confidentiality constitutes, under certain circumstances, a conflict of interest. The duty of lawyers, accountants, and other professionals, for example, precludes the use of information acquired in confidence from a client to advance personal interests—even if the interests of the client are unaffected. Similarly, because a director of a company is privy to much information, it would be wrong to use it for personal gain or other business interests.

The case of R. Foster Winans also illustrates a conflict of interest involving a breach of confidentiality. A reporter with information prior to publication who attempts to capitalize on the expected results is using that information for his or her own personal gain. Specifically, the courts found Mr. Winans guilty of *misappropriating* confidential information that properly belonged to his employer. In the Supreme Court decision affirming the conviction of Mr. Winans, Justice Byron White observed,

> Confidential business information has long been recognized as property. "Confidential information acquired or compiled by a corporation in the course and conduct of its business is a species of property to which the corporation has the exclusive right and benefit."[25]

Justice White further noted,

> The District Court found, and the Court of Appeals agreed, that Winans had knowingly breached a duty of confidentiality by misappropriating prepublication information regarding the timing and the contents of the "Heard" column, information that had been gained in the course of his employment under the understanding that it would not be revealed in advance of publication and that if it were, he would report it to his employer.

Managing Conflict of Interest

Conflict of interest is not merely a matter of personal ethics. A person in a conflict of interest, either potential or actual, may be in the wrong, but conflicts usually occur in the course of being a professional or a member of an organization. Often, these conflicts result from structural features of a profession or an organization and must be managed through carefully designed systems.

Professions, such as medicine, law, and accounting, are highly vulnerable to conflict of interest because of their strong duty to serve the interests of others as patients or clients. Business firms in particular industries also face conflicts because of their need to provide many different kinds of services to many different clients or customers. In some cases, both professional and organizational factors are involved. Accountants, for example, sometimes own stock in the companies that they audit, and the firm they work for may also provide consulting services to its auditing clients. Obviously, accounting firms need to employ a variety of means for managing these kinds of conflicts of interest.

Fortunately, there are many means for managing conflict of interest. Most corporations have a section in their code of ethics that specifically addresses the problem. In some industries, especially financial services, companies have comprehensive compliance programs for ensuring the utmost integrity. For example, an obvious conflict of interest exists when the portfolio manager of a mutual fund also engages in personal trading for his or her own account. Securities and Exchange Commission Rule 17j-1 requires mutual fund companies to develop policies and procedures to prevent inappropriate personal investing. In response, companies have adopted very extensive systems that prohibit certain kinds of trades (e.g., short-selling), require preclearance of other trades, and ban participation in initial public offerings (IPOs). In addition, mutual funds closely monitor portfolio managers and prepare periodic reports of violations.

As these examples indicate, the management of conflict of interest requires a variety of approaches. The following is a list of the major means by which professional groups and business organizations can manage conflicts of interest.

1. *Objectivity.* A commitment to be objective serves to avoid being biased by an interest that might interfere with a person's ability to serve another. Virtually all professional codes require objectivity. Indeed, the code for certified public accountants, which requires objectivity and independence, identifies objectivity (the obligation to be impartial and intellectually honest) with avoiding actual conflicts of interest and independence (avoiding relations that would impair objectivity) with potential conflicts.

2. *Avoidance.* The most direct means of managing conflicts of interest is to avoid acquiring any interests that would bias one's judgment or otherwise interfere with serving others. Avoidance is easier said than done, however. First, it may be difficult to anticipate or identify a conflicting interest. For example, law firms typically conduct a review of new clients to avoid conflicts of interest, but when the number of relations on both sides are numerous, such a review may miss some potentially conflicting interests.

Second, acquiring conflicting interests may be unavoidable due to the nature of the business. This is especially true of investment banking, where conflicts of interest are built into their structure. For example, a large investment bank routinely advises clients on deals that affect other companies which the bank also advises or whose securities the bank holds. Investment banks have been accused of modifying research reports on stocks in order to avoid antagonizing companies from which they solicit business. As one person notes, "The biblical observation that no man can serve two masters, if strictly followed, would make many of Wall Street's present activities impossible."[26]

Where adverse interests cannot be avoided, they can be countered by introducing new interests in a process known as *alignment*. For example, a problem in corporate governance is that CEOs, who are supposed to serve the interests of shareholders, have personal interests that often interfere. One solution is the use of pay-for-performance measures, such as stock options, that align the CEO's personal interest with that of shareholders. Stockbrokers are in a conflict-of-interest situation when their compensation is tied to the number of trades that a customer makes and not to the quality of these trades. The solution in this case is to base the broker's compensation on the customer's portfolio return, thus aligning the broker's interest more closely to the client's.

3. *Disclosure.* Disclosure serves to manage conflict of interest primarily because whoever is potentially harmed by the conflict has the opportunity to disengage or at least to be on guard. For example, a stockbroker who is paid more to sell a firm's in-house mutual funds faces a conflict of interest in recommending a fund to a client. A client who knows of the potential bias can seek out another broker who is uninfluenced by the difference in compensation or can evaluate more carefully the broker's advice to detect any bias. In short, forewarned is forearmed. In legal ethics, a conflict of interest is permissible if three conditions are satisfied: (1) the lawyer discloses the conflict to the client, (2) the lawyer is confident that he or she can provide wholly adequate representation so that the client will be unaffected by the conflict, and (3) the client accepts the lawyer's service under those conditions.[27]

In addition to adverse interests, disclosure may include all kinds of information. The greater the transparency—that is, openness of information—the less opportunity there is for conflict of interest to occur. For example, conflict of interest in government is managed in part by requiring officials to disclose financial holdings, but disclosure in the press of officials' activities also reduces conflicts. Thus, we are better able to judge whether a legislator has a conflict of interest if we know not only how much stock he or she owns in a company affected by a bill but also how that person voted on the bill.

4. *Competition.* Strong competition provides a powerful incentive to avoid conflicts of interest, both actual and potential. For example, at one time commercial banks gave their brokerage business to firms that were already bank customers. This practice, known as reciprocation or "recip," has virtually disappeared because of the need for returns on trust accounts to compare favorably with alternative investments. Competition dictates that the allocation of brokerage commissions be based on the "best execution" of trades and not on keeping bank customers happy. Of course, no firm would use increased competition as a means for managing conflict of interest, but industry regulators should recognize that the power of competition to reduce conflict of interest is another reason to encourage competition.

5. *Rules and Policies.* As already noted, most companies have policies concerning conflicts of interest. These typically require employees to avoid acquiring adverse interests by not accepting gifts or investing in potential suppliers, for example. Rules and policies may also prohibit the kind of conduct that would constitute a conflict, as when a broker trades ahead of a large customer, a practice known as "frontrunning." Conflict of interest may be managed by other rules and policies that do not address conflict of interest directly and have other purposes. For example, controls on the flow of information that affect who has access to what information are necessary for many reasons, but the rules and policies in question also limit conflict of interest. Thus, a portfolio manager of a particular mutual fund who has no knowledge of pending purchases by other funds in the firm has fewer possibilities for conflict.

Priority rules are an especially useful means for managing conflict of interest. For example, an investment bank that advises outside investment funds faces a conflict of interest in deciding which investment opportunities to bring to each fund. This problem is especially acute if the bank also operates its own in-house funds. Generally, in such cases, the bank establishes priority rules so that each client knows the order of favor. A client who knows in advance that the better opportunities will be allocated to other funds cannot complain of unfair treatment.

6. *Independent Judgment.* Insofar as a conflict of interest results in biased judgment, the problem can be corrected by utilizing a third party who is more independent. In courts of law, a judge who, say, owns stock in a company affected by a case is generally obligated to *recuse* himself or herself and allow the decision to be rendered by other judges. Companies usually require an executive with a conflicting interest to pass the decision to the next level. Independent appraisers are often utilized in cases where an insider, such as an executive or a director, is engaging in a property transaction with a corporation. In firms with frequent conflict-of-interest problems, such as investment banks, in which the conflict exists among various units, a standing independent advisory board is often formed to consider matters referred to it.

7. *Structural Changes.* Because conflicts of interest result from providing many different services to different customers or clients, they can be reduced by compartmentalizing these services. Advertising agencies, for example, form separate creative teams for each account; accounting firms separate auditing and advisory services; and commercial banks split trust management from the retail side of the business. Within multifunction institutions, conflicts can be reduced by strengthening the independence and integrity of each unit. For example, instead of treating the investment research division as an arm of their brokerage units, investment banks are being urged to upgrade their status and insulate them from pressure.

Some structural features of American business are dictated by law. Because of the potential conflicts of interest, Congress mandated that commercial banks could not also sell stocks or insurance, thereby making investment banking and insurance separate businesses. Pressure is building among federal regulators to force accounting firms to form separate auditing and consulting companies. Addressing the problem of conflict of interest by structural changes is probably unwise overall, however, because of the many advantages of combining different services in one firm. Separating the functions of an investment bank, for example, might reduce conflicts of interest, but a firm that underwrites corporate securities needs the sales capacity of its brokerage unit and the skills of its research department. On the whole, we probably gain much more than we lose by having firms that provide multiple services.

CONCLUSION

Like whistle-blowing, trade secrets and conflict of interest involve a delicate balancing of the rights and interests of employers and employees, as well as the public at large. Especially in the case of trade secret protection, we see how different kinds of arguments—for property rights, fair competition, and a duty of confidentiality—underlie the law in this area and support our views about what is morally right. For the most part, the language of rights and the obligations of agents have dominated our discussion, although utilitarian considerations about the harm and benefit of protecting trade secrets have been introduced. In the next chapter we examine another right, namely, the right of employees and consumers to privacy. Utilitarian and Kantian arguments are used to explain the concept of privacy and provide a foundation for it. Unlike trade secrets and conflict of interest, privacy is an area where the law has yet to develop very far, and so we can focus mainly on ethical issues.

CASE 5.2 ✳ Explore the Concept on mythinkinglab.com

The Conflict of an Insurance Broker

I work for an insurance brokerage firm, Ashton & Ashton (A&A), which is hired by clients to obtain the best insurance coverage for their needs.[28] To do this, we evaluate a client's situation, keep informed about insurance providers, negotiate on the client's behalf, and present a proposal to the client for approval. Our compensation comes primarily from a commission that is paid by the client as part of the premium. The commission is a percentage of the premium amount, and the industry average for commissions is between 10 percent and 15 percent. A secondary source of compensation is a contingency payment that is made annually by insurance providers; the amount of this payment is based on the volume of business during the past year.

One of our clients, a world-class museum in a major American city, has been served for years by Haverford Insurance Company. Haverford is a financially sound insurer that has provided the museum with reliable coverage at reasonable prices and has gone out of its way on many occasions to be accommodating. Haverford has also built good relations with A&A by allowing a 17 percent commission—a fact that is not generally known by the clients. When the museum's liability insurance policy was up for renewal, A&A was asked to obtain competitive proposals from likely insurers. We obtained quotations from four comparable insurance companies with annual premiums that ranged between $90,000 and $110,000. A fifth, unsolicited proposal was sent by a small, financially shaky insurance company named Reliable. The annual premium quoted by Reliable was $60,000.

There is no question that the museum is best served by continuing with Haverford, and our responsibility as an insurance broker is to place clients with financially sound insurers who will be able to honor all claims. The museum has a very tight operating budget, however, and funding from public and private sources is always unpredictable. As a result, the museum is forced to be extremely frugal in its spending and has always chosen the lowest bid for any service without regard for quality. The dilemma I faced, then, was, Do I present the Reliable bid to the museum? If I do, it will almost certainly accept it given its priority of saving money. Because the market indicates that the value of the needed policy is around $100,000, the Reliable proposal is definitely an attempt to "low-ball" the competition, and the company would probably raise the premium in future years. Is this honest competition? And if not, should A&A go along with it? Allowing a client to accept a low-ball bid might also jeopardize our relations with the reputable insurers who submitted honest proposals in good faith. If relations with Reliable are not successful, the museum is apt to blame us for not doing our job, which is not merely to pass along proposals but to evaluate them for suitability.

On the other hand, A&A will receive a higher commission and a larger contingency payment at the end of the year if the museum is presented with only the four solicited proposals and never learns of the Reliable bid. Because of our financial stake in the outcome, however, do we face a conflict of interest? Could we be accused of choosing a course of action that benefits us, even though in reality the client is also better served?

CASE 5.3   ✳ Explore the Concept on mythinkinglab.com

Procter & Gamble Goes Dumpster Diving

According to *Competitive Intelligence Magazine*, John Pepper, the chairman of Procter & Gamble, told a group that competitive intelligence was "of singular importance" to a consumer-products company and that P&G had shifted "from collecting, analyzing and disseminating information, to acquiring and using knowledge to create winning strategies."[29] Despite these strong words, Mr. Pepper was apparently alarmed to hear that competitive intelligence sleuths hired by P&G had obtained some documents from its European-based rival, Unilever, through questionable means. At least one person sorted through the trash bins at Unilever's Chicago office, a practice known as "dumpster diving." After learning how P&G's competitor intelligence had been obtained, Mr. Pepper informed Unilever of the misdeeds and personally called the Unilever chairman to settle the matter.

In the highly competitive business of shampoo and other hair-care products, information about new lines, launch dates, pricing, advertising plans, and production figures is carefully guarded. Like many companies, P&G attempts to gather all publicly available information about its competitors' activities for what the company calls "competitive analysis." Competitive-analysis executives at P&G contracted with an outside firm, which in turn hired several subcontractors to investigate competitors. A budget estimated at $3 million was allotted to the project, which began in the fall of 2000. The operation was run out of a safe house, called the "Ranch," located in P&G's home town of Cincinnati, Ohio. Among the secrets gained from dumpster diving in Chicago were detailed plans for a product launch in February. In addition to dumpster diving, which P&G admitted, Unilever believed that some rogue operators also misrepresented themselves to competitors in efforts to gain access, a charge that P&G denies.

Although P&G claims that nothing illegal was done, the dumpster diving violated the company's own code of ethics and its policies for competitive intelligence contractors. The ethics code of the Society of Competitive Intelligence Professionals also prohibits dumpster diving when the bins are on private property. In April 2001, when the company became aware that the spying operation had spun out of control, three executives overseeing the project were fired. Mr. Pepper then contacted Unilever with full disclosure and a promise not to use any of the information gained. P&G had, in effect, blown the whistle on itself. Mr. Pepper hoped perhaps that this gesture would put the matter to rest. However, Unilever had just begun to seek a settlement.

In the ensuing negotiations, Unilever proposed that P&G compensate Unilever between $10 million and $20 million for possible losses incurred from the unethical acquisition of information. In addition, Unilever wanted P&G to reassign key personnel in its hair-care division who had read the documents to other positions in which they could not utilize the information they had gained. Perhaps the most unusual remedy was that P&G allow an independent third party to investigate the company's hair-care business for several years and to report to Unilever any situations in which improperly gained information might have been used. Unilever suggested that if a satisfactory settlement could not be reached, then the company might sue in court, with uncertain results.

If John Pepper thought that notifying Unilever and firing the people involved were the right things to do, then Unilever's proposals might seem to be an unwarranted punishment that would discourage others from being so forthright. On the other hand, aside from any monetary payment, P&G could continue to compete as vigorously as it would have had it not gained the information from dumpster diving. A settlement on Unilever's terms might effectively restore fair competition. On August 28, 2001, Mr. Pepper flew to London for final negotiations, knowing that he would soon have to make a decision.

Notes

1. Cleveland Horton, "Ethics at Issue in Lotus Case," *Advertising Age*, 21 December 1987, 6.
2. Alan Farnham, "How Safe Are Your Secrets?" *Fortune*, 8 September 1997, 114–20; Chaim A. Levin, "Economic Espionage Act: A Whole New Ballgame," *New York Law Journal*, 2 January 1997, 5.
3. These are essentially the facts in the classic case *Peabody* v. *Norfolk*, 98 Mass. 452 (1868).
4. *Wexler* v. *Greenberg*, 160 A. 2d 430 (1960).
5. For a discussion of the Lockean view as well as the utilitarian argument discussed later, see Edwin C. Hettinger, "Justifying Intellectual Property," *Philosophy and Public Affairs*, 18 (1989), 36–51.
6. This point is made by Robert E. Frederick and Milton Snoeyenbos, "Trade Secrets, Patents, and Morality," in *Business Ethics*, ed. Milton Snoeyenbos, Robert Almeder, and James Humber, (Buffalo: Prometheus Books, 1983), 165–66.
7. For a discussion of the ethical issues, see Mark Michael, "Patent Rights and Better Mousetraps," *Business and Professional Ethics Journal*, 3 (1983), 13–23.
8. For a summary of the law in other countries, see Stanley H. Lieberstein, *Who Owns What Is in Your Head?* (New York: Hawthorne Books, 1979), 225–32.
9. *International News Service* v. *Associated Press*, 248 U.S. 215 (1918).
10. See Kevin McManus, "Who Owns Your Brain?" *Forbes*, 6 June 1983, 178.
11. See Harlan M. Blake, "Employee Covenants Not to Compete," *Harvard Law Review*, 73 (1960), 625–91.
12. *Dunn* v. *Frank Miller Associates, Inc.*, 237 Ga. 266 (1976).
13. All employees are regarded in law as agents, at least while acting within the scope of their assigned responsibilities, but their specific obligations, including those with respect to confidentiality, are determined by the amount of trust placed in them and any understandings, such as company policies or professional ethics.
14. Michael S. Baram, "Trade Secrets: What Price Loyalty?" *Harvard Business Review*, 46 (November–December 1968), 66–74.
15. Lynn Sharp Paine, "Corporate Policy and the Ethics of Competitor Intelligence Gathering," *Journal of Business Ethics*, 10 (1991), 423–36.
16. Much of the material in this paragraph and the one following is contained in Steven Flax, "How to Snoop on Your Competitors," *Fortune*, 14 May 1984, 28–33.
17. Diana B. Henriques with Kurt Eichenwald, "A Fog over Enron, and the Legal Landscape," *New York Times*, 27 January 2002, sec 3, p. 1.
18. *Second Restatement of Agency*, Sec. 385. Emphasis added.
19. This distinction is made in Thomas M. Garrett and Richard J. Klonosky, *Business Ethics*, 2nd ed. (Upper Saddle River, NJ: Prentice Hall, 1986), 55; and in Manual G. Velasquez, *Business Ethics: Concepts and Cases*, 5th ed. (Upper Saddle River, NJ: Prentice Hall, 2002), 449.
20. Michael Davis, "Conflict of Interest," *Business and Professional Ethics Journal*, 1 (1982), 17–27, makes a threefold distinction between actual, latent, and potential conflicts of interest. Latent conflict of interest involves conflict situations that can reasonably be foreseen, whereas potential conflict of interest involves conflict situations that cannot reasonably be foreseen.
21. The rule reads, "A lawyer shall not represent a client if the representation of that client will be directly adverse to another client unless: (1) the lawyer reasonably believes the representation will not adversely affect the relationship with the other client; and (2) each client consents after consultation."
22. See Abraham J. Briloff, "Do Management Services Endanger Independence and Objectivity?" *CPA Journal*, 57 (August 1987), 22–29.
23. National Society of Professional Engineers, *Code of Ethics for Engineers*, 1987, III, 2(b).
24. "Media Policies Vary on Preventing Employees and Others from Profiting on Knowledge of Future Business Stories," *Wall Street Journal*, 2 March 1984, A12.
25. *Carpenter et al.* v. *United States*, 484 U.S. 19 (1987).
26. Warren A. Law, "Wall Street and the Pubic Interest," in *Wall Street and Regulation*, ed. Samuel L. Hayes (Boston, MA: Harvard Business School Press, 1987), 169.
27. American Bar Association, *Model Rules of Professional Conduct*, Rule 1.7.
28. This case is based on actual events, but the names of the companies have been disguised. The case was prepared by Michael Streett under the supervision of Professor John R. Boatright. Copyright 1995 by John R. Boatright.
29. This case is based on Andy Serwer, "P&G Comes Clean on Spying Operation," www.fortune.com, 30 August 2001; Julian E. Barnes, "Unilever Wants P&G Placed under Monitor in Spy Case," *New York Times*, 1 September 2001, C1; Andrew Edgecliffe-Johnson and Adam Jones, "Unilever Seeks Review after P&G 'Spying'," *Financial Times*, 1 September 2001, 14; Julian E. Barnes, "P&G Said to Agree to Pay Unilver $10 Million in Spying Case," *New York Times*, 7 September 2001, C7; Andy Serwer, "P&G's Covert Operation," www.fortune.com, 17 September 2001.

6

Privacy

((•—Listen to the **Chapter Audio** on **mythinkinglab.com**

CASE 6.1 ✳—Explore the **Concept** on **mythinkinglab.com**
Psychological Testing at Dayton Hudson

Answer each of the following questions True or False:
I feel sure there is only one true religion.

My soul sometimes leaves my body.
I believe in the second coming of Christ.
I wish I were not bothered by thoughts about sex.
I am very strongly attracted by members of my own sex.
I have never indulged in any unusual sex practices.

In April 1989, Sibi Soroka answered these questions satisfactorily and was hired as a Store Security Officer (SSO) at a Target store in California. Afterward, Soroka felt "humiliated" and "embarrassed" at having to reveal his "innermost beliefs and feelings." So he joined with two rejected job applicants in a class-action suit, charging the Dayton Hudson Corporation, the owner of the Target store chain, with invasion of privacy.[1]

Psychological testing is one of many means for enabling employers to evaluate applicants and select the best employee for a job. In the 1920s, the owner of Frank Dry Goods Company in Fort Wayne, Indiana, noticed that some salesgirls sold two to four times as much merchandise as others.[2] Further investigation revealed that the top sellers came from large working-class families with savings accounts, whereas the low performers were from small families that did not need the money and were opposed to the employment. Accordingly, the company developed a set of test questions for job applicants that asked about family size, the occupations of family members, the amount of income needed for an average family, the attitude of the family about working in the store, and the existence of savings accounts.

Dayton Hudson defended the use of the psychological test, called Psychscreen, on the grounds that an SSO, whose main function is to apprehend suspected shoplifters, needs good judgment, emotional stability, and a willingness to take direction. Psychscreen is a combination of two standard tests that have been administered to applicants for such public safety positions as police officers, prison guards, air traffic controllers, and nuclear power-plant operators. The completed Psychscreen test is interpreted by a firm of consulting psychologists which rates an applicant on five traits (emotional stability, interpersonal style, addiction potential, dependability, and rule-following behavior) and offers a recommendation on whether to hire the applicant. Dayton Hudson does not receive the answers to any specific questions.

Dayton Hudson admitted in court that it had not conducted any studies to show that Psychscreen was a reliable predictor of performance as a security officer, except to administer the test to 18 of its most successful SSOs. The company could not document any improvement in the performance of SSOs after adopting the test or any reduction in shoplifting. An expert witness for the plaintiffs contended that the test had not been proven to be reliable or valid for assessing job applicants in this particular setting. An expert witness for Dayton Hudson admitted that the use of Psychscreen resulted in a 61 percent rate of false positives. Thus, even if every unqualified applicant were identified by the test, more than six in ten qualified applicants would also be rejected as unfit.

Dayton Hudson conceded that the intimate questions in Psychscreen constitute an invasion of privacy but added that the intrusion was minor and was justified by the company's needs. Employment application forms ask for some job-related personal information. Even though questions about religion and sex are not themselves job-related, they enable the interpreters of the test to evaluate psychological traits that are related to the job. Dayton Hudson was no more interested than Frank Dry Goods in the personal life of its applicants for employment. The information gained by intimate questions was merely a means to an end. Left unanswered by this response are whether the company's need to administer the test offset the invasion of the applicants' privacy and if so, whether some less invasive means to achieve this end could have been found.

Some critics argue that psychological testing is an invasion of privacy not only because of the intimate nature of the questions but also because the tests seek personal information, namely psychological traits, in ways that the person does not understand and is unable to control. That is, not only the means but also the end is intrusive. Thus, even if a test could be constructed without questions about religion, sex, or any other intimate subject, these critics hold that the test would still be an invasion of privacy.

INTRODUCTION

Early in the twentieth century, the Ford Motor Company set up a "Sociological Department" in order to make sure that workers, in Henry Ford's words, were leading "clean, sober, and industrious" lives.[3] Company inspectors checked bank accounts to keep Ford employees from squandering their munificent $5-a-day wages. They visited employees' living quarters to see that they were neat and healthful, and they interviewed wives and acquaintances about the handling of finances, church attendance, daily diet, drinking habits, and a host of other matters. Workers who failed to live up to Henry Ford's standards of personal conduct were dismissed.

Employers today would scarcely dare to intrude so openly into the private lives of their employees, but they possess less obvious means for acquiring the information sought by Ford's teams of snooping inspectors—and some information that Henry Ford could not have imagined! Among the tools available to present-day employers are quick and inexpensive drug tests, pencil-and-paper tests for assessing honesty and other personality traits of employees, extensive computer networks for storing and retrieving information about employees, and sophisticated telecommunication systems and concealed cameras and microphones for supervising employees' work activities. By administering medical insurance plans and providing on-site healthcare and counseling, employers are now in a position to know about employees' medical conditions. Some employers have also conducted genetic testing to screen employees for genes that make them more vulnerable to chemicals in the workplace.

Consumers have joined employees as targets for information gathering by American corporations. The same surveillance techniques that are used to monitor employees are now used to detect theft by store customers. Video cameras are commonplace in retail stores, and some retailers have installed hidden microphones as well. The main threat to consumer privacy comes from the explosive growth of database marketing. The countless bits of information that consumers generate in each transaction can now be combined in vast databases to generate lists for direct-mail and telemarketing solicitations. Public records, such as automobile registrations and real-estate transfers, are also readily available sources of information for the creation of specialized lists. The collection of information about users of the Internet, which is in its infancy, has immense potential for marketers.

Concern about privacy is a relatively recent occurrence. However, a 1979 public opinion survey conducted by Louis Harris for the Sentry Insurance Company revealed that three out of four respondents believed that privacy should be regarded as a fundamental right akin to life, liberty, and the pursuit of happiness and that half of them fear that American corporations do not adequately safeguard the personal information they gather on individuals.[4] Over 90 percent of those who responded said that they favored safeguards to prevent the disclosure of personnel and medical files to outsiders. A law granting employees access to the information collected about them was favored by 70 percent, and 62 percent wanted Congress to pass a law regulating the kind of information that corporations may collect about individuals.

CHALLENGES TO PRIVACY

Privacy has become a major issue in government and business in recent years for many reasons. One is simply the vast amount of personal information that is collected by government agencies. The need to protect this information became especially acute after the passage of the Freedom of Information Act (FOIA) in 1966. Intended by Congress to make government more accountable for its actions, the act had the unforeseen consequence of compromising the confidentiality of information about private individuals. The Privacy Act of 1974 was designed in large part to resolve the conflict between government accountability and individual privacy. So great were the problems that Congress created the Privacy Protection Study Commission to investigate and make recommendations about further action. The National Labor Relations Board has long faced a similar problem with union demands for access to personnel files and other employee records. Unions claim that they need the information in order to engage in fair collective bargaining, but allowing unions to have unlimited access to this information without consent violates the employees' right of privacy.[5]

Employee Privacy

Government is not the only collector of information. Great amounts of data are required by corporations for the hiring and placement of workers, for the evaluation of their performance, and for the administration of fringe-benefit packages, including health insurance and pensions. Private employers also need to compile personal information about race, sex, age, and handicap status in order to document compliance with the law on discrimination. In addition, workers' compensation law and occupational health and safety law require employers to maintain extensive medical records. Alan F. Westin, an expert on privacy issues, observes that greater concern with employee rights in matters of discrimination and occupational health and safety has had the ironic effect of creating greater dangers to employees' right of privacy.[6]

WORKPLACE MONITORING. Monitoring the work of employees is an essential part of the supervisory role of management, and new technologies enable employers to watch more closely than ever before, especially when the work is done on telephones or computer terminals. Supervisors can eavesdrop on the telephone conversations of employees, for example, and call up on their own screens the input and output that appear on the terminals of the operators.[7] Hidden cameras and microphones can also be used to observe workers without their knowledge. A computer record can be made of the number of telephone calls, their duration, and their destination. The number of keystrokes made by a data processor, the number of errors and corrections made, and the amount of time spent away from the desk can also be recorded for use by management. Even the activities of truck drivers can be monitored by a small computerized device attached to a vehicle that registers speed, shifting, and the time spent idling or stopped.

Companies claim that they are forced to increase the monitoring of employees with these new technologies as a result of the changing nature of work. More complex and dangerous manufacturing processes require a greater degree of oversight by employers. The electronic systems for executing financial transactions and transferring funds used by banks and securities firms have a great potential for misuse and costly errors. In addition, employers are increasingly concerned about the use of drugs by workers and the high cost of employee theft, including the stealing of trade secrets. Employers also claim to be acting on a moral and a legal obligation to provide a safe workplace in which employees are free from the risk of being injured by drug-impaired coworkers.[8]

Even efforts to improve employees' well-being can undermine their privacy. Wellness programs that offer medical checkups along with exercise sessions result in the collection of medical data that can be used to terminate employees or defend against workplace injury claims. More than half of all U.S. employees have access to Employee Assistance Plans (EAPs) for help in handling personal problems and drug addictions. Although the information gained is generally held in confidence, it is available for company use when an employee files a workplace injury claim or sues for discrimination, wrongful discharge, or any other wrong. In some instances, employers have used the threat of revealing unrelated embarrassing information in court to dissuade employees from pressing a suit. Although the use of an EAP is usually voluntary, employees are often required to gain approval from an EAP counselor before seeking company-paid mental healthcare. Some employees thus face the choice of revealing their mental health condition to their company or paying for mental health care out of pocket.

PSYCHOLOGICAL TESTING. One particular area of concern has been psychological testing of the kind conducted by Dayton Hudson (Case 6.1). Interest in psychological testing was spurred in the first half of the twentieth century by the "scientific management" ideas of Frederick Taylor and the development of the field of applied or industrial psychology. The massive testing programs of the armed forces in two world wars were carried over into civilian life by large American corporations. In the postwar period, American education became increasingly reliant on standardized testing for admission to colleges and universities, not only to identify qualified students but also to prevent discrimination. Tests that measure job-related abilities and aptitudes have raised little opposition. However, employers have increasingly come to recognize that an employee's psychological traits are important, not only for predicting successful job performance but also for identifying potentially dishonest and troublesome employees.

This latter goal is the appeal of integrity tests, which are sold by a handful of publishers and administered to an estimated 5 million job applicants annually. Use of the pencil-and-paper tests has been spurred by the banning of mechanical polygraph testing in 1988 and by the reluctance of former employers to reveal any but the most basic information. Studies by the congressional Office of Technology Assessment and the American Psychological Association have found that some tests have moderate predictive value but that others are virtually worthless. Large numbers of honest people are denied jobs and suffer a stigma because of faulty testing, and a few rogues slip through.

Some critics have charged that no one can pass an integrity test without a little dishonesty. Ironically, the highly honest may be among the most frequent victims of mistakes because they are more forthcoming in their answers. The use of integrity tests also assumes that people are honest—or not—and ignores the role of the work environment in promoting honesty—or dishonesty. Some employees steal when they believe that they are being cheated or abused, for example. One benefit of integrity tests, therefore, may be to enable employers to recruit a work force that will tolerate shabby treatment without retaliating.

Consumer Privacy

Concern about consumer privacy has focused primarily on the gathering and use of information in database marketing. Businesses have discovered that it pays to know their customers. For example, grocery stores that issue identification cards that are scanned along with the universal product code on each product are able to construct detailed profiles of each customer's purchasing preferences. This information may be used in many ways, including the making of offers that are tailored to appeal to specific customers. However, the main value of a database of consumer information lies in the capacity to generate customized mailing lists. If a company can identify the characteristics of potential customers by age, income, lifestyle, or other measures, then a mailing list of people with these characteristics would enable the seller to reach these customers at relatively low cost. Such targeted selling, known as direct mail, is also potentially beneficial to consumers, because a customized mailing list is more likely to produce offers of interest to consumers than is a random mailing.

The growth in database marketing has been facilitated by computer technology, which is able to combine data from many sources and assemble them in usable form. For example, by merging information about an individual with census data for that person's zip-code-plus-four area, it is possible to make reliable inferences about income, lifestyle, and other personal characteristics. Companies that specialize in data collection can provide direct marketers with customized mailing lists that target groups with the desired characteristics. Although American consumers are concerned about the threat to privacy posed by the use of personal information for this purpose, one survey showed that over two-thirds of respondents approved of the use of customized mailing lists to offer goods and services to people who are likely to be interested.[9] However, when Lotus Development Corporation announced plans in April 1990 for the database program Lotus Marketplace: Households, a set of compact discs containing information on 120 million Americans, a storm of protest ensued. This episode showed that consumers believe that there are limits on the use of personal information for marketing purposes and that this product had crossed a line.

ISSUES IN CONSUMER PRIVACY. One issue in the use of databases to generate mailing lists is the right of control over information. If we reveal some information about ourselves to a company, does that company "own" the information? For example, does a magazine have a right to sell a list of its subscribers to a direct marketer? We voluntarily provide our name and address to the magazine for the purpose of obtaining a subscription, just as we reveal our annual income to a bank in order to obtain a loan. These are examples of the *primary* use of information. The use of information for some other purpose is labeled *secondary*. Some privacy advocates hold that there should be no secondary use of information without a person's knowledge and consent. Thus, some magazines inform subscribers that they make their list available for direct mail and allow subscribers to "opt out" by removing their name and address from the list. In general, the secondary use of any information in a loan application is prohibited by law.

Other issues concern access to information and potential misuse. Although an individual's annual income is generally regarded as personal, people may not be upset to learn that this information is used to generate a mailing list—as long as no one has access to the information itself. A direct marketer has no interest in knowing a particular person's income but only whether that person is a likely prospect, and the fact that a person's name and address is on a list does not reveal to anyone that person's income. However, some information is considered too sensitive to be included in a marketing database. Health information has generally fallen into this category, but pharmaceutical companies now seek mailing lists of patients with particular conditions. For example, *Reader's Digest* succeeded in obtaining completed questionnaires on health problems from 9 million subscribers, and the magazine was planning to make this information available for direct mail on specific pharmaceutical products.[10] Patients' records, prescription data from pharmacies, and even calls to the toll-free numbers of pharmaceutical companies are resources for information gatherers.[11] Companies that sell lists also have a responsibility to screen buyers to ensure that direct mailings are for legitimate purposes and do not involve consumer fraud.

Ethical questions about employee and consumer privacy are unavoidable because obtaining and using personal information is essential in both employment and marketing. But everyone has a legitimate interest in maintaining a private life that is free from unwarranted intrusion by business. Finding the right balance between the rights of everyone concerned is not a simple task. A set of guidelines or a company code on employee and consumer privacy must address an immense number of different questions. Before we make the attempt to find a balance between these competing rights, though, it is necessary for us to inquire into the meaning of privacy as an ethical concept.

THE MEANING AND VALUE OF PRIVACY

A definition of privacy has proven to be very elusive. After two years of study, the members of the Privacy Protection Study Commission were still not able to agree on one. Much of the difficulty is due to the diverse nature of the many different situations in which claims of a right of privacy are made. Even the narrower concept of privacy for employees and consumers is applied in such dissimilar circumstances that it is not easy to find a common thread running through them.

History of the Concept

As a legal concept, privacy dates only from the late nineteenth century. There is no mention of privacy in the original Constitution or the Bill of Rights. Although a number of rights related to privacy have long been recognized in American law, they have generally been expressed in terms of freedom of thought and expression, the right of private property, protection from "unreasonable searches and seizures," and other constitutional guarantees. The first sustained discussion of privacy occurred in an 1890 article in the *Harvard Law Review* written by two young attorneys, Samuel Warren and Louis Brandeis (who later became a famed justice of the Supreme Court).[12]

The theory of privacy presented by Warren and Brandeis was slow to gain acceptance. It was rejected by the courts in a number of cases around the turn of the century in which the names and pictures of prominent persons were used to advertise products. The public uproar over one of these cases prompted the New York legislature to enact a law prohibiting the commercial use of a person's name or likeness without permission.[13] Gradually, most states followed the lead of New York in granting persons a right to be free of certain kinds of intrusion into their private lives. But it was not until 1965 that the Supreme Court declared privacy to be a constitutionally protected right. The decision came in *Griswold* v. *Connecticut*, which concerned the right of married couples to be free of state interference in the use of contraceptives.[14]

Some philosophers and legal theorists have argued that the concept of privacy does not introduce any new rights into the law but merely expresses several traditional rights in a new way. Consequently, our legal system already contains the resources to protect individuals against these wrongs without creating a distinct right of privacy.[15] For example, disclosing embarrassing facts about a person or intruding into his or her solitude might be described as inflicting mental distress; and the publication of false accusations could be said to constitute libel or defamation of character. What, these critics ask, does the concept of privacy add to other, better-established rights?

Definitions of Privacy

The literature contains many attempts to elucidate privacy as an independent right that is not reducible to any other commonly recognized right. Three definitions in particular merit examination. One, which derives from Warren and Brandeis and finds expression in *Griswold* v. *Connecticut*, holds that privacy is the right to be left alone. Warren and Brandeis were concerned mainly with the publication of idle gossip in sensation-seeking newspapers. The aim of privacy laws, they thought, should be to protect "the privacy of private life" from unwanted publicity, and their proposals all deal with limits on the publication of information about the private lives of individuals. In his celebrated dissenting opinion in *Olmstead* v. *United States*, a 1928 case concerning the constitutionality of telephone wiretapping, Brandeis wrote that the right of privacy is "the right to be let alone—the most comprehensive of rights and the right most valued by civilized men."[16]

A similar view of privacy was expressed by the majority in *Griswold*. Laws governing the use of contraceptives intrude into an area of the lives of individuals where they have a right to be let alone. Justice William J. Brennan expressed the view in a subsequent birth control case that

> If the right to privacy means anything, it is the right of the individual, married or single, to be free from unwarranted government invasion into matters so fundamentally affecting a person as the decision whether to bear or beget a child.[17]

Many critics have pointed out that the phrase "to be let alone" is overly broad.[18] Individuals have a right "to be let alone" in matters of religion and politics, for example, but legal restrictions on religious practices, such as snake handling, or on political activities, such as the making of political contributions, do not involve violations of privacy. At the same time, the Warren and Brandeis definition is too narrow, because some violations of privacy occur in situations where there is no right to be let alone. Workers have no right to be free of supervision, for example, even though it can be claimed that their privacy is invaded by the use of hidden cameras to monitor their activity secretly.

These objections, in the view of critics, are merely symptoms of a deeper source of error in the Warren and Brandeis definition, which is the confusion of privacy with liberty. These examples show that a loss of liberty is neither a necessary nor a sufficient condition for a loss of privacy. Perhaps greater clarity is achieved by limiting the concept of privacy to matters involving information and not stretching the concept to include all manner of intrusions into our private lives. Thus, cases in which companies refuse to hire smokers are better analyzed as limitations of liberty rather than invasions of privacy.

This suggestion is reflected in a second definition in which privacy is defined as control over information about ourselves.[19] According to Alan F. Westin, "Privacy is the claim of individuals . . . to determine for themselves when, how, and to what extent information about them is communicated to others."[20] This definition is open to the same charge: It is at once too broad and too narrow. Richard B. Parker observes, "Not every loss or gain of control over information about ourselves is a gain or loss of privacy."[21] Furthermore, all definitions of privacy as exercising control flounder on the fact that individuals can relinquish their own privacy by voluntarily divulging all sorts of intimate details themselves.[22] There is a loss of privacy under such circumstances but not a loss of control. Therefore, privacy cannot be identified with control.

A third, more adequate definition of privacy holds that a person is in a state of privacy when certain facts about that person are not known by others. W. A. Parent, in an important 1983 article, "Privacy, Morality, and the Law," defines privacy as "the condition of not having undocumented personal knowledge about one possessed by others."[23] By the phrase "personal knowledge," Parent does not mean all information about ourselves but only those facts "which most individuals in a given society at any given time do not want widely known."[24] It is necessary that the definition be restricted to *undocumented* personal information, because some facts that individuals commonly seek to conceal are a matter of public record and can be known without prying into their private lives. A person does not suffer a loss of privacy, for example, when a conviction for a crime becomes known to others, because court records are public documents. Similarly, there is no loss of privacy when an easily observable fact, such as a person's baldness, is known to others, even if the person is sensitive about it and prefers that others not be aware of it.

In the remaining discussion, the concept of privacy is limited to matters involving information and, in particular, to the access of others to undocumented personal information, as described by Parent. The two other definitions—as a right to be let alone and to have control over information about ourselves—confuse privacy with other values. Having gained some understanding of the concept of privacy, we can now turn to the question of why privacy is a value.

Utilitarian Arguments

Why do we value privacy so highly and hold that it ought to be protected as a right? Certainly, we desire to have a sphere of our life in which others do not possess certain information about us. But the mere fact that we have this desire does not entail our having a right of privacy; nor does it tell us how far a right of privacy extends. Some arguments are needed, therefore, to establish the value of privacy and the claim that we have a right to it. Most of the arguments developed by philosophers and legal theorists fall into one of two categories. One category consists of utilitarian arguments that appeal to consequences, and the second is Kantian arguments that link privacy to being a person or having respect for persons. To a great extent, these two different kinds of arguments express a few key insights about privacy in slightly different ways.

One of the consequences cited by utilitarians is that great harm is done to individuals when inaccurate or incomplete information collected by an employer is used as the basis for making important personnel decisions. The lives of many employees have been tragically disrupted by groundless accusations in their personnel records, for example, and the results of improperly administered polygraph and drug tests. Even factual information that ought not to be in an employee's file, such as the record of an arrest without a conviction, can cause needless harm. The harm from these kinds of practices is more likely to occur and to be repeated when employees are unable to examine their files and challenge the information (or misinformation) in them.

A drawback to this argument is that it rests on an unproved assumption that could turn out to be false. It assumes that on balance more harm than good will result when employers amass files of personal information, use polygraph machines, conduct drug tests, and so on. Whatever harm is done to employees by invading their privacy has to be balanced, in a utilitarian calculation, against the undeniable benefits that these practices produce for both employers and employees.

Furthermore, the argument considers only the possible harmful consequences of privacy invasions. However, some practices, such as observing workers with hidden cameras and eavesdropping on business conducted over the telephone, are generally considered to be morally objectionable in themselves, regardless of their consequences. Honest workers, for example, have nothing to fear from surveillance that is designed to protect against employee theft, and indeed the use of hidden cameras in a warehouse can even benefit those who are honest by reducing the possibility of false accusations. Still, workers have a right to complain that secret surveillance of their activities on the job violates the right of privacy. It is the fact that they are subjected to constant observation and not any possible consequence of being observed that is morally objectionable.

EXPANDING THE SCOPE OF CONSEQUENCES.   This objection is avoided by more sophisticated utilitarian arguments that do not locate the harmful consequences solely in the harm that occurs when information is misused. According to these arguments, a certain amount of privacy is necessary for the enjoyment of some activities, so that invasions of privacy change the character of our experiences and deprive us of the opportunity for gaining pleasure from them. Monitoring and surveillance in the workplace, for example, affect job satisfaction and the sense of dignity and self-worth of all workers. They send a message to employees that they are not trusted and respected as human beings, and the predictable results are a feeling of resentment and a decline in the satisfaction of performing a job.

An illustration of this point is provided by a truck driver with 40 years' experience with the Safeway Company who reports that he used to love his job because "you were on your own—no one was looking over your shoulder. You felt like a human being." After the company installed a computerized monitoring device on his truck, he decided to take early retirement. He complains, "They push you around, spy on you. There's no trust, no respect anymore." A directory-assistance operator reported, "I've worked all those years before monitoring. Why don't they trust me now? I will continue to be a good worker, but I won't do any more than necessary now."[25]

PRIVACY AND IDENTITY.   Some writers argue that privacy is of value because of the role it plays in developing and maintaining a healthy sense of personal identity. According to Alan F. Westin, privacy enables us to relax in public settings, release pent-up emotions, and reflect on our experiences as they occur—all of which are essential for our mental well-being. A lack of privacy can result in mental stress and even a nervous breakdown.[26] Another common argument appeals to the importance of privacy in promoting a high degree of individuality and freedom of action among the members of a society. Critics of these arguments object, however, that there is little evidence that privacy has the benefits claimed for it or that the predicted harm would follow from limiting people's privacy.[27] Many societies function very well with less room for solitude than our own, and the experiences of human beings in prisons and detention camps are cited by critics to refute these arguments.

Kantian Arguments

Two Kantian themes that figure prominently in defense of a right to privacy are those of autonomy and respect for persons. Stanley I. Benn, for example, notes that utilitarian arguments for a right of privacy are not able to show what is morally wrong when a person is secretly observed without any actual harm being done. "But respect for persons," Benn claims, "will sustain an objection even to secret watching, which may do no actual harm at all." The reason, he explains, is that covert spying "deliberately deceives a person about his world," which hinders his ability to make a rational choice.[28] Benn's argument thus appeals to both Kantian themes by arguing that invading a person's privacy violates the principle of respect for persons *and* prevents a person from making a rational choice as an autonomous being.

Hyman Gross argues in a similar vein that what is morally objectionable about being observed unknowingly through a hidden camera or having personal information in a data bank is that a person loses control over how he or she appears to others.[29] If people form incomplete or misleading impressions of us that we have no opportunity to correct, then we are denied the possibility of autonomous or self-directed activity, which is a characteristic of human beings. Hence, invasions of privacy diminish an essential condition for being human.

In a very influential discussion, Charles Fried argues that privacy is of value because it provides a "rational context" for some of our most significant ends, such as love, friendship, trust, and respect, so that invasions of privacy destroy our very integrity as a person.[30] The reason that privacy is essential for respect, love, trust, and so on is that these are intimate relations, and intimacy is created by the sharing of personal information about ourselves that is not known by other people. In a society without privacy, we could not share information with other people (because they would already know it), and hence we could not establish intimate relations with them. Thus, monitoring, in Fried's view, "destroys the possibility of bestowing the gift of intimacy, and makes impossible the essential dimension of love and friendship."[31] Similarly, trust cannot exist where there is monitoring or surveillance, because trust is the expectation that others will behave in a certain way without the need to check up on them.

The arguments of Benn, Gross, Fried, and others seize upon important insights about the value of privacy, but many critics have found flaws in the details of their arguments. Jeffrey H. Reiman, for one, objects that it is too strong to assert that all instances of people being watched unknowingly result in deceiving people and depriving them of a free choice. Otherwise, we would be violating people's right of privacy by observing them strolling down a street or riding a bus.[32] Intimate relations such as love and friendship do not consist solely in the sharing of information but involve, as one writer says, "the sharing of one's total self—one's experiences, aspirations, weaknesses, and values."[33] Consequently, these relations can exist and even flourish in the absence of an exclusive sharing of information.

The Role of Privacy in Socialization

Several philosophers have suggested that the key to a more satisfactory theory of privacy can be constructed by understanding the way in which individuals are socialized in our culture.[34] Privacy, in the view of these philosophers, is neither a necessary means for realizing certain ends nor conceptually a part of these ends. Nevertheless, we are trained from early childhood to believe that certain things are shameful (e.g., public nudity) and others strictly our own business (e.g., annual income). There is no intrinsic reason why our bodies or our financial affairs should be regarded as private matters. People at different times and places have been socialized differently with regard to what belongs to the sphere of the private, and we might even be better off if we had been socialized differently. Still, we have been socialized in a certain way. In our culture, certain beliefs about what ought to be private play an important role in the process by which a newborn child develops into a person and by which we continue to maintain a conception of ourselves as persons.

This argument is broadly utilitarian. The consequences that it appeals to, however, are not the simple pleasures and pains of classical utilitarianism or even the notions of mental health and personal growth and fulfillment of more sophisticated utilitarian arguments. The argument goes deeper by appealing to the importance of privacy for personhood, a concept that is more commonly used by Kantian theorists. Unlike Kantian arguments, though, this one recognizes that privacy is not necessary for all people in all times and places but is merely a value specific to contemporary Western culture. There are societies that function very well with less privacy than we are accustomed to; however, given the role privacy plays in our socialization process, a certain amount is needed for us to develop as persons and have a sense of dignity and well-being.

Both utilitarian and Kantian arguments point to a key insight: Privacy is important in some way to dignity and well-being. They claim too much, however; privacy is not absolutely essential to either one, except insofar as we have come to depend on it. For better or worse, privacy has become an important value in our culture, and now that it has, it needs to be maintained. Privacy is like the luxury that soon becomes a necessity, but "necessary luxuries" are not less valuable just because we could formerly get by without them. The justification of privacy just offered is thus the most adequate one we have.

THE PRIVACY OF EMPLOYEE RECORDS

The arguments in the preceding section show that privacy is of such sufficient value that it ought to be protected. There are many instances, however, in which other persons and organizations are fully justified in having personal information about us and thereby in intruding into our private lives. The task of justifying a right of privacy, then, consists not only in demonstrating the value of privacy but also in determining which intrusions into our private lives are justified and which are not.[35]

As an example, consider the issues that must be addressed in developing the case for a right of privacy in employee records and in formulating a company privacy protection plan for these records. Among the issues are the following:

1. The kind of information that is collected.
2. The use to which the information is put.
3. The persons within a company who have access to the information.
4. The disclosure of the information to persons outside the company.
5. The means used to gain the information.
6. The steps taken to ensure the accuracy and completeness of the information.
7. The access that employees have to information about themselves.

The first three issues are closely related, because the justification for an employer's possessing any particular kind of information depends, at least in part, on the purpose for which the information is gathered. Some information is simply of no conceivable use in company decision making and constitutes a gratuitous invasion of employee privacy. It is more often the case, however, that an employer has a need or an interest that provides some justification for intruding into the private lives of employees. An invasion of employee privacy is justified, however, only when the information is used for the intended purpose by the individuals who are responsible for making the relevant decisions.

Companies are generally justified in maintaining medical records on employees in order to administer benefit plans, for example, and to monitor occupational health and safety. If these are the purposes for which a company gathers this kind of information, then it follows that (1) only medical information that is essential for these purposes can be justifiably collected; (2) only those persons who are responsible for administering the benefit plans or monitoring the health and safety of employees are justified in having access to the information; and (3) these persons must use the information only for the intended purposes. There are three corresponding ways in which employees' right of privacy can be violated. These are when (1) personal information is gathered without a sufficient justifying purpose; (2) it is known by persons who are not in a position that is related to the justifying purpose; and (3) persons who are in such a position use the information for other, illegitimate purposes.

WHAT JUSTIFIES A PURPOSE?   Obviously, the notion of a justifying purpose plays a critical role in determining the exact scope of the right of privacy in employment. There is considerable room for disagreement on the questions of whether any given purpose is a legitimate one for a business firm to pursue, whether a certain kind of information is essential for the pursuit of a particular purpose, and whether the information is in fact being used for the intended purpose. Companies have an interest and, indeed, an obligation to ensure that employees are capable of performing physically demanding work and are not subjected to undue risk, for example. The purposes for which Henry Ford created the Sociological Department, however, went beyond this concern to include a paternalistic regard for the general welfare of his employees, which is not a legitimate purpose. Even to the extent that the work of the inspectors from the Ford Motor Company was justified by a legitimate purpose, there could still be an objection to the excessive amount of information they sought. Information about the handling of finances, church attendance, and eating and drinking habits is more than the company needed to know.

Determining the purpose for which information is being used can raise difficult questions about intentions. A controversy was sparked in 1980, for example, when it became publicly known that the DuPont Company was routinely screening black applicants at a plant in New Jersey for signs of sickle-cell anemia. The company asserted that the purpose for conducting the screening was to protect black workers, because carriers of the disease, who are mostly black, were thought to be more vulnerable to certain chemicals used at the plant. Such a purpose is arguably legitimate, but some critics of DuPont charged that the company was actually using genetic screening for another purpose, namely to prevent liability suits and to avoid having to protect workers from dangerous chemicals.[36]

RESOLVING DISAGREEMENTS ABOUT PURPOSE.   Is there any way in which the notion of a justifying purpose can be clarified so that such disagreements can be resolved? One possibility is to specify the conditions necessary for a business to conduct normal operations. In order to do this, a company must be able to assess the suitability of applicants for employment, supervise their work-related behavior, administer fringe-benefit plans, and so on. In addition, employers must be able to acquire the information necessary for complying with legal requirements about taxes, social security, discrimination, health and safety, and the like. As a result, employers are justified in asking potential employees about their educational background, past employment, and so on, but not, for example, about their marital status, because this information is not necessary in order to make a decision about hiring. Once employees are hired, a company may have a need to inquire about marital status in order to determine eligibility for medical benefits, but only if the employee in question chooses to participate in a medical insurance plan. Even then, this information should be used only for the purpose of determining eligibility for medical benefits.

Joseph R. DesJardins suggests that questions about the extent of the right of privacy in the workplace can be settled by appealing to a contract model of the employer–employee relationship.[37] Viewing employment as a contractual relation between an employer and an employee provides a basis for granting a set of rights to both parties, because the validity of contracts requires that certain conditions be satisfied. Contracts are valid, first, only if they are free of force and fraud. As a result, an employer has a right to require applicants to provide enough information to make an informed decision about hiring and to submit to tests for measuring relevant aptitudes and skills. Once hired, employees have an obligation to permit employers to monitor work performance, for example, and to gather whatever information is necessary to maintain an ongoing contractual relation.

Second, valid contracts also require mutual voluntary consent, so a contract model of employment would not permit employers to collect information without the knowledge and permission of the employees affected. Covert searches, surveillance by hidden cameras, the use of private investigators, and so on would be incompatible with the view of employment as a contractual relation. Similarly, objections could be raised to employer demands that employees either submit to drug tests and interrogation with a polygraph machine or be dismissed, because an employee has little choice but to comply. Union contracts in which employees are able to exercise effective choice often contain provisions prohibiting such practices.

Disclosure to Outsiders

The fourth issue—concerning the disclosure of personal information to persons outside a company—arises because of the practice, once very common, of employers sharing the content of personnel files with landlords, lending agencies, subsequent employers, and other inquiring persons without the consent of the employees involved. Even when there is a legitimate purpose that would justify these various parties having the information, it can be argued that an employer has no right to provide it, because the employer is justified in collecting and using information only for purposes connected with the employer–employee relationship. What is morally objectionable about an employer's disclosing personal information to an outside party, in other words, is not necessarily that the outside party is not justified in having it but that the employer has no justification for giving it out.

Thus, medical records collected by a former employer ought not to be passed along to a subsequent employer without the employee's consent. The former employer presumably had a purpose that justified the gathering of that information, and the new employer might also have a similar purpose in gathering the same information. But with the former employer, the information pertains to that employment relation, and can be justifiably used only for purposes connected with it. The subsequent employer must proceed in the same way as the former employer.

This argument points up an important difference between personal information and other kinds of corporate records. Databases of various kinds are generally regarded as resources that are *owned* by a company. Ownership, however, generally entails an exclusive and unrestricted right of access and control, which employers do not have with respect to personal information. A mailing list, for example, is a kind of property that a company can use in any way it pleases, with no restrictions. Medical records, by contrast, can be compiled by a company only for a specific purpose, and any use unrelated to this purpose is prohibited. The fact that employers bear a burden of proof for justifying the collection and use of personal information shows that the notion of ownership is inappropriate in this case.[38]

It is also inappropriate to describe the information in personnel files as belonging to employees, because they relinquish some rights to it by virtue of entering into the employment relation. Neither an employer nor an employee, therefore, can be said to own the information in a company's personnel files. Such information is simply not property in the usual sense, unlike other kinds of data gathered by corporations. It is necessary, therefore, to develop a conceptual model for personal information other than that of ownership.

The Means Used to Gather Information

Justifying the means used to gather information, which is the fifth issue, involves a different set of considerations. Use of certain means may violate an employee's right of privacy, even when the information gathered is of a kind that an employer is fully justified in possessing. Examples of impermissible means are polygraph testing and pretext interviews. (Pretext interviews are inquiries made under false pretenses, as when an employer seeks information from an applicant's family while posing as a market researcher.) Even if employers are justified in asking certain questions on a job application, they are not, for that reason, justified in using a polygraph machine or a pretext interview to verify the accuracy of a person's responses.

A major consideration in evaluating the means used to gather information is whether less intrusive means are available. In general, less intrusive means are morally preferable to those that are more intrusive. Employers are justified in seeking information about drug use by employees in the workplace, for example, but such means as searches of lockers and desks, hidden cameras in rest rooms, random drug tests, and the like are not justified when sufficient information could be gathered by less intrusive means, such as closer observation of work performance and testing only for cause. (Some means are not justified, of course, even if less intrusive means are not available. Hidden cameras and random drug tests are possible examples.)

What makes some means more intrusive than others depends on several factors. Such practices as conducting strip searches and watching while a urine sample is produced involve an affront to human dignity. An objection to constant monitoring, personality tests, and the use of polygraph machines is that they collect more information than is necessary and that they collect it indiscriminately. Honesty tests, for example, often inquire into personal habits and interests, family relations, and sexual adjustment—matters that are extraneous to the ostensible purpose.[39] Improperly administered polygraph tests can easily become "fishing expeditions," which result in the revelation of information that an employer is not justified in having.

Another reason why some practices such as monitoring and surveillance by hidden cameras and polygraph testing are unusually intrusive is that they deprive persons of an opportunity to exercise control over how they appear to others, which is essential for being an autonomous individual. An employee who is unaware of being observed, for example, might be unwittingly led to reveal facts that he or she would otherwise keep from others. George G. Brenkert argues, very perceptively, that because a polygraph machine measures physical characteristics such as breathing rate, perspiration, and blood pressure over which we have little or no control, it "circumvents the person" and undercuts the "way by which we define ourselves as autonomous persons."[40] As a person, one can shape how one appears to others and create an identity for oneself. A machine that registers involuntary responses denies people the power to do that.

Accuracy, Completeness, and Access

The last two issues are concerned primarily with matters of fairness. If the information in personnel files and other corporate databases is going to be used to make critical decisions about wage increases, promotions, discipline, and even termination of employment, then it is only fair that the information be as accurate and complete as possible and that employees have access to their personnel files so that they can challenge the contents or at least seek to protect themselves from adverse treatment based on the information in them.

Employers who maintain inaccurate or incomplete files and deny employees access to them are not invading the privacy of their employees, as the concept of privacy is commonly defined. What is at issue is not the possession of personal information by an employer but its use in ways that are unfair to employees. The right that employers violate is a right of fair treatment, which is not the same as a right of privacy. Still, because these issues are involved in the handling of personal information, they must be considered in devising policies or laws dealing with employee privacy.

Another objection to drug tests and polygraph machines is their unreliability. A number of factors, including the use of prescription drugs and careless laboratory work, can result in false positives, especially in simpler, less-expensive drug tests. Polygraph machines are inherently unreliable, because they register only bodily responses and not the mental experience that triggers them. An investigator might conclude that a subject is lying when the responses recorded by the machine are actually due to a different kind of association. One study, in which 14 polygraphers were asked to evaluate the charts of 207 criminal suspects, found that 50 percent of the experts thought that innocent suspects gave deceptive answers and 36 percent of them considered the guilty suspects to be telling the truth.[41] After a review of the studies to date, the U.S. Office of Technology Assessment concluded in 1983 that polygraph testing was useless for screening in preemployment contexts.[42]

In summary, determining the exact limits of the right of employees to privacy in the workplace requires that we address a number of issues. Questions about four of these issues—those concerning the kind of information collected, the use to which it is put, and the persons both inside and outside the company who have access to it—can be answered largely by appealing to the notion of a legitimate purpose. The issue of the means used to gain information involves different questions about whether some means are inherently objectionable and whether others are objectionable because less-intrusive means are available. Finally, the remaining issues involve the fair treatment of employees, which is not, strictly speaking, part of a right of privacy but is still related to the handling of personal information.

PRIVACY ON THE INTERNET

Imagine that most of the stores you entered created a record of your visit including not only your purchases but also what merchandise you looked at, how long you took, what route you followed through the store, what other stores you had visited, and what you bought there. Imagine further that, in many instances, the store could connect this information with your name, address, telephone number, and perhaps your age, income level, and lifestyle. You would probably have the feeling that your shopping activity was being closely scrutinized and that you lacked virtually any privacy while browsing.

This situation, which most people would find alarming in a shopping mall, is routine on the Internet. A 1999 study found that 92.8 percent of the websites surveyed collected at least one piece of personal information, such as name and e-mail address, and 56.8 percent collected at least one type of demographic data, such as age, gender, or zip code. Only 6.6 percent of these sites collected no information.[43] Some information is provided *overtly* by the user as a condition of making a purchase or gaining access to Web pages. Other information is obtained *covertly*, without the user's knowledge or consent.

The most common method for obtaining information covertly is the installation of a "cookie," which is a file placed on a user's hard drive that recognizes a repeat user and stores information from past visits. Cookies benefit users by eliminating the need to enter information each time, but they can also provide the site owner with "clickstream" data about what pages are visited and how much time is spent on each one. Because cookies identify only a user's computer (by tagging it with a unique number), this tool is considered to preserve anonymity. However, personal information can be obtained by combining cookie data with larger databases that identify and profile individuals. Once users are identified, site owners can share the information derived from cookies to form more complete profiles in a process know as "cookie synchronization."

A Boston technology company called Pharmatrak places cookies on the computers of visitors to the health-information pages of pharmaceutical companies and records the kind of information they seek.[44] If this information could be combined with individual names, then drugs could be marketed to Web users with specific ailments. To date, Pharmatrak has not taken this extra, morally questionable step, but another company, DoubleClick, aroused a storm of protest when it proposed something similar. DoubleClick, which places banner ads on 1,500 websites using profiles based on information from cookies, purchased Abacus Direct Corporation, which has personal information on more than 80 million households. By merging the two databases, DoubleClick could tailor the banner ads on a website to match the user's purchasing preferences. Stung by vociferous protests, the company announced that it would wait until government and industry agreed on standards.[45] However, one observer said that although the industry was letting DoubleClick take the heat, the company is "not doing anything that anyone else isn't doing."[46]

The explosive growth of the Internet as a consumer marketplace is a benefit to consumers and businesses alike. The success of websites depends crucially on the collection of information. One reason is that anonymous sales with cash are not possible. Furthermore, sites that offer free content depend on advertising, and advertising space is much more valuable if it can be tailored to individual users. However, the collection of information on the Internet appears to pose threats to users' privacy. So we need to ask, first, what is the danger? What harm, if any, is done by websites collecting information? Are any rights violated? Second, given the need for government regulation or industry self-regulation, what standards should be applied, and what should be the goal in setting standards? Finally, by what means should these standards be implemented? A variety of organizations have already been formed to offer resources for developing privacy policies and to certify compliance by awarding seals of approval.

What's Wrong with Information Collection?

Although consumers may feel a lack of privacy when browsing the Internet, is this feeling well-grounded? Scott McNealy, the chairman and CEO of Sun Microsystems, once remarked, "You have zero privacy anyway. Get over it!"[47] Much of the information compiled is publicly available; the Internet only makes its compilation easier and cheaper than in the past. Store owners, if they wish, could follow consumers around to see what merchandise they examined. Computers do not observe us without our knowledge or intrude into our private lives the way psychological tests or hidden cameras do. The Internet is arguably a public arena, so being online is like walking and talking in the town square. The use to which the information is put is primarily to sell us something. Although fraud is a serious concern, we seek mainly to avoid the annoyance of advertising on the Internet.

If privacy is defined as control over personal information or the dissemination of personal information without our consent, then the practices of Internet companies violate our rights. However, this position assumes that we "own" the information about ourselves and thus have a right of control. Moreover, we give up a great deal of information in order to enjoy the benefits of Internet commerce, and so perhaps some loss of privacy is a trade-off that we voluntarily make. So, following Scott McNealy's advice, should we get over it?

The noted expert Lawrence Lessig, in his important book *Code and Other Laws of Cyberspace*, raises two problems that are unique to computers and the Internet.[48] One risk for Lessig is that our initial contacts with information gatherers form a profile of who we are, and this profile will fit us into a particular mold, which may not be accurate to begin with and may inhibit our ability to change and grow. Lessig writes, "The system watches what you do; it fits you into a pattern; the pattern is then fed back to you in the form of options set by the pattern; the options reinforce the pattern; the cycle begins anew."[49] If we develop by selecting from the options available to us, then the choice of options is critical. In life apart from the Internet we can always seek out new options, but to the extent that we are bound on the Internet by the options presented to us, our possibilities for growth are limited.

Lessig's second risk is that information collection by computers, especially on the Internet, could undermine the traditional American value of equality. The American Revolution was in part a rejection of European society in which innumerable distinctions of rank divided people. According to Lessig, "An efficient and effective system for monitoring makes it possible once again to make these subtle distinctions of rank. Collecting data cheaply and efficiently will take us back to the past."[50] For example, by means of frequent flyer programs, airlines identify their better customers and offer them special treatment. Companies with 800 numbers recognize the telephone numbers of favored customers and put them at the head of the queue. As a result, some people suffer a form of discrimination in which they do not get a flight on standby or endure long waits on the telephone. Businesses have always provided better service to select customers, but any discrimination was limited by the cost of the information. Lessig observes, "Whereas before there was relative equality because the information that enabled discrimination was too costly to acquire, now it pays to discriminate."[51]

Neither of these concerns involves privacy per se; the first affects autonomy, the second, equality. Moreover, the effect may be slight and insignificant. Perhaps Lessig's greatest insight is that the way in which technology is configured, specifically the way in which computer code is written, has social consequences. Furthermore, to the extent that computer code has consequences, it can be rewritten so as to achieve more desirable results. One of the solutions discussed later is Lessig's suggestion that we develop special software that will act as an electronic butler, negotiating with websites the kind of privacy protection that we desire.

Principles for Protecting Privacy

The appropriate standards or principles that should be applied to information gathering on the Internet depend on what we want to achieve or avoid. Three camps can be identified.[52] Those who worry about a "dossier" society, in which every facet of our lives is available to those with power, want strict limits on the kinds and amounts of data collected and on the availability of these data. Those who view personal data as a kind of property that can be "traded" in a market for certain benefits want to ensure that consumers do not trade too cheaply and that this valuable commodity is fairly priced. In the view of this camp, personal information is currently too "cheap" and hence is being overutilized.

The dominant camp consists of people in industry, government, and public interest groups who want to balance people's concerns about privacy—well-founded or not—with the growth of the Internet as a consumer marketplace. They seek to provide consumers with a voice in the development of this important commercial medium. The danger is that the Internet will firmly fix some practices before the public is aware of what is happening. Their goal is primarily to prevent the most egregious abuses by developing standards or principles that safeguard consumers.

In 1972, the Department of Health, Education, and Welfare developed guidelines for its own handling of information called "fair information practices," which formed the basis for much subsequent action. In 1980, the Organization for Economic Cooperation and Development (OECD) adopted a set of guidelines that underpin most international agreements and self-regulatory policies of multinational corporations. The European Parliament adopted the European Union Privacy Directive, which took effect on October 25, 1998. This law binds not only member countries but also nonmember states doing business in the European Union. Already some major American multinational corporations are being investigated for violations of the EU Privacy Directive. Although many American laws address various aspects of Internet privacy, the United States has preferred a piecemeal legal response instead of adopting an omnibus piece of legislation like the EU Privacy Directive. The Federal Trade Commission, in particular, has attempted to protect Internet privacy by using various consumer-protection laws. Principles of privacy on the Internet have also been developed by industry associations, such as the Online

Privacy Alliance (OPA), and public interest groups, most notably the Electronic Privacy Information Center (EPIC).

Despite this great diversity of sources, a remarkably similar set of standards has emerged. The Federal Trade Commission list of five principles is representative of the many documents on Internet privacy.

1. *Notice/Awareness.* Disclose the identity of the collecting party, the information collected, the means for collecting it, and the uses to which the information will be put. This notice usually consists of a privacy policy that should be prominently displayed and easily understood. Ideally, the home page and every page that asks for information should include a link to the policy. Notice should also be given if the privacy policy is not the same for all linked sites or if data will be shared with other parties with different policies.

2. *Choice/Consent.* Provide a mechanism for choosing whether to allow information to be collected. The mechanism may either require explicit consent (opt-in) or assume consent if a person takes no action (opt-out). One could choose to permit the collection of some information (name and address, for example) but not other (e.g., medical information), or one could consent to some uses of information (to select banner ads, for example) but not others (e.g., providing information to a third party).

3. *Access/Participation.* Allow consumers access to the information collected about them and the opportunity to contest the accuracy or completeness of the data. The right of access may exclude information that a company collects from sources other than the website and any results from processing website data.

4. *Integrity/Security.* Inform users of the steps taken to protect against the alteration, misappropriation, or destruction of data and of the action that will be taken in the event of a breach of security. Also, maintain information so that it is accurate and up-to-date.

5. *Enforcement/Redress.* Assure consumers that the company follows responsible information practices and that there are consequences for failing to do so. Consumers should also have some means for resolving disputes and for receiving an appropriate remedy. One way to ensure enforcement and redress is by contracting with an organization that monitors and certifies the information practices of websites.

Although substantial agreement exists on these five principles, much depends on their interpretation and implementation. In particular, how stringently should the principles be interpreted, and what are the most effective and efficient means for implementing them? Other questions include the responsibility of internet service providers (ISPs). For example, Yahoo! was criticized for revealing to the navy the identity of a sailor who used the pseudonym "Boysrch" in gay chat rooms. (The navy used this information in an attempt to oust the sailor from the service for homosexuality.) The principles do not specify whether they apply to information that websites acquire from sources other than the Internet which are then aggregated with data obtained from users. The most contentious issues are whether the weaker opt-out provision is satisfactory in most instances and in what cases, if any, opt-in ought to be required. Finally, few proposals have been developed for handling enforcement and redress.

Implementing Internet Privacy

Principles are of little value if they cannot be successfully implemented, and the Internet presents unique challenges for implementation. Its decentralized, democratic structure makes centralized, authoritarian approaches ineffective, as does its global reach. Because the Web is worldwide, so too must be any successful regulatory scheme. Although government regulation, as represented by the EU Privacy Directive, creates a powerful incentive to protect privacy, laws must still grapple with the difficult question of the appropriate means. In considering the problem of protecting Internet privacy, we must ask, first, who should be involved and, second, what means should be used?

Obviously, the principal parties are Internet firms (websites and ISPs), computer companies (both hardware and software suppliers), industry associations, governments and regulatory agencies, public interest groups, and, of course, individual users. The main approach to date has focused on government regulation and self-regulation by the industry, designed in large part to prevent further intrusion by government. Self-regulation has largely taken the form of developing privacy policies and, in some instances, creating the post of chief privacy officer (CPO) to direct company efforts. In this task, websites have been aided by public interest groups which offer resources and certification. Organizations, such as TRUSTe and BBBOnline (a service of the Council of Better Business Bureaus), monitor a firm's compliance with its privacy policy and award a seal that can be displayed on its website.

The most effective solution to a problem created by runaway technology might very well be more technology. We can protect privacy through both *formal* and *material* means.[53] Regulation and certification as described earlier utilize rules or norms that are designed to influence behavior. Such formal means can be supplemented with changes in material conditions that prevent certain kinds of behavior. Although we need laws against theft (formal), we also protect property with locks (material). The suggestion, then, is that we develop technology that will enable Internet users to protect their privacy to the extent they desire. To be effective, this technology must be usable by even the most unsophisticated in order to overcome the problem of the "blinking twelve" (which refers to the number of people who cannot even set the clock on a VCR).

A material solution consists in the development of various privacy enhancing technologies (PETs). Among such means are services that permit "proxy surfing" by hiding the identity of the user's computer and remailers that forward e-mail stripped of any identifying markers. Cookie-management software exists that can block or disable cookies. Intel caused controversy by encoding a unique Processor Serial Number (PSN) in its Pentium III processor, but the company later offered software that would enable a user to suppress this number.[54] These PETs are likely to be used, however, only by very sophisticated users, and so we encounter the "blinking twelve" problem.

The most promising technology follows Lessig's suggestion of creating an electronic butler or a Cyber-Jeeves. This is a software program that would allow a user to answer a few questions about the desired features of a website's privacy policy and then determine whether sites to be visited fit the user's preferences. Such software is the goal of the Platform for Privacy Preferences Project (P3P), which is being conducted by the World Wide Web Consortium. If installed on most personal computers, a Cyber-Jeeves would force websites to adopt the privacy policies that the majority of Internet users desire.

Conclusion

Although privacy is a relatively recent concept—dating in American law to the 1890s—public concern is clearly increasing, primarily in response to privacy-invading technologies. The problems facing employees, consumers, and Internet users are similar, as are the solutions. There is greater agreement, however, on the ends than on the means, but even the ends are in dispute. Americans say that they value privacy, and yet they give up a great deal for convenience and material gain. Without question, the technologies that threaten privacy have brought us many benefits. Finding the right means is a great challenge to business firms which must meet employee and consumer expectations as they utilize new technologies. More than many business ethics problems, protecting privacy requires a coordinated solution involving many parties. Until a solution is found, though, the focus of businesses will remain on developing and implementing privacy policies.

CASE 6.2 ✳ Explore the Concept on mythinkinglab.com

Information Handling at ChoicePoint

As the chief executive officer and chairman of ChoicePoint, Derek V. Smith believed that the company's business of collecting information on virtually every American and providing it to customers was a great public service. He asserted that "ChoicePoint is built on the premise that the responsible use of information will reduce risk and make the world safer and more secure."[55] However, some critics think that ChoicePoint and the information collection industry as a whole pose great hazards.

Based in Alpharetta, Georgia, a suburb of Atlanta, ChoicePoint was formed in 1997 as a spin-off from Equifax, the giant credit reporting company. Under Mr. Smith's leadership, ChoicePoint bought more than 70 information-gathering companies over the next seven years to amass billions of pieces of data on individual Americans. This information included motor vehicle records, credit histories, insurance claims, birth and death certificates, marriage and divorce decrees, criminal actions, civil judgments, and real-estate transactions. Among the customers for ChoicePoint's services were banks, insurance companies, debt collectors, landlords, private investigators, law enforcement agencies, and the federal Department of Homeland Security. By 2004, the company provided more than 100,000 individual, corporate, and government customers with reports, which generally cost between $5 and $15 each and which generated around $1 billion in annual revenues.[56]

Aside from generating profits for ChoicePoint and its main competitors, Acxiom and Lexis-Nexis, computerized data collection and dissemination produces many benefits that are expressed in the company's motto, "smarter decisions, safer world." Business transactions are quicker and more secure when both parties know each other. In Mr. Smith's view, easy access to reliable personal information helps restore a lost America in which neighbors in small towns knew each other and could conduct business with confidence.[57] With the advent of centralized computer databases of personal information, the approval of applications for jobs, loans, credit cards, insurance policies, housing rentals, and the like can be done much more quickly than in the past. In addition, ready information enables banks and credit card companies to combat fraud, which benefits consumers by reducing costs. Costs are also reduced when companies use information in ChoicePoint reports to avoid hiring problem employees. Although law enforcement agencies have their own databases, which include nonpublic information gained by eavesdropping and other kinds of surveillance, they can prevent or solve crimes more effectively when they have access to the additional public information offered by commercial firms. ChoicePoint and other private companies are useful to law enforcement and Homeland Security officials because they can collect some information that government agencies cannot because of public sector privacy laws.[58]

These benefits of the data collection industry are offset by some possible harms. Many critics point to the contribution of the industry to the problem of identity theft, which claimed 8.3 million victims in 2005 or 3.7 percent of all American adults.[59] Identity theft, which some call "data rape," affects people's sense of security as well as their pocketbook. In addition to incurring out-of-pocket losses, which may include lost wages, legal fees, and the payment of fraudulent debts, victims of identity theft may also encounter delays in accessing bank accounts, denial of credit, harassment from debt collectors, and the hassle of clearing credit records. It is difficult to determine the extent to which identity thieves obtain personal information from data collection companies. A 2005 report found that more than half of all victims did not know how the thieves had obtained their personal information, and that the information in 16 percent of identity theft cases was stolen by family members and acquaintances.[60] Still, the few breaches of security that have occurred at data collection companies result in the unauthorized release of personal information on large numbers of people.

Critics also charge that commercial data collection is a threat to privacy. Most of the information provided by ChoicePoint and other companies is drawn from records in government offices and courthouses, which have long been available to the public. However, people's privacy has been preserved in the past by the fact that the personal information from these scattered sources has been costly and time-consuming to acquire. With the advent of large computers, though, it is possible to make information about individuals readily available in one place for anyone with a legitimate need to know. One consequence of this development is that damaging information, such as an arrest record, may follow an individual throughout life, thereby creating what some critics call a "scarlet letter" society, in which people's transgressions are publicly displayed for all to see. However, defenders of the data collection industry question whether the inability to escape from one's past constitutes a violation of privacy. Mr. Smith argues that there is a big difference between privacy and anonymity. "Yes we have a right to privacy. But in this society we can't have a right to anonymity."[61]

In February 2005, ChoicePoint acknowledged that serious security breaches had occurred. The company notified 163,000 people that data thieves, posing as representatives of legitimate businesses, had gained unfettered, round-the-clock access to the company's computerized records.[62] Although ChoicePoint employs sophisticated technology to keep hackers out of their computer system, the thieves exploited gaps in the company's verification procedures to register as customers. At least 800 cases of identity theft were known to have resulted from these data losses.[63] In their defense, ChoicePoint executives argued that the rogue customers were sophisticated enough to get business licenses and other credible documents. However, a report by the Federal Trade Commission (FTC) concluded that the company was lax in its procedures and had overlooked obvious "red flags."[64] For example, ChoicePoint did not question applications that had incomplete or contradictory information, that listed residences or commercial mail services as addresses and cellular telephone numbers as contacts, and that were sent from fax machines in public locations, such as Kinko's stores. In some instances, the submitted documents showed that the company's incorporation or tax registration had been suspended or cancelled.[65] One information security consultant observed, "It was a well-known fact back then that ChoicePoint would do business pretty much with anyone who came along."[66]

Following this acknowledgment of security breaches, ChoicePoint was severely criticized by privacy groups. The human rights organization Privacy International bestowed its 2005 Lifetime Menace Award on the company.[67] The Electronic Privacy Information Center (EPIC) filed a complaint with the FTC and called for a congressional investigation, which was subsequently undertaken. Faced with this outpouring of criticism, Mr. Smith and other ChoicePoint executives were forced to consider their response. How should the company deal with the 163,000 individuals whose personal information has been improperly released to data thieves? What steps should ChoicePoint take to improve its security and ensure that the personal information of every American is safe? And, finally, could the company defend its business model of collecting and disseminating personal information for paying customers?

CASE 6.3 ✳ Explore the Concept on mythinkinglab.com
Plugging Leaks at HP

Hewlett-Packard, a leading manufacturer of computers, printers, and peripherals, takes privacy very seriously. The company proclaims that it "has set the bar high when it comes to privacy" and asserts, "We make privacy protection integral to our business operations."[68] This high regard for privacy was apparently cast aside in 2006 when H.P.'s chairwoman sought to discover the source of leaks to the press from the company's own board of directors.[69]

In January and February of 2005, when the board was considering the future of then-CEO Carleton S. Fiorina, who was eventually ousted from her position, articles in the *Wall Street Journal* and the *New York Times* reported extensive details of confidential board deliberations. These unauthorized disclosures exacerbated the existing tensions among board members and led some directors to pressure chairwoman Patricia C. Dunn to find the source of the leaks. Later, in January 2006, a news article on the Web-based CNET Networks on the strategic plan of H.P. under its new CEO, Mark V. Hurd, suggested that leaks were still coming from one or more board members. In Ms. Dunn's view the leaks were doing great harm to the company and had to be stopped.

Because she was a possible subject of suspicion, Ms. Dunn felt that she could not direct an investigation, and so she contracted with a Massachusetts-based firm named Security Outsourcing Solutions, which, in turn, hired a subcontractor, Action Research Group, based in Florida, to do much of the detective work. However, Ms. Dunn was kept apprised of some of the contractors' operations. The investigators managed to obtain telephone records of several board members and journalists for the *Wall Street Journal, New York Times*, and CNET by posing as the individuals in question and requesting copies of their telephone bills, which contained lists of all calls made. This practice is known as "pretexting" because a pretext—this is, a misrepresentation of the identity and purpose of the requester—is employed to obtain information. In all, the outside contractors analyzed 33 months of telephone calls involving 24 people under investigation and 590 of the people they contacted.[70]

In addition, some board members and journalists were put under active surveillance, and videos were examined for signs of meetings between directors and journalists. In at least one instance, an investigator, posing as an anonymous tipster, sent an e-mail message to a CNET reporter with a piece of Trojan software that was intended to send back information about any addresses to which the message was forwarded.[71] This ruse apparently failed to work, though. H.P. also conducted a feasibility study for planting undercover agents in the San Francisco news bureaus of the *Wall Street Journal* and CNET in the guise of clerical workers or cleaning staff.[72] There is no evidence, however, that the plan was ever implemented.

The investigation succeeded in identifying the leaker. It was George A. Keyworth II, the longest-sitting H.P. board member, who had also served as director of the White House Office of Science and Technology Policy from 1981 to 1986 during the Reagan administration. When confronted in a board meeting on May 18, 2006, Mr. Keyworth is reported to have said, "I would have told you all about this. Why didn't you just ask?"[73] In his defense, he explained that he was "frequently asked by H.P. corporate communications officials to speak with reporters—both on the record and on background."[74] He said he often met with reporters to promote the company and denied ever divulging any confidential or damaging information. During the meeting, Keyworth was asked by a majority of the other directors to resign. He refused but later left voluntarily when Ms. Dunn agreed to step down as chair. Another director, Thomas J. Perkins, resigned to protest the way that Ms. Dunn had handled the matter. It was Mr. Perkin's insistence that the reasons for his resignation be explained publicly that led to the disclosure of the investigation.

In the ensuing uproar, the Securities and Exchange Commission and the U.S. House of Representatives requested information in order to determine whether any laws had been broken or any new regulations were needed. The California state attorney general launched a criminal inquiry in the belief that pretexting violated existing law. Although H.P. had obtained a legal opinion that pretexting was legal, the opinion of lawyers was divided. To date, Congress has not passed any legislation that explicitly outlaws the practice. Although the California legislature passed and the governor has signed a bill to forbid pretexting, the law did not take effect until January 1, 2007, after the H.P. investigation.

To the end, Ms. Dunn refused to take responsibility for the investigation or admit that she had done anything wrong. Before a congressional House committee, she declared, "I do not accept personal responsibility for what happened."[75] Although she admitted that the investigation "wasn't implemented well" and that "it looks like there was sloppy work along the way," she still called it a "noble cause" and said that she had "no choice" but to respond to the leaks.[76] In contrast, Mark Hurd, the CEO, stated, "I am taking action to ensure that inappropriate investigative techniques will not be employed again. They have no place at H.P."[77]

Notes

1. *Soroka* v. *Dayton Hudson*, 1 Cal. Rptr. 2d 77 (Cal. App. 1 Dist. 1991).
2. Frank H. Williams, "Selecting Best Type of Salespeople Easy with This Set of Test Questions," *Dry Goods Economist*, 21 April 1923, 15.
3. For information on the Sociological Department, see Robert Lacey, *Ford: The Men and the Machine* (Boston, MA: Little, Brown, 1986), 117–25.
4. See Al Noel, "Privacy: A Sign of Our Times," *Personnel Administrator*, 26 (March 1981), 59–62.
5. For a discussion of this problem, see Karl J. Duff and Eric T. Johnson, "A Renewed Employee Right to Privacy," *Labor Law Journal*, 34 (1983), 747–62.
6. Alan F. Westin, "The Problem of Privacy Still Troubles Management," *Fortune*, 4 June 1979, 120–26. See also Joyce Asher Gildea, "Safety and Privacy: Are They Compatible?" *Personnel Administrator*, 27 (February 1982), 80–83.
7. These new technologies are described in Gary T. Marx and Sanford Sherizen, "Monitoring on the Job: How to Protect Privacy as Well as Property," *Technology Review*, 89 (November–December 1986), 63–72. See also Gary T. Marx, "The New Surveillance," *Technology Review*, 88 (May–June 1985), 42–48.
8. See John C. North, "The Responsibility of Employers for the Actions of Their Employees: Negligent Hiring Theory of Liability," *Chicago-Kent Law Review*, 53 (1977), 717–30; and Marian M. Extejt and William N. Bockanic, "Theories of Negligent Hiring and Failure to Fire," *Business and Professional Ethics Journal*, 8 (Winter 1989), 21–34.
9. John A. Baker, "An Issue of Consumer Privacy . . . and Corporate Retreat," *New York Times*, 31 March 1991, sec. 3, p. 9.
10. Sally Beatty, "Reader's Digest Targets Patients by Their Ailments," *Wall Street Journal*, 17 April 1998, B1.
11. Michael W. Miller, "Patients' Records Are Treasure Trove for Budding Industry," *Wall Street Journal*, 27 February 1992, A1.
12. Samuel Warren and Louis D. Brandeis, "The Right to Privacy," *Harvard Law Review*, 4 (1890), 193–220. Two earlier discussions are in James Fitzjames Stephen, *Liberty, Equality, and Fraternity* (New York: Henry Holt, 1873); and E. L. Godkin, "Rights of the Citizen, Part IV—To His Own Reputation," *Scribner's Magazine*, 8 (1890), 58–67.
13. The case is *Robertson* v. *Rochester Folding Box Co.*, 171 N.Y. 538 (1902).
14. *Griswold* v. *Connecticut*, 381 U.S. 479 (1965).
15. William L. Prosser, "Privacy," *California Law Review*, 48 (1960), 389. Other writers who argue that privacy is a complex of rights are Frederick Davis, "What Do We Mean by 'Right to Privacy'?" *South Dakota Law Review*, 4 (1959), 1–24; and Judith J. Thomson, "The Right to Privacy," *Philosophy and Public Affairs*, 4 (1975), 295–315. For criticism of Prosser, see Edward J. Bloustein, "Privacy as an Aspect of Human Dignity: An Answer to Dean Prosser," *New York University Law Review*, 39 (1964), 962–1007.
16. *Olmstead* v. *United States*, 277 U.S. 438 (1928).
17. *Eisenstadt* v. *Baird*, 405 U.S. 438 (1972).
18. See W.A. Parent, "Privacy, Morality, and the Law," *Philosophy and Public Affairs*, 12 (1983), 269–88; H. J. McCloskey, "Privacy and the Right to Privacy," *Philosophy*, 55 (1980), 17–38; and Joseph R. DesJardins, "Privacy in Employment," in *Moral Rights in the Workplace*, ed. Gertrude Ezorsky (Albany, NY: State University of New York Press, 1987), 127–39.
19. See Charles F. Fried, *An Anatomy of Values* (Cambridge, MA: Harvard University Press, 1970), 141; Richard A. Wasserstrom, "Privacy," in *Today's Moral Problems* (2nd ed.), ed. Richard A. Wasserstrom (New York: Macmillan, 1979), 393; Elizabeth L. Beardsley, "Privacy: Autonomy and Selective Disclosure," in *Privacy*, ed. J. Roland Pennock and John W. Chapman (New York: Atherton Press, 1971), 65; and Arthur Miller, *The Assault on Privacy* (Ann Arbor, MI: University of Michigan Press, 1971), 25.
20. Alan F. Westin, *Privacy and Freedom* (New York: Atheneum, 1967), 7.
21. Richard B. Parker, "A Definition of Privacy," *Rutgers Law Review*, 27 (1974), 279.
22. This point is made by Parent, "Privacy, Morality, and the Law," 273.
23. Ibid., 269.
24. Ibid., 269–70.
25. Both of these cases are contained in Marx and Sherizen, "Monitoring on the Job," 67.
26. Westin, *Privacy and Freedom*, 31–42.
27. For criticisms of these arguments, see McCloskey, "Privacy and the Right to Privacy," 34–35; and Parent, "Privacy, Morality, and the Law," 275–76.
28. Stanley I. Benn, "Privacy, Freedom, and Respect for Persons," in Pennock and Chapman, *Privacy*, 10–11.
29. Hyman Gross, "Privacy and Autonomy," in Pennock and Chapman, *Privacy*, 174.
30. Fried, *An Anatomy of Values*, 9. A similar account is given in James Rachels, "Why Privacy Is Important," *Philosophy and Public Affairs*, 4 (Summer 1975), 295–333.
31. Fried, *An Anatomy of Values*, 148.
32. See Jeffrey H. Reiman, "Privacy, Intimacy, and Personhood," *Philosophy and Public Affairs*, 6 (1976), 26–44.
33. Parent, "Privacy, Morality, and the Law," 275. A similar point is expressed in Reiman, "Privacy, Intimacy, and Personhood," 33.
34. Arguments of this kind are presented in Wasserstrom, "Privacy," and Reiman, "Privacy, Intimacy, and Personhood."
35. This point is made by Parent, "Privacy, Morality, and the Law," 280. Much of the argument in this section is derived from Parent's analysis of wrongful invasion of privacy.
36. See Thomas H. Murray, "Thinking the Unthinkable about Genetic Screening," *Across the Board*, 20 (June 1983), 34–39.
37. DesJardins, "Privacy in Employment."
38. This point is made by Donald Harris, "A Matter of Privacy," *Personnel*, 64 (February 1987), 38.

39. See Anne E. Libbin, Susan R. Mendelssohn, and Dennis P. Duffy, "The Right to Privacy, Part 5: Employee Medical and Honesty Testing," *Personnel*, 65 (November 1988), 47.

40. George G. Brenkert, "Privacy, Polygraphs and Work," *Business and Professional Ethics Journal*, 1 (1981), 30.

41. David T. Lykken, "Polygraphic Interrogation," *Nature*, 23 (February 1984), 681.

42. "Scientific Validity of Polygraph Testing: A Research Review and Evaluation," Technical Memorandum OTA-TM-H-15 (Washington, DC: Office of Technology Assessment, November 1983).

43. Mary J. Culnan, "Georgetown Internet Privacy Policy Survey: Report to the Federal Trade Commission," June 1999.

44. Marcia Stepanek, "Surf at Your Own Risk," *BusinessWeek*, 30 October 2000, 143.

45. Hiawatha Bray, "DoubleClick Backs off on Net Data," *Boston Globe*, 3 March 2000, C1.

46. Matt Richtel, "Yahoo Says It Is Discussing Internet Privacy with the F.T.C.," *New York Times*, 31 March 2000, C5.

47. Polly Sprenger, "Sun on Privacy: 'Get Over It,'" *Wired News*, 26 (January 1999).

48. Lawrence Lessig, *Code and Other Laws of Cyberspace* (New York: Basic Books, 1999).

49. Ibid., 154.

50. Ibid., 155.

51. Ibid., 156.

52. These camps are described and analyzed in Karl D. Belgum, "Who Leads at Half-time? Three Conflicting Views on Internet Privacy," *Richmond Journal of Law & Technology*, 6 (1999), http://law.richmond.edu/jolt/index.asp.

53. Shawn C. Helms, "Translating Privacy Values with Technology," *Boston University Journal of Science and Technology Law*, 7 (2001), 156.

54. Declan McCullagh, "Intel Nixes Chip-Tracking ID," *Wired News*, 27 April 2000.

55. *Inside ChoicePoint*, 2007, company publication.

56. Robert O'Harrow, Jr., "ChoicePoint Data Cache Became a Powder Keg: Identity Thief's Ability to Get Information Puts Heat on Firm," *Washington Post*, 5 March 2005, A1.

57. Derek V. Smith, *The Risk Revolution: Threats Facing America & Technology's Promise for a Safer Tomorrow* (Atlanta, GA: Longstreet Press, 2004), 9.

58. Robert O'Harrow, "In Age of Security, Firm Mines Wealth of Personal Data," *Washington Post*, 20 January 2005, A1.

59. Federal Trade Commission, *2006 Identity Theft Survey Report*, November 2007.

60. Ibid.

61. Steven Brill in the foreword to Smith, *The Risk Revolution*, xi.

62. Robert O'Harrow, Jr., "ID Data Conned from Firm: ChoicePoint Case Points to Huge Fraud," *Washington Post*, 17 February 2005, E1. The figure of 163,000 is contained in the Complaint for *United States* v. *ChoicePoint, Inc.*, United States District Court for the Northern District of Georgia, Civil Action No. 106-CV-0198.

63. Complaint for *United States* v. *ChoicePoint, Inc.*

64. Federal Trade Commission, "ChoicePoint Settles Security Breach Charges; to Pay $10 Million in Civil Penalties, $5 Million for Consumer Redress," Press Release, 26 January 2006.

65. Complaint for *United States* v. *ChoicePoint, Inc.*

66. Gary Rivlin, "Keeping Your Enemies Close," *New York Times*, 12 November 2006, A1.

67. Ibid.

68. "Respecting Privacy at H.P.," company document.

69. This case is based largely on Damon Darlin, "H.P. Chairwoman Aims Not to Be the Scapegoat," *New York Times*, 9 September 2006, C1; Damon Darlin and Matt Richtel, "Spying Uproar Causes Shuffle in Boardroom," *New York Times*, 13 September 2006, A1; and Damon Darlin, "Deeper Spying Is Seen in Hewlett Review," *New York Times*, 18 September 2006, A1.

70. Damon Darlin, "Ex-Chairwoman among 5 Charged in Hewlett Case," *New York Times*, 5 October 2006, A1.

71. Darlin, "Deeper Spying Is Seen in Hewlett Review."

72. Damon Darlin, "H.P. Is Said to Study Infiltrating Newsrooms," *New York Times*, 20 September 2006, C1.

73. David A. Kaplan, "Suspicions and Spies in Silicon Valley," *Newsweek*, 18 September 2006, 40.

74. Darlin and Richtel, "Spying Uproar Causes Shuffle in Boardroom."

75. Darlin, "Ex-Chairwoman among 5 Charged in Hewlett Case."

76. Darlin, "H.P. Chairwoman Aims Not to Be the Scapegoat."

77. Darlin and Richtel, "Spying Uproar Causes Shuffle in Boardroom."

Discrimination and Affirmative Action

((•—[**Listen** to the **Chapter Audio** on **mythinkinglab.com**

CASE 7.1   ✳—[**Explore** the **Concept** on **mythinkinglab.com**

Race Discrimination at Texaco

On November 4, 1996, the *New York Times* disclosed the contents of a secretly recorded conversation in which three senior Texaco executives discussed plans to destroy documents that were being sought in a class-action lawsuit for racial discrimination.[1] Also on the tape were derogatory comments about black employees and ridicule of the company's efforts at diversity. One executive was heard to say, "This diversity thing. You know how all the jelly beans agree." Another said, "That's funny. All the black jelly beans seemed to be glued to the bottom of the bag." To this the first executive responded, "You can't just have black jelly beans and other jelly beans. It doesn't work."

The public reaction was fast and furious. Irate Texaco customers threatened to cut up their credit cards. The trustee of a large pension fund with 1.3 million Texaco shares wrote that the taped conversation suggests "a corporate climate of disrespect." Civil rights leaders, including the Reverend Jesse Jackson, threatened a nationwide boycott of Texaco service stations. Three days after the *New York Times* article appeared, Texaco CEO Peter I. Bijour issued an apology, saying, "The statements on the tapes arouse a deep sense of shock and anger among all the members of the Texaco family and decent people everywhere." Less than 10 days later, Texaco abruptly settled the discrimination lawsuit, which had dragged on for $2^1/_2$ years. The company agreed to pay $141 million in compensation to 1,350 black employees and to spend another $35 million for improvements in the diversity program at Texaco.

The lawsuit was filed in March 1994 by six employees on behalf of 1,500 salaried African Americans employed by Texaco. Although these employees reported numerous examples of racist incidents, the suit focused on a pervasive pattern of discrimination in promotion and pay. The petroleum industry had never fully shed its "good old boy" culture that prevented the advancement of women and racial minorities, but an industry-wide survey conducted annually showed that Texaco lagged behind every other major oil company. As a percentage of employees in each salary bracket in the survey, blacks at Texaco trailed the competition in every one, and the percentage of blacks declined more sharply than at other companies as the salary brackets increased. Of employees earning between $51,100 and $56,900 in 1993, 5.9 percent were black at Texaco versus 7.2 percent at the other major oil companies. In the highest bracket, above $128,800, only 0.4 percent of the income earners were black compared to 1.8 percent elsewhere. On average, blacks in each job category were paid 10 to 15 percent less than their white counterparts. Promotions were slower in each job category. A study by the U.S. Department of Labor in 1995 found that it took 6.1 years for minority employees to rise to the position of accountant and 4.6 years for minority employees at the other major oil companies to achieve the same position. Whites who were promoted to assistant accounting supervisor at Texaco took an average of 9.8 years, but blacks in that position had waited 15.0 years for promotion.

The plaintiffs decided to file the suit, *Roberts* v. *Texaco*, after they discovered striking similarities in the tactics that had been used to prevent their advancement. The lead plaintiff in the suit, Bari-Ellen Roberts, was a pension analyst who had been wooed from Chase Manhattan Bank, where she supervised the Texaco pension account as a vice president. At Texaco, she quickly discovered that she had been hired mainly to improve the racial percentages. She once had a superior evaluation reduced to unsatisfactory because a higher executive had found her "uppity" for openly disagreeing in a meeting. When the position above her in the pension department became open, a white male with no experience in pensions was brought in with the explanation that "Bari will help train him." Another plaintiff complained that he was assigned less capable staff members, whose poor performance reduced his own evaluation. One member of his staff, a white male, was allowed to report directly to the plaintiff's superior to avoid reporting to a black.

Widespread discrimination flourished at Texaco despite an explicit company policy and an established diversity program. The booklet "Texaco's Vision and Values" states, "Each person deserves to be treated with respect and dignity in appropriate work environments, without regard to race, religion, sex, age, national origin, disability or position in the company." The company had an affirmative action plan that set diversity goals and provided for diversity training. In fact, the idea of different-colored jelly beans was taken from a diversity training session attended by the executives in the taped conversation.

The problem, according to the observers of Texaco's culture, was the lack of high-level oversight. Implementation of the diversity program was left to middle- and low-level managers, with little guidance from above. Complaints of racist treatment were generally dismissed, and seldom was any action taken against the offenders. Texaco conducted no audits to measure the success of its own affirmative action plan nor any studies to determine whether its personnel practices discriminated against women or racial minorities. The results of government investigations seldom reached top executives. Promotion was heavily determined by a secret list of "high-potential" employees, which was not formally scrutinized for its possible discriminatory effects. Indeed, no official criteria existed for the inclusion of people on the list—or their removal. (Bari-Ellen Roberts inadvertently discovered after her lowered evaluation that her name had also been removed from the high-potential list.)

The settlement ended Texaco's legal woes, but the task of changing the corporate climate remained. How should the company spend the $35 million that was committed to improving diversity? CEO Peter Bijour denied that the programs that Texaco had in place "were flawed in any way." The solution, in his view, was to expand and improve the initiatives already underway. These efforts included higher goals (but not quotas) for the percentages of black employees, more diversity training, greater emphasis on mentoring and career counseling, an increase in the use of minority suppliers, advertising in black publications, and support for black causes.

Critics contend that Texaco had incorrectly diagnosed the cause of the problems and consequently had failed to devise effective solutions. Some employees believe that the environment at the company is still racist and that such remedies as diversity training and mentoring simply increase the racial friction. Some other efforts are more show than substance. More attention should be given, they say, to punishing offenders and tying more of managers' bonuses to the achievement of goals. Determining who is right on these issues is of great importance for addressing the problems of discrimination in the workplace. In an era of setbacks for affirmative action, Texaco's actions will be closely watched by corporate America and by civil rights groups to gain some vision of the future.

INTRODUCTION

Many racial and ethnic groups have been subject to discrimination, and the treatment of women by American business constitutes another prominent form of discrimination. Discrimination is not simply a matter of the number of blacks, women, and other groups who are hired by an employer. In the early 1970s, for example, more than one-half of the employees of American Telephone & Telegraph Company (AT&T) were women, and racial minorities constituted over 10 percent of the AT&T workforce.[2] Women employees were largely concentrated in low-paying clerical and telephone operator jobs, however, and blacks, Hispanics, and members of other racial minorities were employed chiefly in unskilled job categories, such as maintenance workers and janitors. As a result, AT&T was charged with discriminating against women and racial minorities by using sex and race as factors in making job assignments. Eventually, the company agreed to increase the representation of these groups in job categories from which they had previously been excluded.

This chapter is concerned primarily with the steps that can be taken to prevent discrimination and rectify past wrongs. Some of these measures, such as nondiscriminatory hiring and promotion procedures, are widely implemented in the American workplace, but others, especially affirmative action, remain controversial. In order to address the ethical issues in discrimination and affirmative action, it is useful to begin with a definition of discrimination in its many forms and a discussion of the ethical arguments against it.

WHAT IS DISCRIMINATION?

The term "discrimination" describes a large number of wrongful acts in employment, housing, education, medical care, and other important areas of public life. Although discrimination in each of these areas takes different forms, what they have in common is that a person is deprived of some benefit or opportunity because of membership in some group toward which there is substantial prejudice. Discrimination in employment, which is our concern here, generally arises from the decisions employers make about hiring, promotion, pay, fringe benefits, and the other terms and conditions of employment that directly affect the economic interests of employees. There is nothing unjust about such decisions as long as they are made for reasons that are reasonably job-related, but singling out a person for adverse treatment merely because of that person's race or sex is generally an act of discrimination.

Although discrimination is a form of unequal treatment, not all unequal treatment is discrimination. An employer who shows favoritism in deciding on promotions, for example, is guilty of violating the principle of equality in dealing with employees but not necessarily of discriminating against them. Two further elements are necessary. First, discrimination involves decisions that directly affect the employment status of individuals or the terms and conditions of their employment; that is, discrimination occurs in what are generally regarded as *personnel* decisions, such as those involving hiring and firing, promotion, pay, advancement opportunities, and the like. Second, the unequal treatment results from prejudice or some other morally unjustified attitude against members of the group to which an individual belongs. In cases of discrimination, individuals are not treated on the basis of individual merit but on the basis of membership in a group.

The 1964 Civil Rights Act

These two elements can be observed in Title VII of the 1964 Civil Rights Act. Section 703(a) reads as follows:

> It shall be an unlawful employment practice for an employer—(1) to fail or refuse to hire or to discharge any individual, or otherwise to discriminate against any individual with respect to his compensation, terms, conditions, or privileges of employment, because of such individual's race, color, religion, sex, or national origin; or (2) to limit, segregate, or classify his employees or applicants for employment in any way which would deprive or tend to deprive any individual of employment opportunities or otherwise adversely affect his status as an employee, because of such individual's race, color, religion, sex, or national origin.[3]

Notice that Title VII first describes the kinds of employment decisions that are governed by the statute and then lists five factors—race, color, religion, sex, and national origin—that employers are not legally permitted to take into consideration. These factors define groups that are called in law *protected classes.* In subsequent legislation, Congress extended the list of protected classes in order to prevent discrimination against older people (Age Discrimination in Employment Act of 1967), the handicapped (Rehabilitation Act of 1973 and the Americans with Disabilities Act of 1990), and pregnant women (Pregnancy Discrimination Act of 1978).

Section 703(e) of Title VII allows exceptions for sex, religion, and national origin when these are a "bona fide occupational qualification [BFOQ] reasonably necessary to the normal operation of that particular business or enterprise." Race and color are not included in Section 703(e) as a BFOQ and thus cannot be used legally to make distinctions for purposes of employment. The courts have interpreted the BFOQ exception very narrowly, so that employers must show that the qualification is absolutely essential for the conduct of business and not merely useful. Airlines are legally permitted to force pilots to stop flying at the age of 60 for safety reasons, but a federal appeals court rejected an airline's argument against male flight attendants on the grounds that the job of reassuring anxious passengers and giving courteous personalized service not only could be performed by men but were also peripheral to Pan Am's main business of transporting passengers safely.[4]

One of the few cases in which the Supreme Court has held sex to be a BFOQ concerned a rule adopted by the Alabama Board of Corrections excluding women from positions in a maximum-security male prison requiring close contact with the inmates.[5] The majority opinion argued, first, that women employees are likely to be the victims of sexual assaults in a prison characterized by "rampant violence" and a "jungle atmosphere." Second, the likelihood of sexual assaults would reduce the ability of a woman to maintain order in the prison, which is the main function of a prison employee. The presence of women in a male prison poses a threat, therefore, "not only to the victim of the assault but also to the basic control of the penitentiary and protection of its inmates and other security personnel."

Several members of the Court disagreed. It is not clear, they said, that women are exposed to significantly greater risk of attack than men who are employed in the same positions at the prison. Even if a job is more dangerous for some individuals than others, it is less discriminatory to allow individuals to decide voluntarily the degree of risk to assume rather than bar those at greater risk. Also, Justice Thurgood Marshall observed, "It is women who are made to pay the price in lost job opportunities for the threat of depraved conduct by male prison inmates." A better solution, perhaps, would be to make the workplace safer for women instead of limiting their employment opportunities because of the threatened conduct of others.

Disparate Treatment and Disparate Impact

Employment policies that do not explicitly involve classifying employees by race, sex, or other impermissible characteristics can still serve to exclude members of these groups in disproportionate numbers. In interpreting Title VII, the courts have generally held that employers are guilty of discrimination in the absence of any intent *when the effects are the same as if there had been an intent to discriminate.* Discrimination is thus not solely a matter of intention but also of consequences. A distinction is made in law between *disparate treatment*, which is discrimination of the first kind, involving an express intention, and *disparate impact*, which is discrimination of the second kind.

GRIGGS V. DUKE POWER COMPANY.   A landmark case in discrimination law that illustrates the distinction between disparate treatment and disparate impact is *Griggs* v. *Duke Power Company.*[6] Before the passage of Title VII of the Civil Rights Act of 1964, Duke Power Company openly practiced discrimination against blacks. At the Dan River Plant in Draper, North Carolina, blacks were employed only in the labor department, the lowest paying of the five operating divisions. In order to comply with Title VII, the company revised its hiring and promotion policies in 1965 so as to eliminate distinctions between blacks and whites. All applicants for jobs in any department except labor were now required to have a high school diploma and pass two standardized tests, the Wonderlic Personnel Test, which is designed to measure general intelligence, and the Bennett Mechanical Comprehension Test.

Thirteen black employees in the labor department brought suit against Duke Power Company, contending that the education and test requirements were discriminatory for two reasons. First, according to the 1960 census, 34 percent of white males in North Carolina had graduated from high school compared with only 12 percent for black males. The requirement of a high school diploma, therefore, served to exclude black applicants in proportionately greater numbers than white applicants. Second, the passing scores on the two standardized tests were set by the company at the national median of high school graduates, with the result that 58 percent of whites taking the test passed, whereas only 6 percent of the blacks succeeded in doing so. Again, a requirement imposed by the company had a disproportionate impact on blacks applying for employment.

The difference between blacks and whites in the percentages graduating from high school and the performance of the two groups on the standardized tests is largely attributable to the segregated school system in the state. Thus, the requirements, although ostensibly color-blind, served to perpetuate the effects of discrimination in schooling. Chief Justice Warren Burger asserted, in the majority opinion, that "practices, procedures, and tests neutral on their face, and even neutral in terms of intent, cannot be maintained if they operate to 'freeze' the status quo of prior discriminatory employment practices." Duke Power Company responded to the charge of discrimination by holding that Title VII does not require employers to treat workers without regard for qualifications. The requirement of a minimal educational attainment is reasonable, and intelligence and aptitude tests are specifically sanctioned by Section 703(h) of the Civil Rights Act. This section authorizes the use of "any professionally developed ability test" that is not "designed, intended, or used to discriminate because of race."

THE COURT DECISION.   The position of the Supreme Court was that neither requirement had been shown by the company to be related to successful job performance. According to the majority opinion,

> On the record before us, neither the high school completion requirement nor the general intelligence test is shown to bear a demonstrable relationship to successful performance of the jobs for which it was used. . . . The evidence, however, shows that employees who have not completed high school or taken the tests have continued to perform satisfactorily and make progress in departments for which the high school and test criteria are now used. The promotion record of present employees who would not be able to meet the new criteria thus suggests the possibility that the requirements may not be needed even for the limited purpose of preserving the avowed policy of advancement within the company.

The decision in *Griggs* v. *Duke Power Company* interprets Title VII as prohibiting employment practices that involve no intent to discriminate (disparate treatment) but still operate to exclude members of protected classes unnecessarily (disparate impact). Companies are free to hire and promote workers on the basis of defensible requirements. But in the words of the Court: "The touchstone is business necessity. If an employment practice which operates to exclude Negroes cannot be shown to be related to job performance, the practice is prohibited." Moreover, the burden of proof in showing business necessity rests on the employer.[7]

The Forms of Discrimination

A definition cannot answer all the difficult questions about discrimination in the workplace, and some further clarification is necessary for understanding each form of discrimination.

DISCRIMINATION ON THE BASIS OF SEX.   In the interpretation of Title VII, sex discrimination is discrimination based on the fact that a person is male or female and not on sex-related matters, such as sexual orientation or marital status. Although some local governments have passed laws barring discrimination in employment and other matters against homosexuals, discrimination of this kind is not covered by the Civil Rights Act of 1964. Employers are permitted by Title VII to treat married and single employees differently as long as no distinction is made between men and women. An employer can give a preference in hiring to married applicants, for example, but it would be discriminatory to prefer married men and single women in filling jobs. Because of uncertainty over the legality of discrimination against pregnant women, Congress passed the Pregnancy Discrimination Act of 1978, which amends the phrase in Title VII "because of sex" to include decisions made on the basis of "pregnancy, childbirth, or related medical conditions." Sexual harassment has also been ruled by the courts to constitute a form of sex discrimination.

RELIGIOUS DISCRIMINATION.   Religious discrimination is substantially different from discrimination based on race or sex. There are instances, to be sure, of religious discrimination in which employers refuse to hire or promote individuals simply because of prejudice against members of certain religious groups, such as Catholics and Jews. Most charges of religious discrimination in employment, however, involve conflicts between the religious beliefs and practices of employees and workplace rules and routines. Employees sometimes request revised work schedules for Sabbath observance or time off to observe religious holidays. Members of some religious groups have special dress or grooming requirements, such as a yarmulke for Jewish men and a turban and a beard for Sikh men.[8] Some employees have religious objections to performing certain kinds of work or to submitting to medical examinations; others request prayer breaks and special foods in the company cafeteria.

In 1972, Congress amended Title VII by adding Section 701(j), which states that there is no religious discrimination if "an employer demonstrates that he is unable to reasonably accommodate an employee's or prospective employee's religious observance or practice without undue hardship on the conduct of the employer's business." As a result of this amendment, the bulk of the court cases involving charges of religious discrimination raise questions about what constitutes "reasonable accommodation" and "undue hardship." In addition, the courts have held that religious objections can be dismissed by an employer when they interfere with employee safety.

NATIONAL ORIGIN DISCRIMINATION.   National origin discrimination overlaps discrimination based on race, color, and, to some extent, religion. It is conceptually distinct, however, because an employer could have employment policies that exclude Mexican immigrants but not other Hispanics, or Vietnamese but not other Asians. It is not discriminatory under Title VII for an employer to require U.S. citizenship as a condition for hiring or promotion as long as the requirement is reasonably job-related and is not a pretext for excluding members of some nationality group. Similarly, an employer is permitted by Title VII to impose a requirement that employees be fluent in English, even if it excludes recent immigrants, as long as the requirement is dictated by legitimate business reasons and is uniformly applied.

AGE DISCRIMINATION.　Age discrimination results largely from the benefits that employers perceive in shunting older employees aside to make room for younger employees whom they believe have more up-to-date skills and innovative ideas. Younger employees are less expensive to employ, because older employees generally have higher salaries and make more extensive use of fringe benefits. Young people are sometimes preferred by employers for marketing reasons, for example, when hiring clerks in a youth-oriented clothing store. The Age Discrimination in Employment Act (ADEA), passed by Congress in 1967, follows the form of Title VII in prohibiting employers from discriminating in the hiring, promotion, discharge, compensation, or other terms and conditions of employment because of age. Exceptions to the ADEA are permitted when age is a BFOQ and in cases where a company has a bona fide seniority system. Highly paid corporate executives are also generally excluded from protection under the ADEA.

DISCRIMINATION AGAINST THE HANDICAPPED.　In many respects, discrimination against the handicapped is like religious discrimination rather than discrimination on the basis of race or sex. Employing the handicapped often requires that they be treated differently in order to compensate for their disabilities. It may be argued that employers ought to be willing to make reasonable accommodations for the impairments or disabilities of the handicapped just as they are obligated to make reasonable accommodations for the religious beliefs of their employees.

SEXUAL HARASSMENT

Improper sexual conduct in the workplace—which includes lewd and suggestive comments, touching and fondling, persistent attention, and requests for sexual favors—has long been a problem for women, and occasionally for men. All too often, such sexual harassment has been regarded by employers as a personal matter beyond their control or as an unavoidable part of male–female relations. However, increased attention to the problem and developments in the law have made employers aware of their responsibilities—and women, of their rights!

What Is Sexual Harassment?

Surveys of employee attitudes reveal substantial agreement on some of the activities that constitute sexual harassment and differences on others. In particular, most of the respondents in a 1980 poll conducted by *Harvard Business Review* and *Redbook* magazine consistently rated a supervisor's behavior as more serious than the same action by a coworker, thereby recognizing that sexual harassment is mainly an issue of power.[9] Barbara A. Gutek has found that over 90 percent of both men and women consider socializing or sexual activity as a job requirement to be sexual harassment. However, 84 percent of the women surveyed, but only 59 percent of the men, identified "sexual touching" as sexual harassment.[10] In general, women are more likely than men to label the same activity as sexual harassment.

In 1980, the Equal Employment Opportunity Commission (EEOC) issued guidelines on sexual harassment that included the following definition:

> Unwelcome sexual advances, requests for sexual favors, and other verbal or physical conduct of a sexual nature constitute sexual harassment when (1) submission to such conduct is made either explicitly or implicitly a term or condition of an individual's employment, (2) submission to or rejection of such conduct by an individual is used as the basis for employment decisions affecting such individual, or (3) such conduct has the purpose or effect of unreasonably interfering with an individual's work performance or creating an intimidating, hostile, or offensive working environment.

This definition makes a distinction between two kinds of harassment. One is *quid pro quo* harassment, in which a superior, who is usually a man, uses his power to grant or deny employment benefits to exact sexual favors from a subordinate, who is usually a woman. The other kind is *hostile working environment* harassment, in which the sexual nature of the conduct of coworkers and others causes a woman (or a man) to be very uncomfortable. What constitutes discomfort is not easy to specify, but the judge in the Jacksonville Shipyards case (Case 7.2) ruled that the display of pinup calendars and pornographic pictures constitutes an unrelenting "visual assault on the sensibilities of female workers" and that such a situation constitutes sexual harassment under the "hostile working environment" provision.

Sexual Harassment as a Form of Sex Discrimination

Title VII of the 1964 Civil Rights Act and other legislation protect women against many forms of discrimination. The Equal Pay Act of 1963 forbids an employer to offer different wages to men and women who perform the same or substantially similar work unless the difference is based on some valid factor other than sex, such as seniority or productivity. Unlike race and color, sex can be a BFOQ. Many of the problems about what constitutes sexual discrimination arise in cases where a person's sex can arguably be taken into consideration, such as in hiring guards for a male prison. In some other cases, sex is not a BFOQ, but the stated qualifications serve to exclude virtually all women. Examples are tests for police officers and firefighters that require considerable strength and endurance. Whether the qualifications are discriminatory depends largely on whether they are reasonably necessary for the performance of the job.

QUID PRO QUO HARASSMENT.   Quid pro quo harassment clearly violates the Title VII provision that men and women should not be treated differently in their "compensation, terms, conditions, or privileges of employment." A woman who is promised a promotion or a raise—or threatened with demotion, termination, or loss of pay—based on whether she submits to the sexual demands of her boss is being held to a different standard, merely because of her sex.

Some observers contend that quid pro quo harassment, while unfortunate, is not sexual discrimination but merely a wrongful act committed by one employee against another. It is not uncommon for workers of both sexes to encounter personal problems on the job, and harassment, in this view, is one of these personal problems. However, Catharine A. MacKinnon has argued that sexual harassment in the workplace is more than "personal"; it has a connection to "the female condition as a whole" because it deprives women "of opportunities that are available to male employees without sexual conditions." When harassment is present, the willingness to endure it becomes a condition of employment to which men are not subject.[11]

In *Meritor Savings Bank* v. *Vinson* (1986), the U.S. Supreme Court declared that "without question" both quid pro quo harassment and hostile working environment harassment constitute sexual discrimination under Title VII.[12] The decision in the Jacksonville Shipyards case further upheld the EEOC view that a hostile working environment constitutes sexual harassment. Even when there is no demand for sexual favors, conditions in a workplace can produce a form of stress that interferes with a person's ability to work and erodes that person's sense of well-being. Not only does a visual display of pornographic pictures produce stress, but the need to be diligent to avoid the next incident may induce more stress; and the feeling that their complaints will not produce any change further compounds the stress that harassed women have.

HOSTILE WORKING ENVIRONMENT HARASSMENT.   In reaching its decision in the Jacksonville Shipyards case, the court relied on testimony about sexual (and racial) stereotyping. Stereotyping is likely to occur when members of a group are few in number and when members of another group are in power. The stereotypes in sexual harassment cases are those that prevail outside the workplace where some men view women as sex objects. The conditions for stereotyping thus permit "sex role spillover," in which women's roles outside of employment "spill over" or become central in an environment where other roles, such as the job to be performed, ought to be the only ones relevant.[13] A good welder who is also a husband and father can be treated on the job only as a good welder, whereas a woman like Lois Robinson cannot escape the stereotypes that the men bring with them to the workplace. She cannot be, in their eyes, only a good welder. Stereotyping becomes more prevalent when there are "priming" elements, such as pictures that create a stimulus for harassing treatment. One effect of stereotyping is selective interpretation, whereby complaints may be perceived in accord with a stereotype, such as that women are "overly emotional." The failure of Lois Robinson's supervisors to take her complaints seriously may have been due to that effect.

Hostile working environment harassment is both more pervasive and more difficult to prove. Studies have shown that quid pro quo harassment is relatively rare, but in surveys about one-third of working women (33 percent) report incidents of sexual remarks and jokes and around a fourth cite staring and suggestive leers (27 percent) and unwanted sexual touching (24 percent).[14] Not all of this conduct is considered to be sexual harassment, however, even by the women who report it. Still, a line must be drawn somewhere. One possibility is a *reasonable person* standard, whereby conduct that is offensive to a person of average sensibilities would be impermissible. However, one court has rejected this approach on the grounds that it "tends to be male-biased and tends to systematically ignore the experiences of women." This court has proposed, instead, a *reasonable woman* standard, which requires that the alleged harassment be judged from the recipient's point of view.[15]

FURTHER ISSUES.   Initially, the courts were reluctant to recognize sexual harassment as discrimination unless a woman suffered some economic loss, such as a reduction in pay or the loss of her job. If this position is accepted, however, then any amount of harassment is legal as long as the woman's employment status is not affected. In 1981, though, a court held that sexual harassment is illegal even when there is no economic loss, as long as there is psychological harm. No woman, the court declared, should be forced to endure the psychological trauma of a sexually intimidating workplace as a condition of employment.[16] This position was expanded by the decision in *Harris* v. *Forklift Systems, Inc.* (1993), in which the victim could not establish even psychological harm.

Theresa Harris's employer made disparaging comments about women, suggested that she negotiate a raise at a local motel, publicly announced (falsely) that she had slept with a client to get an account, and required her to retrieve change from his pants pocket. The employer claimed that he was only joking. A lower court found that the employer, the president of a Nashville-based truck-leasing company, was "a vulgar man" but contended that his behavior was not so egregious as to seriously affect her "psychological well-being."[17] In *Harris* v. *Forklift Systems, Inc.*, the U.S. Supreme Court ruled that no psychological harm needs to be shown as long as a reasonable person would find the conduct offensive.[18] In the words of one observer, "You don't have to have a nervous breakdown, but one joke does not make a case."[19] The High Court had an opportunity in the *Harris* case to affirm the reasonable *woman* standard, but the justices relied instead on the reasonable *person* standard.

The most intractable issue for the courts has been the responsibility of an employer for the conduct of an employee, especially when the employer is unaware of the harassment by an employee. In *Meritor Savings Bank*, Mechelle Vinson charged that her supervisor, Sidney Taylor, made repeated sexual advances and raped her on several occasions, but she did not report this to anyone at the bank or use the bank's formal complaint procedure. The bank held that it was not responsible, therefore, because of the lack of knowledge. The Supreme Court disagreed, however, and held that an employer has a responsibility to ensure that the workplace is free of sexual harassment. But how far does this responsibility extend?

In two 1998 cases, *Burlington Industries* v. *Ellerth* and *Faragher* v. *City of Boca Raton*, the U.S. Supreme Court established a two-step test.[20] First, if the harassment is by a superior and results in a "tangible employment action, such as discharge, demotion, or undesirable assignment," then the employer is liable, regardless of whether the employer knew about the harassing activity. Second, if there is no "tangible employment action," the employer is still liable unless the employer can show (1) that reasonable care was exercised to prevent and correct sexual harassment and (2) that the employee unreasonably failed to take advantage of the opportunities provided by the employer to correct or avoid the harassing conduct. In the decision, the Court declined to consider who is at fault in cases of harassment and focused instead on how to prevent them. Employers are now on notice that they must anticipate the possibility of harassment and take demonstrable steps to address the problem. Employees have also been told that they have a responsibility to use whatever means an employer has made available for dealing with harassment.

ARGUMENTS AGAINST DISCRIMINATION

That discrimination is wrong can be shown by a variety of arguments. There are, first, straight-forward utilitarian arguments that cite the ways discrimination harms individuals, business firms, and society as a whole. A second kind of argument appeals to the Kantian notions of human dignity and respect for persons. Arguments of a third kind are based on various principles of justice. Any one of these arguments is sufficient to establish the point, but it is still worthwhile to examine them all because each brings out some important aspects of the problem of discrimination.

Utilitarian Arguments

One standard utilitarian argument favored by economists is that discrimination creates an economically inefficient matching of people to jobs. The productivity of individual businesses and the economy as a whole is best served by choosing the most qualified applicant to fill any particular position. When applicants are evaluated on the basis of characteristics, such as race and sex, that are not job-related, productivity suffers. Similarly, it is economically disadvanta-geous for employees to discriminate by refusing to work with blacks or women and for customers to discriminate by refusing to patronize minority-owned businesses.

There are a number of difficulties with this argument. First, not all forms of discrimination produce economic inefficiencies. This is especially true of religious discrimination and discrimi-nation against the handicapped where complying with the law imposes some cost. It is often cheaper for employers to dismiss employees with troublesome religious beliefs and practices and to avoid hiring handicapped people who have special needs. Second, it is not clear that even racial and sexual discrimination are always inefficient. Under the assumptions of classical economic theory, employers who discriminate on the basis of race or sex are expressing a "taste for discrimi-nation," which they pay for by imposing a higher cost on themselves.[21] For example, when a more productive black applicant is passed over by an employer who prefers to hire whites merely because of race, the output of that employer will be lower. The difference is a cost that the employer is presumably willing to assume in order to satisfy a preference for a white workforce. In a free market, then, employers with a taste for discrimination are liable to be driven out of business, and discrimination should be reduced over time.[22] This theoretical result is not always borne out in practice, and economists have offered a variety of explanations for the discrepancy.[23]

Another utilitarian argument focuses on the harm that discrimination does to the welfare of society as a whole by perpetuating the effects of racism and sexism. When racial discrimination in employment is combined with discrimination in education, housing, medical care, and other areas of life, the result is poverty with all its attendant social ills. Sexism also serves to disadvantage women as a group and create social problems. Employers who discriminate on the basis of race and sex thus impose an external cost on society. An externality is also imposed when employers attempt to cut costs by refusing to hire the handicapped; the savings to employers may be more than offset by the cost to the handicapped themselves and to the society that is forced to care for them.

Kantian Arguments

From a nonconsequentialist point of view, discrimination can be shown to be wrong by appealing to the Kantian notions of human dignity and respect for persons. This is especially true of discrim-ination based on contempt or enmity for racial minorities or women. Discrimination of this kind typically involves a racist or sexist attitude that denies individuals in these groups the status of fully developed human beings who deserve to be treated as the equals of others. The victims of racial and sexual discrimination are not merely disadvantaged by being forced to settle for less desirable jobs and lower pay. They are also deprived of a fundamental moral right to be treated with dignity and respect.

This moral right is also denied when individuals are treated on the basis of group charac-teristics rather than individual merit. Much of the discrimination against women, older workers, and the handicapped does not result from the belief that they are less deserving of respect and equal treatment. It results instead from the stereotypes that lead employers to overlook significant differences among individuals. Stereotypes, which are a part of racism and sexism, clearly result in a denial of dignity and respect. But stereotyping by its very nature is morally objectionable because it leads employers to treat individuals only as members of groups.

Arguments Based on Justice

Perhaps the strongest arguments against discrimination are those that appeal to some principle of justice. Fundamental to many principles of justice is the requirement that we be able to justify our treatment of other people by giving good reasons, but to discriminate is to treat people differently when there is no good reason for doing so. According to Aristotle's principle of justice as proportional equality—that like cases should be treated alike, and unlike cases should be treated differently in proportion to the relevant differences—discrimination is unjust because characteristics such as race and sex are generally irrelevant to the performance of a job. Even when the differences between individuals constitute genuinely job-related characteristics, the difference in pay, for example, should still be in proportion to that difference.

The contract theory of John Rawls provides the basis for yet another argument against discrimination. One of the principles that would be adopted in the original position is described by Rawls as follows: "Social and economic inequalities are to be arranged so that they are . . . attached to offices and positions open to all under conditions of fair equality of opportunity."[24] Even if it were to the advantage of everyone to exclude some groups from certain positions, such a denial of opportunity could not be justified because individuals would be deprived of an important human good, namely, the opportunity for self-development.

AVOIDING DISCRIMINATION AND HARASSMENT

Being a truly nondiscriminatory employer is not an easy task. In addition to good-faith compliance with the law, employers must be aware of some subtle and surprising sources of discrimination. This section discusses what is involved in pursuing a policy of nondiscrimination by examining three basic steps in the hiring and promotion process: analyzing the job to be performed, recruiting applicants, and assessing the applicants for suitability.

Job Analysis

In order to ensure that decisions on hiring and promotion consider only job-related characteristics and result in finding the best person for the job, it is necessary to conduct a *job analysis*. A job analysis consists of two parts: (1) an accurate *job description* that details the activities or responsibilities involved in a position, and (2) a *job specification* listing the qualifications required to perform the job as described. Virtually every job in any present-day corporation has been analyzed in this way, because job analysis is a standard management tool for organizing work and appraising performance.

Because a job description focuses on the specific activities or responsibilities of a position rather than on the people who have traditionally held it, certain kinds of work are less likely to be stereotyped as belonging to one group or another. Even when the qualifications for a job favor one sex over another, a job description that lists only the qualifications will not serve to exclude the members of the other sex who meet them. Because the qualifications must be related to the description, it is easier to determine whether they are really needed for the satisfactory performance of a job. A job analysis need not be confined to traditional job categories. If a job is unnecessarily identified with one sex or another, it can be redesigned, perhaps by combining the activities of one or more other jobs, so that the newly created job is attractive to both men and women. Jobs can also be narrowed so as to avoid excluding some groups unnecessarily. A desk job that involves some moving and lifting can be redesigned to exclude these tasks in order to accommodate the handicapped.

Recruitment and Selection

After a job analysis is done, a company is faced with the task of recruiting applicants in a nondiscriminatory manner. An obvious first step is to make sure that information about an opening is widely disseminated, especially to nontraditional groups. Employers who are serious about not discriminating will place listings of job opportunities with minority publications and educational institutions and employment agencies serving minorities. Also, applications from members of nontraditional groups are more likely to be received if significant numbers of minorities and women are involved in the company's recruitment effort and if a number of nontraditional applicants are hired at one time.[25]

Once a sufficient number of applicants have been recruited, the next task is to select the person who is best suited to fill the job. Discrimination can enter into this stage of hiring in many different ways. The selection process itself, which often includes a battery of tests and rounds of interviews, can be discouraging for many nontraditional applicants. Employers can address this problem by simplifying the application procedure or providing instruction on how to proceed. Small differences in treatment can also make racial minorities and women feel uncomfortable. A company can further reduce the barriers to nontraditional applicants by reducing the number of promotion lines and increasing their flexibility so that minorities and women have more opportunities for advancement.

Objective Tests and Subjective Evaluations

Two other important sources of discrimination in both the hiring and the promotion processes are objective tests and subjective evaluations formed on the basis of personal interviews or the recommendations of supervisors. Three kinds of objective tests are commonly used to make decisions on hiring and promotion: (1) tests that measure specific knowledge and skills, such as those needed to be a bookkeeper or a typist; (2) tests that measure intelligence and general aptitude for performing certain kinds of work; and (3) tests that attempt to gauge an applicant's suitability for employment generally and the extent to which an applicant will fit into a specific work environment.

Objective tests of these kinds are permissible under Title VII of the 1964 Civil Rights Act as long as they are not used as a cover for discrimination. One condition laid down in *Griggs* v. *Duke Power Company*, however, is that a test not unnecessarily exclude a disproportionate number of members of protected classes, which is to say it should not have disparate impact. A second condition is that a test be validated; that is, an employer must be able to show that a test for any given job is a reliable predictor of successful performance in that job. The two tests administered by Duke Power Company, the Wonderlic Personnel Test and the Bennett Mechanical Comprehension Test, are professionally prepared instruments that presumably provide an accurate measure of general intelligence and mechanical ability, respectively. What the company failed to prove, however, is that passing scores on these tests are closely correlated with successful job performance. They failed, in other words, to validate the tests that they used.

The Supreme Court has held employers to very high standards of proof in validating tests. It is not sufficient merely to show that employees who successfully perform a certain job also attain high scores on any given test. An employer must be able to show, further, that applicants with lower scores would not be capable of performing just as well. A biased test that results in the exclusion of a substantial percentage of blacks or women, for example, might still be a reliable predictor of successful performance for those who pass but not a reliable predictor of the lack of success of those who fail the test. Further, comparing the scores of employees who are currently performing a job successfully with the scores of inexperienced applicants is not sufficient proof of the reliability of a test. In order to draw a significant conclusion, it would be necessary to know how the current jobholders would have scored on the test before they were hired.[26]

Objective tests are ethically and legally permissible, then, as long as they do not have disparate impact and are validated. Do the same two conditions apply to subjective evaluations based on personal interviews or the recommendations of supervisors? On the one hand, evaluations of this kind are made by experienced employees who are well acquainted with the job to be filled and have an opportunity to assess qualities in an applicant that do not lend themselves to objective testing. On the other hand, the evaluations of interviewers and supervisors are apt to be influenced by irrelevant factors, such as a person's appearance or manner, and by conscious or unconscious prejudice. This is especially true when the evaluator is not well trained for the task.

The Clara Watson Case

The first opportunity for the Supreme Court to decide on the conditions for an acceptable subjective evaluation system came in 1988 with the suit of Clara Watson against the Fort Worth Bank and Trust Company. In 1976, Clara Watson was one of the few blacks ever employed as a teller by the Fort Worth Bank and Trust. Her ambition, though, was to become a supervisor in charge of other tellers at the bank despite the fact that only one other black person had ever held this position.[27] She applied to be a supervisor on four separate occasions, and each time she was denied the position. The bank claimed that all promotion decisions were based strictly on evaluations of fitness for the job and that race was not a factor in filling any of the vacancies for which Clara Watson applied. However, a study showed that during a four-year period, white supervisors at the bank hired 14.8 percent of the white applicants and only 3.5 percent of the black applicants. The same supervisors rated black employees 10 points lower than white employees on a scale used for annual salary evaluations. As a result, blacks were promoted more slowly from one salary grade to another and earned less. In 1981, Clara Watson left the bank, but not before she went to the Equal Employment Opportunity Commission and filed a charge of racial discrimination.

The Fort Worth Bank and Trust Company used three common types of subjective evaluation procedures: interviews, rating scales, and experience requirements. Rating scales differ from interviews in that they record evaluations derived from observations made over a long period of time while an employee is actively at work. Typically, an evaluator is asked to rank an employee on a numerical scale with respect to certain qualities, such as drive and dependability. Experience requirements involve an inventory of specific jobs performed that provide a basis on which to make judgments about future performance.

The American Psychological Association (APA) submitted an *amicus curiae*, or "friend of the court," brief in the Watson case in order to support the claim that these three types of subjective evaluation procedures are capable of validation.[28] Each procedure is open to bias. The most common bias in interviews and rating scales is the "halo effect," in which a single trait exercises an inordinate influence on an evaluator. Closely related to the halo effect is stereotyping, in which assumptions about members of certain groups influence an evaluator. Interviewers are also subject to the "similar-to-me" phenomenon, in which they are inclined to be more favorable to people who have the same traits as themselves. Among the problems with rating scales are the tendencies of evaluators to place persons toward the center of a scale, thereby avoiding the extremes, and to be lenient, scoring most people favorably. The APA brief also cites considerable evidence to show that scores on rating scales are affected by racial factors.

All of these biases can be avoided by subjective evaluation procedures that are designed and carried out according to the APA's *Standards for Educational and Psychological Testing and the Principles for the Validation and Use of Personnel Selection Procedures*. The key in each type of procedure is to relate it to a thorough analysis of the job to be filled. The interview should be carefully structured with questions designed to elicit information that is relevant only to the qualifications and performance criteria of the job. The traits on the rating scale and the kinds of experience used as experience requirements should be similarly selected. As much as possible, the results of evaluation procedures should reflect the personal characteristics of the person being evaluated and not the person doing the evaluating, so that differences between evaluators are kept to a minimum. Interviewers, supervisors, and other persons involved in the process should be thoroughly trained in performing their roles in the hiring and promotion process.

The APA brief faults Fort Worth Bank and Trust for failing to meet the generally accepted standards for subjective evaluation procedures and for the lack of any validation of the procedures used. Interviews were conducted by only one person, a white male, and there is no evidence that the questions were carefully designed with job-related qualifications in mind. No job analysis was done in order to guide the selection of questions in the interview and the traits on the rating scale. Moreover, the traits on the rating scale were vaguely defined and not clearly related to job performance. The supervisors who performed the ratings were not specifically trained for that task, and no steps were taken to avoid the effect that race is known to have on the results of rating scales. Finally, it would be impossible without a job analysis of the position to determine what prior experience would enable her superiors to judge the success of Clara Watson in that position.

In an 8–0 decision, the Supreme Court found in favor of Clara Watson and established that the theory of disparate impact applied to subjective evaluation procedures as well as to objective tests of the kind at issue in *Griggs*.

Preventing Sexual Harassment

Although sexual harassment is usually committed by one employee against another, employers bear both a legal and an ethical obligation to prevent harassment and to act decisively when it occurs. Harassment is more likely to occur when management has not prescribed clear policies and procedures with regard to conduct of a sexual nature. Employers who display an insufficient concern or have inadequate procedures for detecting harassment in the workplace bear some responsibility for individuals' harassing conduct. In addition, companies cannot fully evade responsibility by blaming the victim for not reporting sexual harassment in accord with established procedures. The way in which employers respond to claims of sexual harassment sends a powerful message about the seriousness with which management takes its own policies and procedures. The legal duty of an employer also extends to harassment by nonemployees, such as customers and clients.

Aside from the law—including the cost of litigating and paying settlements—employers have strong financial incentives to avoid sexual harassment. Tolerating sexual harassment can result in hidden costs to companies. A 1988 study of 160 *Fortune* 500 companies calculated that sexual harassment costs an average company with about 24,000 employees a stunning $6.7 million annually.[29] This figure does not include litigation and settlement costs but merely the losses that result from absenteeism, low morale, and employee turnover. According to the study, productivity suffers when women are forced to waste time avoiding uncomfortable situations or to endure the stress of coping with them. The stress induced by sexual harassment leads to health problems, loss of self-confidence, and a lack of commitment, all of which may reduce career prospects and deprive employers of valuable talent. Women who have been harassed are more likely to seek transfers or to quit, thereby increasing the cost of employee training.

Sexual Harassment Programs

Most corporations have recognized the cost of sexual harassment and accepted their responsibility to prevent it by establishing programs to deal with it on the job. The major features of these programs are (1) developing a firm policy against harassment; (2) communicating this policy to all employees and providing training, where necessary, to secure compliance; (3) setting up a procedure for reporting violations and investigating all complaints thoroughly and fairly; and (4) taking appropriate action against the offenders.

1. *A Sexual Harassment Policy.* The first step in a corporate program to eliminate sexual harassment is a firm statement from a high level in the organization that certain conduct will not be tolerated. The policy statement should not only convey the serious intent of management but also describe the kinds of actions that constitute sexual harassment. A good policy should educate as well as warn.

2. *Communicating the Policy.* No policy can be effective unless it is effectively communicated to the members of the organization, and effective communication is not merely a matter of making the policy known but of gaining understanding and acceptance of the policy. Many corporations include sexual harassment awareness in their initial training and ongoing education programs, often utilizing videos of situations and simulation games to heighten employee sensitivity to the issues.

3. *Setting up Procedures.* A complete policy should include a well-publicized procedure for handling incidents of sexual harassment with assurances of nonretaliation against an accuser. Employees should be informed of the procedure to follow in making a complaint, including the specific person or office to which complaints should be made and preferably offering several alternatives for making complaints. In addition, those who handle complaints should be aware of the procedure they should follow. The policy should assure all parties—the accuser as well as the accused—of confidentiality. The investigation itself should seek to ascertain all the relevant facts and to observe the rules of due process, especially in view of the harm that could result from false accusations. Although companies should have a formal complaint procedure, some also make use of an informal process through which a situation may be resolved to the victim's satisfaction. An informal procedure is well suited for less-serious, infrequent incidents among peers where there is some misunderstanding or insensitivity; it is inappropriate for repeat offenses with multiple victims and for harassment by a victim's superior.

4. *Taking Appropriate Action.* Any disciplinary action—which may include a reprimand, job transfer, demotion, pay reduction, loss of a bonus, or termination—should aim, at a minimum, to deter the offender and perhaps to deter others in the organization (although the deterrent effect on others will depend on publicizing the penalty). Because the victims of harassment may have suffered some job loss or been deprived of some opportunities, a proper resolution may also include compensating the victims for any harm done.

AFFIRMATIVE ACTION

After the passage of the 1964 Civil Rights Act, employers scrutinized their hiring and promotion practices and attempted to eliminate sources of discrimination. However, even the best efforts of companies did not always succeed in increasing the advancement opportunities for women and racial minorities. As a result, many companies and other organizations established affirmative action plans in order to address the problem of discrimination more effectively. In some instances, these plans were adopted in order to be in compliance with Title VII; in others, the intent was to go beyond what the law requires.

Although the goal of eliminating discrimination in employment has generally been accepted in business, people are still divided over the appropriate means. Advocates of affirmative action argue that special programs are required as a matter of "simple justice." Victims of discrimination, they say, deserve some advantage. Preferential treatment is necessary to ensure equality of opportunity. Opponents counter that if it is unjust to discriminate against racial minorities and women on account of their race or sex, then it is similarly unjust to give them preference for the same reason. People who are passed over in favor of a black or a woman are victims of discrimination in reverse. Who is right in this debate?

Examples of Affirmative Action Plans

In 1974, at a plant operated by the Kaiser Aluminum Company in Grammercy, Louisiana, only five skilled craft workers (out of 273) were black. Kaiser had long sought out qualified black workers, but few met the requirement of five years of prior craft experience, in part because of the traditional exclusion of blacks from craft unions. In an effort to meet this problem, Kaiser Aluminum and the local union, the United Steelworkers of America, developed an innovative program to train the company's own employees to become skilled craft workers. The plan set up a training program that admitted blacks and whites in equal numbers based on seniority until the proportion of blacks in the skilled craft category equaled the percentage of blacks in the area workforce, which was approximately 39 percent.

In 1978, Santa Clara County in California undertook a similar effort. According to the 1970 census, women constituted 36.4 percent of local workers. Only 22.4 percent of county employees were women, and these were concentrated in two areas: paraprofessionals (90 percent female) and office and clerical workers (75.9 percent female). Out of 238 skilled craft workers, not one was a woman. In order to correct these imbalances, the county board adopted an Equal Employment Opportunity Policy that set broad goals and objectives for hiring and promotion in each agency. Specifically, the policy stated,

> It is the goal of the County and Transit District to attain a work force which includes in all occupational fields and at all employment levels, minorities, women and handicapped persons in numbers consistent with the ratio of these groups in the area work force.

To carry out the board's policy, the Santa Clara Transportation Agency, the agency responsible for road maintenance in the county, developed a detailed plan for increasing the percentages of women and minorities in job categories where they were underrepresented.

The programs adopted by Kaiser Aluminum and Santa Clara County are examples of *affirmative action*. The idea behind affirmative action is that merely ceasing to discriminate is not enough. Employers, if they choose to do so, ought to be permitted to take more active steps to ensure a balanced workforce, including plans that give preference to job applicants on the basis of race or sex. In response to the plan at Kaiser Aluminum, however, a white employee, Brian Weber, sued both the company and his own union.[30] Weber had insufficient seniority to be admitted as a white trainee, even though he had worked longer at the Kaiser plant than any of the blacks who were selected. He charged, therefore, that he himself was a victim of discrimination in violation of Title VII of the 1964 Civil Rights Act.

A suit also arose as a result of the plan adopted by the Transportation Agency of Santa Clara County when a white male, Paul Johnson, was passed over for promotion and the job went to a woman.[31] In December 1979, Paul Johnson and Diane Joyce applied along with 10 other employees for promotion to the position of dispatcher for the road division of the transportation agency. Dispatchers, who assign road crews, equipment, and materials for road maintenance and keep records of the work done, are classified as skilled craft workers. Applicants for the position were required to have four years of dispatch or road maintenance experience with Santa Clara County. The eligible candidates were interviewed by two different boards. The first board, using a numerical scale, rated Johnson slightly above Joyce (75 to 73), and the second board, although rating both candidates "highly qualified," also recommended Johnson over Joyce. The director of the agency was authorized to select any eligible candidate, however, and in order to implement the affirmative action plan, he gave the nod to Joyce. Johnson, like Weber, believed himself to be a victim of discrimination and sued.

Another kind of affirmative action plan that has been challenged in the courts is a "set-aside" provision for minority contractors. The Public Works in Employment Act, passed by Congress in 1977, required that at least 10 percent of the funds granted to state and local governments for construction be set aside for "minority business enterprise." Some municipalities have enacted similar legislation. The city of Richmond, Virginia, for example, adopted a Minority Business Utilization Plan that required recipients of city construction contracts to subcontract at least 30 percent of the dollar amount of each contract to minority-owned businesses. Some white contractors have charged that set-aside provisions are an illegal form of discrimination.[32]

COURT ACTIONS.   In *Weber* v. *Kaiser Aluminum* and *Johnson* v. *Transportation Agency*, the Supreme Court held that the affirmative action plans in question were not discriminatory under Title VII. In its decisions, the court used a standard of "strict scrutiny," which means that any affirmative action plan must serve a "compelling state interest" and must be "narrowly tailored" to achieve that interest. These plans met this standard, and both Brian Weber and Paul Johnson thus lost their suits. However, after approving set-asides for minority-owned contractors in a 1980 decision, *Fullilove* v. *Klutznick*, the Court cast all such programs into doubt in *City of Richmond* v. *J. A. Croson* (1989) and subsequently *Adarand* v. *Peña* (1995).

In 2003, the Supreme Court revisited affirmative action and, for the most part, reaffirmed the status quo. In two cases, both involving the University of Michigan, the justices upheld an affirmative action program in the law school while striking down a similar plan in an undergraduate college.[33] The main difference between the two plans was that the law school admissions process considered race as one of many factors in achieving a diverse student body, whereas the undergraduate college assigned a point value for race as part of a numerical scale. The principle emerging from these two decisions seems to be that diversity is a valid objective for universities but that it matters how diversity is achieved. The end is not in question, but the means are.

The University of Michigan Law School official admissions policy requires that each applicant be evaluated on the basis of all information that is available in the files with a view to obtaining a diverse student body "with varying backgrounds and experiences who will respect and learn from each other." This policy does not identify all the factors that might contribute to diversity, nor does it assign a specific weight to any one factor. However, the policy does reaffirm the law school's long-standing commitment to "racial and ethnic diversity" for groups that have been "historically discriminated against." This kind of diversity is only one component, though, of a broader conception of diversity that is sought for the school's student body.

The law school's admission procedure thus satisfies the court's requirement of "strict scrutiny." The decision recognizes that diversity, broadly conceived, is a legitimate goal for an educational institution and that the law school's flexible, "holistic" admissions process is well designed to achieve that goal. The school maintains that if a purely "race-blind" procedure had been used in 2000, minority students would have comprised only 4 percent of the entering class instead of the actual 14.5 percent. The undergraduate college admissions process, by contrast, while designed to achieve the same kind of diversity, merely added 20 points for minority status to the 100 points required for admission (out of a possible 150 points). This rather mechanical procedure, the court held, was not tailored narrowly enough; same end, wrong means.

The court's approval of the Michigan Law School admissions plan was greeted with great relief by business. Many corporations, including 3M, General Motors, and Microsoft, had filed "friend of the court" briefs in support of affirmative action because of their leaders' belief that diversity is also important for business, especially in an era of globalization. The majority opinion noted, "These benefits are not theoretical but real, as major American businesses have made clear that the skills needed in today's increasingly global marketplace can only be developed through exposure to widely diverse people, cultures, ideas, and viewpoints." As one executive observed, diversity is "something that business has been highly committed to for at least the last decade and has made tremendous strides in improving. The belief in diversity is not something that is argued anymore in business. It's a factor of being in business."[34]

The Compensation Argument

One argument for giving preferential treatment to members of certain groups is that it is owed to them as *compensation* for the injustice done by discrimination directed against them personally or against other members of a group to which they belong. The root idea in this argument derives from Aristotle's discussion in Book V of the *Nicomachean Ethics*, in which he distinguished between justice in the distribution of goods (distributive justice) and justice where one person has wrongfully inflicted some harm on another (corrective justice). In the latter case, justice requires that the wrong be corrected by providing compensation. For example, if A, while driving carelessly, crashes into B's new car, then B suffers a loss that is A's fault. An injustice has been done. It can be corrected, though, if A compensates B for the amount of the loss, say the cost of repairs plus any inconvenience. Similarly, if A has a right not to be discriminated against and B discriminates, thereby harming A unjustifiably, then it is only just that B compensate A to correct the harm done.

Aristotle's analysis perfectly fits the situation, for example, of an employer who has been found guilty of discriminating against women or racial minorities by assigning them to lower-paying jobs and bypassing them in promotions. The law in such cases is guided by the dictum "No right without a remedy," which is to say that a person cannot be said to have a right unless there is also some means of correcting a violation of that right. If we have a right not to be discriminated against, then the courts should be able to provide some remedy when that right is violated. The remedy is often to require the employer to pay the victims the difference between what they actually earned and what they would have earned had no discrimination taken place and to advance them to the positions that they would have attained.

WHO DESERVES COMPENSATION?   Critics of affirmative action charge that not all affirmative action plans are justified by the compensation argument because the individuals who are given preferential treatment are often not the same as those who are victims of discrimination. Affirmative action plans almost always single out persons as members of a group that has suffered discrimination without requiring any evidence that the persons themselves have been victimized in any way. A person may be a member of a disadvantaged group and yet lead a rather privileged life, relatively free of the effects of discrimination.

Defenders of affirmative action respond that racial and sexual discrimination have subtle psychological effects despite the profound changes that have taken place in our society, and racial and sexual discrimination affect all members of that group to some degree. Bernard R. Boxill observes that the critics' objection involves a non sequitur. From the premise that better-qualified blacks or women are less deserving of compensation than some who have been more severely handicapped by discrimination, we cannot conclude that no compensation is owed. "Because I have lost only one leg," he argues, "I may be less deserving of compensation than another who has lost two legs, but it does not follow that I deserve no compensation at all."[35] Nor does it follow, according to Boxill, that victims of discrimination who succeed in overcoming the harm done to them are any less deserving of compensation than those who are unable to succeed to the same degree.[36]

This response still does not answer the question, Why should preference not be given to those who most deserve compensation, the people who have most suffered the effects of racial discrimination and who are consequently among the least qualified? One reply is that giving preference in hiring is only one way of compensating individuals for past discrimination, and it is a way that is of greater help to those who are better qualified for the jobs available. Those who have been more disadvantaged by discrimination may be less able to benefit from affirmative action and may derive greater benefit from other forms of help, such as job-training programs.

A defender of affirmative action can also argue that claims of compensatory justice must be balanced against another principle of justice, the principle that hiring should be done on the basis of competence.[37] Giving preference to the best qualified of those who are deserving of compensation, according to this argument, is the best way of accommodating these two conflicting principles. Another argument cites the practical difficulty of evaluating each case to determine the extent to which an individual has been harmed by discrimination and hence deserves compensation. Giving preference to members of groups without regard for the particulars of individual cases, therefore, is a matter of administrative convenience.[38]

DOES COMPENSATION PUNISH THE INNOCENT?   A second objection to the compensation argument is that in affirmative action the burden of providing compensation often falls on individuals who are not themselves guilty of acts of discrimination. In the competition for admission into colleges and universities and for hiring and promotion in jobs, it is largely white males who are asked to pay the price of correcting injustices that are not of their making. Critics ask, Why should a few white males bear such a disproportionate burden?

One answer to this question is that white males, even when they are not themselves guilty of discrimination, are still the beneficiaries of discrimination that has occurred and thus are merely being asked to give back some ill-gotten gain. This response does not fully meet the critics' point, however. Even if all white males have benefited to some degree, it still needs to be shown that what is given up by the few white males who are passed over when preference is given to others is equal to the benefit they have obtained by living in a discriminatory society. Furthermore, it would still seem to be unjust to place the full burden in such an arbitrary manner on a few when so many other members of society have also benefited from discrimination.[39]

A second answer to the critics' question is that white males are typically asked not to give up gains they have already made but to forgo a future benefit to which no one has an undisputed right.[40] Brian Weber and Paul Johnson, for example, were not deprived of any gains they had made but only of an opportunity for advancement. Although this is a real loss, neither one had a right to be selected but only a right not to be discriminated against in the selection process. If the compensation argument is correct, then those who were selected *deserved* the advantage given by their race or sex and hence no discrimination took place. (Ironically, the opportunity for Brian Weber to receive on-the-job training for a skilled craft position would not have existed had Kaiser Aluminum not adopted an affirmative action plan in order to hire more blacks.) Still, if the job prospects of white males are substantially reduced by affirmative action, then they have suffered a loss. There is surely some limit on the amount of compensation any individual or group of individuals can justifiably be required to pay.

Accordingly, the courts have laid down three conditions for permissible affirmative action plans to protect those adversely affected by them. They are (1) that a plan does not create an absolute bar to the advancement of any group, (2) that the plan does not unnecessarily trammel the rights of others, and (3) that it be temporary. The training program in the Weber case was open to black and white workers in equal numbers. Although Brian Weber failed to gain admittance to the first class, his seniority would have assured him a place eventually. In addition, he had other opportunities for realizing his ambition of becoming a skilled craft worker. Finally, the training program was scheduled to terminate when the proportion of black craft workers reached 39 percent, the percentage of blacks in the local workforce.

Equality Arguments

We noted in Chapter 3 that, according to Aristotle, justice is a kind of equality. Whether affirmative action is just, therefore, can be decided, perhaps, by the principle that people ought to be treated equally or treated as equals. Two quite different concepts of equality are relevant to the debate over affirmative action, however. These are *equality of opportunity* and *equality of treatment*.

Justice, in the first interpretation of equality, requires that everyone have an equal opportunity to succeed in life and that no one be held back by arbitrarily imposed restraints or barriers. Better enforcement of the laws against discrimination can help to equalize the opportunities for everyone, but the effects of past discrimination also need to be neutralized in some way.

President Lyndon B. Johnson expressed the argument graphically in a 1965 speech on an executive order requiring every federal contractor to be an "equal opportunity employer":

> Imagine a hundred yard dash in which one of the two runners has his legs shackled together. He has progressed 10 yards, while the unshackled runner has gone 50 yards. How do they rectify the situation? Do they merely remove the shackles and allow the race to proceed? Then they could say that "equal opportunity" now prevailed. But one of the runners would still be forty yards ahead of the other. Would it not be the better part of justice to allow the previously shackled runner to make up the forty yard gap; or to start the race all over again? That would be affirmative action towards equality.[41]

The equal opportunity argument addresses not only the harm done to individuals from past discrimination but also the barriers posed by discrimination in present-day society. Many fully qualified blacks and women have not been disadvantaged by past discrimination but are still at a competitive disadvantage because of lingering racism and sexism on the part of employers.

Giving preferential treatment may be necessary under such circumstances simply to ensure that people are considered equally. Whether this is true depends, in part, on what we mean by equal opportunity.

THE MEANING OF EQUAL OPPORTUNITY.   What does equal opportunity mean? To say that every child born today has an equal opportunity to become a surgeon, for example, has two distinct senses. One interpretation is that each child initially has an equal chance in the same way that every ticket holder is equally likely to win the lottery. The other is that the means for pursuing the career of a surgeon are open to all. Following Douglas Rae in his book *Inequalities,* let us call these two possibilities the *prospect-regarding* and the *means-regarding* interpretations of the concept of equal opportunity.[42] Prospect-regarding equality aims at eliminating *all* factors affecting the distribution of goods in a society except for mere chance. Means-regarding equality, by contrast, is compatible with considerable inequality of prospects. The only requirement for equality of opportunity in this latter interpretation is that the results reflect only differences in personal attributes and not differences in the means available to persons.

Equality of prospects is an ideal of egalitarians who want to minimize the effect of "accidents" of birth on people's success in life. Just as our race or sex should have no bearing on what we are able to achieve, so too should it not matter whether we are born into wealth or poverty or whether we are born with certain mental or physical endowments. There are a number of difficulties with interpreting equal opportunity as equality of prospects. First, because people begin life with vastly different prospects, steps would have to be taken to equalize these prospects. Achieving an equality of prospects would entail considerable remedial education and a reallocation of resources to schools with disadvantaged students. Second, how are we to know when unequal prospects have been offset? One way might be to look at equality of outcomes, but equality of prospects need not result in equal outcomes if people make different choices. So there must be some way of determining when prospects are equal without looking at the outcomes.

The interpretation of equal opportunity as equality of means entails that rewards should be distributed on the basis of some relevant criteria. Artificial barriers to advancement, such as racial or sexual characteristics, are irrelevant and should be removed, but justice does not require the removal of inequalities in prospects resulting from differences in a person's various physical and mental characteristics. Equal opportunity, on this view, means a chance to compete under fair conditions.

One difficulty with this interpretation is that it requires only that all discrimination cease; it does nothing to address President Johnson's concern about the head start provided by discrimination in the past. A further difficulty is that the conditions for fair competition are highly suspect. What is commonly called talent is largely the acquisition of the expertise and skills provided by education and certified through formal procedures. If access to education or certification is affected by racial or sexual discrimination, then we can scarcely be said to have equal access to the means for achieving success in life.

EQUAL OPPORTUNITY OR EQUAL TREATMENT?   Some defenders of affirmative action have argued that the goal ought not to be equal opportunity but equal treatment. This concept, too, is ambiguous, with two distinct senses. Ronald Dworkin points out that when we say that certain white males have been denied a right to equal treatment, we might have in mind two different rights.[43]

> The first is the right to *equal treatment*, which is the right to an equal distribution of some opportunity or resource or burden. . . . The second is the right to *treatment as an equal*, which is the right, not to receive the same distribution of some burden or benefit, but to be treated with the same respect and concern as anyone else.[44]

The right to equal treatment in the sense of a right to receive an equal share applies only to a few things, such as the right that each person's vote shall count equally. In the distribution of most things, it is a right to the same respect and concern that is at stake. Affirmative action is objectionable, then, only if the alleged victims are not treated as equals.

Dworkin argues that any selection process advantages some people and disadvantages others. Admitting students to medical school on the basis of academic preparation, for example, serves to exclude some applicants. Such a selection process is justified, however, by a social good that outweighs any harm done to those who are turned away. Affirmative action plans are adopted to serve an important social good, namely, overcoming the effects of racism. In so doing, it must be recognized that some white applicants who are denied admission to medical school would be admitted in the absence of a plan. As long as the interests of these unsuccessful applicants are taken into consideration with the same respect and concern as those of others in adopting rules for medical school admission that best meet the needs of society, and as long as these rules are applied impartially, showing the same respect and concern to every applicant, then no one has cause to complain. Everyone has been treated as an equal.

This argument is open to serious objections.[45] In Dworkin's interpretation, the right to equal treatment is the right to equal respect and concern as rational calculations are made about the social good. According to Robert L. Simon, "So understood, the right to treatment as an equal looks suspiciously like the utilitarian requirement that everyone count for one and only one in computing social benefits and burdens."[46] Simon suggests that placing more emphasis on *respect* for other persons rather than on concern that their *welfare* be given equal weight would make affirmative action programs less compatible with equal treatment interpreted as treatment as an equal.

The conclusion to be drawn from the discussion in this section is that the concept of equal opportunity is too vague and ambiguous to provide conclusive support for any particular position on the justification of affirmative action. Those who favor preferential treatment programs and those who oppose them can find a meaning of "equal opportunity" to fit their particular position. Equality of treatment, by contrast, provides a more solid basis for affirmative action. This principle demands, however, that we think carefully about the reasons for affirmative action and make sure that the goals to be achieved are worthwhile and cannot be attained by means that do not involve taking race or sex into account.

Utilitarian Arguments

Unlike the two previous arguments for affirmative action, arguments based on utility do not hold that programs of preferential treatment are morally *required* as a matter of justice but that we are morally *permitted* to use them as means for attacking pressing social problems. Utilitarian arguments stress that preferential treatment programs are necessary to eradicate lingering racial and sexual discrimination and to accelerate the pace of integrating certain groups into the mainstream of American society. The underlying assumption of these arguments is that racism and sexism are deeply embedded in the major social, political, and economic institutions of our society and in people's attitudes, expectations, and perceptions about social realities. If this assumption is correct, then antidiscrimination legislation addresses only the surface manifestations of racism and sexism and does not penetrate to the root causes. Action must be taken to change the institutions of society and the ways people think about themselves and their world. Otherwise, the goal of a discrimination-free society will come only slowly, if at all.

Preferential treatment programs serve to combat the effects of discrimination, first, by making more jobs available to racial minorities, women, and others through lowering the stated qualifications and formal accreditation required for hiring and promotion. Opportunities for groups subject to discrimination are further increased by breaking down stereotypes in the eyes of employers and the rest of society and by creating role models for people who would not otherwise consider certain lines of work. The long history of sexual and racial stereotyping of jobs in this country has hampered the acceptance of women and members of some racial minorities into desirable positions in our society, and this history has also affected the very people who were excluded by limiting their career aspirations. Finally, affirmative action increases opportunities by heightening awareness about discrimination and changing the hiring and promotion process. When business firms make a commitment to achieve a certain racial and sexual mix in their workforce with established goals, the officials responsible for hiring and promoting employees cannot help but be sensitive to the issue of discrimination in every decision they make.

Affirmative action also provides a direct economic benefit to corporations themselves by increasing the pool of job applicants and generally improving community relations. Discrimination introduces inefficiency into the job market by excluding whole groups of people on the basis of race or sex, some of whom are highly qualified. The result is that people in these groups tend to be "underutilized" in jobs that do not make full use of their abilities and training, and employers are deprived of the best possible workforce. The following statement by an executive of Monsanto Corporation testifies to the benefit that affirmative action can have for employers: "We have been utilizing affirmative action plans for over 20 years. We were brought into it kicking and screaming. But over the past 20 years we've learned that there's a reservoir of talent out there, of minorities and women that we hadn't been using before. We found that it works."[47]

Some Problems with Affirmative Action

Affirmative action has some significant undesirable consequences that must be balanced against the undeniable utilitarian benefits of preferential treatment programs. Three arguments in particular are commonly used by opponents of affirmative action. These are (1) that affirmative action involves hiring and promoting less qualified people and lowering the quality of the workforce, (2) that it is damaging to the self-esteem of employees who are favored because of race or sex, and (3) that it produces race consciousness, which promotes rather than fights discrimination. Let us examine these in turn.

THE QUALITY ARGUMENT.   The first argument—the quality argument—can be expressed in the following way. The most qualified person for a position has no need for special considera-tion. Therefore, a person who is given preference on the basis of race or sex cannot be the most qualified person and cannot perform as well in a job as someone who is more qualified. The result is a decline in the quality of goods and services, which has an adverse effect on the whole of society.

A supporter of affirmative action can question, first, how much quality is given up. Preferential treatment does not involve the hiring or promotion of people who are *un*qualified but who are (at worst) *less* qualified to some degree. And the degree can be so slight as to be of no significance. Many jobs require only minimal qualifications and can readily be mastered by persons of normal abilities. Even occupations requiring considerable ability and expertise involve many tasks that can satisfactorily be performed by people who are not the best available. In many instances, "qualified" means "already trained," which brands as unqualified those people who are capable of being fully competent with some training.

Also, whether a person is qualified for a certain job depends on how qualifications are recognized or determined. Conventional measures, such as standardized tests and academic records, are often criticized for containing a bias against women and racial minorities. The credentials used to certify competence in various fields, such as licenses, certificates, union cards, diplomas, and the like, have been accused of containing a similar bias. More complications emerge when we ask, what are the relevant qualifications for the performance of any given job? It is some-times argued, for example, that a black police officer can be more effective in a black community and that an applicant's race is, therefore, a legitimate consideration in the hiring of a police force.[48] In education, a largely male college faculty may not provide a learning environment that is as beneficial to women students as one with a substantial number of female professors.

THE INJURY DONE BY AFFIRMATIVE ACTION.   A second utilitarian argument against affirma-tive action is that it injures the very people it is designed to help. The effect of hiring and promoting blacks and women because of their race or sex is to draw attention to their lack of qualifications and create an impression that they could not succeed on their own. Another effect of affirmative action is to reduce the respect of society for the many hard-won achievements of blacks and women and to undermine their self-confidence and self-esteem. The stigma attached by preferential treatment may even have the unintended consequence of impeding racial integration if qualified minority applicants avoid jobs where race is a factor in selection.

This is an argument to be taken seriously. It rests, however, on the questionable assumption that programs of preferential treatment have not significantly helped some people. Insofar as affirmative action has boosted some racial minorities and women into higher-level positions of prestige and responsibility, there is bound to be an increase in their pride and self-respect as well as their financial well-being. Success in life is often unearned, but there is little evidence that the beneficiaries of good fortune are psychologically damaged by it. Manuel Velasquez observes, "For centuries white males have been the beneficiaries of racial and sexual discrimination without apparent loss of their self-esteem."[49]

THE IMPORTANCE OF RACE.   The third and final utilitarian argument against preferential treatment programs is that they increase rather than decrease the importance of race and other factors in American society. If the ideal of an equal society is one in which no one is treated differently because of color, ethnic origin, religion, or any other irrelevant factor, then preferential treatment defeats this ideal by heightening our consciousness of these differences. To some critics of affirmative action, all uses of racial, ethnic, and religious classifications are abhorrent and ultimately destructive of the fabric of a society.

One response by proponents of affirmative action is that the use of racial classifications is a temporary expedient, necessary only to eradicate racism before we can realize the ideal of an equal society. Justice Harry Blackmun wrote in an opinion:

> I suspect that it would be impossible to arrange an affirmative action program in a racially neutral way and have it successful. To ask that this be so is to demand the impossible. In order to get beyond racism, we must first take account of race. There is no other way. And in order to treat some persons equally, we must treat them differently.[50]

The Supreme Court has long held that distinctions based on race and ethnic origin are "by their very nature odious to a free people whose institutions are founded upon the doctrine of equality."[51] Nevertheless, they are permissible when the conditions warrant their use.

Others argue that there is nothing inherently wrong with race consciousness and the awareness of sexual, religious, ethnic, and other differences. What makes any of these wrong is their use to degrade and oppress people with certain characteristics. There is a great difference between the racial distinctions that were an essential element of the institution of slavery, for example, and the race consciousness that is a part of the present-day attack on racism. Any utilitarian analysis of affirmative action must take into account the history of racial minorities and women in this country and current social realities. All things considered, the race consciousness engendered by affirmative action may be socially beneficial.

Conclusion

The ethical issues surrounding discrimination and affirmative action are very problematic. Rights figure prominently in these issues—both the rights of people who have been victimized by discrimination and the rights of people who now bear the burden of correcting past wrongs. Considerations of justice also play a role. Justice requires that people who have been wronged be compensated in some way and that all people be treated equally, but the concepts of just compensation and of equal opportunity or equal treatment are subject to differing interpretations. Finally, arguments based on utility provide strong support for antidiscrimination and affirmative-action policies, although the benefits of any given policy must be weighed against the harms. The ideal of a nondiscriminatory society is clear, but the pathway to it is strewn with formidable obstacles.

CASE 7.2 ✳ Explore the Concept on mythinkinglab.com

Jacksonville Shipyards

Lois Robinson was a first-class welder at Florida-based Jacksonville Shipyards, Inc. (JSI).[52] Women in any skilled craft job are a rarity in the largely men's world of shipbuilding and repair. JSI records show that between 1980 and 1987 less than 5 percent of shipyard workers were female, and no woman had ever held a supervisory or executive position at the company. Starting out as a third-class welder in 1977, Lois Robinson had steadily increased her skill so that she was the equal of any male welder. Still, she never quite fit in at JSI, which has been characterized as "a boys' club," where a woman could be admitted only as a sex object. She could not be accepted merely as a good welder.

None of Lois Robinson's coworkers or supervisors had ever solicited her for sex, nor had any of them offered some benefit for her sexual favors or threatened to retaliate if she refused. Lois Robinson was occasionally ridiculed, as when one coworker handed her a pornographic magazine while those around laughed at her response, or when another coworker passed around a picture of a nude woman with long blond hair and a whip. (Because she has long blond hair and uses a welding tool known as a whip, she thought that the picture was being displayed to humiliate her.) It was not these incidents that infuriated her, however; it was rather the pervasive presence of calendars, magazines, pictures, graffiti, and other visual displays of nude women that she found intolerable.

The workplace was plastered with pinup calendars from suppliers that featured nude or partially clad women in sexually submissive poses, often with breasts and genital areas exposed. The suppliers' calendars were distributed by JSI to its employees with permission to display them wherever they pleased. Employees were required to get permission to post any other material in the workplace—and permission was denied in some instances for requests to post material of a commercial or political nature—but pictures of nude women from magazines or other sources were displayed with the full knowledge of management, from the president of JSI down. The pictures observed by Lois Robinson included one with a woman's pubic area exposed and a meat spatula pressed against it and another of a nude woman in full-frontal view and the words "USDA Choice." A drawing on a dartboard pictured a woman's breast with the nipple as the bull's eye. Lois Robinson also became aware that the sexually suggestive comments increased when her male coworkers noticed that she had seen one of the pornographic pictures. Although crude sexual jokes were sometimes told in her presence, she was often warned to "take cover" or leave so that the men could exchange jokes out of her hearing.

In January 1985, Lois Robinson complained to JSI management about the visual displays. Afterward, the pictures became more numerous and more graphic and the number of sexually suggestive comments to her and the other women increased. The complaints to her supervisors were apparently passed to higher levels of management, and a few pictures were removed only to be replaced by others. Some of the pictures to which she objected were in the shipfitter's trailer, where she and other workers reported to receive instructions, and she sometimes entered the trailer to check on paperwork. One day the words "Men Only" appeared on the door of the trailer, and though the sign was soon painted over, the words could still be observed. One supervisor pointed out that the company had no policy against the posting of pictures and claimed that the men had a constitutional right to do so. The supervisor's superior declined to order the pictures removed. Another supervisor suggested that Ms. Robinson "was spending too much time attending to the pictures and not enough time attending to her job."

As a federal contractor (JSI performed repairs on ships for the U.S. Navy), the company is obligated by presidential order to be nondiscriminatory and to have an affirmative action plan. In 1980, JSI adopted a policy entitled "Equal Employment Opportunity." The policy stated in part:

> . . . we should all be sensitive to the kind of conduct which is personally offensive to others. Abusing the dignity of anyone through ethnic, sexist, or racist slurs, suggestive remarks, physical advances or intimidation, sexual or otherwise, is not the kind of conduct that can be tolerated.

The policy asked that any violations be reported to the EEO coordinator at the facility. The policy was not generally known to the supervisors at the shipyards, nor was it incorporated in the standard JSI rule book. The supervisors received no training on how to deal with reports of sexual harassment or other problems, and the name of the EEO coordinator was not given in the policy and was not widely known to employees in the company. In any event, the experience of Lois Robinson was not likely to encourage any victim of harassment to make a report to anyone at JSI.

On September 2, 1986, Lois Robinson filed a suit against Jacksonville Shipyards, Inc., for sexual harassment. In the suit she cited the pervasive presence of sexually explicit pictures, the sexually suggestive and humiliating comments of her male coworkers, and the "Men Only" sign on the shipfitter's trailer.

CASE 7.3   ✳ Explore the Concept on mythinkinglab.com

Sex Discrimination at Wal-Mart

Betty Dukes was hired in May 1994 as a part-time cashier at a Wal-Mart store in Pittsburg, California. Within a year she became a full-time employee, and two years later she was promoted to Customer Service Manager. Shortly thereafter, Ms. Dukes complained to the District Manager about discriminatory treatment from the head of her department and the store manager. After complaining, she was written up for a series of rules violations that were seldom enforced. In August 1999, she was demoted back to cashier, and her hours and wages were reduced. Despite this retaliation, Ms. Dukes aspired to a higher position, but each time the open position was filled without being posted, usually with a man. "Opportunities seemed to come and go, positions were filled," she said, but managers would not provide any support or encouragement. "No one would talk to you."[53]

On June 19, 2001, Betty Dukes joined with five other female workers to file a suit against Wal-Mart for discriminating against them as women.[54] These women charged not only that local Wal-Mart stores had discriminated against them personally but that the whole company had discriminated against all female employees during the previous five-year period. Since women employees at Wal-Mart comprised more than 65 percent of hourly workers in a workforce of over one million people, the potential members of a class-action suit on behalf of all alleged victims of sex discrimination totaled at least 700,000 and possibly as high as 1.6 million women who had worked at the company for any length of time between 1996 and 2001. If the suit is granted class-action status by the courts, *Dukes, et al.* v. *Wal-Mart* will be the largest class-action suit ever brought against an American company.

Although the six women who filed the suit cited instances of discriminatory acts against themselves personally, the evidence that Wal-Mart as a company is guilty of sex discrimination is based, in large part, on a statistical analysis of personnel data. The suit alleges that female employees in Wal-Mart stores were less likely than men to be promoted and that when they were promoted, women's advancement came more slowly. Despite holding roughly two-thirds of all hourly jobs, women filled only one-third of salaried managerial positions during the 1996–2001 period. At Wal-Mart's 20 main competitors, 56.5 percent of managerial positions were held by women. More than 90 percent of store managers were men; all but 4 percent of district managers were men, and there was only one woman among the company's top 20 executives. It took women an average of 4.38 years to be promoted to assistant manger compared with 2.86 years for men, and 10.2 years to become store managers and only 8.64 years for men. Women's pay also lagged behind that of men. Women who worked at least 45 hours per week earned 6.2 percent less than men, and the pay for women managers at Wal-Mart was 15.5 percent lower than that of their male colleagues.[55]

According to Wal-Mart executives, the company has a firm policy against discrimination, and there is little evidence that individual store managers are consciously biased. The suit filed by Betty Dukes and the five other women alleged that the cause of the statistical disparities was the company's pay and promotion practices and the discretion that store managers had in decisions about pay and promotion. Both of these factors allowed store managers to exercise an unconscious bias.[56] There is an extensive psychological research on unconscious bias, which includes studies of stereotyping and in-group favoritism. Sex stereotyping occurs when managers evaluate female employee using traditional conceptions of the characteristics of women and the appropriate roles for them. According to one psychologist, "There are studies that show that the strongest predictor of whether an opening is filled by a man or a woman is whether the previous incumbent was a man or a woman."[57] In-group favoritism is a tendency of human beings to favor those who are considered like themselves in certain respects, such as gender.

At Wal-Mart, pay and promotion decisions were left largely to individual store managers' discretion. This discretion on the local level is in sharp contrast to decisions on other matters, which were highly centralized at Wal-Mart's headquarters in Bentonville, Arkansas. The company had uniform personnel policies and procedures for all stores in the United States on hiring, orientation, training, job assignments, pay, promotion, and discipline. The same departments, job categories, and management hierarchy were employed at all stores. Stores were linked by a sophisticated information technology system through which personnel data as well as daily reports on inventory and sales were submitted. The Bentonville headquarters carefully monitored all aspects of store operations down to temperature setting for heating and cooling systems and the music that is played in each store. The company developed a distinct corporate culture, called the "Wal-Mart Way" that it aggressively fostered among its employees. Employees began each day with the "Wal-Mart cheer" ("Give me a W! Give me an A! . . ."), which was introduced by Sam Walton, after he observed this practice in a Korean factory. The company culture was reinforced by evaluating employees and managers on their understanding of and commitment to the Wal-Mart Way.

In many stores, promotion opportunities were not usually made known, and open positions were often filled with employees previously identified and groomed by store managers, whose decisions were based on vague criteria that were inconsistently applied. Many job categories and departments were identified as male or female lines of work. Women workers were typically assigned to departments such as kitchenware and children's clothing, which were considered less important, and they were not rotated through different departments, in which they could gain valuable experience and recognition. Women who knew of vacancies said that they were not encouraged to apply, and many declined to submit an application in the belief that they stood little chance of being selected. It is alleged that men were promoted more often to positions in the same store whereas promotions involving a transfer elsewhere were offered disproportionately to women. Workers, such as Betty Duke, who complained about sex discrimination or other matters were often subjected to retaliation by store managers, which included demotions and loss of eligibility for promotions.

Wal-Mart has vigorously defended itself against the charge of discrimination and has objected, in particular, to the attempt to bring a lawsuit on behalf of all women employees.[58] The company has argued that if the six women were victims of discrimination, then the suit should seek to redress the wrongs incurred in these cases. Moreover, the circumstances in each of the six cases are different, and so the company should be allowed to defend its conduct given the particulars of each case. Wal-Mart has further argued that as the largest private employer in the United States, with approximately 3,400 domestic stores, employing more than 1 million people, in as many as 53 departments and 170 job classifications, it is necessary to allow store managers leeway to make decisions on a case-by-case basis in response to local situations. With so many decisions to be made, some mistakes may have occurred, but Wal-Mart insists that these are local problems which do not necessarily indicate a problem with the company's policies and procedures.

In addition, one cannot justly extrapolate from the wrongs in these six cases to the conduct of the whole company. It does not follow that because some women suffered discrimination, all women employed by the company from 1997 to 2001 were victims. This is especially true if, as the women argue in the suit, that the discrimination occurred because of the discretion allowed to local store managers. As one observer asked, "How can a court treat 4,000 store managers as acting identically for purposes of a class action when the plaintiff's whole theory of the case is that those store managers are being granted too much autonomy?"[59] Wal-Mart has submitted evidence from its own studies that show that there are no statistically significant gender disparities in 92.8 percent of stores. These studies found that men were favored to a statistically significant degree in only 5.2 percent of stores, and that in the remaining 2.0 percent of cases, women were favored.[60] Thus, Wal-Mart concludes, "The evidence establishes that, if anything, any discrimination that may have occurred was *not* system-wide, and indeed was sporadic and varied widely."

Finally, Wal-Mart argues that discrimination is, in large part, a problem in the larger society that the company cannot be reasonably expected to solve alone. For example, the assignment of women to certain departments, such as kitchenware and children's clothing, may be due to their own preferences. A company spokesperson said about such cases, "Societal issues should not be confused with Wal-Mart practices."[61] In addition, women may have less interest than men in assuming a managerial position. One Wal-Mart study further found that from 1999 to 2002, women constituted 12 percent of applicants but were offered 17 percent of the open positions.[62] The low ratio of women store managers may be due, then, not to company offers of the position but to women's willingness to accept them. Furthermore, statistical disparities have many causes, some of which a company cannot easily identify and correct. Supreme Court justice Sandra Day O'Connor observed in another discrimination case, "It is completely unrealistic . . . to suppose that employers can eliminate, or discover and explain, the myriad of innocent causes that may lead to statistical imbalances in the composition of their workforces."[63]

Notes

1. Material for this case is drawn from Bari-Ellen Roberts, *Roberts* v. *Texaco* (New York: Avon Books, 1998); Amy Myers Jaffe, "At Texaco, the Diversity Skeleton Still Stalks the Halls," *New York Times*, 11 December 1994, sec. 3, p. 5; Peter Fritsch, "Trustee of Big Fund with Texaco Stock Says Tape Shows 'Culture of Disrespect,'" *Wall Street Journal*, 6 November 1996, A15; Kurt Eichenwald, "The First Casualties in Scandal at Texaco," *New York Times*, 7 November 1996, D1; Kurt Eichenwald, "The Two Faces of Texaco," *New York Times*, 10 November 1996, sec. 3, pp. 1, 10–11; Adam Bryant, "How Much Has Texaco Changed?" *New York Times*, 2 November 1997, sec. 3, pp. 1, 16–17.

2. The information on AT&T is taken from Earl A. Molander, "Affirmative Action at AT&T," in *Responsive Capitalism: Case Studies in Corporate Conduct* (New York: McGraw-Hill, 1980), 56–70.

3. 42 U.S.C. 2000e-2.

4. *Diaz* v. *Pan American World Airways, Inc.*, 442 F.2d 385 (1971).

5. *Dothard* v. *Rawlinson*, 433 U.S. 321 (1977).

6. *Griggs* v. *Duke Power Company*, 401 U.S. 424 (1970). Some material is also taken from a case prepared by Nancy Blanpied and Tom L. Beauchamp, *Ethical Theory and Business*, 3rd ed., ed. Tom L. Beauchamp and Norman E. Bowie (Upper Saddle River, NJ: Prentice Hall, 1988), 383–85.

7. The precedent of *Griggs* was altered by several subsequent court decisions, most notably *Wards Cove Packing Co.* v. *Antonio*, 490 U.S. 642 (1988), which made it more difficult for employees to sue for discrimination. A 1991 civil rights bill largely restored the interpretation of *Griggs* that had prevailed before.

8. For a discussion of these and other problems, see James G. Frierson, "Religion in the Workplace," *Personnel Journal*, 67 (July 1988), 60–67; and Douglas Massengill and Donald J. Petersen, "Job Requirements and Religious Practices: Conflict and Accommodation," *Labor Law Journal*, 39 (July 1988), 402–10.

9. Eliza G. C. Collins and Timothy B. Blodgett, "Sexual Harassment: Some See It . . . Some Won't," *Harvard Business Review*, 59 (March–April 1981), 76–95.

10. Barbara A. Gutek, *Sex and the Workplace* (San Francisco, CA: Jossey-Bass, 1985), 43–44.

11. Catharine A. MacKinnon, *Sexual Harassment of Working Women* (New Haven, CT: Yale University Press, 1979), 193.

12. *Meritor Savings Bank* v. *Vinson*, 477 U.S. 57 (1986).

13. The expert witness in *Robinson* v. *Jacksonville Shipyards, Inc.*, who made this point was Susan Fiske. The term "sex role spillover" was developed by Veronica F. Nieva and Barbara A. Gutek, *Women and Work: A Psychological Perspective* (New York: Praeger, 1981).

14. Robert C. Ford and Frank McLaughlin, "Sexual Harassment at Work: What Is the Problem?" *Akron Business and Economic Review*, 20 (Winter 1988), 79–92.

15. *Ellison* v. *Brady*, 924 F.2d 872 (1991). See also Howard A. Simon, "*Ellison* v. *Brady*: A 'Reasonable Woman' Standard for Sexual Harassment," *Employee Relations Law Journal*, 17 (Summer 1991), 71–80.

16. *Bundy* v. *Jackson*, 641 F.2d 934 (D.C. Cir. 1981).

17. Linda Greenhouse, "High Court to Decide Burden of Accusers in Harassment Cases," *New York Times*, 2 March 1993, A1.

18. *Harris* v. *Forklift Systems, Inc.*, 510 U.S. 17 (1993).

19. Barbara Presley Noble, "Little Discord on Harassment Ruling," *New York Times*, 13 November 1993, sec. 5, p. 25.

20. *Burlington Industries* v. *Ellerth*, No. 97–569, and *Faragher* v. *City of Boca Raton*, No. 97–282.

21. This analysis and the phrase "taste for discrimination" are due to Gary S. Becker, *The Economics of Discrimination*, 2nd ed. (Chicago, IL: University of Chicago Press, 1971).

22. This point is also made in Milton Friedman, *Capitalism and Freedom* (Chicago, IL: University of Chicago Press, 1962), 109–10. Ironically, Friedman uses the analysis to argue *against* legislation curbing discrimination on the grounds that competition alone is sufficient to bring discrimination to an end.

23. See Kenneth J. Arrow, "The Theory of Discrimination," in *Discrimination in Labor Markets*, ed. Orley Ashenfelter and Albert Rees (Princeton, NJ: Princeton University Press, 1973), 3–33; Lester C. Thurow, *Generating Inequality* (New York: Basic Books, 1975); Dennis J. Aigner and Glen G. Cain, "Statistical Theories of Discrimination in Labor Markets," *Industrial and Labor Relations Review*, 30 (1977), 175–87; and Barbara R. Bergmann and William Darity, Jr., "Social Relations, Productivity, and Employer Discrimination," *Monthly Labor Review*, 104 (April 1982), 47–49.

24. John Rawls, *A Theory of Justice* (Cambridge, MA: Harvard University Press, 1971), 83.

25. Rosabeth Moss Kanter, in *Men and Women of the Corporation* (New York: Basic Books, 1977), chap. 8, proposes "batch" promotions of two or more individuals from excluded groups so that they can support each other and break down barriers.

26. These points are made in *Albemarle Paper Company* v. *Moody*, 422 U.S. 405 (1975).

27. *Clara Watson* v. *Fort Worth Bank and Trust*, 487 U.S. 977 (1988).

28. "In the Supreme Court of the United States: *Clara Watson* v. *Fort Worth Bank and Trust*," *American Psychologist*, 43 (1988), 1019–28. See also an accompanying explanation by Donald N. Bersoff, "Should Subjective Employment Devices Be Scrutinized? It's Elementary, My Dear Ms. Watson," *American Psychologist*, 43 (1988), 1016–18.

29. The study by Freada Kelin is reported in Susan Crawford, "A Wink Here, a Leer There: It's Costly," *New York Times*, 28 March 1993, sec. 5, p. 17.

30. *United Steelworkers and Kaiser Aluminum* v. *Weber*, 443 U.S. 193 (1979).

31. *Johnson* v. *Transportation Agency, Santa Clara County*, 480 U.S. 616 (1987).

32. The landmark cases are *Fullilove* v. *Klutznick*, 448 U.S. 448 (1980); *City of Richmond* v. *J. A. Croson Company*, 488 U.S. 469 (1989); and *Adarand* v. *Peña*, 115 S. Ct. 896 (1995).

33. *Grutter* v. *Bollinger*, 539 U.S. 982 (2003), and *Gratz* v. *Bollinger*, 539 U.S. 244 (2003).

34. James P. Hackett, quoted in Steven Greenhouse and Jonathan D. Glater, "Companies See Law School Ruling as a Way to Help Keep the Diversity Pipeline Open," *New York Times*, 24 June 2003, A25.

35. Bernard R. Boxill, "The Morality of Preferential Hiring," *Philosophy and Public Affairs*, 7 (1978), 247.

36. Ibid., 248.

37. For a defense of this principle, see Alan H. Goldman, "Justice and Hiring by Competence," *American Philosophical Quarterly*, 14 (1977), 17–26.

38. For an argument of this kind, see James Nickel, "Classification by Race in Compensatory Programs," *Ethics*, 84 (1974), 147–48.

39. These points are made by George Sher, "Preferential Hiring," in *Just Business: New Introductory Essays in Business Ethics*, ed. Tom Regan (New York: Random House, 1984), 48.

40. Boxill, "The Morality of Preferential Hiring," 266.

41. Quoted in Lewis D. Solomon and Judith S. Heeter, "Affirmative Action in Higher Education: Towards a Rationale for Preference," *Notre Dame Lawyer*, 52 (October 1976), 67.

42. Douglas Rae, *Inequalities* (Cambridge, MA: Harvard University Press, 1981), 66–68.

43. Ronald Dworkin, *Taking Rights Seriously* (Cambridge, MA: Harvard University Press, 1978), 223–39; and Ronald Dworkin, *A Matter of Principle* (Cambridge, MA: Harvard University Press, 1985), 293–331.

44. Dworkin, *Taking Rights Seriously*, 227.

45. For criticism of Dworkin's argument, see Robert L. Simon, "Individual Rights and 'Benign' Discrimination," *Ethics*, 90 (1979), 88–97.

46. Ibid., 91.

47. Quoted in Peter Perl, "Rulings Provide Hiring Direction: Employers Welcome Move," *Washington Post*, 3 July 1986, A1.

48. The example and much that follows is taken from Alan Wertheimer, "Jobs, Qualifications, and Preferences," *Ethics*, 94 (1983), 99–112. A different kind of argument for the relevance of race as a qualification is presented by Michael Davis, "Race as Merit," *Mind*, 42 (1983), 347–67. For a criticism of the kind of argument presented by Wertheimer, see Robert K. Fullinwider, *The Reverse Discrimination Controversy: A Moral and Legal Analysis* (Totowa, NJ: Rowman and Littlefield, 1980), 78–86; and Alan H. Goldman, *Justice and Reverse Discrimination* (Princeton, NJ: Princeton University Press, 1979), 167–68.

49. Manuel G. Velasquez, *Business Ethics: Concepts and Cases*, 5th ed. (Upper Saddle River, NJ: Prentice Hall, 2002), 423–24.

50. *Regents of the University of California* v. *Bakke*, 438 U.S. 265 (1978).

51. *Hirabayashi* v. *United States*, 320 U.S. 81 (1943).

52. Material for this case is taken from *Lois Robinson* v. *Jacksonville Shipyards, Inc.*, No. 86–927-Civ-J-12 (1991).

53. Reed Abelson, "Suing Wal-Mart but Still Hoping to Move Up," *New York Times*, 23 June 2004, C1.

54. Plaintiff's Third Amended Complaint, *Betty Dukes, et al.* v. *Wal-Mart Stores, Inc.*, United States District Court, Northern District of California, Case No. C-01–2252 MJJ.

55. Steven Greenhouse, "Wal-Mart Faces Lawsuit over Sex Discrimination," *New York Times*, 16 February 2003, A22.

56. Robert Parloff, "The War over Unconscious Bias," *Fortune*, 15 October 2007, 90.

57. Ibid.

58. Principal Brief for Wal-Mart Stores, Inc., *Betty Dukes, et al.* v. *Wal-Mart Stores, Inc.*, U.S. Court of Appeals for the Ninth Circuit, Nos. 04–16688 and 04–16720.

59. Parloff, "The War over Unconscious Bias."

60. Ibid.

61. Reed Abelson "6 Women Sue Wal-Mart, Charging Job and Promotion Bias," *New York Times*, 20 June 2001, C1.

62. Parloff, "The War over Unconscious Bias."

63. *Clara Watson* v. *Fort Worth Bank and Trust*, 992.

8

Employment Rights

CASE 8.1 ✳—[Explore the **Concept** on **mythinkinglab.com**

The Firing of Robert Greeley

On May 22, 1987, Robert Greeley was abruptly dismissed from his job as a laborer at Miami Valley Maintenance Contractors, Inc., in Hamilton, Ohio.[1] This was a blow not only to the 30-year-old, recently divorced father of two young children, but also to his ex-wife, who was relying on his job for child support payments. Three weeks earlier, a county court judge had ordered that Mr. Greeley's employer withhold the child support payments from his paycheck as permitted under Ohio law, but his bosses at Miami Valley Maintenance Contractors decided that the bookkeeping involved was too much trouble. Firing him was much easier.

Divorced fathers often fail to make court-ordered child support payments, and judges have limited means for making deadbeat dads pay. To address this problem, the U.S. Congress enacted the Child Support Enforcement Amendments of 1984, which require states to provide income withholding as a means of collecting payments. The federal law also mandates that states make provisions for fining employers who refuse to withhold such payments. The Ohio General Assembly complied with this federal law by passing legislation the following year. An employer who violates the Ohio law is subject to a $500 fine.

Miami Valley Maintenance Contractors readily admitted that it fired Mr. Greeley to avoid complying with the Ohio law, and it did not contest the $500 fine. The company contended, however, that Robert Greeley, who was not a union member under a contract, was an at-will employee. Accordingly, he could leave his employment at any time, for any reason, and his employer could terminate him with the same ease.

The law in some states prohibits employers from firing for certain kinds of reasons—such as for refusing to break the law or for serving on a jury—because permitting them to do so conflicts with important matters of public policy. However, Ohio was, at the time, a strict employment-at-will state. Employers could hire and fire at will, with virtually no legal restrictions. In 1986, for example, the state supreme court upheld the firing of a Toledo-area chemist who reported illegal dumping of toxic wastes, even though the employer was eventually found guilty and fined $10 million by the Ohio Environmental Protection Agency. By comparison, Mr. Greeley's employer got off cheaply: The company had to pay a paltry $500 fine for the privilege of firing him.

INTRODUCTION

At first glance, there is nothing remarkable about the case of Robert Greeley. In the United States, employers are generally regarded as having the right to make decisions about hiring, promotion, and discharge, as well as wages, job assignments, and other conditions of work. Employees have the corresponding rights to accept or refuse work on the terms offered and to negotiate for more favorable terms. But in the absence of a contract that spells out the conditions under which employment can be terminated, employees can be legally dismissed for any reason—or for no reason at all. Against this position, some critics hold that certain reasons for dismissal are morally unacceptable, while others go further to argue that employees should be dismissed only for good reasons and that, whatever the reason, they should be afforded due process, which includes being informed of the reasons for dismissal and offered a fair hearing.

In addition to protection against unjust dismissal, the rights of employees in the employment relation that have been advocated include the right to freedom of thought and expression in the workplace, a right to participate in decisions, especially those that affect employees, and certain rights with regard to compensation. Among the moral issues in compensation practices are the adoption of a legal minimum wage and the higher standard of a fair or "living" wage, as well as the controversy over executive compensation. This list of employee rights is not exhaustive. However, other rights that employees have in the workplace, including rights involving privacy, discrimination, whistle-blowing, and occupational health and safety, are covered in other chapters. Indeed, the subject of employee rights is a major focus of this book.

UNJUST DISMISSAL

Losing a job is one of the most traumatic occurrences in people's lives. Aside from the interruption of income and benefits, dismissed workers typically lose a valued social network and an important source of satisfaction and meaning. Even when a terminated worker finds another job quickly, the new position may pay less than the old one, with the result that lifetime earnings are reduced. Thus, job security is an important aspect of employment that workers value and often seek in a job.

Workers lose their jobs for a variety of reasons, many of which are considered to be just grounds for dismissal. Among these just reasons or grounds are economic adjustments, as when an employer has too many workers or workers without the right skills, inadequate job performance, and inappropriate or disruptive behavior on the job. Many people believe not only that employees should be dismissed only for a just reason or good cause but also that they should have an opportunity to know the grounds for dismissal and to offer a defense. Dismissal is widely considered to be unjust, then, under two conditions: when an employee is dismissed without a good cause and when the dismissal occurs without a fair hearing. These two elements together constitute *due process*.

Although due process is a requirement of the criminal justice system, in which the state prosecutes persons for crimes, it is less clear that justice requires due process in employment. A person should not be sentenced to prison or otherwise punished by the state without due process, but is the same true in employment when a worker is dismissed? In general, American labor law has adopted a doctrine of *employment at will* that gives employers wide latitude in dismissing or terminating workers. Thus, the issue of unjust dismissal raises two questions. One question concerns the conditions under which the dismissal of employees is morally justified. Is due process a *moral* requirement for just dismissal? The other question is, even if it is a moral right, should due process be a *legal* requirement and thus have the force of law?

Employment at Will

In the American legal system, a cornerstone of labor law is the doctrine of employment at will, according to which an employer may terminate an employee at any time and for any reason unless an employment contract specifies otherwise. Employment, according to this doctrine, is an "at-will" relation that comes into existence when two parties willingly enter into an agreement, and the relation continues to exist only as long as both parties will that it does so. Both employers and employees have the right to enter into any mutually agreeable arrangement without outside interference. Each party is also free to end an arrangement at any time without violating the rights of the other, as long as doing so is in accord with the terms that they have agreed on.

The first explicit statement that employment is an at-will relation occurred in an 1877 work by Horace G. Wood entitled *A Treatise on the Law of Master and Servant.*[2] The doctrine was first given legal force by an 1884 Tennessee Supreme Court decision in the case *Paine* v. *Western & A.R.R.* In an often-quoted sentence, the court declared,

> Men must be left, without interference . . . to discharge or retain employees at will for good cause or for no cause, or even for bad cause without thereby being guilty of an unlawful act per se. It is a right which an employee may exercise in the same way, to the same extent, for the same cause or want of cause as the employer.[3]

Other state courts followed the example of Tennessee, as did the U.S. Supreme Court, so that shortly after the turn of the century, the doctrine of employment at will was firmly established in American law. However, the United States is virtually alone among the countries of the world in its adoption of employment at will; most other parts of the world, most notably Europe and Japan, place narrow limits on the legal power of employers to terminate employment.

Three arguments are commonly used to justify employment at will. One argument holds that the doctrine is entailed by the rights of property owners; the second argument appeals to the notion of freedom of contract; and the third argument is based on considerations of efficiency.

PROPERTY RIGHTS ARGUMENT.   The property rights argument begins with the assumption that both employers and employees have property of some kind. The owner of a factory, for example, owns the machinery and raw materials for the manufacture of a product, along with a certain amount of money for wages. The remaining resource is labor for operating the machinery and turning the raw materials into a finished product. Labor, or more precisely the productivity of labor, thus has an economic value and can be said to be a kind of "property" that is "owned" by the worker. Employment can be described, therefore, as an exchange of a worker's productive power for the wages that are given out in return by the factory owner.

In this exchange, both parties are free to exercise the rights of property ownership. The owner of the factory is free to utilize the productive resources of the factory and to pay out money as wages in any way that workers are willing to accept. Workers are free to accept work under the conditions and at the wages offered or to seek work elsewhere on more favorable terms. It follows that any restriction on the kinds of agreements that employers and employees can make is a violation of the property rights of both parties. Just as consumers are under no obligation to continue buying a product, employers are free to stop "buying" the labor of an employee. Although the loss of a job may create some hardship for the person dismissed, no rights are violated according to the property rights argument; indeed an important right, the right to property, is respected.

The historical roots of the property rights argument are contained in John Locke's idea that there is a natural right to property, by which he meant a morally fundamental right that exists apart from any particular legal system. Accepting the biblical belief that God gave the bounty of the earth to all persons in common for the purposes of life, Locke went on to observe that we can make use of this bounty only by appropriating it and making it our own. The fruit of a tree cannot nourish us, for example, until we pluck and eat it, but when one person eats a piece of fruit, that person deprives another of its use. Locke's argument for property as a natural right is based, therefore, on the role that property, including labor, plays in satisfying human needs.

FREEDOM OF CONTRACT ARGUMENT.   In the second argument, from freedom of contract, employment is viewed as a contractual arrangement between employers and employees. This arrangement arises in some instances from an explicit contract, a legal document signed by both parties, in which a business firm states the terms under which it is willing to hire a person and that person signifies by his or her acceptance a willingness to work under those terms. Union employees are typically covered by a company-wide contract that is agreed to by both the management of a company and the union rank and file. In the absence of an explicit contract, we can still understand the employment relation as involving an implicit contract insofar as the conditions of employment are understood and tacitly accepted by both parties.

To place a limit, then, on the kinds of agreements that can be made between an employer and an employee is to violate the freedom of contract of both parties. Just as it would be a violation of an employee's freedom to contract to force an employee to remain in a job, so it would be a violation of the employer's freedom to contract to prevent an employer from terminating an employee who voluntarily entered into an at-will employment relation. This reasoning is employed in a Supreme Court decision upholding the right of an employer to fire an employee for belonging to a labor organization. The majority opinion in this case, *Adair* v. *United States* (1907), held:

> [I]t is not within the functions of government—at least in the absence of contract between the parties—to compel any person, in the course of his business and against his will, to accept or retain the personal services of another, or to compel any person, against his will to perform personal services for another. The right of a person to sell his labor upon such terms as he deems proper is, in its essence, the same as the right of the purchaser of labor to prescribe the conditions upon which he will accept such labor from the person offering to sell it. So the right of the employee to quit the service of the employer for whatever reason is the same as the right of the employer, for whatever reason, to dispense with the services of such employee. . . . In all such particulars the employer and the employee have equality of right, and any legislation that disturbs that equality is an arbitrary interference with the liberty of contract which no government can legally justify in a free land.[4]

In another case the Court held, "This right is as essential to the laborer as to the capitalist, to the poor as to the rich; for the vast majority of persons have no other honest way to begin to acquire property, save by working for money."[5]

In the British and American legal traditions, the philosophical basis for the freedom of contract argument, as for the property rights argument, derives from John Locke, who considered the exercise of property rights to be only one part of a more general freedom of action. On the Continent, however, the philosophical basis for freedom of contract derives not from Locke but from Immanuel Kant and his concept of autonomy. The Kantian argument can be sketched briefly as follows: Autonomy involves the capacity and opportunity to make meaningful choices about matters that bear most significantly on our lives. That is, we are autonomous insofar as it is we who make the important decisions affecting our lives and not others. An essential part of acting autonomously in this sense is the possibility of making mutually binding voluntary agreements. Therefore, autonomy entails freedom of contract.

THE EFFICIENCY ARGUMENT.   The third argument for employment at will is a utilitarian one that relies not on property rights or the freedom of contract but on the importance of this doctrine for the efficient operation of business for the benefit of both employers and employees. Although employment at will is often thought to be something that employers impose upon employees without their consent, the contractual nature of employment requires that the terms of employment be mutually advantageous. Given freedom of contract, employers and employees who find mutual benefit in job security and protection from dismissal will contract away from employment at will. However, when both parties agree to employment at will, we must assume that such an arrangement benefits both employers and employees. The mere fact that employment at will persists when employers and employees could contract on other terms demonstrates its advantages for all concerned.

The utilitarian advantages of employment at will to employers are straightforward.[6] The success of any business enterprise depends on the efficient use of all resources, including labor. For this reason, employers should generally be accorded considerable leeway to determine the number of workers needed, to select the best workers available, to assign them to the jobs for which they are best suited, and to discipline and dismiss workers who perform inadequately. Under employment at will, business decisions can be made quickly and at low cost. By contrast, legal restrictions on employment decisions not only add costs, including those of forgone opportunities and the expenses of litigation, but they also put legislatures and courts in the position of making business decisions, which increases the complexity of business operations. Furthermore, an employer with an inflexible workforce must plan more carefully for the future and attempt to anticipate changing circumstances and new opportunities, which may be difficult due to lack of foreknowledge. Overall, the intrusion of factors other than the most efficient allocation of resources into business decision making can only impair efficiency, according to this argument, and thereby harm everyone concerned.

How do employees benefit from employment at will? First, workers at efficient companies will have better job prospects with higher pay due to the ability of the employer to adapt to changing circumstances and exploit new opportunities. Such firms will better utilize the talents and skills of their employees, which makes them more productive and hence able to earn higher compensation. Second, without employment at will, legal restrictions on dismissal will create a rigid workforce in which employees cannot easily change jobs and become trapped in the ones they have. Such job immobility, which is prevalent today in Japan and Europe, has several adverse consequences for employees.

One consequence of low job mobility is that employers can make greater demands on and even abuse workers who cannot readily move to another job. In a more open job market, where employees can simply quit, the freedom of employers to be overly demanding or abusive is sharply limited. High job mobility also restricts the freedom of employers to fire without due process because valued employees who perceive any dismissals to be arbitrary or unfair may respond by reducing their commitment to the company and seeking jobs elsewhere. Any employer who abuses the legal right to dismiss at will pay a high price in the market, and this market price may deter such abusive behavior more effectively than any legal sanction can. Another consequence of reduced job mobility is that workers are less able to switch jobs and migrate to better job opportunities in which they can be more productive. If a worker is likely to stay at any job for a lifetime, then the choice of a first job is critical, and yet no worker has the ability to predict how he or she could be best employed far in the future. The job mobility provided by employment at will thus protects workers from being disadvantaged by their lack of foreknowledge.

Exceptions to Employment at Will

These three arguments not only provide some grounds for justifying employment at will, but they also support some limitations or restrictions. The rights to own property and to contract freely are not unlimited; when they conflict with other rights or goods, some adjustments must be made. Furthermore, the utilitarian benefits of employment at will may be outweighed, in some instances, by the harms resulting from the unrestricted application of this legal doctrine. Accordingly, the courts have carved out exceptions to employment at will under three broad heads: public policy, implied contract, and bad faith and malice.

The courts have held on grounds of good public policy, first, that employees ought not to be subject to discipline, demotion, or discharge for refusing to violate the law. If anything is contrary to public policy, it is a doctrine that permits employers to use the threat of dismissal to force an employee to commit illegal acts. In a 1959 California case, *Petermann* v. *International Brotherhood of Teamsters*, the business manager for a local of the Teamsters union was fired by the union after he refused an order to commit perjury before an investigative committee of the state legislature.[7] The California Court of Appeals held that in order to make the law against perjury effective, some restriction had to be placed on an employer's right of discharge.

Second, employers ought not to prevent employees from receiving the full benefit of their legal rights and entitlements relating to employment. The legislation creating many employee rights includes antiretaliation provisions, so there is no need for the courts to create a separate public-policy exception. Thus, the National Labor Relations Act and the Occupational Safety and Health Act, among others, not only forbid retaliation but also provide for legal remedies. However, some employees have been dismissed for asserting legal rights for which the law does not provide antiretaliation protection. One such right is filing workers' compensation claims for injuries suffered on the job. In one workers' compensation case, the court ruled, "When an employee is discharged solely for exercising a statutorily conferred right, an exception to the general rule [of employment at will] must be recognized."[8]

Third, an employer's right to dismiss at will should not interfere unduly in the ability of government to promote social welfare. For example, when an employee was dismissed for being away from work to serve on a jury, an Oregon court held that the discharge was for "a socially undesirable motive" that tended to "thwart" the jury system, thus undermining the administration of justice.[9] In the case of Robert Greeley (Case 8.1), the Ohio state supreme court held that ensuring that the children of divorced parents are properly supported is an important matter of public policy, and that the means devised by the Ohio state legislature—namely, ordering employers to withhold child support payments from a parent's paycheck—is a reasonable means of achieving this policy objective. Allowing employers to ignore a court order merely by paying a small fine would undermine the child support enforcement mechanism created by the state legislature. The state legislature established a policy, and a justice of the state supreme court said, "It is our job to enforce, not frustrate, that policy."[10]

A second set of exceptions to employment at will involves the existence of an implied contract that contains different terms. In some instances, prospective employees are given assurances in job interviews that dismissal is only for cause, that attempts are made to work through any problems before the company resorts to dismissal, and that due process is followed in all cases. These assurances are conveyed in other instances by employee manuals, policy statements, personnel guidelines and procedures, and other company documents. The claim that an implied contract exists as a result of different kinds of assurances makes an appeal, not to a utilitarian justification based on public policy, but to the law of contracts.

In two Michigan cases that were decided together, *Toussaint* v. *Blue Cross and Blue Shield of Michigan* and *Ebling* v. *Masco Corporation*, the plaintiffs were given assurances of job security by their employers as long as they performed satisfactorily.[11] Charles Toussaint testified that he was told by his employer that he would be with the company until the mandatory retirement age of 65 "as long as I did my job." The supervisory manual at Blue Cross and Blue Shield stipulated that employees could be dismissed only for just cause and that specific disciplinary proceedings were to be used. The court found that his supervisor, in asking him to resign, had not observed these provisions in the manual. Furthermore, the court held,

> While an employer need not establish personnel policies or practices, where an
> employer chooses to establish such policies and practices and makes them known to

its employees, the employment relation is presumably enhanced. The employer secures an orderly, cooperative and loyal work force, and the employee the peace of mind associated with job security and the conviction that he will be treated fairly.

Even without an implied contract, a commonly accepted principle in business is acting in good faith. This concept is applied widely as both a moral and a legal requirement in collective bargaining, contract negotiations, consumer relations, and indeed virtually all commercial dealings. An example of conspicuous bad faith is the case of a 25-year veteran employee of the National Cash Register Company, named Fortune, who was dismissed the next business day after he had secured an order for $5 million worth of equipment to be delivered over the next four years. The court found that the dismissal was motivated by a desire to deprive Fortune of the very substantial commission he would receive as the equipment was sold. The Massachusetts court held that Fortune had an implied contract with his employers and stated that

> in every contract there is an implied covenant that neither party shall do anything which will have the effect of destroying or injuring the right of the other party to receive the fruits of the contract, which means that in every contract there exists an implied covenant of good faith and fair dealing.[12]

In general, the courts have been reluctant to make exceptions to the doctrine of employment at will, placing limits only in cases where employer behavior significantly impacts good public policy or violates recognized legal norms. Although these exceptions reduce the freedom of employers to dismiss at will, they strengthen the doctrine of employment at will by making it more acceptable and predictable.

Right to Due Process

Objections to employment at will have been raised on many different grounds. Some critics would merely modify the doctrine by creating more exceptions, such as protection for freedom of speech in the workplace, which is considered in the next section. Indeed, many other laws, such as those prohibiting discrimination and unsafe working conditions, already restrict the right of employers to dismiss at will by specifying reasons for which an employee cannot be dismissed. Other critics question whether the arguments for employment at will based on property rights and freedom of contract support the doctrine. However, the main source of opposition to employment at will has come from critics who maintain that employees have a moral right to due process in employment decisions that is incompatible with this legal doctrine. Thus, the main alternative to employment at will is a legally recognized right to due process.

RIGHTS-BASED ARGUMENTS. The arguments for employment at will that are based on property rights and freedom of contract assume that these values have supreme importance and benefit both employers and employees. All rights are limited, however, for the simple reason that they inevitably come into conflict with each other and with important societal interests. Thus, it may be argued that employment at will, far from enhancing employee's property rights and freedom of contract, undermines these values or otherwise works to the detriment of employees' well-being.

In particular, property rights are fundamental in Locke's political theory because of the role they play in satisfying our basic needs and securing liberty. It can be argued, however, that instead of serving these Lockean ends, the doctrine of employment at will has the opposite effect, namely, impoverishing workers and subjecting them to the will of others. Property rights have the potential to enable employers to benefit at the expense of employees and to exercise not merely economic but also political power over them. Philip J. Levine argues that this "subjugation of the working class" is made worse by the fact that a job is often a person's only means of support and

170 Chapter 8 • Employment Rights

the basis for his or her position in society. He continues, "The essential elements of life are all dependent on his ability to derive income."[13]

This objection rejects the basic assumptions of the property rights argument for employment at will, namely, that employment at will works to the benefit of employees as well as employers and that employees are able to contract away from this system should it not be to their advantage. Critics also question an underlying assumption of the property rights argument, namely, that employment involves an exercise of property rights at all. As previously noted, employment at will is a distinctively American doctrine, and the law in Japan and most countries of Europe gives workers considerably more job security. Clyde W. Summers notes, "In other countries, employees are viewed as members of the business enterprise." In the United States, he observes, "the employee is only a supplier of labor who has no legal interest or stake in the enterprise other than the right to be paid for labor performed."[14]

For critics like Summers, the flaw in the doctrine of employment at will is the framing of the employment relation as an economic transaction involving an exchange of property between employers and employees. More appropriate, in their view, is a conception, common in Japan and Europe, of a firm as a community to which employees belong as members. As members of a community, employees cannot be dismissed unilaterally by an employer but must be allowed some fair procedure in cases of termination.

The rights-based argument for employment at will is also criticized for overemphasizing freedom of contract. Taken to an extreme, freedom of contract is incompatible with any worker-protective legislation, including laws that limit workers' hours and require a minimum wage. This conflict between freedom of contract and worker protection was at issue in *Lochner* v. *New York*, which involved an 1897 New York statute limiting the work of bakers to 10 hours a day and 60 hours a week.[15] The law was intended to protect the health of bakers, which was being undermined by the long, exhausting hours they were required to work. This piece of protective legislation was struck down by the U.S. Supreme Court in 1905 on the grounds that it violated the right of bakers and bakery owners alike to contract on mutually agreeable terms. According to the majority opinion, "the freedom of master and employee to contract with each other in relation to their employment . . . cannot be prohibited or interfered with, without violating the Federal Constitution."

The freedom of contract argument for employment at will is problematic because of the immense difference in bargaining power that usually prevails between employers and employees. Bargaining almost always takes place between parties of different strengths, and the stronger side usually gains at the expense of the weaker. The outcome need not be unjust for this reason. But is there some point at which employers ought not to be permitted to take advantage of their superior bargaining position? The decision in *Lochner* v. *New York* denied that there was any morally significant difference in bargaining strength between bakery workers and their employers. However, the *Lochner* era came to an end in 1937 with the decision in *West Coast Hotel* v. *Parrish*.[16] Chief Justice Hughes, who delivered the majority opinion, cited "an additional and compelling consideration which recent economic experience has brought into a strong light." This consideration is the "exploitation of a class of workers who are in an unequal position with respect to bargaining power and are thus relatively defenseless against the denial of a living wage." The doctrine of employment at will cannot be justified by a right to freedom of contract, according to Chief Justice Hughes, when the result is to deprive employees of the ability to protect their most vital interests. This decision was followed by a series of federal and state worker-protection laws that addressed the most serious abuses of employment at will.

Except for the position that the employment relation should not be viewed as a matter of contact at all, these objections to rights-based arguments do not undermine the doctrine of employment at will but only support restrictions or conditions on its application. Employment at will is a default legal rule, which is to say that it applies unless employers and employees contract differently. Many American employees, including all union workers, have employment contracts that specify the conditions for termination and the procedure to be followed. Employment at will does not, in any way, hinder such contracts and, indeed, invites them. Moreover, there is much legislation that limits the power of employers over employees. If employers gain too much power over employees because of employment at will, legislators can offset this power, either directly by regulating working conditions or indirectly by promoting collective bargaining, for example. Such remedial legislation might be a better solution to the undesirable consequences of employment at will than the elimination of the doctrine outright.

ARGUMENTS FOR DUE PROCESS.   Aside from their objections to the rights-based arguments for employment at will, proponents of a right to due process argue more directly that employees have such a right and that this right carries greater weight in the employment relation than either property rights or freedom of contract. They also counter the efficiency argument for employment at will by offering evidence that providing due process for employees in matters of discipline, demotion, and dismissal promotes efficiency. Three broad arguments may be offered as justification for a right to due process.

First, it may be argued that a terminated employee suffers some substantial harm that ought not to be inflicted without an adequate reason and a fair hearing. If comparable jobs were readily available, then no employee would be harmed by being forced to change, but when jobs are scarce and the alternatives are less desirable, the loss of a job is a significant financial blow. In addition, our social standing and self-esteem are closely linked to our work, so that a job loss may also result in some psychological harm. Because a job is so essential to our well-being, it should not be subject to the arbitrary power of an employer. Employers have great power over us, and this power should be exercised responsibly. A law that requires employers to have a good reason and provide a fair hearing for any dismissal is reasonable, then, in view of power that they hold.

A second argument for a right to due process is that this right is owed out of respect for the dignity of workers. Tara J. Radin and Patricia H. Werhane argue,

> Employees are human beings, with dignity and emotional attachments, not feelingless robots. This is not to say that inadequate employees should not be replaced with better performers, but employees at least deserve to find out the reasons for underlying employment changes. And if employees are to take charge of their careers, they should receive good reasons for employment decisions and full information.[17]

Some writers argue that employers ought to enable workers to keep their knowledge and skills up to date so that they can easily move to other jobs in the event of job loss. Rosabeth Moss Kanter contends that although employers cannot and should not be expected to provide job security, they have a duty to give workers what she calls "employability security," which is a matter of providing work that "will enhance the person's value in terms of future opportunities."[18]

Third, some proponents of a right to due process argue that treating employees fairly is simply good management practice that pays off in increased productivity. Although job security alone is unlikely to have much effect, there is considerable evidence to show that worker participation in all aspects of a firm's operations enhances productivity and that some measure of job security is essential for gaining the benefits of greater employee involvement.[19] One objection to this efficiency-based argument is that if according employees due process has productivity gains, then employers do not need a legal requirement to do this; the market alone will provide adequate incentives to secure due process. Thus, if employment at will is the default legal rule, employers and employees will contract away from this situation in order to gain the benefits of greater job security. John J. McCall addresses this objection by arguing that the efficacy of such contracting depends on what is the default legal rule, and that having employment at will "as the background default rule may actually inhibit an efficient bargaining outcome."[20] The debate over the efficiency of employment at will and due process or job security as default rules is not easily resolved. In general, the argument that employment at will is a more efficient default rule rests on the assumption that employers and employees are fully rational and well-informed and so can bargain effectively, whereas the argument for due process questions whether the two parties can bargain rationally with full information.

A LAW OF DUE PROCESS. The effect of a law that ensured due process would be to introduce the legal right not to be dismissed without cause and a fair hearing into every employment relation. This right would be guaranteed for all employees and would not depend on an explicit contract and the implied covenant of good faith and fair dealing that currently constitute exceptions to employment at will. Such a right is meaningful only if there are mechanisms in place for hearing employee complaints and providing a remedy. The remedy should not only provide full compensation for an employee's loss but also constitute an effective deterrent to employers' dismissing employees unjustly. In short, a right against unjust dismissal is effective only if any wrong committed in discharging an employee is rectified and the incidence of such wrongdoing is minimized.

The Model Employment Termination Act has been proposed as a guide for the development of state laws.[21] Since its drafting in 1991, no state has chosen to follow the lead of this document. Montana had previously adopted a just-cause statute in 1987 and today remains the only state to depart from employment at will. This model act can serve to illustrate the difficulties involved in legislating a right to due process in the termination of employment.

The key proposal in the Model Employment Termination Act is that an employer may not terminate the employee without "good cause," which is defined as:

> (i) a reasonable basis for the termination of an individual's employment in view of the relevant factors and circumstances, which may include the individual's conduct, job performance and employment record; and the appropriateness of termination for the conduct involved; or (ii) the good faith exercise of business judgment, which may include setting economic goals and determining methods to achieve those goals, organizing or reorganizing operations, discontinuing or divesting operations or parts of operations, determining the size and composition of the workforce, and determining and changing performance standards for positions.

This definition conforms to the concept of "good cause" that has evolved in decades of labor union arbitration, and it does not interfere with decision making on the basis of legitimate business considerations, as long as these are in good faith. Among the potential difficulties of the definition is determining whether an exercise of business judgment is in good faith. For example, an employer might raise the standards of performance merely in order to dismiss a particular employee. In a unionized setting, any raising of standards would be subject to negotiation, but a nonunion worker would have no similar protection.

The model act also contains a waiver provision under which an employee can waive the right not to be dismissed without cause in exchange for the employer's agreement to make a severance payment equal to one month's salary for every year of service. The danger of this provision is that an employer might require all employees to sign a waiver as a condition of employment. Doing so would effectively deprive employees of the option to pursue legitimate termination complaints in court, with the possibility of obtaining a high award, and, at the same time, it would protect employers from court litigation and the risk of paying high awards.

Two final issues concern the method of resolving disputes and the remedy. The Model Employment Termination Act recommends arbitration as the preferred dispute-resolution method and reinstatement with lost pay as the preferred remedy. Arbitration works well in a unionized setting, where it often serves as an extension of union–management negotiation and involves the terms of a master contract. Without this context, arbitrators would have little guidance for resolving disputes. Reinstatement, too, is an appropriate remedy only in a unionized setting where the union is able to protect reinstated employees from subsequent retaliation. In addition, reinstatement with lost pay would not constitute a significant deterrent to employers. An alternative to state laws that follow the model act is a federal statute modeled on Title VII and other antidiscrimination laws, which provides for court action and monetary compensation.

EXPRESSION AND PARTICIPATION

Two rights that we cherish as citizens are the right to freedom of speech or expression and the right to participate in decisions that affect us. Both of these rights, which are enshrined in the U.S. Constitution, have been embodied in legislation and vigilantly enforced by the courts. Although these rights protect citizens and, in the case of expression, public employees from the actions of government, they are not constitutionally guaranteed to private-sector employees in their dealings with corporate employers. In general, there is no legal right to express one's views in the private workplace, whether related to the job or not, or uttered at work or away. Nor are corporations democracies in which employees have a legally mandated voice in the decision-making process.

Despite the lack of any broad legal recognition of workplace rights with regard to expression and participation, some people hold that there are still moral free-speech and participation rights, which employers have a moral, if not a legal, obligation to respect. Some argue, further, that these moral rights, if indeed they exist, ought to be enacted into law by legislatures and recognized by the courts. However, critics of these positions hold that there is no moral right to expression and participation and that the current lack of legal recognition of such rights is morally justified. This section considers the main positions and arguments concerning these two controversial rights.

Freedom of Expression

Expressing one's views at work or even away from the job can be hazardous. Employees have been dismissed or disciplined for their opinion of their bosses and their decisions, for complaints about compensation or working conditions, for their support or lack of support for political candidates or issues, for a refusal to make political contributions, for their advocacy of a union, for their published writings, for holding public office, and, indeed, for the expressions of almost any views that offend their superiors. Related to freedom of expression is freedom of conscience, which has led some employees to refuse to perform parts of their job which they consider to be morally wrong. For example, some pharmacists have cited a right of conscience in refusing to fill prescriptions for birth control drugs or the so-called "morning after" pill.[22]

David C. Yamada argues that there are "disturbing signs of a severe chill" on expression in today's business world, which are due to a number of features in the new, postindustrial workplace.[23] He writes,

> In essence, today's American workplace is evolving into an institution in which the expression of an individual employee is severely devalued. The unstable, downsizing nature of today's economy has made workers feel insecure about keeping their jobs, contributing to self-censorship in the workplace and a reluctance to initiate collective action. . . . Workers generally are spending more time on the job, thus taking away time that could be devoted to cultural self-expression and civic activities. This is occurring at a time when companies themselves are becoming *more* vocal about issues of social concern, often in ways that suggest that going along with an employer's social views help to guarantee one's continued employment.[24]

Issues about freedom of expression overlap with those in whistle-blowing, which is covered in Chapter 4, since whistle-blowers issue warnings about potentially harmful corporate activities. Firing or disciplining employees for their expression of views outside the workplace might also be considered a violation of a right to privacy, which is the subject of Chapter 6. When at-will employees suffer adverse personnel consequences for expressing themselves, then questions arise about the justification of such treatment under the legal doctrine of employment at will, which is discussed earlier in this chapter. Any legal protection for at-will employees who speak out would add a further exception to the rights of employees under this doctrine. Still, freedom of expression raises issues that extend beyond these other matters and merit a separate discussion.

DEFINING FREEDOM OF EXPRESSION.   A definition of freedom of expression includes four elements: (1) the nature of the expression (whether it is speech, writing, or symbolic acts); (2) the subject or topic of the expression (whether it is about the workplace or unrelated matters); (3) the location or venue of the expression (whether it takes place in or outside the workplace); and (4) the audience of the expression (whether it is made in private to a few people or publicly declared to many).[25]

First, one can express oneself not only in speech and writing but also through symbolic acts, such as wearing a campaign button or refusing to participate in certain activities. For example, a factory worker for a defense contractor was fired for stomping on an American flag and then blowing his nose into it after refusing to display the flag at his workstation during a Gulf War celebration.[26] The Connecticut Supreme Court ruled that the employee's symbolic actions were not protected by the state's free speech law. Second, an employee can express views about not only the workplace but matters wholly unrelated to it, such as social or political affairs or current events. Third, the expression, whether work related or not, may take place completely away from the workplace on an employee's own time. And, finally, the expression may be made only to one or a few people in or out of the workplace or to the public at large in a publication or other public forum. The possibilities for public dissemination of one's views have been greatly expanded by advances in information technology, including e-mail and Web-based communication. For example, a number of people have been fired for comments about an employer in personal blogs posted on the Internet.[27]

Freedom of expression can be defined narrowly or broadly. It might be restricted to the expression of views about the workplace in the workplace. A broad definition, offered by Bruce Barry, is that workplace freedom of expression is the ability to engage in acts of expression, which may be written, spoken or symbolic, made in public or private, "at or away from the workplace, on subjects related or unrelated to the workplace, free from the threat of formal or informal workplace retribution, discipline, or discharge."[28]

LEGAL PROTECTION FOR EXPRESSION.   Legal protection or the lack of protection for freedom of expression in the workplace in the United States is due to two separate provisions of American law. One is the First Amendment guarantee of free speech and the other is the doctrine of employment at will. In addition, freedom of expression for whistle-blowers is provided by many federal, state, and municipal legislative acts concerning such matters as collective bargaining, environmental protection, worker health and safety, government procurement, and securities fraud. Some states have passed so-called "privacy laws" that prohibit an employer from firing or refusing to hire a person for engaging in legal activities away from the job.[29]

Although free speech is guaranteed by the U.S. Constitution and the constitution of every state, this right protects only citizens against state action and not the action of private individuals or organizations. Thus, it is illegal for the government to limit people's expression, but the Constitution places no restriction on the actions of private businesses. As a result, public and private employers and employees are treated differently under the law. Government employees have recourse in federal and state courts when their employer, which is to say the government, dismisses or otherwise sanctions them for expressing their views, but employees of corporations in the private sector have no constitutionally guaranteed free-speech protection.

The courts have recognized a right of free speech for public employees under the First Amendment. For example, a public school teacher in Illinois wrote a letter to the editor of a local newspaper, criticizing the school board for favoring athletics at the expense of the academic program. The teacher, named Marvin Pickering, was fired on the grounds that writing the letter was "detrimental to the efficient operation and administration of the schools of the district." Pickering charged in reply that writing the letter was an exercise of the First Amendment right of free speech that cannot be denied citizens just because they are government employees. The U.S. Supreme Court agreed with Pickering and thereby established free-speech protection for government employees.[30] *Holodnak v. Avco Corporation* (1975) extended the precedent set by *Pickering* to private employers who do extensive work for the federal government.[31]

The free-speech right of government employees is not unlimited. In general, the courts have employed a balancing test that weighs the value of freedom of expression when a government employee speaks out on a matter of public concern with the need of government agencies to maintain order and efficiency in the workplace. In *Connick* v. *Myers*, a New Orleans prosecutor was fired when she distributed a questionnaire to her coworkers to protest a personnel matter. The U.S. Supreme Court ruled that the "speech" in question, namely the distribution of the questionnaire, did not address a matter of "public concern" sufficient to override the interest of the employer in maintaining control and efficiency in the workplace.[32] However, along with greater freedom of expression on some matters, government employees face some restrictions on partisan political activity that are not placed on private-sector employees.

Employees in the private sector have a right to expression insofar as such a right is contained in employment contracts. Tenured university professors have perhaps the strongest contractually guaranteed right to express their views, though some instances of free speech (proselytizing in the classroom, for example) are not protected. Contracts with due-process provisions, which are typical of union contracts, do not usually specify freedom of expression, but an exercise of free speech would usually not constitute a "good cause" for dismissal or discipline. In a fair hearing that would occur when a contract has a due-process provision, there is usually the same kind of balancing test that is applied in public-sector employment, in which the value of expression is weighed against the needs of the employer. However, the doctrine of employment at will precludes any legal protection for at-will employees who are dismissed or disciplined for expressing their view, no matter the subject, location, or audience.

ARGUMENTS OVER EXPRESSION.   The arguments against a right for workplace expression are, for the most part, the same as the arguments for employment at will. Private corporations are the property of the owners, who have a right to use their property, make contracts, and generally run their businesses as they see fit. In addition to a right to earn profits by operating efficiently, corporations have legitimate interests in building and maintaining a loyal, committed workforce, preserving the confidentiality of information, and protecting their reputations.[33] Although these rights and interests would generally lead corporations to respect employees' views and, in most cases, not seek to suppress them, some expressions can create discord in the workplace, undermine loyalty and commitment, release confidential information, or tarnish a corporation's reputation.

The arguments for a right to freedom of expression in the workplace generally parallel those for the corresponding right for citizens in a state, which underlie the First Amendment guarantee of free speech. These arguments divide into two groups, depending on whether freedom of expression benefits individuals or society. Individualist justifications, which are similar to arguments for a right to privacy, emphasize the importance of free speech for our development as persons. The freedom to express ourselves is an essential component of individual autonomy and liberty, and it contributes to a sense of worth and dignity.[34] Although these benefits can be gained by expressing ourselves outside of the workplace, the long hours that employees spend at work reduce the opportunities for free expression, and the workplace itself may counteract some of these benefits by, for example, limiting our autonomy or dignity.

The social arguments for freedom of speech or expression generally cite its importance for the search for truth and the operation of a free, democratic society. John Stuart Mill's famous *Essay on Liberty* justifies freedom of speech on the grounds that the competition of truth and falsehood in a marketplace of ideas is the surest method for allowing truth to emerge and become stronger in the process. Although a marketplace of ideas can operate outside the workplace, the efforts by the business community to advance its ideas and beliefs cannot be effectively countered if voices inside corporations are silenced. Bruce Barry contends, "Where suppression of one's power to think, speak, and dissent is conventionally accepted in workplaces, the ideology of management is given license to run free, not just at work, but everywhere."[35] Furthermore, a modern democratic society requires that people with disparate interests and desires find ways of cooperating and living together harmoniously. This cooperation and harmony is possible only if people can express their interests and desires freely as part of a democratic decision-making process.[36] Because so much of people's interaction with others and the development of sociability occur in the workplace, a democratic society cannot function if free expression is limited to the time spent away from work. Cynthia L. Estlund observes, "The sheer amount of sociability and cooperation that takes place every day in workplaces should place them at the center of any account of what holds a complex, modern democratic society together."[37]

Although these arguments for a right to expression in the workplace have merit, they must be weighed against the legitimate rights and interests of employers. Some acts of expression in the workforce, such as derogatory insults, disruptive criticism, and disclosure of confidential information, are, arguably, just grounds for dismissal or discipline. Crafting legal remedies that strike the right balance is difficult. The main options of extending the First Amendment right to free speech to the private sector and making an additional public-policy exception to employment at will might unduly restrict private employers. The other alternative is for employers to respect employees and allow, even encourage, responsible expression in the workplace.

Workplace Democracy

The typical workplace is organized as a top-down hierarchy, in which most employees merely follow orders from above. Many workers participate in decision making within a limited sphere of responsibility, but business organizations are not democracies in which everyone has a voice in the decisions that most affect them. Corporations bear a greater resemblance to military organizations, which exhibit a rigid chain of command and an unquestioning acceptance authority. However, a central tenet of the theory of democracy is that the exercise of state power by a government is legitimate only if the citizens subject to this power have a right to participate in decision making, including the democratic election of leaders. Otherwise, the government is an illegitimate dictatorship. So, are corporations more like an army or a political state? And can the exercise of power by corporate leaders be legitimate if there is no participation in decision making by employees?

PARTICIPATION AND DEMOCRACY.   The terms "worker participation" and "workplace democracy," which are often used interchangeably, cover a variety of arrangements. Worker participation may be defined as "a process that allows employees to exercise some influence over their work and the conditions under which they work."[38] Sample forms of participation include works councils, which are shop-floor worker organizations that are mandated in many Western European countries; codetermination, in which workers elect one or more board directors to represent them; grievance, mediation, and arbitration proceedings, which may be stipulated in employee contracts; collective bargaining by unions; quality circles and other employee involvement in total quality management programs; and self-directed teams. Workplace democracy includes participation but also involves more substantial control. According to one definition, "Workplace democracy exists when employees have some real control over organizational goal-setting and strategic planning, and can thus ensure that their own goals and objectives, rather than only those of the organization, can be met."[39] There are few examples of workplace democracy outside of employee-owned firms or worker cooperatives, which are not uncommon.[40] In general, the implementation of participation and democracy is much more extensive in Europe and Japan than in the United States.[41]

ARGUMENTS FOR DEMOCRACY. Although participation and democracy in the workplace have been proposed and implemented for reasons of increased organizational effectiveness and productivity,[42] the concern here is with moral arguments. Some advocates cite the same benefits as freedom of expression, such as the promotion of autonomy, dignity, personal development, and even physical and mental health.[43] However, the main moral or ethical arguments, especially for workplace democracy, involve the contribution that it makes to political democracy and, further, the need for democracy in order to legitimize power or authority in economic organizations.

The first argument, about the contribution to political democracy, holds that in the workplace, where people spend a great portion of their adult life, people develop the attitudes, interests, and skills of citizenship that are critical for being an active citizen.[44] Consequently, if people do not participate in workplace decisions, they may lack the ability to engage in outside political activity. Thus, Richard Sobel observes,

> Perhaps those empowered by activities within the workplace pursue analogous political involvement outside because they learn to be political on the job. Those who do not participate in work decisions . . . do not learn skills that carry over to the political sphere: avoiding office or shop politics may lead to avoiding politics outside, while being political at work encourages being political in the community. The quality of political life may, then, depend on the quality of work life.[45]

Although workplace participation is likely to have some impact on civic involvement, the evidence of any significant effect is weak.[46]

The second argument, the need for legitimacy, is theoretical rather than empirical. That is, it is based on considerations of democratic theory rather than factual evidence about the impact of workplace democracy. Although theoretical arguments have been developed in many forms,[47] the best-known version is that presented by the noted political theorist Robert A. Dahl. In *A Preface to Economic Democracy*, Dahl develops an argument with three premises: (1) the state is only one kind of association, (2) the argument for democracy in a state can be generalized for any association, and (3) an economic organization is an association to which the argument for democracy applies. Hence, it follows, in Dahl's words, that "*if* democracy is justified in governing the state, then it must *also* be justified in governing economic enterprises."[48]

First, what is the argument for democracy in an association? Any association is composed of persons with different and, sometimes, incompatible interests who join together in order to further their own interests. However, associations must make some rules that are binding on all members and may affect their interests differently. Because these rules affect people's interests, they should be made by those who are bound by them. If the members of an association are equal in their claims that their interests be satisfied, then they should have an equal vote in all decisions about mutually binding rules. According to this argument, members of an association have a right to a democratic vote as compensation for forgoing their interests, in some instances, for the benefit of others. Dahl's argument is thus based on distributive justice: The right to democratic rule-making ensures a just distribution of benefits and burdens in a cooperative endeavor.

This argument supports democracy in a state, but does it apply to business organizations? Dahl addresses this second question by attempting to refute claims that corporations are different from states. Specifically, there are two possible objections: (1) that members of corporations are not bound by rules, and (2) these members do not have equal claims. First, unlike citizens of a state, who are compelled by force to obey laws, members of a firm join voluntarily and are free to leave. The sanction for a citizen who violates a law may be imprisonment, but the worst a company can do to a disobedient employee is dismissal. Second, the members of a corporation are not equal, either in their decision-making abilities or in their claims on the firm. Corporations are not associations within which we live our lives, as is the state, but special-purpose entities created for economic production. Engaging in production requires considerable knowledge and many specialized skills that are possessed by only a few, so that most decisions in business cannot be made effectively by everyone in an organization.

Moreover, the goal of a corporation is not a good life for its members, as in a state, but efficient economic production. In the productive process, people bring different resources that form the basis of their claims. These resources are the private property of the different parties, and these parties exercise their property rights by making economic transactions. The claims that people have on a corporation are principally for the economic return on the resources provided. Employees' claims are, in part, for wages, though other groups such as shareholders, suppliers, and customers also have claims. Specifically, the basis for control of corporations by shareholders and management acting for their benefit is property rights: Shareholders are the owners of a corporation and, as such, have a right to operate it in their own interest.

To the objection that employees of a corporation are not bound by rules, Dahl replies that the sanctions for violating a rule need not be as severe as imprisonment by the state.[49] Losing one's job for disobedience is sufficiently severe to qualify as an exercise of coercive power by a business organization. Such coercive power is not justified unless the rule violated was adopted by a democratic process. As to whether employees are equal in their ability to make decisions, Dahl argues that employees, like citizens, do not have the competence to make every decision, but they have enough interest in the success of the firm to delegate decision-making power about matters outside their competence to others.[50] Moreover, Dahl cites the experience of employee-owned firms, which manage to make rational economic decisions.[51]

The most difficult problem in Dahl's argument is the claim that employees in a corporation have equal claims. First, the argument overlooks the point that many groups, including shareholders, customers, and suppliers, have claims on a corporation. A business organization as an association does not consist solely of employees; it encompasses all groups who contribute to production. Second, workplace democracy seems to violate property rights, especially the rights of the shareholder-owners of a firm.[52] In an employee-owned firm, the employees, in effect, buy the company, which gives them the right to make decisions. But why should employees of a firm owned by others have a right to operate it as if they owned it?

Dahl's response to this objection is to deny that the right to property is a moral right at all.[53] Property rights, as they exist, are themselves allotments made through a democratic process. They are merely conventional rights, and as such they are subordinate to the moral right of workplace democracy and must give way when there is a conflict. In the words of one commentator, "In economic associations it is democracy that is trumps, not the ownership of assets, because power over people is morally non-negotiable."[54] However, given that the right to property is an essential element of capitalism, it may be questioned whether Dahl's argument for workplace democracy is compatible with a capitalist economic system.

The ideas of participation in decision making and workplace democracy have been the subject of limited experimentation with slight success. Some forms of employee voice that appear to enhance productivity have been widely adopted, and most employees have some say about their work. If the efficiency gains of employee voice were greater, then more of it would have already been adopted by businesses. The implication is that additional participation and democracy could not be achieved without some loss of productivity. However, if the moral arguments are sufficiently compelling, then more participation and democracy would be worth the price. Countries in Western Europe that have mandated works councils, codetermination, and other means of worker involvement in decision making apparently believe that the moral benefits outweigh the economic costs. In the end, perhaps the extent to which employees have a right to participation and democracy in the workplace is a decision to be made in the political sphere by a democratic process.

JUST COMPENSATION

Compensation or pay is one of the most important aspects of employment. The level of compensation influences people in their selection of an occupation and in their decision to accept a particular job. On the job, employees are motivated by pay and are intensely concerned with whether their pay is just or fair.

Asking whether compensation is just or fair invites the further question: Compared to what? Most employees are concerned about how their pay compares with others in the organization and elsewhere who hold similar or comparable jobs. This kind of comparative justice may be determined by a comparison of jobs and pay scales. However, on this conception of fairness, all workers could be underpaid or overpaid, but the pay would be perceived as fair as long as there was a rough parity of similar jobs and differences in pay were proportional to the effort and ability required. Another kind of justice or fairness involves the factors that ought to determine the absolute level of pay for any job. What factors are relevant in judging whether any given level of pay is just? This question leads to many more specific ones such as whether it is unjust to pay wages below a certain level and whether the high pay of executives is justified. These questions are among those considered of this section on just compensation.

Workers' Wages

The compensation systems of large corporations are designed and operated by human resource professionals and compensation consultants in order to ensure that pay scales are both fair and efficient. In small companies the pay-setting process is often rather informal but follows the patterns set by larger firms. Determining the appropriate level of pay for each employee and the appropriate distribution of wages among all employees is vitally important for the success of any business. Although compensation is determined largely by market forces, employers must consider not only the market price of labor but also the effect of pay on attracting, retaining, and motivating their employees. In addition to the level of pay, employers must also consider the form in which employees are compensated. Besides wages, compensation takes other forms, including bonuses, profit sharing, employee stock ownership plans (ESOPs), fringe benefits (especially health insurance and pension plans), and employee stock options.

The level and the form of pay are determined mostly with a view to efficient production, which includes worker motivation and satisfaction, but they may also be linked to decisions about a company's strategy. For example, while Wal-Mart has pursued a strategy of low-priced products that depends on low wages and few benefits for a heavily part-time labor force, Starbucks pays relatively high wages with generous benefits to its workers as part of a strategy of providing a special ambience for customers. The higher compensation at Starbucks is offset by the benefits of a more skilled workforce with lower turnover and an experience for customers that enables the company to charge high prices for coffee. The differences in compensation at Wal-Mart and Starbucks are due not merely to the cost of labor in the market but also to these companies' different strategies.

Compensation is not only a matter of concern in production and strategy, but it is also a moral issue. First, the attitudes of employees, who depend on a paycheck for their livelihood, are affected by perceptions of fairness in the pay-setting process and in the overall distribution of pay in an organization. Even well-paid employees may be resentful if they perceive some unfairness. Second, society, which is concerned with people's welfare, has a strong interest in the justice of compensation. Among the conditions for a just society are that people's basic needs be met and that income and wealth be distributed justly. If the income that people receive from working enables them to meet their basic needs, then compensation helps to create a just society. However, if some people cannot support themselves from their earnings in a job or have no job at all, then an unjust society may result, and it may fall to society to provide for their well-being and secure justice.

Defenders of a market distribution of income and wealth argue that people deserve whatever they can gain in a market, and that the existence of poverty or inequality of income and wealth is not in itself unjust. If a market distributes income and wealth in ways that society considers to be unjust, any injustice can be corrected in one of two ways. One is to place legal limits on the operation of the market by, for example, minimum wage laws that mandate a certain level of pay. The other way is to provide for basic needs and to redistribute wealth through government programs, such as the welfare system and progressive taxation. If the latter course is taken, then the justice of compensation need not be a concern for companies, as long as the state corrects for any injustice that occurs in compensation. It is an open question, therefore, whether justice in compensation is a task for private employers or government—or perhaps both.

In a free-market economy, the compensation of employees is determined largely by market forces. Any discussion of justice in compensation must include, therefore, an understanding of how pay is set in a market and an assessment of whether the pay so set is just.

THE MARKET MECHANISM.   Economists view the level of wages as a reflection of the market price for labor. On this economic view, labor is simply one input into the productive process, and just as raw materials and equipment have a market price, so too does labor. In general, the price of an input or good is a function of supply and demand. Supply and demand are in equilibrium when at any given price, the supply of a good equals the demand for it, so that all of that good sells and no demand goes unsatisfied. If, at any given price, demand exceeds supply, buyers offer to pay more for a good and hence raise the price. Similarly, if the demand drops, then sellers will be forced to reduce the price until a sufficient number of buyers is found. In the case of employment, a shortage of workers will lead employers to raise the wages offered until enough workers accept a job; and a surplus of workers will result in a drop in wages until only the desired number remain.

The wage at which exactly the desired number of workers is employed is called the *market-clearing price*. In an efficient market, all workers employed will receive at least the market-clearing price for the reason that if an employer offers wages below it, a sufficient number of workers cannot be induced to take a job with that employer (because better paying jobs are available elsewhere), and the employer will lose an opportunity to employ the desired number of workers productively. However, if wages are above the clearing price, employers will have an opportunity to cut the cost of labor and still have the desired number of workers. Any employer who does not take advantage of such a cost-cutting opportunity will be at a competitive disadvantage to competitors who do.

Another way to put the economist's account is that in an efficient market, wages will equal the *marginal product* of a worker's labor. Each incremental increase of any input in production will, up to a certain point, increase the value of the output. That is, if a product is in demand, hiring additional workers and buying more raw materials and equipment will yield more sales and hence more profit. The marginal product is the value that each incremental increase of an input adds in the production of any good. Employers will seek to add inputs as long as the marginal product exceeds the cost of the input. For example, if each worker hired by an employer leads to an additional revenue of $1 for each unit produced, then the employer will keep adding workers and attracting them, if necessary, with higher wages up to $1 for the time needed to produce that unit. Wages will continue to rise until workers receive the full value of what they add to the productive process, which is to say the marginal product.

Are the wages set by market forces just? The economist's answer is that market transactions result from voluntary contracting, in which every party willingly consents to an exchange. Thus, workers are free to work on their own or otherwise seek the most lucrative employment. A plumber, for example, can work as an independent contractor, offering his or her services to whoever is willing to pay. A plumber who is able to make more income working for an employer is merely putting his or her productive potential to its most valued use. Thus, workers seek to sell their labor at the highest price they can—whether they work for themselves or others—and whatever price they can get is fair because it represents the best bargain that can be struck between economic actors.

Furthermore, all input providers receive as a return some portion of the revenues of a business firm. The input providers collectively cannot receive more than a firm earns from engaging in productive activity. Consequently, if one group receives more than the market value of its input, then some other group must receive less. Thus, if employees are paid more than the market-clearing rate or marginal product, then some other group receives less than the market price of its input. For example, customers may end up paying more for products than they would otherwise. Since workers are also consumers, what they receive in higher-than-market wages, they may have to spend buying higher-than-market products. In addition, the price system is critical in ensuring that the economy operates efficiently so that resources are used most efficiently and the greatest amount of total wealth is created. If any input, including labor, is not accurately priced, then the whole economy suffers. One possible consequence of distorted prices is that employers might not create jobs that would otherwise be created in an efficient economy.

Finally, the wages set in a free-market economy reward people in proportion to the knowledge and skills that they have acquired and the effort expended. Workers make an investment in the factors that make them productive—what economists call *human capital*. It is only fair that those who have made a greater contribution to productivity receive a proportionately greater return. Conversely, it would be unfair to pay everyone the same without regard for their contribution. In summary, the arguments for justifying wage-setting by a market rest on the ethical principles of *freedom* (in market exchange), *welfare* (the greater wealth produced), and *desert* (receiving in proportion to one's contribution).

These arguments may be challenged. First, if there were a large number of potential workers in jobs that require few skills, the market-clearing rate would be so low that employers could exploit the opportunity to offer unconscionably low wages. This possibility was identified by Karl Marx as the "reserve army of labor," which he thought would drive down wages in a capitalist economy to poverty levels. Although such a situation prevails in some developing countries (see the section Wages and Working Conditions in Chapter 14), it is not the case in developed economies, and the best remedy for a mass of unemployed workers is raising the productivity of workers so that they can command higher wages. Second, the bargaining that takes place in labor markets may be among parties with unequal economic power, so that workers do not receive the true market value of their labor. This objection may be used to support labor unions as a necessary counterweight to the power of employers. Political power may also hamper workers in bargaining effectively when companies influence the government to obtain favorable laws and regulations.

Third, the wealth created by a firm may not be distributed equitably in proportion to each group's contribution. That is, the market may be skewed in favor of one group over another. Among the causes of such inequitable distribution are well-recognized instances of market failures. For example, the bias in a market economy for private over public goods (which is discussed in Chapter 2) helps to explain why investment bankers are paid much more than school teachers, despite the similar contribution of their services to society. Market economies also produce "winner-take-all" competitions in which a few "superstars" in any industry (e.g., sports and entertainment) are able to gain outsized rewards.[55] Finally, capitalist economies produce significant degrees of inequality in the distribution of income and wealth that may undermine social welfare and stability. Thus, even if economic exchanges are purely voluntary and enhance the overall welfare of a society, low- and middle-income workers who do not benefit from increasing wealth creation in society might rightly claim that benefits of the economy are not being justly distributed. This consequence is one reason for a legally mandated minimum wage.

MINIMUM WAGE.   A minimum wage is the lowest wage that an employer may legally pay to employees. Minimum wage laws have been enacted in virtually all developed and most developing countries. Related to the minimum wage is the call for a "living wage," which is commonly defined as a wage for a full-time worker that would enable that person to attain a standard of living that is above the poverty level or some other measure of well-being.[56] In the United States, organized support for a living wage law has focused predominantly on municipalities. By 2006, 134 cities in the United States had adopted a living wage ordinance.[57] A living wage is invariably higher than a legal minimum wage, though the arguments for and against the two concepts are generally the same.

Two rationales have been offered for minimum wage legislation. Some proponents contend that it is exploitative for employers to offer unconscionably low wages to workers who have few employment options. Richard T. DeGeorge writes, "A just legal and political system must at least provide an income floor and must keep desperation out of the market by providing alternatives to forced acceptance of any wage offered, regardless of conditions."[58] On this view, the absence of a minimum wage permits an impermissible kind of coercion that violates people's dignity and autonomy. Such a state of affairs is morally wrong and presumably should not be permitted regardless of the economic consequences.

A second, and more common, rationale for a minimum wage is that it serves to redistribute income in society so that the lives of workers at the lowest income levels are improved. Although a redistribution of income may be sought for many reasons, including a compassion for the poor and social and political stability, an important reason, no doubt, is a sense that a just society should provide for everyone's basic needs. If this is a moral obligation, then the redistribution argument for a minimum wage is founded on morality, as is the exploitation argument. There are two important differences between these two rationales, however. First, if the absence of a minimum wage permits exploitation, then a law should be adopted regardless of the economic consequences. However, if a minimum wage is intended to redistribute income, then it matters whether it, in fact, achieves this goal, and there is no reason to have a minimum wage if it fails to do so. Second, there are many means besides a minimum wage for redistributing income, and so there is no moral imperative to have a minimum wage if other means of distribution work as well or better. If exploitation would occur in the absence of a minimum wage, though, then it is morally imperative to have one.

The exploitation argument is questionable. First, the experience in developed countries is that workers without skills are not coerced into accepting jobs at extremely low wages. Jobs in the informal, unregulated economy, such as illegal clothing factories, and in agriculture, which is not covered by the minimum wage law, typically pay very low wages, and the people who take these jobs have few other opportunities and work under uncomfortable conditions. However, they choose these jobs in preference to the alternatives, and so it is not evident that their dignity or autonomy is denied. Second, if no higher-paying jobs are available (and a worker would surely take one if it were), then it is difficult to see how a minimum wage that would deny them any job at all improves their situation. Indeed, that denial might be a violation of their dignity and autonomy.

If the purpose of a minimum wage is redistribution, then there is the moral question of whether income ought to be distributed for the benefit of low-income workers, and the empirical questions of whether a minimum wage has that effect or is the most effective means. Although the moral question is debatable, some amount of redistribution has been an accepted goal in all industrialized countries for more than a century, especially in view of the great increase in inequality that has accompanied modern industrialization. This question is moot, however, in the debate over the minimum wage if legally prescribed minimum wages do not have a redistributive effect. Economists generally argue that a minimum wage does not redistribute income to low-wage earners and, in fact, harms them by reducing the number of jobs. However, the empirical evidence for this position is inconclusive.

Economists commonly argue that employers create jobs only when the marginal product of new workers—which is to say, the value that a new worker adds to production—is equal to or less than a new worker's wage.[59] Any employer who hires a new worker at more than that worker's marginal product will lose money unless the cost can be passed on to others. Consequently, there are new jobs that would be created at a lower wage that will not be created if an employer is required by law to pay a higher wage. If the cost is passed on, the result will be some combination of lower wages for higher-earning workers, higher prices to consumers for products, and lower profits for investors. In addition, a minimum wage may attract more teenagers, many from affluent families, into low-paying jobs, which will reduce the number of jobs available to adults without skills. Some of these consequences may result in a redistribution downward, but low-wage workers and especially the unemployed are likely to bear the brunt of the losses. To the extent that prices are distorted, decisions by businesses, consumers, investors, and workers themselves may not result in the greatest possible wealth creation. For example, a minimum wage may reduce the incentive for low-wage workers to improve their job skills and seek higher-paying jobs.

The empirical evidence for the economist's theoretical argument is inconclusive.[60] In a much-discussed study, David Card and Alan B. Krueger examined the effect on employment in the fast-food industry after a rise in the New Jersey minimum wage in 1992 compared with nearby Pennsylvania, which did not change the law.[61] Card and Krueger found no significant difference and detected even a slight rise in employment in New Jersey after the change in the minimum wage. Another study found that a rise in the minimum wage can have a slight distributional effect, especially if it is linked with other policies and programs to help the poor.[62] These conclusions have been challenged.[63] Virtually all economists agree, though, that, whatever the distributional effect, which is small at best, the minimum wage is a very inefficient way to raise the income of the poor.[64] Other means can do this more effectively with less harm to the economy.

Executive Compensation

Few business practices have drawn as much moral criticism as the compensation lavished on the top executives of large corporations and especially on the chief executive officer (CEO). The total pay of American CEOs is comprised of not only a base salary but also bonuses, incentive plans, generous fringe benefits, and, most valuable of all, stock grants and stock options. In 2000, executive compensation peaked in S&P 500 companies at $17.4 million, though the amount had dropped to $9.1 million by 2003.[65] Although the rapid rise in CEO pay occurred between 1995 and 2000, the criticism began around 1990 when many companies were shedding jobs and workers' wages were stagnant. The combination of increasing wealth for CEOs and declining worker fortunes struck many people as unfair.

CRITICISM OF CEO PAY. Aside from the huge CEO pay packages, which have exceeded $400 million for a few recipients, critics have noted that some of the companies awarding high executive compensation performed poorly, so that pay seemed to be unrelated to performance. In some cases, CEOs received handsome rewards upon departure from a company, after their value to the company had ended. Another concern is the lack of proportion between executive compensation and the pay of lower-level employees. The top CEOs make 400 to 500 times the income of the average worker. In addition, CEO pay has grown much faster than the average paycheck. From 1993 to 2000, the average total compensation of an S&P 500 company CEO increased 470 percent, while the pay of average workers increased a mere 42 percent, six percentage points above the rate of inflation.[66] At the same time, workers were receiving a declining portion of increases in productivity. Between 2000 and 2006, the productivity of workers increased 18 percent, but their inflation-adjusted wage hike was only 1 percent.[67]

One justification for high executive compensation is its incentive effect to induce CEOs to perform at their best. Some critics argue, though, that the same effect could be achieved at lower cost. As Derek Bok, a former president of Harvard University observes, "But there is no reason to suppose that American executives would work less hard if they were paid several hundred thousand dollars a year instead of several million."[68] Critics also note that CEOs in Europe and Japan are paid much less but still seem to be effective. Moreover, too much compensation might have unintended consequences. CEOs who are intent on raising stock price, upon which most incentives are based, may pursue short-term strategies that harm the company in the long run or pursue excessively risky, bet-the-farm strategies in hopes of a high payoff. Strong monetary incentives may also lead to questionable accounting practices and even fraud.

JUSTIFYING CEO PAY. The total compensation of a CEO is set by the compensation committee of the board of directors, which is acting on behalf of the shareholders. Directors have a fiduciary duty to make all decisions, including those about CEO pay, in the best interests of the shareholders.

The value of a CEO to the corporation and its shareholders is determined, in part, by a market for CEOs that operates like any labor market on the basis of supply and demand. One factor in the amount of pay offered by a board to a CEO is the value that that person can bring to a firm, which is to say, his or her marginal product. The decisions that CEOs make have profound consequences for a company and the whole of society. If the difference in performance of the very best CEO and the second-best choice is, for example, $100 million in profit, then it benefits the shareholders to pay up to that amount to get the best person available.

In addition to the marginal product of a CEO, the board must consider two other factors. One is that the CEO must be motivated to achieve the maximal results. However, unlike most workers, who need to be motivated only to accomplish specific tasks, a CEO must conceive and implement the best strategy for a company. This is best done by tying CEO pay to some measure of corporate success, such as stock price. Thus, bonuses, stock grants, and stock options, which are responsible for much of the recent increase in CEO pay, are a distinctively effective way of motivating a CEO, as well as measuring success. Second, in addition to motivating a CEO, compensation must be designed to overcome an agency problem. The interests of CEOs may not be the same as those of shareholders, and so a chief executive must be induced to become a loyal agent of the shareholder principals. One function of CEO pay in stock and stock options is to align the interests of a CEO with those of the shareholders by making that person a special kind of shareholder. Put simply, in setting CEO pay, the board of directors is "buying" not merely a CEO's services but also that person's loyalty.

The standard justification for CEO compensation is that it represents a bargain struck between a CEO and the board over the value of a CEO to a corporation and its shareholders. When a CEO is hired, it is difficult to determine what value the CEO will bring to a firm. However, both the CEO and the board make their best estimates. One reason for compensating CEOs with bonuses and stock options is that the pay becomes contingent on performance. A poorly performing CEO may get little, while a successful one is richly rewarded. Thus, whatever amount is agreed to in arm's-length negotiation between the two parties is just, no matter the amount. Even though some CEOs produce disappointing results, they deserve the amount offered because of the initial agreement in which both sides made a good faith attempt to predict the CEO's value to the firm. And CEOs who produce superlative results deserve what they receive because much of their pay has been tied to performance.

Still, are some CEOs worth tens or even hundreds of millions of dollars? Warren Buffett has been quoted as saying, "You'll never pay a really top-notch executive . . . as much as they are worth. A million, $3 million, or $10 million, it's still peanuts."[69] However, Graef Crystal, a persistent critic of executive compensation, questions the linkage between pay and performance.[70] Although sports and entertainment figures negotiate multimillion-dollar contracts, Crystal finds that at least 70 percent of those amounts can be explained by the extra revenue these stars generate. Crystal's studies have never been able to account for more than 40 percent of CEO pay by such factors as company size, performance, business risk, or industry type. Crystal concludes that the pay of top executives is highly arbitrary, with some CEOs receiving two to three times what his model indicates as "rational."

Other evidence indicates that much of the high pay in recent years has been due to strong performance in a robust economy. Michael Jensen and Kevin Murphy found that CEOs typically receive about $3.25 for each $1,000 increase in shareholder wealth.[71] At this rate, the amount of wealth created by American corporations since 1990 would result in very high compensation. In addition, two other researchers, Xavier Gabaix and Augustin Landier, calculated that the sixfold increase in executive compensation in S&P 500 corporations between 1983 and 2003 was accompanied by a corresponding sixfold increase in the market capitalization of these firms.[72] These figures suggest that the increase in compensation was proportional to the wealth that was created.

PROBLEMS WITH JUSTIFICATION. One objection to the standards justification of CEO compensation is that its core assumption—that the agreement results from arm's-length negotiation between a CEO and the board, acting for shareholders—is not entirely true. Lucien

Bebchuk and Jesse Fried in their book *Pay Without Performance* argue that CEOs have undue influence over the process with the result that boards are unable or unwilling to engage in tough negotiations.[73] They contend that CEOs have power over the selection of directors, who are consequently beholden to the CEO. Board members are also linked to the CEO and each other by social ties, and they are often CEOs themselves, with a vested interest in high compensation. Even board members who might be inclined to bargain aggressively typically lack the skill, time, and information to do so. Boards are often advised by compensation consultants who serve the company as well, and so have little incentive to alienate the CEO.

The Bebchuk and Fried thesis has many skeptics.[74] First, the thesis would apply only to incumbent CEOs, but incoming chiefs, who have had no opportunity to influence the board, receive similar pay packages. Second, high compensation also occurs in privately held companies where shareholders have greater control. Third, some boards are more independent of the CEO than others, but there is no evidence that pay varies with the degree of board independence. Finally, it may be better for boards not to negotiate aggressively with a CEO with whom the board must work closely. Thus, it may be in the shareholders' interest that CEOs be paid generously in order to avoid strife. In sum, although CEOs undoubtedly have some power over the setting of their own pay, it is not clear that their influence has produced the current high level of executive compensation.

Another group of critics object that even if CEO compensation results from arm's-length bargaining with the board, and even if selecting and motivating a CEO who will create maximal wealth for shareholders and thereby benefit society, the inequality of income and wealth that high compensation produces is morally objectionable. Just as low compensation below a minimum or a living wage creates social problems, so, too, does very high compensation. The problems resulting from great inequality in wealth and income include less social cohesion and increased strife and resentment both in business organizations and among members of society. Critics who object in this way generally hold that justice requires a certain distribution of income and wealth that differs from that produced by markets. One reason for the comparatively higher pay of executives in the United States, with its emphasis on individualism and freedom, may be that in Europe and Japan there is less acceptance of market outcomes and more concern for the common good.

Conclusion

Employee rights are important because so much of people's lives is spent at work, and injustice on the job seriously impacts people's lives. Justice is also a great concern to employers because workers are very sensitive to perceptions of unfair or unjust treatment and act accordingly. Employers violate employee's rights at their peril. However, the extent of employee rights is uncertain. Some rights, such as the alleged rights to expression, participation, and a living wage, are arguably "manifesto rights," which is to say ideals perhaps worth striving toward. Other rights, especially due process in termination, have more solid moral grounding. A key question about employee rights, though, is the extent to which they should be enforced by law. There is a considerable body of labor law that ensures fair or just treatment of workers, but on many matters, such as termination, it is questionable whether justice should be legally mandated or be achieved by more informal processes in the workplace.

CASE 8.2 ✳ Explore the Concept on mythinkinglab.com
Worker Participation at Saturn

A study undertaken by General Motors in 1982 concluded that the American automobile industry could not successfully challenge the Japanese in producing small, fuel-efficient cars without a radical overhaul of traditional manufacturing processes.[75] Out of this study came a proposal not just for a new automobile but for a new company, separate from G.M.'s other units. The resulting

Saturn Corporation, a wholly owned G.M. subsidiary, would utilize the advanced technology and management practices that had enabled the Japanese to gain a $2,000 per car cost advantage over their American competitors. The Saturn factory would also make a radical break from the past by involving assembly workers in company decision making. The new president of the Saturn Corporation declared, "Saturn is not a car, and it is not a manufacturing process. It is a new way of doing business with everyone."[76] Roger B. Smith, the chairman of G.M., said, "The Saturn process is going to institute technology and business and management procedures so advanced that they don't exist anywhere in the world today, not even in Japan."[77]

Between 1983 and 1991, when the first car rolled off the assembly line, G.M. negotiated a revolutionary contract with the United Auto Workers union (UAW) that did away with conventional, hierarchical labor–management relations. The Saturn Philosophy set forth in the contract stated,

> We believe that all people want to be involved in decisions that affect them, care about their job and each other, take pride in themselves and in their contributions, and want to share in the success of their efforts.

In accord with the union agreement, Saturn workers, initially 6,000 in number, were organized into self-directed work units of 6 to 15 people with responsibility for a particular part of the production process. The work groups performed a series of operations taking several minutes and requiring some skill, instead of the quick repetition of a single task involving little skill on the typical assembly line. Among various other tasks, members determined job assignments, set work schedules, maintained equipment, and ordered supplies. In contrast to the dozens of job classifications used in traditional assembly-line production, there was one classification for production workers and three to five for skilled workers. Each team also elected one member to be a "counselor" to represent the union.

At the next level, three to six work units were formed into work modules, led by a company work unit adviser. Workers had union representation on all committees, including the Business Unit Committee that coordinated plant-level operations and the top-level Manufacturing Advisory Committee and Strategic Advisory Committee. Decisions at the plant were to be made by consensus to the extent possible. The agreement stated that any party may block a potential decision, but adds, "In the event an alternative solution is not found, the blocking party must reevaluate the position in the context of the philosophy and mission."[78] Although management reserved the right to make the final decision on any matter, employees still had considerable voice in the decision-making process.

In addition to participation in decision making, the Saturn contract provided for variable pay. There were no time clocks, and workers were paid a salary instead of an hourly wage. In the first year of operation, absenteeism at the plant was less than 1 percent, which is one-tenth of the rate at other G.M. plants and about the same as Japanese factories. The base pay for workers was set at 80 percent of the average compensation at other unionized G.M. factories, and the difference was to be made up by bonuses based on productivity. Job security was provided by a guarantee that 80 percent of the workforce would be protected from layoff except in the case of "catastrophic events," and even then, layoff could be avoided by a consensus decision to substitute reduced work hours or temporary shutdowns.

To produce the Saturn, G.M. built a state-of-the-art plant in Spring Hill, Tennessee, 25 miles south of Nashville. However, by the time the factory began operations, the American automobile industry was in a slump, and the demand for small cars was declining. The goal of producing 500,000 cars annually was cut in half, and because of production problems, the company did not make a profit the first year. During the 1980s, G.M. workers at any facility in the country could apply for a job at the Spring Hill plant, and many who moved were attracted by the prospect of worker participation. However, in 1990, applicants were restricted to workers who had been laid off at other G.M. plants. These workers were, on the whole, less enthusiastic about the new system and were more suspicious of management. Although the first workers were given 700 hours of training to prepare them for Saturn's cooperative work methods, the amount of training for subsequent hires was reduced to 175 hours.

By 1997, Saturn workers were becoming dissatisfied with the new system. The sales of the Saturn dropped almost 10 percent that year, and unsold cars were piling up at dealerships. Production was halted one day a week, and workers were put to other tasks around the plant. Workers' bonuses fell to $2,200 in 1997 from $10,000 in each of the two previous years. Workers blamed some of the problems on mistakes by management. G.M. had ignored workers' suggestions that Saturn produce small sport-utility vehicles. Although the Saturn was popular, the automobile itself was rather conventional in design, and G.M. had been slow to make improvements. In order to cut costs, G.M. was trying to reduce the number of frames and parts of its automobiles by designing Saturns with components from other G.M. lines made at plants with traditional labor contracts. The Saturn was intended to be a unique product, built entirely at the Spring Hill plant. However, the local union head complained, "They are just looking at basically outsourcing everything they can, and run it through a lean assembly and still call it a Saturn."[79] It appeared to workers that G.M. was trying to fold Saturn back into the parent company.

Despite their participation in decision making, some Saturn workers felt that they had lost the power of unionized workers in traditional plants. Historically, worker participation has been viewed as an effort by companies to reduce the power of unions. Even when well intentioned, worker participation programs are difficult to implement because they can be successful only if power is meaningfully shared. Such programs have also been short-lived. According to one expert, "only 25 percent of all programs, meaningful or not, last beyond five years."[80] Workers complained that their union leaders had become too close to management. In 1998, a proposal to abandon the Saturn agreement and replace it with the standard UAW labor contract was rejected by a margin of two to one, which means that a third of all workers supported the change. The next year, in 1999, the local union leaders who had guided the Saturn experiment from the beginning were voted out of office and replaced by new leadership that favored more traditional labor relations. Although worker participation continues at Saturn, the early dreams have not been realized. Whether the setbacks have occurred because of adverse economic conditions, company sabotage or the impracticability of worker participation remains to be determined.

CASE 8.3   ✳ Explore the Concept on mythinkinglab.com

Health Benefits at Wal-Mart

Wal-Mart, the world's largest private employer with 1.3 million store workers or "associates," has long been criticized for its low level of health benefits.[81] Wal-Mart reported in 2005 that only 43 percent of its associates received company-sponsored health insurance. Approximately 27 percent of its workforce had not been employed long enough to be eligible for health benefits, although many would eventually qualify. Of the remaining 73 percent who were eligible, only 60 percent chose to enroll in Wal-Mart's health insurance plan. Some of those not enrolled had health insurance from a spouse or parent, a previous job, the military, or some other source. Wal-Mart estimated that in 2005, 75 percent of its associates had health insurance of some kind, but that the remaining 25 percent were completely uninsured.

The lack of health insurance extended to the children of Wal-Mart associates. Among these dependents, 27 percent relied on government funded healthcare (Medicaid and the State Children's Health Insurance Program), and 19 percent of associates' children had no healthcare benefits at all. Prior to 2006, only full-time associates could obtain coverage for children. In total, only 54 percent of the children of Wal-Mart associates were enrolled in a Wal-Mart health insurance plan. Medicaid was the principal source of healthcare payments for 4 percent of Wal-Mart associates (compared with 5 percent of workers nationally). When adult workers and their children rely on government programs and hospital emergency rooms, the cost of healthcare is transferred from employers to taxpayers.

The criticism of Wal-Mart focused on not only the numbers covered by health insurance but also the cost of insurance to employees, which deterred many associates from enrolling. Wal-Mart offered several health insurance plans with different premium costs and levels of coverage. However, on average, associates with Wal-Mart health insurance spent 8 percent of their income on healthcare, including premiums, deductibles, and out-of-pocket expenses. This figure is nearly double the national average. Associates with coverage for a spouse spent, on average, 13 percent of their income for healthcare.

In 2005, Wal-Mart sought to make insurance more affordable by introducing a Value Plan, with premiums as low as $11 a month. The $11 premium was available in only a few states, however. For most workers the costs were, on average, $25 for an individual, $37 for a single parent, and $65 for a family. The plan had a deductible of $1,000, although three doctor visits were allowed before the deductible was applied. In addition, the insured were required to pay $300 out of pocket for drugs and $1,000 for a hospital stay before insurance took over payment for these items. Thus, in a year, a family paying $780 for insurance might have to pay $2,300 in deductibles and out-of-pocket expenses. Critics questioned the value of the Value Plan for Wal-Mart associates, most of whom earn less than $20,000 annually.

Wal-Mart and other retail employers face a number of obstacles to providing health benefits. First, in 2005, approximately 20 percent of the company's workforce consisted of part-time workers, and many others were new hires. Generally, the health benefits costs are the same whether a worker is full- or part-time. This factor increases the total cost to employers with a large percentage of part-time workers, if they are offered health benefits. Second, worker turnover, which is typical in retail, increases the number of workers employed over the course of a year. Enrolling workers who leave after a short period of enrollment imposes an administrative burden on employers and provides little benefit for employees. Most employers deal with this problem by imposing waiting periods before workers can enroll in a health insurance plan. At Wal-Mart, full-time employees were eligible after six months of employment, and part-time employees, after two years. However, the longer the waiting period is, the larger will be the number of uninsured workers. Third, the design of the health insurance plan affects the number of workers who enroll. Plans that cover most costs with few deductibles and co-pays require large premiums, which tend to discourage low-wage workers from enrolling. Low premiums boost enrollment by low-wage workers but may create financial hardship when serious illness or injury leads to considerable out-of-pocket expenses.

Consequently, Wal-Mart and other retailers who want to maximize the enrollment percentage must consider such questions as whether to offer health insurance for part-time employees, how long to make the waiting periods for full- and part-time workers, and what trade-offs to make between the cost of premiums on the one hand and the amount of deductibles and co-pays on the other. Generally, the trade-offs will be different for industries with a low-wage, heavily part-time workforce than for those with highly paid full-time employees.

Because the retail industry employs a workforce with different characteristics than many other industries, the question also arises whether the health benefits offered by Wal-Mart should be compared with its other retail competitors or with all employers. Critics generally cite figures from all industries, while Wal-Mart and other retailers contend that they should be compared only with each other. For example, the 60 percent of eligible associates who participate in the Wal-Mart health insurance plan is only slightly below the 63 percent figure for all retailers, but significantly below the 83 percent national average. And the 73 percent of associates who were eligible for health insurance in 2005 is less than other large employers (79 percent) but well above the 61 percent average in the retail industry.

The cost of health benefits at Wal-Mart, as at most companies, is substantial and increasing. In 2005, Wal-Mart spent $1.5 billion on health insurance, which is $2,660 per insured associate. From 2002 to 2005, this cost rose 19 percent each year. This increase was due not only to rising healthcare costs but also to greater utilization of healthcare services by associates, which was increasing at a rate of 10 percent per year. Among the factors contributing to this increase in utilitzation were that the Wal-Mart workforce was aging faster than the general population and was becoming less healthy, due mainly to diseases related to obesity. In addition, Wal-Mart associates tended to utilize healthcare inefficiently, in part by skimping on preventive medicine and relying too much on emergency rooms and hospital services. Compounding these problems was the fact that the least healthy associates were more satisfied with their benefits and more inclined to stay with the company.

The challenge facing Wal-Mart in 2005 was twofold: to reduce the rate of increase in health benefits and to spend the money available in the best way. This task fell to Wal-Mart's vice-president for benefits, M. Susan Chambers, who produced a confidential memo with a number of controversial proposals. The memo proposed that the waiting time for part-time employees to be eligible for health insurance be reduced from two years to one and that the waiting time for all new employees be changed from a fixed period of time to the number of hours worked. Another proposal was to assist new employees in finding private health insurance until they were eligible for the company's plan. The problem of inefficient utilization of healthcare services was addressed by proposals to educate associates about healthcare and health insurance and to avoid emergency room visits by putting health clinics in stores.

The memo also proposed to cut costs by reducing enrollment of spouses, hiring more part-time workers, and discouraging unhealthy people from working at Wal-Mart. The percentage of workers enrolled in the company's health insurance plan would not be affected if spouse coverage—which is an expensive option—were made less attractive. Increasing the percentage of part-time workers would decrease the enrollment in the company's health insurance plan. Additional cost savings would be realized if already insured full-time associates worked longer hours, since this would reduce the total number of full-time associates required. Workers in poor health could be discouraged from applying for a job or, once hired, from remaining at Wal-Mart if some moderate physical activity were incorporated into all jobs. For example, ordinarily sedentary checkout clerks might also be required to gather shopping carts in the parking lot. The memo observed, "It will be far easier to attract and retain a healthier work force than it would be to change behavior in an existing one."[82]

Postscript

In April 2006, Susan Chambers was replaced as vice president for benefits, and her successor was told by Wal-Mart CEO H. Lee Scott, Jr., "We need you to go make a difference in health care."[83] The eligibility waiting period for part-time workers was reduced to one year, and for 2008, associates could choose from a broad range of more affordable plans to suit many different needs. Wal-Mart claimed at the beginning of 2008 that the percentage of eligible employees enrolled in a company plan was 50.2 percent and that 92.7 percent of its eligible associates were covered by some form of health insurance. Wal-Mart has announced a study of why 7.3 percent of eligible associates declined to enroll. Critics complained that the company's health insurance was still too expensive for low-wage workers. However, Wal-Mart's health benefits are now more generous than most of its competitors in the retail industry, though they continue to lag behind the health insurance offered by most major American employers.

Notes

1. *Greeley* v. *Miami Valley Maintenance Contractors, Inc.*, 49 Ohio St. 3d 228 (1990); 551 N.E. 2d 981 (1990).

2. H. G. Wood, *A Treatise on the Law of Master and Servant* (Albany, NY: John D. Parsons, Jr., 1877), 134.

3. *Paine* v. *Western & A.R.R.*, 81 Tenn. 507, 519–20 (1884).

4. *Adair* v. *United States*, 208 U.S. 161, 28 S.Ct. 277 (1907).

5. *Coppage* v. *Kansas*, 26 U.S. 1, 35 S.Ct. 240 (1914).

6. The efficiency argument for employment at will is presented in Richard Epstein, "In Defense of the Contract at Will," *University of Chicago Law Review*, 51 (1984), 947–82.

7. *Petermann* v. *International Brotherhood of Teamsters*, 174 Cal. App. 2d 184, 344 P. 2d 25 (1959).

8. *Frampton* v. *Central Indiana Gas Company*, 260 Ind. 249, 297 N.E. 2d 425 (1973). In addition, see *Kelsay* v. *Motorola*, 74 Ill. 2d 172, 384 N.E. 2d 353 (1978); *Sventko* v. *Kroger Co.*, 69 Mich. App. 644, 245 N.W. 2d 151 (1976).

9. *Nees* v. *Hocks*, 272 Or. 210, 536 P. 2d 512 (1975).

10. *Greeley* v. *Miami Valley Maintenance Contractors, Inc.*

11. *Toussaint* v. *Blue Cross and Blue Shield of Michigan* and *Ebling* v. *Masco Corporation*, 408 Mich. 579, 272 N.W. 2d 880 (1980).

12. *Fortune* v. *National Cash Register Company*, 364 N.E. 2d 1251 (1977).

13. Philip J. Levine, "Towards a Property Right in Employment," *Buffalo Law Review*, 22 (1973), 1084.

14. Clyde W. Summers, "Employment at Will in the United States: The Divine Right of Employers," *University of Pennsylvania Journal of Labor and Employment Law*, 65 (2000–2001), 65.

15. *Lochner* v. *New York*, 198 U.S. 45, 25 S.Ct. 539 (1905).

16. *West Coast Hotel* v. *Parrish*, 300 U.S. 379 (1937). In a landmark decision, *Nebbia* v. *New York*, 291 U.S. 502 (1934), the Supreme Court had previously ruled that states have the power to regulate business—and thereby limit the property rights of owners—for the sake of the public welfare. The decision in *West Coast Hotel* thus extends the precedent of *Nebbia*, which concerned the setting of prices, to matters of employment.

17. Tara J. Radin and Patricia H. Werhane, "Employment-at-Will, Employee Rights, and Future Directions for Employment," *Business Ethics Quarterly*, 13 (2003), 115.

18. Rosabeth Moss Kanter, *When Giant's Learn to Dance* (New York: Free Press, 1990), 321.

19. See Casey Ichniowski, "Human Resource Management and Productive Labor-Management Relations," in *Research Frontiers in Industrial Relations and Human Resources*, ed., David Lewis, et al. (Madison, WI: Industrial Relations Research Association, 1992); David Levine and Laura D'Andrea Tyson, "Participation, Productivity and the Firm's Environment," in *Paying for Productivity: A Look at the Evidence*, ed. Alan Blinder (Washington, DC: Brookings Institution, 1990); Jeffrey Pfeffer, *The Human Equation: Building Profits by Putting People First* (Cambridge, MA: Harvard Business School Press, 1998).

20. John J. McCall, "A Defense of Just Cause Dismissal Rules," *Business Ethics Quarterly*, 13 (2003), 159. For further discussion of the effect of default rules, especially in employment, see Pauline Kim, "Bargaining with Imperfect Information: A Study of Worker Perceptions of Legal Protection in an At-Will World," *Cornell Law Review*, 83 (1997), 105–60; David Millon, "Default Rules, Wealth Distribution and Corporate Law Reform: Employment at Will versus Job Security," *University of Pennsylvania Law Review* 146 (1998), 975–1041; Cass Sunstein, "Switching the Default Rule," *New York University Law Review*, 77 (2001), 106–43.

21. Uniform Commissioners' Model Employment Termination Act, *Uniform Laws Annotated*, 7A Cumulative Annual Pocket Part (St. Paul, MN: West Publishing, 1997), Prefatory Note.

22. Jill M. Dieterle, "Freedom of Conscience, Employee Prerogatives, and Consumer Choice," *Journal of Business Ethics*, 77 (2008), 191–203; Richard Lippke, "Speech, Conscience, and Work," *Social Theory and Practice*, 18 (1992), 237–58.

23. David C. Yamada, "Voice from the Cubicle: Protecting and Encouraging Private Employee Speech in the Post-Industrial Workplace," *Berkeley Journal of Employment and Labor Law*, 19 (1998), 1–59.

24. Ibid., 21.

25. These distinctions are made in Bruce Barry, "The Cringing and the Craven: Freedom of Expression In, Around, and Beyond the Workplace," *Business Ethics Quarterly*, 17 (2007), 263–96.

26. "Court Upholds Ruling on Free Speech Law," *New York Times*, 5 October 1999, B8.

27. Todd Wallack, "Beware If Your Blog Is Related to Work," *San Francisco Chronicle*, 24 January 2005, C1.

28. Barry, "The Cringing and the Craven," 265.

29. As of 2006, 26 states had enacted such laws, mainly in response to employers who prohibit smoking, even away from work. See Karen L. Chadwick, "Is Leisure-Time Smoking a Valid Employment Consideration?" *Albany Law Review*, 70 (2006), 117–41.

30. *Pickering* v. *Board of Education*, 391 U.S. 563 (1968).

31. *Holodnak* v. *Avco Corporation*, 423 U.S. 892 (1975). In other Supreme Court decisions, the right to speak out on matters of public concern was upheld in cases involving a police officer, a firefighter, and a public health nurse. *Muller* v. *Conlisk*, 429 F. 2d 901 (7th Cir. 1970); *Dendor* v. *Board of Fire and Police Commissioners*, 11 Ill. App. 3d 582, 297 N.E. 2d 316 (1973); *Rafferty* v. *Philadelphia Psychiatric Center*, 356 F. Supp. 500 (E.D.Pa. 1973).

32. *Connick* v. *Myers*, 461 U.S. 138 (1983).

33. For one presentation of these arguments, see Lucy Vickers, *Freedom of Speech and Employment* (Oxford: Oxford University Press, 2002).

34. See C. Edwin Baker, *Human Liberty and Freedom of Speech* (New York: Oxford University Press, 1989); Cynthia L. Estlund, "Free Speech and Due Process in the Workplace," *Indiana Law Journal*, 71 (1995), 101–51; Kent Greenawalt, "Free Speech Justifications," *Columbia Law Review*, 89 (1989), 119–55.

35. Barry, "The Cringing and the Craven," 287–88.

36. See Greenawalt, "Free Speech Justifications," 141–42.

37. Estlund, "Free Speech and Due Process in the Workplace," 13.

38. Frank Heller, Eugen Pusic, George Strauss, and Bernhard Wilpert, *Organizational Participation: Myth and Reality* (Oxford: Oxford University Press 1998), 15.

39. Janice R. Foley and Michael Polanyi, "Workplace Democracy: Why Bother?" *Economic and Industrial Democracy*, 27 (2006), 173–91.

40. Although employee ownership is rare in industrial firms, which require extensive financial capital, they are common in businesses that involve mainly human capital, such as professional services. If partnerships in accounting, law, and other services are regarded as employee owned, then they are very common indeed. Employee-owned firms are more prevalent in Italy, France, and Spain. See Henry Hansmann, *The Ownership of Enterprise* (Cambridge, MA: Harvard University Press, 1996), 66–69.

41. For examples of workplace democracy in the United States, see Jaclyne Badal, "Can a Company Be Run as a Democracy?" *Wall Street Journal*, 32 April 2007, B1.

42. Abraham Sagie and Meni Koslowsky, *Participation and Empowerment in Organizations: Modeling, Effectiveness, and Applications* (Thousand Oaks, CA: Sage Publications, 2000).

43. Foley and Polanyi, "Workplace Democracy" offers a health-based argument. For other arguments, see John J. McCall, "Employee Voice in Corporate Governance: A Defense of Strong Participation Rights," *Business Ethics Quarterly*, 11 (2001), 195–213; and Patricia H. Werhane, *Persons, Rights, and Corporations* (Englewood Cliffs, NJ: Prentice Hall, 1985).

44. Carol Pateman, *Participation and Democratic Theory* (Cambridge: Cambridge University Press, 1970).

45. Richard Sobel, "From Occupational Involvement to Political Participation: An Exploratory Analysis," *Political Behavior*, 15 (1993), 349.

46. Neil Carter, "Political Participation and the Workplace: The Spillover Thesis Revisited," *British Journal of Politics and International Relations*, 8 (2006), 412–26.

47. For one form of the argument, see George G. Brenkert, "Freedom, Participation and Corporations: The Issue of Corporate (Economic) Democracy," *Business Ethics Quarterly*, 2 (1992), 251–79. Another important argument is offered in Christopher McMahon, *Authority and Democracy: A General Theory of Government and Management* (Princeton, NJ: Princeton University Press, 1994).

48. Robert A. Dahl, *A Preface to Economic Democracy* (Berkeley and Los Angeles, CA: University of California Press, 1985), 111.

49. Ibid., 115.

50. Ibid., 118.

51. Ibid., 122–33.

52. Jan Narveson, "Democracy and Economic Rights," *Social Philosophy and Policy*, 9 (1992), 45–49.

53. Dahl, *A Preface to Economic Democracy*, 73–83.

54. Robert Mayer, "Robert Dahl and the Right to Workplace Democracy," *Review of Politics*, 63 (2001), 230.

55. See Rosen, Sherwin, "The Economics of Superstars," *American Economic Review*, 71 (1981), 845–58; Robert H. Frank and Philip J. Cook, *The Winner-Take-All Society* (New York: Free Press, 1995).

56. Robert Pollin and Stephanie Luce, *The Living Wage: Building a Fair Economy* (New York: New Press, 1998).

57. Jon Gertner, "What Is a Living Wage?" *New York Times Magazine*, 15 January 2006, 38.

58. Richard T. DeGeorge, *Moral Issues in Business*, 6th ed. (Upper Saddle River, NJ: Prentice Hall, 2006), 364.

59. For a classic statement of the economist's argument, see George J. Stigler, "The Economics of Minimum Wage Legislation," *American Economic Review*, 36 (1946), 358–65. A fuller presentation is contained in Charles Brown, Curtis Gilroy, and Andrew Kohen, "The Effect of the Minimum Wage on Employment and Unemployment," *Journal of Economic Literature*, 20 (1982), 487–528.

60. Brown, Gilroy, and Kohen, "The Effect of Minimum Wage on Employment and Unemployment."

61. David Card and Alan B. Krueger, *Myth and Measurement: The New Economics of the Minimum Wage* (Princeton, NJ: Princeton University Press, 1995).

62. Richard B. Freeman, "The Minimum Wage as a Redistributive Tool," *Economic Journal*, 106 (1996), 639–49.

63. John Keenan, "The Elusive Effects of Minimum Wages," *Journal of Economic Literature*, 33 (1995), 1949–65; and Marvin H. Kosters, ed., *The Effect of the Minimum Wage on Employment* (Washington, DC: The AEI Press, 1996).

64. Marvin H. Kosters, "Employment and the Minimum Wage: What Does the Evidence Show?" in *The Effect of the Minimum Wage on Employment* (Washington, DC: The AEI Press, 1996), 104.

65. Lucian Bebchuk and Yaniv Grinstein, "The Growth of Executive Pay," *Oxford Review of Economic Policy*, 21 (2005), 283–303.

66. Ibid.

67. Scott Klinger, Chris Hartman, Sarah Anderson, John Cavanagh, and Holly Sklar, "Executive Excess 2002: CEOs Cook the Books, Skewer the Rest of Us," Ninth Annual CEO Compensation Survey, Institute for Policy Studies and United for a Fair Economy, 2002, 14.

68. Derek Bok, *The Cost of Talent: How Executives and Professionals Are Paid and How It Affects America* (New York: The Free Press, 1993), 102.

69. Stuart D. Wechsler, "Would Adam Smith Pay Them So Much?" *Forbes*, 28 May 1990, 210.

70. Graef S. Crystal, *In Search of Excess* (New York: W. W. Norton, 1991).

71. Brian J. Hall and Jeffrey B. Liebman, "Are CEOs Really Paid Like Bureaucrats?" *Quarterly Journal of Economics*, 113 (1998), 653–91.

72. Xavier Gabaix and Augustin Landier, "Why Has CEO Pay Increased So Much?" Unpublished Manuscript, 21 July 2006.

73. Lucian Bebchuk and Jesse Fried, *Pay without Performance: The Unfulfilled Promise of Executive Compensation* (Cambridge, MA: Harvard University Press, 2004).

74. Most notably, William Bratton, "The Academic Tournament over Executive Compensation," *California Law Review*, 93 (2005), 1557–84; John E. Core, Wayne R. Guay, and Randall S. Thomas, "Is U.S. CEO Compensation Inefficient Pay without Performance?" *Michigan Law Review*, 103 (2004–2005), 1142–85; and Stephen M. Bainbridge, "Executive Compensation: Who Decides?" *Texas Law Review*, 83 (2004–2005), 1615–62.

75. Information in this case is taken from John Holusha, "G.M. Pact Seeks High Degree of Cooperation," *New York Times*, 28 July 1985, sec. 1, p. 25; William Serrin, "Bold G.M. Pact Draws Praise, and Some Caveats," *New York Times*, 3 August 1985, sec. 1, p. 6; John Holusha, "Saturn Division Finds a Home in the Heartland," *New York Times*, 4 August 1985, sec. 4, p. 5; Maralyn Edid, "How Power Will be Balanced on Saturn's Shop Floor," *BusinessWeek*, 5 August 1985, 65; Doron P. Levin, "Saturn: An Outpost of Change in G.M.'s Steadfast Universe," *New York Times*, 17 March 1991, sec. 4, p. 4; Doron P. Levin, "At Saturn Plant, a Vote on Innovation," *New York Times*, 14 November 1991, D1; David Woodruff, "Saturn: Labor's Love Lost?" *BusinessWeek*, 8 February 1993, 122; Robyn Meredith, "Many at the Saturn Auto Factory Are Finding Less to Smile About," *New York*

Times, 6 March 1998, A1; Robyn Meredith, "Saturn Union Votes to Retain Its Cooperative Company Pact," *New York Times*, 12 March 1998, D1; Keith Bradsher, "Labor's Peace with G.M. Unraveling at Saturn," *New York Times*, 22 July 1998, A1; Frank Swoboda, "Saturn Experiment in Jeopardy," *Washington Post*, 6 March 1999, E1; Keith Bradsher, "Saturn's Plant's Union Leaders Are Voted Out," *New York Times*, 26 February 1999, C1; Saul A. Rubenstein and Thomas A. Kochan, *Learning from Saturn* (Ithaca, NY: Cornell University Press, 2001).

76. Holusha, "Saturn Division Finds a Home in the Heartland."

77. Serrin, "Bold G.M. Pact Draws Praise, and Some Caveats."

78. Holusha, "G.M. Pact Seeks High Degree of Cooperation."

79. Bradsher, "Labor's Peace with G.M. Unraveling at Saturn."

80. William Serrin, "Giving Workers a Voice of Their Own," *New York Times Magazine*, 2 December 1984, 126.

81. Information for this case is taken from Michael Barbaro, "Wal-Mart to Expand Health Plan for Workers," *New York Times*, 24 October 2005, C1; Steven Greenhouse and Michael Barbaro, "Wal-Mart Memo Suggests Ways to Cut Employee Benefit Costs," *New York Times*, 26 October 2005, C1; Michael Barbaro, "Wal-Mart to Expand Health Plan," *New York Times*, 24 February 2006, C1; Michael Barbaro and Reed Abelson, "Wal-Mart Says Health Plan Is Covering More Workers," *New York Times*, 11 January 2007, C13; Michael Barbaro and Reed Abelson, "A Health Plan for Wal-Mart: Less Stinginess," *New York Times*, 13 November 2007, A1; Michael Barbaro, "Wal-Mart Crosses a Health Insurance Threshold," *New York Times*, 23 January 2008, C2; "Supplemental Benefits Documentation," Board of Directors Retreat FY06, Wal-Mart Stores, Inc., company document, 2005; "Wal-Mart's Health Care Benefits Are Competitive in the Retail Sector," company document, n.d.

82. Greenhouse and Barbaro, "Wal-Mart Memo Suggests Ways to Cut Employee Benefit Costs."

83. Barbaro and Abelson, "A Health Plan for Wal-Mart."

9

Occupational Health and Safety

CASE 9.1   ✳─[Explore** the **Concept** on **mythinkinglab.com**

When Is an Accident a Crime?

On June 14, 2002, a 22-year-old plumber's apprentice, Patrick Walters, was installing a sewer pipe at the bottom of a 10-foot-deep trench when the rain-soaked walls gave way and he was buried alive under the heavy mud.[1] The company he worked for, Moeves Plumbing (pronounced MAY-vis), had a contract to run water and sewer lines to new houses in a development about 40 miles north of Cincinnati, Ohio. Walters and a backhoe operator, John Kehrer, pumped rainwater out of the trench dug the previous day, and after further digging, Walters entered the trench to cut the sewer pipe. As the trench collapsed, Kehrer felt his backhoe slide toward the trench, but he had no time to shout out a warning. It took seven hours to recover the body.

Charles Shelton, an official from the Occupational Safety and Health Administration (OSHA), who watched as the body was pulled from the mud, was familiar with the plumbing company and the dead apprentice. Two weeks before, on Friday, May 31, Shelton had responded to a complaint about an unsafe trench being dug by Moeves Plumbing and ordered the work to stop. Because trench walls can easily give way, OSHA law requires that trenches over five feet deep be sloped at a safe angle or else shored up with braces. If a metal trench box is used, it must be large enough to protect a worker and strong enough to withstand the force of collapsing walls. A person trained in excavation safety must examine the trench before workers may enter it. None of these conditions were met at this site.

The following Monday, Shelton returned with a tape recorder and interviewed the workers, including Patrick Walters. Walters admitted for the record that the company did not always observe the rules for trench safety and made little effort to enforce them. He also reported in the interview that he didn't like getting down into trenches, but he had explained to his family that the attitude of the company was "either do it or go home." Walters had reason to be grateful for this job since Moeves, a small, family-owned company with 50 employees, was paying for his four-year apprenticeship program. Shelton later learned that the company's safety manager had left over three months ago, but that person confessed that he could not recall ever giving any training in trench safety during his two years at Moeves. After his departure, three Moeves supervisors did attend a course on trench safety, but two of them supervised the trench that Shelton now found to be unsafe. John Kehrer, the backhoe operator working with Walters on the day he died, said that he had taken a 10-hour training session on trench safety with a former employer but had forgotten most of it, and that in six years with Moeves he had received no safety training.

Patrick Walter was not the first person to die working for Moeves Plumbing. Thirteen years earlier in 1989, a worker named Clint Daley died in a similar accident in a 12-foot-deep trench that was neither sloped nor shored. Prior to this accident, the company had been warned three times about trench safety—in 1984, 1985, and 1986—and fined $700. The owner of the company, Linda Moeves, claimed to know none of this. She took over in 1987 upon the death of her husband, and before this time, she had little involvement with the operations of the company. After Clint Daley's death, though, Linda Moeves promised to make sweeping changes. She resolved that all supervisors and backhoe operators would learn trench safety, that there would be regular safety meetings, and that a safety director would be appointed. A written safety policy was adopted that required all trenches over four feet deep to be sloped or shored and to be inspected daily. Until Patrick Walter's death in 2002, Moeves Plumbing had been cited for nothing more than minor safety violations.

The parents of Patrick Walters and his young wife were understandably enraged. His father considered the conduct of Moeves Plumbing to be "flat-out criminal." OSHA law makes it a criminal offense for an employer to cause a worker's death through "willful" violations of safety standards. A "willful" violation means that the employer displayed either "intentional disregard" of safety standards or "plain indifference" toward them. A criminal charge could be brought only if OSHA could persuade the Justice Department that Linda Moeves and Moeves Plumbing had engaged in such a "willful" violation of OSHA law.

INTRODUCTION

Without question, workers have a right to be protected against workplace hazards that can cause injury, illness, and even death. Some accidents and exposures are unavoidable, however, and others can be prevented only at considerable cost. Working in a trench, such as the one that killed Patrick Walters, is inherently dangerous, but we can still establish safety standards that an employer ought to meet. Similarly, when exposure to dangerous chemicals cannot be avoided, it is possible to establish permissible exposure limits (PELs). Safety always comes at a price, though, and the costs of complying with safety standards or exposure limits must be weighed against their benefit.

Questions can also be raised about the right of employees to be given information about the workplace hazards to which they are exposed and their right to refuse to perform dangerous work without fear of dismissal or other reprisals. An especially difficult kind of case is posed by the fact that certain jobs pose a health threat to the fetus of a pregnant woman and to the reproductive capacities of both men and women. Some pregnant women and women of childbearing age are demanding the right to transfer out of jobs thought to pose reproductive hazards. On the other hand, employers who exclude pregnant women or women of child-bearing age from certain jobs because of reproductive hazards are open to charges of illegal sexual discrimination, especially when they do not show an equal concern for the reproductive risk to men.

This chapter is concerned with determining how questions about the rights of workers in matters of occupational health and safety ought to be answered. At issue in these questions is not only the obligation of employers with respect to the rights of workers but also the justification for government regulation of the workplace, especially by the Occupational Safety and Health Administration (OSHA). As a result, many of the questions discussed in this chapter deal with specific regulatory programs and policies which are the subject of intense controversy.

THE SCOPE OF THE PROBLEM

Many Americans live with the possibility of serious injury and death every working day. For some workers, the threat comes from a major industrial accident, such as the collapse of a mine or a refinery explosion, or from widespread exposure to a hazardous substance, such as asbestos, which is estimated to have caused more than 350,000 cancer deaths since 1940.[2] The greatest toll on the workforce is exacted, however, by little-publicized injuries to individual workers, some of which are gradual, such as hearing loss from constant noise or nerve damage from repetitive motions. Some of the leading causes of death, such as heart disease, cancer, and respiratory conditions, are thought to be job-related, although causal connections are often difficult to make. Even stress on the job is now being recognized as a workplace hazard that is responsible for headaches, back and chest pains, stomach ailments, and a variety of emotional disorders.

The Distinction between Safety and Health

Although the term "safety" is often used to encompass all workplace hazards, it is useful to make a distinction between *safety* and *health*.[3] Safety hazards generally involve loss of limbs, burns, broken bones, electrical shocks, cuts, sprains, bruises, and impairment of sight or hearing. These injuries are usually the result of sudden and often violent events involving industrial equipment or the physical environment of the workplace. Examples include coming into contact with moving parts of machinery or electrical lines, getting hit by falling objects or flying debris, chemical spills and explosions, fires, and falls from great heights.

Health hazards are factors in the workplace that cause illnesses and other conditions that develop over a lifetime of exposure. Many diseases associated with specific occupations have long been known. In 1567, Paracelsus identified pneumoconiosis, or black lung disease, in a book entitled *Miners' Sickness and Other Miners' Diseases*. Silicosis, or the "white plague," has traditionally been associated with stonecutters. Other well-known occupational diseases are caisson disease among divers, cataracts in glassblowers, skin cancer among chimney sweeps, and phosphorus poisoning in matchmakers. Mercury poisoning, once common among felt workers, produces tremors, known as "the hatters' shakes," and delusions and hallucinations, which gave rise to the phrase "mad as a hatter."

In the modern workplace, most occupational health problems result from routine exposure to hazardous substances. Among these substances are fine particles, such as asbestos, which causes asbestosis, and cotton dust, which causes byssinosis; heavy metals, such as lead, cadmium, and beryllium; gases, including chlorine, ozone, sulfur dioxide, carbon monoxide, hydrogen sulfide, and hydrogen cyanide, which damage the lungs and often cause neurological problems; solvents, such as benzene, carbon tetrachloride, and carbon disulfide; and certain classes of chemicals, especially phenols, ketones, and epoxies. Pesticides pose a serious threat to agricultural workers, and radiation is an occupational hazard to x-ray technicians and workers in the nuclear industry.

Because occupationally related diseases result from long-term exposure and not from identifiable events on the job, employers have generally not been held liable for them, and they have not, until recently, been recognized in workers' compensation programs. The fact that the onset of many diseases occurs years after the initial exposure—30 or 40 years in the case of asbestos—hides the causal connection. The links are further obscured by a multiplicity of causes. The textile industry, for example, claims that byssinosis among its workers results from their own decision to smoke and not from inhaling cotton dust on the job.[4] Lack of knowledge, especially about cancer, adds to the difficulty of establishing causal connections.

Regulation of Occupational Health and Safety

Prior to the passage of the Occupational Safety and Health Act (OSH Act) in 1970, government regulation of occupational health and safety was almost entirely the province of the states. Understaffed and underfunded, the agencies charged with protecting workers in most states were not very effective.[5] Only a small percentage of workers in many states were even under the jurisdiction of regulatory agencies; often, powerful economic interests were able to influence their activities. Because the agencies lacked the resources to set standards for exposure to hazardous substances, they relied heavily on private standard-setting organizations and the industries themselves. The emphasis in most states was on education and training, and prosecutions for violations were rare. State regulatory agencies were also concerned almost exclusively with safety rather than with health.

States still play a major role in occupational health and safety through workers' compensation systems, but in 1970, primary responsibility for the regulation of working conditions passed to the federal government. The "general duty clause" of the OSH Act requires employers "to furnish to each of his employees employment and a place of employment which are free from recognized hazards that are causing or are likely to cause death or serious injury."[6] In addition, employers have a specific duty to comply with all the occupational safety and health standards that OSHA is empowered to make. Employees also have a duty, under Section 5(b), to "comply with occupational safety and health standards and all rules, regulations, and orders issued pursuant to this Act which are applicable to his own actions and conduct." OSHA regulates occupational health and safety primarily by issuing standards, which are commonly enforced by workplace inspections. Examples of standards are permissible exposure limits for toxic substances and specifications for equipment and facilities, such as guards on saws and the height and strength of railings.

The Right to a Safe and Healthy Workplace

At first glance, the right of employees to a safe and healthy workplace might seem to be too obvious to need any justification. This right—and the corresponding obligation of employers to provide working conditions free of recognized hazards—appears to follow from a more fundamental right, namely, the right of survival. Patricia H. Werhane writes, for example, "Dangerous working conditions threaten the very existence of employees and cannot be countenanced when they are avoidable." Without this right, she argues, all other rights lose their significance.[7] Some other writers base a right to a safe and healthy workplace on the Kantian ground that persons ought to be treated as ends rather than as means. Thus, Mark MacCarthy argues that a right to work free from job-related diseases and injury follows from a more basic right people have to protect themselves from those who would use them for their own ends.[8]

Congress, in passing the OSH Act granting to all employees the right of a safe and healthy workplace, was apparently relying on a cost–benefit analysis, balancing the cost to industry with the savings to the economy as a whole. Congress, in other words, appears to have been employing essentially utilitarian reasoning. Regardless of the ethical reasoning used, though, workers have an undeniable right not to be injured or killed on the job.

It is not clear, though, what specific protection workers are entitled to or what specific obligations employers have with respect to occupational health and safety. One position, recognized in common law, is that workers have a right to be protected against harm resulting directly from the actions of employers where the employer is at fault in some way. In most workplace accidents, however, employers can defend themselves against the charge of violating the rights of workers with two arguments. One is that their actions were not the *direct cause* of the death or injury and the other is that the worker *voluntarily assumed the risk*. These defenses are considered in turn.

The Concept of a Direct Cause

Two factors enable employers to deny that their actions are a direct cause of an accident in the workplace.[9] One factor is that industrial accidents are typically caused by a combination of things, frequently including the actions of workers themselves. When there is such a multiplicity of causes, it is difficult to assign responsibility to any one person.[10] The legal treatment of industrial accidents in the United States incorporates this factor by recognizing two common-law defenses for employers: A workplace accident was caused in part by (1) lack of care on the part of the employee (the doctrine of "contributory negligence"), or by (2) the negligence of coworkers (the "fellow-servant rule"). As long as employers are not negligent in meeting minimal obligations, they are not generally held liable for deaths or injuries resulting from industrial accidents.

The second factor is that it is often not practical to reduce the probability of harm any further. It is reasonable to hold an employer responsible for the incidence of cancer in workers who are exposed to high levels of a known carcinogen, especially when the exposure is avoidable. But a small number of cancer deaths can statistically be predicted to result from very low exposure levels to some widely used chemicals. Is it reasonable to hold employers responsible when workers contract cancer from exposure to carcinogens at levels that are considered to pose only a slight risk? The so-called Delaney amendment, for example, forbids the use of any food additive found to cause cancer.[11] Such an absolute prohibition is practicable for food additives, because substitutes are usually readily available. But when union and public interest groups petitioned OSHA in 1972 to set zero tolerance levels for 10 powerful carcinogens, the agency refused on the ground that workers should be protected from carcinogens "to the maximum extent practicable *consistent with continued use*."[12] The position of OSHA, apparently, was that it is unreasonable to forgo the benefit of useful chemicals when there are no ready substitutes and the probability of cancer can be kept low by strict controls. This is also the position of philosopher Alan Gewirth, who argues that the right of persons not to have cancer inflicted on them is not absolute. He concluded, "Whether the use of or exposure to some substance should be prohibited should depend on the degree to which it poses the risk of cancer. . . . If the risks are very slight . . . and if no substitutes are available, then use of it may be permitted, subject to stringent safeguards."[13]

THE BENZENE CASE.   This issue arose again in 1977 in a case involving benzene, a hazardous chemical with well-documented effects. Because of its toxicity, a PEL of 10 parts per million (ppm) was set by OSHA. The assumption that exposure below the level of 10 ppm is safe was challenged in 1977 when a disproportionate number of leukemia deaths occurred at two rubber pliofilm plants in Ohio.[14] On the evidence contained in a report by the National Institute for Occupational Safety and Health (NIOSH), OSHA declared benzene to be a leukemia-causing agent and issued an emergency temporary standard ordering that the PEL for benzene in most work sites be reduced to 1 ppm until a hearing could be conducted on setting a new limit. OSHA was acting under a section of the law that requires the PEL for a known carcinogen (cancer-causing agent) to be set at the lowest technologically feasible level that will not impair the viability of the industries being regulated.

In the resulting uproar, the American Petroleum Institute, a trade association of domestic oil companies, contended that the evidence linking benzene to leukemia was not conclusive and that the exposure standard should take into account the cost of compliance. Previous studies had documented the incidence of leukemia only at exposures above 25 ppm. One study of exposure below 10 ppm, conducted by Dow Chemical Company, found three leukemia deaths in a group of 594 workers, where 0.2 deaths would be expected, but it was impossible to rule out other causes, because the workers who developed leukemia had been exposed to other carcinogens during their careers. OSHA was unable to demonstrate, therefore, that exposure to benzene below the level of 10 ppm had ever caused leukemia.

According to OSHA figures, complying with the 1-ppm standard would require companies to spend approximately $266 million in capital improvements, $187 million to $205 million in first-year operating costs, and $34 million in recurring annual costs. The burden would be least in the rubber industry, where two-thirds of the workers exposed to benzene are employed. The petroleum-refining industry, by contrast, would be required to incur $24 million in capital costs and $600,000 in first-year operating expenses. The cost of protecting 300 petroleum refinery workers would be $82,000 each, compared with a cost of only $1,390 per worker in the rubber industry.

The main legal issue faced by the Supreme Court is the authority of the Secretary of Labor under the OSH Act to set standards. An "occupational safety and health standard" is defined in Section 3(8) of the OSH Act as "a standard which requires conditions, or the adoption or use of one or more practices, means, methods, operations, or processes, reasonably necessary or appropriate to provide safe or healthful employment and places of employment." Section 6(b)(5) states,

> The Secretary, in promulgating standards dealing with toxic materials or harmful physical agents under this subsection, shall set the standard which most adequately assures, to the extent feasible, on the basis of the best available evidence, that no employee will suffer material impairment of health or functional capacity even if such employee has regular exposure to the hazard dealt with by such standard for the period of his working life. Development of standards under this subsection shall be based upon research, demonstrations, experiments, and such other information as may be appropriate. In addition to the attainment of the highest degree of health and safety protection for the employee, other considerations shall be the latest available scientific data in the field, the feasibility of the standards, and experience gained under this and other health and safety laws.

Two specific issues raised by the language of the OSH Act are (1) What is meant by "to the extent feasible"? Should all technologically possible steps be taken? Or should some consideration be given to the economic burden on employers? Should the agency, in determining what is "reasonably necessary and appropriate," also weigh costs and benefits? (2) What amount of evidence is required? To what extent should the agency be required to provide valid scientific studies to prove that a standard addresses a genuine problem and will, in fact, achieve the intended result? On the one hand, the power to set emergency standards on the basis of flimsy evidence that turns out later not to warrant action exposes businesses to the possibility of heavy and unpredictable expenses. On the other hand, adequate scientific research is very costly and time-consuming. Lack of funding for research and the time lag between suspicion and proof that a substance is carcinogenic, for example, could result in the needless deaths of many workers. A high level of proof exposes workers to preventable harm, therefore, but at the price of a possibly unnecessary cost to employers. Where does the balance lie?

A plurality of justices agreed with a lower court opinion that OSHA does not have "unbridled discretion to adopt standards designed to create absolutely risk-free workplaces regardless of the cost." But no consensus was achieved on how the level of risk is to be determined and, in particular, whether OSHA is required to use cost–benefit analysis in setting standards. By a bare majority, though, the Supreme Court struck down the 1-ppm standard because the agency was unable to prove that exposure to benzene below concentrations of 10 ppm is harmful. Ample evidence existed at the time to justify a 10-ppm standard, but little evidence indicated that a lower standard would achieve any additional benefits. The Court's answer to the second question, then, is that a rather high level of proof is needed to impose a highly restrictive standard.

In a subsequent case, however, the Court ruled that OSHA is not required to take cost into account but only technological feasibility. The case, *American Textile Manufacturers Institute Inc.* v. *Raymond J. Donovan, Secretary of Labor*, concerned an established standard for cotton dust, which is the primary cause of byssinosis, or "brown lung" disease. The evidence linking cotton dust to byssinosis was not in dispute, but OSHA relied on cost–benefit studies that, as the agency itself admitted, underestimated the cost of compliance. The reason given for not requiring OSHA to consider costs and benefits is that Congress, in passing the OSH Act, had already made a cost–benefit analysis.[15] According to the majority opinion,

> Not only does the legislative history confirm that Congress meant "feasible" rather than "cost-benefit" when it used the former term, but it also shows that Congress understood that the Act would create substantial costs for employers, yet intended to impose such

costs when necessary to create a safe and healthful working environment. . . . Indeed Congress thought that the *financial costs* of health and safety problems in the workplace were as large as or larger than the *financial costs* of eliminating these problems.

Cost–benefit analysis is the proper instrument for striking a balance on issues of worker health and safety, in other words, but this instrument was used by Congress as a justification for empowering OSHA to set standards without regard for costs. OSHA, therefore, should base its decisions solely on technological feasibility.

As a postscript to the benzene case, OSHA announced, in March 1986, a new standard based on subsequent research. The new standard, which took effect in February 1988, set a permissible exposure limit of 1 ppm for an eight-hour workday, with a short-term limit of 5 ppm. By this time, however, improvements in equipment and the monitoring of airborne pollutants required by the Environmental Protection Agency (EPA) had already reduced the level of exposure to benzene close to the 1-ppm standard. Consequently, the initial capital expenditures for meeting the new standard were considerably less than in 1977, 10 years earlier, when the controversy first erupted.

The Voluntary Assumption of Risk

A further common-law defense is that employees voluntarily assume the risk inherent in work. Some jobs, such as coal mining, construction, longshoring, and meatpacking, are well known for their high accident rates, and yet some individuals freely choose these lines of work even when safer employment is available. The risk itself is sometimes part of the allure, but more often the fact that hazardous jobs offer a wage premium in order to compensate for the greater risk leads workers to prefer them to less hazardous, less-well-paying jobs. Like people who choose to engage in risky recreational activities, such as mountain climbing, workers in hazardous occupations, according to the argument, knowingly accept the risk in return for benefits that cannot be obtained without it. Injury and even death are part of the price they may have to pay. And except when an employer or a fellow employee is negligent in some way, workers who have chosen to work under dangerous conditions have no one to blame but themselves.

A related argument is that occupational health and safety ought not to be regulated because it interferes with the freedom of individuals to choose the kind of work that they want to perform. Workers who prefer the higher wages of hazardous work ought to be free to accept such employment, and those with a greater aversion to risk ought to be free to choose other kinds of employment or to bargain for more safety, presumably with lower pay. To deny workers this freedom of choice is to treat them as persons incapable of looking after their own welfare.[16] W. Kip Viscusi, who served as a consultant to OSHA during the Reagan administration, adds an extra twist by arguing that programs designed to keep workers from being maimed and killed on the job effectively deprive them of the opportunity to select risky but good-paying jobs and thus are a form of class oppression in which the rich impose their risk preferences on the poor.[17]

The argument that employees assume the risk of work can be challenged on several grounds. First, workers need to possess a sufficient amount of information about the hazards involved. They cannot be said to assume the risk of performing dangerous work when they do not know what the risks are. Also, they cannot exercise the right to bargain for safer working conditions without access to the relevant information. Yet, employers have generally been reluctant to notify workers or their bargaining agents of dangerous conditions or to release documents in their possession. Oftentimes, hazards in the workplace are not known by the employer or the employee until after the harm has been done. In order for employers to be relieved of responsibility for injury or death in the workplace, though, it is necessary that employees have adequate information *at the time they make a choice.*

Second, employees' choices must be truly free. When workers are forced to perform dangerous work for lack of acceptable alternatives, they cannot be said to assume the risk. For many people with few skills and limited mobility in economically depressed areas, the only work available is often in a local slaughterhouse or textile mill, where they run great risks. Whether they are coerced into accepting work of this kind is a controversial question. Individuals are free in one sense to accept or decline whatever employment is available, but the alternatives of unemployment or work at poverty-level wages may be so unacceptable that people lack freedom of choice in any significant sense.

Risk and Coercion

In order to determine whether workers assume the risk of employment by their free choice, we need some account of the concept of coercion. A paradigm example is the mugger who says with a gun in hand, "Your money or your life." The "choice" offered by the mugger contains an undesirable set of alternatives that are imposed on the victim by a threat of dire consequences. A standard analysis of coercion that is suggested by this example involves two elements: (1) getting a person to choose an alternative that he or she does not want, and (2) issuing a threat to make the person worse off if he or she does not choose that alternative.

Consider the case of an employer who offers a worker who already holds a satisfactory job higher wages in return for taking on new duties involving a greater amount of risk.[18] The employer's offer is not coercive because there is no threat involved. The worker may welcome the offer, but declining it leaves the worker still in possession of an acceptable position. Is an employer acting like a mugger, however, when the offer of higher pay for more dangerous work is accompanied by the threat of dismissal? Is "Do this hazardous work or be fired!" like or unlike the "choice" offered by the mugger? The question is even more difficult when the only "threat" is not to hire a person. Is it coercive to say, "Accept this dangerous job or stay unemployed!" because the alternative of remaining out of work leaves the person in exactly the same position as before? Remaining unemployed, moreover, is unlike getting fired, in that it is not something that an employer inflicts on a person.

In order to answer these questions, the standard analysis of coercion needs to be supplemented by an account of what it means to issue a threat. A threat involves a stated intention of making a person worse off in some way. To fire a person from a job is usually to make that person worse off, but we would not say that an employer is coercing a worker by threatening dismissal for failure to perform the normal duties of a job. Similarly, we would not say that an employer is making a threat in not hiring a person who refuses to carry out the same normal duties. A person who turns down a job because the office is not provided with air conditioning, for example, is not being made worse off by the employer. So why would we say that a person who chooses to remain unemployed rather than work in a coal mine that lacks adequate ventilation is being coerced?

The answer of some philosophers is that providing employees with air conditioning is not morally required; however, maintaining a safe mine is. Whether a threat is coercive because it would make a person worse off can be determined only if there is some baseline that answers the question: Worse off compared with what? Robert Nozick gives an example of an abusive slave owner who offers not to give a slave his daily beating if the slave will perform some disagreeable task the slave owner wants to be done.[19] Even though the slave might welcome the offer, it is still coercive, because the daily beating involves treating the slave in an immoral manner. For Nozick and others, what is *morally required* is the relevant baseline for determining whether a person would be made worse off by a threatened course of action.[20]

It follows from this analysis that coercion is an inherently ethical concept that can be applied only after determining what is morally required in a given situation.[21] As a result, the argument that the assumption of risk by employees relieves employers of responsibility involves circular reasoning. Employers are freed from responsibility for workplace injuries on the ground that workers assume the risk of employment only if they are not coerced into accepting hazardous work. But whether workers are coerced depends on the right of employees to a safe and healthy workplace—and the obligation of employers to provide it.

In conclusion, the right of employees to a safe and healthy workplace cannot be justified merely by appealing to a right not to be injured or killed. The weakness of this argument lies in the difficulty of determining the extent to which employers are *responsible* for the harm that workers suffer as a result of occupational injuries and diseases. The argument applies only to dangers that are directly caused by the actions of employers; however, industrial accidents result from many causes, including the actions of coworkers and the affected workers themselves. The responsibility of employers is also problematical when the probability of harm from their actions is low. Moreover, the responsibility of employers is reduced insofar as employees voluntarily assume the risk inherent in employment. Whether the choice to accept hazardous work is voluntary, though, depends in part on difficult questions about the concept of coercion, which, on one standard analysis, can be applied only after the rights of employees in matters of occupational health and safety have been determined.

CASE 9.2 ✳ Explore the Concept on mythinkinglab.com

Whirlpool Corporation

The Whirlpool Corporation operated a plant in Marion, Ohio, for the assembly of household appliances.[22] Components for the appliances were carried throughout the plant by an elaborate system of overhead conveyors. To protect workers from the objects that fall from the conveyors, a huge wire mesh screen was installed approximately 20 feet above the floor. The screen was attached to an angle-iron frame suspended from the ceiling of the building. Maintenance employees at the plant spent several hours every week retrieving fallen objects from the screen. Their job also included replacing paper that is spread on the screen to catch dripping grease from the conveyors, and sometimes they did maintenance work on the conveyors themselves. Workers were usually able to stand on the frame to perform these tasks, but occasionally it was necessary to step onto the screen.

In 1973, several workers fell partway through the screen, and one worker fell completely through to the floor of the plant below but survived. Afterward, Whirlpool began replacing the screen with heavier wire mesh, but on June 28, 1974, a maintenance employee fell to his death through a portion of the screen that had not been replaced. The company responded by making additional repairs and forbidding employees to stand on the angle-iron frame or step onto the screen. An alternative method for retrieving objects was devised using hooks.

Two maintenance employees at the Marion plant, Virgil Deemer and Thomas Cornwell, were still not satisfied. On July 7, 1974, they met with the maintenance supervisor at the plant to express their concern about the safety of the screen. At a meeting with the plant safety director two days later, they requested the name, address, and telephone number of a representative in the local office of the Occupational Safety and Health Administration. The safety director warned the men that they "had better stop and think about what they were doing," but he gave them the requested information. Deemer called the OSHA representative later that day to discuss the problem.

When Deemer and Cornwell reported for the night shift at 10:45 p.m. the next day, July 10, they were ordered by the foreman to perform routine maintenance duties above an old section of the screen. They refused, claiming that the work was unsafe, whereupon the foreman ordered the two employees to punch out. In addition to losing wages for the six hours they did not work that night, Deemer and Cornwell received written reprimands, which were placed in their personnel files.

THE RIGHT TO KNOW ABOUT AND REFUSE HAZARDOUS WORK

The Whirlpool case illustrates a cruel dilemma faced by many American workers. If they stay on the job and perform hazardous work, they risk serious injury and even death. On the other hand, if they refuse to work as directed, they risk disciplinary action, which can include loss of wages, unfavorable evaluation, demotion, and even dismissal. Many people believe that it is unjust for workers to be put into the position of having to choose between safety and their job. Rather, employees ought to be able to refuse orders to perform hazardous work without fear of suffering adverse consequences. Even worse are situations in which workers face hazards of which they are unaware. Kept in the dark about dangers lurking in the workplace, employees have no reason to refuse hazardous work and are unable to take other steps to protect themselves.

Features of the Right to Know and Refuse

The right to refuse hazardous work is different from a right to a safe and healthy workplace. If it is unsafe to work above the old screen, as Deemer and Cornwell contended, then their right to a safe and healthy workplace was violated. A right to refuse hazardous work, however, is only one of several alternatives that workers have for securing the right to a safe and healthy workplace. Victims of racial or sexual discrimination, for example, also suffer a violation of their rights, but it does not follow that they have a right to disobey orders or to walk off the job in an effort to avoid discrimination. Other means are available for ending discrimination and for receiving compensation for the harm done. The same is true for the right to a safe and healthy workplace.

The right to know is actually an aggregation of several rights. Thomas O. McGarity classifies these rights by the correlative duties that they impose on employers. These are (1) the duty to *reveal* information already possessed; (2) the duty to *communicate* information about hazards through labeling, written communications, and training programs; (3) the duty to *seek* out existing information from the scientific literature and other sources; and (4) the duty to *produce* new information (e.g., through animal testing) relevant to employee health.[23] Advocates of the right of workers to know need to specify which of these particular rights are included in their claim.

Disagreement also arises over questions about what information workers have a right to know and which workers have a right to know it. In particular, does the information that employers have a duty to reveal include information about the past exposure of workers to hazardous substances? Do employers have a duty to notify past as well as present employees? The issue at stake in these questions is a part of the "right to know" controversy commonly called *worker notification.*

The main argument for denying workers a right to refuse hazardous work is that such a right conflicts with the obligation of employees to obey all reasonable directives from an employer. An order for a worker to perform some especially dangerous task may not be reasonable, however. The foreman in the *Whirlpool* case, for example, was acting contrary to a company rule forbidding workers to step on the screen. Still, a common-law principle is that employees should obey even an improper order and file a grievance afterward, if a grievance procedure is in place, or seek whatever other recourse is available. The rationale for this principle is that employees may be mistaken about whether an order is proper, and chaos would result if employees could stop work until the question is decided. It is better for workers to obey now and correct any violation of their rights later.

The fatal flaw in this argument is that later may be too late. The right to a safe and healthy workplace, unlike the right not to be discriminated against, can effectively provide protection for workers only if violations of the right are prevented in the first place. Debilitating injury and death cannot be corrected later; neither can workers and their families ever be adequately compensated for a loss of this kind. The right to refuse hazardous work, therefore, is necessary for the existence of the right to a safe and healthy workplace.

The Justification for Refusing Hazardous Work

A right to a safe and healthy workplace is empty unless workers have a right in some circumstances to refuse hazardous work, but there is a tremendous amount of controversy over what these circumstances are. In the *Whirlpool* case, the Supreme Court cited two factors as relevant for justifying a refusal to work. These are (1) that the employee reasonably believes that the working conditions pose an imminent risk of death or serious injury, and (2) that the employee has reason to believe that the risk cannot be avoided by any less disruptive course of action. Employees have a right to refuse hazardous work, in other words, only as a last resort—when it is not possible to bring unsafe working conditions to the attention of the employer or to request an OSHA inspection. Also, the hazards that employees believe exist must involve a high degree of risk of serious harm. Refusing to work because of a slight chance of minor injury is less likely to be justified. The fact that a number of workers had already fallen through the screen at the Whirlpool plant, for example, and that one had been killed strengthens the claim that the two employees had a right to refuse their foreman's order to step onto it.

The pivotal question, of course, is the proper standard for a reasonable belief. How much evidence should employees be required to have in order to be justified in refusing to work? Or, should the relevant standard be the actual existence of a workplace hazard rather than the belief of employees, no matter how reasonable? A minimal requirement, which has been insisted on by the courts, is that employees act in *good faith*. Generally, acting in good faith means that employees have an honest belief that a hazard exists and that their only intention is to protect themselves from the hazard. The "good-faith" requirement serves primarily to exclude refusals based on deliberately false charges of unsafe working conditions or on sabotage by employees. Whether a refusal is in good faith does not depend on the reasonableness or correctness of the employees' beliefs about the hazards in the workplace. Thus, employees who refuse an order to fill a tank with a dangerous chemical in the mistaken but sincere belief that a valve is faulty are acting in good faith, but employees who use the same excuse to conduct a work stoppage for other reasons are not acting in good faith, even if it should turn out that the valve is faulty.

THREE STANDARDS FOR REASONABLE BELIEF.   Three standards are commonly used for determining whether a good-faith refusal is based on a reasonable belief. One is the *subjective* standard, which requires only that employees have evidence that they sincerely regard as sufficient for their belief that a hazard exists or that most workers in their situation would regard as sufficient. At the opposite extreme is the *objective* standard. This standard requires evidence that experts regard as sufficient to establish the existence of a hazard. In between these two is the *reasonable person* standard, which requires that the evidence be strong enough to persuade a reasonable person that a hazard exists.

The subjective standard provides the greatest protection for worker health and safety. Employees cannot be expected to have full knowledge of the hazards facing them in the workplace. They may not be told what chemicals they are using, for example, or what exposure levels are safe for these chemicals. Safe exposure levels for the chemicals may not even have been scientifically determined. Employees may also not have the means at the moment to measure the levels to which they are exposed. Yet, the objective standard forces employees to bear the consequences if their beliefs about the hazards present in the workplace cannot be substantiated. The reasonable person standard is less exacting, because it requires only that employees exercise reasonable judgment. Still, this standard places a strong burden of proof on workers who have to make a quick assessment under difficult circumstances. A wrong decision can result in the loss of a job or possibly the loss of a worker's life.

On the other hand, the subjective standard allows employees to make decisions that are ordinarily the province of management. Management is usually better informed about hazards in the workplace, along with other aspects of the work to be performed, and so its judgment should generally prevail. To allow workers to shut down production on the basis of unsubstantiated beliefs, and thereby to substitute their uninformed judgment for that of management, is likely to result in many costly mistakes. The subjective standard creates no incentive for workers to be cautious in refusing hazardous work because the cost is borne solely by the company. The reasonable person standard, therefore, which places a moderate burden of proof on employees, is perhaps the best balance of the competing considerations.

The Justification of a Right to Know

Unlike the right to refuse hazardous work, the right to know about workplace hazards is not necessary for the right to a safe and healthy workplace. This latter right is fully protected as long as employers succeed in ridding the workplace of significant hazards. Some argue that the right to know is still an effective, if not an absolutely essential, means for securing the right to a safe and healthy workplace. Others maintain, however, that the right to know is not dependent for its justification on the right to a safe and healthy workplace; that is, even employees who are adequately protected by their employers against occupational injury and disease still have a right to be told what substances they are handling, what dangers they pose, what precautions to take, and so on.

THE ARGUMENT FROM AUTONOMY. The most common argument for the right to know is one based on autonomy. This argument begins with the premise that autonomous individuals are those who are able to exercise free choice in matters that affect their welfare most deeply.[24] Sometimes this premise is expressed by saying that autonomous individuals are those who are able to *participate* in decision making about these matters. One matter that profoundly affects the welfare of workers is the amount of risk that they assume in the course of earning a living. Autonomy requires, therefore, that workers be free to avoid hazardous work, if they so choose, or have the opportunity to accept greater risks in return for higher pay, if that is their choice. In order to choose freely, however, or to participate in decision making, it is necessary to possess relevant information. In the matter of risk assumption, the relevant information includes knowledge of the hazards present in the workplace. Workers can be autonomous, therefore, only if they have a right to know.

In response, employers maintain that they can protect workers from hazards more effectively than workers can themselves, without informing workers of the nature of those hazards. Such a paternalistic concern, even when it is sincere and well-founded, is incompatible, however, with a respect for the autonomy of workers. A similar argument is sometimes used to justify paternalism in the doctor–patient relationship. For a doctor to conceal information from a patient even in cases where exclusive reliance on the doctor's greater training and experience would result in better medical care is now generally regarded as unjustified. If paternalism is morally unacceptable in the doctor–patient relationship where doctors have an obligation to act in the patient's interest, then it is all the more suspect in the employer–employee relationship where employers have no such obligation.[25]

Although autonomy is a value, it does not follow that employers have an obligation to further it in their dealings with employees. The autonomy of buyers in market transactions is also increased by having more information, but the sellers of a product are not generally required to provide this information except when concealment constitutes fraud.[26] The gain of autonomy for employees must be balanced, moreover, against the not inconsiderable cost to employers of implementing a "right to know" policy in the workplace. In addition to the direct cost of assembling information, attaching warning labels, training workers, and so on, there are also indirect costs. Employees who are aware of the risk they are taking are more likely to demand either higher wages or safer working conditions. They are more likely to avail themselves of workers' compensation benefits and to sue employers over occupational injury and disease. Finally, companies are concerned about the loss of valuable trade secrets that could occur from informing workers about the hazards of certain substances.

BARGAINING OVER INFORMATION.   An alternative to a right-to-know policy that respects the autonomy of both parties is to allow bargaining over information. Since acquiring information involves some cost, the employees must be willing to pay for it. However, economic theory suggests that employees would be willing to pay, perhaps in reduced wages, for any information that would protect them in the workplace as long as the benefit exceeds the cost.

Although promising in theory, this alternative is not practical. It creates a disincentive for employers, who possess most of the information, to yield any of it without some concession by employees, even when it could be provided at little or no cost. Bargaining is feasible for large unions with expertise in safety matters, but reliance on it would leave members of other unions and nonunionized workers without adequate means of protection. In the absence of a market for information, neither employers nor employees would have a basis for determining the value of information in advance of negotiations. Finally, there are costs associated with using the bargaining process to decide any matter—what economists call "transaction costs"—and these are apt to be quite high in negotiations over safety issues. It is unlikely, therefore, that either autonomy or worker health and safety would be well served by the alternative of bargaining over matters of occupational health and safety.

UTILITARIAN ARGUMENTS FOR A RIGHT TO KNOW   There are two arguments for the right to know as a means to greater worker health and safety. Both are broadly utilitarian in character. One argument is based on the plausible assumption that workers who are aware of hazards in the workplace will be better equipped to protect themselves. Warning labels or rules requiring protective clothing and respirators are more likely to be effective when workers fully appreciate the nature and extent of the risks they are taking. Also, merely revealing information about hazardous substances in the workplace is not apt to be effective without extensive training in the procedures for handling them safely and responding to accidents. Finally, workers who are aware of the consequences of exposure to hazardous substances will also be more likely to spot symptoms of occupational diseases and seek early treatment.

The second utilitarian argument is offered by economists who hold that overall welfare is best achieved by allowing market forces to determine the level of acceptable risk. In a free market, wages are determined in part by the willingness of workers to accept risks in return for wages. Employers can attract a sufficient supply of workers to perform hazardous work either by spending money to make the workplace safer, thereby reducing the risks, or by increasing wages to compensate workers for the greater risks. The choice is determined by the marginal utility of each kind of investment. Thus, an employer will make the workplace safer up to the point that the last dollar spent equals the increase in wages that would otherwise be required to induce workers to accept the risks. At that point, workers indicate their preference for accepting the remaining risks rather than suffering a loss of wages in return for a safer workplace.

Unlike the autonomy argument, in which workers bargain over risk information, this argument proposes that workers bargain over the trade-off between risks and wages. In order for a free market to determine this trade-off in a way that achieves overall welfare, it is necessary for workers to have a sufficient amount of information about the hazards in the workplace. To the extent that workers lack this information, they will undervalue the risks they face and accept lower wages, which in turn will create no incentive for employers to increase the level of safety. The end result, according to Thomas O. McGarity, will be a loss of wealth as society covers the cost of more disease and injury.[27]

Although these two utilitarian arguments provide strong support for the right to know, they are both open to the objection that there might be more efficient means, such as more extensive OSHA regulation, for securing the goal of worker health and safety. Could the resources devoted to complying with a right-to-know law, for example, be better spent on formulating and enforcing more stringent standards on permissible exposure limits and on developing technologies to achieve these standards? Could the cost of producing, gathering, and disseminating information be better borne by a government agency than by individual employers? These are difficult empirical questions for which conclusive evidence is largely lacking.

The Problem of Trade Secrets

One issue that remains to be addressed is the protection of trade secrets. Occasionally, information about the chemical composition of the substances used in industrial processes cannot be disclosed to workers without compromising the ability of a company to maintain a legally protected trade secret. When this is the case, is it justifiable to place limits on the right to know? These two rights—the right of workers to know about the hazards of substances that they use and the right of employers to maintain trade secrets—are not wholly incompatible, however. So it may be possible to implement the right to know in a way that maximizes the amount of information available to workers while at the same time minimizing the risk of exposing trade secrets.

Before limiting the right of employees to know, we need to be sure, first, that a genuine trade secret is involved and that it cannot be protected by any less restrictive means, such as obtaining a patent. Also, employers do not have a right to conceal *all* information connected with a trade secret but only the portion that cannot be revealed without jeopardy. Even when an employer is justified in not disclosing the chemical identity of a critical ingredient in a formula or a process, for example, there may be no justification for not providing workers with information about some of the physical characteristics and special hazards of that ingredient. Finally, information can sometimes be revealed in ways that preserve secrecy. It might be possible, for example, to reveal information about hazardous substances to union representatives or to the employees' own private physicians under a pledge of confidentiality without endangering valuable trade secrets.

CASE 9.3 ✳ Explore the Concept on mythinkinglab.com

Johnson Controls, Inc.

Based in Milwaukee, Wisconsin, Johnson Controls was the largest manufacturer of automobile batteries for the U.S. replacement market.[28] Known chiefly for the production of control instruments for heating, lighting, and other electrical functions, Johnson Controls was also the largest independent supplier of automobile seating, and the company provided many small components for cars and light trucks. In 1978, Johnson Controls purchased Globe Union, Inc., a battery manufacturer. By 1990, the Globe Battery Division of Johnson Controls was operating 14 plants nationwide and employed approximately 5,400 people. Batteries accounted for roughly 18 percent of Johnson Controls' sales and 17 percent of operating income.

Lead plates, which are essential for an automobile battery, are formed by compressing a paste of lead oxide. In this process, lead dust and lead vapor are released into the work area. Lead has been known for centuries to cause extensive neurological damage, and recent studies have shown that it affects the body's cardiovascular system, leading to heart attacks and strokes. Children who are exposed to lead, through eating peeling lead-based paint, for example, exhibit hyperactivity, short attention span, and learning difficulties. Lead in a pregnant woman's bloodstream can affect the neurological development of an unborn child, resulting in mental retardation, impaired motor control, and behavioral abnormalities. Pregnant women exposed to lead also run an increased risk of spontaneous abortion, miscarriage, and stillbirth. Although the effects of lead on men are less well understood, studies have shown some genetic damage to sperm that might cause birth defects.

Prior to Johnson Controls' purchase of Globe Union, the battery manufacturer had instituted a comprehensive program to minimize lead exposure in the workplace and to keep employees from carrying lead home on their bodies and clothing. Although no legal standards for lead exposure existed at the time, Globe Union routinely tested employees' blood lead levels and transferred employees with readings of 50 µg/dl of blood to other jobs without loss of pay until their levels had dropped to 30 µg/dl. In 1978, the Occupational Safety and Health Administration (OSHA) set a permissible exposure limit for lead of 50 micrograms per deciliter of blood (µg/dl). OSHA did not establish a separate standard for pregnant women but recommended that both men and women who planned to conceive maintain blood levels below 30 µg/dl. OSHA concluded that there is no reason to exclude women of childbearing age from jobs involving lead exposure.

In 1977, as more women began working in battery production, Globe Union informed women employees of the hazards of lead and asked them to sign a statement that they had been told of the risks of having a child while exposed to lead in the workplace. Between 1979 and 1983, after Johnson Controls acquired Globe Union, eight women with blood lead levels in excess of 30 µg/dl became pregnant. In response, Johnson Controls changed its policy in 1982 to exclude fertile women from all jobs where lead is present. Specifically, the policy stated, "It is [Johnson Controls'] policy that women who are pregnant or who are capable of bearing children will not be placed into jobs involving lead exposure or which could expose them to lead through the exercise of job bidding, bumping, transfer or promotion rights." The policy defined women "capable of bearing children" as "all women except those whose inability to bear children is medically documented." In defending this policy, Johnson Controls maintained that a voluntary approach had failed and that to permit lead poisoning of unborn children was "morally reprehensible." Undoubtedly, the company was also concerned with its legal liability.

In April 1984, a class-action suit was filed by several workers and their union, the United Auto Workers, charging that Johnson Controls' fetal-protection policy violated the Title VII prohibition against sex discrimination. The policy is discriminatory, the employees complained, because it singled out fertile women for exclusion, when evidence indicates that lead also poses a hazard to the reproductive capacities of men. Although Title VII permits exceptions for bona fide occupational qualifications (BFOQs), the inability to bear children has no relevance to the job of making a battery and therefore cannot be a legitimate BFOQ. Johnson Controls' fetal-protection policy applied to women who had no intention of becoming pregnant and those who might choose to accept the risk for the sake of keeping their jobs. The policy also offered women a choice of becoming sterile or losing their job, which some regarded as coercive. Among the employees suing were a woman who had chosen to be sterilized in order to keep her job, a 50-year-old divorcée who had been forced to accept a demotion because of the policy, and a man who had requested a leave of absence in order to reduce his blood lead level before becoming a father.

THE PROBLEM OF REPRODUCTIVE HAZARDS

The problem of reproductive hazards puts companies such as Johnson Controls in a very difficult position. On one hand, fetal-protection policies are open to the charge of being discriminatory because they limit the job opportunities of fertile women while ignoring the substantial evidence of risk to men. Employees also claim that the policies are adopted by employers as a quick and cheap alternative to cleaning up the workplace. On the other hand, employers have a responsibility not to inflict harm, and this obligation extends, presumably, to the fetus of a pregnant employee. Asking employees to sign waivers releasing a company from responsibility is no solution, however, because employees cannot waive the right of their future children to sue for prenatal injuries. Employers seem to face a choice, therefore, between discriminating against their female employees and allowing fetuses to be harmed, with potentially ruinous consequences for the company.

The Issue of Who Decides

A number of employers have resolved this dilemma by adopting fetal-protection policies similar to that of Johnson Controls. However, many women are claiming the right to decide for themselves whether to work at jobs that involve reproductive risks. Although they have a strong maternal interest in the health of an unborn child, they are also concerned about their own economic well-being and want to be free to choose the level of risk to themselves and their offspring that they feel is appropriate. With regard to the problem of reproductive hazards, the usual positions of employers and employees have been reversed. Typically, workers have been more concerned than companies to respond quickly to new evidence of hazards. On fetal protection, however, business has taken an almost alarmist posture, whereas labor has urged a go-slow approach.[29]

This reversal is not hard to understand. Protecting unborn children from harmful chemicals in the workplace and coping with the consequences of occupationally related birth defects involve substantial costs. The struggle between employers and employees is over who will exercise the choice about assuming the risk of reproductive hazards and who will bear the burden of responsibility. Fetal-protection policies are adopted by corporate managers who assume the right to make crucial decisions about how the fetus of an employee will be protected. The cost of these decisions is borne largely by women, however, who find that their economic opportunities are sharply limited. According to estimates by the federal government in 1980, at least 100,000 jobs were closed to women because of fetal-protection policies already in place,[30] and as many as 20 million jobs would be closed if women were excluded from all work involving reproductive hazards.[31] The women most affected by the reduction in the number of jobs available are those with the fewest skills and the least education, who are already near the bottom of the economic ladder. Because they bear the heavy cost, women argue that they should be the ones to make the decisions involved in protecting their own offspring.

Are Women Forced to Undergo Sterilization?

The debate over fetal-protection policies takes on a tragic dimension when women undergo sterilization for fear of losing a job. When five women were laid off by the Allied Chemical Company in 1977 because of concern for fetal damage by a substance known as Fluorocarbon 22, two of them underwent surgical sterilization in order to return to work. Shortly afterward, the company determined that Fluorocarbon 22 posed no threat to a developing fetus, so the women's loss of fertility was needless.[32] When the American Cyanamid Company announced the adoption of a fetal-protection policy at a plant in Willow Island, West Virginia, in 1978, five women between the ages of 26 and 43 submitted to sterilization in order to retain jobs that involved exposure to lead chromate, an ingredient of paint pigments. Two years later, American Cyanamid stopped producing paint pigments because of a decreased demand for the lead-based product.[33]

Certainly, no person, man or woman, should be put in the position of having to choose between holding a job and being able to bear children unless there is no acceptable alternative. Employers insist that they do not encourage women to take the drastic step of undergoing sterilization, but they also maintain that they have no control over such an intimate decision by employees or women seeking employment and that there is no reason to exclude women who undergo sterilization from jobs involving exposure to reproductive hazards. According to critics of fetal-protection policies, however, companies that exclude fertile women from such jobs effectively force sterilization on those who have no other satisfactory employment opportunities. The problem is one of intentions versus results. Although there is no intention to force women to become sterile, employers create situations that precisely have this result.

Issues in the Charge of Sex Discrimination

Whether employers have a right to adopt fetal-protection policies depends in part on whether excluding fertile women from certain jobs is a form of sex discrimination. The point at issue is not whether women are vulnerable to reproductive hazards (they certainly are), but whether men are vulnerable as well. If they are, then it is discriminatory for employers to adopt a policy that applies only to women and not to men. In order to evaluate the scientific evidence, it is necessary to understand more about the nature of reproductive hazards.

THE SCIENTIFIC BACKGROUND.   Substances harmful to a fetus are of three kinds. First, there are *fetotoxins*. These are toxic substances that affect a fetus in the same way that they affect an adult, although a fetus, because of the smaller size, may be harmed by exposure to substances below the permissible limits for adults. *Teratogens*, the second group of substances, interfere with the normal development of the fetus in utero. These may pose no danger to a fully developed person outside the womb. Finally, some substances are *mutagens*, which damage genetic material before conception. The effects of fetotoxins, teratogens, and mutagens are similar. They include spontaneous abortion, miscarriage, stillbirth, and congenital defects. Some defects, such as deformities, are visible at birth, whereas others may be latent conditions that manifest themselves later, as in the case of childhood cancers.

Fetotoxins and teratogens (many substances are both) must be transmitted to the fetus through the mother. This can occur, however, when the father is exposed to a hazardous substance in the workplace. Studies show that the nonworking wives of men exposed to lead, beryllium, benzene, vinyl chloride, and anesthetic gases, for example, have higher-than-normal rates of miscarriage. Children of fathers exposed to asbestos and benzene are shown in studies to have a greater incidence of cancer. The most likely explanation for these correlations is that the hazardous substances are brought home on the father's body or on his clothing and other belongings.

The main reproductive hazard to men is posed by mutagenic substances, because these are capable of altering the chromosomal structure of both the ovum and the sperm. Although the mutagenic effect of many suspected substances is not firmly established, some researchers theorize that most teratogens are also mutagens and that there is a strong connection between the three phenomena: teratogenesis, mutagenesis, and carcinogenesis (i.e., the development of cancers). The reason is that all three operate on the cellular level by altering the DNA molecule.[34] If these relationships exist, then virtually any substance that poses a reproductive hazard to a woman is also hazardous to the reproductive capacity of a man and ultimately the health of a fetus.

ARE FETAL-PROTECTION POLICIES DISCRIMINATORY?   The research on reproductive hazards, although inconclusive, suggests that fetal harm can result when either parent is exposed to hazardous substances. If that is in fact the case, then fetal-protection policies should apply to both sexes. Wendy W. Williams argues, "There is simply no basis for resolving doubts about the evidence by applying a policy to women but not to men on the unsubstantiated generalization that the fetus is placed at greatest risk by workplace exposure of the pregnant woman."[35]

Fetal-protection policies are also discriminatory if they are applied only to women who occupy traditionally male jobs and not to women in female-dominated lines of work where the hazard is just as great. Some critics charge that fetal-protection policies have been used to discriminate by reinforcing job segregation through their selective application to women with jobs in areas formerly dominated by men, whereas the reproductive risks to other women have been ignored.

American Cyanamid, for example, identified five substances in use at the Willow Island plant as suspected fetotoxins and notified 23 women in production jobs that they were exposed to reproductive hazards and would be transferred if they became pregnant. However, the fetal-protection policy was applied only to the nine women who held comparatively high-paying jobs in the paint pigments department, which had formerly been reserved for men. Barbara Cantwell, one of the four women who submitted to sterilization in order to retain her job, remarked, "I smelled harassment when the problem was suddenly narrowed to the area where women worked."[36]

Among the women in traditionally female lines of work who are exposed to reproductive hazards are nurses in operating rooms, who have twice as many miscarriages as other women because of anesthetic gases; female X-ray technicians, who are twice as likely to bear defective children; and women who work in dry-cleaning operations, where petroleum-based solvents are used.[37] Yet there has been no movement in the industries employing these women to implement fetal-protection policies similar to those in the male-dominated chemical, petroleum, and heavy-manufacturing industries.

Defenses to the Charge of Sex Discrimination

Distinctions based on sex are not always discriminatory. They are morally permissible if they have an adequate justification, and Title VII of the 1964 Civil Rights Act recognizes this by allowing employers two defenses. These are the claims that a sex-based policy serves a proper business purpose (the business necessity defense) and that a person's sex is a bona fide occupational qualification (the BFOQ defense). A BFOQ is defined as a qualification "reasonably necessary to the normal operation" of a business. As we saw in Chapter 7 on discrimination, this exception has been narrowly limited by the courts. The business necessity defense is less stringent. Generally, an employer must establish that a policy is needed for achieving a proper business objective in a safe and efficient manner and that the objective cannot reasonably be achieved by less discriminatory means.

The lower courts ruled that the fetal-protection policy adopted by Johnson Controls was permissible under Title VII. The Court of Appeals for the Seventh Circuit held that the policy passed a three-step business necessity defense because the company had established (1) there is a substantial risk to a fetus; (2) this risk occurs only through women; and (3) there is no less discriminatory alternative. Although not required to do so, the court addressed the question of whether sex is a BFOQ in this case and concluded that it is. The crucial phrase in the BFOQ defense, "reasonably necessary for the normal operation" of a business, has been interpreted by the courts to include "ethical, legal, and business concerns about the effects of an employer's activities on third parties." Simply put, a qualification is a BFOQ if it is necessary for conducting business without greatly endangering other people. Under this interpretation, the courts had ruled that age was a BFOQ for being an airline flight engineer because the safety of passengers depended on that person's performance.[38] By the same line of reasoning, sex is a BFOQ because a woman working in a battery factory is liable to expose a third party—namely, a fetus—to harm.

The U.S. Supreme Court, in a landmark 9–0 decision, overruled the lower courts and held Johnson Controls' fetal-protection policy to be discriminatory in violation of Title VII. The policy is discriminatory for reason that it excludes women based only on their childbearing capacity and ignores the risk to men. Thus, the policy does not protect "effectively and equally" the offspring of all employees. Further, the Court ruled that sex is not a BFOQ in this case. All evidence indicates that fertile and even pregnant women are as capable of manufacturing batteries as anyone else. According to the unanimous opinion, the claim that the safety of third parties ought to be taken into consideration is inapplicable because this exception concerns only the ability of an employee to perform a job in a safe manner, and a fetus, in this case, is not endangered by the manner in which the job is performed. The workers at Johnson Controls, in other words, are not manufacturing batteries in ways that are unsafe for children. "No one can disregard the possibility of injury to future children," the opinion states, but the BFOQ defense "is not so broad that it transforms this deep social concern into an essential aspect of batterymaking."[39]

Remaining Issues

The decision in *Johnson Controls* clearly establishes that fetal-protection policies constitute illegal sex discrimination, and the ruling is a victory for working women. It gives women the right not to have their job opportunities limited because of their ability to conceive and bear children. Still, two important issues remain. One is how to balance this right with the desirable social goal of fetal protection. The other is whether the right established in *Johnson Controls* conflicts with another desirable goal, namely, protecting corporations against liability in the event that a person is harmed before birth from exposure to reproductive hazards in the workplace.

The ruling in *Johnson Controls* does not leave the unborn without protection. In the words of the Court, "Decisions about the welfare of future children must be left to the parents who conceive, bear, support, and raise them rather than to the employers who hire those parents." There is little reason to believe that employees are any less concerned than employers about the well-being of their offspring. Indeed, they have a far more compelling interest. This is not to say that some parents-to-be (both men and women) will not continue to choose work that exposes them to reproductive hazards. However, they, rather than their employers, will be making the crucial decision about the reasonableness of that choice. Employees may decide—all things considered—that the risk is worth the price. Parents also choose where to live with their children, thereby deciding whether they can afford to live farther away from sources of pollution and other hazards. Because parents in our society make choices in other matters that bear on the welfare of their children, why should an exception be made in the case of reproductive hazards? What is unfortunate is that any parents are required to choose between making a living and protecting their children.

Whether the *Johnson Controls* ruling exposes corporations to heavy tort liability is an open question. The view expressed in the Court's opinion is that the prospect is "remote at best," provided that employers (1) fully inform employees of the risks they face and (2) do not act negligently. If employees are to make rational choices in cases of exposure to reproductive hazards, then they must have sufficient information, which employers have an obligation to provide. Employers can protect themselves from suits by cleaning up the workplace and reducing the risk as much as possible. The issue of tort liability, then, is hypothetical but nonetheless important for that reason.

Conclusion

This chapter shows that workers have a right to a safe and healthy workplace and that employers have a moral and, in many cases, a legal obligation to secure this right. The controversial questions concern two matters: What is the morally required level of health and safety, and how this level can be achieved? Increasing the level of health and safety usually involves trade-offs with other goods, including higher wages for employees and greater profits for employers. The commonly accepted standard for making such trade-offs is cost–benefit analysis, in which the benefits of increased workplace protection are balanced against the costs. In general, employees, employers, and society at large are best served when cost-effective decisions are made. However, the rights to know about and refuse hazardous work and the problem of reproductive hazards raise the different issue of the extent to which employees should be involved in protecting themselves. Not only may a right to employee involvement in matters of health and safety be morally justified, but such involvement may also be an effective means for achieving workplace health and safety that complements the protections offered by employers.

CASE 9.4 ✳ Explore the Concept on mythinkinglab.com

Genetic Testing at Burlington Northern

Gary Avary, a 45-year-old track and maintenance worker for the Burlington Northern Santa Fe Railroad (BNSF), returned to work in October 2000 after successfully undergoing surgery for carpel tunnel syndrome (CTS).[40] A few days later the railroad's medical department requested all records of his treatment for CTS, and in December he was asked to report for a mandatory medical examination that would include blood tests. When his wife, a registered nurse, inquired about the need for blood, she inadvertently learned that a genetics test was included. Gary Avary was subsequently told that if he did not submit to the test, he would be fired.

The previous March, BNSF had introduced a policy of secret genetic testing of workers with CTS in order to determine whether any of them has a DNA defect known as Chromosome 17 deletion. This was thought to be associated with a condition called Hereditary Neuropathy with liability to Pressure Palsies (HNPP), which can make a person susceptible to nerve injuries, including CTS. HNPP is a rare condition that is estimated to occur in one in every 2,500 people.[41] Although approximately 90 percent of people with HNPP develop CTS, this defect can scarcely begin to account for the vast majority of CTS cases, especially among railroad workers whose lives have been spent in bone-jarring labor.

Gary Avary's union filed a suit, charging that BNSF had tested or had sought to test 36 employees who had filed claims for job-related CTS.[42] The suit was based on the Americans with Disabilities Act (ADA), which reads in part, "Medical examinations of existing employees must be job-related and consistent with business necessity." The company claimed, however, that the testing was a matter of business necessity. Injuries to railroad workers are subject to a 1908 law, the Federal Employers Liability Act (FELA), which allows jury trials. Because of the heavy potential liability, BNSF claimed that it has a right to defend itself, especially if the injury is due to genetic rather than workplace factors. In the words of the company's general counsel: "Any time an employee comes to us and says, 'I have an injury, and it's your fault,' we have a right to request and conduct the medical examination."[43]

Critics of BNSF's genetic testing discount this business necessity defense. First, the connection between Chromosome 17 deletion and CTS is not scientifically established and thus would probably not be admissible as evidence in any trial under FELA. Second, according to critics, the real aim of the railroad was to discourage any injured employee from bringing a suit. An attorney for the union observed, "They show a guy a piece of paper that says, 'This is your genetic test, and this condition wasn't caused from your work,' and they hope he will believe them."[44] Many of the affected employees had no more than a seventh-grade education, and some did not speak English, making it more likely that they would accept the company's claims.

Few employers will admit to genetic testing. A study conducted by the American Management Association in 2001 found only two among the 1,627 companies surveyed, although 16 percent said that they performed some medical tests to determine employees' susceptibility to workplace hazards.[45] One company, Brush Wellman, which tested prospective employees for a genetic condition that increases the danger of exposure to beryllium, did not look at the results but gave them to the applicants so that they could decide for themselves whether to accept employment.[46] Although Brush Wellman thought that this was an innovative approach, critics question the value of this information if it is not based on valid science and if job applicants lack the ability to understand the risks. The result may be only unfounded fears.

In April 2001, Burlington Northern settled the suit by agreeing to halt genetic testing and to pay 36 employees $2.2 million. The settlement short-circuited an opportunity for the courts to rule on whether genetic testing is prohibited by the ADA. Approximately half of the states have passed laws governing genetic testing, although their effectiveness is questionable; President Clinton issued an executive order banning genetic testing of federal employees; but none of the many bills introduced in the U.S. Congress has secured passage. As science and technology advance, the issue of genetic testing is sure to become more pressing.

Notes

1. Information for this case is taken from David Barstow, "A Trench Caves In; A Young Worker Is Dead: Is It a Crime?" *New York Times*, 21 December 2003, A1.

2. The estimate is made in William J. Nicholson, "Failure to Regulate—Asbestos: A Lethal Legacy," U.S. Congress, Committee of Government Operations, 1980.

3. Much of the following description of health and safety problems is adapted from Nicholas Askounes Ashford, *Crisis in the Workplace: Occupational Disease and Injury* (Cambridge, MA: MIT Press, 1976), chap. 3.

4. For a review of the controversy that discredits the industry claim, see Robert H. Hall, "The Truth about Brown Lung," *Business and Society Review*, 40 (Winter 1981), 15–20.

5. For a critical assessment of state efforts, see Joseph A. Page and Mary-Win O'Brien, *Bitter Wages* (New York: Grossman, 1973), 69–85.

6. Sec. 5(a)(1). This clause is the subject of much legal analysis. See Richard S. Morley, "The General Duty Clause of the Occupational Safety and Health Act of 1970," *Harvard Law Review*, 86 (1973), 988–1005.

7. Patricia H. Werhane, *Persons, Rights, and Corporations* (Upper Saddle River, NJ: Prentice Hall, 1985), 132.

8. Mark MacCarthy, "A Review of Some Normative and Conceptual Issues in Occupational Safety and Health," *Environmental Affairs*, 9 (1981), 782–83.

9. These two factors are discussed by Alan Gewirth, who cites them as exceptions to his claim that persons have a right not to have cancer inflicted on them by the actions of others. See Alan Gewirth, "Human Rights and the Prevention of Cancer," in *Human Rights: Essays on Justification and Applications* (Chicago, IL: University of Chicago Press, 1982), 181–96. For an evaluation, see Eric Von Magnus,

"Rights and Risks," *Journal of Business Ethics*, 2 (February 1983), 23–26.

10. See H. L. A. Hart and A. M. Honoré, *Causation in the Law* (Oxford: Oxford University Press, 1959), 64–76.

11. U.S. Code 21, 348(c) (3).

12. *Federal Register*, 39, no. 20 (29 January 1974), 3758. Emphasis added.

13. Gewirth, "Human Rights and the Prevention of Cancer," 189.

14. *AFL-CIO v. American Petroleum Institute*, 448 U.S. 607 (1980).

15. *American Textile Manufacturers Institute Inc. v. Raymond J. Donovan, Secretary of Labor*, 452 U.S. 490 (1981).

16. For an argument of this kind, see Tibor R. Machan, "Human Rights, Workers' Rights, and the Right to Occupational Safety," in *Moral Rights in the Workplace*, ed. Gertrude Ezorsky (Albany, NY: State University of New York Press, 1987), 45–50.

17. W. Kip Viscusi, *Risk by Choice* (Cambridge, MA: Harvard University Press, 1983), 80.

18. The following argument is adapted from Norman Daniels, "Does OSHA Protect Too Much?" in *Moral Rights in the Workplace,* ed. Ezorsky, 51–60.

19. Robert Nozick, "Coercion," in *Philosophy, Science and Method*, ed. Sidney Morgenbesser, Patrick Suppes, and Morton White (New York: St. Martin's Press, 1969), 440–72.

20. In considering whether a person voluntarily chooses undesirable work when all of the alternatives are even worse as a result of the actions of other people, Nozick says that the answer "depends upon whether these others had the right to act as they did." Robert Nozick, *Anarchy, State, and Utopia* (New York: Basic Books, 1974), 262.

21. Some philosophers have attempted to give a morally neutral analysis of coercion that involves no assumptions about what is morally required. See David Zimmerman, "Coercive Wage Offers," *Philosophy and Public Affairs*, 10 (1981), 121–45.

22. Information on this case is contained in *Whirlpool Corporation v. Marshall*, 445 U.S. 1 (1980).

23. Thomas O. McGarity, "The New OSHA Rules and the Worker's Right to Know," *The Hastings Center Report*, 14 (August 1984), 38–39.

24. For a version of this argument, see ibid. Much of the following discussion of the autonomy argument is adapted from this article.

25. This point is made in Ruth R. Faden and Tom L. Beauchamp, "The Right to Risk Information and the Right to Refuse Health Hazards in the Workplace," in *Ethical Theory and Business* , 7th ed., ed. Tom L. Beauchamp and Norman E. Bowie (Upper Saddle River, NJ: Prentice Hall, 204), 204–11.

26. This exception suggests a further argument for the right to know based on fairness. Employers who knowingly place workers at risk are taking unfair advantage of the workers' ignorance. See McGarity, "The New OSHA Rules and the Worker's Right to Know," 40.

27. Ibid., 41.

28. This case is based on *United Automobile Workers et al. v. Johnson Controls, Inc.*, 449 U.S. 187, 111 S.Ct. 1196 (1991). Other sources include Linda Greenhouse, "Court Backs Right of Women to Jobs with Health Risks," *New York Times*, 21 March 1991, A1; Stephen Wermiel, "Justices Bar

'Fetal Protection' Policies," *Wall Street Journal*, 21 March 1991, B1; and Anne T. Lawrence, "Johnson Controls and Protective Exclusion from the Workplace," *Case Research Journal*, 13 (1993), 1–14.

29. This point is made in Ronald Bayer, "Women, Work, and Reproductive Hazards," *The Hastings Center Report*, 12 (October 1982), 14–19.

30. Wendy W. Williams, "Firing the Woman to Protect the Fetus: The Reconciliation of Fetal Protection with Employment Opportunity Goals under Title VII," *The Georgetown Law Journal*, 69 (1981), 647.

31. Equal Employment Opportunity Commission and Office of Federal Contract Compliance Programs, "Interpretive Guidelines on Employment Discrimination and Reproductive Hazards," *Federal Register*, 1 February 1980, 7514.

32. Gail Bronson, "Issue of Fetal Damage Stirs Women Workers at Chemical Plants," *Wall Street Journal*, 9 February 1979, A1.

33. "Company and Union in Dispute as Women Undergo Sterilization," *New York Times*, 4 January 1979, A1; "Four Women Assert Jobs Were Linked to Sterilization," *New York Times*, 5 January 1979, A1; Philip Shabecoff, "Job Threats to Workers' Fertility Emerging as Civil Liberties Issue," *New York Times*, 15 January 1979, A1; and Bronson, "Issue of Fetal Damage Stirs Women Workers at Chemical Plants."

34. See Williams, "Firing the Woman to Protect the Fetus," 659–60.

35. Ibid., 663.

36. Cited in Bronson, "Issue of Fetal Damage Stirs Women Workers at Chemical Plants."

37. These examples are cited in Lois Vanderwaerdt, "Resolving the Conflict between Hazardous Substances in the Workplace and Equal Employment Opportunity," *American Business Law Journal*, 21 (1983), 172–73.

38. *Western Airlines v. Criswell*, 472 U.S. 400 (1985).

39. The Supreme Court did not consider the business necessity defense, because only the BFOQ defense was held to be applicable in this case. The reason is that the fetal-protection policy adopted by Johnson Controls was considered by the Court to be "facial" discrimination, which is to say that a distinction was made explicitly on the basis of sex, and "facial" discrimination requires the more demanding BFOQ defense rather than the weaker business necessity defense.

40. U.S. House of Representatives, Committee on Education and the Workforce, Subcommittee on Employer–Employee Relations, Testimony of Mr. Gary Avary, 24 July 2001.

41. http://www.hnpp.org/whatis.htm, last visited 8 January 2005.

42. *EEOC v. Burlington Northern Santa Fe Railroad Co.*, No. C01-4013 (N.D. Iowa, filed 9 February 2001).

43. David Rubenstein, "Burlington Northern Discovers a Third Rail: Burned by a Genetic Test," *Corporate Legal Times*, July 2001, 68.

44. Ibid.

45. Darryl van Duch, "EEOC Goes After Genetic Testing," *National Law Journal*, 7 May 2001, B1.

46. Karen Long, "Can Genes Cost You Your Job? Experts Ponder the Ethics of Genetic Tests in Workplace," *Cleveland Plain Dealer*, 16 December 2001, *Sunday Life*, p. L1.

Marketing, Advertising, and Product Safety

CASE 10.1 ✳─ **Explore** the **Concept** on **mythinkinglab.com**

Selling Hope

In 1986, an outdoor billboard in a depressed community on the west side of Chicago offered hope. The message was, "Your way out." The promised ticket for these desperately poor people? The Illinois state lottery.[1] Although most lottery advertising is less blunt, the appeal of a life-changing event is a common theme. Although many consumer products are promoted as the fulfillment of people's deepest longings, state lotteries cruelly disappoint all but a few lucky winners. Still, as one New York state ad declared, "Hey, you never know."

Lotteries are a big business for the 43 states (plus the District of Columbia) that operate them.[2] These games produce approximately $34 billion in revenue, which, after an average payout of 55 percent, leaves more than $15 billion, less expenses, for state coffers. Among the expenses are approximately $400 million that are spent on marketing, which is necessary for the lotteries' success. As one lottery official explained, "To survive and prosper, it is essential that lotteries practice the business techniques of the private sector, particularly in the area of marketing."[3]

Lotteries present a marketing challenge. As a legal monopoly, they have no competitors, and so they cannot attract consumers away from competing brands, which is a major aim of much advertising. This leaves two objectives: recruiting new players and encouraging existing players to increase their activity. Lottery advertising focuses mainly on the latter, inducing confirmed gamblers to play more games and spend more money on each one. Marketing begins with the development of a product mix because different games appeal to different groups. Marketers regularly develop new games with different features, such as the number and size of the payouts, the degree of complexity, and the length of time (from instant scratch cards and daily numbers to months-long, high-jackpot lotteries).

To aid them in product development and advertising, marketers use focus groups, telephone surveys, and other research tools to learn people's preferences and responses to proposed games. They also engage in target marketing by identifying specific demographic groups and learning which are more likely to participate in lotteries and what appeals to each one. Research shows that African Americans play more than Hispanics, and that non-Hispanic whites play less than either group; that men play more than women; that playing increases with age; and that playing correlates with lower education and income (with education a stronger factor than income).[4] In addition to the standard demographics of race, sex, age, and income, marketers also use lifestyle categories, such as Belongers, Achievers, Emulators, Socially Conscious, and so on. For example, Belongers are not ordinarily attracted to gambling but find lotteries acceptable because they are state sponsored. Their attitude is, "It's okay if the government says so." Belongers also like consistency and regularity and so are attracted to games that require repeated participation, like collecting letters to spell a word.[5]

State sponsorship of lotteries is widely criticized, first, for being a regressive form of taxation that takes a disproportionate amount from those who can least afford to lose the money, and, second, for being an improper role for government. Although lottery revenue supports other state services, it is the only state activity that is not aimed directly at improving people's lives. Given that the objective of lottery commissions is to maximize revenues, it is understandable that they should engage in extensive advertising, and the amount spent is not out of line with consumer products companies in the private sector. However, lottery advertising is not regulated by the Federal Trade Commission, as is all private-sector advertising, and critics complain that ads for state lotteries could not meet federal standards.

Some of the criticism is directed at the social impact of advertising. Aside from enticing people to squander their limited income on lottery games instead of the basics of food, shelter, and the like (lottery ads are concentrated around paydays), lottery advertising promotes a get-rich-quick mentality that deters people, critics charge, from making investments in education and other ways of improving their life prospects. In a New York State television ad that was widely criticized, a mother was telling a daughter that she did not need to study so hard because Mom was playing the lottery, suggesting that luck could substitute for hard work.[6] Lottery advertising also relies heavily on fantasy. Some ads feature people who worry about how they will tell a boss that they are quitting and who dream about owning the company they work for. Critics question whether encouraging such unrealistic aspirations is good public policy.

The main criticism of lottery advertising focuses on the question of deception. Although many ads highlight the maximum award, they seldom disclose the odds of winning it. In one Connecticut ad, the odds of winning any prize was correctly listed as 1 in 30, but the 1 in 13 million odds of winning the prominently displayed jackpot were nowhere to be found. Large jackpots are usually paid out over a 20-year period, and the present value of a multimillion-dollar prize may be barely half the face amount—and even less after taxes, which are not mentioned in the ads. Prizes may also be divided among several winners.

To counter awareness of the long odds, lottery advertising often includes profiles of winners and slogans like (from Arizona) "Every single second, someone is cashing a winning ticket." Psychological research shows that people's perceptions of probabilities are increased by tangible examples of successful outcomes.[7] Although some ads mention the good uses to which lottery revenue is put ("When Colorado plays, everyone wins"), such appeals may be deceptive because the benefits are usually so small. For example, the California lottery provides only 2 percent to 3 percent of school budgets, and even that amount is reduced if legislators use this source as a reason to cut other funding. Worse, the (false) idea that lottery revenues provide significant support may lead people to vote against increased taxes for education. In any event, advertising the social benefits of lottery revenue is not common because studies show that people do not respond to such appeals.[8]

Defenders of lotteries and lottery marketing argue that the poor are heavier users of games because they have more to gain, and that for this reason any restrictions would deprive them of life-changing opportunities. Winning the lottery, for some, may be the "way out" of poverty. Much of life depends on chance, so how is the lottery any different from other factors in success?

If more lottery outlets are in poor areas, they are there to better serve the larger number of customers. A great deal of lottery advertising is merely instructional, explaining to people how to play the games (advertising also stresses the fun and excitement). One study suggests that lottery advertising receives more attention from the more affluent, which, if true, would reduce the percentage of poor players by increasing the absolute numbers.[9] Although some people have gambling addictions, there is little evidence that lotteries severely impact the lives of typical players.[10] Finally, if lotteries are a regressive form of taxation, they are relatively painless and purely voluntary. Players apparently value the chance of winning and the excitement of the game, while the "tax" benefits everyone by supporting necessary state services. And "Hey, you never know."

INTRODUCTION

Marketing is an essential function in any business. As the marketing theorist Theodore Levitt observes, "There can be no effective corporate strategy that is not marketing oriented, that does not in the end follow this unyielding prescription: The purpose of business is to create and keep a customer."[11] However, Levitt should add that businesses must also develop products and services that customers want at prices they are willing to pay. Marketing broadly conceived includes, then, making decisions about what products or services to put on the market, who are the potential customers for these goods, how to reach the target markets and induce them to buy, how to price the product or service to make it attractive to these customers, and how to deliver the goods physically to the ultimate consumers.

These matters are often expressed as the four Ps of marketing: product, price, promotion, and placement. The decisions that marketing managers must make about each of these Ps involve numerous ethical issues. Product, for example, raises obvious concerns about product safety, but the social impact of some products has drawn moral criticism. Aside from alcohol and tobacco, which are frequent targets of complaints, objections have been raised about unhealthful foods, gas-guzzling SUVs, and poor-value financial products aimed at the poor. Ethical issues about price include price gouging, predatory pricing (which undercuts the competition unfairly), price discrimination (charging more to some customers than others), and misleading prices (e.g., pricing that makes it difficult for consumers to make comparisons and markdowns from an unrealistic regular price), and price-fixing (colluding with competitors to keep prices high).

Promotion is the most visible face of marketing, and for this reason it draws the greatest moral scrutiny. Much of the criticism of promotion focuses on questionable sales techniques and possible deception and manipulation in advertising. Many people are also concerned about the intrusiveness of direct marketing and the alleged social harm of some advertisements. Finally, placement raises ethical issues about anticompetitive practices, such as controlling the channels of distribution, paying so-called slotting allowances for shelf space in stores, and so-called gray marketing, which is the diversion of goods outside officially sanctioned channels.

This chapter begins with a section on three of the Ps, price, promotion, and placement, except for advertising, which is covered in the second section. The section on advertising considers not only the central problem of deceptive advertising but also the ethical issues involved in using the powers of persuasion that advertisers possess, the social consequences of particular advertisements, and pervasive advertising in general. The final section, on the remaining P, product, treats the ethical issues in product safety of the kind involved in the Ford Explorer and Firestone tires (see Case 10.3) with particular attention to the theories of product liability.

MARKETING

Since everyone is a consumer, marketing is an area of life where we all come into contact with businesses. The other main point of contact is the employment relation, which arguably raises more ethical issues, but only marketing affects everyone. Marketing is also an area where the conflict inherent in the marketplace is most acute. Marketers have strong incentives to sell products and services as well as powerful means for doing so. Despite the doctrine of *consumer sovereignty*—the notion that consumers are "kings" in the economy because they ultimately decide whether to buy a company's products—individual consumers are still vulnerable given the vast power of companies to determine what goods are offered and, through advertising, what consumers want. Because selling is so important for business and such powerful means are available, ethical problems are inevitable. This section focuses on four broad areas, namely, sales practices, labeling, pricing, and distribution. First, though, we need to establish a framework for marketing ethics.

A Framework for Marketing Ethics

Most of the ethical problems in marketing involve three ethical concepts: fairness (or justice), freedom, and well-being. Fairness is a central concern because it is a basic moral requirement of any market transaction—and the result of successful marketing is always a market transaction. In a market transaction, each party gives up something of value in return for something they value more. And such exchanges are fair (and mutually beneficial) as long as each party acts freely and has adequate information. The requirement of acting freely rules out exchanges in which there is coercion or manipulation or when one party lacks competence (children and other vulnerable populations, for example), and the adequate information requirement excludes the making of false or deceptive statements (which is also a kind of manipulation). These two requirements are often expressed as the absence of force and fraud.

The need for information in a fair market transaction is problematic, though, because a seller does not have an obligation to provide *all* relevant information to a buyer, and a buyer has some obligation to become informed about what is being bought. The question of who has the obligation to disclose or acquire what information leads to two traditional doctrines in marketing, namely, *caveat emptor* (let the buyer beware) and *caveat venditor* (let the seller beware). Under caveat emptor the buyer has full responsibility to judge the quality of the goods absent any warranty or representation made by the seller. By contrast, the doctrine of caveat venditor places a responsibility on the seller to fully reveal the quality of the goods sold.

In practice, the responsibility for ensuring adequate information is divided between buyers and sellers. Buyers have good economic reasons to become informed (to protect themselves) and sellers, to provide information (to attract buyers). Beyond this, the main principle is who can provide the information at the lowest cost. A great deal of consumer law assumes that because sellers can provide the necessary information more cheaply than consumers can acquire it, the responsibility rests largely with the sellers. To the questions of how much information to provide and of what kind, the guiding principle is the extent to which a lack of information is harmful to consumers. Generally, consumer laws require only the disclosure of information that buyers need to make rational purchasing decisions.

Freedom is at issue in marketing with respect to having a range of consumer options. Freedom is denied when marketers engage in deceptive or manipulative practices and, in particular, take advantage of vulnerable populations, such as children, the poor, and the elderly. In channels of distribution, large retailers, such as Wal-Mart, have been accused of using their power to force small suppliers into accepting unfavorable agreements, and similarly large suppliers can take advantage of size to disadvantage small retailers. Freedom is also an issue in marketing research that invades the privacy of subjects against their will. Finally, well-being is a consideration in evaluating the social impact of products and advertising, as well as product safety.

These three principles of fairness, freedom, and well-being can be expressed in the four-point bill of rights for consumers that President John F. Kennedy proclaimed in 1962, as a movement for consumer rights was developing in American society. These rights are as follows:

1. The right to be protected from harmful products (well-being).
2. The right to be provided with adequate information about products (fairness).

3. The right to be offered a choice that includes the products that consumers truly want (well-being and freedom).

4. The right to have a voice in the making of major marketing decisions (freedom).

These rights are needed, according to consumer advocates, because the mere right not to buy (consumer sovereignty) provides inadequate opportunities for consumers to satisfy their needs and desires. Also, the burden of protecting their own interests is often too heavy for consumers to bear, especially in view of the unequal relation between buyers and sellers in present-day markets.

The first two of these rights are now embodied to some extent in consumer protection legislation. The Consumer Product Safety Act (1972), for example, created an independent regulatory body, the Consumer Product Safety Commission, which has the power to issue standards, require warnings, and even ban dangerous products entirely. The Fair Packaging and Labeling Act (1966) requires that containers disclose the ingredients of the product, the amount, and other pertinent information, including nutritional content in the case of food. The Magnuson-Moss Warranty Act (1975) specifies the information and the minimum conditions that must be included in a full warranty and requires that all warranties be written in comprehensible language. The latter two rights, especially the right to a voice, have not been addressed by the law and remain unrealized goals of the consumer movement.

Sales Practices and Labeling

Although companies rely on advertising to reach mass markets, most transactions are completed by personal selling. More than 16 million people in the United States are employed as sales personnel, 30 times the number who work in advertising.[12] Most people experience personal selling as part of sales to individual customers (B2C marketing), but business to business selling (B2B marketing) also involves personal selling insofar as sales-force members call on the people at other businesses who are responsible for buying. Sales personnel are typically put under great pressure to sell by such means as commissions, quotas, and other sales-force management techniques. They may be led by this pressure to lie to customers, conceal information, make unrealistic promises, disparage the competition, and oversell (pushing products the customer does not need). Salespeople may also be tempted to cultivate customers with lavish entertainment or other perks and to close deals by offering or agreeing to pay kickbacks or outright bribes, with or without the company's knowledge. Because sales people often work away from the office without close supervision, they have the opportunity to misrepresent their work, pad their expense accounts, or otherwise cheat their employers.

With respect to customers, the main moral obligation of a salesperson is to facilitate the conditions for a fair transaction, which, we have noted, are that the customer act freely and with adequate knowledge.[13] Although this duty can be violated in many ways, most of the attention given to unethical sales practices focuses on deception and manipulation. Roughly, sales practices are deceptive when consumers are led to hold false beliefs about a product.[14] The most straight-forward way to deceive, of course, is to lie by knowingly making a false statement, but one can also deceive without lying. For example, a piano salesperson may say that the "special sale" ends today but fail to add that another "special sale" will begin the next day.[15] Examples of some common deceptions in sales are markdowns from a "suggested retail price" that is never charged, "introductory offers" that incorrectly purport to offer a savings, and bogus clearance sales in which inferior goods are brought in for the "sale." Packaging and labeling are deceptive when the size or shape of a container, a picture or description, and terms such as "economy size" and "new and improved" mislead consumers in some significant way. Warranties that cannot easily be understood by the average consumer are also deceptive.

Manipulation is distinguished from deception in that it typically involves no false or misleading claims. Instead, it consists of taking advantage of consumer psychology to make a sale.

More precisely, manipulation is noncoercively shaping the alternatives open to people or their perception of those alternatives so that they are effectively deprived of a choice.[16] An example of manipulation is "bait and switch," a generally illegal practice in which a customer is lured into a store by an advertisement for a low-cost item and then sold a higher-priced version. Often the low-cost item is not available, but even when it is, the advertised product may be of such low quality that customers are easily "switched" to a higher-priced product. Bait and switch is manipulative not only because consumers are tricked into entering the store but also because they enter in a frame of mind to buy.

Manipulation can also take place when salespeople use high-pressure tactics. The sales force of one encyclopedia company used deception to gain entry to the homes of prospects by claiming to be conducting advertising research (the questionnaires were thrown away afterward). Another company offered to place a set of encyclopedias "free," provided the family bought a yearly supplement for a certain number of years at a price that exceeded the cost of the encyclopedia set alone. Some groups of people are more vulnerable to manipulation than others, most notably children, the elderly, and the poor.[17] Special care needs to be taken, therefore, in marketing aimed at those groups.

The moral case against deceptive and manipulative marketing needs little explanation because it rests on the requirement that markets be free of force and fraud. The difficult ethical questions in this area concern the definition of deception and manipulation. Few consumers are adequately informed, but how much information is a seller obligated to provide? All selling involves the use of persuasive techniques, but when does good salesmanship cross over into manipulation? These questions are examined more fully in the section on advertising.

LABELING.   Many consumer purchases occur without any contact with a salesperson. When a consumer merely takes a product off a shelf, the main contact between that consumer and the manufacturer is the print on the package. The label becomes a means not only for selling a product but also for informing the consumer. What appears on a label is important, therefore, in judging the fairness of the transaction.

Consider the plight of a consumer examining a frozen apple pie in a sealed, opaque cardboard box. Without information on the label, consumers have no practical means for determining the size of the frozen pie, the ingredients used, the nutritional content, or the length of time the product has been sitting in the freezer case. Health-conscious consumers are especially disadvantaged by the welter of claims about low fat and salt content and the unregulated use of words such as "light" and "healthy." Certainly, the more information consumers have, the better they can protect themselves in the marketplace. The ethical question, though, is, how much information is a manufacturer obligated to provide? To what extent are consumers responsible for informing themselves about the products for sale?

The Fair Packaging and Labeling Act was passed by Congress in 1966 to enable consumers to make meaningful value comparisons. Specifically, the act requires that each package list the identity of the product; the name and location of the manufacturer, packer, or distributor; the net quantity; and, as appropriate, the number of servings, applications, and so on. There are detailed requirements for many specific kinds of products in the Fair Packaging and Labeling Act and other statutes. The rationale for this legislation is that certain information is important for making an informed consumer choice, and consumers have few means for securing the information if it is not provided by the manufacturer.

The Nutrition Labeling and Education Act (NLEA) of 1990 further requires that the labels on packaged food products contain information about certain ingredients, expressed by weight and as a percentage of the recommended daily diet in a standardized serving size. The total number of calories and the number of calories from fat must also be listed along with the percentage of the recommended daily intake of certain vitamins and minerals. In addition, the NLEA lists the health claims that are permissible and defines such terms as "low fat," "light," and "healthy." Previously, food manufacturers were able to manipulate the information on labels.

The amount of fat or salt could be reduced, for example, merely by decreasing the listed serving size. A product labeled "light" could contain a substantial amount of fat.

Manufacturers offer a number of reasons for not providing more information. A detailed listing of amounts of ingredients might jeopardize recipes that are trade secrets; listing the kind of fat would prevent them from switching ingredients to take advantage of changes in the relative prices of different oils; product dating is often misunderstood by consumers, who reject older products that are still good; and packaging has to be designed with many considerations in mind, such as ease in filling, the protection of goods in transit, the prevention of spoilage, and so on. Therefore, the objectives of the Fair Packaging and Labeling Act and the Nutrition Labeling and Education Act, manufacturers argue, need to be balanced against a number of practical constraints. Still, the bottom line is that consumers should have sufficient information to make rational buying decisions.

Pricing and Distribution

Prices are critical for efficient markets. The price of any good should reflect all available information about its value and thus enable market participants to make rational economic choices. Generally, inaccurate prices—which is to say prices that do not reflect the value of the goods in question—distort economic decision making. For example, manipulation of stock prices or stock market bubbles cause stocks to be overpriced with the result that capital is not allocated to its most profitable use. Therefore, there are strong economic reasons to ensure that the prices of all goods accurately reflect their value.

The moral (and legal) issues in pricing fall into two categories. The first category involves the use of prices to engage in anticompetitive behavior that can seriously harm other firms. The prevention of such anticompetitive behavior is the subject of antitrust law, which seeks to ensure low, accurate prices by preventing monopolies. When a single company (a monopoly) or a few companies (an oligopoly) dominate a market, the lack of competitors allows such firms to charge artificially high prices. The second category concerns fairness in pricing, which can be violated when prices are used to deceive or manipulate consumers and when goods are overpriced in ways that consumers cannot easily detect.

ANTICOMPETITIVE PRICING.   Most anticompetitive marketing practices are also illegal under the Sherman Act (1890), the Clayton Act (1914), the Federal Trade Commission Act (1914), and the Robinson–Patman Act (1936). Many states also have antitrust statutes that prohibit the same practices. The major anticompetitive marketing practices prohibited by these acts follow.

1. *Price-Fixing.* Price-fixing is an agreement, either explicit or implicit, among two or more companies operating in the same market to sell goods at a set price. Such an agreement is contrary to the usual practice whereby prices are set in a free market by arm's-length transactions. The effect of price-fixing, obviously, is to raise prices above what they would be in a free market. Most commonly, price-fixing is horizontal, among different sellers at the same level of distribution, but price-fixing can also be vertical, when it occurs between buyers and sellers at different levels, such as an agreement between a manufacturer and a wholesaler. Price-fixing occurs not only when there is an explicit or implicit agreement among competitors to charge similar prices, but also when the same result is achieved by other means. Among these are an implicit agreement to follow an industry standard (parallel pricing) or the lead of a dominant seller (price leadership); a situation in which one company effectively controls the prices of competitors (administered price); and market allocation, in which competitors agree not to compete in certain geographical areas or with certain buyers.

2. *Resale Price Maintenance.* This is a practice whereby products are sold on the condition that they be resold at a price fixed by the manufacturer or distributor. Resale price maintenance is thus a form of vertical price-fixing as described earlier. There are various reasons for imposing resale price maintenance on retailers, including fostering a prestige image, enabling a larger number of retailers to carry a product, and providing an adequate margin for promotion or service. As a form of price-fixing, resale price maintenance prevents prices from being set by the forces of a competitive market.

3. *Price Discrimination.* Sellers engage in price discrimination when they charge different prices or offer different terms of sale for goods of the same kind to different buyers. Often this occurs when buyers are located in different geographical regions or vary in size or proximity to other sellers. Thus, a seller who gives a discount to large buyers solely by virtue of their size is guilty of discriminating against small buyers. However, bulk discounts and other price differences are legal as long as the same terms are available to all buyers or if they are good-faith attempts to meet competition in particular markets. Price discrimination can be practiced not only by sellers but also by large buyers. The Robinson–Patman Act prevents large buyers, such as chain stores, from demanding and receiving preferential treatment from manufacturers and wholesalers to the detriment of smaller buyers.

4. *Predatory Pricing.* Predatory pricing consists of reducing prices to unreasonably low or unprofitable levels in order to drive competitors out of business. Once this occurs, the company is in a monopoly position and can recoup its losses by charging above-market rates. Predatory pricing is often difficult to prove because, first, a company like Wal-Mart with a low cost structure might be able to make a profit selling goods at prices that would be unprofitable for competitors. Second, a company might sell goods at a loss in order to reduce inventory that otherwise would not be sold at all. Department store clearance sales are often of this character. Third, some companies may sell at a loss in order to gain market share and become competitive. Some computer software is distributed free for this reason. The key factors are intent and consequences: whether low prices are offered with a view to raising prices later and whether prices, in fact, do rise later. Wal-Mart, for example, does aim to drive competitors out of business, but not so that Wal-Mart can raise prices, which remain low even where its stores are in a monopoly position. Wal-Mart's low prices are precisely what healthy competition is supposed to achieve.

UNFAIR PRICING.   Pricing can be done in ways that treat consumers unfairly. The main types of such unfair pricing are unconscionably high prices (price gouging) and misleading prices, including prices that are difficult to determine and compare.

The adage "Charge what the market will bear" is good advice under ordinary market conditions but not in all circumstances. For one, temporary shortages of critical goods, such as occur during natural disasters, create opportunities for charging very high prices. Oil companies have been accused of price gouging during periods of shortage, which are sometimes due to war, and airline prices during peak periods are similarly criticized. Charges of price gouging have also been leveled against pharmaceutical companies, especially in the pricing of AIDS drugs, and against lenders who prey on the poor by charging exorbitant rates of interest and piling on high fees. So-called payday loans, for example, can carry annual interest rates above 500 percent, and interest combined with late fees and other charges have resulted in some people owing more than 10 times the original loan amount.[18]

In the absence of shortages, it is difficult for companies to sell overpriced products to well-informed consumers with ample choices. However, there are some products that are difficult to evaluate and that people can be persuaded to buy. Unless force or fraud is employed, the sale of these products is generally legal, but consumer advocates still object that they are overpriced. Examples include highly profitable extended warranties for appliances and collision damage waivers for rental cars (which are sometimes pushed on renters with high-pressure tactics).

Psychological research shows that people make nuanced judgments about when it is fair to raise prices.[19] Taking advantage of natural disasters is generally regarded as unfair. Because of this perception, Home Depot did not raise prices of building materials during Hurricane Andrew (see Case 1.2). Tickets to sports events, for example, could vary according to the expected demand, but teams do not do this for fear that charging high prices for popular games would be viewed as taking unfair advantage, even though people willingly pay a premium to scalpers without feeling cheated. Airlines seek to counter the perception that charging full last-minute rates to travelers attending family funerals is unfair by offering special bereavement rates. These examples show that, to some extent, people's perceptions of fairness in pricing affect companies' pricing behavior.

Misleading prices are a form of deception in which customers are induced to buy because they believe the good is a bargain. Perhaps the most common form of misleading prices is selling goods at prices reduced from a supposed regular price or the manufacturer's suggested retail price (MSRP). In order to get around state laws, some stores offer goods at full price for a short period of time before reducing them to "sale" prices for the rest of the selling season. A mark-down from an MSRP that is never charged also creates a false impression of savings. The main principle used by the courts in determining whether such "high–low" pricing is deceptive is the extent to which the seller makes a good-faith attempt to sell at full or MSRP price.

When customers are accustomed to paying a certain price for a product, such as a candy bar, manufacturers often reduce the size in order to maintain the same price, a practice known as customary pricing. The size of one popular brand of tuna, for example, was reduced without any fanfare from the industry standard of $6^1/_2$ ounces to $6^1/_8$ ounces. Although the same price was maintained per can, this constituted a nearly invisible 5.8 percent price increase for the tuna.[20]

The proliferation of products at different quantities and prices makes it difficult for consumers to compare even those from the same manufacturer. For example, mattress manufacturers produce constantly shifting lines at different prices so that price comparisons between lines and mattresses from other manufacturers are virtually impossible to make. It is generally difficult for consumers to compare packaged-food items to determine how much they cost per ounce or other measure. For this reason, some municipalities and states require unit pricing, in which the cost of packaged food in some standardized unit is displayed on the shelf. To ensure that consumers are aware of the price of goods, there are laws in some parts of the country that require prices to be displayed on each item (item marking) and not merely on the shelf.

In addition, some products have hidden costs. The price of tires, for example, often excludes mounting, balancing, extended warranties, and other extras, which are often mentioned to consumers after a decision has been made to buy (a sales technique known as "low-balling"). Consumers cannot compare two air conditioners without knowing the cost of operating them, because a cheaper but less-efficient air conditioner can cost more in the long run. Manufacturers of household electrical appliances are now required by law, therefore, to disclose the amount of energy used in a year and the range of energy consumption for products of the same kind. Comparisons are facilitated by standard units for measuring the relevant factors. Thus, tires are required by federal law to be graded with a tread-wear index and a rating for traction, and insulating materials have an R-value that enables consumers to compare different grades of insulation. All of these requirements enable consumers to make sense of prices and make rational consumer choices.

DISTRIBUTION.   Distribution, which is the means by which products are delivered from the manufacturer to the ultimate consumer, is a necessary function of marketing that is of increasing importance. Once regarded merely as a matter of logistics, distribution is now a source of competitive advantage as large retailers seek to cut costs in the distribution chain and manufacturers find means of doing so. In the process, distribution relations have become more complex and competitive, thereby increasing the number of ethical problems. The main ethical issues in distribution are abuse of power in channeling relations, slotting allowances to gain access to shelf space in stores, and gray markets that arise from diverting and parallel importing.[21] Another problem area in distribution is direct marketing, which is not considered here because the main concern, the violation of privacy through the use of databases of personal information, is covered in Chapter 6 on privacy.

Whenever manufacturers have greater power than retailers or vice versa, the stronger party can use its power to force agreements that the other party would not otherwise make. Such use of market power can lead to anticompetitive practices, some of which are prohibited by law. Three illegal abuses of power in distribution are reciprocal dealing, exclusive dealing, and tying arrangements. *Reciprocal dealing* involves a sale in which the seller is required to buy something in return, as when an office supply firm agrees to buy a computer system only on the condition that the computer firm agrees to purchase supplies from the office supply firm. In an *exclusive dealing* agreement, a seller provides a product—a brand of sportswear, for example—on the condition that the buyer not handle competing brands. These practices are anticompetitive because they force transactions that do not make economic sense (otherwise the transactions would be freely made).

A *tying arrangement* exists when one product is sold on the condition that the buyer purchase another product as well. An example of a tying arrangement is an automotive supply firm that requires as a condition for selling tires to a service station that the buyer also purchase batteries from the seller. A kind of tying arrangement but one that is generally legal is *full-line forcing*, in which a retailer is forced to carry a manufacturer's full line of products as a condition for carrying any product from that manufacturer. Full-line forcing is ethically questionable because it freezes out other manufacturers when a retailer can reasonably carry only one or a few lines, and it limits consumer choice at any given retailer. Manufacturers often employ this practice to take advantage of the popularity of a few products and to secure outlets for products with a higher margin.

One of the most controversial practices in distribution is the payment of *slotting allowances*, which are payments by manufacturers to retailers to secure space on store shelves. Carried to an extreme, this practice makes store shelves a kind of real estate that retailers lease to the highest bidder. Manufacturers have been shifting resources from advertising to trade promotions of various kinds in part because large retailers increasingly have the power to demand such payments. However, another reason for favoring trade promotions over advertising is that harried consumers are more likely to buy a product because it is conveniently displayed, and hence easy to buy, than because it has been heavily advertised.

Some critics of slotting allowances regard the practice as a kind of shakedown of manufacturers, made possible by retailers' increasing power. In addition, the fees, which can total tens of thousands of dollars, prevent smaller manufacturers from getting stock on retailers' shelves, and the added savings to retailers are not always passed along to consumers, who may end up paying higher prices. Retailers argue in reply that the fees cover the added costs of purchasing, stocking, and labeling, especially of new products, and provide a means for manufacturers to get new products to market quickly. Although slotting allowances are currently legal, Congress and state legislatures are looking into the matter, and the reluctance of people in the industry to discuss the practice suggests that it is ethically questionable.

Gray markets result when products are sold outside the channels of distribution authorized by a manufacturer. This may be due to *diverting*, which occurs when a wholesaler sells goods to unauthorized intermediaries who in turn sell them to unauthorized retailers in the same market area. Another cause of gray markets is *parallel importing*, in which goods intended for one market (say Asia) are distributed without authorization in another market (say Europe). In both cases, a company may find that the products sold through authorized channels are competing with the same products sold in a gray market, almost always at a lower price. The lower price of gray market goods is possible because authorized channels include extra costs, such as creating and maintaining a reliable distribution system and providing after-sale support service, which are avoided by diverting or parallel importing. Although the buyers in a gray market may enjoy a savings on the purchased goods, they may lack the warranty protection and after-sale service that are provided when the same goods are sold by an authorized retailer.

Gray markets have several undesirable effects. First, they make it more difficult for manufacturers to maintain channels of distribution with reliable and responsible distributors.

Second, they force manufacturers to unbundle warranties and after-sale service, which deprives consumers of these benefits as well as the manufacturers, for whom these are often profitable items. Third, gray markets create consumer dissatisfaction and erode brand value when buyers of gray market goods blame the company for lack of warranty and after-sale service. On the other hand, gray markets drive down prices, and for mass-market goods that do not require the benefits of authorized channels of distribution, this may be in the consumers' and ultimately the manufacturers' interest. To some extent, gray markets serve to wring excess costs out of distribution systems.

ADVERTISING

Advertising pervades our lives. It is impossible to read a newspaper or magazine, watch a television show, or travel the streets of our cities without being bombarded by commercial messages. Although some ads may be irritating or offensive, the better efforts of Madison Avenue provide a certain amount of entertainment. We also derive benefit from information about products and from the boost that advertising gives to the economy as a whole. On the other side of the fence, companies with products or services to sell regard advertising as a valuable, indeed indispensable marketing tool. Approximately two percent of the gross national product is currently devoted to advertising. So whether we like it or not, advertising is a large and essential part of the American way of doing business.

A typical definition of advertising, from a marketing textbook, is that it is "a paid nonpersonal communication about an organization and its products that is transmitted to a target audience through a mass medium."[22] So defined, advertising is only one kind of promotional activity. The others are publicity, sales promotion, and personal selling. Although most advertising is for a product or a service, some of it is devoted to enhancing the image of a corporation or advancing some issue or cause. Thus, a distinction is commonly made between product advertising on one hand and advocacy or cause-related advertising, including political campaign ads, on the other.[23] Advertising is also used to "sell" ideas, attitudes, and behaviors in order to benefit the targeted individuals and society generally. This kind of advertising on behalf of better health, environmental protection, and the like is called social marketing.

Advertising is widely criticized. Exaggerated claims and outright falsehoods are the most obvious targets for complaints, followed closely by the lack of taste, irritating repetition, and offensive character. More recently, questions have been raised about the morality of specific kinds of advertising, such as advertising for alcohol and tobacco products and ads aimed at children. Particular ads are also faulted for their use of excessive sex or violence or for presenting negative stereotypes of certain groups. Other critics complain about the role advertising plays in creating a culture of consumerism. Advertising encourages people not only to buy more but also to believe that their most basic needs and desires can be satisfied by products. Finally, there is great concern about the potential of advertising for behavior control.

These objections to advertising have led to calls for government regulation and industry self-regulation. Deceptive advertising is subject to regulation by the Federal Trade Commission (FTC), but many questions still arise about the definition of deception in advertising. The other objections to advertising are generally controlled by public opinion, to which advertisers must pay heed. Particularly offensive ads, for example, usually draw critical attention. The American Association of Advertising Agencies has adopted a code of ethics that addresses the more subtle issues of fairness and good taste in advertising.

This section examines three broad areas of ethical concern about advertising, namely, deceptive advertising, irrational persuasion, and the impact of advertising.

Deceptive Advertising

Roughly, an advertisement is deceptive if it has a tendency to deceive. On this definition, the deceptiveness of an ad does not depend solely on the truth or falsity of the claims it makes, but also on the impact the ad has on the people who see or hear it. It is possible for advertising to contain false claims without being deceptive and for advertising to be deceptive without containing any false claims. A patently false claim for a hair restorer, for example, might not actually deceive anyone. Furthermore, there are other advertising claims that are false if taken literally but are commonly regarded as harmless exaggerations or bits of puffery. Every razor blade, for example, gives the closest, most comfortable shave; every tire, the smoothest, safest ride; and every pain reliever, the quickest, gentlest relief. Some ad copy has no determinate meaning at all and cannot be characterized as either true or false.

Some writers even defend the literal falsehoods and meaningless babble of advertising as legitimate and even socially desirable. Perhaps the best known of these defenders is Theodore Levitt, who compares advertising to poetry:

> Like advertising, poetry's purpose is to influence an audience; to affect its perceptions and sensibilities; perhaps even to change its mind. . . . [P]oetry's intent is to convince and seduce. In the service of that intent, it employs without guilt or fear of criticism all the arcane tools of distortion that the literary mind can devise.[24]

In order to see that true claims can still be deceptive, consider an ad for Anacin that prompted a complaint by the FTC in 1973. The ad asserted that Anacin has a unique painkilling formula that is superior to all other nonprescription analgesics. Anacin is composed of two active ingredients, aspirin (400 mg) and caffeine (32.5 mg), but the sole pain-relieving component is aspirin. Aspirin itself is unique in the way that all chemical compounds are different from each other, and aspirin was superior to any other pain reliever available at that time without a prescription. Therefore, it is literally true that Anacin contains a unique and superior painkilling formula: aspirin. The impression that the ad conveyed, however, was that only Anacin has this superior pain-relieving ingredient (false) and that consequently Anacin itself is superior to competing brands of analgesics containing aspirin (also false).

The basis of the FTC complaint, therefore, was not that the claims made for Anacin are literally false but that they gave rise to, or were likely to give rise to, false beliefs in the minds of consumers. Ads for Anacin also claimed that it causes less-frequent side effects. The position of the FTC is that the deceptiveness of this claim does not depend solely on whether it is true or false but also on whether the manufacturer, American Home Products, had sufficient evidence to back it up. That is, unsupported claims that turn out to be true are still deceptive, because, in the words of the court, "a consumer is entitled to assume that the appropriate verification has been performed." Even if Anacin does cause less-frequent side effects, the consumer is deceived by being led to believe that there is evidence for the claim when there is not. Whether a claim is deceptive, therefore, depends, in some cases, on whether there is evidence for it.

THE DEFINITION OF DECEPTION.   The rough definition of deception that has been developed so far—namely, an ad is deceptive if it has a tendency to deceive—is not adequate, either for increasing our understanding of the ethical issues in deceptive advertising or for enforcing a legal prohibition against it. Unfortunately, the FTC has yet to offer a precise legal definition, and none of the attempts by marketing theorists and others to define deception in advertising has been entirely successful.[25] An adequate definition of deception must overcome several obstacles.

First, we need to consider whether the deception is due to the ad or the person. Is an ad deceptive if it creates a false belief in relatively few, rather ignorant consumers or only if it would deceive more numerous, reasonable consumers? Ivan Preston recounts the story of a customer who failed to catch the joke in an ad for a novelty beer, Olde Frothingslosh, that proclaimed it to be the only beer with the foam on the bottom and was outraged to discover that the foam was on the top, like all other beers.[26] Or consider whether it was deceptive for Clairol to advertise in the 1940s that a dye will "color hair permanently."[27] Only a few ignorant people would fail to realize the need to dye new growth. Yet the FTC, employing an ignorant consumer standard, found this claim deceptive.

Second, an ad may not actually create a false belief but merely take advantage of people's ignorance. Consider health claims in food advertising. The word "natural," which usually means the absence of artificial ingredients, evokes images of wholesomeness in the minds of consumers. Yet many food products advertised as natural contain unhealthy concentrations of fat and sugar and are deficient in vitamins and minerals.[28] The makers of some brands of peanut butter advertise their products as cholesterol-free even though cholesterol is present only in animal fats, so no brand of peanut butter contains any cholesterol. Is it deceptive for food advertising to make use of terms such as "natural" and "no cholesterol"? Even though the advertisers' claims may not create false beliefs, they still depend for their effect on people's lack of full understanding.

Central to any definition of deception in advertising is the concept of rational choice. Deception is morally objectionable because it interferes with the ability of consumers to make rational choices, which requires adequate information. But advertising is not intended to produce knowledgeable consumers, and so it should not be faulted for every failure to do so. Also, not every false belief is of such importance that consumers should be protected from it. But there is still a certain standard of rational consumer behavior, and advertising is deceptive when it achieves its effect by false beliefs that prevent consumers from attaining this standard. A proposed definition of deception is the following:

> Deception occurs when a false belief, which an advertisement either creates or takes advantage of, substantially interferes with the ability of people to make rational consumer choices.

Whether an ad "substantially interferes" with the ability of people to make rational consumer choices assumes some view of what choices they would make if they were not influenced by an ad. At least two factors are relevant to the notion of substantial interference. One is the ability of consumers to protect themselves and make rational choices despite advertising that creates or takes advantage of false beliefs. Thus, claims that are easily verified or not taken seriously by consumers are not necessarily deceptive. The second factor is the seriousness of the choice that consumers make. False beliefs that affect the choices we make about our health or financial affairs are of greater concern than false beliefs that bear on inconsequential purchases. Claims in life insurance advertising, for example, ought to be held to a higher standard than those for chewing gum.

APPLICATION OF THE DEFINITION.   Both of these factors can be observed in two cases involving the Campbell Soup Company. Campbell ran afoul of the FTC in 1970 when it ran television ads showing a bowl of vegetable soup chock-full of solids.[29] This effect was achieved by placing clear-glass marbles on the bottom of the bowl to hold the solids near the surface. How does this case differ from one in which clear-plastic cubes are used instead of real ice in ads for cold drinks? In each case, false beliefs are created in consumers' minds. The false beliefs that viewers have about the contents of a glass of iced tea as a result of using plastic cubes have no bearing on a decision to purchase the product (an iced tea mix, for example), whereas a decision to purchase a can of Campbell's vegetable soup can definitely be influenced by the false belief created by the glass marbles. The consumers who buy the soup in the belief that the bowl at home will look like the one in the ad will be disappointed, but not the consumers who buy the iced tea mix. The soup ads have the potential, therefore, to interfere with the ability of consumers to make rational choices.

In 1991, the Campbell Soup Company was charged again by the FTC for ads stressing the low-fat, low-cholesterol content of some of its soups and linking these qualities to a reduced risk of heart disease.[30] The soups in question have reduced amounts of fat and cholesterol, but the ads failed to mention that they are high in sodium, which increases the risk of some forms of heart disease. In the FTC's judgment, Campbell was implying that its soups could be part of a diet that reduces heart disease, while at the same time refusing to tell consumers how much sodium the soups contain or that salt should be avoided by people concerned about heart disease. Consumers who are unaware of the salt content of canned soups might purchase Campbell products as part of a diet aimed at reducing the risk of heart disease. In so doing, they would be better off buying these products than high-salt soups that are also high in fat and cholesterol. But health-conscious consumers who are aware of the salt content might well make different, more rational consumer purchases instead.

Although these ads may not directly cause consumers to have false beliefs about certain Campbell products, the campaign depends for its success on consumer ignorance about the salt content of its soups and the link between salt and heart disease and thus takes advantage of this ignorance. Whether Campbell would have an obligation to reveal the sodium content of its soups if it did not make health claims is debatable, but having made claims designed to lead people concerned about heart disease to buy its products, Campbell definitely has such an obligation. (Campbell eventually agreed to reveal the sodium content in ads for soups with more than 500 milligrams of sodium in an eight-ounce serving.)[31] The health claims made on behalf of some Campbell soups also involve the two factors that are a part of substantial interference. The salt content of a soup, unlike the amount of vegetable solids, cannot easily be verified by consumers, and the decisions consumers make to protect their health are of great importance. Accordingly, the FTC rigorously scrutinizes health claims in ads and holds them to a higher standard.

Irrational Persuasion

In 1957, Vance Packard frightened Americans with his best-selling book *The Hidden Persuaders*, which revealed how advertisers were turning to motivational research to discover the subconscious factors that influence human action. A pioneer in this area, Dr. Ernest Dichter, declared in 1941 that advertising agencies were "one of the most advanced laboratories in psychology" and that a successful advertiser "manipulates human motivations and desires and develops a need for goods with which the public has at one time been unfamiliar—perhaps even undesirous of purchasing."[32] The key to success in advertising, according to Dr. Dichter, is to appeal to feelings "deep in the psychological recesses of the mind" and to discover the right psychological "hook."[33]

These claims are disturbing because of the possibility that advertisers have means of influence that we are powerless to resist. We now know that advertising and propaganda—advertising's political cousin—have limited power to change people's basic beliefs and attitudes. Still, there is evidence that the techniques of modern advertising are reasonably successful in playing on natural human desires for security, acceptance, self-esteem, and the like so as to influence consumer choices. In particular, inducing fear is a proven advertising technique.[34] Advertisers have also discovered that visual images are more powerful than written words, in part because they bypass our rational thought processes. Finally, advertising pervades our daily environment, and this constant exposure is bound to have some cumulative psychological effect.

The main concern of philosophers with advertising is whether the influence it exerts on consumers is consistent with a respect for personal freedom or autonomy. Persuasion is a broad category that ranges from the laudable (e.g., guidance by parents and teachers) to the sinister (psychoactive drugs, psychosurgery, and torture, for example). Advertising does not involve extreme, sinister methods, of course. Still, advertising that cynically exploits deep-seated emotions or short-circuits logical thought processes can be criticized on the ground that it wrongfully deprives people of a certain amount of freedom in the making of consumer choices.

POSSIBLE THREATS TO FREE CHOICE. An advertising technique that might be faulted for interfering with freedom of choice is *subliminal communication*. There is a story, probably apocryphal, of an experiment in which a movie theater in New Jersey boosted sales of ice cream by flashing split-second messages on the screen during the regular showing of a film.[35] Several studies have reported a decrease in shoplifting in department stores when exhortations against stealing were mixed with the background music being piped over speakers.[36] Although many people believe that subliminal communication is a commonly used technique in advertising, there is little evidence to establish either its frequency or its effectiveness.[37]

The ethical argument against the use of subliminal communication in advertising, if it were effective in influencing consumer behavior, is quite simple. Richard T. DeGeorge expressed it in the following way:

> Subliminal advertising is manipulative because it acts on us without our knowledge, and hence without our consent. If an ad appears on TV, we can tune it out or change stations if we do not want to be subject to it. If an ad appears in a magazine, we are not forced to look at it. In either case, if we do choose to look and listen, we can consciously evaluate what we see and hear. We can, if we wish, take a critical stance toward the advertisement. All of this is impossible with subliminal advertising, because we are unaware that we are being subjected to the message. The advertiser is imposing his message on us without our knowledge and consent.[38]

Related forms of unconscious, if not subliminal, communication are *product placement*, which is the conspicuous placement of brand-name products in movies,[39] and *buzz marketing*, in which people who are natural trendsetters volunteer to create "buzz" about a product by casually talking about it, without revealing their purpose.[40] Because people are unaware that advertising is being directed at them by product placement or buzz marketing, they may not be prepared to evaluate it critically. Ads in newspapers and magazines and on television are clearly identified as such, so that we can separate them from news, entertainment, and other elements and treat them accordingly. Plugs in movies or conversations in bars catch us unawares, without our critical faculties at work, so to speak. We are not able to subject them to the same scrutiny as other ads because we do not recognize them for what they are.[41]

In all of these cases, the main complaint is that certain advertising techniques—namely, subliminal communication, product placement, and buzz marketing—do not allow people to use their capacity for critical evaluation, which is essential for freedom of choice. In the view of many philosophers, a choice is free to the extent that a person makes it on the basis of reasons that are considered by that person to be good reasons for acting. Freedom, in this view, is compatible with persuasion, but only as long as the techniques used do not undermine the ability of people to evaluate reasons for or against a course of action.

THE DEPENDENCE EFFECT.   Another way in which advertising might involve nonrational persuasion is described by the economist John Kenneth Galbraith. He coined the term *dependence effect* to describe the fact that present-day industrial production is concerned not merely with turning out goods to satisfy the wants of consumers but also with creating the wants themselves. He has written,

> As a society becomes increasingly affluent, wants are increasingly created by the process by which they are satisfied. This may operate passively. Increases in consumption . . . act by suggestion or emulation to create wants. Or producers may proceed actively to create wants through advertising and salesmanship. Wants thus come to depend on output.[42]

If wants depend on output, then production cannot be justified by the familiar claim of producers, "We only give the public what it wants." These words are hollow if, as Galbraith claims, these same producers determine what the public wants. Thus, he continues,

> If the individual's wants are to be urgent they must be original with himself. They cannot be urgent if they must be contrived for him. And above all they must not be contrived by the process of production by which they are satisfied. For this means that the whole case for the urgency of production, based on the urgency of wants, falls to the ground. One cannot defend production as satisfying wants if that production creates the wants. . . . Production only fills a void that it has itself created.[43]

The dependence effect, in Galbraith's formulation, involves a distinction between wants that originate in a person and those that are created by outside forces. F. A. von Hayek has pointed out that almost all wants beyond the most primitive needs for food, shelter, and sex are the result of cultural influences.[44] Thus, desires for art, music, and literature are no less created than desires for any consumer product. The creation of the former desires, moreover, is due in part to efforts by painters, composers, and novelists to earn a living. It is a non sequitur, therefore, to hold that wants that are created by the forces that also satisfy them are less urgent or important for that reason.

Even if it is not morally objectionable to create wants, advertising can still be criticized for creating desires by making irrational appeals. Consider, for example, advertising that creates desires for expensive brands of liquor or designer clothing by appealing to people's yearning for status. Any clearheaded person should see the absurdity of thinking that status could be achieved merely by what one drinks or wears. A defender of advertising can reply that people do not really believe (irrationally) that they are "buying" status in making certain consumer purchases. Rather, advertising has succeeded in surrounding some products with an aura of status, so that people derive a certain satisfaction from purchasing and using those products and so (rationally) desire them.

Consumer behavior suggests, however, that people really do make certain purchases because they want status. Vance Packard reported that in the 1950s, people expressed reluctance to buy small cars because they were less safe. Research showed, however, that a process of rationalization was taking place.[45] People wanted large cars for reasons of status but disguised their true motivation as a concern for safety. Today, many ads for luxury cars stress safety so that buyers can assure themselves of the rationality of their decisions, even though status is uppermost in their minds. (The headline of one ad asked, "How important is the elegance of Chrysler Fifth Avenue if it can't protect you in an emergency?")

Defenders of advertising point out that nonrational appeals are not necessarily unethical. A suitor, for example, is unlikely to win the heart of his beloved with logical arguments alone; a romantic setting with candlelight and soft music improves the chances of success. Courtroom lawyers do not rely solely on strong legal arguments to win cases but also on their ability to play on the feelings of jurors.[46] Similarly, good advertising appeals on many levels; it is aesthetically pleasing, intellectually stimulating, and often humorous or heartwarming. In many ads, both rational and nonrational elements are combined for greater effect without reducing people's freedom of choice.

The Impact of Advertising

Advertising has a single aim: to get us to buy. In doing so, it is inevitable that advertisers will produce other effects, without intending to do so and perhaps without even being aware that they do. Since advertisers have no reason to study the impact of advertising beyond its success in selling products and services, this task is left to advertising's many critics. Drawn from such diverse fields as psychology, sociology, communications studies, cultural history, and philosophy, these critics go beyond the generally beneficial economic function of advertising to explore its effects on individuals and society. Although critics of advertising offer wide-ranging observations,[47] their main points can be grouped under three headings: the impact of advertising on us as persons, the impact on society, and the ethical challenges of social marketing.

THE IMPACT ON PERSONS.   In getting us to buy, advertising also shapes us as persons—in our beliefs, attitudes, and values. Its impact on personality formation rivals that of parents, teachers, and religious leaders. American children watch an average of three to five hours of television daily, during which time they are exposed to dozens of ads day in and day out. Although advertising to children has been criticized mostly for taking advantage of their lack of development,[48] both television advertising and television programming have an enormous impact on children's cognitive and emotional development.[49] As we mature, advertisements continue to shape our personalities.

What kind of person is created by this relentless barrage of advertising? Obviously, avid consumers. Beyond this, advertisers claim merely to be reflecting who we are. To this defense, the writer and critic Marya Mannes charges that advertising may be reflecting us incorrectly. She continues:

> And if you reflect us incorrectly, as I believe you are doing, you are raising a generation of children with cockeyed values as to what men and women and life and family really are.[50]

But even as consumers, how are we being trained?

First, critics charge that advertising does not merely lead us to consume more than we would otherwise, leading to increasing indebtedness without an increase in happiness,[51] but makes us into consumers who work in order to spend. The media critic Richard W. Pollay writes, "At the least, advertising is seen as inducing us to keep working in order to be able to keep spending, keeping us on a treadmill, chasing new and improved carrots with no less vigor, even though our basic needs may be well met."[52] The impetus for this overconsumption comes, in part, from advertisers' ability to present goods as components of the good life and also as solutions to life's enduring problems. As another writer observes, "In consuming certain products, one buys not only a 'thing' but also an image, an image which invokes the belief and the hope of having the good rather than the bad, happiness rather than misery, success rather than failure, life rather than death."[53] In short, advertising has successfully identified products with our conception of the good life so that consumption becomes an end in itself. To live is to consume.

A second charge is that advertising does not educate people to grapple with the complex problems of life. Life as presented in advertisements consists of simple, stereotypical situations for which the solution is some product. This is far different from the novel and complicated challenges of life that require interaction with other people in social settings. Admittedly, it is not the purpose of advertising to equip people with life skills, but in the absence of other training, people may fall back on the lessons that advertising teaches.

Third, critics allege that advertising has harmful effects on people's conception of themselves, which in turn affect their self-esteem and confidence. This charge has been leveled especially against ads that depict an ideal of female beauty that few women can meet. The authors of *Measuring Up: How Advertising Affects Self-Image* write,

> Throughout the history of advertising, messages detailing the perfect female—her beauty, her societal roles, and her sexuality—have occupied a central role. These images . . . provide prescriptions for how we should look and be looked at, how we should feel and be made to feel, and how we should act.[54]

This kind of advertising, called "image advertising," has been blamed for a sense of inadequacy in women that has led to eating disorders, diet obsessions, unnecessary plastic surgeries, and various other psychological disorders. Some critics of advertising also hold image advertising responsible for violence against women.[55] Although some depiction of persons in advertising is unavoidable and even necessary, advertisers should be aware of the impact of image advertising and select images accordingly.[56]

Finally, some psychologists find that a society with pervasive advertising leads people to view themselves as marketable commodities in a process called the "objectification of the self." This phenomenon is known in personality theory as a "marketing orientation," in which a person thinks of himself or herself as an asset to be deployed for maximum gain. In this orientation, personality traits such as friendliness and kindness are developed, not for their own sake but for the advantages that they bring in a market for personality. Although the "marketing orientation" is a personality disorder that cannot be blamed on advertising alone, an increasingly competitive economy that places a greater emphasis on personality forces people to "sell" themselves in the marketplace.

Whatever the merit of these charges, advertising does affect us in ways both large and small, and what the effects are and whether they make us better or worse as persons are questions worth exploring.

THE IMPACT ON SOCIETY.   Advertising has the power to affect not only persons individually but also groups in society. Thus, particular ads have been criticized for presenting damaging stereotypes of the elderly, women, and racial and ethnic groups. The sociologist Erving Goffman observed that many ads of the 1970s portrayed women as inept and childlike. One small example is that women's hands were often shown barely touching objects while men grasped things firmly, suggesting that women are weak and in need of a man's care.[57] Consumers are now quick to complain about such stereotypes, causing advertisers to be much more careful. More recently, criticism has been directed against advertising that encourages poor eating habits that cause obesity and preventable diseases and the purchase of gas-guzzling vehicles that harm the environment.

The greatest area of concern about the social impact of advertising has been in marketing to the poor, who, as a group, are targeted not only with harmful products but also with advertising that heavily promotes them. The products in question are mostly tobacco and alcohol. Thus, inner-city areas contain more billboards than do suburbs, and more of the billboards in the inner city advertise cigarettes and alcohol. A 1987 survey in St. Louis, for example, revealed that 62 percent of the billboards in predominantly black neighborhoods advertised cigarettes and alcohol compared with 36 percent in white neighborhoods.[58] The target marketing of the poor generally and the African American poor in particular is illustrated by a new cigarette brand from R. J. Reynolds Tobacco Company and a malt liquor from G. Heileman Brewing Company.

In 1990, R. J. Reynolds, a division of RJR Nabisco, developed Uptown, a cigarette designed to appeal to blacks. The introduction was scuttled after protests from outraged civil rights groups. The Secretary of Health and Human Services, Dr. Louis W. Sullivan, who is an African American physician, charged that Uptown was "deliberately and cynically targeted toward black Americans," and he urged the company to cancel plans to test-market the new brand. "At a time when our people desperately need the message of health promotion," he said, "Uptown's message is more disease, more suffering, and more death for a group already bearing more than its share of smoking-related illness and mortality."[59]

The development of Uptown was based on extensive marketing research. A light menthol flavor was selected because 69 percent of black smokers prefer menthol-flavored cigarettes compared with 27 percent for all smokers. Many blacks open a package from the bottom, and so the cigarettes were to be packed with the filter end pointing down. Researchers discovered that the name Uptown, which evokes images of sophisticated nightlife, drew the most favorable response from blacks in test groups, and the theme of elegance was reinforced by lettering in black and gold, which were chosen instead of the green that is more commonly used for menthol brands. The market testing for Uptown, which was scheduled to begin on February 5, 1990, in Philadelphia, involved print ads in black-focused magazines and newspapers and billboards and point-of-sale displays in black neighborhoods.

In June 1991, G. Heileman Brewing Company, no longer in business, announced the introduction of a new malt liquor called PowerMaster, which would compete in the growing "up-strength" malt liquor category.[60] With 5.9 percent alcohol (31 percent higher than the company's top-selling Colt 45 at 4.5 percent alcohol), this new product was launched in Heileman's unsuccessful attempt to emerge from bankruptcy. Since malt liquor is the drink of choice of many inner-city black males, Heileman's planned advertising focused on this group, with posters and billboards showing black male models. The name PowerMaster and the slogan "Bold Not Harsh" were designed to emphasize the high alcoholic content as well as mastery and boldness.

Like Uptown, PowerMaster incited a storm of protest for obvious reasons. Not only do inner-city blacks suffer higher rates of alcohol-related diseases, but the inner city experiences higher rates of violence and crime as a result of alcohol abuse. The ads might also be regarded as deceptive because of their appeal to mastery and boldness. One reporter for the *Los Angeles Times* quoted activists who charged that "alcoholic beverage manufacturers are taking advantage of minority groups and exacerbating inner-city problems by targeting them with high-powered blends."[61] And another reporter for the same newspaper wrote that "at issue is growing resentment by blacks and other minorities who feel that they are being unfairly targeted—if not exploited—by marketers of beer, liquor and tobacco products."[62]

Although Uptown and PowerMaster were never marketed, the controversies surrounding these failed products show the need to be concerned with the social impact of advertising and the products themselves. The deleterious impacts of tobacco and alcohol on poor communities are due to factors beyond any single product or advertising campaign and may not add significantly to these problems. R. J. Reynolds denied that it was attempting to attract new smokers among blacks and maintained that the company was merely trying to take away business from its competitors. A spokesperson for the Beer Institute claimed that PowerMaster was not being unfairly marketed to the poor. He said, "Everyone sells his product to the people who prefer them. . . . People can make up their own minds about what products they prefer."[63] However, as George G. Brenkert argues, marketers have a responsibility to consider not only the impact of individual products and advertisements but also the overall impact of their activities and those of others in the industry on groups that may suffer from problems related to other causes.[64] In considering the social impact of advertising, then, any one company must look at consequences in the context of all the forces operating in a community.

SOCIAL MARKETING.   Advertising has the potential to impact society positively as well as negatively. Aside from the useful economic role that advertising plays in promoting products and service, its techniques of persuasion can also be used to address social problems. Beginning in the 1970s, social welfare organizations turned to marketers to conduct advertising campaigns to raise money for charities, to support educational and cultural institutions, to promote healthy lifestyles, and to protect the environment, among other worthy aims. This development is known as *social marketing*,[65] which may be defined as "the application of commercial marketing technologies to the analysis, planning, execution, and evaluation of programs designed to influence the voluntary behavior of target audiences in order to improve their personal welfare and that of their society."[66] Insofar as many of the causes promoted by social marketing are morally desirable, this movement puts advertising in the service of ethics.

The admirable aims of social marketing do not make it free of ethical concerns. Indeed, whereas conventional marketers need to consider only the avoidance of deception, manipulation, and undesirable social impacts, social marketers must address a number of ethical concerns. Ironically, social marketing may be more ethically problematic precisely because of its good intentions. The main ethical challenges of social marketing are the following.[67]

First, since social marketers seek to change people's beliefs, attitudes, and behaviors in ways that benefit themselves and society, they must evaluate the desirability of these changes and be sure that an advertising campaign will produce them. For example, the goal of preventing heart disease is uncontroversial, although the social marketers must be sure that the recommended preventive measures are effective. However, on controversial matters, such as preventing AIDS or teen pregnancy, the ends in question, as well as the means, need to be carefully justified. At issue is some conception of people's welfare, and on this there may be reasonable disagreement.

Second, the social problems addressed by social marketing are ones on which public discussion may be desirable. For example, there are many important issues about protection of the environment that need informed debate and understanding. Insofar as advertising uses standard techniques of persuasion, people may be led to change their behavior with regard to the environment (recycling, for example) without any real public discussion taking place (say, becoming informed about greenhouse gases). By forestalling public discussion, social marketers may produce short-term benefits at the expense of long-term gains.

Third, social marketing may be effective in changing individuals' behavior, but the solutions to many social problems require more sweeping social, political, and economic change. For example, obesity can be reduced by persuading people to eat less, but significant reductions can be achieved only if fast-food companies and food manufacturers offer more healthy products. By focusing primarily on individual behavior, social marketing neglects broader social change.

Fourth, since advertising techniques are designed to persuade without necessarily enabling the target audience to understand what they are being asked to do or why, social marketing runs the risk of being manipulative. Instead of a two-sided conversation in which the people exposed to advertising participate, social marketing operates paternalistically and undemocratically.

None of these four ethical challenges suggests that social marketing ought not to be done. Indeed, social marketers have provided a great public service. Nevertheless, social marketing involves ethical questions that must be satisfactorily answered for each advertising campaign.

PRODUCT SAFETY

The right of consumers to be protected from harmful products raises innumerable problems for manufacturers. Many products can injure and even kill people, especially if the products are used improperly. Every dangerous product can be made safer at some cost, but is there a limit to the safety improvements that a manufacturer ought to provide? Do manufacturers also have a responsibility to ensure that a product is safe before it is placed on the market? If a product, like the Firestone tire, is used on an automobile designed by another company, in this case Ford, who is responsible for ensuring safety (see Case 10.3)? Three theories are commonly used to determine when a product is defective and what is owed to the victims of accidents caused by defective products.[68] These are the due care theory, the contractual theory, and the strict liability theory. Each of these theories appeals to a different ground for its ethical justification, and as legal doctrines, they each have a different source in the law.

The Due Care Theory

Generally, manufacturers have an obligation to exercise *due care*, which means that they should take all reasonable precautions to ensure that products they put on the market are free of defects likely to cause harm. According to this due care theory, manufacturers are liable for damages only when they fail to carry out this obligation and so are at fault in some way. One ethical justification for this view is the Aristotelean principle of corrective justice: Something is owed by a person who inflicts a wrongful harm upon another. By failing to exercise due care, a manufacturer is acting wrongly and hence ought to pay compensation to anyone who is injured as a result.

The legal expression of this theory is the view in the law of torts that persons are liable for acts of negligence. Negligence is defined in the *Second Restatement of Torts* (Section 282) as "conduct which falls below the standard established by law for the protection of others against unreasonable risk of harm." The usual standard established by law is the care that a "reasonable person" would exercise in a given situation. Accordingly, a reckless driver is negligent (because a reasonable person would not drive recklessly), and the driver can be legally required to pay compensation to the victims of any accident caused by the negligent behavior.[69] In the case of persons with superior skill or knowledge, the standard is higher. A manufacturer can be assumed to know more than the average person about the product and, hence, can be legally required to exercise a greater degree of care.

STANDARDS OF DUE CARE.   The standards of due care for manufacturers or other persons involved in the sale of a product to a consumer, including wholesalers and retailers, cover a wide variety of activities. Among them are the following.

1. *Design.* The product ought to be designed in accord with government and industry standards to be safe under all foreseeable conditions, including possible misuse by the consumer.

A toy with small parts that a child could choke on, for example, or a toy that could easily be broken by a child to reveal sharp edges is badly designed. Similarly, due care is not taken in the design of a crib or a playpen with slats or other openings in which a child's head could become wedged.

2. *Materials.* The materials specified in the design should also meet government and industry standards and be of sufficient strength and durability to stand up under all reasonable use. Testing should be done to ensure that the materials withstand ordinary wear and tear and do not weaken with age, stress, extremes of temperature, or other forces. The wiring in an appliance is substandard, for example, if the insulation cracks or peels, posing a risk of electrical shock.

3. *Production.* Due care should be taken in fabricating parts to specifications and assembling them correctly, so that parts are not put in the wrong way or left out. Screws, rivets, welds, and other ways of fastening parts should be properly used, and so on. Defects due to faulty construction can be avoided, in part, by giving adequate training to employees and creating conditions that allow them to do their job properly. Fast assembly lines, for example, are an invitation to defects in workmanship.

4. *Quality Control.* Manufacturers should have a systematic program to inspect products between operations or at the end to ensure that they are of sufficient quality in both materials and construction. Inspections may be done either by trained personnel or by machines. In some programs every product is inspected, whereas in others inspection is done of samples taken at intervals. Records of all quality control inspections should be maintained, and the inspectors themselves should be evaluated for effectiveness.

5. *Packaging, Labeling, and Warnings.* The product should be packaged so as to avoid any damage in transit, and the packaging and handling of perishable foodstuffs, for example, should not create any new hazard. Also, the labels and any inserts should include instructions for correct use and adequate warnings in language easily understood by users.

6. *Notification.* Finally, the manufacturers of some products should have a system of notifying consumers of hazards that only become apparent later. Automobile manufacturers, for example, maintain lists of buyers, who can be notified of recalls by mail. Recalls, warnings, and other safety messages are often conveyed by paid notices in the media.

One question that arises in the due care theory is whether manufacturers have an obligation to ensure that a product is safe to use as intended or to anticipate all the conditions under which injury could occur. The driver of a 1963 Chevrolet Corvair, for example, was severely injured in a head-on collision when the steering column struck him in the head. In the model of the car he was driving, the steering column was a rigid shaft that extended to the front end of the car. Although this design did not cause the accident, the victim claimed that his injuries were greater as a result of it. General Motors contended that its cars were intended to be used for driving on streets and highways and not for colliding with other objects. Consequently, it had no obligation to make them safe for this latter purpose. A U.S. court of appeals held, however, that due care includes "a duty to design the product so that it will fairly meet any emergency of use which can reasonably be anticipated."[70]

THE PROBLEM OF MISUSE.   This duty also extends to foreseeable misuse by the consumer. The owner's manual for the 1976 Mercury Cougar, for example, explicitly stated that the original-equipment Goodyear tires should not be used "for continuous driving over 90 miles per hour."[71] A U.S. court of appeals determined that the tread separation on the right-rear tire of a Cougar being driven in excess of 100 miles per hour was not the result of any flaw in the tire. However, the Ford Motor Company should have known that a car designed for high performance and marketed with an appeal to youthful drivers would occasionally be driven at speeds above the safe operating level of the tires. Accordingly, Ford should have warned owners of the Cougar more effectively or else equipped the car with better tires.

Some courts have held companies responsible not only for foreseeable misuse but also for misuse that is actively encouraged in the marketing of a product.[72] General Motors, for example, marketed the Pontiac Firebird Trans Am by entering specially reinforced models in racing competitions and by featuring the car in crash scenes in "antihero scofflaw" motion pictures. A promotion film that had spliced together stunt scenes from these movies was used for promotions in dealers' showrooms. In a suit brought on behalf of the driver of a 1978 Trans Am who was injured when the car went out of control while traveling more than 100 miles per hour, the court found for the plaintiff by invoking a doctrine of "invited misuse."[73]

THE CONCEPT OF NEGLIGENCE.   The major difficulty with the due care theory is establishing what constitutes due care. Manufacturers have an obligation to take precautions that are more stringent than the "reasonable person" standard, but no means exist for determining exactly how far the obligation of manufacturers extends. The courts have developed a flexible standard derived from Justice Learned Hand's famous formulation of the negligence rule.[74] In this rule, negligence involves the interplay of three factors: (1) the probability of harm, (2) the severity of the harm, and (3) the burden of protecting against the harm. Thus, manufacturers have a greater obligation to protect consumers when injury in an accident is more likely to occur, when the injury is apt to be greater, and when the cost of avoiding injury is relatively minor. These are relevant factors in formulating a standard of due care, but they are not sufficient by themselves to decide every case.

Some standards for design, materials, inspection, packaging, and the like have evolved through long experience and are now incorporated into engineering practice and government regulations. However, these standards reflect the scientific knowledge and technology at a given time and fail to impose an obligation to guard against hazards that are discovered later. Asbestos companies claimed that the danger of asbestos exposure was not known until the 1960s, at which time they instituted changes to make handling asbestos safer. This so-called "state-of-the-art" defense—in which a company contends that it exercised due care as defined by the scientific knowledge and technology at the time—was flatly rejected by the New Jersey Supreme Court decision in *Bashada* v. *Johns-Manville Products Corp.* in 1982.[75] The court reasoned that Johns-Manville ought to have made a greater attempt to discover the hazards of asbestos. In the words of the court, "Fairness suggests that manufacturers not be excused from liability because their prior inadequate investment in safety rendered the hazards of their products unknowable."

As a legal doctrine, the due care theory is difficult to apply. The focus of the theory is on the *conduct* of the manufacturer rather than on the *condition* of the product. So the mere fact that a product is defective is not sufficient for holding that a manufacturer has failed in an obligation of due care; some knowledge is needed about specific acts that a manufacturer performed or failed to perform. Lawsuits based on the theory thus require proof of negligence, which the victims of accidents caused by defective products are often not able to provide. In addition, common law allows for two defenses under the due care theory: *contributory negligence* and *assumption of risk*. Just as a manufacturer has an obligation to act responsibly, so too does a consumer. Similarly, if consumers know the dangers posed by a product and use it anyway, then to some extent they assume responsibility for any injury that results.

The Contractual Theory

A second theory is that the responsibility of manufacturers for harm resulting from defective products is that specified in a sales *contract*. The relation between buyer and seller is viewed in this theory as a contractual relation, which is subject to the terms of a contract. Even in the absence of an explicit, written contract, there may still be an implicit, understood contract between the two parties that is established by their behavior. This fact is recognized by the Uniform Commercial Code (UCC), Section 2-204(1), which states, "A contract for sale of goods may be made in any manner sufficient to show agreement, including conduct by both parties which recognizes the existence of such a contract."

One of the usual understandings is that a product be of an acceptable level of quality and fit for the purpose for which it is ordinarily used. These implicit contractual provisions are part of what is described in Section 2-314 of the UCC as an *implied warranty of merchantability*. Manufacturers have both a moral and a legal obligation, therefore, by virtue of their contractual relation, to offer only products free from dangerous defects. A person who buys a new automobile, for example, is entitled to assume that it will perform as expected and that nothing in the design makes it especially hazardous in the event of an accident.

There is also an *implied warranty of fitness* for a particular purpose when the buyer is relying on the seller's expertise in the selection of the product. In addition, an *express warranty* is created, according to Section 2-313 of the UCC, as follows:

> Any affirmation of fact or promise made by the seller to the buyer which relates to the goods and becomes part of the basis of the bargain creates an express warranty that the goods shall conform to the affirmation or promise.

The notion of an affirmation is very broad and includes any description or illustration on a package or any model or demonstration of the product being used in a certain way.

The ethical basis for the contractual theory is fairness in commercial dealings. Agreements to buy or sell a product are fair only when they are entered into freely by the contracting parties. Freedom in such agreements entails, among other things, that both buyers and sellers have adequate information about the product in question. Consumers know that the use of many products involves some danger, and they voluntarily assume the risk when the nature and extent of the hazards are revealed to them. Manufacturers may not take unfair advantage of consumers by exposing them to the risk of harm from hazards that are not disclosed. Selling a product that the manufacturer knows to be dangerous, without informing consumers, is a form of deception because crucial information is either suppressed or misrepresented. Even when the manufacturer is unaware of a defect, the cost of any accident caused by a defective product still ought to be borne by the manufacturer, because the product was sold with the understanding that it posed no hazards except those already revealed to consumers.

OBJECTIONS TO THE CONTRACTUAL THEORY.   One objection to the contractual theory is that the understandings in a sales agreement, which are the basis for implied and express warranties, are not very precise. Whether a product is of an acceptable level of quality or is fit for the purpose for which it is ordinarily used is an extremely vague standard. In practice, the theory leaves consumers with little protection, except for grossly defective products and products for which the manufacturer makes explicit claims that constitute express warranties.

Second, a sales agreement may consist of a written contract with language that sharply limits the right of an injured consumer to be compensated. If buyers and sellers are both free to contract on mutually agreeable terms, then the sales agreement can explicitly disclaim all warranties, express or implied. Section 2-316 of the UCC provides for the exclusion or modification of an implied warranty of merchantability as long as (1) the buyer's attention is drawn to the fact that no warranty is being given, with expressions such as "with all faults" or "as is"; (2) the buyer has the opportunity to examine the goods; and (3) the defect is one that can be detected on examination. If a consumer signs a contract with limiting language or explicit disclaimers, then, according to the contractual theory, the terms of that contract are binding.

HENNINGSEN V. BLOOMFIELD MOTORS.   Both of these objections are illustrated in the classic court case in warranty law *Henningsen* v. *Bloomfield Motors, Inc.*[76] Claus Henningsen purchased a new 1955 Plymouth Plaza "6" Club Sedan for use by his wife, Helen. Ten days after taking delivery of the car from a Chrysler dealer in Bloomfield, New Jersey, Mrs. Henningsen was traveling around 20 miles per hour on a smooth road when she heard a loud noise under the hood and felt something crack. The steering wheel spun in her hands as the car veered sharply to the right and crashed into a brick wall. Mrs. Henningsen was injured and the vehicle was declared a total wreck by the insurer. At the time of the accident, the odometer registered only 468 miles.

In the sales contract signed by Mr. Henningsen, the Chrysler Corporation offered to replace defective parts for 90 days after the sale or until the car had been driven 4,000 miles, whichever occurred first, "if the part is sent to the factory, transportation charges prepaid, and if examination discloses to its satisfaction that the part is defective." The contract further stipulated that the obligation of the manufacturer under this warranty is limited to the replacement of defective parts, which is "in lieu of all other warranties, expressed or implied, and all other obligations or liabilities on its part." By this language, liability for personal injuries was also excluded in the contract.

The question, as framed by the court, is simple:

> In return for the delusive remedy of replacement of defective parts at the factory, the buyer is said to have accepted the exclusion of the maker's liability for personal injuries arising from the breach of warranty, and to have agreed to the elimination of any other express or implied warranty. An instinctively felt sense of justice cries out against such a sharp bargain. But does the doctrine that a person is bound by his signed agreement, in the absence of fraud, stand in the way of any relief?

In giving an answer, the court decided that considerations of justice have greater force than an otherwise valid contract. Furthermore, the main conditions for a valid contract—namely, that the parties have roughly equal bargaining power and are able to determine the relevant facts for themselves—were absent in this case.

First, there is a gross inequality of bargaining power between consumers and manufacturers. Virtually all American cars at the time were sold using a standardized form written by the Automobile Manufacturers Association which the dealer was prohibited from altering. Due to the lack of competition among manufacturers with respect to warranties, consumers had no choice but to buy a car on the manufacturer's terms—or else do without, which is not a genuine alternative in a society where an automobile is a necessity. Hence, consumers did not have freedom of choice in any significant sense, and manufacturers were not offering consumers what they truly wanted. Consumers would most likely prefer to buy cars with better warranties.

Second, consumers are also at a profound disadvantage in their ability to examine an automobile and determine its fitness for use. They are forced to rely, for the most part, on the expertise of the manufacturer and the dealer to ensure that a car is free of defects. Further, the relevant paragraphs in the contract itself were among the hardest to read, and there was nothing in them to draw the reader's attention. "In fact," the court observed, "a studied and concentrated effort would have to be made to read them."

The Strict Liability Theory

A third theory, now gaining wider acceptance in the courts, holds that manufacturers are responsible for all harm resulting from a dangerously defective product even when due care has been exercised and all contracts observed. In this view, which is known in law as *strict liability*, a manufacturer need not be negligent nor be bound by any implied or express warranty to have responsibility. The mere fact that a product is put into the hands of consumers in a defective condition that poses an unreasonable risk is sufficient for holding the manufacturer liable.

A more precise account of the theory of strict liability is given in Section 402A of the *Second Restatement of Torts* as follows:

1. One who sells any product in a defective condition unreasonably dangerous to the user or consumer or to his property is subject to liability for physical harm thereby caused to the ultimate user or consumer, or to his property, if (a) the seller is engaged in the business of selling such a product, and (b) it is expected to and does reach the user or consumer without substantial change in the condition in which it is sold.

   2. The rule stated in Subsection (1) applies although (a) the seller has exercised all possible care in the preparation and sale of his products, and (b) the user or consumer has not bought the product from or entered into any contractual relation with the seller.

IS PRIVITY NECESSARY?   The provision of 2(b) addresses an important legal issue in both the due care and the contractual theories. Generally, lawsuits under either theory have required that the victim of an accident be in a direct contractual relation with the manufacturer. This relation is known in law as *privity*. Suppose an accident is caused by a defective part that is sold to a manufacturer by a supplier, and the finished product is sold to a wholesaler, who sells it to a retailer. The consumer, under a requirement of privity, can sue only the retailer, who can sue the wholesaler, who in turn can sue the manufacturer, and so on.

The requirement of privity developed as a way of placing reasonable limits on liability, because the consequences of actions extend indefinitely. In a simpler age when goods were often bought directly from the maker, this rule made sense. With the advent of mass production, however, most goods pass through many hands on the way to the ultimate consumer, and the requirement of a direct contractual relation greatly restricts the ability of consumers to collect compensation from manufacturers. In the landmark case *MacPherson* v. *Buick Motor Company* (1916), the New York State Court of Appeals ruled that privity was not necessary when there is negligence.[77] Negligence was present, according to the decision, because the defect in the wooden wheel supplied by another manufacturer should have been detected during the assembly of the car.

The main blow to privity in the contractual theory came in *Baxter* v. *Ford Motor Company* (1934).[78] The Supreme Court of Washington State held that a driver who was injured by flying glass when a pebble struck the windshield had a right to compensation because all Ford cars were advertised as having Triplex shatterproof glass—"so made that it will not fly or shatter under the hardest impact." Because the truth of this claim could not easily be determined by an ordinary person, buyers have a right to rely on representations made by the Ford Motor Company. Hence, the wording of Ford's advertisements creates a warranty, in the view of the court, even without a direct contractual relation.

LEGAL ISSUES IN STRICT LIABILITY.   Strict liability as a legal doctrine did not make much headway in the courts until 1963, when the California State Supreme Court ruled in *Greenman* v. *Yuba Power Products*.[79] The relevant facts are that for Christmas 1955, Mr. Greenman's wife gave him a multipurpose power tool, called a Shopsmith, which could be used as a saw, a drill, and a lathe. Two years later, while using the machine as a lathe, the piece of wood he was turning flew out of the machine and struck him on the forehead. Expert witnesses testified that some of the screws used to hold parts of the machine together were too weak to withstand the vibration.

The court declined to consider whether Yuba Power Products was negligent in the design and construction of the Shopsmith or whether it breached any warranties, either express or implied. The only relevant consideration, according to the decision, was the fact that the tool was unsafe to use in the intended way. Specifically, the court held,

> To establish the manufacturer's liability it was sufficient that the plaintiff proved that he was injured using the Shopsmith in a way it was intended to be used as a result of a defect in design and manufacture of which plaintiff was not aware that made the Shopsmith unsafe for its intended use.

Section 402A was formulated a year later in 1964. Since that time, all 50 states and the District of Columbia have adopted the doctrine of strict liability as expressed in the *Second Restatement of Torts*.

The wording of Section 402A raises two questions of definition: What is a "defective condition," and what does it mean to say that a product is "unreasonably dangerous"? Generally, a product is in a defective condition either when it is unsuitable for use as it is intended to be used or when there is some misuse that can reasonably be foreseen and steps are not taken to prevent it. A ladder that cannot withstand the weight of an ordinary user is an example of the first kind of defect; a ladder without a label warning the user against stepping too high is an example of the second. A defect in a product can include a wide range of problems—from poor design and manufacture to inadequate instructions or warnings.

The definition of "unreasonably dangerous," offered in a comment on Section 402A, is, "The article sold must be dangerous to an extent beyond that which would be contemplated by the ordinary consumer who purchases it, with the ordinary knowledge common to the community as to its characteristics." This definition is inadequate, however, because it implies that a product is not unreasonably dangerous if most consumers are fully aware of the risks it poses. All power lawnmowers are now required by federal law to be equipped with a "kill switch," which stops the engine when the handle is released. Although the dangers of power mowers are obvious to any user, a machine without a "kill switch" is (arguably) unreasonably dangerous.

THE ETHICAL ARGUMENTS FOR STRICT LIABILITY.   The ethical arguments for strict liability rest on the two distinct grounds of efficiency and equity. One argument is purely utilitarian and justifies strict liability for securing the greatest amount of protection for consumers at the lowest cost. The second argument is that strict liability is the fairest way of distributing the costs involved in the manufacture and use of products.

Both of these arguments recognize that there is a certain cost in attempting to prevent accidents and in dealing with the consequences of accidents that do occur. Preventing accidents requires that manufacturers expend greater resources on product safety. Consumers must also expend resources to avoid accidents by learning how to select safe products and how to use them correctly. Insofar as manufacturers avoid the cost of reducing accidents and turn out defective products, this cost is passed along to consumers who pay for the injuries that result. A manufacturer may save money, for example, by using a cheaper grade of steel in a hammer, but a user who suffers the loss of an eye when the head chips ends up paying instead. When product safety is viewed as a matter of cost, two questions arise: (1) How can the total cost to both manufacturers and consumers be reduced to the lowest possible level? (2) How should the cost be distributed between manufacturers and consumers?

The efficiency argument holds, in the words of one advocate, that "responsibility be fixed wherever it will most effectively reduce the hazards to life and health inherent in defective products that reach the market."[80] By this principle, manufacturers ought to bear this responsibility, because they possess greater expertise than consumers about all aspects of product safety. They also make most of the key decisions about how products are designed, constructed, inspected, and so on. By giving manufacturers a powerful incentive to use the advantages of their position to ensure that the products they turn out are free of dangerous defects, strict liability protects consumers at a relatively low cost. The alternatives, which include placing primary responsibility on government and consumers, generally involve comparatively higher costs.

The principle involved in the equity argument is expressed by Richard A. Epstein as follows: "[T]he defendant who captures the entire benefit of his own activities should . . . also bear its entire costs."[81] Insofar as manufacturers are the beneficiaries of their profit-making activity, it is only fair, according to this principle, that they be forced to bear the cost—which includes the cost of the injuries to consumers as a result of defective products. Much of the benefit of a manufacturer's activity is shared by consumers, however. But they also share the cost of compensating the victims of accidents through higher prices, and it is also just that they do so insofar as they reap some benefit. The distribution of the cost of compensating the victims of product-related injuries is fair, then, if this cost is distributed among all who benefit in the proportion that they benefit, so that it is not borne disproportionately by accident victims.

THE PROBLEM OF FAULT.   The major stumbling block to the acceptance of strict liability is that the theory ignores the element of fault, which is a fundamental condition for owing compensation on the Aristotelean conception of compensatory justice.[82] We all benefit from automotive travel, for example, but we can justly be required to pay only for accidents that are our fault. Any system of liability that makes us pay for the accidents of others is unjust—or so it seems. Similarly, it is unjust to hold manufacturers liable to pay large sums to people who are injured by defective products in the absence of negligence or a contractual obligation to compensate. It is equally unjust to force consumers to pay indirectly through higher prices the settlements in product liability suits.

The response of some advocates of strict liability is that it is not unjust to require those who are faultless to pay the cost of an activity *if everyone benefits by the use of an alternative method of paying compensation*. After all, the victims of accidents caused by defective products are not necessarily at fault either, and everyone is potentially a victim who deserves to be compensated for injuries received from defective products. Thus, those who "pay" under a system of strict liability are also protected. Furthermore, if manufacturers were not held strictly liable for the injuries caused by defective products, then they would take fewer precautions. As a result, consumers would have to spend more to protect themselves—by taking more care in the selection of products, by using them more carefully, and perhaps by taking out insurance policies—and to make up the losses they suffer in product-related accidents where no one is at fault. In either case, the lower prices that consumers pay for products under a negligence system based on the due care theory would not be sufficient to offset the higher cost of insurance, medical care, and so on.

Under a system of strict liability, consumers give up a right they have in the due care theory—namely, the right not to be forced to contribute to the compensation of accident victims when they (the consumers) are not at fault. Prices are also higher under a strict liability system in order to cover the cost of paying compensation. But consumers gain more than they lose by not being required to spend money protecting themselves and making up their own losses. They also acquire a new right: the right to be compensated for injuries from defective products without regard to fault. Thus, everyone is better off under a strict liability system than under a negligence system.

OBJECTIONS TO STRICT LIABILITY.   Critics reject many key assumptions in the two arguments for strict liability. First, product liability covers many different kinds of accidents, and the most efficient or equitable system for one kind may not be efficient or equitable for another. Careful studies need to be made of the consequences of competing theories for each kind of accident. Some proposals for reform have recommended strict liability for defects in construction and a negligence system for design defects, for example.[83]

Second, the view that corporations are able to distribute the burden of strict liability to consumers effortlessly is not always true. Multimillion-dollar awards in product liability suits and the high cost of insurance premiums place a heavy burden on manufacturers, driving some out of business and hindering the ability of others to compete. Other complaints of critics are that the threat of liability suits stifles innovation because new and untested products are more likely to be defective, and that a patchwork of state laws with differing theories and standards creates uncertainty for manufacturers. For these reasons, many business leaders have pressed for uniform product liability laws, upper limits on awards, restrictions on class-action lawsuits, and other steps to ease the impact of product liability on manufacturers.

Which theory of liability ought to be adopted? The theories rest on different ethical foundations. The due care theory is based on the Aristotelean principle of compensatory justice; the contractual theory, on freedom of contract; and strict liability, largely on utilitarian considerations. Each one embodies something we consider morally fundamental, and yet the three theories are ultimately incompatible. The contractual theory is the least satisfactory because of the power of manufacturers to write warranties and other agreements to their own advantage and to offer them to consumers on a "take it or leave it" basis. The main shortcoming of the due care theory is the difficulty of deciding what constitutes due care and whether it was exercised. Strict liability, despite the absence of fault, is arguably the best theory. It provides a powerful incentive for manufacturers to take great precautions and creates a workable legal framework for compensating consumers who are injured by defective products. For strict liability to be just, however, the costs have to be properly distributed, so that they are fair to all parties.

Conclusion

The ethics of marketing is concerned chiefly with how producers treat their customers. What goods to produce and how to sell them are among the most basic decisions that businesses make, and the impacts of these decisions on the well-being of consumers are many and varied. However, the interactions between producers and consumers take place primarily in a market, and so much of the ethics of marketing is the ethics of the buyer–seller relationship, in which honesty and fair dealing are the main moral requirements. Much of this chapter deals with marketing practices in which sales techniques and the pricing, labeling, and advertising of products are manipulative, deceptive, or otherwise unfair to consumers. In addition, marketing, especially advertising, has social consequences that producers must handle responsibly. Finally, some products on the market pose risks to consumers. Because of the importance of compensating the victims of hazardous products, questions about product safety revolve mainly around the standards for legal liability. That is, under what conditions should manufacturers be legally required to compensate people who are injured by their products? The legal standards for liability also answer the question of how safe should products be, and they play an important role in ensuring the safety of products on the market.

CASE 10.2   ✴ Explore the Concept on mythinkinglab.com

Volvo's "Bear Foot" Misstep

The television ad showed a monster truck riding atop the roofs of cars lined up in its path.[84] The truck, named "Bear Foot" because of its oversized, six-foot tires, crushed every car but one—a Volvo station wagon. The scene of devastation around the still-standing Volvo vividly illustrated the company's advertising message of strength and safety. The TV and print ads both appeared in October 1990 and received immediate critical acclaim for their effectiveness. The monster truck campaign was quickly dropped, however, amid charges of deceptive advertising.

The idea for the ad came from a monster truck rally in Vermont in which a Volvo was the only survivor of a similar stunt. In re-creating the scene at a Texas arena, the production crew employed by the advertising agency Scali, McCabe, Sloves reinforced the roof of the Volvo with lumber and steel and partially sawed through the roof supports of the other cars. When word leaked out, the attorney general of Texas began an investigation that confirmed the rigging and led to a lawsuit for consumer fraud. Volvo quickly settled the suit by running corrective ads and by reimbursing the state of Texas for the cost of the investigation and the legal fees incurred. Scali, McCabe, Sloves also resigned its Volvo account, which generated $40 million a year in revenues.

In apologizing for the ads, Volvo insisted that the company was unaware of the rigged demonstration but defended the rigging all the same. The reasons for the alterations to the cars, the company explained, were to enable the production crew to conduct the demonstration safely and to allow the Volvo to withstand the repeated runs of the monster truck that were required for filming. The claim being made was not false: Volvo engineers had determined that the roof could withstand the weight of a five-ton monster truck. The mistake was in not revealing to consumers that the ad was not an actual demonstration but a dramatization of the event in Vermont.

This was not the first time that Volvo and Scali, McCabe, Sloves had been criticized for questionable ads. The year before, an ad was produced that showed a large truck perched atop a Volvo with the tag line "How well does your car stand up to heavy traffic?" This ad was similar to one from the 1970s showing a Volvo withstanding the weight of six other Volvos stacked one on top of another. In both ads, the Volvo on the bottom was supported by jacks. The reason for the jacks, according to the company, was that the ads were intended to show only the strength of the main body; no claim was being made about the tires and suspension system, which, in any event, could not withstand such a load. The tires would blow out and the suspension system would collapse.

CASE 10.3   ✳• Explore the Concept on mythinkinglab.com

The Ford–Firestone Brawl

For almost 100 years, Firestone Tire and Rubber Company had supplied tires to Ford Motor Company. This venerable business relationship, which sprang from the close friendship of Harvey Firestone and Henry Ford at the beginning of the automotive age, was being sorely strained by a dispute between these longtime partners over problems with the Firestone tires installed on Ford's popular Explorer sport utility vehicle (SUV). By 2001, 203 deaths and over 700 injuries had resulted from rollovers in the Ford Explorer after the tread of Firestone tires separated. The showdown came at a meeting on May 21, 2001, when three senior Ford executives flew to Firestone's Nashville, Tennessee, headquarters to discuss the cause of these tragic incidents with Firestone's chief executive John Lampe.

Both Ford and Bridgestone/Firestone (Firestone merged with the Japanese tire manufacturer Bridgestone in 1988) had long been aware of safety problems with the Ford Explorer equipped with Firestone tires. When the development of a new SUV was begun in 1986, Ford executives insisted that the vehicle be cheap to produce and in production quickly. The solution that Ford engineers proposed was to bolt a passenger cabin to the chassis of the existing Ranger pickup truck. For additional cost and time savings, the vehicle could be built on the available Ranger assembly line. Initial tests on the prototype, code-named UN46, showed the vehicle to be unstable. It was prone to tipping when cornering or changing lanes and to rolling over in the event of a tire failure.

Road performance could be improved by widening the wheelbase and lowering the center of gravity, but instead of these costly improvements, Ford engineers proposed softening the suspension system and lowering the pressure on the tires. Rather than the prescribed 30 to 35 pounds per square inch (psi), the engineers recommended 26, even though low-pressure tires create more heat, especially in hot climates. In February 1989, tests of Firestone tires at 29 psi showed "a severe 'tread package' separation from the tire carcass."[85] The soft suspension system as well as the heavier weight of the Explorer compared to the Ranger truck (600 pounds more) further contributed to the heat buildup. When the lower tire pressure reduced fuel efficiency, Ford ordered Firestone to cut the weight of the tires by 3 percent in order to meet federal Corporate Average Fuel Economy (CAFE) standards.[86]

Soon after the Ford Explorer hit the market in March 1990, reports of tire failure followed by rollovers were received by both Ford and Firestone. The first complaints came from the Middle East and Venezuela, where rough road conditions were common. Drivers in Saudi Arabia and other Persian Gulf countries often lowered the tire pressure to gain traction on sand and neglected to add air for highway driving. Ford quietly replaced the original Firestone tires on thousands of vehicles outside the United States without calling the action a recall or reporting it to the National Highway Traffic Safety Agency (NHTSA). Reports of tire failure in the United States involving Firestone tires came largely from Florida, Texas, Arizona, and other warm-weather states.

On August 9, 2000, Firestone, which had been tracking warranty claims and other reports of tire failure, announced a recall of all 15-inch ATX and ATX II tires, as well as all Wilderness AT tires made at Firestone's Decatur, Illinois, plant. This recall covered an estimated 6.5 million tires still in use. Firestone engineers determined that a design flaw in the ATX tires resulted in cracking in the so-called shoulder pockets, which are scalloped areas on the side of the tire that give traction in snow and soil.[87] In addition, the Decatur plant, which endured a bitter strike in the years 1994 to 1996 that led to the production of inferior tires, used rubber pellets, which did not fuse as well as the rubber sheets used at other Firestone facilities. Despite these defects, there were few reports of tire failures involving Firestone ATX tires installed on the lighter Ranger pickup truck.

By the time of the recall, it was evident that whatever the design flaws in the Ford Explorer and the Firestone ATX tires, the combination of the two—an Explorer equipped with Firestone tires—was a dangerously defective product. Firestone executives insisted that its tires were safe when installed on appropriate vehicles but that Ford was at fault in installing them on the

Explorer. Tire failures on Explorers would not be so severe, they added, if the vehicle were not so prone to rollovers. Moreover, they held that the search for causes should focus, to some extent, on the design of the Explorer. In testimony to Congress, Mr. Lampe noted that there had been 16,000 rollovers of Explorers and that tire failure had been the cause of less than 10 percent of those accidents.[88] He also observed that more than 80 percent of the failures occurred on the rear wheels and more than half of those on the left rear tire.[89] Firestone also faulted Ford for addressing the Explorer's instability by recommending the lower tire pressure and also for steadily increasing the weight of the Explorer during the mid-1990s, which further eroded the tires' margin of safety. Consumers were also at fault, they claimed, for not maintaining proper inflation and making repairs correctly.[90]

Jacques Nasser, the CEO of Ford, countered, "This is a tire issue, not a vehicle issue."[91] Ford released data showing that during a five-year period, Firestone tires on 1996 Explorers were involved in 30 fatal accidents per million tires produced while Explorers equipped with Goodyear tires were involved in only three fatal accidents per million tires produced, one-tenth the number.[92] Although automobile manufacturers dictate tire specifications to their suppliers, Firestone still chose to provide the tires for the Explorer that Ford demanded. Interestingly, Goodyear stopped supplying tires to Ford in 1997 because executives decided that they could not meet their own quality standards at the price that Ford was willing to pay.[93] Despite numerous warranty claims, though, Firestone failed to recognize the seriousness of the problem and to share the information with Ford. One reason for these failures is that after the merger of Firestone with Bridgestone, the database of warranty claims remained in Akron, where Firestone was located, while the database on damages was moved to Nashville, the home of Bridgestone.[94] Once the problem was recognized, Firestone issued a recall for the 15-inch ATX and ATX II tires but not the 16- and 17-inch tires, which some believed were also defective.

Prior to the May 21 meeting, each side had provided the other with some of the auto safety data they had collected. It soon became apparent that each company was interpreting the data differently and using them to place responsibility on the other.[95] The Ford executives would not comment on a report that the company was preparing to replace virtually all suspect Firestone tires on its Explorers, and they refused a request to conduct a joint investigation into the safety of the vehicle. What they wanted to talk about instead was data that suggested problems with yet other Firestone tires. At that point, John Lampe handed the Ford executive a letter he had composed in advance, severing all relations between Firestone and Ford. The next day, Ford announced the company would replace 13 million Firestone tires at a cost of $3 billion.[96] Jacques Nasser was surprised that Firestone would walk away from $7.5 billion in annual sales, which was 40 percent of Bridgestone/Firestone's global revenues. Mr. Lampe, in his letter addressed to Mr. Nasser, wrote, "Business relationships, like personal ones, are built on trust and mutual respect." He explained, "We have come to the conclusion that we can no longer supply tires to Ford since the basic foundation of our relationship has been seriously eroded."[97] Thus, the relationship forged by Harvey Firestone and Henry Ford a century ago came to an end amid mutual recriminations.

Notes

1. Iris Cohen Selinger, "The Big Lottery Gamble," *Advertising Age*, 10 May 1993, 22.
2. Charles T. Clotfelter and Philip J. Cook, *Selling Hope: State Lotteries in America* (Cambridge, MA: Harvard University Press, 1989). Most of the information in this case is derived from this study and from Charles T. Clotfelter, Philip J. Cook, Julie A. Edell, and Marian Moore, "State Lotteries at the Turn of the Century: Report to the National Gambling Impact Study Commission," 23 April 1999.
3. Clotfelter and Cook, *Selling Hope*, 186.
4. Clotfelter et al., "State Lotteries at the Turn of the Century."
5. John Koza, "Who Is Playing What? A Demographic Study," *Public Gaming*, 12 (March–June 1984), 31–40.
6. Selinger, "The Big Lottery Gamble."

7. Amos Tversky and Daniel Kahneman, "Judgment under Uncertainty: Heuristics and Biases," *Science* 185 (1974), 1124–31.

8. Selinger, "The Big Lottery Gamble."

9. James M. Stearns and Shaheen Borna, "The Ethics of Lottery Advertising: Issues and Evidence," *Journal of Business Ethics*, 14 (1995), 43–51.

10. The average lottery expenditure of families with annual incomes under $25,000 is less than $600. Clotfelter, et al., "State Lotteries at the Turn of the Century."

11. Theodore Levitt, *The Marketing Imagination* (New York: Free Press, 1986), 19.

12. Michael J. Etzel, Bruce J. Walker, and William J. Stanton, *Marketing*, 13th ed. (New York: McGraw-Hill/Irwin, 2004), 511.

13. David Holley, "A Moral Evaluation of Sales Practices," *Business and Professional Ethics Journal*, 5 (1986), 3–21, see p. 5.

14. Thomas Carson, "Deception and Withholding Information in Sales," *Business Ethics Quarterly*, 1 (2001), 275–306.

15. Holley, "A Moral Evaluation of Sales Practices," 7.

16. Tom L. Beauchamp, "Manipulative Advertising," *Business and Professional Ethics Journal*, 3 (1984), 1–22.

17. Manipulative sales practices that exploit the poor are well documented in David Caplovitz, *The Poor Pay More* (New York: Free Press, 1963), and the report by the National Advisory Commission on Civil Disorders, better known as the Kerner Commission, in 1968. Another study is Alan R. Andreasen, *The Disadvantaged Consumer* (New York: Free Press, 1975).

18. Cheryl L. Reed, "The 'Wild, Wild West' in Loans," *Chicago Sun-Times*, 15 August 2004, 20.

19. See Daniel Kahneman, Jack L. Knetch, and Richard Thaler, "Fairness as a Constraint on Profit-Seeking: Entitlements in the Market," *American Economic Review*, 76 (1986), 728–41.

20. John B. Hinge, "Critics Call Cuts in Package Size Deceptive Move," *Wall Street Journal*, 5 February 1991, B1.

21. Much of this discussion is adapted from Frank V. Cespedes, "Ethical Issues in Distribution," in *Ethics in Marketing*, ed. N. Craig Smith and John A. Quelch (Burr Ridge, IL: Irwin, 1993).

22. William M. Pride and O. C. Ferrell, *Marketing: Basic Concepts and Decisions*, 10th ed. (Boston, MA: Houghton Mifflin, 1997), 40.

23. See Harry L. Darling, "How Companies Are Using Corporate Advertising," *Public Relations Journal*, 31 (November 1975), 26–29; William S. Sachs, "Corporate Advertising: Ends, Means, Problems," *Public Relations Journal*, 37 (November 1981), 14–17; and S. Prakash Sethi, "Institutional/Image Advertising and Idea/Issue Advertising as Marketing Tools: Some Public Policy Issues," *Journal of Marketing*, 47 (January 1983), 68–78.

24. Theodore Levitt, "The Morality (?) of Advertising," *Harvard Business Review*, 48 (July–August 1970), 85.

25. For examples, see David M. Gardner, "Deception in Advertising: A Conceptual Approach," *Journal of Marketing*, 39 (January 1975), 40–46; and Thomas L. Carson, Richard E. Wokutch, and James E. Cox, Jr., "An Ethical Analysis of Deception in Advertising," *Journal of Business Ethics*, 4 (1985), 93–104.

26. Ivan L. Preston, "Reasonable or Ignorant Consumer? How the FTC Decides," *Journal of Consumer Affairs*, 8 (1974), 132.

27. *Gelb* v. *FTC*, 144 F. 2d 580 (2nd Cir. 1944).

28. See Bonnie Liebman, "Nouveau Junk Food: Consumers Swallow the Back-to-Nature Bunk," *Business and Society Review*, 51 (Fall 1984), 47–51.

29. *Campbell Soup*, 77 FTC 664 (1970).

30. See Jeanne Saddler, "Campbell Soup Will Change Ads to Settle Charges," *Wall Street Journal*, 9 April 1991, B6.

31. "F.T.C. in Accord with Campbell," *New York Times*, 10 April 1991, D4.

32. Vance Packard, *The Hidden Persuaders* (New York: David McKay, 1957), 20–21.

33. Ibid., 25.

34. Herbert J. Rotfeld, "Fear Appeals and Persuasion," *Current Issues and Research in Advertising*, 11 (1989), 21–40.

35. Ibid., 35.

36. For one example, see "Secret Voices: Messages That Manipulate," *Time*, 10 September 1979, 71.

37. A researcher who claims to find evidence for both the frequency and the effectiveness of subliminal advertising is Wilson Brian Key, who has written three books: *Subliminal Seduction* (Upper Saddle River, NJ: Prentice Hall, 1974); *Media Sexploitation* (Upper Saddle River, NJ: Prentice Hall, 1976); and *The Clam-Plate Orgy and Other Subliminal Techniques for Manipulating Your Behavior* (Upper Saddle River, NJ: Prentice Hall, 1980). A generally negative appraisal of the effectiveness of the technique is offered in Norman F. Dixon, *Subliminal Perception* (London: McGraw-Hill, 1971). For evidence specifically on advertising, see Stephen G. George and Luther B. Jennings, "Effect of Subliminal Stimuli on Consumer Behavior: Negative Evidence," *Perceptual and Motor Skills*, 41 (1975), 847–54; Del I. Hawkins, "The Effects of Subliminal Stimulation on Drive Level and Brand Preference," *Journal of Marketing Research*, 8 (1970), 322–26; and Timothy E. Moore, "Subliminal Advertising: What You See Is What You Get," *Journal of Marketing*, 46 (Spring 1982), 38–47.

38. Richard T. DeGeorge, *Business Ethics*, 6th ed. (Upper Saddle River, NJ: Prentice Hall, 2006), 343.

39. See Michael Schudson, *Advertising, The Uneasy Persuasion: Its Dubious Impact on Society* (New York: Basic Books, 1984), 102–13.

40. Rob Walker, "The Hidden (in Plain Sight) Persuaders," *New York Times Magazine*, 5 December 2004, 69.

41. This is not the only ground for objecting to product placement. Critics also cite the element of deception and the corrupting effect of product placement on the artistic integrity of movies.

42. John Kenneth Galbraith, *The Affluent Society* (New York: Houghton Mifflin, 1958), 128.

43. Ibid., 124–25.

44. Friedrich August von Hayek, "The Non Sequitur of the 'Dependence Effect,'" *Southern Economic Journal*, 27 (April 1961), 346–48. Similar points are made in Levitt, "The Morality(?) of Advertising," 84–92.

45. Packard, *The Hidden Persuaders*, 110.

46. Although this practice is generally accepted as legitimate persuasion, an interesting issue is posed by the increasing use of market research in jury selection and the formation of legal strategy. If lawyers start adopting the techniques of advertisers, then they could open themselves up to many of the same criticisms. See Scott M. Smith, "Marketing Research and Corporate Litigation . . . Where Is the Balance of Ethical Justice?" *Journal of Business Ethics*, 3 (1984), 185–94.

47. For a comprehensive summary of advertising's critics, see Richard W. Pollay, "The Distorted Mirror: Reflections on the Unintended Consequences of Advertising," *Journal of Marketing*, 50 (1986), 18–36. Much of this section is drawn from this article.

48. Lynn Sharp Paine, "Children as Consumers: The Ethics of Children's Television Advertising," *Business and Professional Ethics Journal*, 3 (1984), 119–45.

49. For a critique of television's impact on children, see Marie Winn, *The Plug-In Drug*, 2nd rev. ed. (New York: Penguin Books, 2002).

50. Marya Mannes, *But Will It Sell?* (New York: Lippincott, 1964), 32.

51. See Juliet B. Schor, *The Overspent American: Why We Want What We Don't Need* (New York: Basic Books, 1998).

52. Pollay, "The Distorted Mirror," 25.

53. Varda Langholz Leymore, *Hidden Myth: Structure and Symbolism in Advertising* (New York: Basic Books, 1975), x.

54. Vickie Rutledge Shields and Dawn Heinecken, *Measuring Up: How Advertising Affects Self-Image* (Philadelphia, PA: University of Pennsylvania Press, 2002), x.

55. This case is made in documentary films by Jean Kilbourne, *Still Killing Us Softly: Advertising Images of Women* (Cambridge, MA: Cambridge Documentary Films, 1987); and *Slim Hopes* (Amherst, MA: Media Education Foundation, 1999).

56. For ethical guidelines, see John Douglas Bishop, "Is Self-Identity Image Advertising Ethical?" *Business Ethics Quarterly*, 10 (2000), 371–98.

57. Erving Goffman, *Gender Advertisements* (London: Marion Boyars, 1978), 17.

58. "Media Uproar Over Billboards in Poor Areas," *New York Times*, 1 May 1989, D32.

59. Philip J. Hilts, "Health Chief Assails Reynolds Co. for Ads That Target Blacks," *New York Times*, 19 January 1990, A1.

60. George G. Brekert, "Marketing to Inner-City Blacks: PowerMaster and Moral Responsibility," *Business Ethics Quarterly*, 8 (1998), 1–18. Much of the information about this case is taken from this article.

61. Marc Lacey, "Marketing of Malt Liquor Fuels Debate," *Los Angeles Times*, 15 December 1992, A32.

62. Bruce Horovitz, "Brewer Faces Boycott Over Marketing of Potent Malt Liquor," *Los Angeles Times*, 25 June 1991, D6.

63. Paul Farhi, "Surgeon General Hits New Malt Liquor's Name, Ads," *Washington Post*, 26 June 1991, A4.

64. Brenkert, "Marketing to Inner-City Blacks," 14–15.

65. The seminal work is Philip Kotler and Eduardo L. Roberto, *Social Marketing: Strategies for Changing Public Behavior* (New York: Free Press, 1989).

66. Alan R. Andreasen, *Marketing Social Change* (San Francisco, CA: Jossey-Bass, 1995), 7.

67. George G. Brenkert, "Ethical Challenges of Social Marketing," *Journal of Public Policy and Marketing*, 21 (2002), 14–25. Much of the following discussion is taken from this article. See also Alan R. Andreasen, ed., *Ethics in Social Marketing* (Washington, DC: Georgetown University Press, 2001).

68. For the sake of simplicity, the discussion in this section focuses only on manufacturers, but a responsibility for product safety extends to wholesalers, distributors, franchisers, and retailers, among others, although their responsibility is generally less than that of manufacturers.

69. The conditions under which a negligent act is a cause of injury to another person (known in law as proximate cause) are complicated. See any standard textbook on business law for an explanation.

70. *Larsen v. General Motors Corporation*, 391 F. 2d 495 (8th Cir. 1968).

71. *LeBouef v. Goodyear Tire and Rubber Co.*, 623 F. 2d 985 (5th Cir. 1980).

72. See Ed Timmerman and Brad Reid, "The Doctrine of Invited Misuse: A Societal Response to Marketing Promotion," *Journal of Macromarketing*, 4 (Fall 1984), 40–48.

73. *Commercial National Bank of Little Rock, Guardian of the Estate of Jo Ann Fitzsimmons v. General Motors Corporation*, U.S. Dist. Ct. E.D.Ark., No. LR-C-79-168 (1979).

74. *United States v. Carroll Towing Co.*, 159 F. 2d 169 (2nd Cir. 1947).

75. *Bashada v. Johns-Manville Products Corp.*, 90 N.J. 191, 447 A. 2d 539 (1982). The "state-of-the-art" defense has been accepted in other cases. See, for example, *Boatland of Houston, Inc. v. Bailey*, 609 S.W. 2d 743 (Tex. 1980). For an overview, see Jordan H. Leibman, "The Manufacturer's Responsibility to Warn Product Users of Unknowable Dangers," *American Business Law Journal*, 21 (1984), 403–38.

76. *Henningsen v. Bloomfield Motors, Inc. and Chrysler Corporation*, 161 A. 2d 69 (1960).

77. *MacPherson v. Buick Motor Company*, 217 N.Y. 382 (1916).

78. *Baxter v. Ford Motor Company*, 168 Wash. 456, 12 P. 2d 409 (1932); 179 Wash. 123, 35 P. 2d 1090 (1934).

79. *Greenman v. Yuba Power Products*, 59 Cal. 2d 57, 377 P. 2d 897, 27 Cal. Rptr. 697 (1963). The theory was enunciated 19 years earlier in *Escola v. Coca-Cola Bottling Co.*, 24 Cal. 2d 453, 150 P. 2d 436 (1944).

80. *Escola v. Coca-Cola Bottling Co.*

81. Richard A. Epstein, *Modern Products Liability Law* (Westport, CT: Quorum Books, 1980), 27. Epstein holds, however, that this principle has limited application in product liability cases.

82. George P. Fletcher, "Fairness and Utility in Tort Theory," *Harvard Law Review*, 85 (1972), 537–73; Richard A. Epstein, "A Theory of Strict Liability," *Journal of Legal Studies*, 2 (1973), 151–204; and Jules L. Coleman, "The Morality of Strict Tort Liability," *William and Mary Law Review*, 18 (1976), 259–586. Richard Posner argues that the Aristotelean principle of compensatory justice in a negligence system, correctly understood, is the same as the principle of efficiency that underlies strict liability. See Richard Posner, "A Theory of Negligence," *Journal*

of Legal Studies, 1 (1972), 29–96; and Richard Posner, "The Concept of Corrective Justice in Recent Theories of Tort Law," *Journal of Legal Studies*, 10 (1981), 187–206.

83. This proposal was contained in S. 44, an unsuccessful bill introduced in the 98th Congress.

84. Material for this case is from Barry Meier, "For This Pounding, Volvo Had Help," *New York Times*, 6 November 1990, D1; Kim Folz, "Scali Quits Volvo Account, Citing Faked Commercial," *New York Times*, 14 November 1990, D1; Krystal Miller and Jacqueline Mitchell, "Car Marketers Test Gray Area of Truth in Advertising," *Wall Street Journal*, 19 November 1990, B1.

85. "Chronology of Firestone/Ford Knowledge of Tire Safety Defect," http://www.citizen.org, last accessed January 31, 2005.

86. John Greenwald, "Tired of Each Other," *Time*, 22 June 2001, 50–56.

87. Keith Bradsher, "Firestone Engineers Offer a List of Causes for Faulty Tires," *New York Times*, 19 December 2000, C1.

88. Matthew L. Wald, "Rancor Grows between Ford and Firestone," *New York Times*, 13 September 2000, C1.

89. Mark Truby, "Firestone CEO Quits, New Chief Rips Ford," *Detroit News*, 11 October 2000.

90. Ibid.

91. Francisco Toro and Frank Swoboda, "Venezuela Puts Blame on Ford, Firestone," *Washington Post*, 1 September 2000, Al.

92. James V. Grimaldi and Frank Swoboda, "Ford Offers Tire Data Comparison," *Washington Post*, 18 September 2000, A10.

93. Ibid.

94. Bradsher, "Firestone Engineers Offer a List of Causes of Faulty Tires."

95. Caroline E. Mayer and Frank Swoboda, "A Corporate Collision," *Washington Post*, 20 June 2001, E1.

96. Ibid.

97. Keith Bradsher, "Firestone Stops Sales to Ford, Saying It Was Used as Scapegoat," *New York Times*, 22 May 2001, A1.

11

Ethics in Finance

CASE 11.1 ✳─Explore the Concept on mythinkinglab.com

Merrill Lynch and the Nigerian Barge Deal

The investment bankers at Merrill Lynch were considering an unusual offer from the treasurer at Enron.[1] Daniel Bayly, the global head of the investment banking division at Merrill Lynch, had been approached by Jeffrey McMahon at Enron about the purchase of three electrical generating barges in the waters of Nigeria. Enron was coming to the end of 1999 and desperately needed to book more revenue to keep up the company's high-flying stock price, and this deal would earn Enron a much-needed $12 million profit.

Merrill Lynch was not in the electrical generating business, but the deal did not require the investment banking giant to operate the barges, which, in any event, were not yet up and running. The plan, as conceived by Enron executives, was for Merrill Lynch to purchase the three barges for $28 million. Three-quarters of this amount, $21 million, would be loaned to Merrill Lynch by Enron, so that Merrill Lynch would need to put up only $7 million of the purchase price. In return, Enron would promise to find a buyer for the barges or else buy them back within six months with a guaranteed return of 15 percent on Merrill Lynch's $7 million outlay. Ordinarily, a return of this size would require the assumption of considerable risk, but Enron was offering the Merrill Lynch bankers an outsized, risk-free return—almost too good an offer to turn down. All that was needed was for Daniel Bayly to sign off on the deal.

Mr. Bayly had some reasons for concern. If Enron was committed to buying back the barges with no risk for Merrill, then was this a true sale? Would Merrill Lynch be the real owner during this time? If not, then the "sale" would be more a disguised loan. Such a loan should be recorded in Enron's books as debt, but the purpose of the deal was clearly to enable Enron to report $12 million in revenue. Enron might thus be engaging in accounting fraud, but, if so, was this Merrill Lynch's responsibility? Enron did not promise to repurchase the barges itself but only to ensure that a buyer would be found. If that buyer were a third party, then the transaction would be a legitimate sale. In the meantime, Merrill Lynch would be providing what is called "bridge equity," which is a short-term investment that is used until a long-term investor can be found. Enron had, in fact, been negotiating to sell the barges to a Japanese firm, the Marubeni Corporation. The negotiations were not proceeding fast enough to complete a sale before the end of the year, but perhaps a sale could be concluded within six months' time.

The repurchase could also be made by one of the many off-balance-sheet partnerships, or special purpose entities (SPEs), that Enron had set up. One partnership, called LJM2, which was controlled by Enron CFO Andrew Fastow, had engaged in a number of rapid sales and repurchases that created revenues for Enron and kept debt off its balance sheet. If the commitment to buy back the barges came from Mr. Fastow on behalf of the LJM2, then it would not be coming from Enron itself. Moreover, the Enron plan did not call for Merrill Lynch to directly buy the barges. Instead, an SPE would be created that would be funded with $21 million from Enron and $7 million from Merrill. Accounting standards permitted such a shell entity to be off Enron's balance sheet if it had 3 percent outside ownership, which would be provided by Merrill's investment. Since Enron would still have control of the SPE, the effect would be Enron buying from and selling to itself. After six months, Enron would not be buying the barges back from Merrill but merely closing down the partnership and returning to Merrill its investment plus the guaranteed return.

The deal was submitted to Merrill's Debt Market Commitments Committee, where Robert Furst, a managing director of Merrill Lynch, and the Enron relationship manager at the time apparently supported it. The head of the Asset Lease and Finance Group, James A. Brown, was concerned, though, about Enron manipulating earnings. Others apparently thought that the amount was too small to be material given Enron's total revenues. Concern was also expressed about the firmness of Enron's commitment, and so Mr. Bayly talked directly with Andrew Fastow, who has testified that he said unequivocally that Merrill would not lose money on the deal and would receive a guaranteed return. Both Mr. Bayly and Mr. Brown insist that the Enron CFO promised only to make a "best effort" to find a buyer. According to other testimony, Mr. Bayly asked for Enron's commitment in writing but was told that Enron could not do that and get "the right accounting treatment." In the meantime, there was no due diligence in examining the three Nigerian barges and no bargaining over the price that Merrill would pay or the return, both of which would be expected in a real investment.

In the end, the deal was accepted. Merrill Lynch invested $7 million; Enron recorded $12 million in revenues; and six months later Fastow's partnership LJM2 repurchased the barges for $7.525 million, which represents Merrill's $7 million investment plus a 15 percent annualized return. In 2003, the Securities and Exchange Commission (SEC) brought a suit alleging fraud. Messrs. Bayly, Brown, and Furst were convicted in 2004 along with another Merrill Lynch employee and one low-level Enron employee. Before these individuals were tried, Merrill Lynch settled with the SEC, paying $80 million for the Nigerian barge deal and another transaction with Enron. In 2006, the convictions of the three former Merrill Lynch bankers were overturned on the grounds of a legal technicality over the interpretation of the federal fraud statute under which they were originally tried.

INTRODUCTION

Some cynics jokingly deny that there is any ethics in finance, especially on Wall Street. This view is expressed in a thin volume, *The Complete Book of Wall Street Ethics*, which claims to fill "an empty space on financial bookshelves where a consideration of ethics should be."[2] Of course, the pages are all blank! However, a moment's reflection reveals that finance would be impossible without ethics. The very act of placing our assets in the hands of other people requires immense trust. An untrustworthy stockbroker or insurance agent, like an untrustworthy physician or attorney, finds few takers for his or her services. Financial scandals shock us precisely because they involve people and institutions that we should be able to trust.

Finance covers a broad range of activities, but the two most visible aspects are financial markets, such as stock exchanges, and the financial services industry, which includes not only commercial banks but also investment banks, mutual fund companies, both public and private pension funds, and insurance companies. Less visible to the public are the financial operations of a corporation, which are the responsibility of the chief financial officer (CFO). This chapter focuses first on ethics in financial markets and the financial services industry by examining market regulation, which is the subject of securities law and regulation by the Securities and Exchange Commission (SEC), and the treatment of customers by financial services firms. Because Wall Street was shaken in the 1980s by instances of insider trading by prominent financiers and by hotly contested battles for corporate control by some of the same financiers, this chapter also covers the topics of insider trading and hostile takeovers.

FINANCIAL SERVICES

The financial services industry still operates largely through personal selling by stockbrokers, insurance agents, financial planners, tax advisers, and other finance professionals. Personal selling creates innumerable opportunities for abuse, and although finance professionals take pride in the level of integrity in the industry, misconduct still occurs. However, customers who are unhappy over failed investments or rejected insurance claims are quick to blame the seller of the product, sometimes with good reason.

For example, two real estate limited partnerships launched by Merrill Lynch & Co. in 1987 and 1989 lost close to $440 million for 42,000 investor-clients.[3] Known as Arvida I and Arvida II, these highly speculative investment vehicles projected double-digit returns on residential developments in Florida and California, but both stopped payments to investors in 1990. At the end of 1993, each $1,000 unit of Arvida I was worth $125, and each $1,000 unit of Arvida II, a mere $6.

The Arvida partnerships were offered by the Merrill Lynch sales force to many retirees of modest means as safe investments with good income potential. The brokers themselves were told by the firm that Arvida I entailed only "moderate risk," and company-produced sales material said little about risk while emphasizing the projected performance. Left out of the material was the fact that the projections included a return of some of the investors' own capital, that the track record of the real estate company was based on commercial, not residential projects, and that eight of the top nine managers of the company had left just before Arvida I was offered to the public.

This case raises questions about whether investors were deceived by the brokers' sales pitches and whether material information was concealed. In other cases, brokers have been accused of churning client accounts in order to generate higher fees and of selecting unsuitable investments for clients. Other abusive sales practices in the financial services industry include twisting, in which an insurance agent persuades a policy holder to replace an older policy with a newer one that provides little if any additional benefit but generates a commission for the agent, and flipping, in which a loan officer persuades a borrower to repay an old loan with a new one, thereby incurring more fees. In one case, an illiterate retiree, who was flipped 10 times in a four-year period, paid $19,000 in loan fees for the privilege of borrowing $23,000.

This section discusses three objectionable practices in selling financial products to clients, namely, deception, churning, and suitability.

Deception

The ethical treatment of clients requires salespeople to explain all of the relevant information truthfully in an understandable, nonmisleading manner. One observer complains that brokers, insurance agents, and other salespeople have developed a new vocabulary that obfuscates rather than reveals.

Walk into a broker's office these days. You won't be sold a product. You won't even find a broker. Instead, a "financial adviser" will "help you select" an "appropriate planning vehicle," or "offer" a menu of "investment choices" or "options" among which to "allocate your money." . . . [Insurance agents] peddle such euphemisms as "private retirement accounts," "college savings plans," and "charitable remainder trusts." . . . Among other linguistic sleights of hand in common usage these days: saying tax-free when, in fact, it's only tax-deferred; high yield when it's downright risky; and projected returns when it's more likely in your dreams.[4] Salespeople avoid speaking of commissions, even though they are the source of their compensation. Commissions on mutual funds are "front-end" or "back-end loads"; and insurance agents, whose commissions can approach 100 percent of the first year's premium, are not legally required to disclose this fact—and they rarely do. The agents of one insurance company represented life insurance policies as "retirement plans" and referred to the premiums as "deposits."[5]

Deception is often a matter of interpretation. Promotional material for a mutual fund, for example, may be accurate but misleading if it emphasizes the strengths of a fund and minimizes the weaknesses. Figures of past performance can be carefully selected and displayed in ways that give a misleading impression. Deception can also occur when essential information is not revealed. Thus, an investor may be deceived when the sales charge is rolled into the fund's annual expenses, which may be substantially higher than the competition's, or when the projected hypothetical returns do not reflect all charges. As these examples suggest, factually true claims may lead typical investors to hold mistaken beliefs. Deception aside, what information ought to be disclosed to a client? The Securities Act of 1933 requires the issuer of a security to disclose all material information, which is defined as information about which an average prudent investor ought reasonably to be informed or to which a reasonable person would attach importance in determining a course of action in a transaction. The rationale for this provision of the Securities Act is both fairness to investors, who have a right to make decisions with adequate information, and the efficiency of securities markets, which requires that investors be adequately informed. Most financial products, including mutual funds and insurance policies, are accompanied by a written prospectus that contains all of the information that the issuer is legally required to provide.

The analysis of deception by a financial service provider is similar to that provided for deceptive advertising in Chapter 10. In general, a person is deceived when that person is unable to make a rational choice as a result of holding a false belief that is created by some claim made by another. That claim may be either a false or misleading statement or a statement that is incomplete in some crucial way.

Consider two cases of possible broker (mis)conduct:

1. A brokerage firm buys a block of stock prior to issuing a research report that contains a "buy" recommendation in order to ensure that enough shares are available to fill customer orders. However, customers are not told that they are buying stock from the firm's own holdings, and they are charged the current market price plus the standard commission for a trade.

2. A broker assures a client that an initial public offering (IPO) of a closed-end fund is sold without a commission and encourages quick action by saying that after the IPO is sold, subsequent buyers will have to pay a seven percent commission. In fact, a seven percent commission is built into the price of the IPO, and this charge is revealed in the prospectus but will not appear on the settlement statement for the purchase.

In the first case, one might argue that if an investor decides to purchase shares of stock in response to a "buy" recommendation, it matters little whether the shares are bought on the open market or from a brokerage firm's holdings. The price is the same. An investor might appreciate the opportunity to share any profit that is realized by the firm (because of lower trading costs and perhaps a lower stock price before the recommendation is released), but the firm is under no obligation to share any profit with its clients. On the other hand, the client is buying the stock at the current market price and paying a fee as though the stock were purchased at the order of the client. The circumstances of the purchase are not explained to the client, but does the broker have any obligation to do so? And would this knowledge have any effect on the client's decision?

In the second case, however, a client might be induced to buy an initial offering of a closed-end mutual fund in the mistaken belief that the purchase would avoid a commission charge. The fact that the commission charge is disclosed in the prospectus might ordinarily exonerate the broker from a charge of deception except that the false belief is created by the broker's claim, which, at best, skirts the edge of honesty. Arguably, the broker made the claim with an intent to deceive, and a typical, prudent investor is apt to feel that there was an attempt to deceive.

Churning

Churning is defined as excessive or inappropriate trading for a client's account by a broker who has control over the account with the intent to generate commissions rather than to benefit the client. Although churning occurs, there is disagreement on the frequency or the rate of detection. The brokerage industry contends that churning is a rare occurrence and is easily detected by firms as well as clients. No statistics are kept on churning, but complaints to the SEC and various exchanges about unauthorized trading and other abuses have risen sharply in recent years.

The ethical objection to churning is straightforward: It is a breach of a fiduciary duty to trade in ways that are not in a client's best interests. Churning, as distinct from unauthorized trading, occurs only when a client turns over control of an account to a broker, and by taking control, a broker assumes a responsibility to serve the client's interests. A broker who merely recommends a trade is not acting on behalf of a client or customer and is more akin to a traditional seller, but a broker in charge of a client's portfolio thereby pledges to manage it to the best of his or her ability.

Although churning is clearly wrong, the concept is difficult to define. Some legal definitions offered in court decisions are as follows: "excessive trading by a broker disproportionate to the size of the account involved, in order to generate commissions,"[6] and a situation in which "a broker, exercising control over the frequency and volume of trading in the customer's account, initiates transactions that are excessive in view of the character of the account."[7] The courts have held that for churning to occur a broker must trade with the intention of generating commissions rather than benefiting the client. The legal definition of churning contains three elements, then: (1) the broker controls the account; (2) the trading is excessive for the character of the account; and (3) the broker acted with intent.

The most difficult issue in the definition of churning is the meaning of "excessive trading." First, whether trading is excessive depends on the character of the account. A client who is a more speculative investor, willing to assume higher risk for a greater return, should expect a higher trading volume. Second, high volume is not the only factor; pointless trades might be considered churning even if the volume is relatively low. Third, churning might be indicated by a pattern of trading that consistently favors trades that yield higher commissions. Common to these three points is the question of whether the trades make sense from an investment point of view. High-volume trading that loses money might still be defended as an intelligent but unsuccessful investment strategy, whereas investments that represent no strategy beyond generating commissions are objectionable, no matter the amount gained or lost.

A 1995 SEC report concluded that the compensation system in brokerage firms was the root cause of the churning problem.[8] The report identified some "best practices" in the industry that might prevent churning, including ending the practice of paying a higher commission for a company's own products, prohibiting sales contests for specific products, and tying a portion of compensation to the size of a client's account, regardless of the number of transactions. However, an SEC panel concluded that the commission system is too deeply rooted to be significantly changed and recommended better training and oversight by brokerage firms.

Suitability

In general, brokers, insurance agents, and other salespeople have an obligation to recommend only suitable securities and financial products. However, suitability, like churning, is difficult to define precisely. The rules of the National Association of Securities Dealers include the following:

> In recommending to a customer the purchase, sale, or exchange of any security, a member shall have reasonable grounds for believing that the recommendation is suitable for such customer upon the basis of the facts, if any, disclosed by such customer as to his other security holding and as to his financial situation and needs.[9]

The most common causes of unsuitability are (1) unsuitable types of securities, that is, recommending stocks, for example, when bonds would better fit the investor's objectives; (2) unsuitable grades of securities, such as selecting lower-rated bonds when higher-rated ones are more appropriate; (3) unsuitable diversification, which leaves the portfolio vulnerable to changes in the markets; (4) unsuitable trading techniques, including the use of margin or options, which can leverage an account and create greater volatility and risk; and (5) unsuitable liquidity. Limited partnerships, for example, are not very marketable and are thus unsuitable for customers who may need to liquidate the investment.

The critical question, of course, is, When is a security unsuitable? Rarely is a single security unsuitable except in the context of an investor's total portfolio. Investments are most often deemed to be unsuitable because they involve excessive risk, but a few risky investments may be appropriate in a well-balanced, generally conservative portfolio. Furthermore, even an aggressive, risk-taking portfolio may include unsuitable securities if the risk is not compensated by the expected return.

Ensuring that a recommended security is suitable for a given investor thus involves many factors, but people in the financial services industry offer to put their specialized knowledge and skills to work for us. We expect suitable recommendations from physicians, lawyers, and accountants. Why should we expect anything less from finance professionals?

FINANCIAL MARKETS

Financial transactions typically take place in organized markets, such as stock markets, commodities markets, futures or options markets, currency markets, and the like. These markets presuppose certain moral rules and expectations of moral behavior. The most basic of these is a prohibition against fraud and manipulation, but, more generally, the rules and expectations for markets are concerned with fairness, which is often expressed as a level playing field. The playing field in financial markets can become "tilted" by many factors, including unequal information, bargaining power, and resources.

In addition to making one-time economic exchanges, participants in markets also engage in financial contracting whereby they enter into long-term relationships. These contractual relationships typically involve the assumption of fiduciary duties or obligations to act as agents, and financial markets are subject to unethical conduct when fiduciaries and agents fail in a duty. In the standard model of contracting, the terms of a contract specify the conduct required of each party and the remedies for noncompliance. In short, there is little "wiggle room" in a well-written contract. However, many contractual relationships in finance and other areas fall short of this ideal, because actual contracts are often vague, ambiguous, incomplete, or otherwise problematic. The result is uncertainty and disagreement about what constitutes ethical (as well as legal) conduct.

Much of the necessary regulatory framework for financial markets is provided by law. The Securities Act of 1933, the Securities Exchange Act of 1934, their many amendments, and the rules adopted by the SEC constitute the main regulatory framework for markets in securities. In addition, financial investment institutions, such as banks, mutual funds, and pension and insurance companies, are governed by industry-specific legislation.

Equity and Efficiency

The main aim of financial market regulation is to ensure efficiency, but markets can be efficient only when people have confidence in their fairness or equity. Efficiency is itself an ethical value because achieving the maximum output with the minimum input—which is a simple definition of efficiency—provides an abundance of goods and services and thereby promotes the general welfare. A society is generally better off when capital markets, for example, allocate the available capital to its most productive uses. People will participate in capital markets, however, only if the markets are perceived to be fair; that is, fairness has value as a means to the end of efficiency.

We also value fairness as an end in itself, and because fairness can conflict with efficiency, some choice or trade-off between the two must often be made. This unfortunate fact of life is commonly described as the equity/efficiency trade-off. Painful choices between efficiency and fairness (or equity), or between economic and social well-being, are at the heart of many difficult public-policy decisions, but we should not lose sight of the fact that fairness contributes to efficiency even as the two conflict.

Fairness in Markets

What constitutes fairness in financial markets?[10] Fairness is not a matter of preventing losses. Markets produce winners and losers, and in many cases the gain of some persons comes from an equal loss to others (although market exchanges are typically advantageous to both parties). In this respect, playing the stock market is like playing a sport: The aim is not to prevent losses but only to ensure that the game is fair. Still, there may be good reasons for seeking to protect individual investors from harm, even when the harm does not involve unfairness. Just as bean balls are forbidden in baseball (but playing hardball is okay!), so too are certain harmful practices prohibited in the financial marketplace.

The regulation of financial markets protects not only individual investors but also the general public. The stock market crash of 1929, which prompted the first securities legislation, profoundly affected the entire country. Everyone is harmed when financial markets do not fulfill their main purpose but become distorted by speculative activity or disruptive trading practices. The deleterious effect of stock market speculation is wryly expressed by John Maynard Keynes's famous quip: "When the capital development of a country becomes a by-product of the activities of a casino, the job is likely to be ill-done."[11] More recently, the question of whether junk bonds or program trading poses risks to the stability of the financial markets has been a subject of dispute.

The possible ways in which individual investors and members of society can be treated unfairly by the operation of financial markets are many, but the main kinds of unfairness are the following.

FRAUD AND MANIPULATION. One of the main purposes of securities regulation is to prevent fraudulent and manipulative practices in the sale of securities. The common-law definition of fraud is the willful misrepresentation of a material fact that causes harm to a person who reasonably relies on the misrepresentation. Section 17(a) of the 1933 Securities Act and Section 10(b) of the 1934 Securities Exchange Act both prohibit anyone involved in the buying or selling of securities from making false statements of a material fact, omitting a fact that makes a statement of material facts misleading, or engaging in any practice or scheme that would serve to defraud.

Investors—both as buyers and as sellers—are particularly vulnerable to fraud because the value of financial instruments depends almost entirely on information that is difficult to verify. Much of the important information is in the hands of the issuing firm, and so antifraud provisions in securities law place an obligation not only on buyers and sellers of a firm's stock, for example, but also on the issuing firm. Thus, a company that fails to report bad news may be committing fraud, even though the buyer of that company's stock buys it from a previous owner who may or may not be aware of the news. Insider trading is prosecuted as a fraud under Section 10(b) of the Securities Exchange Act on the grounds that any material, nonpublic information ought to be revealed before trading.

Manipulation generally involves the buying or selling of securities for the purpose of creating a false or misleading impression about the direction of their price so as to induce other investors to buy or sell the securities. Like fraud, manipulation is designed to deceive others, but the effect is achieved by the creation of false or misleading appearances rather than by false or misleading representations.

Fraud and manipulation are addressed by mandatory disclosure regulations as well as by penalties for false and misleading statements in any information released by a firm. Mandatory disclosure regulations are justified, in part, because they promote market efficiency: Better-informed investors will make more rational investment decisions, and they will do so at lower overall cost. A further justification, however, is the prevention of fraud and manipulation under the assumption that good information drives out bad. Simply put, fraud and manipulation are more difficult to commit when investors have easy access to reliable information.

EQUAL INFORMATION.   A "level playing field" requires not only that everyone play by the same rules but also that they be equally equipped to compete. Competition between parties with very unequal information is widely regarded as unfair because the playing field is tilted in favor of the player with superior information. When people talk about equal information, however, they may mean that the parties to a trade actually possess the same information or have equal access to information.

That everyone should posses the same information is an unrealizable ideal, and actual markets are characterized by great information asymmetries. The average investor cannot hope to compete on equal terms with a market pro, and even pros often possess different information that leads them to make different investment decisions. Moreover, there are good reasons for encouraging people to acquire superior information for use in trade. Consider stock analysts and other savvy investors who spend considerable time, effort, and money to acquire information. Not only are they ordinarily entitled to use this information for their own benefit (because it represents a return on an investment), but they perform a service to everyone by ensuring that stocks are accurately priced.

The possession of unequal information strikes us as unfair, then, only when the information has been illegitimately acquired or when its use violates some obligation to others. One argument against insider trading, for example, holds that an insider has not acquired the information legitimately but has stolen (or "misappropriated") information that rightly belongs to the firm. In this argument, the wrongfulness of insider trading consists not in the possession of unequal information but in violating a moral obligation not to steal or a fiduciary duty to serve others. Insider trading can also be criticized on the grounds that others do not have the same access to the information, which leads us to the second sense of equal information, namely, equal access.

The trouble with defining equal information as having equal access to information is that the notion of equal access is not absolute but relative. Any information that one person possesses could be acquired by another with enough time, effort, and money. An ordinary investor has access to virtually all of the information that a stock analyst uses to evaluate a company's prospects. The main difference is that the analyst has faster and easier access to information because of an investment in resources and skills. Anyone else could make the same investment and thereby gain the same access—or a person could simply "buy" the analyst's skilled services. Therefore, accessibility is not a feature of information itself but a function of the investment that is required in order to obtain the information.

We also hold that some information asymmetries are objectionable to the extent that they reduce efficiency. In particular, markets are more efficient when information is readily available, so we should seek to make information available at the lowest cost. To force people to make costly investments in information—or to suffer loss from inadequate information—is a deadweight loss to the economy if the same information could be provided at little cost. Thus, the requirement that the issuance of new securities be accompanied by a detailed prospectus, for example, is intended not only to prevent fraud through the concealment of material facts but also to make it easier for buyers to gain certain kinds of information, which benefits society as a whole.

Although efficiency and fairness both support attempts to reduce information asymmetries in financial markets, exactly what fairness or justice requires is not easy to determine. Consider, for example, whether a geologist who concludes after careful study that a widow's land contains oil would be justified in buying the land without revealing what he knows.[12] A utilitarian could argue that without such opportunities, geologists would not search for oil, and so society as a whole is better off if such advantage taking is permitted. In addition, the widow herself, who would be deprived of a potential gain, is better off in a society that allows some exploitation of superior knowledge. A difficult task for securities regulation, then, is drawing a line between fair and unfair advantage taking when people have unequal access to information.

EQUAL BARGAINING POWER.　　Generally, agreements reached by arm's-length bargaining are considered to be fair, regardless of the actual outcome. A trader who negotiates a futures contract that results in a great loss, for example, has only himself or herself to blame. However, the fairness of bargained agreements assumes that the parties have relatively equal bargaining power. Unequal bargaining power can result from many sources—including unequal information, which is discussed earlier—but other sources include the following factors.

1. *Resources.* In most transactions, wealth is an advantage. The rich are better able than the poor to negotiate over almost all matters. Prices of groceries in low-income neighborhoods are generally higher than those in affluent areas, for example, because wealthier customers have more options. Similarly, large investors have greater opportunities. They can be better diversified; they can bear greater risk and thereby use higher leverage; they can gain more from arbitrage through volume trading; and they have access to investments that are closed to small investors.

2. *Processing Ability.* Even with equal access to information, people vary enormously in their ability to process information and to make informed judgments. Unsophisticated investors are ill-advised to play the stock market and even more so to invest in markets that only professionals understand. Fraud aside, financial markets can be dangerous places for people who lack an understanding of the risks involved. Securities firms and institutional investors overcome the problem of people's limited processing ability by employing specialists in different kinds of markets, and the use of computers in program trading enables these organizations to substitute machine power for gray matter.

3. *Vulnerabilities.* Investors are only human, and human beings have many weaknesses that can be exploited. Some regulation is designed to protect people from the exploitation of their vulnerabilities. Thus, consumer protection legislation often provides for a "cooling off" period during which shoppers can cancel an impulsive purchase. The requirements that a prospectus accompany offers of securities and that investors be urged to read the prospectus carefully serve to curb impulsiveness. Margin requirements and other measures that discourage speculative investment serve to protect incautious investors from overextending themselves, as well as to protect the market from excess volatility. The legal duty of brokers and investment advisers to recommend only suitable investments and to warn adequately of the risks of any investment instrument provides a further check on people's greedy impulses.

Unequal bargaining power that arises from these factors—resources, processing ability, and vulnerabilities—is an unavoidable feature of financial markets, and exploiting such power imbalances is not always unfair. In general, the law intervenes when exploitation is unconscionable or when the harm is not easily avoided, even by sophisticated investors. The success of financial markets depends on reasonably wide participation, and so if unequal bargaining power were permitted to drive all but the most powerful from the marketplace, then the efficiency of financial markets would be greatly impaired.

EFFICIENT PRICING.   Fairness in financial markets includes efficient prices that reasonably reflect all available information. A fundamental market principle is that the price of securities should reflect their underlying value. The mandate to ensure "fair and orderly" markets—set forth in the Securities Exchange Act of 1934—has been interpreted to authorize interventions to correct volatility or excess price swings in stock markets. Volatility that results from a mismatch of buyers and sellers is eventually self-correcting, but in the meantime, great harm may be done by inefficient pricing. Individual investors may be harmed by buying at too high a price or selling at too low a price during periods of mispricing. Volatility also affects the market by reducing investor confidence, thus driving investors away, and some argue that the loss of confidence artificially depresses stock prices. At its worst, volatility can threaten the whole financial system, as it did in October 1987.

INSIDER TRADING

Insider trading is commonly defined as trading in the stock of publicly held corporations on the basis of material, nonpublic information. In a landmark 1968 decision, executives of Texas Gulf Sulphur Company were found guilty of insider trading for investing heavily in their own company's stock after learning of the discovery of rich copper ore deposits in Canada.[13] The principle established in the *Texas Gulf Sulphur* case is that corporate insiders must refrain from trading on information that significantly affects stock price until it becomes public knowledge. The rule for corporate insiders is, reveal or refrain!

Much of the uncertainty in the law on insider trading revolves around the relation of the trader to the source of the information. Corporate executives are definitely "insiders," but some "outsiders" have also been charged with insider trading. Among such outsiders have been a printer who was able to identify the targets of several takeovers from legal documents that were being prepared; a financial analyst who uncovered a huge fraud at a high-flying firm and advised his clients to sell; a stockbroker who was tipped off by a client who was a relative of the president of a company and who learned about the sale of the business through a chain of family gossip; a psychiatrist who was treating the wife of a financier who was attempting to take over a major bank; and a lawyer whose firm was advising a client planning a hostile takeover.[14] The first two traders were eventually found innocent of insider trading; the latter three were found guilty (although the stockbroker case was later reversed in part). From these cases, a legal definition of insider trading is slowly emerging.

The key points are that a person who trades on material, nonpublic information is engaging in insider trading when (1) the trader has violated some legal duty to a corporation and its shareholders; or (2) the source of the information has such a legal duty and the trader knows that the source is violating that duty. Thus, the printer and the stock analyst had no relation to the corporations in question and so had no duty to refrain from using the information that they had acquired. The stockbroker and the psychiatrist, however, knew or should have known that they were obtaining inside information indirectly from high-level executives who had a duty to keep the information confidential. The corresponding rule for outsiders is: Don't trade on information that is revealed in violation of a trust. Both rules are imprecise, however, and leave many cases unresolved.

Arguments against Insider Trading

The difficulty in defining insider trading is due to disagreement over the moral wrong involved. Two main rationales are used in support of a law against insider trading. One is based on property rights and holds that those who trade on material, nonpublic information are essentially stealing property that belongs to the corporation. The second rationale is based on fairness and holds that traders who use inside information have an unfair advantage over other investors and that, as a result, the stock market is not a level playing field. These two rationales lead to different definitions, one narrow and the other broad. On the property rights or "misappropriation" theory, only corporate insiders or outsiders who bribe, steal, or otherwise wrongfully acquire corporate secrets can be guilty of insider trading. The fairness argument is broader and applies to anyone who trades on material, nonpublic information no matter how it is acquired.

INSIDE INFORMATION AS PROPERTY.   One difficulty in using the property rights or misappropriation argument is to determine who owns the information in question. The main basis for recognizing a property right in trade secrets and confidential business information is the investment that companies make in acquiring information and the competitive value that some information has. Not all insider information fits this description, however. Advance knowledge of better-than-expected earnings would be an example. Such information still has value in stock trading, even if the corporation does not use it for that purpose. For this reason, many employers prohibit the personal use of any information that an employee gains in the course of his or her work. This position is too broad, however, since an employee is unlikely to be accused of stealing company property by using knowledge of the next day's earning report for any purpose other than stock trading.

A second difficulty with the property rights argument is that if companies own certain information, they could then give their own employees permission to use it, or they could sell the information to favored investors or even trade on it themselves to buy back stock. Giving employees permission to trade on insider information could be an inexpensive form of extra compensation that further encourages employees to develop valuable information for the firm. Such an arrangement would also have some drawbacks; for example, investors might be less willing to buy the stock of a company that allowed insider trading because of the disadvantage to outsiders. What is morally objectionable about insider trading, according to its critics, though, is not the misappropriation of a company's information but the harm done to the investing public. So the violation of property rights in insider trading cannot be the sole reason for prohibiting it. Let us turn, then, to the second argument against insider trading, namely, the argument of fairness.

THE FAIRNESS ARGUMENT.   Fairness in the stock market does not require that all traders have the same information. Indeed, trades will take place only if the buyers and sellers of a stock have different information that leads them to different conclusions about the stock's worth. It is only fair, moreover, that a shrewd investor who has spent a lot of time and money studying the prospects of a company should be able to exploit that advantage; otherwise there would be no incentive to seek out new information. What is objectionable about using inside information is that other traders are barred from obtaining it no matter how diligent they may be. The information is unavailable not for lack of effort but for lack of access. Poker also pits card players with unequal skill and knowledge without being unfair, but a game played with a marked deck gives some players an unfair advantage over others. By analogy, then, insider trading is like playing poker with a marked deck.

The analogy may be flawed, however. Perhaps a more appropriate analogy is the seller of a home who fails to reveal hidden structural damage. One principle of stock market regulation is that both buyers and sellers of stock should have sufficient information to make rational choices. Thus, companies must publish annual reports and disclose important developments in a timely manner. A CEO who hides bad news from the investing public, for example, can be sued for fraud. Good news, such as an oil find, need not be announced until a company has time to buy the drilling rights, and so on; but to trade on that information before it is public knowledge might also be described as a kind of fraud.

Insider trading is generally prosecuted under SEC Rule 10b-5, which merely prohibits fraud in securities transactions. In fraudulent transactions, one party, such as the buyer of the house with structural damage, is wrongfully harmed for lack of knowledge that the other party concealed. So too—according to the fairness argument—are the ignorant parties to insider-trading transactions wrongfully harmed when material facts, such as the discovery of copper ore deposits in the *Texas Gulf Sulphur* case, are not revealed.

The main difficulty in the fairness argument is to determine what information ought to be revealed in a transaction. The reason for requiring a homeowner to disclose hidden structural damage is that doing so makes for a more efficient housing market. In the absence of such a requirement, potential home buyers would pay less because they are not sure what they are getting, or they would invest in costly home inspections. Similarly—the argument goes—requiring insiders to reveal before trading makes the stock market more efficient.

The trouble with such a claim is that some economists argue that the stock market would be more efficient without a law against insider trading.[15] If insider trading were permitted, they claim, information would be registered in the market more quickly and at less cost than the alternative of leaving the task to research by stock analysts. The main beneficiaries of a law against insider trading, critics continue, are not individual investors but market professionals who can pick up news "on the street" and act on it quickly. Some economists argue further that a law against insider trading preserves the illusion that there is a level playing field and that individual investors have a chance against market professionals.

Economic arguments about market efficiency look only at the cost of registering information in the market and not at possible adverse consequences of legalized insider trading, which are many. Investors who perceive the stock market as an unlevel playing field may be less inclined to participate or will be forced to adopt costly defensive measures. Legalized insider trading would have an effect on the treatment of information in a firm. Employees whose interest is in information that they can use in the stock market may be less concerned with information that is useful to the employer, and the company itself might attempt to tailor its release of information for maximum benefit to insiders. More importantly, the opportunity to engage in insider trading might undermine the relation of trust that is essential for business organizations.[16] A prohibition on insider trading frees employees of a corporation to do what they are supposed to be doing—namely, working for the interests of the shareholders—not seeking ways to advance their own interests.

The harm that legalized insider trading could do to organizations suggests that the strongest argument against legalization might be the breach of fiduciary duty that would result. Virtually everyone who could be called an "insider" has a fiduciary duty to serve the interests of the corporation and its shareholders, and the use of information that is acquired while serving as a fiduciary for personal gain is a violation of this duty. It would be a breach of professional ethics for a lawyer or an accountant to benefit personally from the use of information acquired in confidence from a client, and it is similarly unethical for a corporate executive to make personal use of confidential business information.

The argument that insider trading constitutes a breach of fiduciary duty accords with recent court decisions that have limited the prosecution of insider trading to true insiders who have a fiduciary duty. One drawback of the argument is that "outsiders," whom federal prosecutors have sought to convict of insider trading, would be free of any restrictions. A second drawback is that insider trading, on this argument, is no longer an offense against the market but the violation of a duty to another party. And the duty not to use information that is acquired while serving as a fiduciary prohibits more than insider trading. The same duty would be violated by a fiduciary who buys or sells property or undertakes some other business dealing on the basis of confidential information. That such breaches of fiduciary duty are wrong is evident, but the authority of the SEC to prosecute them under a mandate to prevent fraud in the market is less clear.

THE O'HAGAN DECISION. In 1997, the U.S. Supreme Court ended a decade of uncertainty over the legal definition of insider trading. The SEC has long prosecuted insider trading using the misappropriation theory, according to which an inside trader breaches a fiduciary duty by misappropriating confidential information for personal trading. In 1987, the High Court split 4–4 on an insider-trading case involving a reporter for the *Wall Street Journal* and thus left standing a lower court decision that found the reporter guilty of misappropriating information.[17] However, the decision did not create a precedent for lack of a majority. Subsequently, lower courts rejected the misappropriation theory in a series of cases in which the alleged inside trader did not have a fiduciary duty to the corporation whose stock was traded. The principle applied was that the trading must itself constitute a breach of fiduciary duty. This principle was rejected in *U.S.* v. *O'Hagan.*[18]

James H. O'Hagan was a partner in a Minneapolis law firm that was advising the British firm Grand Metropolitan in a hostile takeover of Minneapolis-based Pillsbury Company. O'Hagan did not work on Grand Met business but allegedly tricked a fellow partner into revealing the takeover bid. O'Hagan then reaped $4.3 million by trading in Pillsbury stock and stock options. An appellate court ruled that O'Hagan did not engage in illegal insider trading because he had no fiduciary duty to Pillsbury, the company in whose stock he traded. Although O'Hagan misappropriated confidential information from his own law firm—to which he owed a fiduciary duty—trading on this information did not constitute a fraud against the law firm or against Grand Met. Presumably, O'Hagan would have been guilty of insider trading only if he were an insider of Pillsbury or had traded in Grand Met stock.

In a 6–3 decision, the Supreme Court reinstated the conviction of Mr. O'Hagan and affirmed the misappropriation theory. According to the decision, a person commits securities fraud when he or she "misappropriates confidential information for securities trading purposes, in breach of a fiduciary duty owed to the source of the information." Thus, an inside trader need not be an insider (or a temporary insider, like a lawyer) of the corporation whose stock is traded. Being an insider in Grand Met is sufficient in this case to hold that insider trading occurred. The majority opinion observed that "it makes scant sense" to hold a lawyer like O'Hagan to have violated the law "if he works for a law firm representing the target of a tender offer, but not if he works for a law firm representing the bidder." The crucial point is that O'Hagan was a fiduciary who misused information that had been entrusted to him. This decision would also apply to a person who receives information from an insider and who knows that the insider source is violating a duty of confidentiality. However, a person with no fiduciary ties who receives information innocently (by overhearing a conversation, for example) would still be free to trade.

HOSTILE TAKEOVERS

Since its founding in the nineteenth century, Pacific Lumber Company had been a model employer and a good corporate citizen. As a logger of giant redwoods in northern California, this family-managed company had long followed a policy of perpetual sustainable yield. Cutting was limited to selected mature trees, which were removed without disturbing the forests, so that younger trees could grow to the same size. Employees—many from families who had worked at Pacific Lumber for several generations—received generous benefits, including an overfunded company-sponsored pension plan. With strong earnings and virtually no debt, Pacific Lumber seemed well-positioned to survive any challenge.

However, the company fell prey to a hostile takeover. In 1986, financier Charles Hurwitz and his Houston-based firm Maxxam, Inc., mounted a successful $900 million leveraged buyout of Pacific Lumber. By offering $40 per share for stock that had been trading at $29, Hurwitz gained majority control. The takeover was financed with junk bonds issued by Drexel Burnham Lambert under the direction of Michael Milken, the junk-bond king. Hurwitz expected to pare down the debt by aggressive clear-cutting of the ancient stands of redwoods that Pacific Lumber had protected and by raiding the company's overfunded pension plan.

Using $37.3 million of $97 million that Pacific Lumber had set aside for its pension obligations, Maxxam purchased annuities for all employees and retirees and applied more than $55 million of the remainder toward reducing the company's new debt. The annuities were purchased from First Executive Corporation, a company that Hurwitz controlled. First Executive was also Drexel's biggest junk-bond customer, and the company purchased one-third of the debt incurred in the takeover of Pacific Lumber. After the collapse of the junk-bond market, First Executive failed in 1991 and was taken over by the state of California in a move that halted pension payments to Pacific Lumber retirees. Today, Charles Hurwitz and Maxxam are mired in lawsuits by former stockholders, retirees, and environmentalists.

Hostile takeovers—which are acquisitions opposed by the management of the target corporation—appear to violate the accepted rules for corporate change. Peter Drucker observed that the hostile takeover "deeply offends the sense of justice of a great many Americans."[19] An oil industry CEO charged that such activity "is in total disregard of those inherent foundations which are the heart and soul of the American free enterprise system."[20] Many economists—most notably Michael C. Jensen—defend hostile takeovers on the grounds that they bring about needed changes that cannot be achieved by the usual means.[21]

The ethical questions in hostile takeovers are threefold. First, should hostile takeovers be permitted at all? Insofar as hostile takeovers are conducted in a market through the buying and selling of stocks, there exists a "market for corporate control." So the question can be expressed in the form, should there be a market for corporate control? Or, should change-of-control decisions be made in some other fashion? Second, ethical issues arise in the various tactics that have been used by raiders in launching attacks as well as by target corporations in defending themselves. Some of these tactics are criticized on the grounds that they unfairly favor the raiders or incumbent management, often at the expense of shareholders. Third, hostile takeovers raise important issues about the fiduciary duties of officers and directors in their responses to takeover bids. In particular, what should directors do when an offer that shareholders want to accept is not in the best interests of the corporation itself? Do they have a right, indeed a responsibility, to prevent a change of control?

The Market for Corporate Control

Defenders of hostile takeovers contend that corporations become takeover targets when incumbent management is unable or unwilling to take steps that increase shareholder value. The raiders' willingness to pay a premium for the stock reflects a belief that the company is not achieving its full potential under the current management. "Let us take over," the raiders say, "and the company will be worth what we are offering." Because shareholders often find it difficult to replace the current managers through traditional proxy contests, hostile takeovers are an important means for shareholders to realize the value of their investment. Although restructurings of all kinds cause some hardships to employees, communities, and other groups, society as a whole benefits from the increased productivity of better-run companies.

Just the threat of a takeover serves as an important check on management, and without this constant spur, defenders argue, managers would have less incentive to secure full value for the shareholders. With regard to the market for corporate control, defenders hold that shareholders are, and ought to be, the ultimate arbiters of who manages the corporation. If the shareholders have a right to replace the CEO, why should it matter when or how shareholders bought the stock? A raider who bought the stock yesterday in a tender offer has the same rights as a shareholder of long standing. Any steps to restrict hostile takeovers, the defenders argue, would entail an unjustified reduction of shareholders' rights.

Critics of hostile takeovers challenge the benefits and emphasize the harms. Targets of successful raids are sometimes broken up and sold off piecemeal or downsized and folded into the acquiring company. In the process, people are thrown out of work and communities lose their economic base. Takeovers generally saddle companies with debt loads that limit their options and expose them to greater risk in the event of a downturn. Critics also charge that companies are forced to defend themselves by managing for immediate results and adopting costly defensive measures.

The debate over hostile takeovers revolves largely around the question of whether they are good or bad for the American economy. This is a question for economic analysis, and the evidence, on the whole, is that takeovers generally increase the value of both the acquired and the acquiring corporation.[22] However, there is little evidence that newly merged or acquired firms outperform industry averages in the long run.[23] The effect on the economy aside, the benefit of hostile takeovers must be viewed with some caution.

First, not all takeover targets are underperforming businesses with poor management. Other factors can make a company a takeover target. The "bust-up" takeover operates on the premise that a company is worth more sold off in parts than retained as a whole. Large cash reserves, expensive research programs, and other sources of savings enable raiders to finance a takeover with the company's own assets. The availability of junk-bond financing during the 1980s permitted highly leveraged buyouts with levels of debt that many considered to be unhealthy for the economy. Finally, costly commitments to stakeholder groups can be tapped to finance a takeover. Thus, Pacific Lumber's pension plan and cutting policy constituted commitments to employees and environmentalists, respectively. Both commitments were implicit contracts that had arguably benefited shareholders in the past but that could be broken now with impunity.

Second, some of the apparent wealth that takeovers create may result from accounting and tax rules that benefit shareholders but create no new wealth. For example, the tax code favors debt over equity by allowing a deduction for interest payments on debt while taxing corporate profits. Rules on depreciation and capital gains may result in tax savings from asset sales following a takeover. Thus, taxpayers provide an indirect subsidy in the financing of takeovers. Some takeovers result in direct losses to other parties. Among the losers in hostile takeovers are bondholders, whose formerly secure, investment-grade bonds are sometimes downgraded to speculative, junk-bond status.

Takeover Tactics

In a typical hostile takeover, an insurgent group—often called a "raider"—makes a *tender offer* to buy a controlling block of stock in a target corporation from its present shareholders. The offered price generally involves a premium, which is an amount in excess of the current trading price. If enough shareholders tender their shares in response to the offer, the insurgents gain control. In the usual course of events, the raiders replace the incumbent management team and proceed to make substantial changes in the company. In some instances, a tender offer is made directly to the shareholders, but in others, the cooperation of management is required.

The officers and directors of firms have a fiduciary duty to consider a tender offer in good faith. If they believe that a takeover is not in the best interests of the shareholders, then they have a right, even a duty, to fight the offer with all available means. Corporations have many resources for defending against hostile takeovers. These tactics—collectively called "shark repellents"—include poison pills, white knights, lockups, crown jewel options, the Pac-Man defense, golden parachutes, and greenmail (see Exhibit 11.1). Some of the defensive measures (e.g., poison pills and golden parachutes) are usually adopted in advance of any takeover bid, while others (white knights and greenmail) are customarily employed in the course of fighting an unwelcome offer. Many states have adopted so-called antitakeover statutes that further protect incumbent management against raiders. Because of shark repellents and antitakeover statutes, a merger or acquisition is virtually impossible to conduct today without the cooperation of the board of directors of the target corporation.

All takeover tactics raise important ethical issues, but three, in particular, have elicited great concern. These are unregulated tender offers, golden parachutes, and greenmail.

TENDER OFFERS. Ethical concern about the tactics of takeovers has focused primarily on the defenses of target companies, but unregulated tender offers are also potentially abusive.

Crown Jewel Option A form of lockup in which an option on a target's most valuable assets (crown jewels) is offered to a friendly firm in the event of a hostile takeover.

Golden Parachute A part of the employment contract with a top executive that provides for additional compensation in the event that the executive departs voluntarily or involuntarily after a takeover.

Greenmail The repurchase by a target of an unwelcome suitor's stock at a premium in order to end an attempted hostile takeover.

Lockup Option An option given to a friendly firm to acquire certain assets in the event of a hostile takeover. Usually, the assets are crucial for the financing of a takeover.

Pac-Man Defense A defense (named after the popular video game) in which the target makes a counteroffer to acquire the unwelcome suitor.

Poison Pill A general term for any device that raises the price of a target's stock in the event of a takeover. A common form of poison pill is the issuance of a new class of preferred stock that shareholders have a right to redeem at a premium after a takeover.

Shark Repellant A general term for all takeover defenses.

White Knight A friendly suitor who makes an offer for a target in order to avoid a takeover by an unwelcome suitor.

EXHIBIT 11.1   Takeover Defenses

Before 1968, takeovers were sometimes attempted by a so-called "Saturday night special," in which a tender offer was made after the close of the market on Friday and set to expire on Monday morning. The "Saturday night special" was considered to be coercive because shareholders had to decide quickly whether to tender their shares, with little information.[24] Shareholders would generally welcome an opportunity to sell stock that trades at $10 a share on a Friday afternoon for, say, $15. If, on Monday morning, however, the stock sells for $20 a share, then the shareholders who tendered over the weekend gained $5 but lost the opportunity to gain $10. With more information, shareholders might conclude that $15 or even $20 was an inadequate price and that they would be better off holding on to their shares—perhaps in anticipation of an even better offer.

Partial offers for only a certain number or percentage of shares and two-tier offers can also be coercive. In a two-tier offer, one price is offered for, say, 51 percent of the shares and a lower price is offered for the remainder. Both offers force shareholders to make a decision without knowing which price they will receive for their shares or indeed whether their shares will even be bought. Thus, tender offers can be structured in such a way that shareholders are stampeded into tendering quickly lest they lose the opportunity. The payment that is offered may include securities—such as shares of the acquiring corporation or a new merged entity—and the value of these securities may be difficult to determine. Without adequate information, shareholders may not be able to judge whether a $15-per-share noncash offer, for example, is fairly priced.

Congress addressed these problems with tender offers in 1968 with the passage of the Williams Act. The guiding principle of the Williams Act is that shareholders have a right to make important investment decisions in an orderly manner and with adequate information. They should not be stampeded into tendering for fear of losing the opportunity, or forced to decide in ignorance. Under Section 14(d) of the Williams Act, a tender offer must be accompanied by a statement detailing the bidder's identity, the nature of the funding, and plans for restructuring the takeover target. A tender offer must be open for 20 business days, in order to allow shareholders sufficient time to make a decision, and tendering shareholders have 15 days in which to change their minds—thereby permitting them to accept a better offer should one be made. The Williams Act deals with partial and two-tier offers by requiring proration. Thus, if more shares are tendered than the bidder has offered to buy, then the same percentage of each shareholder's tendered stock must be purchased. Proration ensures the equal treatment of shareholders and removes the pressure on shareholders to tender early.

GOLDEN PARACHUTES. At the height of takeover activities in the 1980s, between one-quarter and one-half of major American corporations provided their top executives with an unusual form of protection—golden parachutes.[25] A golden parachute is a provision in a manager's employment contract for compensation—usually, a cash settlement equal to several years' salary—for the loss of a job following a takeover. In general, golden parachutes are distinct from severance packages because they become effective only in the event of a change of control and are usually limited to the CEO and a small number of other officers and executives.

The most common argument for golden parachutes is that they reduce a potential conflict of interest. Managers who might lose their jobs in the event of a takeover cannot be expected to evaluate a takeover bid objectively. Michael C. Jensen observes, "It makes no sense to hire a realtor to sell your house and then penalize your agent for doing so."[26] A golden parachute protects managers' futures, no matter the outcome, and thus frees them to consider only the best interests of the shareholders. In addition, golden parachutes enable corporations to attract and retain desirable executives because they provide protection against events that are largely beyond managers' control. Without this protection, a recruit may be reluctant to accept a position with a potential takeover target, or a manager might leave a threatened company in anticipation of a takeover bid.

Critics argue, first, that golden parachutes merely entrench incumbent managers by raising the price that raiders would have to pay. In this respect, golden parachutes are like poison pills; they create costly new obligations in the event of a change of control. All such defensive measures are legitimate if they are approved by the shareholders, but golden parachutes, critics complain, are often secured by executives from compliant boards of directors that they control. If golden parachutes are in the shareholders' interests, then executives should be willing to obtain shareholder approval. Otherwise, they appear to be self-serving defensive measures that violate a duty to serve the shareholders.

Second, some critics object to the idea of providing additional incentives to do what they are being paid to do anyway.[27] Philip L. Cochran and Steven L. Wartick observe that managers are already paid to maximize shareholder wealth. "To provide additional compensation in order to get managers to objectively evaluate takeover offers is tantamount to management extortion of the shareholders."[28] One experienced director finds it "outrageous" that executives should be paid after they leave a company. Peter G. Scotese writes, "Why reward an executive so generously at the moment his or her contribution to the company ceases? The approach flies in the face of the American work ethic, which is based on raises or increments related to the buildup of seniority and merit."[29]

The principle for justifying golden parachutes is clear, even if its application is not. The justification for all forms of executive compensation is to provide incentives for acting in the shareholders' interests. If golden parachutes are too generous, they entrench management by making the price of a takeover prohibitive—or else they motivate managers to support a takeover against the interests of shareholders. In either case, the managers enrich themselves at the shareholders' expense. The key is to develop a compensation package with just the right incentives, which, as Michael Jensen notes, will depend on the particular case.[30]

GREENMAIL. Unsuccessful raiders do not always go away empty-handed. Because of the price rise that follows an announced takeover bid, raiders are often able to sell their holdings at a tidy profit. In some instances, target corporations have repelled unwelcome assaults by buying back the raiders' shares at a premium. After the financier Saul Steinberg accumulated more than 11 percent of Walt Disney Productions in 1984, the Disney board agreed to pay $77.50 per share, a total of $325.3 million, for stock that Steinberg had purchased at an average price of $63.25. As a reward for ending his run at Disney, Steinberg pocketed nearly $60 million. This episode and many like it have been widely criticized as greenmail.

The play on the word "blackmail" suggests that there is something corrupt about offering or accepting greenmail. A more precise term that avoids this bias is *control repurchase.* A control repurchase may be defined as a "privately negotiated stock repurchase from an outside shareholder, at a premium over the market price, made for the purpose of avoiding a battle for control of the company making the repurchase."[31] Although control repurchases are legal, many people think that there ought to be a law. So we need to ask first why control repurchases are considered to be unethical.

There are three main ethical objections to control repurchases.[32] First, control repurchases are negotiated with one set of shareholders, who receive an offer that is not extended to everyone else. This is a violation, some say, of the principle that all shareholders should be treated equally. The same offer should be made to all shareholders—or none. To buy back the stock of raiders for a premium is unfair to other shareholders.

This argument is easily dismissed. Managers have an obligation to treat all shareholders according to their rights under the charter and bylaws of the corporation and the relevant corporate law. This means one share, one vote at meetings, and the same dividend for each share. There is no obligation for managers to treat shareholders equally otherwise. Moreover, paying a premium for the repurchase of stock is a use of corporate assets that presumably brings some return to the shareholders, and the job of managers is to put all corporate assets to their most productive use. If the $60 million that Disney paid to Saul Steinberg, for example, brings higher returns to the shareholders than any other investment, then the managers have an obligation to all shareholders to treat this one shareholder differently.

Second, control repurchases are criticized as a breach of the fiduciary duty of management to serve the shareholders' interests. Managers have a strong interest in maintaining their own jobs, but their fiduciary duty to shareholders requires them to disregard this interest in all matters involving corporate assets, which properly belong to the shareholders.

Therefore, if managers use shareholders' money to pay raiders to go away merely to save their own jobs, they have clearly violated their fiduciary duty. However, this may not be the intent of managers in all cases of greenmail. Managers of target corporations may judge that an offer is not in the best interests of shareholders and that the best defensive tactic is a repurchase of the raiders' shares. With $60 million, Disney might have made another movie that would bring a certain return. However, Disney executives might also have calculated that the costs to the company of continuing to fight Saul Steinberg—or allowing him to gain control—would outweigh this return. If so, then the $60 million that Disney paid in greenmail is shareholder money well spent. So there is no reason to believe that greenmail or control repurchases necessarily involve a breach of fiduciary duty.

Third, some critics object to greenmail or control repurchases on the grounds that the payments invite pseudobidders who have no intention of taking control and mount a raid merely for the profit.[33] The ethical wrong, according to this objection, lies with the raiders' conduct, although management may be complicitous in facilitating it. At a minimum, pseudobidders are engaging in unproductive economic activity, which benefits no one but the raiders themselves; at their worst, pseudobidders are extorting corporations by threatening some harm unless the payments are made.

Is pseudobidding for the purpose of getting greenmail a serious problem? The effectiveness of pseudobidding depends on the credibility of the threatened takeover. No raider can pose a credible threat unless an opportunity exists to increase the return to shareholders. Therefore, the situations in which pseudobidders are likely to emerge are quite limited. Even if a pseudobidder or a genuine raider is paid to go away, that person has pointed out some problem with the incumbent management and paved the way for change. Unsuccessful raiders who accept greenmail may still provide a service for everyone.[34]

The Role of the Board of Directors

In 1989, Paramount Communications made a tender offer for all outstanding stock in Time Incorporated. Many Time shareholders were keen to accept the all-cash, $175-per-share bid (later raised to $200 per share), which represented about a 40 percent premium over the previous trading price of Time stock. However, the board of directors refused to submit the Paramount offer to the shareholders. Time and Warner Communications, Inc., had been preparing to merge, and the Time directors believed that a Time–Warner merger would produce greater value for the shareholders than an acquisition by Paramount. Disgruntled Time shareholders joined Paramount in a suit that charged the directors with a failure to act in the shareholders' interests.

This case raises two critical issues. First, who has the right to determine the value of a corporation in a merger or acquisition? Is this a job for the board of directors and their investment banking firm advisors? Both boards and their advisors have superior information about a company's current financial status and future prospects, but they also have a vested interest in preserving the status quo. Should the task of evaluation be left to the shareholders, whose interests are the ultimate arbiter but whose knowledge is often lacking? Some of the shareholders are professional arbitragers, who are looking merely for a quick buck. Second, does the interest of the shareholders lie with quick, short-term gain or with the viability of the company in the long run? Acceptance of the Paramount offer would maximize the immediate stock price for Time shareholders but upset the long-term strategic plan that the board had developed.

The Delaware State Supreme Court decision in *Paramount Communications, Inc. v. Time Inc.* addressed both issues by ruling that the Time board of directors had a right to take a long-term perspective in evaluating a takeover bid and had no obligation to submit the Paramount proposal to the shareholders.[35] The court recognized that increasing shareholder value in the long run involves a consideration of interests besides those of current shareholders, including other corporate constituencies, such as employees, customers, and local communities. One concern of the Time directors was to preserve the "culture" of *Time* magazine because of the importance of editorial integrity to the magazine's readers and journalistic staff.

The *Paramount* decision is an example of a so-called other constituency statute. A majority of states have now adopted (either by judicial or legislative action) laws that permit (and, in a few states, require) the board of directors to consider the impact of a takeover on a broad range of nonshareholder constituencies.[36] Other constituency statutes reflect a judgment by judges and legislators that legitimate nonshareholder interests are harmed by takeovers and that directors faced with a takeover do not owe allegiance solely to the current shareholders.[37] As a result of other constituency statutes, decisions about the future of corporations depend more on calm deliberations in boardrooms and less on the buying and selling of shares in a noisy marketplace.

Conclusion

Ethical issues in finance are important because they bear on our financial well-being. Ethical misconduct, whether it be by individuals acting alone or by financial institutions, has the potential to rob people of their life savings. Because so much money is involved in financial dealings, there must be well-developed and effective safeguards in place to ensure personal and organizational ethics. Although the law governs much financial activity, strong emphasis must be placed on the integrity of finance professionals and on ethical leadership in our financial institutions. Some of the principles in finance ethics are common to other aspects of business, especially the duties of fiduciaries and fairness in sales practices and securities markets. However, such activities as insider trading and hostile takeovers raise unique issues that require special consideration.

CASE 11.2 ❋ Explore the Concept on mythinkinglab.com

Strong Capital Management Mutual Funds

When Richard S. Strong founded Strong Capital Management (SCM) in 1974, he wanted it to be "the Nordstrom's of the financial industry," believing that this store provided the very best customer service.[38] With this goal in mind, he built SCM into an investment company that by 2004 managed $33.8 billion in mutual fund and pension investments. In that year, though, SCM and Richard Strong came under scrutiny by the Securities and Exchange Commission (SEC) and the New York Attorney General for permitting market timing—not only by an outside investor but by Mr. Strong himself.

Although stocks are difficult to predict, some investors make money by market timing, which is selling stocks within a few days of buying. Market timers are able to exploit inefficiencies in the market that occur when new information has not yet been reflected in stock prices. Such inefficient or "stale" prices are especially common with foreign stocks because of the large time difference between markets. Mutual funds are attractive to market timers because, unlike trades of individual stocks, which incur a broker's fee, many mutual funds charge little or nothing to put money in and take it out since they receive their return from a management fee on the amount invested.

Rapid in-and-out trading (called "round trips") hurts long-term mutual fund investors in several ways. For one, if a fund rises from the day before, when the market timer's investment was made, and the trader cashes out quickly, the effect is to dilute the return to the other investors in a fund. If the market timer's infusion of cash has not yet been invested in stocks, the earnings of the fund are due entirely to the money provided by the other investors. The market timer thus contributes nothing to the holdings that generate a fund's earnings, and yet by putting millions of dollars into a fund for a day or two, the market timer gets a portion of that return. In addition, large inflows and outflows add trading and overhead costs, and if a fund manager has to sell stocks when a market timer withdraws funds, this could trigger taxable capital gains for all fund investors.

Market timing is not illegal, but most mutual funds discourage or prohibit the practice because of the harm to long-term investors. SCM, like most mutual fund companies, encouraged long-term holding of five years or more and advised that market timing does not work. Beginning in 1997, SCM warned shareholders that frequent traders could be banned: "Since an excessive number of exchanges may be detrimental to the Funds, each Fund reserves the right to discontinue the exchange privilege of any shareholder who makes more than five exchanges in a year or three exchanges in a calendar quarter." Like most other mutual fund companies, SCM also had "timing police," who monitored trading activity for frequent activity, and from 1998 through 2003, hundreds of market timers were identified and barred from investing in Strong funds. When it was discovered that some SCM employees were market timing in their own accounts, the company issued a clear directive that the Strong funds were not to be used for short-term trading and that violators could have their trading privileges restricted.

Any activity by SCM employees that would harm fund shareholders was also prohibited by the company's code of ethics, which was distributed to all employees. In his introduction to the code, Richard Strong summed up the "three most important principles" for dealing with clients:

- You must deal with our clients fairly and in good faith;
- You must never put the interests of our firm ahead of the interests of our clients; and
- You must never compromise your personal ethics or integrity, or give the appearance that you may have done so.

Moreover, as chairman and chief investment officer of SCM[39] and as chairman of the board of directors of the 27 investment companies that managed the 71 SCM mutual funds,[40] Richard Strong had a fiduciary duty to serve the interests of all shareholders in the SCM family of funds.

A fiduciary duty prohibits a person in a position of trust from gaining a benefit at the expense of those to whom the duty is owed.

Despite the company's policy on market timing, the code of ethics, and a fiduciary duty, Richard Strong engaged in market timing in SCM mutual funds, making 1,400 quick trades between 1998 and 2003, including 22 round trips in 1998 in a fund for which he was also a portfolio manager. In 2000, SCM's timing police detected the chairman's trading activity, and the general counsel spoke to him, noting that his trading was inconsistent with the company's stated position on market timing and its treatment of other market timers. After agreeing to quit market timing, he increased his activity, making a record 510 trades in 2001. In total, he netted $1.8 million and obtained higher returns than ordinary investors in the same SCM funds.

In late 2002, Mr. Strong was presented with another opportunity. Canary Capital, a hedge fund headed by Edward J. Stern, sought permission to make market-timing trades in SCM funds. In return, Canary would make large investments in other SCM funds, including SCM's own hedge fund. Between 2000 and 2003, market timing in mutual funds and also late trading—an illegal activity in which traders were permitted to place orders after the official 4:00 P.M. close of the market—became epidemic, and Canary was one of the biggest operators. An SEC survey of the 88 largest fund companies found that half admitted to allowing market timers in their funds.[41] By one estimate, market timing during this period cost long-term mutual fund investors $5 billion a year, which reduced the return to other investors by 1 percentage point.[42]

Hedge funds like Canary sought an agreement (called a "capacity" arrangement) to make a certain number of trades involving an agreed-upon amount of money during a fixed period of time. In return, the hedge fund would turn over a large amount of money (called a "sticky asset") to be managed by the investment company. Canary had obtained a capacity arrangement with a large number of investment companies and banks, including Pimco Advisors, Alliance Capital Management, Invesco, Bank One, and, most famously, Bank of America, which provided Canary with its own computer terminal to place late trades. In addition, Canary gained access to the list of stock holdings in these companies' mutual funds. This information, which was provided to other investors only twice a year, was essential for determining how a fund would perform.

In 2001 and 2002, Canary was making so much money and attracting so many new investors that it was finding it more difficult to obtain sufficient "capacity," that is, mutual funds that would permit market-timing trades. This success led to the firm's downfall. In an effort to get the attention of Goldman Sachs, Canary hired a former employee, Noreen Harrington. Goldman Sachs was uninterested, and Harrington left in dismay when she discovered how Canary's money was made. She was not intending to blow the whistle until her sister complained about how much money she was losing in her mutual fund and how she would never be able to retire. "I didn't think about this from the bottom up until then," Harrington said.[43] A telephone call to the New York State Attorney General's office started the investigation that eventually led to Richard Strong.

CASE 11.3 ✳ Explore the Concept on mythinkinglab.com
Martha Stewart: Inside Trader?

On December 27, 2001, Martha Stewart was en route with a friend from her home in Connecticut to a post-Christmas holiday in Mexico when her private plane landed for refueling in San Antonio, Texas.[44] While standing on the tarmac, she listened to a telephone message from her assistant, Ann Armstrong, reporting a call from Peter Bacanovic, her stockbroker at Merrill Lynch. The message relayed by her assistant was brief: "Peter Bacanovic thinks ImClone is going to start trading down." Stewart immediately returned the call, and at some point during the 11-minute conversation was put through to her broker's office at Merrill Lynch. Bacanovic was on vacation in Florida, and so she talked instead with his assistant, Douglas Faneuil. Faneuil later testified that, on orders from Bacanovic, he told Stewart that he had no information on the company but that the Waksal family was selling their shares in ImClone. Although Stewart denied being told this, she instructed Faneuil to sell all of her ImClone stock. Her 3,928 shares sold within the hour at an average price of $58.43 a share, netting her approximately $228,000. Stewart then made one more phone call, to Sam Waksal's office, leaving a message that Waksal's secretary scribbled as "Martha Stewart something is going on with ImClone and she wants to know what." During her vacation in Mexico, she reportedly told her friend, "Isn't it nice to have brokers who tell you those things?"

Martha Stewart became a national celebrity and self-made billionaire through her print and television presence and the many household products bearing her brand name. After a brief career on Wall Street as a stockbroker, she started a successful catering business that led to a succession of books on cooking and household decorating. The magazine *Martha Stewart Living* followed, along with a television series and a partnership with Kmart. In 1999, her company, Martha Stewart Living Omnimedia (MSLO) went public, with Stewart as the CEO and chairman. MSLO was unique in that Martha Stewart herself was the company's chief marketable asset.

Sam Waksal was the founder, president, and CEO of ImClone Systems, Inc., a biopharmaceutical company that sought to develop biologic compounds for the treatment of cancers. Martha Stewart and Sam Waksal were close friends, having been introduced in the early 1990s by Stewart's daughter Alexis, who had dated Waksal for a number of years. It was also through Alexis that her mother and Waksal came to know Peter Bacanovic, who attended Columbia University in the mid-1980s while Alexis was enrolled at nearby Barnard College. Bacanovic worked briefly at ImClone before joining Merrill Lynch in 1993 as a broker, and Stewart and Waksal became two of his most important clients. Waksal helped Stewart achieve an advantageous split from her then-publisher Time Warner in 1997, and in gratitude, she invested an initial $80,000 in ImClone stock. With a net worth of over $1 billion, her investment in 2001 represented three-hundredths of 1 percent of her total holdings.

In 2001, the future of ImClone rested on the uncertain prospects of a single drug, Erbitux, for the treatment of advanced colon cancer. Erbitux was a genetically engineered version of a mouse antibody that showed great promise in early tests. In October, ImClone submitted a preliminary application to the Food and Drug Administration (FDA) for approval of Erbitux. This application was merely the first step that allowed the FDA to determine whether the research submitted by the company was sufficiently complete to begin a full FDA review. A decision on the application was expected by the end of December. On December 28, 2001, ImClone announced that the FDA had found the application to be incomplete and would not proceed to the next stage. After the news was announced, ImClone stock dropped 16 percent to $46 a share. The previous day, on the morning of December 27, Sam Waksal and his daughter asked Peter Bacanovic to sell all of their ImClone shares held at Merrill Lynch, which were worth over $7.3 million. Merrill Lynch sold the ImClone stock of the daughter for approximately $2.5 million but declined to sell Sam Waksal's shares, citing concern about insider trading. An attempt by Waksal to have his shares transferred to his daughter so that they could be sold by her failed. Separately, Sam Waksal's father sold shares worth more than $8 million, and smaller amounts were sold by another daughter and a sister of Sam Waksal.

The Securities and Exchange Commission (SEC) quickly opened an investigation into suspected insider trading in ImClone stock. Faneuil later testified that Bacanovic initially told him that dumping Stewart's stock was part of a tax-loss selling plan. After being informed by Faneuil that Stewart had made a profit, Bacanovic changed the story, explaining that Stewart had placed a stop-loss order to sell the stock if it dropped below $60 a share. Stewart affirmed to federal investigators that she had given this instruction to Bacanovic and gave as a reason that she did not want to be bothered about the stock during her vacation. This conversation, she claimed, was with Bacanovic, though she had in fact talked only with Faneuil. She also said that she was unable to recall whether Sam Waksal had been discussed in the December 27 telephone conversation or whether she had been informed about stock sales by the Waksal family. Before meeting with investigators, Stewart accessed the phone message log on her assistant's computer and changed the entry "Peter Bacanovic thinks ImClone is going to start trading downward" to "Peter Bacanovic re imclone," but afterward told her assistant to restore the original wording. Meanwhile, Bacanovic altered a worksheet that contained a list of Stewart's holdings at Merrill Lynch with notations in blue ballpoint ink to include "@$60" by the entry for ImClone. An expert later testified in court that the ink for this entry was different from that used in the other notations.

In March 2003, Sam Waksal pleaded guilty to charges of securities fraud for insider trading, obstruction of justice, and perjury. He was later sentenced to seven years and three months in prison and ordered to pay $4 million. The Department of Justice accepted a proposal from Martha Stewart's attorneys that she plead guilty to a single felony count of making a false statement to federal investigators that would probably avoid any prison time. However, Stewart decided that she could not do this and would take her chances in court. A justice department official said, "We had no desire to prosecute this woman" but indicated that the lying was too egregious to ignore.[45] Stewart and Bacanovic were charged with conspiracy, obstruction of justice, and perjury—but not insider trading. On March 5, 2004, a jury found both parties guilty. Stewart and Bacanovic were each sentenced to five months in prison, five months of home confinement, and two years of probation. Stewart was fined $30,000 and Bacanovic, $4,000. By selling her ImClone stock when she did, Stewart avoided a loss of approximately $46,000. She estimated the total loss from her legal troubles to be $400 million, including a drop in the value of MSLO stock and missed business opportunities.

In June 2003, the SEC brought a civil action for insider trading, which was separate from the criminal charges of which Stewart was found guilty. To convict Stewart of insider trading, the SEC would have to show that she had received material nonpublic information in violation of a fiduciary duty. The information that she received from Faneuil in the December 27 phone call was that the members of the Waksal family were selling their ImClone stock. Neither Faneuil nor Bacanovic had information about the FDA rejection of the Erbitux application that prompted the sell-off. Neither one had a fiduciary duty to ImClone. However, Bocanovic owed a fiduciary duty to Merrill Lynch that he breached in ordering that information about the Waksal's sales conveyed to Stewart. Merrill Lynch had an insider trading policy that prohibited the disclosure of material nonpublic information to anyone who would use it to engage in stock trading. A confidentiality policy also prohibited employees from discussing information about a client with other employees except on a "strict need-to-know basis," and further stated, "We do not release client information, except upon a client's authorization or when permitted or required by law."

Since the information that the Waksals were selling was obtained by Bacanovic in his role as their broker, he breached his duty to Merrill Lynch. However, Martha Stewart denied that she was aware that Bacanovic was their broker. Moreover, as a former stockbroker who understood the law on insider trading, she knew that she could not act on information received from an insider like Waksal. But could she trade on information provided by Bacanovic, even if he was violating a fiduciary duty to Merrill Lynch? Stewart was apparently unconcerned about her first interview with federal investigators because, according to a close associate, "All she thought they wanted to talk about was whether Waksal himself had tipped her about the F.D.A. decision. She knew she was in the clear on that one."[46]

Postscript

On August 7, 2007, the SEC announced a settlement with Martha Stewart and Peter Bacanovic.[47] Stewart agreed to pay a $195,000 penalty and accept a five-year ban on serving as an officer or director of a public company. Bacanovic was ordered to pay $75,000; he had previously received a permanent bar from work in the securities industry. The SEC's Director of Enforcement declared, "It is fundamentally unfair for someone to have an edge on the market just because she has a stockbroker who is willing to break the rules and give her an illegal tip. It's worse still when the individual engaged in the insider trading is the Chairman and CEO of a public company."[48]

CASE 11.4 ✳ Explore the Concept on mythinkinglab.com
Oracle's Hostile Bid for PeopleSoft

At a quickly convened board meeting on June 8, 2003, the directors of PeopleSoft considered their response to an unsolicited takeover offer from Oracle Corporation. Two days prior, Oracle's CEO, Lawrence J. (Larry) Ellison, announced that the company would seek to buy all of PeopleSoft's stock in a deal worth $5.1 billion. Because the PeopleSoft executives who sat on the board had a vested interest in rejecting the offer, the board's independent directors, who had no stake in the outcome, formed a committee to address the issues. In deciding whether to accept the offer and how to repel it if need be, their fiduciary duty was to act solely in the interest of PeopleSoft's shareholders.

Oracle and PeopleSoft were companies that developed and installed software for Enterprise Resource Planning (ERP), which enables business customers to integrate all data processing in a company across functions. Instead of separate computer software for accounting, finance, human resources, manufacturing, supply chain management, customer orders, and the like, ERP provides a unified system that operates from a common database. A few companies dominated the ERP business, with SAP, Siebel, and J. D. Edwards being the other major providers. Typically, an ERP system represents a very large investment by a company, and the installation may take a year or more. During the three to four years' period before a change to a next-generation system, support from the ERP provider is critical. Consequently, the choice of ERP systems is a matter of great importance to companies.

The 1990s was a period of growth in the ERP industry, but by 2003, the sales of systems were declining, and price competition was reducing profitability. Companies were able to expand primarily by branching out into new applications, which could be done most quickly by acquiring smaller companies. Accordingly, PeopleSoft entered into an agreement to purchase J. D. Edwards for $1.8 billion. Not only did the two companies' products fit well together, but the merger of PeopleSoft and J. D. Edwards, which had 10 percent and 5 percent of the market, respectively, would enable the combined companies to exceed the 13 percent market share of Oracle. PeopleSoft announced the acquisition of J. D. Edwards on June 2, 2003.

Oracle had long considered PeopleSoft for an acquisition or merger. A year before the hostile bid, the two companies had engaged in talks that were eventually abandoned. However, Oracle anticipated a possible PeopleSoft acquisition of J. D. Edwards and had prepared a plan to be put into effect as soon as an acquisition was announced. Ellison was quoted in the *Wall Street Journal* as saying, "We've got this war game in the box. This has all been pre-scripted. If they launched on J. D. Edwards, we were going to launch on them."[49] The Oracle bid was unusual, though, in that the offer of $16 per share represented a mere 6 percent premium over the current price of PeopleSoft stock. Typically, a serious raider offers a premium of 20 percent or more. Furthermore, Oracle announced that it would not offer PeopleSoft applications to its customers but would seek to convert PeopleSoft's customers to Oracle's E-Business Suite. Although the merger would make Oracle the number two ERP, next only to SAP, Oracle seemed interested only in PeopleSoft's customers and not its software or employees.

The PeopleSoft CEO, Craig Conway, saw the takeover bid merely as a ploy for preventing the company's acquisition of J. D. Edwards and, at the same time, damaging PeopleSoft's business. The deal for acquiring J. D. Edwards, which involved the trade of stock, depended on the ability of PeopleSoft to maintain its stock price. However, the Oracle offer was likely to deter new customers from purchasing PeopleSoft applications because of the uncertainty over the future of the company. In a press release, Conway said, "By making an offer with the acknowledged intent of eliminating PeopleSoft's business, Oracle seeks to disrupt PeopleSoft's efforts to complete new sales, thus effectively damaging PeopleSoft's business even if Oracle never buys a single share of PeopleSoft Stock."[50] In private, Conway was more candid, deriding the bid as "classic Larry bad behavior" from "a company with a history of atrociously bad behavior."[51]

Conway was firmly against a consideration of Oracle's hostile bid. He told reporters that "there is no condition that I can even remotely imagine where PeopleSoft would be sold to Oracle."[52] However, the committee of independent board directors recognized that there were conditions under which it would be in the shareholders' interest to sell the company. The relevant questions for their decision were, what are those conditions, and have they been met?

First, there was the matter of price. Was $16 per share a fair price for the company's stock, or should the board hold out for a higher offer? In takeovers, a better price might be offered not only by the original suitor but by a rival raider. This rival might be a "white knight," who makes a friendly offer to save the company from the clutches of an undesirable suitor. In takeovers, a bidder, like a house buyer, typically makes a low bid with the intent of raising the price eventually. On June 18, Oracle raised its offer to $19.50 a share, a 22 percent increase in the bid price and a 29 percent premium over the price on the day Oracle announced its hostile bid.

Second, what were Oracle's intentions in making an offer for PeopleSoft? Larry Ellison strenuously denied that his intent was merely to harm PeopleSoft and derail the J. D. Edwards acquisition. To his critics Ellison replied, "I'm a rich guy, and I think $5 billion is serious money." He added, "We absolutely think this is going to happen."[53] Moreover, many analysts thought that an acquisition would strengthen Oracle by giving the company new products, new employees, and new customers. According to one observer, "Ellison has a vision of ensuring that Oracle is, to a large extent, a vertically integrated company that is equipped to offer virtually any business software product or service to customers."[54] However, if the price that Oracle is willing to pay were high enough to induce PeopleSoft shareholders to sell, should Oracle's plans for the acquired company be of any concern to the board? If Oracle is not serious in acquiring and does not successfully absorb PeopleSoft, then it is Oracle's shareholders who bear the loss, not the former PeopleSoft shareholders.

Third, what would be the impact of selling PeopleSoft to Oracle on the company's existing customers? Even if its customers eventually migrate to Oracle's E-Business Suite, Oracle might not provide adequate maintenance and upgrades for the PeopleSoft applications that they are currently running. One solution to this problem that the board of directors considered was a Customer Assurance Plan (CAP) that would reimburse customers from two to five times the original cost of their software if an acquirer failed to provide adequate service during the life of a system. Such a guarantee would reassure not only customers who had already purchased PeopleSoft applications but also companies shopping for new software. CAP would also be a costly commitment that would increase the cost of a takeover for the acquirer. Although CAP would be a benefit to PeopleSoft's customers, the board had to consider whether it was in the best interest of the shareholders. Once in place, it probably could not be withdrawn by the board, and it might reduce the price that the shareholders could get for the company.

Fourth, the board had to assess the effect of Oracle's bid on J. D. Edwards. If the acquisition of J. D. Edwards were not completed quickly, the opportunity might be lost, and J. D. Edwards shareholders would not be able to realize the gain they expected from the deal. The J. D. Edwards CEO declared, "Oracle's unsolicited offer for PeopleSoft will only destroy value for our companies' shareholders, customers and employees and the technology community overall."[55] After the announcement of Oracle's bid, J. D. Edwards filed a suit against Oracle alleging that Oracle had wrongfully interfered in the sale of J. D. Edwards to PeopleSoft. Because the purchase agreement involved payment with PeopleSoft stock, the deal required the approval of the PeopleSoft shareholders, which could not be gained quickly. However, the board had the option of buying J. D. Edwards for cash, which could be done without shareholder approval, and so the acquisition could be completed promptly. The question for the board, then, was whether to proceed with the J. D. Edwards acquisition, and if so, how to do it.

If the PeopleSoft board were to accept Oracle's offer, then it would need to rescind a "poison pill" that it had previously adopted as protection against a hostile takeover. The poison pill provided that in the event of an acquirer purchasing 20 percent of the stock, new shares would be issued to the shareholders at a low price. The effect of such a provision is to reduce the acquirer's percentage below 20 percent, and this provision would be triggered each time an acquirer increased its stake above that level. If the board decided to accept a bid for the company, the poison pill could be eliminated by board action. Although this protection effectively ensured that a takeover could not occur through the purchase of stock without board approval, a hostile raider could still take the difficult and more time consuming route of a proxy battle to elect its own members to the board, who would then rescind the poison pill.

At the board meeting on June 8, the directors concluded that they needed more information before making a decision, and so they adjourned and scheduled at meeting for June 11, at which time the board would address all of the issues facing them in responding to Oracle's hostile bid.

Postscript

At the board meeting on June 11, the PeopleSoft directors rejected Oracle's $16-per-share offer as too low and adopted a Customer Assurance Plan. In August 2003, PeopleSoft completed the acquisition of J. D. Edwards. Oracle and PeopleSoft engaged in extensive court battles over many issues, including the poison pill and CAP. During 18 month of skirmishing, Oracle raised its bid price five times, eventually offering $26.50 per share.[56] On December 13, 2004, the PeopleSoft board announced that it would accept this offer. In the end, PeopleSoft was acquired by Oracle for $10.3 billion.

Notes

1. Information for this case is taken from reporting by Kurt Eichenwald for the *New York Times* and Tom Fowler and Mary Flood for the *Houston Chronicle*. Kurt Eichenwald, "4 at Merrill Accused of an Enron Fraud," *New York Times*, 18 March 2003, C1; Kurt Eichenwald, "An Enron Trial with Big Stakes for Ones Ahead," *New York Times*, 20 September 2004, C1; Kurt Eichenwald, "First Criminal Trial to Examine Enron Deal Begins," *New York Times*, 22 September 2004, C4; Kurt Eichenwald, "Witness Tells of Hearing about Merrill-Enron Side Deal," *New York Times*, 24 September 2004, C3; Kurt Eichenwald, "Former Executive Testifies, Offering Insider's Look at Enron's Deal Making," *New York Times*, 28 September 2004, C1; Kurt Eichenwald, "Ex-Enron Treasurer Describes Discomfort with Barge Deal," *New York Times*, 7 October 2004, C2. Tom Fowler and Mary Flood, "Merrill Lynch to Settle with SEC," *Houston Chronicle*, 21 February 2003, B1; Tom Fowler and Mary Flood, "Prosecutors: E-mail Show Enron Deal on Barges Was Sham," *Houston Chronicle*, 6 October 2004, B1; Mary Flood, "Enron Trial Is Wrapping Up Today," *Houston Chronicle*, 27 October 2004, B4.

2. Jay L. Walker [pseudonym], *The Complete Book of Wall Street Ethics* (New York: William Morrow and Company, 1987).

3. Mark Maremont, "Burned by Merrill," *BusinessWeek*, 25 April 1994, 122–25.

4. Ellen E. Schultz, "You Need a Translator for Latest Sales Pitch," *Wall Street Journal*, 14 February 1994, C1.

5. Michael Quint, "Met Life Shakes Up Its Ranks," *New York Times*, 29 October 1994, C1.

6. *Marshak v. Blyth Eastman Dillon & Co.*, Inc., 413 F. Supp. 377, 379 (1975).

7. *Kaufman v. Merrill Lynch, Pierce, Fenner & Smith*, 464, F. Supp. 528, 534 (1978).

8. Report of the Committee on Compensation Practices, issued by the Securities and Exchange Commission, 10 April 1995.

9. NASD Rules of Fair Practice, art. III, sec. 2.

10. This question is addressed in Hersh Shefrin and Meir Statman, "Ethics, Fairness and Efficiency in Financial Markets," *Financial Analysts Journal* (November–December 1993), 21–29, from which portions of this section are derived.

11. John Maynard Keynes, *The General Theory of Employment, Interest, and Money* (New York: Harcourt Brace & Co., 1936), 159.

12. The example is taken from Anthony Kronman, "Contract Law and Distributive Justice," *Yale Law Journal*, 89 (1980), 472–79.

13. *SEC v. Texas Gulf Sulphur*, 401 F.2d 19 (1987).

14. *Chiarella v. U.S.*, 445 U.S. 222 (1980); *Dirks v. SEC*, 463 U.S. 646 (1983); *U.S. v. Chestman*, 903 F.2d 75 (1990); *U.S. v. Willis*, 737 F. Supp. 269 (1990); *U.S. v. O'Hagen*, 117 S.Ct. 2199 (1997).

15. Henry Manne, *Insider Trading and the Stock Market* (New York: Free Press, 1966).

16. This point is argued in Jennifer Moore, "What Is Really Unethical about Insider Trading?" *Journal of Business Ethics*, 9 (1990), 171–82.

17. *Carpenter et al. v. U.S.*, 484 U.S. 19 (1987).

18. *U.S. v. O'Hagen*.

19. Peter Drucker, "To End the Raiding Roulette Game," *Across the Board* (April 1986), 39.

20. Michel T. Halbouty, "The Hostile Takeover of Free Enterprise," *Vital Speeches of the Day* (August 1986), 613.

21. See Michael C. Jensen, "The Takeover Controversy," *Vital Speeches of the Day* (May 1987), 426–29; Michael C. Jensen,

"Takeovers: Folklore and Science," *Harvard Business Review* (November–December 1984), 109–21.

22. Jensen, "Takeovers"; Michael C. Jensen and Richard S. Ruback, "The Market for Corporate Control: The Scientific Evidence," *Journal of Financial Economics*, 11 (1983), 5–50; and Douglas H. Ginsburg and John F. Robinson, "The Case Against Federal Intervention in the Market for Corporate Control," *The Brookings Review* (Winter–Spring 1986), 9–14.

23. F. M. Scherer, "Takeovers: Present and Future Dangers," *The Brookings Review* (Winter–Spring 1986), 15–20.

24. For a discussion of coercion in tender offers, see John R. Boatright, "Tender Offers: An Ethical Perspective," in *The Ethics of Organizational Transformation: Mergers, Takeovers, and Corporate Restructuring*, ed. W. Michael Hoffman, Robert Frederick, and Edward S. Petry, Jr. (New York: Quorum Books, 1989), 167–81.

25. Philip L. Cochran and Steven L. Wartick, "'Golden Parachutes': A Closer Look," *California Management Review*, 26 (1984), 113.

26. Michael C. Jensen, "The Takeover Controversy: Analysis and Evidence," in *Knights, Raiders, and Targets: The Impact of the Hostile Takeover*, ed. John C. Coffee, Jr., Louis Lowenstein, and Susan Rose-Ackerman (New York: Oxford University Press, 1988), 340.

27. Peter G. Scotese, "Fold Up Those Golden Parachutes," *Harvard Business Review* (March–April 1985), 170.

28. Cochran and Wartick, "Golden Parachutes," 121.

29. Scotese, "Fold Up Those Golden Parachutes," 168.

30. Jensen, "The Takeover Controversy," 341.

31. J. Gregory Dees, "The Ethics of 'Greenmail,'" in *Business Ethics: Research Issues and Empirical Studies*, ed. William C. Frederick and Lee E. Preston (Greenwich, CT: JAI Press, 1990), 254.

32. These arguments are developed and evaluated in Dees, "The Ethics of 'Greenmail.'"

33. John C. Coffee, Jr., "Regulating the Market for Corporate Control: A Critical Assessment of the Tender Offer's Role in Corporate Governance," *Columbia Law Review*, 84 (1984), 1145–1296.

34. This is argued in Roger J. Dennis, "Two-Tiered Tender Offers and Greenmail: Is New Legislation Needed?" *Georgia Law Review*, 19 (1985), 281–341.

35. *Paramount Communications, Inc.* v. *Time Inc.*, 571 A.2d 1140 (1990).

36. See Eric W. Orts, "Beyond Shareholders: Interpreting Corporate Constituency Statutes," *George Washington Law Review*, 61 (1992), 14–135.

37. Roberta S. Karmel, "The Duty of Directors to Non-shareholder Constituencies in Control Transactions—A Comparison of U.S. and U.K. Law," *Wake Forest Law Review*, 25 (1990), 68.

38. Most of the information in this case is taken from Verified Complaint, Supreme Court of the State of New York, Plaintiff, against, Strong Financial Corporation et al.,

defendants; and Securities and Exchange Commission, Administrative Proceeding, File No. 3–11498, In the Matter of Strong Capital Management, Inc. et al., Respondent.

39. Richard Strong was also chairman and chief executive officer of the parent company Strong Financial Corporation. To simplify the complex corporate structure of the Strong enterprises, all references are to Strong Capital Management.

40. Each mutual fund operates as a separate company with its own board of directors and contracts with an investment company, such as SCM, to serve as an investment advisor.

41. Peter Elkind, "The Secrets of Eddie Stern," *Fortune*, 19 April 2004, 106.

42. The estimate is by Stanford University business professor Eric Zitzewitz. Janice Revell and David Stires, "Making Sense of the Mutual Fund Scandal," *Fortune*, 24 November 2003, 237.

43. Elkind, "The Secrets of Eddie Stern."

44. Information on this case is taken from the following sources: *United States of America* v. *Martha Stewart and Peter Bacanovic*, United States District Court, Southern District of New York, Superseding Indictment S1 03 Cr. 717 (MGC); U.S. Securities and Exchange Commission, Plaintiff against Martha Stewart and Peter Bacanovic, Defendants, United States District Court, Southern District of New York, Complaint 03 CV 4070 (NRB); Jeffrey Toobin, "Lunch at Martha's," *New Yorker*, 3 February 2003, 38–41; Jeffrey Toobin, "A Bad Thing," *New Yorker*, 22 March 2004, 60–72.

45. Toobin, "A Bad Thing."

46. Ibid.

47. U.S. Securities and Exchange Commission, "Martha Stewart and Peter Bacanovic Settle SEC's Insider Trading Charges," press release 2006, 134.

48. U.S. Securities and Exchange Commission, "SEC Charges Martha Stewart, Broker Peter Bacanovic with Illegal Insider Trading," press release 2003, 69.

49. Mylene Mangalindan, Don Clark, and Robin Sidel, "Software Assault: Oracle's Bid for PeopleSoft Offers Possible Taste of Future," *Wall Street Journal*, 9 June 2003, A1.

50. "PeopleSoft CEO Comments on Oracle Offer," PeopleSoft press release, 6 June 2003.

51. Andrew Ross Sorkin and Laurie Flynn, "Oracle Takes a $5 Billion Jab at PeopleSoft," *New York Times*, 7 June 2003, C1.

52. Carrie Kirby, "Oracle Gets a Run for Its Money: Hostile Bid for PeopleSoft Turns into a Battle," *San Francisco Chronicle*, 22 December 2003.

53. Mangalindan, Clark, and Sidel, "Software Assault."

54. "What's Behind Oracle's Unwelcome Bid for PeopleSoft," Knowledge@Wharton, 17 June 2003.

55. Andrew Ross Sorkin, "PeopleSoft Rejects Bid from Oracle," *New York Times*, 13 June 2003, D1.

56. Oracle was able to offer so much more than the price in its original offer because, once it gained access to PeopleSoft's books, Oracle discovered that the revenue from maintenance contracts was significantly higher than the company had previously estimated.

CHAPTER 12

Corporate Social Responsibility

((•┤Listen to the Chapter Audio on mythinkinglab.com

CASE 12.1 ✴┤Explore the Concept on mythinkinglab.com

Competing Visions at Malden Mills

The tragic fire that struck Malden Mills in 1995 and made its owner, Aaron Feuerstein, an American folk hero was the beginning of a struggle that eventually pitted Mr. Feuerstein against the might of GE Capital over competing visions of how to run the company.

After three of the Malden Mills' eight buildings in Lawrence, Massachusetts, burned to the ground on the night of December 11, Aaron Feuerstein, the patriarch of this family-owned firm, announced that wages and benefits for the 3,100 affected workers would be continued and that the facilities would be rebuilt on the same site. This heartfelt concern for the company's workers and the community won Mr. Feuerstein widespread acclaim as an exemplar of corporate social responsibility. Many business people wondered why he would not use the $300 million in insurance to move overseas to a low-wage country as his competitors were doing—or simply take the money and retire. Instead, the rebuilding of the plants required an additional $100 million investment. For his compassionate response, Mr. Feuerstein received numerous awards, invitations to speak, and honorary degrees at a time when Americans were disturbed by massive layoffs ordered by highly paid CEOs. President Bill Clinton invited him to a conference on corporate social responsibility and mentioned him in his 1996 State of the Union address.

However, heavy debt from the rebuilding forced Malden Mills into bankruptcy in November 2001, and when the company emerged from bankruptcy in October 2003, it was owned and operated by its former creditors, led by investment giant GE Capital. Aaron Feuerstein held the largely ceremonial posts of president and nonexecutive chairman and retained a 5 percent stake, but majority ownership and operational control of the company was in the hands of the investors who had come to the company's aid. Now, Mr. Feuerstein wanted to repurchase the company that his grandfather founded in 1906 in order to keep the much-needed jobs in Lawrence. The plan of the current owners, though, was to keep control and cut costs by sending operations to Asia. The company's CFO wrote, in August 2003, that management would probably move "a substantial part of Malden's operations overseas in the next few years."[1]

Aaron Feuerstein's response to the fire—which also included generous support for the injured workers and their families—was motivated by his religion (he is an observant Jew), by a sense of responsibility as the head of a family-owned business, and by a certain pride in his ability to overcome obstacles. As he watched the blaze, he was heard to say, "This is not the end."[2] According to a *Boston Globe* reporter, he told himself with "incredible confidence," "I know I can find a way."[3] He later explained his decision as a matter of responsibility. "I have a responsibility to the worker. . . . I have an equal responsibility to the community. It would have been unconscionable to put 3,000 people on the streets and deliver a death blow to [the city of Lawrence]."[4] He described his view of corporate social responsibility as follows:

> Corporate responsibility to me means yes, you must . . . take care of the shareholder, but that is not your exclusive responsibility. The CEO has responsibility to his workers, both white collar and blue collar, as well, and he has responsibility to his community and city. And he has to be wise enough to balance out these various responsibilities and . . . to act justly for the shareholder, as well as the worker.[5]

Although Mr. Feuerstein's decision to rebuild and even expand in Lawrence has been criticized from a business point of view, some observers see in his decision an astute business logic—that he is "crazy like a fox."[6] In the highly competitive fabric industry, where most production now takes place in low-wage countries, Malden Mills had managed to survive and even prosper in the United States by focusing on quality and customer satisfaction. After a bankruptcy in 1982 caused by the collapse of the market for the faux-fur fabric on which Malden Mills depended, the company developed Polartec and Polarfleece, two widely used materials for outer garments that it sold to companies like L.L. Bean, Lands' End, Patagonia, North Face, and Eddie Bauer. Using equipment that requires skilled workers, the company turned out consistently high-quality fabric that was highly valued by these apparel manufacturers—and by *their* customers.

Aaron Feuerstein himself worked closely with customers to achieve a high degree of loyalty. He saw that if the company were to rebuild quickly, he would have to keep his highly skilled workers ready to return to production. He also recognized, though, that layoffs are sometimes necessary, especially when technological advances improve worker productivity. However, he said that at Malden Mills, they had always tried to combine cutbacks in one area with an expansion in another so as to keep workers. Furthermore, he explained,

> And we concentrate less on . . . the cuttable expense of the labor and more on research and development to make better quality products . . . and to differentiate ourselves from our competitors in the market place. We pay more than the average mill does, and so that's fine, because we don't concentrate on pay, we concentrate on where the real profit is in making the product better.[7]

Although Aaron Feuerstein deserves credit for leading Malden Mills through turbulent times, who should lead going forward? The current CEO, who is a career textile executive installed by GE Capital and the other major investors, does not have the same vision.[8] But what vision does Malden Mills need at this point in time? There is a certain irony that chief among the investors who came to the company's rescue was GE Capital because GE's former CEO Jack Welch is considered to be a ruthless, profit-minded executive, the opposite of Aaron Feuerstein. The case for Jack Welch's vision is expressed in the following dissenting observation:

> Feuerstein's pledge to continue paying his workers eventually cost them their jobs, and cost Feuerstein his company. Feuerstein ran out of money, and Malden Mills was forced to declare bankruptcy. Welch, on the other hand, turned GE from a sleepy

home-appliance company into an international mega-corporation that today is a leader in several industries. For every job slashed, he eventually created dozens of new ones. For all the praise heaped on Feuerstein and scorn heaped on Welch, it is Welch, not Feuerstein, whose . . . management style did the most good for the most people.[9]

The choice between these two competing visions will be made largely by a calculation of the market worth of Malden Mills under the leadership of Aaron Feuerstein versus that under GE Capital.

INTRODUCTION

Although corporations are primarily business organizations run for the benefit of shareholders, they have a wide-ranging set of responsibilities—to their own employees, to customers and suppliers, to the communities in which they are located, and to society at large. Most corporations recognize these responsibilities and make a serious effort to fulfill them. Often, these responsibilities are set out in formal statements of a company's principles or beliefs. Many companies have institutionalized corporate social responsibility (CSR) as an integral part of their operations. In addition, there are many outside groups, including nongovernmental organizations (NGOs), socially responsible investors, and consultancy firms, that monitor companies' CSR activities and provide their services. This public demand for social responsibility has led a number of rankings of CSR by outside groups and to formal reporting by corporations of their CSR performance. Today, CSR is a worldwide movement that is gaining increasing acceptance and visibility.

At issue in the discussion of CSR are three questions: First, why do corporations have a social responsibility? That is, what is the basis for such a responsibility? Second, what is the extent of this responsibility, or what exactly do corporations have a responsibility to do? Third, and perhaps most important, how should corporations decide what CSR activities to undertake, and what is required to implement CSR programs effectively? As CSR has gained increasing acceptance, attention has moved away from the first two questions to the third. The focus of business today is no longer on *whether* to engage in corporate social responsibility but *how* to do it.[10] As companies have come to accept a social responsibility, they have also recognized the benefits of CSR activities for themselves as well as society. The most progressive companies effectively use CSR to protect their reputations and to develop and implement corporate strategy. These companies are viewing CSR less as philanthropy and more as savvy corporate-community involvement or as profitable corporate social initiatives.[11]

This chapter examines the concept of corporate social responsibility and the CSR movement. It begins with the debate over the question of whether corporations have a social responsibility and why, and then moves into the reasons why corporations have come increasingly to accept CSR and how they are implementing it effectively. The concept of CSR is closely linked to two other prominent movements: corporate social performance and corporate citizenship. The meaning and implication of these concepts are also considered in this chapter.

THE DEBATE OVER CSR

Although some elements of CSR can be traced back to the mid-nineteenth century, the concept of corporate social responsibility originated in the 1950s when American corporations rapidly increased in size and power, thus creating a concern for their legitimacy in a democracy.[12] The concept continued to figure prominently in public debate during the 1960s and 1970s as the nation confronted pressing social problems such as poverty, unemployment, race relations, urban blight, and pollution. Corporate social responsibility became a rallying cry for diverse groups demanding change in American business during a time of great social unrest. Although CSR did not receive much attention in Europe until the 1980s, the concern for the subject and organized activity surrounding it are more prominent there today than in the United States.[13] Among the factors at work in Europe are the integration of countries into the European Union, the deregulation of the economy, and the decline of the welfare state. Many governments in Europe have promoted CSR as a way of replacing the traditional role of the state in regulating business and providing for people's well-being.

In the last two decades of the twentieth century, American corporations generally recognized a responsibility to society, but that responsibility was weighed against the changes brought about by technology and the demands of being competitive in a rapidly changing global economy. Strong market pressures to be profitable constrained the ability of companies to expend significant resources for CSR. At the same time, however, the increasing globalization of business made corporations more vulnerable to criticism for their operations abroad. Especially corporations with valuable brand names, such as Nike, needed to protect their reputations in the face of adverse publicity and organized protests. In the early years of the new century, CSR is firmly established. As the *Economist* magazine observed in 2004, "CSR is thriving. It is now an industry in itself, with full-time staffs, websites, newsletters, professional associations and massed armies of consultants. This is to say nothing of the NGOs [nongovernmental organizations] that started it all."[14]

Some contend that corporate social responsibility is altogether a pernicious idea. The well-known conservative economist Milton Friedman writes, in *Capitalism and Freedom*, "Few trends could so thoroughly undermine the very foundations of our free society as the acceptance by corporate officials of a social responsibility other than making as much money for their stockholders as possible."[15] He continues,

> The view has been gaining widespread acceptance that corporate officials . . . have a "social responsibility" that goes beyond serving the interest of their stockholders. . . . This view shows a fundamental misconception of the character and nature of a free economy. In such an economy, there is one and only one social responsibility of business—to use its resources and engage in activities designed to increase its profits so long as it stays within the rules of the game, which is to say, engages in open and free competition, without deception or fraud. . . . It is the responsibility of the rest of us to establish a framework of law such that an individual pursuing his own interest is, to quote Adam Smith . . . , "led by an invisible hand to promote an end which was no part of his intention."[16]

At the other extreme are critics who would like corporations to be more socially responsible but are mistrustful. They consider talk about corporate social responsibility to be a public relations ploy designed to legitimize the role of corporations in present-day American society, to divert attention away from the destructive social consequences of corporate activity, and to forestall more appropriate government action.[17] Even those who are more favorably disposed to the idea have reservations about the ability of corporations to respond effectively to social issues. Businesses are single-purpose institutions, conceived, organized, and managed solely in order to engage in economic activity. As such, they lack the resources and the expertise for solving major social problems, and some add that they lack the legitimacy as well. Corporate executives are not elected officials with a mandate from the American people to apply the resources under their control to just any ends that they deem worthwhile.

Furthermore, the idea that corporations should be more socially responsible fails to give adequate ethical guidance to the executives who must decide which causes to pursue, how much to commit to them, and how to evaluate their effectiveness. Much CSR activity is undertaken in response to outside pressures, and so the leaders of a company need to decide which pressures to respond to and how to address them effectively. These problems are especially acute in view of the fact that all choices involve trade-offs. A program to increase minority employment, for example, might end up reducing wages for employees or raising prices for consumers. Or such a program might be adopted at the expense of achieving improvements in worker health and safety or reductions in the amount of pollution. Corporations committed to exercising greater social responsibility need more specific moral rules or principles to give them reasons for acting in one way rather than another.

The Meaning of CSR

All accounts of corporate social responsibility recognize that business firms have not one but many different kinds of responsibilities, including economic and legal responsibilities. Corporations have an *economic* responsibility to produce goods and services and to provide jobs and good wages to the workforce while earning a profit. Economic responsibility also includes the obligation to seek out supplies of raw materials, to discover new resources and technological improvements, and to develop new products. In addition, business firms have certain *legal* responsibilities. One of these is to act as a fiduciary, managing the assets of a corporation in the interests of shareholders, but corporations also have numerous legal responsibilities to employees, customers, suppliers, and other parties. The vast body of business law is constantly increasing as legislatures, regulatory agencies, and the courts respond to greater societal expectations and impose new legal obligations on business.

The concept of corporate social responsibility is often expressed as the voluntary assumption of responsibilities that go beyond the purely economic and legal responsibilities of business firms.[18] More specifically, social responsibility, according to some accounts, is the selection of corporate goals and the evaluation of outcomes not solely by the criteria of profitability and organizational well-being but by ethical standards or judgments of social desirability. The exercise of social responsibility, in this view, must be consistent with the corporate objective of earning a satisfactory level of profit, but it implies a willingness to forgo a certain measure of profit in order to achieve noneconomic ends.

Archie B. Carroll views social responsibility as a four-stage continuum.[19] Beyond economic and legal responsibilities lie ethical responsibilities, which are "additional behaviors and activities that are not necessarily codified into law but nevertheless are expected of business by society's members."[20] At the far end of the continuum are discretionary responsibilities. These responsibilities are not legally required or even demanded by ethics, but corporations accept them in order to meet society's expectations. S. Prakash Sethi notes that social responsibility is a relative concept: What is only a vague ideal at one point in time or in one culture may be a definite legal requirement at another point in time or in another culture. In most of the advanced nations of the world, fulfilling traditional economic and legal responsibilities is no longer regarded as sufficient for legitimizing the activity of large corporations. Corporate social responsibility can thus be defined as "bringing corporate behavior up to a level where it is congruent with the prevailing social norms, values, and expectations of performance."[21]

In 1971, the Committee for Economic Development issued an influential report that characterized corporate social responsibility in a similar fashion but without an explicit mention of legal responsibilities. The responsibilities of corporations are described in this report as consisting of three concentric circles.

> The *inner circle* includes the clear-cut basic responsibilities for the efficient execution of the economic function—products, jobs, and economic growth.
>
> The *intermediate circle* encompasses responsibility to exercise this economic function with a sensitive awareness of changing social values and priorities: for example, with respect to environmental conservation; hiring and relations with employees; and more rigorous expectations of customers for information, fair treatment, and protection from injury.
>
> The *outer circle* outlines newly emerging and still amorphous responsibilities that business should assume to become more broadly involved in actively improving the social environment. Society is beginning to turn to corporations for help with

major social problems such as poverty and urban blight. This is not so much because the public considers business singularly responsible for creating these problems, but because it feels large corporations possess considerable resources and skills that could make a critical difference in solving these problems.[22]

EXAMPLES OF SOCIAL RESPONSIBILITY.   Although there are some disagreements about the meaning of corporate social responsibility, there is general agreement on the types of corporate activities that show social responsibility. Among these are the following:

1. *Choosing to operate on an ethical level that is higher than what the law requires.* For example, Motorola's code of ethics prohibits payments of any kind to a government official, even when the payments are permitted by U.S. and local law; and Mattel closely monitors its factories in China to ensure that its high labor standards are observed.

2. *Making contributions to civic and charitable organizations and nonprofit institutions.* American companies contribute, on average, 1 percent of pre-tax net revenues to worthy causes, and many larger corporations operate nonprofit foundations that fund grant applications from worthy philanthropic organizations.

3. *Providing benefits for employees and improving the quality of life in the workplace beyond economic and legal requirements.* Examples include family-friendly programs such as flexible work and childcare, and time off for volunteer work (see Case 12.3 on Timberland).

4. *Taking advantage of an economic opportunity that is judged to be less profitable but more socially desirable than some alternatives.* For example, Starbucks pays an above-market rate for fair-trade coffee that benefits growers in poor countries (see Case 12.2); and Home Depot ensures that none of the wood it sells comes from old growth or endangered forests.

5. *Using corporate resources to operate a program that addresses some major social problem.* AT&T devotes substantial resources to promoting diversity among its employees, suppliers, and local communities; and major pharmaceutical firms supply drugs for public health programs in less-developed countries. For example, Merck developed and now gives away in Africa a drug for the treatment of the disease river blindness.

Although these activities are all beyond the economic and legal responsibilities of corporations and may involve some sacrifice of profit, they are not necessarily antithetical to corporate interests. For example, corporate philanthropy that makes the community in which a company is located a better place to live and work results in direct benefits. The "goodwill" that socially responsible activities create makes it easier for corporations to conduct their business. High standards and socially responsible products also serve to protect and even enhance a company's reputation and to attract and retain loyal employees and customers. It should come as no surprise, then, that some of the most successful corporations are also among the most socially responsible. They are led by executives who see that even the narrow economic and legal responsibilities of corporations cannot be fulfilled without the articulation of noneconomic values to guide corporate decision making and the adoption of nontraditional business activities that satisfy the demands of diverse constituencies.

CORPORATE SOCIAL RESPONSIVENESS.   An important aspect of corporate social responsibility is the responsiveness of corporations—that is, the ability of corporations to respond in a socially responsible manner to new challenges.[23] William C. Frederick explains that the concept of *corporate social responsiveness* "refers to the capacity of a corporation to respond to social pressures."[24] The emphasis of corporate social responsiveness, in other words, is on the *process* of responding or the readiness to respond, rather than on the *content* of an actual response. Thus, a socially responsive corporation uses its resources to anticipate social issues and develop policies, programs, and other means of dealing with them. The management of social issues in a socially responsive corporation is integrated into the strategic planning process, instead of being handled as an ad hoc reaction to specific crises.

The *content* of a response is also important because it represents the outcome of being socially responsible. Donna Wood has combined all three elements—the *principle* of being socially responsible, the *process* of social responsiveness, and the socially responsible *outcome*—in the concept of *corporate social performance*.[25] Using the example of environmental concerns about packaging, the *principles* of corporate social responsibility would be those that lead the company to recognize an obligation to change its packaging in order to protect the environment. The *processes* might consist of establishing an office of environmental affairs or working with environmentalists to develop new packaging. The *outcomes* could include the switch to environmentally responsible packaging and perhaps building facilities to recycle the packaging.

CORPORATE CITIZENSHIP.   The term "corporate citizenship," which gained currency in the 1990s, especially in Europe, is often used interchangeably with "corporate social responsibility" and "corporate social performance," but it sometimes has a broader meaning to include the impacts of a business organization on all groups in society, on society as a whole, and on the environment. According to one definition, "corporate citizenship is the process of identifying, analyzing and responding to the company's social, political and economic responsibilities as defined through law and public policy, stakeholder expectations, and voluntary acts flowing from corporate values and business strategies."[26]

In contrast to CSR, which is often conceived to be voluntary activities of a company that are in addition to its core business, corporate citizenship focuses on the integration of social and environmental concerns into a company's policies and practices, so that all business is done as a "good citizen." The language of citizenship implies a set of obligations that arises in virtue of membership in a larger community to which something is "owed" in return for enjoying certain privileges. The popular idea that society gives corporations a "license" to operate fits well with the idea of citizenship. The language of citizenship generally has greater appeal to businesses and NGOs than the terminology of CSR, which may also account for its widespread adoption in recent years. However, corporations are not citizens in the sense of having all the rights and obligations of the citizens of a state, and so the term "corporate citizenship" may be misleading and unhelpful in understanding the responsibilities of corporations.[27]

The Normative Case for CSR

The initial debate over CSR in the 1950s and 1960s was largely over the normative question of whether CSR was something that corporations were morally obligated or, at least, morally permitted to do. Opponents of the idea, such as Milton Friedman, argued on moral grounds that corporations ought not to engage in CSR at all, unless doing so benefited shareholders, while proponents offered arguments for the position that corporations were morally permitted to engage in some voluntary socially responsible activity and, in some situations, could be morally faulted for not doing so. The starting point for most of the arguments for and against corporate social responsibility is what has been called the "classical view" of the corporations, which is the dominant conception, at least in the United States.

THE CLASSICAL VIEW.   The classical view, which prevailed in the nineteenth century, is still very influential today, especially among economists. It is expressed by James W. McKie in three basic propositions.

1. Economic behavior is separate and distinct from other types of behavior, and business organizations are distinct from other organizations, even though the same individuals may be involved in business and nonbusiness affairs. Business organizations do not serve the same goals as other organizations in a pluralistic society.

2. The primary criteria of business performance are economic efficiency and growth in production of goods and services, including improvements in technology and innovations in goods and services.

3. The primary goal and motivating force for business organizations is profit. The firm attempts to make as large a profit as it can, thereby maintaining its efficiency and taking advantage of available opportunities to innovate and contribute to growth.[28]

In the classical view, corporations should engage in purely economic activity and be judged in purely economic terms. Social concerns are not unimportant, but they should be left to other institutions in society.

The classical view is part of a larger debate about the legitimate role of the corporation in a democracy. In his introduction to the influential volume *The Corporation in Modern Society*, Edward Mason described the problem of the modern corporation as follows: America is a "society of large corporations . . . [whose] management is in the hands of a few thousand men. Who selected these men, if not to rule over us, at least to exercise vast authority, and to whom are they responsible?"[29] The classical view is a response to this problem that recognizes that corporate power must be harnessed to a larger social good if it is not to become tyrannical. Confining corporations to economic ends is intended, in part, to limit their role in society so as to preserve other kinds of institutions, both public and private.

Business activity, in the classical view, is justified partly on the ground that it secures the well-being of society as a whole. The crux of this argument is the efficacy of Adam Smith's invisible hand in harmonizing self-interested behavior to secure an end that is not a part of anyone's intention. This justification also depends on the ability of the rest of society to create the conditions necessary for the invisible hand to operate and to address social problems without the aid of business. The debate over the workings of the invisible hand cannot be settled here (it is examined at some length in Chapter 2), but the invisible hand argument, upon which the classical view depends, is not incompatible with certain arguments for corporate social responsibility.

THE MORAL MINIMUM OF THE MARKET.   First, a certain level of ethical conduct is necessary for the invisible hand to operate, or indeed for business activity to take place at all. Milton Friedman speaks of the "rules of the game," by which he means "open and free competition, without deception or fraud." Theodore Levitt, in his article "The Dangers of Social Responsibility," says that aside from seeking material gain, business has only one responsibility, and that is "to obey the elementary canons of everyday face-to-face civility (honesty, good faith, and so on)."[30] The "rules of the game" and "face-to-face civility" impose not inconsequential constraints on business. Presumably, the prohibition against deception and fraud obligates corporations to deal fairly with employees, customers, and the public and to avoid sharp sales practices, misleading advertising, and the like.

The moral minimum of the market also includes an obligation to engage in business without inflicting injury on others. Critics of Levitt's position observe,

> Levitt presents the reader with a choice between, on the one hand, getting involved in the management of society . . . and, on the other hand, fulfilling the profitmaking function. But such a choice excludes another meaning of corporate responsibility: the making of profits in such a way as to minimize social injury. Levitt at no point considers the possibility that business activity may at times injure others and that it may be necessary to regulate the social consequences of one's business activities accordingly.[31]

Thus, corporations in a free market have an obligation not to pollute the environment and to clean up any pollution they cause.

It may also be in the best interests of a corporation to operate above the moral minimum of the market. Corporations that adhere only to the moral minimum leave themselves open to pressure from society and regulation by government. One of the major reasons advanced for corporations to exercise greater social responsibility is to avoid such external interference. By "internalizing" the expectations of society, corporations retain control over decision making and avoid the costs associated with government regulation.

POWER AND RESPONSIBILITY.   Second, corporations have become so large and powerful that they are not effectively restrained by market forces and government regulation, as the invisible hand argument assumes. Some self-imposed restraint in the form of a voluntary assumption of greater social responsibility is necessary, therefore, for corporate activity to secure the public welfare. Keith Davis expressed this point succinctly in the proposition "*social responsibility arises from social power.*"[32] He also cited what he calls the Iron Law of Responsibility: "In the long run, those who do not use power in a manner which society considers responsible will tend to lose it."[33] The need for greater social responsibility by corporations, then, is an inevitable result of their increasing size and influence in American society.

Holders of the classical theory argue in reply that precisely because of the immense power of corporations, it would be dangerous to unleash it from the discipline of the market in order to achieve vaguely defined social goals.[34] Kenneth E. Goodpaster and John B. Matthews, Jr., concede that this is a matter for serious concern, but they argue in response:

> What seems not to be appreciated is the fact that power affects when it is used as well as when it is not used. A decision by [a corporation] . . . not to exercise its economic influence according to "non-economic" criteria is inevitably a moral decision and just as inevitably affects the community. The issue in the end is not whether corporations (and other organizations) should be "unleashed" to exert moral force in our society but rather how critically and self-consciously they should choose to do so.[35]

GIVING A HELPING HAND TO GOVERNMENT.   Third, the classical view assumes that business is best suited to provide for the economic well-being of the members of a society, whereas noneconomic goals are best left to government and the other noneconomic institutions of society. This sharp division of responsibility is true at best only as a generalization, and it does not follow that corporations have *no* responsibility to provide a helping hand. Corporations cannot attempt to solve every social problem, of course, and so some criteria are needed for distinguishing those situations in which corporations have an obligation to assist other institutions. John G. Simon, Charles W. Powers, and Jon P. Gunnemann propose the following four criteria:

1. The urgency of the need;
2. The proximity of a corporation to the need;
3. The capability of a corporation to respond effectively;
4. The likelihood that the need will not be met unless a corporation acts.[36]

Accordingly, a corporation has an obligation to address social problems that involve more substantial threats to the well-being of large numbers of people, that are close at hand and related in some way to the corporation's activity, that the corporation has the resources and expertise to solve, and that would likely persist without some action by the corporation.

FRIEDMAN'S ARGUMENT AGAINST CSR.   Perhaps the best-known critic of corporate social responsibility is Milton Friedman. Friedman's main argument against CSR is that corporate executives, when they are acting in their official capacity and not as private persons, are agents of the shareholders of the corporation. As such, executives of a corporation have an obligation to make decisions in the interests of the shareholders, who are ultimately their employers. He has asked,

> What does it mean to say that the corporate executive has a "social responsibility" in his capacity as businessman? If this statement is not pure rhetoric, it must mean that he is to act in some way that is not in the interest of his employers. For example, that he is to refrain from increasing the price of the product in order to contribute to the social objective of preventing inflation, even though a price increase would be in the best interests of the corporation. Or that he is to make expenditures on reducing pollution beyond the amount that is in the best interests of the corporation or that is

required by law in order to contribute to the social objective of improving the environment. Or that, at the expense of corporate profits, he is to hire "hardcore" unemployed instead of better-qualified available workmen to contribute to the social objective of reducing poverty.

In each of these cases, the corporate executive would be spending someone else's money for a general social interest. Insofar as his actions in accord with his "social responsibility" reduce returns to stockholders, he is spending their money. Insofar as his actions raise the price to customers, he is spending the customers' money. Insofar as his actions lower the wages of some employees, he is spending their money.[37]

When corporate executives act in the way Friedman describes, they take on a role of imposing taxes and spending the proceeds that properly belongs only to elected officials. They become, in effect, civil servants with the power to tax, and as civil servants, they ought to be elected through the political process instead of being selected by the stockholders of private business firms.[38]

CRITICISM OF FRIEDMAN'S ARGUMENT.   The classical view does not sanction an unrestrained pursuit of profit. Friedman himself acknowledges that business must observe certain essential limitations on permissible conduct, which he describes as the "rules of the game." Presumably, he would also grant the necessity of government with limited powers for setting and enforcing rules. Business activity requires, in other words, a minimal state in order to prevent fraud and anticompetitive practices and to enforce contracts and the basics of commercial law. Friedman recognizes, further, that many supposed socially responsible actions are really disguised forms of self-interest. Contributions to schools, hospitals, community organizations, cultural groups, and the like are compatible with the classical view insofar as corporations receive indirect benefits from the contributions. All Friedman asks is that corporations recognize these as effective means for making a profit and not as philanthropic activities.

In addition, holders of the classical view generally admit the legitimacy of three other functions of government that place limits on business activity.[39] First, business activity generates many *externalities*, that is, social harms, such as worker injury and pollution, which result indirectly from the operation of business firms. In order to prevent these harms or to correct them after they occur, it is proper for government to act—by requiring safer working conditions and pollution controls, for example.[40] Second, the operation of a free-market economy results in considerable *inequalities* in the distribution of income and wealth. Insofar as it is desirable as a matter of public policy to reduce these inequalities, it is appropriate for government to undertake the task by such means as progressive taxation and redistribution schemes. It is the job of government, in other words, and not business, to manage the equity/efficiency trade-off.[41] Third, free markets are prone to *instability* that manifests itself in inflation, recessions, unemployment, and other economic ills. Individual firms are too small to have much effect on the economy as a whole, and so government must step in and use its powers of taxation, public expenditure, control of the money supply, and the like to make the economy more stable.

The classical view is compatible, then, with some intervention in business activity by government in order to secure the public welfare. The important point to recognize is that the restraints are almost entirely *external*. The primary burden for ensuring that corporations act in a way that is generally beneficial rests on society as a whole, which is charged by Friedman with the task of creating a framework of law that allows business firms to operate solely in their self-interest. The classical theory, therefore, does not permit corporations to *act* in a socially irresponsible manner; it only relieves them of the need to *think* about matters of social responsibility. In a well-ordered society, corporations attend to business while government and other institutions fulfill their proper roles.

It is questionable, however, whether such a neat division of responsibility between business and government can be realized in practice. First, if it is the role of government to set the "rules of the game," it is difficult to see how, on Friedman's account, any lobbying or other interference in government decision making can be justified. How can one claim that business has no responsibility except to play within the rules of the game set by government and then allow business to also set the rules? Once business assumes part of the role of government in setting rules, then it assumes some of the responsibilities of government to provide for society's welfare. Second, it may not be possible for government to address the problems of externalities, inequality, and stability without the cooperation of business. If so, then it is reasonable to expect corporations to take some responsibility for reducing pollution, for example, and not rely solely on government regulation.

Friedman's points that company leaders who take on social responsibilities are acting as unelected civil servants with the power to tax and that they may lack the necessary expertise deserve serious consideration. The same view is expressed by Robert B. Reich:

> Corporate executives are not authorized by anyone—least of all by their consumers or investors—to balance profits against the public good. Nor do they have the expertise for making such moral calculations. That's why we live in a democracy, in which government is supposed to represent the public in drawing such lines.[42]

In contrast to Friedman, who believes that CSR infringes on the proper role of business, Reich's complaint is that the promotion of CSR diverts attention from a role that government ought to play.

However, both concerns can be allayed by observing that, in truth, company executives have very little discretion is pursuing CSR. The CSR agenda is set largely by outside groups, which exert the pressure of public opinion on companies, and by a company's own consumers and employees, who express their desire for socially responsible behavior by their market decisions to buy a company's products or to accept employment. In both a democracy and a market, the people are the ultimate decision makers; in the one they make decisions with their vote, and in the other, with their buying choices. Although companies may lack expertise on some matters, on others they have a great deal of expertise upon which government must rely. Furthermore, any company can acquire expertise by making the necessary investment, and many companies have discovered that new challenges require the acquisition of nontraditional kinds of expertise. For example, in recent years, companies in polluting industries have developed their own in-house expertise in pollution control.

THE "TAXATION" ARGUMENT. The objections to Friedman's argument against corporate social responsibility discussed so far do not address his point that in exercising corporate social responsibility, managers are spending someone else's money. Investors, according to the "taxation" argument, entrust their money to the managers of corporations in order to make profits for the shareholders. Spending money to pursue social ends is thus a form of taxation. Many things are wrong with the "taxation" argument. To say, as Friedman does, that corporate assets belong to the shareholders, that it's *their* money, is not wholly accurate. The role of shareholders in corporate governance is a rather complex issue, however, that is examined in the next chapter. Even if Friedman's assumption is accepted, though, it does not follow that corporations have no social responsibility.

First, managers of a corporation do not have an obligation to earn the greatest amount of profit for shareholders without regard for the means used. A taxi driver hired to take a passenger to the airport as fast as possible, for example, is not obligated to break traffic laws and endanger everyone else on the road. Similarly, money spent on product safety or pollution control may reduce the potential return to shareholders, but the alternative is to conduct business in a way that threatens the well-being of others in society. Friedman would insist, of course, that managers carry out their responsibility to shareholders within the rules of the game, but the moral obligation of managers to be sensitive to the social impact of their actions is more extensive than the minimal restraints listed by Friedman.

Second, the obligation of managers is not merely to secure the maximum return but also to preserve the equity invested in a corporation. Securing the maximum return for shareholders consistent with the preservation of invested capital requires managers to take a long-term view that considers the stability and growth of the corporation. For corporations to survive, they must satisfy the legitimate expectations of society and serve the purposes for which they have been created. Friedman admits the legitimacy of acts of social responsibility as long as they are ultimately in the self-interest of the corporation. The main area of disagreement between proponents and critics of social responsibility is, How much socially responsible behavior is in a corporation's long-term self-interest?

Third, the interests of shareholders are not narrowly economic; corporations are generally expected by their owners to pursue some socially desirable ends. Shareholders are also consumers, environmentalists, and citizens in communities. Consequently, they are affected when corporations fail to act responsibly. In fact, shareholders may be morally opposed to some activities of a corporation and in favor of some changes. One writer contends that "there are conventionally motivated investors who have an interest in the social characteristics of their portfolios *as well as* dividends and capital gains."[43] If so, managers who exercise social responsibility are not "taxing" shareholders and spending the money contrary to their interests but quite the opposite; managers who do not act in a socially responsible manner are using shareholders' money in ways that are against the interests of their shareholders. Friedman's response is that if shareholders want certain social goals, let them use their dividends for that purpose. However, it may be more efficient for corporations to expend funds on environmental protection, for example, than for shareholders to spend the same amount in dividends for the same purpose.

For these reasons, then, the "taxation" argument against corporate social responsibility is not very compelling. Although the rights of shareholders place some limits on what businesses can justifiably do to address major social concerns, they do not yield the very narrowly circumscribed view of Friedman and others. The managers of a business must attend to matters beyond their immediate tasks. Serving the shareholders' interests well requires some attention to a corporation's social responsibilities, although managers have considerable discretion in deciding how to respond to demands of other constituencies or stakeholder groups.

THE BUSINESS CASE FOR CSR

Although moral arguments over CSR still have intellectual interest, they are largely irrelevant to today's corporate executives, who have, for the most part, accepted the business necessity of addressing issues of social responsibility. The *Economist*, which has been critical of CSR in the past, now admits, "Clearly, CSR has arrived." A 2008 special report in the magazine concludes that CSR is a source of competitive advantage by enabling companies to meet society's heightened expectations and protect their reputations in ways that are more focused and vigorous than those in the past.[44] The business case for CSR, in contrast to the moral or ethical case, does not claim that it is the right thing to do but only that it is to a company's advantage to adopt CSR. In considering this prudential argument, though, some skepticism might be in order. At its core, the business case for CSR is the proposition that "being socially responsible is good business." But is this always true?

There are two related arguments for the business case for CSR. One argument is that CSR contributes to profitability because the market rewards responsible behavior and punishes a company's lapses. The second argument is that CSR can be a source of competitive advantage. These two arguments are examined in turn.

The Market for Virtue

If CSR is profitable, then the profit opportunities in CSR should be sufficient to induce managers to lead socially responsible companies—assuming, of course, that managers are aware of the link between CSR and profitability. One obstacle to greater CSR activity may be a lack of awareness of this link. However, the profitability of CSR or the difficulties of implementing it profitably may be overestimated. David Vogel calls the power of market forces to produce CSR activities "the market for virtue," and in his view there is a limited market in support of CSR, but it "is not sufficiently important to make it in the interest of all firms to behave more responsibly."[45] The existence and potential of a market for virtue can be ascertained by identifying the specific market forces that induce managers to undertake CSR activities and measuring their power.

In economic terms, if CSR is the supply in a market for virtue, then there must be some demand for it. The demand, if it exists, comes from customers, employees, investors, and other groups that are willing to express their desire for CSR in the marketplace. A number of studies show that many consumers in the United States and Europe say that they would pay more for products that meet some social test, such as being made without sweatshop labor or environmental pollution.[46] Some companies have responded by certifying their products as socially or environmentally responsible. For example, the Rugmark label informs consumers that a hand-made carpet was not woven with child labor, and the FSC label, issued by the Forest Stewardship Council, attests that lumber was harvested from sustainable forests. Certified conflict-free diamonds can be purchased by consumers who want to avoid supporting wars in Africa that are financed by the diamond trade. Similarly, some employees seek jobs that are socially constructive. Many college students upon graduation have taken the Graduation Pledge of Social and Environmental Responsibility, which reads, "I pledge to explore and take into account the social and environmental consequences of any job I consider and will try to improve these aspects of any organization for which I work." Companies that are known for social responsibility may be more attractive to the job candidates that they seek.

Investors are registering their concerns about the social impact of business by engaging in *socially responsible investment* (SRI). SRI mutual and retirement funds screen their investments to remove companies in objectionable industries, commonly tobacco, alcohol, and gambling (negative screens) and, sometimes, to select exemplary companies (positive screens). Some SRI funds also practice *investor advocacy*, whereby they use their position as shareholders to pressure companies' management and also to seek change through shareholder resolutions. A few funds engage in *community investment*, whereby they invest in worthwhile community activities that may not easily obtain conventional financing. The amount of investment in SRI in the United States was estimated in 2005 to be $2.3 trillion out of total personal investment of $24 trillion.[47]

Perhaps the most significant market force pushing companies toward greater CSR is the explosive growth of nongovernmental organizations or NGOs. These advocacy groups, which range in size from such giant international organizations such as Greenpeace and Oxfam to very small local operations, are generally focused on specific issues, mainly human rights, the environment, and public health. Some NGOs monitor particular industries or companies. For example, Wal-Mart's activities are closely followed by Wal-Mart Watch, which is a project of The Center for Community and Corporate Ethics. NGOs are supported largely by contributions from private individuals and organizations who want corporations to be more socially responsible, and much of their success results from the ability of NGOs to create adverse publicity about corporate targets.

Some companies and industries have organized to support CSR. The organization Business for Social Responsibility, whose membership is open only to companies, serves to help its members "integrate sustainability into business strategy and operations." Companies That Care is an organization of businesses that encourages employers to act responsibly toward employees and the community. One example of industry CSR efforts is Responsible Care, which was established by chemical companies to improve the health, safety, and environment performance of the industry. Some NGOs are collaborations between companies in certain industries and other groups. For example, the membership of the Fair Labor Association, which grew out of concerns over working conditions in contract factories in the shoe and garment industry, includes companies (among them, Nike, Liz Claiborne, and Patagonia), NGOs, and universities. (The latter are involved because of concerns about the conditions under which apparel with university logos is made.)

Finally, CSR is being driven by governments, which also serve as a conduit for public concerns. Government-driven CSR may be viewed as a form of company and industry self-regulation that seeks to avoid more direct government regulation. Not only may business want to avoid government regulations, but governments themselves may also promote CSR in lieu of direct regulation. For example, the Fair Labor Association grew out of the Apparel Industry Partnership, which was convened by President Bill Clinton to address public concerns about conditions in contract factories overseas without resorting to increased government regulation. In 2002, the government of Great Britain, under Prime Minister Tony Blair, established the post of Minister for Corporate Responsibility in an effort to make the promotion of CSR a major governmental objective.

All of these forces in support of CSR—consumers, employees, investors, NGOs, peer companies, and government—are present in the marketplace, as well as in the social and political environment in which corporations operate. In the contemporary world, corporate managers are forced, more than ever before, to deliver value to shareholders. Their discretion to devote corporate resources to good causes is very limited. However, the pressures for CSR are among the factors that managers must respond to in their pursuit of profit. Insofar as there is a market for virtue, the question confronting managers is not whether to make a trade-off between social responsibility and profitability but the extent to which attending to CSR is necessary for making a profit. Ironically, Milton Friedman's fear was that unrestrained managers would use their discretion to squander corporate resources for feel-good causes. The reality today is that highly constrained managers with little discretion are being forced by the market to engage in some socially responsible behavior.

How effective is the market for virtue in promoting CSR? There is scant evidence that the economic choices of consumers, employees, or investors have much influence on corporate decision making. The most powerful factor is the ability of activists to damage the reputation and brand name of companies. The companies most likely to be targets of activists and hence to respond to market forces are those with valuable brands that are engaged in activities that raise concerns about human rights, the environment, and public health. These companies are concentrated in certain industries, such as shoe and apparel and household products, in which goods are manufactured in contract factories overseas (Nike, Gap, Wal-Mart); petroleum, timber, and mining, which raise environment issues (Shell, Home Depot, Rio Tinto); food and beverage, in which raw materials are sourced from less-developed countries (Starbucks, Nestlé, Coca-Cola); and tobacco and fast foods, which are blamed for tobacco-related deaths and obesity, respectively (Philip Morris, Kraft, McDonald's). Although the impact of the market for virtue is limited in both power and scope, the effect is not insignificant, and for many of the companies most affected, the change in their attitude and approach to CSR has been profound.

Competitive Advantage

In mature efficient markets, it is very difficult for companies, especially those producing basic commodities, to gain a significant, long-term competitive advantage. Any difference that will enhance a company's products in a crowded, noisy market is a valuable corporate asset. Although competitive advantage has many sources, a strategy that incorporates social responsibility is one. Even for companies that are responding to outside pressures in the market for virtue, competitive advantage can be gained if a CSR program is also integrated into the company's strategy so as to confer a competitive advantage.

As Michael E. Porter and Mark R. Kramer observe, "A firm that views CSR as a way to placate pressure groups often finds that its approach devolves into a series of short-term defensive reactions—a never-ending public relations palliative with minimal value to society and no strategic benefit for the business."[48] The alternative is to be strategic about CSR and to find ways to gain a corporate benefit along with a public good. CSR can provide a win-win opportunity, in which a company and society can create shared value. This can be done, Porter and Kramer claim, if companies bring to CSR the same analytical tools they bring to the rest of their operations. They write,

> The fact is, the prevailing approaches to CSR are so fragmented and so disconnected from business and strategy as to obscure many of the greatest opportunities for companies to benefit society. If, instead, corporations were to analyze their prospects for social responsibility using the same frameworks that guide their core business choices, they would discover that CSR can be much more than a cost, a constraint, or a charitable deed—it can be a source of opportunity, innovation, and competitive advantage.[49]

The importance of CSR as a source of competitive advantage is all the more important given the difficulty in the present-day global economy of finding any means to differentiate a company and its products from competitors. As traditional sources of competitive advantage such as financial capital, technology, and location become less significant, David Hess, Nikolai Rogovsky, and Thomas Dunfee observe that in response, "senior management is searching for new, hard-to-imitate, less-tangible sources of competitive advantage." These "soft sources," they note, "may include the benefits achieved through the successful implementation of corporate social initiatives."[50]

Companies may be able to gain a competitive advantage from engaging in CSR activities either by locating opportunities in their standard business operations or by transforming the competitive environment to create new opportunities. As an example of the former, Porter and Kramer cite the experience of Nestlé in India, where the company built a dairy in an area of severe poverty. Finding that the supply of milk from local farmers was of low quality and uneven quantity, Nestlé sent specialists to help the farmers produce better milk in higher quantities by improving their cow's health and diet. The company also provided financing and technical assistance to dig wells for irrigation and to increase crop yields. The result was not only to provide the dairy with an abundant, stable supply of high-quality milk but also to improve the standard of living in the area's villages significantly. A program that enabled Nestlé to operate successfully also had a collateral benefit for the communities on which the company depended. Nestlé has applied the lessons it learned from its dairy in India to the sourcing of other commodities, such as coffee and cocoa, in other parts of the world.

Whole Foods Market is an example of a company that created a successful business model with social values at its core. Founded in 1980 as a single organic food store in Austin, Texas, Whole Foods Market is unlike a conventional grocery chain that sells basic commodities at low margin. With the motto "Whole Foods, Whole People, Whole Planet," the company seeks to implement a "new vision of the future by changing the way we think about the relationships between our food supply, the environment, and our bodies."[51] Implementing this vision consists of meeting the needs of all its stakeholders. For customers this means not only satisfying but "delighting" them by providing them with wholesome food at good value and educating them about nutrition and the benefits of organic foods. Whole Foods employees, who work in self-directed teams, are encouraged to take responsibility for the success of the business and develop their own potential. The company is committed to supporting local growers and to sourcing from organic farmers who practice sustainable agriculture. Among the steps Whole Foods takes to protect the environment are a reduction in the use of packaging and the sale of less toxic cleaning products. The company supports local communities by contributing 5 percent of its after-tax profits to worthy causes.

In contrast to Nestlé in India, where the company found a way to benefit itself and the community in the ordinary course of doing business, Whole Foods Market has promoted important social values by making them a part of their strategy for attracting customers to their products, as well as employees to its workforce, and for distinguishing the company from its competitors. By seizing on people's concern for organic food, sustainable agriculture, and environmental protection, Whole Foods has created a business model that allows it to deliver greater value to its customers than its competitors are able to do—and to charge higher prices because of this added value. The strategy of Whole Foods also confers an enduring competitive advantage that other companies cannot easily duplicate. This use of CSR to obtain competitive advantage may not be feasible for many companies and industries; indeed, it may be a niche strategy that is suitable only under limited circumstances. However, most large corporations profess a commitment to CSR and engage in a wide range of activities in the belief that they offer some competitive advantage.

IMPLEMENTING CSR

If either of the two arguments for CSR—the argument from the market for virtue or the argument about competitive advantage—is persuasive to a company's management, a large gulf still remains between making a commitment to CSR on the one hand and formulating and implementing a successful CSR program on the other. Although a few exemplary companies provide inspiring stories and attest to the potential benefits of CSR, their programs may offer little guidance to managers who are trying to decide what their own company should do about CSR. One set of challenges for company managers concerns the specific activities to be selected and the design of these activities. Once companies have developed a significant CSR program, they are further challenged by outside groups about the reporting of their CSR performance. Activists are urging companies to report their CSR performance in much the same way that they report their financial performance. As a result, some companies now engage in so-called triple-bottom-line accounting: financial, social, and environmental. Questions remain, however, about whether such accounting is worth doing and, indeed, whether it can be done meaningfully.

Program Selection and Design

The guiding principles of strategic CSR are that there is an interdependence between business and society and that, as a result, there are opportunities for mutual benefit. The search for opportunities in this realm of mutually beneficial interdependence must be approached like any other business problem. As Porter and Kramer express the point, "To put these broad principles into practice, a company must integrate a social perspective into the core frameworks it already uses to understand competition and guide its business strategy."[52] A survey of corporations with successful CSR programs that produce genuine social benefits while serving corporate interests yields some valuable guidance about the selection and implementation process.

First, one important aspect of CSR is the management of reputation risk. Companies, especially those with strong brand names, need to identify the activities that could be the target of moral criticism. An analysis of these reputation risks should focus specifically on business activities that have impacts on such ethically sensitive matters as human rights, the environment, and public health. Many reputation-threatening issues are easily anticipated, such as the environmental risk of mining, but others are emerging issues that companies fail to anticipate in a timely manner. For example, Nike was slow to accept responsibility for the treatment of workers in its contract factories abroad (see Case 14.1). McDonald's anticipated environmental concerns about food packaging and addressed the subject effectively, but the company was caught off guard by two emerging issues, the alleged destruction of Amazon rain forests from cattle raising and the company's use of trans fats in its products. Even spurious issues are better handled if they are anticipated and addressed quickly. For example, Coca-Cola denies charges that its operations in India have damaged underground water supplies, but its response to this issue has taken considerable effort and has not allayed all criticism.

Second, CSR activities that are closely linked to a company's employment needs or product sales yield easily identifiable and measurable benefits. For example, both McDonald's and Marriott, which have a great need for large numbers of entry-level workers, conduct extensive training programs that help workers who have never held a job to learn valuable work skills and attitudes. Many companies in the computer industry, including Microsoft, IBM, and Intel, have supported projects in computer literacy and science education among students throughout the world. Such efforts are clearly linked to these companies' interest in the spread of computer usage and the development of technology. In a similar manner, Home Depot, whose sales depend on home improvements and repairs, offers many programs to support local communities, including Home Impact Grants to nonprofit organizations that promote affordable housing.

Third, the most successful CSR programs make use of a company's mission and core competencies. United Parcel Service, with its extensive expertise in logistics, is committed to transporting relief supplies to war-torn and disaster-stricken areas. This valuable service not only fits with the company's core competency in shipping goods but also improves the company's capabilities. Coca-Cola, which is Africa's largest employer, announced in 2001 that it would help combat AIDS on that continent by using its expertise in advertising and distribution to educate people about the disease and deliver literature, condoms, and testing kits where needed.[53] In this effort, Coca-Cola is making use of its formidable marketing ability, which is capable of rolling out a new advertising campaign in 50 countries at once, and its extensive distribution system, which operates in every African country except for two and which supplies soft drinks to even remote villages. The company is not acting alone in fighting AIDS but is partnering with existing organizations, including Unaids, a United Nations agency. A Coca-Cola spokesperson observed, "We don't intend to create programs, but we'll help existing ones." He added, "We don't kid ourselves—we're a beverage company."[54]

Fourth, truly strategic CSR identifies opportunities that fit with a company's strategy. Only a few companies can develop a comprehensive strategy around social values in the way that Whole Foods Market has done. However, McDonald's support for Ronald McDonald House Charities, which provide accommodations near hospitals for the families of seriously ill children undergoing treatment, advances the company's strategy of promoting a family-friendly atmosphere in its restaurants. Although many companies have responded to environmental concerns by reducing emissions and energy use, BP, formerly British Petroleum, put the environment at the core of its strategy of reinventing the energy business. Instead of seeking merely to produce oil and gas more efficiently, BP reconceived itself, under the leadership of Sir John Browne, as an energy company, with the motto that BP stood for "Beyond Petroleum," and committed the company to the goal of researching new energy sources. BP proclaims that " 'Beyond petroleum' is a summation of our brand promise and values. It's our way of expressing our brand to the world in the most succinct and focused way possible."

Fifth, successful CSR programs incorporate stakeholder engagement or dialogue. Outside groups can be a resource not only in expanding a company's capabilities—as witness Coca-Cola's decision to partner with other organizations in Africa to fight AIDS—but also in understanding the needs and outlook of others and engaging them in the pursuit of mutual benefit. According to the World Business Council for Sustainable Development, which was formed in 1995 by the CEOs of 200 global companies to address environmental issues,

> The essence of corporate social responsibility is to recognize the value of external stakeholder dialogue. Because of this, we place stakeholder engagement at the center of CSR activity. CSR means more than promulgating a company's own values and principles. It also depends on understanding the value and principles of those who have a stake in its operations.[55]

If strategic CSR involves the discovery of mutually beneficial activities that arise because of the interdependence of business and society, then the mutual benefits are more likely to arise from the interaction of a company and outside groups, with respect on both sides, and not merely from business acting alone.

Reporting and Accountability

CSR has value only if it actually has the social benefits that companies claim and outside groups want. The demand for some measurement of social performance has given rise to a movement that is variously described as social and ethical auditing, accounting, and reporting (SEAAR) and triple-bottom-line accounting (3BL). The impetus for this movement comes from several sources.

First, companies themselves, which are accustomed to measuring all aspects of their performance, seek to evaluate the benefits of their CSR programs. They do this not only to ensure that projects are properly selected and implemented but also to demonstrate the value of CSR activities to shareholders and the public. Second, there are several influential rating organizations that rank companies on social performance. The most prominent rankings are the Dow Jones Sustainability Index, FTSE4Good Index, and the KLD Index. Although these indexes are intended primarily for use by investment managers, they are also widely followed by the public. Third, socially responsible investment funds generally apply their own measures to company performance in addition to using the rankings of rating organizations. Fourth, there is a substantial body of academic research devoted to measuring corporate social performance and comparing this with financial performance. In general, these studies, which use various measurement systems, have found a small but statistically significant positive correlation between social and financial performance.[56] These studies raise issues of method and interpretation, however, especially about the direction of causation. That is, does greater social performance lead to greater profitability or are more profitable companies better able to afford more social performance?

No matter the purpose for which the measurement of CSR is done, the results are only as reliable as the data and their interpretation.[57] The information used for measuring social and environmental performance is very diverse in kind and comes from a variety of sources. Not only may different attempts to measure performance use different data, but also the data may be given different weights and interpretations. As a result, companies are able to select data and interpret them in ways that yield virtually any desired result and prevent meaningful comparison between companies. The root of the problem is that unlike financial data, which are recorded, reported, and verified according to uniform accounting and auditing standards, information about social and environmental performance is not easily subjected to the same kind of precise treatment. Several organizations have attempted to make social reporting more like financial reporting. In particular, the Global Reporting Initiative (GRI) and the Institute of Social and Ethical AccountAbility (ISEA) have developed complex and specific guidelines for measuring social and environmental performance. ISEA also offers a certification, the AA1000, that is similar in concept to awards for quality control, such as the ISO 9000.

Despite the problems with SEAAR and 3BL, corporations annually publish glossy documents that detail their good works, and the various indexes and rankings continue to be produced with great fanfare. Although the amount and reliability of data are increasing and methods of accounting and auditing are growing more sophisticated, social or ethical reporting will never be as meaningful as financial reporting. In particular, the idea of a social bottom line that is comparable to a financial bottom line is unattainable in principle simply because there is no common unit of measurement for social benefits that corresponds to the dollars and cents of financial accounting.[58] Moreover, a financial bottom line subtracts expenses from revenues to yield net income, whereas a social bottom line consists mainly of a number of beneficial activities that represent a sum total of good done by a company. Thus, the idea of 3BL can probably be nothing more than a clever turn of phrase.

Even if social or ethical reporting cannot be fully comparable to financial reporting, the recent interest by companies and the public in gathering information about CSR and publishing the results is probably overall a worthwhile development. Although some companies might be hypocritical in their use of SEAAR or 3BL, most appear to be genuine in their commitment.

Such reporting is likely to encourage greater corporate social performance and also increase the transparency of CSR activities, which permits closer scrutiny of companies' social performance.

Conclusion

The meaning of corporate social responsibility and the arguments for it, as well as the attitudes of business toward it, have changed dramatically over the past 50 years. The vigorous debate over the normative case for CSR gave way eventually to a wary acceptance and then an enthusiastic embrace of the business case. Somewhere along the way, the question about CSR changed from whether to how. However, whether the meaning of CSR also shifted to fit with what business was willing and able to do is an open question. What is undeniable is that, in the words of the *Economist* magazine, "CSR is thriving." CSR has become a virtual industry, with most large corporations proclaiming long lists of activities. The challenge now for corporations is to be strategic about CSR and develop programs that provide the greatest benefit for themselves and society. The challenge for society is to make demands on corporations that best utilize their capabilities and resources.

CASE 12.2   ✳ Explore the Concept on mythinkinglab.com

Starbucks and Fair Trade Coffee

Starbucks has built a fast-growing business on a corporate philosophy that puts people first. Two of the six guiding principles in the company's mission statement are "Provide a great work environment and treat each other with respect and dignity" and "Develop enthusiastically satisfied customers all of the time." To explain this emphasis on employees, Howard Schultz, the leader of the company, who bought it from its founders in 1989, wrote in his book *Pour Your Heart Into It* that if you "treat people like family . . . they will be loyal and give their all."[59] Customer loyalty was built on providing a special ambience in its stores and offering the finest coffee available. Hence, the principle: "Apply the highest standards of excellence to the purchasing, roasting and fresh delivery of our coffee." The mission statement expressed a further commitment to benefit communities and protect the environment. It is characteristic of Starbucks that the principle "Recognize that profitability is essential to our future" comes last.

In 2000, Starbucks was confronted with a demand that the company buy fair trade coffee.[60] Global Exchange, a nongovernmental organization (NGO) that focused on human rights, accused Starbucks of making a profit at the expense of coffee growers in poor countries, who received a small portion of the world price for their beans. The first salvo in the Global Exchange campaign took place in February with a demonstration at a San Francisco Starbucks store. A few days later, leaders from the NGO appeared at the annual meeting of Starbucks and threatened a national boycott if the company refused to buy and promote fair trade coffee.

The fair trade movement, which gained impetus in the 1990s, seeks fair compensation for the producers of basic commodities and mutual respect between producers and buyers. In 1999, the organization TransFair USA began offering a certification for fair trade coffee, and Global Exchange launched an education campaign to persuade consumers to buy coffee with the TransFair USA logo. According to TransFair USA, "Fair Trade Certification empowers growers and farmworkers to lift themselves out of poverty by investing in their farms and communities, protecting the environment, and developing the business skills necessary to compete in the global marketplace."[61] Products, including not only coffee but also tea, cocoa, rice, vanilla, honey, sugar, and flowers, qualify for fair trade certification if six conditions are met:

- **Fair prices:** Democratically organized farmer groups receive a guaranteed minimum floor price and an additional premium for certified organic products. Farmer organizations are also eligible for pre-harvest credit.
- **Fair labor conditions:** Workers on Fair Trade farms enjoy freedom of association, safe working conditions, and living wages. Forced child labor is strictly prohibited.
- **Direct trade:** With Fair Trade, importers purchase from Fair Trade producer groups as directly as possible, eliminating unnecessary middlemen and empowering farmers to develop the business capacity necessary to compete in the global marketplace.
- **Democratic and transparent organizations:** Fair Trade farmers and farmworkers decide democratically how to invest Fair Trade revenues.
- **Community development:** Fair Trade farmers and farmworkers invest Fair Trade premiums in social and business development projects like scholarship programs, quality-improvement trainings, and organic certification.
- **Environmental sustainability:** Harmful agrochemicals and GMOs are strictly prohibited in favor of environmentally sustainable farming methods that protect farmers' health and preserve valuable ecosystems for future generations.

The fair trade movement addresses several factors in global coffee trade that disadvantage small growers in less-developed countries. First, the coffee market consists of a long supply chain with many intermediaries between the growers and the eventual consumer. In 2000, more than 50 percent of all coffee beans were grown on small plots of land. Individual growers and some small cooperatives lacked the machinery for the next stage of hulling the beans, and so they sold their crop to the owners of a local mill. From there, the raw beans passed through many layers of middlemen before they were roasted and offered for sale to consumers. As a result, growers received only a small portion of the world market price.

Second, many growers had difficulty obtaining financing and were often forced to sell their anticipated crop to middlemen for a cash advance. Not only did this arrangement limit their bargaining power over price, but it also kept them mired in a continuous cycle of poverty.

Third, the prices of all agricultural commodities are subject to wide fluctuations based on supply and demand. High prices when supplies are short encourage overproduction, which leads to subsequent low prices; and when the resulting reduction in supply leads to higher prices, the cycle starts over again. By 2000, an oversupply of coffee beans had pushed prices down to the lowest levels in 50 years, and the world price fell to 64 cents per pound. Although in 2000, Starbucks paid an average of $1.24 per pound, which was almost double the basic price, much of the difference was due to the company's purchase of premium beans.

The demand by Global Exchange for Starbucks to purchase and promote fair trade coffee fit with the principles in the company's mission statement, especially the commitment to apply high standards in the purchase of coffee beans. Some customers had requested not only fair trade coffee but also coffee grown in the shade to protect bird habitats and organic coffee grown without chemicals.[62] However, the customer demand for fair trade coffee was unknown. Partners (the Starbucks term for employees) might find more satisfaction in their work if the company were to offer fair trade coffee and might be distressed by a boycott against the company. Moreover, Starbucks had already worked with NGOs on several social and environmental projects. The company contributed to CARE, an international humanitarian organization devoted to fighting global poverty, with instructions that its funds be directed to coffee-growing countries. In 1998, Starbucks joined with Conservation International to promote shade-grown coffee, which brought many benefits to coffee cooperatives in Chiapas, Mexico. In 1994, Starbucks established a department of Environmental Affairs, and created a department of Corporate Social Responsibility in 1999.

Although the demand by Global Exchange fit with Starbucks' mission, company executives were concerned whether it was compatible with Starbucks' successful strategy of offering high-quality coffee at premium prices. The company's reputation was built on meeting customers' expectations of a certain experience. Sourcing fair trade coffee would mean dealing with suppliers whose record for consistent high quality, uniformity in taste, and reliability in delivery was unknown. The head of bean purchasing at Starbucks cautioned, "This was an uncharted category, and, as marketers, we were concerned about endorsing a product that didn't meet our quality standards." Although the price of free trade coffee was only six cents per pound more than Starbucks generally paid, additional costs would be incurred in identifying fair trade growers and working with them, if necessary, to meet Starbucks' high standards. Developing a marketing campaign would entail further costs.

Starbucks executives also needed to consider the impact of sourcing fair trade coffee on the company's relationships with its regular suppliers around the world who had managed to obtain the high price offered by Starbucks only by meeting the company's high standards. As one executive explained,

> The relationships I have with growers were built over the last 20 years. It's taken some of them years before I would use their beans consistently and pay them $1.25 or more. Now I was being asked to use another farmer who I didn't know and pay him the same price without the same quality standards.

Many of Starbucks' suppliers could not meet the criteria for fair trade certification because they are large growers and not individual farmers or cooperatives, and so they cannot be run democratically as the fair trade criteria require.

A further question facing Starbucks executives was how much of the higher price for fair trade coffee actually reached the growers. Critics of the fair trade movement charge that too many fair trade dollars end up in the pockets of middlemen and NGOs.[63] TransFair USA claims that fair trade can eliminate as many as five layers of middlemen by enabling growers to deal directly with American wholesalers and thereby double or triple their income.[64] However, it is difficult for purchasers of fair trade coffee to know how much the growers actually benefit. FairTrade USA and other organizations that certify fair trade products collect a fee for monitoring and licensing growers. In 2005, FairTrade USA collected $1.89 million in fees, spending most of this amount on salaries, travel, and other expenses for its 40 employees.[65] Ensuring that fair trade products meet the criteria for certification involves some monitoring, and so the relevant question is whether this monitoring will be done by third parties, such as TransFair USA, or by the buyer, in this case Starbucks. In any event, monitoring imposes an extra cost that is borne ultimately by the grower due to a lower price for beans or the consumer in higher prices for the brewed coffee—or else by Starbucks shareholders.

A final question is whether the fair trade movement is an effective solution to the economic problem of coffee production by small growers in a world market. The fluctuation of supply and demand due to alternating overproduction and underproduction and the lack of credit that forces growers into a cycle of indebtedness are the inevitable result of too many coffee growers tilling small plots of land. Another solution besides the fair trade movement is to consolidate coffee bean production in larger farms with the capacity to switch to other agricultural products as the market changes. Such a transformation might force some growers off their land and reduce them to laborers for large growers, or else it would send them to the cities in search of other employment. The fair trade movement offers the prospect of improving the lives of one group of growers. However, unless demand for coffee beans increases—and worldwide per capita consumption of coffee has been declining since the 1960s—the main effect of the fair trade movement is that the coffee that is purchased by sellers, such as Starbucks, comes from the growers of fair trade coffee. As a result, the growers of nonfair trade coffee will sell less, and so the welfare of coffee growers worldwide will be unchanged.

CASE 12.3   ✴ Explore the Concept on mythinkinglab.com

Timberland and Community Service

Our company is organized around values. Not out of convenience, but out of necessity.[66]

—Jeffrey Swartz, President and CEO, Timberland Company

Jeffrey Swartz, the President and CEO of Timberland Company, was the third-generation leader of a formerly family-owned business that went public in 1987.[67] In 1955, Swartz's grandfather, a Russian immigrant, bought the Abington Shoe Company, located in South Boston, Massachusetts, and brought his two sons into the business. The iconic Timberland boot was introduced in 1965 when the Swartz family developed a process for fusing rubber soles to leather uppers to form a rugged, waterproof boot that was also less expensive to produce. The success of the Timberland boot led the Swartz family to relocate in 1969 to Stratham, New Hampshire, and to change the name to Timberland Company in 1978. The growing company began to market a variety of casual and work footwear under the Timberland brand, and, later, introduced clothing and accessories for men, women, and children, as the company expanded sales to Europe, Asia, and Latin America. After graduation from Brown University and the Amos Tuck School of Business at Dartmouth, Jeffrey Swartz assumed a variety of positions at Timberland, becoming chief operating officer in 1991 at the age of 31 and president and CEO seven years later.

Under the leadership of Jeffrey Swartz, Timberland Company developed an expanding program of community service in an effort to combine "commerce and justice." The centerpiece of this program was the trademarked Path of Service, launched in 1992, which allowed employees to devote 16 hours of company-paid time each year to community service. Path of Service was expanded to 32 hours in 1994, and to 40 hours in 1997. The purpose, as stated by Swartz, was "to engage the skills and talents of employees to create long-term solutions for critical community needs." Although participation was optional, employees were encouraged to use the hours for their own favored causes or to participate in company-sponsored events. A new Community Enterprise Department was created to support the Path of Service program and other community service initiatives.

The origin of Timberland's commitment to community service was a chance encounter that Swartz made with the Boston-based nonprofit organization City Year. City Year was founded in 1988 to engage young people in a year of full-time service that gave them "the skills and opportunities to change the world."[68] After Timberland responded twice to requests for donations of boots, a founder of City Year called on Swartz to thank him and invited him and other Timberland employees to spend four hours of community service with a group of City Year volunteers. Swartz accepted the invitation and was appalled by the social problems he saw, as well as inspired by the possibilities for change. He reported of his experience:

> And I found myself not a mile from our headquarters, face to face with the stories you read in the newspaper, face to face with a vision for America not unlike the one that drew my grandfather to leave Russia in steerage so many years ago. . . . Behind my desk again, safe no longer, moved by my own sense of purpose having served, albeit briefly, all that mattered was figuring out how service could become part of daily life at Timberland.[69]

Swartz gradually increased Timberland's support for City Year by making an initial pledge of $1 million annually for three years, later extended for another five years, and loaning a Timberland executive to assist in marketing for City Year. Swartz became chairman of City Year's national board. In turn, City Year organized team-building exercises for Timberland employees, aided in creating community service projects, and, in 2000, located an office in Timberland's headquarters. Timberland expanded its community service program with two full days of activities, one in the spring that coincided with Earth Day, and another in the fall called Serv-a-palooza. The company extended its collaboration with nonprofit organizations by establishing a link with Share Our Strength, an antipoverty group, and SkillsUSA, which provided vocational training for young people.

If Timberland had remained a family-owned business, then Swartz could indulge his passion for service because he would be using his own resources. As a public company, however, he was responsible to shareholders. This responsibility was tested in the mid-1990s, when profits fell, and in 1995 the company suffered its first loss in net income. Although he was urged to cut the community service program, Swartz resisted. He believed that instead of being an expense that could be cut in bad times, the cost of community service was an investment of resources that contributed to the company's success. Community service, in his view, was a key part of the strategy at Timberland for fulfilling the company's mission and values, which in turn were integral to the company's main goals that included strong financial performance.

The mission of Timberland was stated in company documents as "To equip people to make their difference in the world." Four core values were identified as guides for all company activity. These were humanity, humility, integrity, and excellence. And five "bold goals" were set forth:

- Become the authentic outdoor brand of choice by providing inventive and practical products to our consumers
- Be the business partner of choice by providing distinctive value to our customers
- Be a top employer of choice globally
- Be the reference for socially accountable business globally
- Deliver exceptional financial performance for shareholders

Swartz believed that these measures of the company's success—its mission, values, and goals—required not only the community service program but also ambitious initiatives to protect the environment and secure human rights in its manufacturing facilities worldwide.

Swartz expressed his belief in this connection of commerce and justice in the following way:

We operate on the core theory, on the belief that doing well and doing good are not separate ideas; they are inseparable ideas. That, in fact, they are inextricably linked and that everything we do, every business decision we make, every strategy we promulgate, every speech we make, or every pair of boots or shoes that we ship, have to be the embodiment of commerce and justice, and that's a different model.

This is a model that has served Timberland well as it has survived and prospered in the highly competitive footwear industry. The questions remain, however, whether this is a model for many companies or industries, and whether it will remain a viable model for Timberland if its competitive environment changes or the company faces another economic downturn.

Notes

1. Gretchen Morgenson, "GE Capital vs. the Small-Town Folk Hero," *New York Times*, 24 October 2004, sec. 3, p. 5.
2. Michael Ryan, "They Call Their Boss a Hero," *Parade Magazine*, 8 September 1996, 4–5.
3. Bruce D. Butterfield, "What Flames Could Not Destroy," *Boston Globe*, 8 September 1996, A1.
4. Ryan, "They Call Their Boss a Hero."
5. "Bridging the Gap," PBS *NewsHour* transcript, 20 March 1996.
6. Thomas Teal, "Not a Fool, Not a Saint," *Fortune*, 11 November 1996, 201.
7. "Bridging the Gap."
8. Ross Kerber, "Future Tense: Feuerstein's Vision for Malden Mills, Commitments to Lawrence are Not Shared by Firm's New Owners," *Boston Globe*, 29 January 2004, F1.
9. Radley Balko, "Altruism? Bah, Humbug," *Apple Daily*, 22 December 2004.
10. N. Craig Smith, "Corporate Social Responsibility: Not Whether but How?" *California Management Review*, 45 (2003), 52–76.

11. David Hess, Nikolai Rogovsky, and Thomas W. Dunfee, "The New Wave of Corporate Community Involvement: Corporate Social Initiatives," *California Management Review*, 44 (2002), 110–25.

12. For a comprehensive account of the historical development of the concept of corporate social responsibility, see Morrell Heald, *The Social Responsibilities of Business: Company and Community, 1900–1960* (Cleveland, OH: Case Western Reserve University Press, 1970). Brief accounts are given in Clarence C. Walton, *Corporate Social Responsibilities* (Belmont, CA: Wadsworth, 1967), 21–53; and James W. McKie, "Changing Views," in *Social Responsibility and the Business Predicament*, ed. James W. McKie (Washington, DC: The Brookings Institution, 1974), 17–40. Among the first advocates was Howard R. Bowen, *Social Responsibilities of the Businessman* (New York: Harper & Brothers, 1953).

13. André Habisch, Jan Jonker, Martina Webner, and René Schmidpeter, eds., *Corporate Social Responsibility Across Europe* (Berlin, Germany: Springer, 2005).

14. "Two-Faced Capitalism," *Economist*, 24 January 2004, 53.

15. Milton Friedman, *Capitalism and Freedom* (Chicago, IL: University of Chicago Press, 1962), 133.

16. Ibid., 133. The quotation by Adam Smith is from *The Wealth of Nations*, Book IV, chap. II. This famous paragraph concludes, "It is an affectation, indeed, not very common among merchants, and very few words need be employed in dissuading them from it."

17. See, for example, Robert B. Reich, *Supercapitalism: The Transformation of Business, Democracy, and Everyday Life* (New York: Knopf, 2007), chap. 5.

18. Joseph W. McGuire, *Business and Society* (New York: McGraw-Hill, 1963), 144. For the point that the assumption of responsibility must be voluntary, see Henry Manne and Henry C. Wallich, *The Modern Corporation and Social Responsibility* (Washington, DC: American Enterprise Institute for Public Policy Research, 1972), 5.

19. Archie B. Carroll, "A Three-Dimensional Conceptual Model of Corporate Performance," *Academy of Management Review*, 4 (1979), 497–505.

20. Ibid., 500.

21. S. Prakash Sethi, "Dimensions of Corporate Social Performance: An Analytical Framework for Measurement and Analysis," *California Management Review*, 17 (Spring 1975), 62. Emphasis in original omitted.

22. Committee for Economic Development, *Social Responsibilities of Business Corporations* (New York: Committee for Economic Development, 1971), 15.

23. The concept of corporate social responsiveness is developed in Robert W. Ackerman and Raymond A. Bauer, *Corporate Social Responsiveness: The Modern Dilemma* (Reston, VA: Reston, 1976).

24. William C. Frederick, "From CSR1 to CSR2: The Maturing of Business-and-Society Thought," *Business and Society Review*, 33 (1994), 150–64.

25. Donna J. Wood, "Corporate Social Performance Revisited," *Academy of Management Review*, 16 (1991), 693.

26. James E. Post and Shawn L. Berman, "Global Corporate Citizenship in a Dot.com World: The Role of Organizational Identity," in *Perspectives in Corporate Citizenship*, ed. Jorg Andriof and Malcolm McIntosh (Sheffield, UK: Greenleaf Publishing, 2001).

27. Pierre-Yves Néron and Wayne Norman, "Citizenship, Inc.: Do We Really Want Businesses to Be Good Corporate Citizens?" *Business Ethics Quarterly*, 18 (2008), 1–26. See the four commentaries on this article in the same issue and the authors' response.

28. McKie, "Changing Views," 18–19.

29. Edward S. Mason, ed., *The Corporation in Modern Society* (New York: Atheneum, 1974), 5.

30. Theodore Levitt, "The Dangers of Social Responsibility," *Harvard Business Review*, 36 (September–October 1958), 49.

31. John G. Simon, Charles W. Powers, and Jon P. Gunnemann, "The Responsibilities of Corporations and Their Owners," in *The Ethical Investor: Universities and Corporate Responsibility* (New Haven, CT: Yale University Press, 1972), 16–17.

32. Keith Davis, "Five Propositions for Social Responsibility," *Business Horizons*, 18 (June 1975), 20. Italics in the original.

33. Keith Davis and Robert L. Blomstrom, *Business and Society: Environment and Responsibility*, 3rd ed. (New York: McGraw-Hill, 1975), 50.

34. This objection is formulated in Kenneth E. Goodpaster and John B. Matthews, Jr., "Can a Corporation Have a Conscience?" *Harvard Business Review*, 60 (January–February 1982), 139–40.

35. Ibid., 140.

36. Simon, Powers, and Gunnemann, "Responsibilities of Corporations and Their Owners," 22–25.

37. Milton Friedman, "The Social Responsibility of Business Is to Increase Its Profits," *New York Times Magazine*, 13 September 1970, 33.

38. Ibid., 122.

39. See, for example, Richard Musgrave, *The Theory of Public Finance* (New York: McGraw-Hill, 1959), in which the three functions of securing efficiency (which includes considerations of externalities), equity, and stability properly belong to government.

40. Holders of the classical view generally favor market solutions over government action in the belief that many externalities result from a lack, rather than an excess, of free-market forces and that regulation is often ineffective. Still, they usually admit the principle that government regulation is appropriate in some instances to deal with externalities.

41. For an explanation and discussion of this concept, see Arthur M. Okun, *Equality and Efficiency: The Big Tradeoff* (Washington, DC: The Brookings Institution, 1975).

42. Reich, *Supercapitalism*, 197.

43. Marvin A. Chirelstein, "Corporate Law Reform," in *Social Responsibility and the Business Predicament*, ed. McKie, 55.

44. "Just Good Business: Special Report on Corporate Society Responsibility," *Economist* 19 January 2008, 24.

45. David Vogel, *The Market for Virtue, The Potential and Limits of Corporate Society Responsibility* (Washington, DC: Brookings Institution, 2005), 17.

46. Ibid., 47–49.

47. Social Investment Forum, *2005 Report on Socially Responsible Investing Trends in the United States*, 24 January 2006.

48. Michael E. Porter and Mark R. Kramer, "Strategy and Society: The Link Between Competitive Advantage and Corporate Social Responsibility," *Harvard Business Review*, December 2006, 82.

49. Ibid., 80.

50. Hess, Rogovsky, and Dunfee, "The New Wave of Corporate Community Involvement," 113.

51. "Sustainability and Our Future," company document, 2003.

52. Porter and Kramer, "Strategy and Society," 84.

53. Donald G. McNeil, Jr., "Coca-Cola Joins AIDS Fight in Africa," *New York Times*, 21 June 2001, A8.

54. Ibid.

55. World Business Council for Sustainable Development, "Corporate Social Responsibility: Making Good Business Sense," January 2000, 15.

56. Joshua D. Margolis and James P. Walsh, *People and Profits? The Search for a Link between a Company's Social and Financial Performance* (Mahwah, NJ: Lawrence Erlbaum, 2001).

57. For a discussion of the problems of evaluating social performance, see Aaron Chatterji and David Levine, "Breaking Down the Wall of Codes: Evaluating Non-Financial Performance," *California Management Review*, 48 (2006), 29–51.

58. This argument is developed in Wayne Norman and Chris McDonald, "Getting to the Bottom of the 'Triple Bottom Line,'" *Business Ethics Quarterly*, 14 (2004), 243–62.

59. Howard Schultz, *Pour Your Heart Into It* (New York: Hyperion, 1997), 127.

60. Information on this case, unless indicated otherwise, comes from Paul A. Argenti, "Collaborating with Activists: How Starbucks Works with NGOs," *California Management Review*, 47 (2004), 91–116.

61. http://transfairusa.org/content/about/mission.php.

62. Sam Dillon, "Seeking a Seal of Approval for Socially Aware Coffee," *New York Times*, 1 April 2000, C2.

63. Jennifer Alsever, "Fair Prices for Growers: Simple Idea, Complex Reality," *New York Times*, 19 March 2006, sec. 3, p. 5.

64. Ibid.

65. Ibid.

66. Jeff Swartz, "Doing Well and Doing Good," *Brookings Review*, 40 (2002), 24.

67. Information on this case, unless otherwise noted, is taken from the Timberland Company Web site www.timberland.com and James Austin, Herman B. Leonard, and James W. Quinn, "Timberland: Commerce and Justice," Harvard Business School, Case 9–305–002, rev. 21 December 2004.

68. www.cityyear.org.

69. Swartz, "Doing Well and Doing Good," 24.

Corporate Governance and Accountability

((•⃝[Listen to the **Chapter Audio** on **mythinkinglab.com**

CASE 13.1 ☀️[Explore the **Concept** on **mythinkinglab.com**

Shareholder Rights at Cracker Barrel

Cracker Barrel Old Country Stores, Inc., based in Lebanon, Tennessee, operated a chain of restaurants and gift shops, mostly in the South and Midwest, that featured southern-style cooking. In 1991, many Cracker Barrel shareholders, along with the company's employees and members of the public, were outraged when at least 11 employees were dismissed for their sexual orientation. The gay and lesbian employees ran afoul of a new company policy that Cracker Barrel would no longer employ individuals whose sexual preferences "fail to demonstrate normal heterosexual values" or whose lifestyle was "contrary to traditional American values." The fired employees had no legal protection since discrimination laws do not cover sexual orientation. The public could only boycott the restaurants by staying away, which many did. However, the outraged shareholders had a power that everyone else lacked: They were the owners of Cracker Barrel, and they could exercise their rights as owners to bring about change—or at least they thought they could.

The $22 billion New York City Employees' Retirement System, known as NYCERS, which owned 121,000 shares of Cracker Barrel stock worth around $4.5 million, proposed a resolution to be voted on at the 1992 annual meeting. NYCER's shareholder resolution was that the two words "sexual orientation" be added to the company's equal employment policy and that the company take steps to ensure compliance with the amended policy. The legal basis of NYCER's action was Rule 14a-8 of the 1934 Securities Exchange Act, which permits shareholders to propose resolutions to be included in the company's proxy materials that are submitted to shareholders for a vote as part of an annual meeting. At the time, the right to propose a resolution was accorded to any shareholder holding stock worth $1,000; this amount has since been raised to $2,000.

However, the shareholders were not allowed to vote on NYCER's proposed resolution. Rule 14a-8 also permits a company to refuse to submit a proposed resolution to a shareholder vote under several conditions, one being that the resolution deals with the "ordinary business operations" of the company.[1] The management of Cracker Barrel judged that this shareholder resolution dealt with ordinary business operations and, thus, could legally be withheld from the company's proxy materials. A company that rejects a proposed resolution is required to notify the Securities and Exchange Commission (SEC) of the action. The SEC agreed with the judgment of the Cracker Barrel management and issued a "no-action" letter affirming management's decision.[2]

This decision by the SEC constituted a significant shift of position and created a storm of protest. In 1976, the SEC interpreted "ordinary business operations" in such a way that a resolution could be rejected only if it involved "business matters mundane in nature" and did not involve "any substantial policy or other considerations."[3] Between 1976 and 1992, the SEC ruled that a number of resolutions dealing with equal employment opportunity had to be submitted to the shareholders because diversity was not a "mundane" matter and it involved a "substantial policy" given the importance of a diverse workforce for a company's competitiveness. Using the same reasoning, the SEC ruled in 1990 that AT&T was required to submit for a shareholder vote a resolution by a white supremacist group that asked AT&T to abandon its entire affirmative action program.[4] The SEC's 1992 Cracker Barrel ruling meant that shareholders had no right to vote on any resolution dealing with a company's employment policies, even when some shareholders believed that the policy, like Cracker Barrel's policy decision not to hire gays or lesbians, was morally objectionable. If shareholders are the owners of a company, do they not have the right to force a vote and make their voice heard? Some people consider the right to vote on important issues a matter of shareholder democracy.

Supporters of the SEC's Cracker Barrel ruling note that the shareholders have already elected the board of directors, which, in turn, selects the management team. If shareholders disapprove of the way in which the board and management are running a company, then they should attempt to vote them out. In the meantime, shareholders should leave the top executives free to run a company as they see fit and not interfere in day-to-day operations. Indeed, boards of directors typically involve themselves only in the selection of management and the overall strategy of the company and leave all other matters to the management team. However, directors are usually nominated by a committee of the board, and federal and state law does not, in general, give shareholders any right to nominate candidates of their own.[5] Usually, the shareholders' only power is to withhold votes from a slate presented to them by the current board. In response to demands for greater shareholder democracy, the SEC announced plans in 2003 to examine whether shareholders should have a greater voice in the nomination of directors.[6] By the end of 2007, though, no changes had been made.

Shareholder activists tend to be state and union pension funds, religious organizations, and other social action groups that use the shareholder resolution process to advance their own causes. For example, in 1971, the Episcopal Church proposed a resolution that General Motors cease operations in South Africa in protest against the country's racial apartheid policy. During the Vietnam War, shareholder resolutions were proposed by antiwar activist to force Dow Chemical Company to stop manufacturing napalm. Typically, shareholder resolutions included in proxy materials are defeated by large margins. However, the aim of activist shareholders is usually not to affect corporate behavior but to effect larger social change by increasing public awareness of issues. Even when such activism is socially beneficial, though, critics charge that shareholder resolutions are a distraction for corporations and that social change ought to be brought about through the political process, not by means of shareholder resolutions. Some argue that people who are citizens in a democratic state do not need shareholder democracy.

Postscript

In 1998, the SEC reversed the Cracker Barrel ruling and reverted to a case-by-case application of the two-part 1976 test that asked whether the resolution involved "business matters mundane in nature" and did not involve "any substantial policy or other considerations." In announcing the change, the SEC observed that since the Cracker Barrel ruling, "the relative importance of certain social issues related to employment has re-emerged as a consistent topic of widespread public debate."[7] As a result of this reversal, the power of shareholders to vote on matters that concern them was increased.

INTRODUCTION

A corporation brings together many different groups—most notably managers, employees, suppliers, customers, and, of course, investors—for the purpose of conducting business. Because these various corporate constituencies have different and sometimes conflicting interests, the question arises: In whose interest should the corporation be run? This question can be answered by establishing who should *control* a corporation. What group or groups ought to have ultimate decision-making power? Any group that has this power is able to run a corporation in its own interest and make its interest the objective of the firm. This question of who should control a corporation is the subject matter of corporate governance.

In addition to some group with ultimate decision-making power or control, a corporation also needs a control environment to ensure that employees do their job well and do not engage in unethical and/or illegal behavior. A control environment requires not only rules and policies for employee behavior but also the means for educating employees about proper conduct and responding to possible misconduct. For this purpose, most corporations have established ethics programs. Finally, to ensure that shareholders and others are protected from corporate malfeasance, controls must be in place to ensure corporate accountability. In particular, the prominent examples of fraud perpetrated by high-level executives at Enron, WorldCom, Adelphia, and Parmalat, to name just a few, show the need for better corporate governance and tighter control systems. These three topics—corporate governance, corporate ethics, and corporate accountability—are addressed in this chapter.

CORPORATE GOVERNANCE

In the standard system of corporate governance, ultimate decision-making power or control is held by the shareholders. In addition to control, shareholders are also entitled to the profits of a corporation. So an initial question is, Why should shareholders have control of a corporation and the right to its profits? To this question, there is a simple answer: Shareholders are by definition the group that has these two rights, namely, the right to control and the right to profits. The possession of these two rights also defines ownership: Ownership of a corporation just means having the right of control and the right to profits. So to say that shareholders are the owners of a corporation is also a matter of definition.

In most corporations, the shareholders—which is to say the group with control and the right to profits—are investors or, more precisely, equity capital providers. Bondholders, for example, are also investors, but their investment is debt, not equity. Equity capital differs from debt in that the investment is not for a fixed period of time—it is for the life of the firm—and has no fixed return like a bond's interest rate; the return on equity capital is the profits of a firm, which may vary. However, equity capital providers are not always the owners of a corporation. Some corporations are owned by employees, while others, called cooperatives, are customer owned or supplier owned. Land O'Lakes, Inc., for example, which markets butter, cheese, and other dairy products, is a producer cooperative that is owned by the dairy farmers who supply it. Mutual insurance companies are owned by their policyholders. Still, the investor-owned corporation is the dominant form of corporate governance in the world today.

So the critical question is not why shareholders have the rights that they do—this is a matter of definition—but why equity capital providers should generally be the shareholders with these rights. The answer to this question requires an extended discussion that begins with some account of the nature of the corporation.

The Nature of the Corporation

Debate has long raged over the nature of the corporation. Is the corporation the private property of the stockholders who choose to do business in the corporate form, or is the corporation a public institution sanctioned by the state for some social good?[8] In the former view, which may be called the *property rights theory*, the right to incorporate is an extension of the property rights and the right of contract that belong to all persons.[9] The latter view—let us call it the *social institution theory*—holds that the right to incorporate is a privilege granted by the state and that corporate property has an inherent public aspect.[10] A third view is the *contractual theory* of the firm. In the contractual theory, shareholders, along with other investors, employees, and the like, each own assets that they make available to the firm. Thus, the firm results from the property rights and the right of contract of every corporate constituency and not from those of shareholders alone. Whether corporations ought to serve only the interests of shareholders or the interests of a wider range of constituencies depends on the theory of the firm that we accept. Even though holders of all three theories generally conclude that the interests of shareholders are primary, the arguments that they provide are different, and it is important to understand the logic of each argument.

The Property Rights and Social Institution Theories

The original form of the modern corporation was the joint stock company, in which a small group of wealthy individuals pooled their money for some undertaking that they could not finance alone. In the property rights theory, this corporate form of business organization is justified on the grounds that it represents an extension of the property rights and the right of contract enjoyed by everyone. Just as individuals are entitled to conduct business with their own assets, so, too, they have a right to contract with others for the same purpose. Although individual shareholders in a joint stock company or a corporation have exchanged their personal assets for shares of stock, they jointly own the common enterprise, and as owners they are entitled to receive the full proceeds. This is the property rights theory.

The social institution theory emphasizes that a corporation is not merely a private association created for the purpose of personal enrichment but also a public enterprise that is intended to serve some larger social good. The earliest joint stock companies were special grants that kings bestowed on favored subjects for specific purposes. Today, corporations are chartered by states, so that the opportunity for individuals to do business in the corporate form is a state-granted privilege. The courts have also held in decisions such as *Munn* v. *Illinois* (1876) that corporate property is "affected with a public interest" so that states have a right to regulate its use.[11] Corporations are thus not wholly private; they have an inherent public aspect.

In a pure expression of the property rights theory, the Michigan State Supreme Court ruled in 1919 that the Ford Motor Company could be forced to pay more dividends to the shareholders in spite of Henry Ford's view that the company had made too much profit and ought to share some of it with the public by reducing prices. In *Dodge* v. *Ford Motor Co.*, the court declared, "A business corporation is organized and carried on primarily for the profit of the stockholders."[12] The profit-making end of a corporation is set forth in its charter of incorporation, which represents a contract among the shareholders who have invested their money, and Henry Ford had no right to substitute another end by using corporate resources for an essentially philanthropic purpose.

The decision in *Dodge* v. *Ford Motor Co.* assumed that shareholders are the owners of a corporation. This assumption was true as long as corporations had relatively few shareholders who actively controlled the business. However, in 1932, a book by Adolf A. Berle, Jr., and Gardiner C. Means, *The Modern Corporation and Private Property*, documented a dramatic shift that had occurred in American business.[13] Stock ownership in large corporations had become dispersed among numerous investors who had little involvement in corporate affairs, and the actual control of corporations had passed to a class of professional managers. The result was a separation of ownership and control, and with this separation came a change in the nature of corporate property.

THE NATURE OF CORPORATE PROPERTY.   Strictly speaking, property is not a tangible thing like land, but a bundle of rights that defines what an owner is entitled to do with a thing. A property right, in the full sense of the term, involves control over the thing owned and an assumption of responsibility. With the separation of ownership and control, shareholders had relinquished both control and responsibility. As a result, shareholders of large, publicly held corporations had ceased to be owners in the full sense and had become merely one kind of provider of the resources needed by a corporation, namely, equity capital.

According to Berle and Means, "The property owner who invests in a modern corporation so far surrenders his wealth to those in control of the corporation that he has exchanged the position of independent owner for one in which he may become merely recipient of the wages of capital."[14] They continued,

> [T]he owners of passive property, by surrendering control and responsibility over the active property have surrendered the right that the corporation should be operated in their sole interest—they have released the community from the obligation to protect them to the full extent implied in the doctrine of strict property rights. At the same time, the controlling groups . . . have in their own interest broken the bars of tradition which require that the corporation be operated solely for the benefit of the owners of passive property.[15]

Because of the separation of ownership and control, managers have assumed the position of trustee for the immense resources of a modern corporation, and in this new position, they face the question: For whom are corporate managers trustees?

THE BERLE–DODD DEBATE.   In a famous 1932 exchange with Berle in the *Harvard Law Review*, E. Merrick Dodd, Jr., argued that the corporation is "an economic institution which has a social service as well as a profit-making function."[16] According to Dodd, the modern corporation had become a public institution, as opposed to a private activity of the shareholders, and as such, it had a social responsibility that could include the making of charitable contributions.[17] Because a corporation is property only in a "qualified sense," it may be regulated by society so that the interests of employees, customers, and others are protected. Corporate managers have a right, even a duty, to consider the interests of all those who deal with the corporation.[18]

Berle cautioned against Dodd's position because of the dangers posed by unrestrained managerial power. In a response to Dodd in the *Harvard Law Review*, Berle wrote, "When the fiduciary obligation of the corporate management and 'control' to stockholders is weakened or eliminated, the management and 'control' become for all practical purposes absolute."[19] It would be unwise, in Berle's estimation, for the law to release managers from a strict accountability to shareholders, not out of respect for their property rights as owners of a corporation but as a matter of sound public policy. He wrote,

> Unchecked by present legal balances, a social-economic absolutism of corporate administrators, even if benevolent, might be unsafe; and in any case it hardly affords the soundest base on which to construct the economic commonwealth which industrialism seems to require.[20]

Corporate law has evolved effective means for restraining managerial power by directing managers to act in the interests of the shareholders, but we lack effective means for ensuring that managers serve the interests of society as a whole. There is no guarantee that managers will exercise their newly acquired control in any interests but their own. Berle described the rise of corporate managers as a "seizure of power without recognition of responsibility—ambition without courage."[21] But in the absence of effective restraints on managerial power, Berle concludes, "[W]e had best be protecting the interests we know, being no less swift to provide for the new interests as they successively appear."[22]

SUBSEQUENT DEVELOPMENTS.   Eventually, the law loosened the restraints that were imposed in *Dodge* v. *Ford Motor Co.* and allowed corporations to expend some corporate funds for the good of society. In *A. P. Smith Manufacturing Co.* v. *Barlow* (1953), the New Jersey State Supreme Court ruled that the managers of the company were permitted by law to give $1,500 to Princeton University despite shareholder objections on the grounds that to bar corporations from making such contributions would threaten our democracy and the free enterprise system. The court agreed with the testimony of a former chairman of the board of U.S. Steel Company that if American business does not aid important institutions such as private universities, then it is not "properly protecting the long-range interests of its stockholders, its employees and its customers." After the decision in *A. P. Smith Manufacturing Co.* v. *Barlow*, Berle conceded defeat in his debate with Dodd. Public opinion and the law had accepted Dodd's contention that corporate powers ought to be held in trust for the whole of society.[23]

Although the separation of ownership and control documented by Berle and Means undermined the property rights theory, a fully developed social institution theory did not replace it. Instead, a conception of the corporation as a quasi-public institution emerged, in which managers have limited discretion to use the resources at their command for the good of employees, customers, and the larger society. In a world of giant corporations, managers are called upon to balance the interests of competing corporate constituencies, and in order to fill this role they have developed a sense of management as a profession with public responsibilities. Managers ceased being the exclusive servants of the stockholders and assumed the mantle of public-spirited leaders, albeit of profit-making business organizations.

In the last several decades, another theory of the firm has emerged that now dominates thinking in financial economics and corporate law. This is the contractual theory, in which the firm is viewed as a nexus of contracts among all corporate constituencies.

The Contractual Theory

The origin of the contractual, or nexus-of-contracts, theory is the work of the economist Ronald Coase, who claimed that firms exist as less costly alternatives to market transactions.[24] In a world where market exchanges could occur without any costs (what economists call *transaction costs*), economic activity would be achieved entirely by means of contracting among individuals in a free market. In the actual world, the transaction costs involved in market activity can be quite high, and some coordination can be achieved more cheaply by organizing economic activity in firms. Thus, there are two forms of economic coordination—firms and markets—and the choice between them is determined by transaction costs.

In the Coasean view, the firm is a market writ small in which parties with economic assets contract with the firm to deploy these assets in productive activity. Generally, an individual's assets are more productive when they are combined with the assets of others in joint or team production. Individuals will choose to deploy their assets in a firm instead of the market when the lower transaction costs of a firm combined with the benefits of team production yield them a higher return.

Deploying assets in a firm involves some risks, however, when those assets are *firm-specific*. Consider the situation of an employee who acquires special skills that are needed by a particular employer. A worker with such skills will generally earn more than one with only generic skills, but only a few employers will value those special skills and be willing to pay the higher wages. An employee with special skills is also tied more closely to the firm because the skills in question are not easily transferable, and the employee would likely suffer a loss if forced to move to another employer. The assets of an employee that can be more profitably employed with one or a few firms are thus firm-specific. Firm-specific assets enable a worker to create more wealth, which makes possible the higher pay, but this wealth can also be appropriated by the firm itself, leaving the employee without adequate compensation for acquiring special skills.

Not only employees but also investors, suppliers, customers, and other groups have firm-specific assets, and these groups will make their assets available to a firm only with adequate safeguards against misappropriation. That is, every group will seek guarantees to ensure that they are adequately compensated for any assets that cannot be easily removed from joint productive activity. Most groups protect themselves by means of contracts. These may be either explicit, legally enforceable contracts or implicit contracts that have no legal standing. Thus, employees are often protected by employment contracts, suppliers by purchase contracts, consumers by warranties, and so on. An implicit contract is created, for example, when an employer creates an expectation about the conditions of employment. In the nexus-of-contracts firm, managers coordinate these contracts with the various corporate constituencies. The contracts with most corporate constituencies are relatively unproblematical, but one group raises special problems, namely shareholders.

THE ROLE OF SHAREHOLDERS. In the usual interpretation of the contractual theory, shareholders along with bondholders and other investors provide capital, but, more significantly, they also assume the residual risk of conducting business. They assume this residual risk by accepting profits as the return on their investment. Since profits represent the residual revenues of a firm—the amount that is left after all fixed claims are paid—profits are not guaranteed and may vary. Thus, every fixed claimant of a firm is guaranteed payment as long as the firm remains solvent, and only shareholders are at risk of not getting paid. Residual risk could be borne by every group that contracts with a firm, but risk-bearing can also be a specialized role in which one group bears the preponderance of risk. In the large, publicly held corporation, shareholders fill the role of residual risk bearer, and it is this role, rather than the role of capital provider, that sets them apart from other groups in the nexus of contracts.

The position of residual risk bearer is difficult to protect by ordinary contractual provisions, such as those available to bondholders, employees, customers, and other constituencies. Some protection is provided by the opportunity to diversify and by the limited liability that shareholders enjoy. Shareholders are also rewarded for their investment with prospects of a higher return than that assured to secured creditors such as bondholders. However, the most important protection for shareholders is corporate control. Corporate control is a package of rights that includes the right to select the board of directors and approve important changes. In addition, shareholders have a claim on management's allegiance. This is commonly expressed by saying that management has a fiduciary duty to operate the corporation in the shareholders' interest and that the objective of the firm is to maximize shareholder wealth.

The contractual theory of the firm itself does not assign this right to shareholders—or to any other group, for that matter. Rather, corporate control is a benefit to be bargained for in the nexus-of-contracts firm, and through bargaining any constituency group could conceivably assume the right of control. Indeed, other groups take control when a corporation becomes employee owned or customer owned. Employees have also successfully bargained for representation on boards of directors, and bond indentures sometimes give bondholders the right to vote on certain risky ventures. When corporations are in bankruptcy, creditors take control from shareholders and the creditors' interests become primary until the firm recovers.

Still, the current system of corporate governance assigns control, for the most part, to shareholders. Some further argument is needed, however, for this assignment of rights. Why should shareholders, as residual risk bearers, control a corporation?

THE ARGUMENT FOR SHAREHOLDER CONTROL.   The starting point of the argument for shareholder control is that this right is of greater value to residual claimants than to other constituencies. First, control is better suited than other kinds of protection for the special situation of shareholders. That is, control is a fitting solution for the problem of protecting the firm-specific assets of residual risk bearers. Second and more importantly, the return to shareholders is wholly dependent on the profitability of a firm, and so they value control as a means to spur a firm to the highest possible level of performance. By contrast, nonshareholder constituencies have little to gain from control because their fixed claims will be satisfied as long as the firm remains solvent. The right of control, therefore, is more valuable to whichever group settles for residual rather than fixed claims.

The contractual theory envisions the corporation as a nexus of contracts that is formed by bargaining among all corporate constituencies. In an actual or hypothetical bargaining situation, shareholders as residual claimants would insist on corporate control and be more willing to pay for this right. Moreover, other constituencies would agree to this arrangement. The reason is that bondholders, employees, and other groups would prefer different contractual terms. Employees, for example, would opt for contracts that assure them a specific wage and other benefits. Bargaining for control rights, such as the right to a seat on the board of directors, would require employees to give up something else, and the reluctance of employees to bargain for such rights suggests that the gain is not worth the price. Employee-owned firms are rather rare because, for the most part, ownership provides few advantages for employees compared to the risks they would be taking.

The contractual theory also holds that society benefits when shareholders control a corporation. Assuming that maximum wealth creation is the goal of business activity, control should go to the group with the appropriate incentives for making wealth-maximizing decisions, and this group—according to the argument—is the shareholders. It has already been observed that bondholders, employees, and other corporate constituencies with fixed claims tend to favor decisions that secure their claims and no more. Therefore, some profitable investment opportunities might not be pursued if these groups had control. Managers, too, lack the incentives to pursue all profitable ventures, especially those that would reduce their power or place them at risk. Wealth-maximizing decisions are more likely to be made by the residual risk bearers, because they incur the marginal costs and gain the marginal benefits of all new ventures. Shareholder control, therefore, is the ideal arrangement for the whole of society.

The contractual theory argument for shareholder control, then, is that corporations will create more wealth if decisions are made with only the shareholders' interests in mind and that, as a result, all groups will benefit. What is important to note about this argument is that the ultimate objective of the firm is the maximization of wealth for the whole of society. The objective of shareholder wealth maximization is merely a means to this larger end. This argument does not neglect other constituencies, such as employees, customers, suppliers, and the larger community. It assumes, rather, that these groups are well protected by other kinds of contracts and that, on the whole, they are well served by shareholder control. In other words, this arrangement is optimal not merely for shareholders but for society as a whole.

Stakeholder Theory

The contractual theory generally supports a stockholder-centered conception of the corporation. A much-discussed alternative to this view is *stakeholder theory*. The central claim of the stakeholder approach is that corporations ought to be operated for the benefit of all those who have a *stake* in the enterprise, including employees, customers, suppliers, and the local community. A stakeholder is variously defined as "those groups who are vital to the survival and success of the corporation"[25] and as "any group or individual who can affect or is affected by the achievement of the organization's objectives."[26] The concept of a stakeholder highlights the fact that a corporation interacts continually with its stakeholder groups, and much of the success of a firm depends on how well all of these stakeholder relationships are managed.

Thomas Donaldson and Lee E. Preston distinguish three uses of the stakeholder theory: descriptive, instrumental, and normative.[27] First, the theory can be used as a *description* of the corporation that can enable us to understand the corporation better. Thus, a researcher who believes that the stakeholder theory accurately describes corporations can use it to answer questions about how corporations are organized and managed. The claim that stakeholder theory provides an accurate description can be confirmed to the extent that the answers to these research questions are put to a test and empirically verified.

Second, the stakeholder theory can be used *instrumentally* as a tool for managers. Even if making a profit for shareholders is the ultimate goal of corporate activity, this point does not provide much help in the daily conduct of business. By contrast, telling managers to handle stakeholder relationships well is a more practical action guide that may actually lead to greater profit. In addition, companies faced with social and political challenges may find that relationships with stakeholder groups are valuable resources. James E. Post, Lee E. Preston, and Sybille Sachs argue that in recent years, corporations have been forced by social and political challenges in their competitive environments to become "extended enterprises," in which relationships with stakeholders become not only necessary for survival but also a source of organizational wealth.[28] They write, "The long-term survival and success of a firm is determined by its ability to establish and maintain relationships within its entire network of stakeholders."[29]

Third, the stakeholder theory can be used as a *normative* account of how corporations *ought* to treat their various stakeholder groups. Normative stakeholder theory would have managers recognize the interests of employees, customers, and others as worth furthering for their own sakes. As Donaldson and Preston explain, "The interests of all stakeholders are of '*intrinsic value*.'"[30] Beyond this, normative stakeholder theory might be developed as a theory for corporate governance that challenges the standard system in which shareholders have control and maximizing shareholder wealth is the objective of the firm. Some stakeholder theorists argue that shareholder control of corporations unjustly neglects the interest of other corporate constituencies. Instead of serving only the interests of shareholders alone, they argue that corporations ought to be run in the interests of all stakeholder groups.[31]

Evaluating Stakeholder Theory

As a normative account of corporate governance, stakeholder theory is sometimes presented as an alternative to the standard shareholder-centered model. The shareholder and stakeholder theories agree on one point: The purpose of the firm is to enable each corporate constituency or stakeholder group to obtain the maximum benefit from its involvement. By providing inputs or resources to a firm, each group contributes to the creation of wealth, and this wealth is then distributed among all participants. There are two main points of disagreement between the two theories. One point concerns how best to secure each group's return from the benefit of joint production in a firm. That is, what are the best means to ensure that each group receives its rightful return? The second point of difference involves the determination of a rightful return. That is, who or what should determine what each group receives in return for participating in the wealth-creating activities of a firm?

The answers of the contractual theory to these two questions are straightforward: The best means for protecting each group's rightful return are contracts and legal rules, and the return that each group has a right to receive is the market value of its contribution. For example, employees typically work under a legally enforceable contract that specifies their wages and other conditions of employment, and any disputes arising from this contract can be litigated in court. In addition, legal rules, mainly those of labor law, supplement employees' contracts to provide further protection. Similarly, suppliers and consumers are protected by sales contracts, as well as the body of commercial law, and securities law and the law of corporate governance protect the interest of shareholders in the operation of a firm. By contrast, stakeholder theory relies on managerial discretion both to protect each group's interests and to determine what return they should receive. In the stakeholder-managed firm, the tasks of protecting group interests and balancing their interests fall to corporate managers.

The first question—how best to protect each stakeholder's interest—is largely a pragmatic one about the effectiveness of the available means. What protections work best in practice? One way to answer this question is by conducting a thought experiment. Suppose that the stakeholder theory were adopted by all firms in an economy. In such a system of corporate governance, all groups would share control of a firm; managers would have a fiduciary duty to act in the interests of all groups; and the objective of the firm would be to maximize the return of every group. The resulting economy would exemplify stakeholder theory. Now, add one more condition: that each group is free to opt out of a stakeholder system of governance and choose other means for protecting its interests. That is, they would have the opportunity to forgo the protection of management acting in their interests and seek contracts with a firm or different legal rules for protecting their interests.

Although opinions may differ on the system of corporate governance that might emerge from this thought experiment, there is good reason to believe that each group would prefer the shareholder model. First, management decision making is a weaker form of protection than legally enforceable contracts or legal rules. When such contracts and rules are available, they are more likely to be preferred than a reliance on management's discretion. Shareholders are forced to rely on the protection of a fiduciary duty imposed on management because of problems that prevent them from utilizing fully specified contracts or precise legal rules. Fiduciary duty should be viewed, accordingly, not as a special privilege that shareholders enjoy but as an imperfect substitute when more effective means for protecting a group's interests are not available.[32]

Second, corporate decision making is more efficient and effective when management has a single, clearly defined objective, and shareholder wealth maximization provides not only a workable decision guide but also one that increases the total wealth creation of the firm.[33] This, in turn, enables each group to obtain a greater share. That is, each group can get a larger piece of pie if the pie itself is larger. Thus, employees who seek greater job security or expanded benefits—which advocates of the stakeholder view would support—are more likely to get these goods if the employing company is prospering. A similar argument can be developed for customers, suppliers, investors, and every other stakeholder group. The benefits of a single objective would be compromised if other groups sought, like shareholders, to protect themselves with claims on management's loyalty.

If, in this thought experiment, each group would prefer to opt out of a system that relies on managerial discretion and to seek the protection of contracts and legal rules, the superiority of the shareholder theory over the stakeholder theory is demonstrated. Another conclusion that can be drawn is that on the shareholder theory, everyone can benefit from corporate activity without the need for management to secure each group's interest. If a firm is like a market, in which everyone gains from economic transacting without anyone being responsible for ensuring this outcome, then it is not necessary for managers to assume responsibility for ensuring that everyone benefits. Therefore, from the premise that corporate activity should benefit all stakeholder groups, it does not follow that ensuring this outcome is a task for *management*. The alternative of contracts and legal rules, which do not involve management action but are secured in a market, may achieve this end more effectively.

The second question about who or what should determine what each group receives in return for participating in the wealth-creating activities of a firm concerns fairness or justice in distribution. Broadly speaking, an economy faces two questions: How to *produce* wealth and how to *distribute* it. Generally, decisions about production are made in a market on the basis of economic considerations. On the shareholder theory, the market also determines how wealth is to be distributed, but the resulting distribution may not be fair. The stakeholder theory makes the just distribution of wealth a task of management by requiring managers to balance competing stakeholder interests. Not only does stakeholder theory give no guidance on how this balancing is to be done, but also managers have neither the ability nor the authority to determine a fair distribution. It is not only unreasonable to expect managers, who have enough responsibility making decisions about how to produce wealth, to handle questions about how it should be distributed, but it is also dangerous in a democracy to allow unelected managers to make such crucial decisions. Decisions about the distribution of wealth that depart from market outcomes should be made, for the most part, by governments through the political process.

The main conclusion to be drawn is that the familiar model of shareholder control of corporations is justified, although the shareholders need not be investors but could be any group, including employees, customers, or suppliers. In the American system of corporate governance, the control of corporations is left largely to the choices that each group makes through contracting with the firm in a market. Through such contracting, each group is able to protect its interest and gain its rightful share of the wealth created by engaging in economic production. The shareholder model of corporate governance is better able than the alternative of a stakeholder firm to best serve all stakeholder groups.

CASE 13.2 ✳ Explore the Concept on mythinkinglab.com

Bath Iron Works

On May 17, 1991, a quick decision by CEO William E. Haggett almost destroyed Bath Iron Works, the largest private employer in Maine.[34] Founded in 1884, Bath Iron Works (BIW) is a major shipbuilder for the U.S. Navy with 10,400 employees. As one of two companies with the capability to build Aegis naval destroyers worth $250 million each, BIW was competing fiercely for contracts with its rival, Ingalls Shipbuilding in Mississippi. At 5:30 that morning, a janitor found a 67-page document stamped "Business Sensitive" in a conference room that had been used the previous day for a meeting with navy officials. Two vice presidents who examined the document realized that it contained a detailed comparison of BIW's and Ingalls's costs for building the Aegis destroyer. They delivered the document to Mr. Haggett at 9:00 A.M. The CEO, who was leaving the office to deliver a luncheon speech, examined it for 15 minutes before making a decision. He ordered the two vice presidents to copy the document, return the original to the conference room, and meet with him late in the afternoon to discuss how they should handle the situation.

During the next few hours, the two executives analyzed the information and did some computer modeling based on it. At 2:15 they decided to notify the president of BIW, Duane D. "Buzz" Fitzgerald, who had a reputation for impeccable integrity. Mr. Fitzgerald immediately recognized that the federal Procurement Integrity Act requires defense contractors to certify that they have not been in unauthorized possession of any proprietary information. In addition, BIW is a signatory to the Defense Industry Initiative on Business Ethics and Conduct (DII), which was formed in 1986 in response to revelations by the Packard Commission of irregularities in defense industry contracting. The six principles of the DII require not only that signatories adopt a written code of ethics, engage in ethics training, and provide mechanisms for internal reporting of possible misconduct but also that they take responsibility for any violation of law. Principle 4 states, "Each company has the obligation to self-govern by monitoring compliance with federal procurement laws and adopting procedures for voluntary disclosure of violations of federal procurement laws and corrective actions taken." Mr. Fitzgerald ordered that all copies be shredded and all data erased from the computer. Upon his return, Mr. Haggett agreed with the action taken and admitted that he had made an "inappropriate business-ethics decision." The CEO personally delivered the original document to navy officials on site. However, Mr. Haggett decided not to reveal that copies had been made but to admit only that "no copies existed."

The navy launched its own investigation and concluded that the bidding process had not been compromised. An adverse decision could have resulted in suspension or debarment as a government contractor, which would have jeopardized the survival of the firm with devastating consequences for its employees and the surrounding community. As part of the settlement with the navy, BIW agreed to establish an ethics program headed by an ethics officer, expand ethics training, create a board committee for ensuring compliance, and report to the navy for three years on the implementation of this agreement. BIW was still competing for contracts to build at least two new Aegis destroyers, and many at the company feared that lingering suspicion about the use of a competitor's information would be an impediment. To allay this concern, the two vice presidents who first handled the discovery of the document were asked to leave the company and William Haggett resigned as CEO. He later severed all connections with BIW, thus ending a 28-year career with a company where his father had worked as a pipe fitter. He lamented that 15 minutes of ethical uncertainty had cost him his job. Buzz Fitzgerald became the new CEO and immediately declared that BIW "must meet the highest ethical standards and avoid even the appearance of impropriety."

CORPORATE ETHICS

Corporations are increasingly paying attention to ethics in the conduct of employees at all levels of the organization. Unlike the emphasis on corporate social responsibility, which focuses on the impact of business activity on society at large, the corporate ethics movement addresses the need to guide individual decision making and to develop an ethical workplace environment. Much of the impetus in the United States has come from a recognition of the dangers posed by individual misconduct. However, unethical business practices are seldom due to a lone rogue employee but usually result from factors in the organization.[35] Ethics programs are designed, therefore, to create an organization that fosters ethical conduct. The case of Bath Iron Works shows that no program can prevent momentary lapses of judgment, much less intentional wrongdoing. The incident occurred in spite of an existing ethics program. The consequences of this incident might have been far worse, though, had the company not implemented the principles of the Defense Industry Initiative. Significantly, the chosen remedy was a strengthening of the program in place in order to prevent a recurrence.

This section examines corporate ethics programs. Specifically, what are the components of an ethics program? What leads corporations to adopt a program, and what do they expect to achieve? Some companies have adopted ethics programs in response to serious scandals, whereas others seek to prevent scandals before they occur. In particular, the corporate ethics movement has been spurred by the Federal Sentencing Guidelines, which offer lenient treatment for convicted organizations with an effective ethics program. These are primarily defensive strategies aimed at legal compliance. However, many corporations strive for a higher level of conduct in the belief that a reputation for integrity provides a strategic advantage. Like all other corporate initiatives, though, ethics programs represent an investment that must be justified, and so we need to take a critical look at their benefits and also at possible objections to them.

The Components of an Ethics Program

Every organization has an ethics program of some kind, although it may not be recognized as such.[36] In the broadest sense, an ethics program consists of the rules and policies of an organization and the procedures and systems for motivating and monitoring ethical performance. Rules and policies include the culture and values of an organization and formal documents, such as mission statements, codes of ethics, policy and personnel manuals, training materials, and management directives. Compliance with rules and policies is secured by various procedures and systems for orientation, training, compensation, promotion, auditing, and investigation. These procedures and systems are essential functions in any business organization. Companies with an identifiable ethics program are distinguished by the emphasis that they place on these functions and the manner in which they address them.

The components of a corporate ethics program generally include a code of ethics, ethics training for employees, means for communicating with employees about matters of ethics, a reporting mechanism for enabling employees to report alleged wrongdoing, an audit system for detecting wrongdoing, and a system for conducting investigations and taking corrective action. In addition, more than 500 U.S. corporations have established the position of ethics officer to oversee all aspects of an ethics program. Many companies without an ethics officer still assign the main responsibilities to one or more high-level executives.

This list of components does not reveal the range of corporate ethics programs. At one end of the spectrum are programs designed merely to secure compliance with the law and with the company's own rules and policies. The goals are to prevent criminal conduct and violation of government regulations on one hand, and to protect the company from self-interested action by employees on the other. Compliance of this kind is essential in any organization, but some corporations take a broader view of ethics. At the other end of the spectrum are ethics programs that communicate the values and vision of the organization, seek to build relations of trust with all stakeholder groups, and emphasize the responsibility of each employee for ethical conduct.

Lynn Sharp Paine describes this latter kind of program as an *integrity strategy* in contrast to the *compliance strategy* that is represented by the former kind.[37] While a compliance approach imposes standards of conduct on employees and attempts to compel acceptable behavior, a program guided by integrity aligns the standards of employees with those of the organization and enables them to act ethically. An integrity strategy seeks to create conditions that foster right action instead of relying on deterrence and detection. These conditions are created by the whole management team rather than being relegated to lawyers or others in compliance, and by employing the whole resources of the organization. In particular, the full range of procedures and policies, the accounting and control systems, and the decision-making structures of the corporation are utilized for the end of fostering right conduct. An integrity strategy also attempts to motivate employees by appealing to their values and ideals, rather than relying solely on material incentives.

The Benefits of an Ethics Program

The main benefit of an ethics program is to prevent ethical misconduct by employees, which is costly to companies not only in direct losses but also in those sustained from a tarnished reputation. The total cost to Sears, Roebuck and Company for settling suits nationwide over allegations that its Sears Auto Centers made unnecessary repairs (see Case 13.3) has been estimated to be $60 million. In addition, the trust of consumers that enabled the company to enter the competitive auto repair market was seriously damaged. The falsification of records by defense contractors, for which the companies were fined and forced to make restitution, led to development of the Defense Industry Initiative.

The financial services industry has produced some examples of very costly misconduct. A bond-trading scandal at Salomon Brothers in 1991 cost the firm almost $1 billion, and in 1994 Prudential Securities agreed to pay fines and penalties in excess of $700 million for crimes committed in the sale of limited partnerships in the 1980s. A Japanese copper trader hid losses estimated at $2.6 billion from his employer, Sumitomo Corporation; and Nicholas Leeson, a 29-year-old, Singapore-based trader for Barings Bank, destroyed this venerable British firm by losing more than $1 billion in unauthorized trading. In 2008, a rogue trader at Société Générale lost more than $7 billion for the French bank. In some instances, the main loss from employee misconduct has been the company's reputation. For example, NYNEX adopted an ethics program after learning that between 1984 and 1988, its purchasing unit had hosted an annual convention in Florida for suppliers and company employees featuring strippers and prostitutes. The public exposure of these events—dubbed "pervert conventions" by the press— came at the same time that the struggling company was seeking an unpopular $1.4 billion rate increase from the New York State Public Service Commission.

Second, ethics programs provide a managerial tool for adapting the organization to rapid change. Among the factors that have led corporations to adopt ethics programs are increased competition, the development of new technologies, increased regulation, recent mergers and acquisitions, and the globalization of business. The problems at NYNEX, for example, were not confined to risqué parties. The breakup of AT&T in 1984 had forced NYNEX and all Baby Bells to compete in an unfamiliar environment that required new ways of doing business. NYNEX needed to provide individual guidance to employees during a period in which all the rules were being rewritten. Mergers and acquisitions also disrupt familiar routines and create the need to develop new ones rapidly. Finally, a formerly domestic company that becomes a global enterprise must not only set the rules for its own employees' behavior abroad but must also mesh its conduct with that of foreign customers, suppliers, and joint venture partners.

A third benefit of ethics programs is managing relations with external constituencies. An ethics program serves to reassure customers, suppliers, investors, and the general public of the serious intent of a corporation to adhere to high ethical standards. It is no accident that the first ethics programs were developed by defense contractors, which have only one customer, namely, the Department of Defense. The Defense Industry Initiative, which commits each signatory to develop an ethics program, was an attempt to assure this all-important customer of its trustworthiness. Problems often develop when a company and its suppliers or vendors operate by different standards, and so a company's ethics program helps make its standards known. For example, some companies notify suppliers of their policy on gift giving and ask them to respect it.

The existence of an ethics program is an assurance not only to socially responsible investors, who look for such indicators, but also to shareholders generally, who want to avoid the cost of major scandals. The shareholders of Caremark International, Inc., a healthcare provider, sued the individual members of the board of directors for failing to prevent criminal violations that cost the company $260 million. In deciding this case, the Delaware Chancery Court held in 1996 that directors have a fiduciary duty to the shareholders to ensure that the corporation's reporting systems are reasonably well designed to provide management with sufficient information to detect violations of law.[38] The *Caremark* decision has been described as a "wake-up call" to directors that they may be personally liable for their failure to ensure that a corporation has an adequate compliance system in place.[39] Of course, an ethics program is only one means for securing compliance. However, the *Caremark* decision, combined with the Federal Sentencing Guidelines, provides a strong incentive for developing one.

The Federal Sentencing Guidelines

In 1984, Congress created the U.S. Sentencing Commission in order to bring greater uniformity and effectiveness to the sentences that judges impose for federal crimes. In developing new guidelines, the Sentencing Commission departed from prevailing practices by holding organizations responsible for the conduct of individual decision makers and creating incentives for organizations to prevent misconduct by their members. Under the Federal Sentencing Guidelines for Organizations, which took effect in 1991, the sentence for an organization that has been convicted of a federal crime depends, in part, on the effort that has been made to prevent and detect criminal wrongdoing, including the adoption of an effective ethics program.

The Federal Sentencing Guidelines have the dual aim of imposing a just sentence on any convicted organization and influencing the conduct of all organizations. The former aim is achieved by guidelines that base the penalty on the seriousness of the offense and the culpability or blameworthiness of the organization. The guidelines provide not only for fines that punish an organization but also for restitution to the victims, and the fines can be set so as to wipe out any gain for an organization from its criminal activity. In addition, the severity of the fines, which can reach $290 million or the higher of the gain to the organization or the loss to the victims, provides a powerful incentive for organizations to take preventive steps and to cooperate in an investigation.

HOW THE GUIDELINES WORK. The first step in applying the guidelines is determining a base fine. This amount is generally taken from a table that ranks crimes according to their seriousness and assigns a monetary amount to each level. The base fine ranges from $5,000 for a level 6 offense or lower (embezzlement, theft, bribery of a public official) to $72.5 million for a level 38 offense or higher. Commercial bribery, for example, is a level 8 offense with a $10,000 base fine, and money laundering is a level 20 offense with a base fine of $650,000.

The base fine may then be either increased or decreased by a multiplier based on a "culpability score." This score, which ranges from 1 to 10, is determined by starting with five points and by subtracting or adding points for certain factors. Five points are added if high-level personnel were involved in the wrongdoing; three points are added if the organization obstructed the investigation or prosecution of the crime; and two points are added if similar misconduct had occurred before. Up to five points are subtracted for reporting an offense, cooperating with the investigation, and accepting full responsibility. The significant factor for the development of an ethics program is that a sentencing judge subtracts three points if the offense occurred "despite an effective program to prevent and detect violation of the law." (This provision does not apply if high-level personnel were involved or if they delayed reporting the offense after becoming aware of it.)

For each culpability score, there is a range from which a judge can choose a multiplier that either reduces or increases the base fine. The minimum multiplier is 0.05, which reduces the fine imposed to 5 percent of the base fine. The maximum multiplier is 4.00, which quadruples the base fine. Hence, the highest fine is $72.5 million (the highest base fine) multiplied by 4.00 (the highest multiplier), or $290 million. The highest fine imposed so far by using the Federal Sentencing Guidelines is $340 million levied against Daiwa Bank in New York, even though the bank was a victim of unauthorized trading by an employee that cost the bank $1.1 billion.[40] The charge against the bank was that officials had failed to inform U.S. officials within 30 days of the discovery of the loss as required by law. The bank officials engaged in the cover-up in part to avoid a decline in the bank's stock price but also because they felt that they needed time to understand what had happened and because the Japanese Ministry of Finance feared that disclosure would have an adverse impact on markets in Japan. However, if the bank had adopted an adequate compliance program, perhaps the loss would have been detected earlier with less severe consequences.

AN EFFECTIVE ETHICS PROGRAM.   The Federal Sentencing Guidelines define an effective ethics program as one "that has been reasonably designed, implemented, and enforced so that it generally will be effective in preventing and detecting criminal conduct."[41] The program need not prevent or detect every instance of wrongdoing, but the organization must have practiced "due diligence," which involves the following steps.[42]

1. The organization must have established compliance standards and procedures that are reasonably capable of reducing misconduct.
2. Specific high-level personnel must have been assigned responsibility for overseeing compliance with the standards and procedures.
3. The organization must take due care not to assign substantial discretionary authority to individuals with a propensity to engage in illegal behavior.
4. Standards and procedures must have been communicated to all employees and agents through such means as publications and training programs.
5. The organization must have taken reasonable steps to ensure compliance by using monitoring and auditing systems and a reporting system that employees may use without fear of retaliation.
6. The standards must have been consistently enforced through appropriate disciplinary measures, including, as appropriate, the punishment of employees who fail to detect an offense by others.
7. After an offense has been detected, the organization must have taken all reasonable steps to respond appropriately and to prevent further similar offenses.

The specific actions involving these steps will depend on many factors, including the size of the organization, the nature of the industry, and the organization's prior history.

Although the Federal Sentencing Guidelines provide a strong incentive for corporations to establish ethics programs and contain a good definition of an effective ethics program, questions have been raised about the overall approach of the guidelines and specific features of the definition. First, there is no solid evidence that ethics programs are more effective than other kinds of compliance systems in preventing illegal behavior. Some evidence indicates that misconduct occurs not because of ignorance about the standards for acceptable conduct but because of organizational pressures and the actions of peers.[43] To be effective, therefore, an ethics program must go beyond setting and enforcing rules and include the goal-setting and reward systems of an organization. Second, to the extent that ethics programs are not effective, the guidelines may encourage corporations to create highly visible "window dressing" programs at the expense of more substantive initiatives. Moreover, most large corporations already have compliance programs that would satisfy the guidelines' requirements, so that little is to be gained by offering a reduction in any fine. But small firms may be penalized for investing their more limited resources in a formal ethics program when other systems of control might be more effective in preventing misconduct.

Codes of Ethics

The first step in developing an ethics program, and the only step that some companies take, is a code of ethics. Codes of ethics vary widely, falling into three main types. The most common is a statement of specific rules or standards for a variety of situations. These are most often called codes of conduct or statements of business standards or practices. A second type is a statement of core values or the vision of an organization, sometimes called a credo or mission statement. These statements frequently include affirmations of the commitments of a company to key stakeholders, such as customers, employees, and the community. Third are corporate philosophies that describe the beliefs guiding a particular company. Perhaps the best known of these is Hewlett-Packard's "The HP Way." Corporate philosophy statements are generally written by the founders of businesses in emerging industries, such as computers, where new ways of doing business are needed.

Most codes of ethics combine elements of the first two types, but at least one firm, Levi Strauss & Company, has adopted all three kinds of statements. An Aspiration Statement describes what kind of company its members want it to be. A Code of Ethics explains the values and ethical principles that guide action. And finally, Levi Strauss has adopted a document entitled "Global Sourcing and Operating Guidelines," which contains very specific rules on working with business partners and choosing countries for operations. A few weeks before the guidelines were officially adopted, Levi Strauss canceled a contract with a supplier in Saipan (a U.S. territory) after reports of human rights violations. Subsequently, the U.S. Department of Labor charged that the contractor worked the employees, mostly Chinese women, up to 11 hours a day in guarded compounds and paid them well below the Saipan minimum wage. The contractor settled the charges for $9 million. One Levi Strauss manager observed, "If anyone doubted the need for guidelines, this convinced them."

In addition to company codes of ethics, there are many industry codes, generally adopted by a trade organization. These include organizations for the advertising, banking, direct marketing, franchising, insurance, and real-estate industries. Because a commitment to high ethical standards and self-regulation is integral to a profession, most professional groups have also developed ethics codes to which their members are generally required to subscribe. Among professions with codes of ethics are physicians, lawyers, accountants and auditors, architects, engineers, financial planners, public administrators, consultants, and journalists. Unlike company and industry codes of ethics, which are of recent origin, some professional codes are as old as the profession, as witness the Hippocratic oath for physicians, which dates from the fourth century B.C.

The development of ethics codes for corporations is a relatively recent phenomenon, with most having been written since 1970.[44] In many instances, these codes replaced other kinds of documents, such as policy manuals, executive directives, and customary practices. An early prominent code of ethics was "The Penney Idea," a set of seven principles set forth by the merchandizing pioneer J.C. Penney in 1913. A major impetus for the development of corporate ethics codes was provided by the influential National Commission on Fraudulent Financial Reporting (the "Treadway Report"), issued in October 1987. This report recommended,

> Public companies should develop and enforce written codes of corporate conduct. Codes of conduct should foster a strong ethical climate and open channels of communication to help protect against fraudulent financial reporting. As a part of its ongoing oversight of the effectiveness of internal controls, a company's audit committee should review annually the program that management establishes to monitor compliance with the code.[45]

Until recently, codes of ethics have primarily been adopted by American companies. A study in 1987 revealed that more than three-quarters of U.S. respondents had a code of ethics, but less than half of the responding European corporations had one.[46] The number of companies abroad with a code of ethics is increasing, however, in part because of the rise of mergers and joint ventures between American and foreign firms.

THE REASONS FOR ADOPTING A CODE. The reasons for adopting a code of ethics include those that lead companies to develop ethics programs. Even without a program, a code of ethics serves a number of valuable functions. A written document enables an organization to clarify standards that may otherwise be vague expectations left to individual interpretation. Where there is disagreement on the appropriate standards, codes can achieve a measure of consensus, and where standards are lacking or in need of revision, codes enable an organization to create new ones. This is especially true for American corporations with foreign operations and relationships, although a code of ethics may need to be modified when applied abroad. Codes of ethics are an effective means for disseminating standards to all employees in an easily understood form. Finally, an effective code of ethics that is enforced in an organization provides employees with a tool for resisting pressure to perform unethical or illegal actions. A code of ethics may enable employees to do what they believe to be right.

Even well-written codes of ethics have limitations, and badly written ones may have some unintended consequences. An emphasis on rules may create a rigid literalness that discourages judicious discretion. An especially dangerous situation is created when employees conclude that whatever is not prohibited is permitted. Some codes focus primarily on employee misconduct that can harm the company, which may lead to cynicism about the purpose of ethics. Some companies do not adopt a code of ethics because they believe that their way of doing business is best achieved by maintaining a strong culture and leading by example. Other companies believe that a code is inappropriate to their situation because extensive government regulation and internal auditing are sufficient to deter both unethical and illegal behavior.

Studies of which companies adopt codes of ethics reflect these advantages and disadvantages. Codes are more prevalent in large companies, in companies with more complex structures, especially those that have grown rapidly or recently merged, and in companies that have high visibility and depend on their reputation.[47] Codes of ethics are less common among financial firms—investment banks, for example—in part because of the extensive government regulation, but also because of the strong incentive to monitor employee behavior closely.

WRITING A CODE. There is no blueprint for writing a code of ethics. Both the procedure and content must arise from specific features of the company in question. However, some values, such as respect of the individual, fair treatment, honesty, integrity, responsibility, trust, teamwork, and quality, are included in typical codes, as are such topics as conflict of interest, use of company resources, gifts and entertainment, confidentiality of information, and workplace behavior. There is one common trait of all successful codes of ethics, namely, that they have the clear support of top-level management. A code is unlikely to be successful, though, if it is imposed from the top down. Ideally, everyone in a company should have "ownership" of the code.

CORPORATE ACCOUNTABILITY

The recent scandals at Enron, WorldCom (Case 2.3), and other companies were not the result of misconduct by a few individuals that might have been deterred by an effective ethics program. They revealed major weaknesses in the systems of corporate control by which corporations are held accountable. Enron had a code of ethics and other elements of an ethics program, and there were no doubt acts by some individuals that violated the Enron code. However, the collapse of Enron, as well as WorldCom, involved fraudulent conduct by high-level executives that evaded the controls ordinarily imposed on corporation by financial reporting requirements and oversight by a board of directors. The Sarbanes-Oxley Act of 2002 (SOX), which was passed in the wake of Enron's collapse, reflected the belief of Congress that there were deep flaws in the American accounting system and the operation of corporate boards. The act also increased the penalties for criminal offenses by corporate executives. The various provisions of SOX thus address the three major components of the American system for holding corporations accountable: financial reporting, boards of directors, and the criminal law. This section examines how each of these three forms of accountability function to prevent fraud and other kinds of corporate misconduct and what weaknesses have permitted major corporate scandals.

Financial Reporting

Enron's filing for bankruptcy on December 2, 2002, followed more than two months of revelations about the company's declining financial situation. When third-quarter earnings were reported on October 16, 2001, Enron announced that it was writing down the value of certain investments by $1.01 billion and that investor equity had shrunk by $1.2 billion. More bad news followed on November 8 when the company revealed that its net income dating back to 1997 was $586 million less than had been previously reported due to improper accounting practices. When investors realized that Enron's reported income had been greatly exaggerated and that large amounts of debt had been hidden in dubious off-balance-sheet partnerships, all trust was eroded and the company's stock lost almost all value.

Enron's collapse was due not merely to bad business decisions that had been hidden from investors but also to a plundering of the company by insiders. The first line of defense against incompetence and outright criminality by corporate executives is a company's financial reports. The law requires that public companies prepare financial statements that present a fair and accurate picture of their financial condition, and these statements must be audited and attested to by a certified public accounting firm. Although audited financial statements are intended primarily to aid investors in making sound investment decisions and to increase the efficiency of financial markets, they also serve as an important check on management by making corporate operations more transparent. The ability of the market to react swiftly to changes in a company's situation makes it an effective monitor of managers' performance. Because investors rely so heavily on them, financial reports are also tempting vehicles for committing fraud. By presenting a false picture of a company's financial condition, executives can cover up poor performance and continue to receive lavish compensation. In many of the recent scandals, fraudulent accounting also enabled executives to dump much of their stock before bad news became public.

ACCOUNTING AND AUDITING.   Accounting is the recording and presentation of the financial transactions of an organization. Any organization, whether it is a business corporation, a not-for-profit organization, or a government unit, must keep track of its revenues and expenditures and compile this information in ways that provide managers with an understanding of the organization's financial condition. Accountants also compile an organization's financial information in reports that are presented to outside parties, such as creditors from whom the organization is seeking loans or the government, which requires that certain information be disclosed. All public companies are required by law to issue an annual report that details all assets, liabilities, revenues, and earnings in a consolidated balance sheet and income statement. In the United States, all accounting must be done in accord with established rules, known as generally accepted accounting principles (GAAP). Each country has its own version of GAAP, and there is an emerging set of International Financial Reporting Standards (IFRS).

Auditing is an inspection of an organization's accounting records to determine their accuracy, completeness, and reliability. This inspection may be conducted inside the organization by managerial accountants or internal auditors, who are employees of the organization, or by outside, independent public auditors, who are certified public accountants (CPAs). In addition to inspecting an organization's financial accounting records, a CPA conducting an independent audit also examines the organization's financial accounting system and offers a report or opinion about both the accounting records and the accounting system. The independent auditor's report or opinion may be *unqualified*, which means that the organization's financial records fairly represent its financial condition and have been prepared according to GAAP, or *qualified*, which indicates either that the audit was not complete in scope or that GAAP was not followed completely. An independent public audit should be conducted in accord with Generally Accepted Auditing Standards (GAAS).

ETHICAL ISSUES. If corporate accounting and auditing were properly done, then fraud and other kinds of financial wrongdoing would be difficult to commit, and detection would be easy. Individual accountants and auditors, being human, are subject to ethical lapses, but, more importantly, there are certain structural problems with the practices of accounting and auditing that impair their effectiveness as a first line of defense against financial scandals.

First, managerial accountants and internal auditors, who are employees of a company, and the outside CPAs, who are engaged by the client company, are subject to intense pressure to achieve the financial picture that top executives want to convey. Often the pressure comes to meet earnings expectations in order to maintain a company's stock price or allow executives to make bonus or stock option targets. Such "earnings management" is possible because accounting rules allow great flexibility in their application. This flexibility is permitted so that companies can choose the accounting treatments that provide the fairest representation of their financial condition. However, a company's own accountants and its CPA firm may be pressured to go along with accounting treatments that give an inaccurate or misleading picture of the company's financial condition but serve management's interest.

Arthur Levitt, a former chairman of the SEC, addressed the abuse of the flexibility in the accounting system with a call for higher ethical standards:

> Our accounting principles weren't meant to be a straitjacket. Accountants are wise enough to know they cannot anticipate every business structure, or every new and innovative transaction, so they develop principles that allow for flexibility to adapt to changing circumstances. That's why the highest standards of objectivity, integrity and judgment can't be the exception. They must be the rule.[48]

Of course, accountants may also be pressured to approve accounting treatments that are not in accord with GAAP, as when WorldCom personnel were ordered to record accruals as revenue and line charges as capital expenses (Case 2.3). Such cases require accountants to have the moral courage to resist. CPAs are not employees who can be fired for failing to please management; but CPA firms are still selected by management, and they have a strong incentive to please the client in order to be retained. Enron, for example, was one of Arthur Andersen's most valued clients, and the company succeeded in having accountants who objected to Enron's accounting removed from the Enron team.[49]

Second, CPA firms have other interests besides a desire to be retained that put them in conflict-of-interest situations. An individual CPA may have a financial relationship with the company being audited by, for example, owning stock in that company or a company doing business with it. The CPA firm may also have other clients which have business relationships with or which are competitors of the company being audited. Any such relationships might impair the objectivity and independence of the CPAs engaged in an audit. For this reason, "The Code of Professional Conduct of the American Institute of Certified Public Accountants" requires CPAs to maintain objectivity and independence and be free of conflicts of interest. The code specifically prohibits having "any direct or material indirect financial interest" in an audit client and any loan from the company or anyone related to it. This prohibition does not address the conflict that results when auditors take positions with a company that he or she formerly audited. The prospect of an attractive job with an audit client might influence an auditor's judgment. Indeed, a number of top executives at Enron had previously been with the Houston office of Arthur Andersen on the Enron account.

CPA firms encounter two other sources of conflicts of interest. One source arises when accounting firms provide both auditing and consulting services to a client. Critics of this arrangement charge that since consulting services are usually more lucrative than auditing, firms have an incentive to avoid alienating clients by conducting aggressive audits in order to maintain the consulting engagements. The other source of conflict results from the dual loyalty of auditors. The word "public" in "certified public accountant" indicates that an audit is conducted to serve shareholders and the investing public. However, CPAs are engaged and compensated by the companies they audit, thus making these companies the clients of the accounting firm.

Since the interests of a client company and the public can be different, should the CPA firm balance these interests in some way or regard the interest of the public as paramount? In 1984, the U.S. Supreme Court declared the public interest paramount:

> By certifying the public reports that collectively depict a corporation's financial status, the independent auditor assumes a public responsibility transcending any employment relationship with the client. The independent public accountant performing this special function owes allegiance to the corporation's creditors and stockholders as well as to the investing public. This "public watchdog" function demands that the accountant maintain total independence from the client at all times and requires complete fidelity to the public trust.[50]

The ideal of total independence from the client and complete fidelity to the public is very difficult to achieve in practice in view of the competition for clients and the high fees they generate. These two sources of conflict of interest have led to proposals—so far unimplemented—that auditing and consulting services be provided by separate firms and that audits be publicly funded.

Third, accountants have a strict duty of confidentiality that prevents them from disclosing any confidential information about a client without that client's consent except when required to do so by law. One such legal requirement is that an accounting firm that withdraws from an auditing engagement because of suspected wrongdoing by the client must file a report with the SEC detailing the reasons for the withdrawal. However, any other information about suspected wrongdoing should not be disclosed to other parties, including any companies that are harmed by the wrongdoing or another accounting firm that takes over the engagement. An example of the difficulties that a duty of confidentiality creates is provided by the experience of Arthur Andersen in the late 1960s. After an Arthur Andersen team audited Fund of Funds and found no problems, the same team began an audit of King Resources, which had business dealings with Fund of Funds. The auditors discovered that King Resources had sold properties to Fund of Funds at inflated prices. If Andersen informed Fund of Funds of the fraud, then King Resources might sue for breach of confidentiality. However, if Andersen said nothing, then Fund of Funds might sue Andersen for concealing the information. Andersen chose the latter course and was successfully sued by Fund of Funds for failing to disclose the inflated prices.[51]

Fourth, the ability of auditors to detect fraud and other wrongdoing is limited by what auditors are expected to do and what they can reasonably accomplish. An audit conducted according to GAAS is not intended to be a forensic audit to uncover fraud but is designed merely to provide reasonable assurances that a company's records are accurate representations. Auditors examine the records prepared by the company's own accountants, and they test only selected transactions. If a company's accounting system is judged to be adequate, then less effort is expended in testing. A "clean" or unqualified opinion attests only the accuracy of the company's books and not to the company's solvency or future prospects. Because the public expects auditors to do more than this and accepts a "clean" opinion as a "clean bill of health," there is an "expectations gap" between what the public expects of auditors and what auditors actually do. The expectations gap could be closed so as to make auditors more effective at detecting fraud, but doing so would involve greater costs and change the nature of auditing. The question from a regulatory point of view is whether auditors or federal and state investigators can better serve as detectors of fraud.

SARBANES-OXLEY ACT.   The Sarbanes-Oxley Act of 2002 contains a number of provisions that address the problems with accounting and auditing. Title I created the Public Company Accounting Oversight Board, which has the power to review audits, set additional auditing standards, and sanction firms for conducting inadequate audits. Title II, titled "Auditor Independence," prohibits the provision of certain nonaudit services to an audit client, requires that the lead audit partner for any client be rotated at least every five years, and imposes a one-year waiting period before accepting employment with an audit client. In signing SOX, President George W. Bush declared, "This law says to corporate accountants: the high standards of your profession will be enforced without exception; the auditors will be audited; the accountants will be held to account."[52]

The Board of Directors

Although the Enron board of directors included many distinguished, competent, and diligent individuals and exemplified many good corporate governance practices, its members twice voted to rescind the company's conflict-of-interest policy so that the chief financial officer, Andrew Fastow, could serve as the managing partner of several special purpose entities. These off-balance-sheet partnerships not only allowed Fastow to enrich himself at the expense of Enron shareholders but also created enormous risks of which the board was apparently unaware. The failure of the board of directors to exercise its proper oversight role in corporate governance is at least one cause of Enron's collapse.

Corporate directors are elected by the shareholders to exercise their right of control in the operation of a corporation. In this role, directors select and monitor the chief executive officer of the corporation, approve the company's overall strategic plan, and ensure that adequate control systems are in place. The board also exercises control through an audit committee that reviews financial reports, a nominating committee that recruits new board members, and a compensation committee that sets the compensation package for the CEO. In addition to its control responsibilities, the members of the board, who have wide experience and extensive connections, also provide advice to the top-management team and offer crucial outside resources. Board members are characterized as inside or outside directors depending on whether they are currently executives of the corporation, and outside directors are designated as independent if they have no relationship with the corporation other than service on the board. In the United States, the chairman of the board is often the CEO, although the two roles may be separated, and they often are in other countries.

PROBLEMS WITH BOARDS.   In most of the recent scandals, boards of directors have not been complicit in any wrongdoing but have been unaware of what was occurring in the companies they supposedly controlled. For some directors, this ignorance was due to a lack of attention, a lack of competence, a lack of independence, conflicts of interest, or some combination of these four factors. Board members are often chosen by the CEO, and probably too many of them were close associates of the CEO, celebrities who brought little but their name to the board or else CEOs themselves who did not have the time to devote their full attention. However, much of the failure of corporate boards to prevent wrongdoing, like the failure of accountants and auditors, was due to structural features, many of which were addressed by SOX.

Among the factors contributing to failed board performance is a low percentage of independent directors. A sign of good board practice is a majority of independent directors with crucial committees, most notably the nomination, compensation and audit committees, constituted entirely by independent directors. Board members cannot be expected to know about misconduct in the organization, but they are responsible for having control systems and accounting procedures capable of detecting it. Some boards had failed to evaluate the adequacy of the systems and procedures in place. Although board members must have the confidence to leave a CEO free to operate a company, they should also exercise greater independence by, for example, conducting some executive sessions without the CEO and other chief officers present. Some have proposed to increase board independence by separating the roles of CEO and chairman or, at least, appointing a designated or lead director to guide the independent members. Good board practice calls for the audit committee to meet with the independent auditors in executive session to satisfy themselves that there are no financial irregularities. Some of the other proposals for reform include reducing the number of boards on which directors sit, reducing the number of members on a board, increasing the number of meetings held annually, and increasing the amount of work done by committees. Increasing the compensation of board members and including stock grants and stock options have been proposed as ways of providing greater incentives for them to focus on protecting shareholder interests.

A number of provisions in the Sarbanes-Oxley Act address the problems of weak boards and control systems. Among the highlights: SOX requires the CEO and the CFO to certify that they have reviewed every report filed with the SEC and that, to the best of their knowledge, the report does not contain any material misstatements. Section 404 requires every public company to assess annually the adequacy of its internal control system and its procedures for financial reporting. The audit committee of the board is required by SOX to be composed entirely of independent directors, and at least one member must be a "financial expert." SOX also requires that the independent auditor meet with the audit committee of the board and that the committee be solely responsible for selecting, compensating, and monitoring the independent auditor. Finally, a significant source of abuse was removed by banning corporate loans to company executives. Although SOX has been subjected to considerable criticism, especially for the cost of complying with Section 404, the act represents a significant effort by Congress to improve the effectiveness of boards of directors in preventing the kinds of misconduct that occurred at Enron and other companies.

Criminal Prosecution

Kenneth L. Lay and Jeffrey K. Skilling, the former chief executives of Enron, were found guilty in May 2006 of multiple counts of fraud and conspiracy. Mr. Skilling was sentenced to 24 years and four months of imprisonment, while Mr. Lay died in July 2006 before a sentence could be imposed. Skilling's sentence was just short of the 25 years handed down to Bernie Ebbers, the CEO of WorldCom. The main offense of all three men was lying to shareholders about the financial condition of their company; at the same time, Lay and Skilling were dumping a large portion of their stock holdings. The criminal law is applied not only to individuals but also to corporations. Arthur Andersen, the accounting firm that had signed off on Enron's faulty financial reports, was indicted on March 14, 2002, for obstruction of justice in shredding documents, and when the firm was found guilty three months later, it, too, collapsed like Enron before it.

Fraud and conspiracy to commit fraud are criminal offenses for which both individuals and corporations can be prosecuted. Other misdeeds for which corporations have been prosecuted criminally include unsafe products and working conditions, bribery and corruption, and willful pollution. The possibility of criminal prosecution, along with financial reporting and corporate boards, serves as a means for holding corporations accountable. Individuals and corporations may instead be prosecuted for civil rather than criminal offenses. Generally, a criminal offense involves some harm to the state, whereas a civil offense arises from the violation of some regulation or a private right. Crimes are generally more serious than civil offenses and usually result in a more severe sanction or penalty. Prosecutors often have the choice of bringing a criminal or a civil indictment against an individual or a corporation. Criminal and civil prosecutions are state actions, but individuals and corporations may also be sued by private parties under tort law for recovery of damages from wrongful harms.

PROBLEMS WITH CRIMINAL LAW.   The problems with prosecuting corporations were neatly stated by an eighteenth-century Lord Chancellor of England who was quoted as saying, "Did you ever expect a corporation to have a conscience, when it has no soul to be damned, and no body to be kicked?"[53] Unlike natural persons, corporations are legal fictions that appear to lack the two essential elements for criminal liability: a mind that has the necessary knowledge and intent and a body that can perform the criminal act. In law, these elements are *mens rea* (a guilty mind) and *actus reus* (the guilty act). In addition, a corporation also lacks a body that can be punished; it cannot be imprisoned, for example. However, corporate decision making exhibits features apart from the actions of the individuals who make up a corporation that may be described by saying the corporation knows, intends, and so on. Similarly, there are actions performed by individuals that may be attributed to a corporation, especially when that person is acting in an organizational role.

Because the ascription of mental states and actions to corporations is speculative, legislators and judges have been ambivalent about the applicability of corporate criminal law. In practice, proving the necessary elements of *mens rea* and *actus reus* is difficult. Corporate criminal action has been traditionally established by the legal doctrine of vicarious liability, by which a principal may be held liable for the actions of his or her agent. However, this doctrine might unfairly hold a corporation liable when an employee acts outside the scope of his or her role. It is often difficult to determine when an employee is acting on behalf of the corporation or on his or her own. Moreover, the main punishment that can be imposed on a corporation is a monetary fine, which is borne by the shareholders, who may be innocent of the crime and victims as well.

In addition to these theoretical problems, prosecutors face enormous difficulty building a case against individuals or a corporation for white-collar crimes given the diffuse nature of corporate decision making and corporate action and the inaccessibility of information. The fraudulent transactions at Enron typically involved many people, each with responsibility for only one small part of the paperwork involved, and none of these participants may have had knowledge of the full scope of any given transaction. Absent a "smoking gun" that shows knowledge and intent by specific individuals, criminal charges against corporations are not easily proven in court. To overcome this problem, the American legal system has shifted emphasis to a corporation's pre- and post-offense behavior. The aim of the law has been to prevent misconduct before it can occur and to encourage cooperation by the corporation to settle charges quickly and expose the individuals responsible.

This new cooperative approach is the result of two developments: the federal Sentencing Guidelines for Organizations, implemented in 1991, and the Principles of Federal Prosecution of Business Organizations, which was promulgated first in 1999. The sentencing guidelines, discussed earlier in this chapter, guide judges in the sentencing of organizations, and the principles, issued by the U.S. Department of Justice, direct federal prosecutors in decisions about whether to charge corporations with crimes. Under the principles, corporations are less likely to be criminally prosecuted if they voluntarily cooperate with investigators and do not shield employees. The main effects of these two influential documents have been to encourage organizations to implement ethics programs, disclose wrongdoing, admit guilt, provide requested documents, fire employees who refuse to testify, and withhold support for employees' legal expenses. Although the cooperative approach may prevent misconduct before it occurs and facilitate the prosecution of crimes that are committed, it may raise ethical issues of its own. John Hasnas has argued that in cooperating with investigators, corporations may violate employees' rights to confidentiality and privacy and destroy the trust that is necessary for corporations to function.[54] If this is the case, then company executives are faced with a choice between protecting the company from legal liability and acting ethically toward their employees.

Conclusion

The modern corporation is a remarkable form of economic organization that enables everyone in society to interact for mutual gain. Ideally, everyone should benefit from the wealth-creating power of business corporations. In order for corporations to function and provide their benefits, several problems must be solved. First, corporations must be controlled so that investors, employees, customers, suppliers, and other groups that participate in productive activity are protected. This is the task of corporate governance. Second, there must be a control environment within the corporation to detect and deter employee misconduct. This is the task of corporate ethics. Third, corporations must be held accountable so that corporate executives do not engage in fraud or other wrongdoing. In addition to corporate governance, this task is addressed by accounting and auditing, a corporation's board of directors, and the criminal law. When an economic system combines all of these elements together—corporate governance, corporate ethics, and corporate accountability—the results can be a prosperous society. Where one or more of the elements is absent, the corporation cannot achieve its full potential.

CASE 13.3   ✳ Explore the Concept on mythinkinglab.com
Sears Auto Centers

On June 11, 1992, the CEO of Sears, Roebuck and Company, Edward A. Brennan, learned that the California Department of Consumer Affairs (DCA) was seeking to shut down the 72 Sears Auto Centers in that state.[55] A yearlong undercover investigation by the DCA had found numerous instances in which Sears employees had performed unnecessary repairs and services. Officials in New Jersey quickly announced similar charges against six local Sears Auto Centers, and several other states, including Florida, Illinois, and New York, opened their own probes into possible consumer fraud. In the wake of this adverse publicity, revenues from the auto centers fell 15 percent, and the public's trust in Sears was badly shaken.

Sears Auto Centers, which were generally connected with a Sears department store, concentrated on basic "undercar" services involving tires, brakes, mufflers, shock absorbers, and steering mechanisms. Investigators from the DCA's Bureau of Automotive Repair purchased old vehicles in need of minor repairs and disassembled the brakes and suspension systems. After examining and photographing each part, the investigators towed the automobiles to a shop where they requested a brake inspection. In 34 of 38 instances, Sears employees recommended unnecessary repairs and services, and some auto centers charged for parts that were not installed or work that was not performed. The average overcharge was $235, but in two cases the amount overcharged exceeded $500.

Brennan had been notified in December 1991 of early results from the investigation, and Sears executives negotiated for six months with California officials. The company objected to the state's position that no part should be replaced unless it had failed and claimed that many repairs were legitimate preventive maintenance. For example, there is disagreement in the industry on whether brake calipers should be reconditioned whenever the pads are replaced. In addition, some of the automobiles used in the investigation showed signs of damage from worn parts that had already been replaced, thus leading mechanics to believe that repairs were needed. The DCA moved to revoke the licenses of all Sears Auto Centers in the state after the negotiations broke down over details of the financial settlement.

California officials charged that the problems at the Sears Auto Centers were not confined to a few isolated events but constituted systemic consumer fraud. According to a deputy attorney general, "There was a deliberate decision by Sears management to set up a structure that made it totally inevitable that the consumer would be oversold." Until 1991, service advisers, who make recommendations to customers, were paid a flat salary, but subsequently their compensation included a commission incentive. The service advisers were also required to meet quotas for a certain number of parts and services in a fixed period of time. The new incentive system also affected the mechanics, who perform the work on the customers' automobiles. Instead of an hourly wage that was paid regardless of how much work was done, mechanics now received a lower hourly wage that was supplemented by an amount based on the time required to install a part or perform a service. The company determined how long it should take to complete each job, and a mechanic could earn the former hourly wage only by finishing the work in the time specified. Under this system, slow workers would earn less than before, but a mechanic could also earn more by working faster than expected.

Commissions and quotas are commonly used in competitive sales environments to motivate and monitor employees. However, critics of Sears charge that there were not enough safeguards to protect the public. One former auto center manager in Sacramento complained that quotas were not based on realistic activity and were constantly escalating. He said that "sales goals had turned into conditions of employment" and that managers were "so busy with charts and graphs" that they could not properly supervise employees. A mechanic in San Bruno, California, alleged that he was fired for not doing 16 oil changes a day and that his manager urged him to save his job by filling the oil in each car only halfway. This illustrated, he said, the "pressure, pressure, pressure to get the dollar."

The changes in the compensation system at Sears Auto Centers were part of a company-wide effort to boost lagging performance. In 1990, net income for all divisions, including Allstate (insurance), Coldwell Banker (real estate), and Dean Witter (brokerage), dropped 40 percent. Net income for the merchandising group, which included the department stores and the auto centers, fell 60 percent. Brennan, CEO since 1985, was under strong pressure to cut costs and increase revenues. Some dissident shareholders were urging the board of directors to spin off the more profitable insurance, real estate, and brokerage divisions and focus on the ailing merchandising group. Brennan's response was to cut jobs, renovate stores, and motivate people. The overall thrust, according to a story in *BusinessWeek*, was to "make every employee, from the sales floor to the chairman's suite focus on profits." Some critics of Sears attribute the problems at the auto centers to an unrealistic strategic plan that sought to wring more revenue out of the auto repair business than was possible. Robert Monk, who unsuccessfully sought a seat on the company's board, said, "Absent a coherent growth strategy, these sorts of things can happen."

At a press conference on June 22, 1992, Edward Brennan announced that, effective immediately, Sears would eliminate its incentive compensation system for automotive service advisers and all product-specific sales goals. Although he admitted that the company's compensation program "created an environment where mistakes did occur," Brennan continued, "We deny allegations of fraud and systemic problems in our auto centers. Isolated errors? Yes. But a pattern of misconduct? Absolutely not." He reaffirmed his belief that the California investigation was flawed and that Sears was practicing responsible preventive maintenance. He further announced that the company would retain an independent organization to conduct random "shopping audits" to ensure that no overcharging would occur. Sears also paid

$8 million to settle claims in California and gave auto center customers $50 coupons that were expected to cost the company another $3 million. The total cost, including legal bills and lost sales, is estimated to have been $60 million.

On September 30, 1992, Sears revealed plans to spin off its three nonretail divisions, Allstate, Coldwell Banker, and Dean Witter, and to reorganize the merchandising group. A new CEO, Arthur C. Martinez, succeeded Brennan and began a turnaround of the company. In describing his vision, Martinez said, "I want to revisit and intensify the theme of our customer being the center of our universe." A cornerstone of Martinez's strategy, according to the *New York Times*, was "clean business ethics."

CASE 13.4 ✳ Explore the Concept on mythinkinglab.com
The Sale of Trans Union

Promptly at noon on Saturday, September 20, 1980, nine members of the board of directors of Trans Union Corporation gathered for a hastily called special meeting.[56] None of the five outside directors had been informed of the meeting's purpose or had been provided with any materials. Only one hour earlier did many of the top executives learn of the plan to be proposed to the board by the chairman and chief executive officer, Jerome W. Van Gorkom. The plan was to sell the company for a price of $688 million to the Marmon Group, headed by Jay A. Pritzker, a prominent takeover specialist and chairman of the Hyatt hotel chain.

Trans Union Corporation was a publicly traded, diversified holding company, located on LaSalle Street in Chicago. Founded in 1968 out of the Union Tank Car Company, Trans Union was engaged primarily in the business of leasing railroad cars. Although the company was doing well, it could not match the lower rates of its competitors in the railroad-car leasing business due to its inability to benefit from an investment tax credit. Because the credit was offered as an offset on the company's taxable income, Trans Union could not realize the full benefit since deductions for depreciation reduced its taxable income below the full amount of the credit. Lobbying efforts in Congress for a change in the tax code to permit the receipt of the credit in cash had proved fruitless. Among the other solutions to this problem examined by company executives were a leveraged buyout by management and a sale to a larger company with more taxable income.

On his own, without consulting the board or any other executives except one, Van Gorkom arranged to meet with Pritzker at the latter's home on Saturday, September 13. The two men had been acquainted socially for more than 10 years and had worked together on the Chicago School Finance Authority to rescue the city school system from a financial crisis. Rather than merely seeking to discern Pritzker's interest, Van Gorkom presented him with a detailed proposal based on a $55-per-share price, which represented a premium of 48 percent over the current price and 62 percent over the average of the high and low prices during 1980. Van Gorkom explained how Pritzker could finance the deal so as to realize the extra value reflected in the premium. Pritzker was interested in the deal, and after several more meetings over the next few days to settle certain details, he announced that he was ready to make a $55-per-share all-cash offer for the company. However, Pritzker insisted that the deal had to be completed by Sunday of that week, September 21.

At an 11:00 meeting of top executives on Saturday, September 20, the reaction was decidedly negative. Van Gorkom gave a verbal account of the proposed agreement but did not provide the executives with written copies. Several of the executives questioned how the $55 price had been determined and whether it was too low. Objections were also made to several conditions that Pritzker had inserted that would discourage any rival bidders for the company. Some executives also expressed concern about the adverse tax consequences of an all-cash buyout for certain shareholders. The executives realized, though, that the decision was not theirs to make: The board of directors had the responsibility of deciding whether to approve the proposed agreement and submit it to the shareholders for a vote.

The five outside directors on the board were very knowledgeable about mergers and acquisitions and had a thorough grasp of Trans Union's financial condition and strategic direction, including the problem with the investment tax credit. Four of them were CEOs of other companies, and the fifth was a former dean of the University of Chicago business school. During the two-hour special board meeting on September 20, Van Gorkom gave a 20-minute oral presentation of the proposed agreement, without providing written copies. He did not provide any analysis to support the $55-per-share price, and he did not claim that this was the highest price that could be obtained but only that it was a fair price which the shareholders should be allowed to accept or reject. It is common in such situations to seek a fairness opinion from an investment advisory firm to attest that the price placed on a company for sale is fair, but no such opinion had been sought in this case. Also, Van Gorkom did not mention that he had proposed the $55 price to Pritzker rather than receiving an offer at this price from him. He defended the price on the ground that once the Pritzker offer was announced, other bidders could come forth, thus allowing the market to determine the highest price that could be obtained.

The chief financial officer of Trans Union, who had not been aware of the proposed agreement until that morning, told the board that he had not attempted to determine the company's value. The studies he had done were aimed, rather, at analyzing the feasibility of a management buyout at different share price levels in the $50 to $60 range. He explained that this methodology would not yield a valid price for the company but would produce a reasonable approximation. He told the board that, in his opinion, $55 was "in the range of a fair price" but "at the beginning of the range." An outside lawyer, who had been retained by Van Gorkom to advise the company on the sale, told the board, correctly, that a fairness opinion was not legally required and that they might be sued by shareholders if they did not allow the shareholders to vote on the offer.

At the end of two hours, the directors voted to accept the proposed agreement, without having read it. The board members later claimed that they had attached two conditions to the agreement that reserved the right to accept a better offer if one were made before the deal was completed, and that committed the company to provide any potential bidder with confidential financial information. However, these conditions were not recorded in the meeting minutes nor incorporated into the final agreement. Moreover, the board did not reserve the important right to actively solicit other bids.

That evening was the opening night of the Chicago Lyric Opera season. Following tradition, Van Gorkom and his wife hosted a formal pre-opera gala party on the twenty-fifth floor penthouse of the Trans Union Building for a large number of Chicago's elite, including the Pritzkers. During the celebration, the two men, attired in tuxedos, slipped down to the floor below where a team of lawyers was putting the final touches on the sale document. Before leaving for the opera—a production of Modest Moussorgsky's "Boris Godunov"—they signed the agreement to sell Trans Union to Pritzker's Marmon Group. This agreement, which still had to be presented for a shareholder vote, was not yet complete, though. Pritzker was forced to make some concessions to keep key executives from leaving, but he also added some provisions that further limited the board's ability to obtain a better offer or withdraw from the deal. Van Gorkom reconvened the board for a meeting on October 8. However, the final agreement, executed on October 10, contained provisions that differed from what Van Gorkom had told the directors. No member of the board had read the final agreement, and Van Gorkom himself apparently failed to appreciate the implications of some of the changes.

On January 26, 1981, the board met and voted to proceed with the sale and approved the information that would be sent to shareholders. The shareholders voted to approve the sale with 69.9 percent in favor, 7.25 percent against, and 22.8 percent not voting. Before the vote, a group of shareholders brought a class-action suit challenging the sale. These shareholders sought to hold the individual board members personally liable for failing to fulfill their fiduciary duty in approving the sale, citing specifically the duty of candor to disclose fully all relevant information and a duty of care to inform themselves fully before taking action. The monetary damages sought was the difference between the sale price of $55 per share and the true value of the company. Although directors and officers of publicly held corporations have a fiduciary duty to shareholders, they also have the benefit of the business judgment rule, which protects them from shareholder suits alleging a breach of fiduciary duty as long they act reasonably and there is no evidence of negligence, bad faith, fraud, or self-dealing. The purpose of the business judgment rule is to insulate corporate decision making from second-guessing by the courts and to avoid unnecessary personal risk for individuals, which might make them unduly cautious. According to this rationale, shareholder interests are better served if the fiduciary duty of directors and officers is not excessively stringent but is tempered by the business judgment rule.

The Delaware Supreme Court reversed a lower court ruling and found that Van Gorkom and the other directors guilty of a breach of their fiduciary duty. The opinion of the judge writing for the majority stated the following:

> Under the business judgment rule there is no protection for directors who have made "an unintelligent or unadvised judgment." A director's duty to inform himself in preparation for a decision derives from the fiduciary capacity in which he serves the corporation and its stockholders. Since a director is vested with the responsibility for the management of the affairs of the corporation, he must execute that duty with the recognition that he acts on behalf of others. Such obligation does not tolerate faithlessness or self-dealing. But fulfillment of the fiduciary function requires more than the mere absence of bad faith or fraud. Representation of the financial interests of others imposes on a director an affirmative duty to protect those interests and to proceed with a critical eye in assessing information of the type and under the circumstances present here.[57]

This decision provoked a strong, immediate reaction, with one critic calling it "surely one of the worst decisions in the history of corporate law."[58] One judge, in dissent, opined that while the board may not have read the material, they were experienced men of business who knew the company thoroughly, had confidence in its top executives, and understood the need, in this case, for quick action. While $55 per share may not have been the highest amount obtainable, it was still a fair price. Other critics have stressed the cost involved in gathering and processing information compared with the benefit for shareholders and the need to rely on the expert opinion of company management and professional advisers. In response to this negative reaction, the Delaware General Assembly passed legislation allowing corporations chartered in the state to adopt an exculpatory provision in their documents of incorporation that protect directors and officers from monetary damages for failure to fulfill the standard of fiduciary duty articulated in the Trans Union case, on the condition that such a provision is approved by shareholders. The effect of this legislation is to permit shareholders to bypass the decision in the Trans Union case if they believe that doing so is to their advantage. Subsequently, virtually all large Delaware-incorporated companies have done this. As a result, successful suits for breach of fiduciary duty today can be brought only for egregious cases of fraud, bad faith, or self-dealing and not merely for the kind of conduct exhibited by the directors of Trans Union Corporation.

Notes

1. The other conditions are that the proposed resolution involves (1) a personal grievance, (2) a personal benefit to the party proposing the resolution that is not shared by other shareholders, (3) vague or misleading statements, and (4) an impractical goal that the company lacks the power to achieve.

2. Cracker Barrel Old Country Store, Inc., SEC No-Action Letter, Fed. Sec. L. Rep. 76,418 (October 13, 1992).

3. Adoption of Amendments Relating to Proposals by Security Holders, Exchange Act Release No. 12,999, 41 Fed. Reg. 52,994 (1976).

4. American Telephone & Telegraph Co., SEC No-Action Letter, 1990 WL 2285776 (5 January 1990).

5. Some corporations have bylaws or charters that permit nomination of directors by shareholders.

6. "Commission to Review Current Proxy Rules and Regulations to Improve Corporate Democracy," Securities and Exchange Commission, press release 2003–46, 14 April 2003.

7. Amendments to Rules on Shareholder Proposals, Exchange Act Release No. 34–40018, 63 Fed. Reg. 29,106 (1998). For a discussion, see Phillip R. Stanton, "SEC Reverses Cracker Barrel No-Action Letter," *Washington University Law Quarterly*, 77 (1999), 979–92.

8. The distinction between the property rights and the social institution conceptions of the corporation is due to William T. Allen, "Our Schizophrenic Conception of the Business Corporation," *Cardozo Law Review*, 14 (1992), 261–81. See also, William T. Allen, "Contracts and Communities in Corporate Law," *Washington and Lee Law Review*, 50 (1993), 1395–1407.

9. Because the right to incorporate is alleged to "inhere" in the right to own property and to contract with others, this view is also known as the *inherence theory*.

10. The view that incorporation is a privilege "conceded" by the state in order to achieve some social good is also known as the *concession theory*.

11. *Munn* v. *Illinois*, 94 U.S. 113, 24 L. Ed. 77 (1876).

12. *Dodge* v. *Ford Motor Co.*, 170 N.W. 668, 685 (1919).

13. Adolf A. Berle, Jr., and Gardiner C. Means, *The Modern Corporation and Private Property* (New York: Macmillan, 1932).

14. Ibid., 3.

15. Ibid., 355.

16. E. Merrick Dodd, "For Whom Are Corporate Managers Trustees?" *Harvard Law Review*, 45 (1932), 1148.

17. Ibid., 1161.

18. Ibid., 1162.

19. Adolf A. Berle, Jr., "For Whom Corporate Managers Are Trustees: A Note," *Harvard Law Review*, 45 (1932), 1367.

20. Ibid., 1372.

21. Ibid., 1370.

22. Ibid., 1372.

23. Adolf A. Berle, Jr., *The 20th Century Capitalist Revolution* (New York: Harcourt, Brace & World, 1954), 169.

24. Ronald M. Coase, "The Nature of the Firm," *Economica*, N.S., 4 (1937), 386–405. The contractual theory has been developed by economists using an agency or transaction cost perspective. See Armen A. Alchian and Harold Demsetz, "Production, Information Costs, and Economic Organization," *American Economic Review*, 62 (1972), 777–95; Benjamin Klein, Robert A. Crawford, and Armen A. Alchian, "Vertical Integration, Appropriable Rents, and the Competitive Contracting Process," *Journal of Law and Economics*, 21 (1978), 297–326; Michael C. Jensen and William H. Meckling, "Theory of the Firm: Managerial Behavior, Agency Costs, and Ownership Structure," *Journal of Financial Economics*, 3 (1983), 305–60; Eugene F. Fama and Michael C. Jensen, "Separation of Ownership and Control," *Journal of Law and Economics*, 26 (1983), 301–25; Steven N. S. Cheung, "The Contractual Theory of the Firm," *Journal of Law and Economics*, 26 (1983), 1–22; and Oliver E. Williamson, *The Economic Institutions of Capitalism* (New York: Free Press, 1985). An authoritative development of the theory of the firm in corporate law is Frank H. Easterbrook and Daniel R. Fischel, *The Economic Structure of Corporate Law* (Cambridge, MA: Harvard University Press, 1991). See also William A. Klein, "The Modern Business Organization: Bargaining under Constraints," *Yale Law Journal*, 91 (1982), 1521–64; Oliver Hart, "An Economist's Perspective on the Theory of the Firm," *Columbia Law Review*, 89 (1989), 1757–73; and Henry N. Butler, "The Contractual Theory of the Firm," *George Mason Law Review*, 11 (1989), 99–123.

25. William M. Evan and R. Edward Freeman, "A Stakeholder Theory of the Modern Corporation: Kantian Capitalism," in *Ethical Theory and Business*, 4th ed., ed. Tom L. Beauchamp and Norman E. Bowie (Upper Saddle River, NJ: Prentice Hall, 1993), 79. See also R. Edward Freeman and David L. Reed, "Stockholders and Stakeholders: A New Perspective on Corporate Governance," in *Corporate Governance: A Definitive Exploration of the Issues*, ed. C. Huizinga (Los Angeles: UCLA Extension Press, 1983), 88–106.

26. R. Edward Freeman, *Strategic Management: A Stakeholder Approach* (Boston, MA: Pitman, 1984), 46. This book provides a useful discussion of the history of the stakeholder concept and the literature on it.

27. Thomas Donaldson and Lee E. Preston, "The Stakeholder Theory of the Corporation: Concepts, Evidence, and Implications," *Academy of Management Review*, 20 (1995), 65–91.

28. James E. Post, Lee E. Preston, and Sybille Sachs, "Managing the Extended Enterprise: The New Stakeholder View," *California Management Review*, 45 (2002), 6–28. See also, James E. Post, Lee E. Preston, and Sybille Sachs, *Redefining the Corporation: Stakeholder Management and Organizational Wealth* (Stanford, CA: Stanford University Press, 2002).

29. Post, Preston, and Sachs, "Managing the Extended Enterprise," 7.

30. Donaldson and Preston, "The Stakeholder Theory of the Corporation," 67.

31. Freeman, *Strategic Management*; R. Edward Freeman and William M. Evan, "Stockholders and Stakeholders: A New Perspective on Corporate Governance," *California Management Review*, 25 (1983), 88–106; and R. Edward Freeman and William M. Evan, "Corporate Governance: A Stakeholder Interpretation," *Journal of Behavioral Economics*, 19 (1990), 337–59.

32. Jonathan R. Macey, "An Economic Analysis of the Various Rationales for Making Shareholders the Exclusive Beneficiaries of Corporate Fiduciary Duties," *Stetson Law Review*, 21 (1999), 23–44; Richard Marens and Andrew C. Wicks, "Getting Real: Stakeholder Theory, Management Practice, and the General Irrelevance of Fiduciary Duties Owed to Shareholders," *Business Ethics Quarterly*, 9 (1999), 273–93.

33. Michael C. Jensen, "Value Maximization, Stakeholder Theory, and the Corporate Objective Function," *Business Ethics Quarterly*, 12 (1992), 235–56; Anant K. Sundaram and Andrew C. Inkpen, "The Corporate Objective Revisited," *Organizational Science*, 15 (2004), 350–63.

34. Material for this case is taken from Rushworth M. Kidder, *How Good People Make Tough Choices* (New York: Fireside, 1995), 35–38; Glenn Adams, "Bath Iron Works CEO Admits Ethics Breach, Steps Down," *The Associated Press*, 16 September 1991; Jerry Harkavy, "Haggett Severs Ties with Shipyard in Aftermath of Photocopy Scandal," *The Associated Press*, 25 September 1991; Suzanne Alexander, "Bath Iron Works Says Haggett Quit as Chief," *Wall Street Journal*, 17 September 1991, B9; and Joseph Pereira and Andy Pasztor, "Bath Chairman, 2 Vice Presidents Quit under Navy Pressure over Secret Data," *Wall Street Journal*, 26 September 1991, A4.

35. Lynn Sharp Paine, "Managing for Organizational Integrity," *Harvard Business Review*, 72 (March–April 1994), 106.

36. Steven N. Brenner, "Ethics Programs and Their Dimensions," *Journal of Business Ethics*, 11 (1992), 391.

37. Paine, "Managing for Organizational Integrity."

38. *In re Caremark International Inc.* Derivative Litigation. Civil Action No. 13670 (Del. Ch. 1996).

39. Dominic Bencivenga, "Words of Warning: Ruling Makes Directors Accountable for Compliance," *New York Law Journal*, 13 February 1997, 5.

40. For an explanation, see Jeffrey M. Kaplan, "Why Daiwa Bank Will Pay $340 Million under the Sentencing Guidelines," *Ethikos*, 9 (May–June 1996).

41. United States Sentencing Commission, *Federal Sentencing Guidelines Manual*, §8A1.2, Commentary, Application Note 3(k).

42. Ibid., Application Note 3(k)(1–7).

43. O. C. Farrell, Debbie Thorne LeClair, and Linda Ferrell, "The Federal Sentencing Guidelines for Organizations: A Framework for Ethical Compliance," *Journal of Business Ethics*, 17 (1998), 353–63.

44. *Corporate Ethics*, The Conference Board, Research Report No. 900 (1987), 14.

45. National Commission on Fraudulent Financial Reporting, *Report of National Commission on Fraudulent Financial Reporting*, 1987, p. 35.

46. *Corporate Ethics*, 13.

47. Messod D. Benish and Robert Chatov, "Corporate Codes of Conduct: Economic Determinants and Legal Implications for Independent Auditors," *Journal of Accounting and Public Policy*, 12 (1993), 3–35.

48. Arthur Levitt, "The 'Numbers Game'," Remarks to New York University Center for Law and Business, 28 September 1998.

49. See Barbara Ley Toffler with Jennifer Reingold, *Final Accounting: Ambition, Greed, and the Fall of Enron* (New York: Broadway Books, 2003); and Kurt Eichenwald, *Conspiracy of Fools* (New York: Broadway Books, 2005).

50. *United States* v. *Arthur Young & Co.*, 79 L.Ed.2d 826, 836; 104 S. Ct. 1495 (1984).

51. Karen Arenson, "Anderson [sic] Firm Is Found Guilty of Fraud," *New York Times*, 5 November 1981, D3. For a discussion of this "Catch 22," see Norman E. Bowie, "Accountants, Full Disclosure, and Conflicts of Interest," *Business and Professional Ethics Journal* 5 (1986), 60–73.

52. "President Bush Signs Corporate Corruption Bill," Office of the Press Secretary, press release, 30 July 2002.

53. Edward, First Baron Thurlow, in H. L. Mencken, *A New Dictionary of Quotations on Historical Principles from Ancient and Modern Sources* (New York: Knopf, 1942), 223.

54. John Hasnas, *Trapped: When Acting Ethically Is Against the Law* (Washington, DC: Cato Institute, 2006).

55. Material for this case is taken from Lynn S. Paine and Michael A. Santoro, "Sears Auto Centers (A)," Boston, MA: Harvard Business School Publishing, 1993; Kevin Kelly, "How Did Sears Blow This Gasket?" *BusinessWeek*, 29 June 1992, 38; Julia Flynn, "Did Sears Take Other Customers for a Ride?" *BusinessWeek*, 3 August 1992, 24–25; Judy Quinn, "Repair Job," *Incentive*, October 1992, 40–46; Jennifer Steinhauer, "Time to Call a Sears Repairman," *New York Times*, 15 January 1998, sec. 3, p. 1; News from Sears, Roebuck and Co. press release, 22 June 1992.

56. Information on this case is taken from *Smith* v. *Van Gorkom*, 488 A.2d 858 (Del. 1985).

57. *Smith* v. *Van Gorkom* at 872.

58. Daniel R. Fischel, "The Business Judgment Rule and the *Trans Union* Case," *Business Lawyer*, 40 (1985), 1455.

14

International Business Ethics

((∙━ Listen to the Chapter Audio on mythinkinglab.com

CASE 14.1 ✳━Explore the Concept on mythinkinglab.com

Mattel's Toy Woes

In 2007, consumers everywhere were alarmed by reports of hazardous Chinese products, ranging from tainted pet food and toothpaste to defective automobile tires.[1] None of these scares, though, matched the concern in the United States over lead paint on toys manufactured for Mattel in China, which led to two highly publicized recalls in August of that year. On August 2, 2007, Mattel jointly announced, with the Consumer Products Safety Commission, a voluntary recall of 1.5 million Chinese-made toys containing impermissible amounts of lead. Shortly before this announcement, the company became aware of lead contamination in another line of toys produced by a different vendor, which became the subject of another voluntary recall on August 14. These two recalls undermined the confidence of consumers not only in all products made in China but also in the ability of a company, even one as diligent as Mattel, to effectively enforce its stringent standards of safety in an extended global supply chain.

Mattel, Inc., with headquarters in El Segundo, California, was the world's largest toy company by revenue. It grew from its modest founding in 1945 to a global giant that by 2007 produced 800 million items a year under more than 100 registered brands, including Fisher-Price toys, Hot Wheels and Matchbox cars, and Barbie and American Girl dolls. Mattel had long experience manufacturing in Asia, with the first Barbie dolls produced in Japan in 1959. Like other toy companies, Mattel sought low-wage labor in developing countries, closing its last U.S. plant in 2002; but unlike its competitors, Mattel recognized the perils of outsourcing production to independent factories, which led it to build ten company-owned plants abroad, five of which were in China. By 2007, 65 percent of Mattel products were made in China, although one-half of its products worldwide were made in company-owned factories. These Mattel factories manufactured the company's most valuable core products, which were vulnerable to counterfeiting and other problems that could affect brand image. The other half, which consisted of less valuable and less vulnerable, noncore products, was manufactured by independent contract factories, 37 of which Mattel dealt directly with in China. However, these 37 factories used subcontractors, which, in turn, had their own subcontractors, so that in 2007, Mattel toy production in China involved an estimated 3,000 companies.

The August 2 recall affected products manufactured by Lee Der Industrial, located in Foshan, China, in Guangdong province, where most toy production was clustered. Mattel had sourced from Lee Der for 15 years, during which time the Chinese vendor had generally observed the stringent guidelines that Mattel had long imposed to ensure safety. Lead paint is a well-recognized hazard due to the serious neurological effects of lead, especially on the bodies of young children, who are apt to ingest it from chewing on toys. Although generally banned, lead paint is still in common use because it has a brighter color, is easier to apply to hard surfaces, and, most important, is 30 percent cheaper than nonlead paint. Mattel vendors were permitted to source paint from only eight approved suppliers, which were required to test paint batches to ensure that they met standards and to link each batch with the certificates of compliance. The vendor was responsible for checking the certification of each batch, and Mattel checked the records and conducted its own tests at least every three months. Once a vendor was approved, it was prohibited from moving production to any new facility without notifying Mattel. Lee Der, which manufactured 83 different products for Mattel, used three of the approved paint suppliers. One of these suppliers apparently ran short of yellow paint and, using the Internet, found a company that provided 330 pounds of yellow pigment for a cost of $1,250, accompanied by falsified documents that the supplier failed to detect. Later attempts to locate this company proved futile, and the individuals involved have disappeared. Although Lee Der had equipment for conducting lead tests, it was not used for the newly supplied paint. The lead paint on some Mattel products manufactured by Lee Der was discovered by a French importer, which immediately notified Mattel headquarters. Mattel executives also received a report of lead on some toys from a mother in the United States using a home test kit. At first, Mattel thought that Lee Der had corrected the problem of lead paint, but the company soon realized that it faced a more serious systemic problem and quickly ceased accepting deliveries from the troubled Chinese vendor.

The August 14 recall involved 460,000 units of the Sarge car in the Pixar line from another vendor, Early Light Industrial Company, which Mattel had used satisfactorily for 20 years. In this case, Early Light had subcontracted the painting of the olive-green roof of the car to another company but provided the paint from an authorized supplier. However, the subcontractor either ran out of paint or else sold the paint and bought a cheaper substitute from an unapproved supplier. Contrary to Mattel rules, the use of the subcontractor had not been disclosed. Following an extensive testing of other products, which revealed more cases of lead paint on toys, Mattel stopped all production in China until the source of the problem could be discovered and corrected, and the company instituted another recall of a few products on September 4, 2007. Lead paint was not the only hazard known to Mattel at this time. Because magnets in some toys could be dislodged and ingested by children, resulting in intestinal blockage and rupture when the magnets joined together, Mattel also instituted a recall of 17.4 million units of some popular magnet-based toys, mostly Polly Pocket, Batman, and Doggie Daycare play sets.

The initial reaction of Mattel was to blame the vendors for violations of long-standing rules that the company had carefully developed and implemented. With decades of experience in Asia, Mattel recognized the risks of operating there, and it insisted that its vendors follow a long list of detailed rules designed to ensure product safety. One observer commented, "Mattel was in China before China was cool, and they learned to do business there in a good way. They understood the importance of protecting their brand, and they invested."[2] Mattel's system involved close monitoring but still depended, to some extent, on the vendors' voluntary compliance, which was subject to failure. Robert A. Eckert, the Mattel CEO, commented that "we wouldn't have faced this problem if our suppliers followed the rules." Another executive explained, "I think it's the fault of the vendor who didn't follow the procedures we've been living with for a long time."[3] In addition to the recalls, Mattel stepped up the enforcement of its rules with a three-stage safety check that involved testing every batch of paint by the vendor, testing samples of finished products by Mattel, and conducting random, unannounced inspections of vendors. Mattel also tightened the rules requiring that vendors notify the company of the use of any subcontractors before engaging them and imposed a new rule that prohibited subcontractors from outsourcing further.

Critics place some of the blame on Mattel and the competitive environment in which the company operates. The toy industry depends heavily on fads in which a few novel items prove extraordinarily popular but sell for very short periods. It is essential that companies constantly innovate and rush new products into production quickly in the right quantities and at the right times (generally in the last two quarters of the year when the vast majority of toys are sold). Above all else, it was important to find the right price point for marginal consumers. Mattel had developed a very rigorous, detailed bidding process that forced vendors to compete not only on quality and delivery but also on price. Although retails customers are price sensitive in buying toys, even more pressure for low prices comes from the giant retailers, such as Wal-Mart, Target, and Toys "R" Us, which together account for 45 percent of Mattel sales. In China, the rising costs of labor and materials and the rising value of the currency, the *yuan*, put tremendous pressure on vendors to cuts corners wherever possible. One critic noted, "There was a lot of scapegoating China, but . . . this was caused by a system that is designed to push down costs and speed up delivery. There are root causes and Mattel is behind those."[4] Although scapegoating China took some pressure off Mattel and made it look like a victim rather than a perpetrator, other critics argued that the vast majority of recalls were due not to manufacturing faults, such as lead paint, but to design flaws that originated with the toy companies themselves. One study found that over the past 20 years, 76 percent of all recalls of toys were due to design problems, such as the loose magnets in Mattel's magnet-based products, and only 10 percent were caused by faulty manufacturing.[5]

Mattel has also been criticized for not treating consumer safety with the same kind of care that the company has devoted to worker protection. Before Christmas 1999, the NBC news program Dateline broadcast a story about Mattel's alleged use of underage workers in Indonesia, and the magazine *U.S. News and World Report* featured a cover story with the headline "Sweatshop Christmas." At the time, workers, mostly young women on three-to four-year contracts, worked 10-hour days, six days a week for around $120 to $175 a month; they generally lived in crowded on-site dormitories, had their meals deducted from their pay, and were often forced into working overtime. In response to this publicity and to pressure from the "anti-sweatshop" movement, Mattel developed a model program that included a set of Global Manufacturing Principles. The company also submitted to monitoring by an independent organization, the International Center for Corporate Accountability (ICCA), which was willing to be engaged only on the condition that its reports be made public. In the view of one observer, Mattel "has gone further than any other company to be a good corporate citizen with regard to its Chinese operations."[6] Although Mattel aggressively addressed problems in the treatment of workers, it did not adopt the same auditing and monitoring processes to product safety. According to the head of ICCA, "The code was designed to protect Chinese workers from being exploited. Nobody was thinking about unsafe products. They were thinking about cheap products."[7]

Mattel's efforts to blame vendors backfired. Chinese government officials and industry leaders were frightened that the public image being conveyed by Mattel threatened the export basis of the Chinese economy. The owner of the Lee Der factory, Zhang Shuhong, aged 52, committed suicide in his empty factory after Mattel ceased accepting deliveries. Mr. Zhang had a reputation for treating workers well, paying wages on time, and not requiring mandatory overtime. He had devoted his life to the company and was preparing, at the time, to open a newly completed $5 million plant. His last act was to order that the machinery be sold so the workers could be paid. To allay Chinese concerns, Mattel met with Chinese officials and issued a press release clarifying that the recall of toys with magnets was a design flaw for which Mattel took full responsibility; and the press release also admitted that some of the toys that had been withdrawn from the market had low levels of lead that did not exceed the standards of the United States or any other country. This press release was perceived by some as an apology that exonerated the Chinese vendors. Senator Charles Schumer complained, "It's like a bank robber apologizing to his accomplice instead of the person who was robbed. . . . They're playing politics in China rather than doing what matters."[8] Mattel responded that its statement had been "mischaracterized" and replied, "Since Mattel toys are sold the world over, Mattel apologized to the Chinese today just as it has wherever its toys are sold."[9]

INTRODUCTION

Increasingly, business is being conducted across national boundaries. As large multinational corporations (MNCs) that have long operated in other countries are expanding their international presence, they are being joined by smaller domestic firms going abroad for the first time. Intense competition and profitable opportunities are forcing companies worldwide to enter the global marketplace, whether they are ready or not.

This development presents a host of ethical problems that managers are often unprepared to address. Some of these problems arise from the diversity of business standards around the world and especially from the lower standards that generally prevail in less-developed countries (LDCs). Companies are able to pay wages and impose working conditions that are shockingly low by U.S. standards, and yet they usually operate well above the standards of local firms. With extended supply chains, companies, such as Mattel (Case 14.1), find it difficult to ensure the integrity of their products. Environmental standards in LDCs are also invariably lower than those of more developed countries. MNCs may also operate in countries with repressive governments that routinely violate human rights and in so doing become complicit in their barbarous deeds. This is especially true in extractive industries, such as oil and minerals, since companies must go where the resources are located. And in countries with pervasive corruption, it may be difficult to conduct business without paying bribes, as witness the situation of Siemens AG (Case 14.3).

Additional problems result from the power of multinational corporations to affect the development of LDCs. MNCs often exploit the cheap labor, lower standards, and natural resources of LDCs without making commensurate investments that would advance local economic development. These problems are exacerbated when companies successfully avoid onerous regulations and their fair share of taxes. Even though LDCs invariably benefit to some extent from the activities of MNCs, the distribution of the gains is usually unequal. Critics ask whether it is fair for corporations from developed countries to return so little to the less-developed parts of the world from which they derive so much.

Operations in foreign countries also raise questions about the proper role of corporations in political affairs. Most multinationals consider themselves to be guests in host countries and refrain from influencing local governments. However, Google (Case 14.4) was widely criticized for enabling the Chinese government to censor the Internet and thereby maintain its dictatorial control. MNCs have an opportunity to play a constructive role in countries making the transition from a socialist, planned economy to a free market. The high levels of repression and corruption in some of these countries, though, present special challenges.

This chapter begins with the problem of determining the appropriate ethical standards for operating globally, especially when multinational companies conduct business in less-developed countries. Applying home country standards in all parts of the world is generally not morally required, but adopting host country standards for wages, working conditions, and other matters may be morally impermissible. What principles can guide us in finding a justifiable middle ground? These principles are then applied to the issue of wages and working conditions, especially in factories with which MNCs contract for the production of their goods. Although bribery is universally recognized as wrong, it, too, is a practice that is viewed differently around the world and may sometimes be an unavoidable condition of operating in some countries. Accordingly, a section is devoted to understanding the critical problem of foreign bribery. Finally, this chapter examines the challenges of dealing with repressive governments that engage in massive violations of human rights and concludes with the development of codes of ethics that attempt to guide responsible business conduct worldwide.

DIFFERENT STANDARDS

The main charge against multinational corporations is that they adopt a double standard, doing in less-developed countries what would be regarded as wrong if done in the developed world. However, many criticized practices are legal in the countries in question and may not be considered unethical by local standards. Should MNCs be bound by the prevailing morality of the home country and, in the case of American corporations, act everywhere as they do in the United States? Should they follow the practices of the host country and adopt the adage "When in Rome, do as the Romans do"? Or are there special ethical standards that apply when business is conducted across national boundaries? If so, what are these appropriate standards for international business?

Unfortunately, there are no easy answers to these questions. In some cases, the standards contained in American law and morality ought to be observed beyond our borders; in other cases, there is no moral obligation to do so. Similarly, it is morally permissible for managers of MNCs to follow local practice and "do as the Romans do" in some situations but not others. Even if there are special ethical standards for international business, these cannot be applied without taking into account differences in cultures and value systems, the levels of economic development, and the social, political, and legal structures of the foreign countries in which MNCs operate.

Absolutism versus Relativism

In answer to the question, "When in Rome, do what?" there are two extremes. The absolutist position is that business ought to be conducted in the same way the world over with no double standards. In particular, U.S. corporations ought to observe a single code of conduct in their dealings everywhere. This view might be expressed as, "When in Rome or anywhere else, do as you would at home."[10] The opposite extreme is relativism, which may be expressed in the familiar adage, "When in Rome, do as the Romans do." That is, the only guide for business conduct abroad is what is legally and morally accepted in any given country where a company operates.

Neither of these positions can be adopted without exception. The generally high level of conduct that follows from "When in Rome, do as you would at home" is not morally required of MNCs in all instances, and they should not be faulted for every departure from home country standards in doing business abroad. However, "When in Rome, do as the Romans do" is not wholly justified either. The mere fact that a country permits bribery, unsafe working conditions, exploitive wages, and violations of human rights does not mean that these practices are morally acceptable, even in that country. Even what is legal in a country may be difficult to determine, but ascertaining the accepted ethical standards is especially problematic. Bribery, for example, is almost universally condemned; but the people in some countries may consider it to be less offensive than those elsewhere, and it may be tolerated (but not approved) as an unavoidable practice. In such situations, what *is* the local standard with regard to bribery? The debates over absolutism and relativism revolve around four important points.

MORALLY RELEVANT DIFFERENCES. First, some conditions in other countries, especially those in less-developed parts of the world, are different in morally relevant ways. As a result, different standards may be morally permitted, indeed required. If Rome is a significantly different place, then standards that are appropriate at home do not necessarily apply there.

For example, pharmaceutical companies have been criticized for adopting a double standard in promoting drugs in less-developed countries with more indications for their use and fewer warnings about side effects. Although such practices may be designed solely to promote sales, some drugs may be medically appropriate in an LDC for a wider range of conditions. With regard to one powerful but dangerous antibiotic, which is prescribed in the United States only for very serious infections, doctors in Bolivia claim that this limited use is a luxury that Americans can afford because of generally better health. "Here," they say, "the people's general health is so poor that one must make an all out attack on illness."[11] Thus, an antibiotic that should be marketed in the United States with one set of indications might be justifiably sold abroad with a more extensive list.

More generally, the relative level of economic development must be taken into account in determining the appropriate standards for different countries. For example, health and safety standards in the developed world are very stringent, reflecting greater affluence and a greater ability and willingness to pay for more safety. The standards of these countries are not always appropriate in poorer, less-developed countries with fewer resources and more pressing needs. For example, the accident at the Union Carbide plant in Bhopal, India, in 1984, which exposed hundreds of thousands of poor local residents to 40 tons of highly toxic methyl isocyanate, resulted from some safety lapses that would be morally wrong in any country. Some low levels of safety may be regarded as violations of basic human rights anywhere. However, the design and operation of the Bhopal plant, which produced a much needed pesticide, Sevin, also resulted from trade-offs that were favored at the time by the Indian government to promote agricultural development. The plant was located in populous Madhya Pradesh state to increase employment there; manual rather than automatic gauges and valves were installed to create more jobs and cut costs; and a less-safe method for producing Sevin in which methyl isocyanate was an intermediate step was used to make the pesticide more affordable to poor farmers.[12] Although these trade-offs had tragic consequences, some of them might be considered reasonable given the urgent need of India for a cheap pesticide to grow sufficient food for its burgeoning population. Such trade-offs would not be made in the wealthier United States, but this country made different trade-offs between safety and other values at earlier stages of its economic development. Thomas Donaldson suggests that in evaluating a standard in a less-developed country, we should ask what standard would be adopted in our home country if it were at a comparable level of economic development.[13]

THE VARIETY OF ETHICAL OUTLOOKS.   Second, the absolutist position assumes that one country's standards are correct and that they should be imposed on people elsewhere, perhaps in conflict with their own moral values and principles. Acting on these assumptions ignores the wide variety of ethical outlooks in the world. Although some bedrock conceptions of right and wrong exist among people everywhere, many variations occur due to historical, political, economic, and cultural factors.

These differences are important, first, because they may affect the *meaning* of acts performed. For example, lavish gifts that would be considered bribes or kickbacks in the United States are an accepted and expected part of business in Japan and some other Asian countries. This difference in perception is due, in part, to the role that gift giving plays in building relationships, which are more critical in Asian business. Thus, giving gifts in Japan and China is usually understood not as an attempt to improperly influence a person's judgment but rather as a means to cement a legitimate relationship.[14] Similarly, whistle-blowing, which is generally viewed favorably in the United States as a moral protest, is regarded unfavorably in Japan and China as an act of disloyalty. In both cases, there are differences among people in various countries about the very meaning of what a person has done in giving a gift or blowing the whistle.

The impact of historical, political, and economic differences can be seen in Russian views of business ethics. The collapse of communism and the chaotic development of free markets in the former Soviet Union have created great uncertainty about ethical business behavior.[15] Although Russians and Americans agree on many matters, such as the importance of keeping one's word, paying debts, competing fairly, and avoiding extortion, they still differ in their ethical assessment of certain other matters. For example, less stigma is attached in Russia to making payments for favors (*blat*), falsifying information, and coordinating prices because of the prevalence of these practices in the previous planned economy and the lack of efficient markets that require arm's-length transactions, truthful information, and accurate prices. The lack of a workable legal system forces Russian managers to ignore senseless and contradictory regulations. Unfortunately, a certain amount of lawlessness is necessary for operating in the current business environment. On the other hand, Russia's socialist tradition leads them to criticize America's tolerance for exorbitant pay differentials and massive layoffs. As in Japan, whistle-blowing is viewed with suspicion, but for a different reason: It reminds Russians of the informer ethos that existed during the communist era.

In addition to historical, political, and economic differences, culture can deeply influence not only basic values but also the nature of a people's moral thinking. The most striking feature of Asian ethics, which is based on the teachings of Confucius or Confucianism, is the central role of long-term relationships. These rest on a high level of trust and reciprocity among all the parties and require careful attention to each party's interests so as to maintain harmony. In a society built on relationships, ethical obligations depend not on universal moral principles that characterize the western Judeo-Christian heritage but on the duties that attend specific roles and relationships. Accordingly, norms in such a society tend to be relative or situational rather than absolute and universal.[16] Instead of known rules that are applied equally to all, moral decisions are made on a case-by-case basis with attention to specifics.

An example of a Confucian-based ethical difference is the Chinese practice of *guanxi*, in which business depends on a web of long-term reciprocal relationships. Foreigners complain that because of *guanxi*, they cannot do business in China without first building the necessary long-term relationships, which may involve payments that appear to be bribes. Relationships are often the result of school and work ties that arise from decades of interactions and mutually beneficial exchanges that cannot be quickly duplicated by outsiders, who consequently feel that they are victims of cronyism. On the other hand, *guanxi* exists not only because of the Confucian emphasis on relationships but also because of the need for trust among business partners in a society without legally enforceable contracts and efficient, transparent markets, which are taken for granted in Europe and the United States. Thus, whether the practice of *guanxi* is ethical depends not only on the ethical value of relationships but also on their usefulness in overcoming a lack of trust in a society that has not yet developed reliable laws and markets.

THE RIGHT OF PEOPLE TO DECIDE. Third, the absolutist position denies the right of the people who are affected to decide on important matters of business conduct. The primary responsibility for setting standards should rest on the government and the people of the country in which business is being conducted. The argument that the people affected have a right to decide is not a form of ethical relativism. The fact that people approve of a certain practice does not make it right. The argument is rather an expression of respect for the right of people to govern their own affairs, rightly or wrongly. Imposing the standards of a developed country on LDCs is criticized by some as a form of "ethical imperialism."

The process of avoiding "ethical imperialism" and allowing the people affected to decide must be approached cautiously. A respect for the right of people to set their own standards does not automatically justify corporations in inflicting grave harm on innocent people, for example, or violating basic human rights. Furthermore, it may be difficult to determine what people have decided. Some countries lack the capacity to regulate effectively the activities of MNCs within their own borders. The governments of developing countries are, in many instances, no less committed than those in the United States and Europe to protecting their people against harm, but they do not always have the resources—the money, personnel, and institutions—to accomplish the task.

Some countries with the capacity to regulate multinationals lack the necessary will. MNCs, through the exercise of economic power, including bribery, are able to influence regulatory measures. The governments of LDCs are also careful not to offend the developed countries on which they depend for aid. Furthermore, the absence of laws against unethical business practices is sometimes part of a pattern of oppression by local elites that exists within the country itself, so that MNCs are taking advantage of the immorality of others when they follow the law of countries with corrupt governments.

Consequently, we need to ask whether a standard in a host country, if it is lower than that at home, truly represents the considered judgment of the people in question. Does it reflect the decision that they would make if they had the capacity to protect their own interests effectively? A genuine respect for the right of people to determine which standards to apply in their own country requires a careful and sympathetic consideration of what people would do under certain hypothetical conditions rather than what is actually expressed in the law, conventional morality, and commonly accepted practices.

REQUIRED CONDITIONS FOR DOING BUSINESS. Fourth, some practices may be justified where local conditions require that corporations engage in them as a condition of doing business. This point may be expressed by saying, "We don't necessarily agree with the Romans, but find it necessary to do things their way." American firms with contracts for projects in the Middle East, for example, have complied in many instances with requests not to station women and Jewish employees in those countries. Although discrimination of this kind is morally repugnant, it is (arguably) morally permissible when the alternative is to risk losing business in the Muslim world. A more complicated case is posed by the boycott of Israel, which was begun by the countries of the Arab League in 1945. In order to avoid blacklisting that would bar them from doing business with participating Arab League countries, many prominent U.S. companies cooperated by avoiding investment in Israel. Other firms, however, refused to cooperate with the boycott for ethical reasons. (Congress addressed this issue in 1977 by amending the Export Administration Act to prohibit American corporations from cooperating with the Arab League boycott against Israel.)

As with the other arguments, "There is no other way of doing business" cannot be accepted without some qualifications. The alternative is seldom to cease doing business; rather, the claim that a practice is "necessary" often means merely that it is the easiest or most convenient way of doing business. For example, the embargo against Israel greatly complicated the problem of doing business in the Middle East, but some companies were able to avoid cooperating with the boycott and still have business relationships in Arab countries. Similarly, during the period of apartheid in South Africa, some American companies defied the government and integrated their workforces. There are some situations, however, in which a company is morally obligated to withdraw if there is no other way to do business. Some companies have refused to do business in certain countries because they believe that involvement in an immoral system cannot be justified. (This matter is discussed later in this chapter in the section on human rights abuses.)

GUIDELINES FOR MULTINATIONALS

If neither home country nor host country standards provide complete guidance, what rules or principles should multinational corporations follow? Three kinds of guidelines have been offered, based on considerations of rights, welfare, and fairness or justice. All of these are relevant moral concepts; the challenge is determining exactly how they apply to international business.

RIGHTS. Thomas Donaldson has proposed that corporations have an obligation to respect certain rights, namely those that ought to be recognized as fundamental international rights.[17] MNCs are not obligated to extend all the rights of U.S. citizens to people everywhere in the world, but there are certain basic rights that no person or institution, including a corporation, is morally permitted to violate. Fundamental international rights are roughly the same as natural or human rights, discussed in Chapter 3, and some of these are given explicit recognition in such documents as the United Nations Universal Declaration of Human Rights, the International Covenant on Social, Economic, and Cultural Rights, and the International Covenant on Civil and Political Rights.

The main problem with a principle to respect fundamental international rights (or fundamental rights, for short) is specifying the rights in question. Even undeniable human rights that create an obligation for some person or institution, such as the government of a country, are not always relevant to a multinational corporation. Moreover, observing a right ranges from merely not depriving people of some protection to ensuring the fulfillment of a right. For example, everyone has a right to subsistence, but a corporation may be under no obligation to feed the hungry in a country where it operates, especially if doing so has no relation to its business activity. It has an obligation, however, not to contribute directly to starvation by, say, destroying farmland. In general, Donaldson claims, a corporation is morally bound only by those minimal duties such that "the persistent failure to observe [them] would deprive the corporation of its moral right to exist" and not by maximal duties whose fulfillment would be "praiseworthy but not absolutely mandatory."[18]

Donaldson suggests the following fundamental rights as a moral minimum:

1. The right to freedom of physical movement
2. The right to ownership of property
3. The right to freedom from torture
4. The right to a fair trial
5. The right to nondiscriminatory treatment
6. The right to physical security
7. The right to freedom of speech and association
8. The right to minimal education
9. The right to political participation
10. The right to subsistence[19]

Sample applications of these rights, according to Donaldson, include failing to provide safety equipment to protect employees from serious hazards (the right to physical security); using coercive tactics to prevent workers from organizing (the right to freedom of speech and association); employing child labor (the right to minimal education); and bribing government officials to violate their duty or seeking to overthrow democratically elected governments (the right to political participation).

Donaldson recognizes that it may be impossible to observe all these rights, especially in less-developed countries where human rights violations are routine. However, insofar as the acceptance of a practice in a host country is due to its low level of economic development, we can perform what he calls the *rational empathy* test: Would we, in our home country, regard the practice as morally permissible under conditions of similar economic development? This test employs home-country standards but asks us to to apply them in a hypothetical situation of a lower level of development, which may have prevailed in the past.[20]

Although Donaldson's list of fundamental rights sets some minimal conditions for ethical behavior, it is not a complete guide for managers. First, the bearing of these rights on controversial questions is not wholly clear. For example, no one disputes that causing starvation by destroying farmland is a human rights violation. But what does the right to subsistence tell us about cases in which multinationals convert land from the production of domestic crops to foods for export? Even though the MNC is acting within its rights within a free market as a property owner, and even though the country may benefit from a more productive use of the land, the ability of local people to feed themselves may be severely curtailed. Has the multinational violated the right of these people to subsistence? To this kind of question, Donaldson's rights-based approach offers little guidance.

Second, many of the most difficult moral questions in international business do not involve rights at all. Although rights violations by corporations receive great public attention, they are relatively infrequent. The critical issues at the forefront of global business today focus more on abuses of power by multinationals and on their failure to aid developing countries. For example, the OECD Guidelines for Multinational Enterprises, adopted by the Organization for Economic

Cooperation and Development (OECD), covers such matters as competing fairly, disclosing information, paying taxes, considering countries' balance-of-payment and credit policies, utilizing appropriate technologies, and aiding economic development. In general, the goal of the OECD guidelines is to achieve a smoothly functioning global economic system that spreads the benefits widely, rather than to protect people's rights.

In sum, guidelines based on human rights provide a bedrock moral minimum. However, the application of rights-based guidelines are uncertain in more controversial situations where we are most in need of guidance, and they are inapplicable to many other pressing matters.

WELFARE. Richard DeGeorge offers seven basic guidelines for multinational corporations that cover a variety of moral considerations, including rights. However, several of these rules concern avoiding harm and providing benefits. His guidelines are as follows:

1. Multinationals should do no intentional direct harm.
2. Multinationals should produce more good than harm for the host country.
3. Multinationals should contribute by their activity to the host country's development.
4. Multinationals should respect the human rights of their employees.
5. To the extent that local culture does not violate ethical norms, multinationals should respect the local culture and work with and not against it.
6. Multinationals should pay their fair share of taxes.
7. Multinationals should cooperate with the local government in developing and enforcing just background institutions.[21]

The first three of these guidelines express in different ways a duty to consider the welfare of people in a host country. The first, do no intentional direct harm, is vacuous if it excludes all actions with a legitimate business purpose. No company intends to do harm; any harm results rather from its regular business activity. However, a company can engage in such activity knowing that harm will result. In some instances, this harm may be wrong, as when a firm produces oil in such a way that the land is polluted. On the other hand, a firm might open a plant that, because of its efficiency, will drive local competitors out of business. This latter result, unlike the former, is not wrong but is merely the working of market forces. In a well-functioning economy, more efficient producers should replace the less efficient. For the same reason, polluting oil production (Is there any other kind?) may be acceptable if the benefits outweigh the costs. What DeGeorge's first guideline presumably excludes is pollution that results from unjustifiably low standards. What standards ought to be adopted, however, is a question not merely about the harm done but about the benefit gained—and also about how these ought to be distributed.

The same problems afflict DeGeorge's second guideline, do more good than harm. Economic theory tells us that all voluntary exchange results in more good than harm for the reason that no one makes a trade that is not beneficial. Thus, as long as a multinational corporation offers employment in a factory and workers in a developing country are willing to accept, then everyone is better off. Controversial cases like that of Nike in Indonesia raise two questions. First, how much more good than harm should a multinational bring to a country like Indonesia? And, second, does it matter that multinationals are often able to use their market power to reap most of the benefit, leaving the host country with a narrow balance of good over harm? The answers to these questions depend not on whether more good than harm is produced but on whether the outcome is obtained justly.

Multinationals are criticized primarily in cases where they take more than a fair share by exploiting their superior position in an imperfect market. A developed country, such as the United States, attempts to maintain perfect markets by preventing monopolies and other conditions that reduce fair competition. However, the marketplace that MNCs encounter in less-developed countries is highly imperfect. Under such circumstances, some outcomes may be criticized for resulting from unfair competition. As Manuel Velasquez observes, DeGeorge's approach "fails to take seriously the importance of justice in evaluating the activities of multinationals."[22]

JUSTICE.   Much of the criticism of multinational corporations rests on considerations of justice. Even when MNCs respect human rights and produce more good than harm, their activities may still be criticized for being unfair or unjust. This is true even for the outcomes of voluntary market exchanges when they occur in imperfect markets, as when a multinational exploits a monopoly position.

One kind of unfairness cited by critics is the often one-sided division of the benefits from foreign investment. Certainly, the gap between rich and poor countries is an urgent moral concern, and multinational corporations have much to offer. Thus, the third of DeGeorge's guidelines is that "[m]ultinationals should contribute by their activity to the host country's development." The main questions, however, are who should act and what should be done? National governments and world organizations are the primary actors, and it is questionable what role multinationals should play. What should they do to aid development other than engage in business activity?

The answer to this question depends, in part, on how we answer the second question about what should be done. What is the most effective strategy for aiding developing countries? The main approach being taken today is to increase foreign investment and export production in an increasingly integrated world economy. If this development—generally called *globalization*— is the most effective strategy, then multinational corporations can contribute best by being efficient—but responsible!—businesses. Indeed, if MNCs are expected to expend resources on development, they may then choose not to invest in poorer countries, thus depriving them of any aid. However, opponents of globalization, such as the protesters at meetings of the World Trade Organization (WTO), propose other strategies for development that would place greater responsibilities on multinational corporations.

Another kind of unfairness is violating the rules of the marketplace, which is to say engaging in unfair competition and otherwise taking unfair advantage. One example is the ability of multinationals to avoid paying taxes by means of *transfer pricing*. Transfer prices are the values assigned to raw materials and unfinished products that one subsidiary of a company sells to another. Because transfer prices are set by the company and not the market, they can be raised or lowered so that most of the profits are recorded in countries with low tax rates. This use of transfer pricing is facilitated by the fact that multinationals are usually able to avoid disclosure of the relevant financial information. As a result, host countries often have little knowledge of a company's true financial situation.

Tax avoidance through transfer pricing is a critical problem for both developed and developing countries. Approximately a third of world trade or $1.6 trillion takes place within firms, so the possible loss of tax revenues is enormous. Consequently, the major countries of the world are trying to tighten accounting standards to prevent abuses. The OECD Guidelines for Multinational Enterprises requires firms to disclose financial statements on a regular basis and provide relevant information requested by taxing authorities. Furthermore, the Guidelines states that an enterprise should "[r]efrain from making use of the particular facilities available to them, such as transfer pricing which does not conform to arm's length standard, for modifying in ways contrary to national laws the tax base on which members of the group are assessed." This arm's-length standard is feasible when a market exists for the good in question, and for other goods a market price can be approximated by calculating the costs of production.[23]

If avoiding taxes by means of transfer pricing violates no laws, why should multinationals not take full advantage of this opportunity? The same question can be asked of paying bribes, offering kickbacks, and similar practices. One answer, offered by Norman E. Bowie, is that these actions violate the rules that are required for markets to operate. The very possibility of market exchanges depends on the general observance of certain rules of honesty, trust, and fair dealing. Because businesses benefit from the marketplace that these rules make possible, they are taking an unfair advantage, being a freeloader so to speak, by simultaneously violating these rules. "Contrary behavior," Bowie writes, "is ultimately inconsistent and self-defeating."[24]

An obvious difficulty is determining the essential rules for markets to operate. That problem aside, is avoiding taxes by means of transfer pricing really a violation of market morality? One might argue that prices, which play a critical role in markets, should be set in ways that have a clear economic purpose. Setting prices for no other purpose than reducing taxes is not a genuine economic activity but a sham transaction. Indeed, whether a transaction serves a reasonable business purpose is a test that U.S. courts use to determine whether a tax shelter is legal.

Individually, the concepts of rights, welfare, and justice do not provide complete guidance for MNCs in addressing the many moral challenges of operating in a global environment; but each one is appropriate for certain problems, and used together they form a powerful resource. The successful use of these guidelines depends on a careful analysis of any given ethical problem to determine the relevant moral considerations and the specific factual details of the situation. These guidelines cannot be applied, moreover, without a deep understanding of and respect for the local context—the history, politics, economy, and culture—of the country in question. The guidelines can gain further force and clarity by being incorporated into international codes of ethics to which multinational corporations can subscribe.

International Codes of Ethics

Given the diversity of ethical outlooks in the world, is it possible to agree on a single code of ethics for business worldwide? Such a goal must be achievable if globalization is to succeed. The theologian Hans Küng has observed that "the very phenomenon of globalization makes it clear that there must also be a globalization of ethics."[25] Substantial agreement is being achieved through a number of codes that have been developed by international organizations involving governments, religious bodies, and private individuals.

The foundational document for human rights is the 1948 United Nations Universal Declaration on Human Rights. In 1966, the United Nations adopted two agreements which have subsequently been ratified by the major countries of the world: the International Covenant on Social, Economic, and Cultural Rights and the International Covenant on Civil and Political Rights. Since 1972, the United Nations has been developing a code of conduct for multinational corporations, which has yet to be completed or adopted. However, in 1999, UN Secretary-General Kofi Annan challenged world business leaders to "embrace and enact" the Global Compact, which consists of ten principles covering human rights, labor, anticorruption, and the environment.

The International Labour Organization, which dates from 1919 and is now a specialized agency of the United Nations, sets many international standards, including those of the Tripartite Declaration of Principles concerning Multinational Enterprises and Social Policy (1977). More recently, the Organization for Economic Cooperation and Development, whose members are the more developed countries of the world, has adopted the OECD Guidelines for Multinational Enterprises. Several interfaith religious bodies have developed codes. The most prominent are the Principles for Global Corporate Responsibility, adopted by the U.S.-based Interfaith Center on Corporate Responsibility and similar organizations in Great Britain, Ireland, and Canada, and the Interfaith Declaration on International Business Ethics, which resulted from a dialog among Christians, Jews, and Muslims.[26] A group of world business leaders, meeting in Caux, Switzerland, developed the Caux Roundtable Principles for Business. These codes have many guidelines in common and cover the areas of employment practices, consumer protection, environmental preservation, involvement in politics, bribery, and basic human rights. The emerging order has been described as a "policy regime" to distinguish it from conventional regulation.[27] Regulation within a state consists of precise, legally-enforced rules that are developed to address most foreseeable circumstances. In the absence of international government, the main alternative is the development of mutually accepted norms that serve to coordinate global business activity. A policy regime provides everyone with a reasonable set of expectations about how others will behave. The various codes that make up a policy regime do not have the force of law but still represent publicly declared commitments that have some binding force.

A policy regime is enforced primarily by the advantages of cooperation and the threat of retaliation for not cooperating. Although compliance is voluntary, countries and companies usually find it in their interest to abide by the major codes. However, these codes also draw strength from their ethical force; that is, the widespread recognition that the guidelines represent universal values further contributes to their observance. Consequently, codes for international business are more likely to be effective when they have considerable moral authority. William C. Frederick finds four sources from which codes derive moral authority. These are (1) *national sovereignty*, which underlies strictures against interfering in the political process of a host country and bribing foreign officials; (2) *equality*, which supports nondiscriminatory treatment on the basis of race, sex, and nationality; (3) *market integrity*, which requires property rights, contracts, fair competition, and the other conditions for free markets to operate; and (4) *human rights*.[28] Any guidelines not supported by these sources—to aid in a country's development, for example—do not have strong moral force and hence are less effective.

The guidelines for multinationals and various international codes of ethics which are discussed in this section are applied in the following sections to the problems of wages and working conditions, foreign bribery, and countries with repressive governments that violate human rights.

WAGES AND WORKING CONDITIONS

In 1998, Nike was the leader in the sports shoe industry, with annual sales of $9.5 billion and a 40 percent share of the American sneaker market, when it became a lightning rod for worldwide protests over alleged "sweatshop" conditions in factories across Southeast Asia. In a May 1998 speech, Phil Knight, the founder and CEO, admitted that "the Nike product has become synonymous with slave wages, forced overtime, and arbitrary abuse."[29] How did a prominent company, whose "swoosh" logo is a symbol for the "Just Do It" spirit, come to be associated with deplorable labor practices?

Nike's phenomenal success is due to a visionary strategy which was developed by Phil Knight during his student days at the Stanford Business School. The strategy involves outsourcing all manufacturing to contractors in low-wage countries and pouring the company's resources into high-profile marketing. One Nike vice president observed, "We don't know the first thing about manufacturing. We are marketers and designers."[30] Central to Nike's marketing effort was placing the Nike "swoosh" on the uniforms of collegiate and professional athletes and enlisting such superstars as Michael Jordan and Tiger Woods.

When Nike was founded in 1964, the company contracted with manufacturers in Japan, but as wages in that country rose, Nike transferred production to contractors in Korea and Taiwan. By 1982, more than 80 percent of Nike shoes were made in these two countries, but rising wages there led Nike to urge its contractors to move their plants to Southeast Asia. By 1990, most Nike production was based in Indonesia, Vietnam, and China. In the early 1990s, young Indonesian women working in plants under contract with Nike started at 15 cents an hour. With mandatory overtime, which was often imposed, more experienced workers might make $2 for a grueling 11-hour day. The Indonesian minimum wage was raised in 1991 from $1.06 for a seven-hour day to $1.24, only slightly above the $1.22 that the government calculated as necessary for "minimum physical needs." The women lived in fear of their often brutal managers, who berated them for failing to meet quotas and withheld pay to enforce discipline. Indonesian labor laws, lax to begin with, were flouted with impunity by contractors, since the government was eager to attract foreign investment. Workers often toiled in crowded, poorly ventilated factories, surrounded by machinery and toxic chemicals. There was little effective union activity in Indonesia, and labor strikes were firmly suppressed by the army.

Nike's initial response to growing criticism was to deny any responsibility for the practices of its contractors. These are independent companies from which Nike merely buys shoes. The workers are not Nike employees, and their wages are above the legal minimum and the prevailing market rate. When asked about labor strife in some factories supplying Nike, John

Woodman, the company's general manager for Indonesia, said that he did not know the causes and added, "I don't know that I need to know."[31] Mr. Woodman defended Nike by arguing, "Yes, they are low wages. But we've come in here and given jobs to thousands of people who wouldn't be working otherwise."[32]

Public concern about multinational corporations has focused in recent years on manufacturing companies, primarily in the footwear, apparel, toy, and electronics industries, and their relations with foreign contractors. Virtually all major manufacturers of consumer and light industrial products have adopted the strategy pioneered by Nike and outsourced the actual assembly to contractors in Southeast Asia and Central America. This development benefits consumers and industrial buyers everywhere by lowering the cost of goods, and jobs are created in countries that desperately need them. Overall, the manufacture of goods in countries with low labor costs is advantageous to developed and developing countries alike.

To many critics, however, the benefits must be weighed against a long list of wrongs that include very low wages and substandard working conditions, as well as the use of child labor, lack of contribution to local development, and association with repressive regimes. Some of the factories operated by multinationals and their foreign contractors are alleged to be "sweatshops" of the kind that operated in developed countries until the passage of protective legislation in the early twentieth century. The critics also question the ability of foreign contracting to advance economic development. Instead of improving the lives of people, they charge, the contracting system leads to greater misery for the bulk of the population and to a wider gap between the rich and the poor. Although outsourcing may benefit developed countries by the cheaper products that are imported, these countries may be harmed when the exported jobs create unemployment at home.

Setting Wage Standards

How should the standards for wages and working conditions be determined? One answer is that these standards should be set by the market. In developed countries, the determination of wages and working conditions results primarily from the competition among employers for desirable workers, which compels them to offer high wages and good working conditions. On this view, there is nothing unjust about jobs with lower pay and poorer working conditions. As long as workers are willing to accept employment on the terms offered, then any arrangement is justified. On this view, no wage can be too low in a free market. However, using the market to determine the standards for wages and working conditions in developing countries encounters two obstacles.

First, developed countries do not rely solely on the market but set certain minimum conditions by law, such as minimum wage laws, fair labor standards, and health and safety regulations. These conditions reflect, in part, the recognition of certain human rights that ought to be observed in all economic activity. Thus, one rationale for minimum wage laws is that it is unjust to pay workers less than a certain amount. That is, some wages are unjustifiably low, even if enough workers would accept them. Although multinational corporations and their foreign contractors generally pay the legal minimum wage in the countries where they operate, this amount often provides only a basic subsistence for one person, if that. Consequently, critics argue that the standard should be a "living wage" that enables a worker to live with dignity and support a family.

The second obstacle to using the market to set wages and working conditions is the possibility that the conditions for a free market are lacking. In particular, the mass of unemployed, desperately poor people in less-developed countries constitutes a pool of laborers willing to accept bare subsistence wages. The market for labor in any given country may also be artificially low because of political repression that prevents workers from organizing. Although the role of correcting such market failures generally falls to national governments—by enacting minimum wage laws, for example—this form of protection is often uncertain in less-developed countries.

Consequently, we need to consider the extent to which market forces should be allowed to operate in the setting of wages and working conditions and the extent to which principles of human rights ought to be applied. Specifically, should multinationals and foreign contractors be guided only by the market as long as they observe local laws? Or, should they observe higher standards than either the law or the market dictates, guided perhaps by certain human rights principles? In some instances, workplace abuses—such as degrading punishment, forced overtime, and confinement to company quarters—have little or no economic justification. Although the wrongness of these abuses is not in question, we still need to ask whether a company such as Nike is responsible for the abusive practices of its foreign contractors and, if it is responsible, what steps a company should take to prevent these abuses.

The wages paid by multinationals and their foreign contractors are usually above the minimum wage and the prevailing market rate. As a result, the jobs in these factories generally pay better than work in local enterprises, and regular employment in the formal economy is vastly superior to work in the informal sector, which includes agriculture, domestic service, and small, unregulated manufacture. Even so, the wages paid for factory work are seldom sufficient to provide what the nation's government calculates as the minimum for a decent standard of living or the minimum physical needs for one person, let alone a family. In many poor countries of Southeast Asia and Central America, the minimum wage set by law is below the official poverty level.

Critics observe that the labor cost for a pair of shoes or a shirt is usually a few cents and that paying a few cents more would add little to the ultimate price. However, this observation overlooks the point that the labor of any one worker may earn only a few cents, but much more labor goes into a pair of shoes or a shirt than that required for assembly. If all the workers who make the raw materials and provide other resources involved in production are considered, then paying each one a few cents more per item for his or her contribution adds up to a considerable amount. Moreover, economists warn that raising the pay scales in a developing country has serious adverse consequences. Well-intentioned efforts to improve the condition of factory workers will ultimately reduce the number of jobs and the level of foreign investment. If a government raises the minimum wage or multinationals and foreign contractors are pressured to pay above-market wages, the result will be a reduced incentive to relocate jobs from higher-wage countries. Because higher-wage countries have more productive workers and a better infrastructure for manufacturing, firms will have little reason to move to a less-developed country unless it offers significantly lower labor costs.

This economic argument shows, first, why less-developed countries should not raise the minimum wage beyond the market value of its labor. In a developed country, raising the minimum wage generally benefits low-wage workers without much effect on others (although some argue that low-wage workers are harmed by reducing the number of jobs available), but the effect in a less-developed country is different. A relatively small minority of urban workers, who already make above-average wages, may benefit, but the vast majority will suffer for lack of jobs, and the economy will not develop for lack of foreign investment. For this reason, the economist Jagdish Bhagwati contends, "Requiring a minimum wage in an overpopulated, developing country . . . may actually be morally wicked."[33]

Low labor costs constitute a competitive advantage for a poor country, and attracting investment on this basis provides jobs that can lead to greater development. Indeed, formerly low-wage countries, such as Korea, Taiwan, and Malaysia, have successfully employed this strategy for creating higher-paying jobs. If firms do not take advantage of the low-cost labor in countries like Indonesia and Vietnam, then they are depriving these countries of the opportunity to use their main competitive edge, namely unemployed workers, to begin the process of development. This competitive advantage is also lost if multinational corporations and their foreign contractors are required, say by public pressure, to pay above-market wages: The result will be that companies facing such pressure will remain in higher-wage countries where labor is generally more productive and the infrastructure better.

This argument about wages also applies to working conditions inasmuch as both are matters of cost. According to a World Bank report, "Reducing hazards in the workplace is costly, and typically the greater the reduction the more it costs. . . . As a result, setting standards too high can actually lower workers' welfare."[34] One reason for this outcome is that investment to improve working conditions may come at the expense of wages. More significantly, if higher standards inhibit foreign investment, then fewer jobs are created and more of those available are in local industries with lower pay and working conditions.

The dispute between those who advocate paying the market rate for labor and those favoring a "living wage" is not over the ultimate end, which is to improve the welfare of people in developing countries. The difference lies in the appropriate means. Economists argue that requiring higher wages is counterproductive; it harms the very people we are trying to benefit. The only path to prosperity is economic development, and this requires an attractive climate for foreign investment. Proponents of a "living wage" believe, on the other hand, that payment of wages above a certain level is morally required. To offer less than a "living wage" is to unjustly exploit an opportunity for cheap labor.

One difficulty with the economists' position is that it fails to consider the possibility of exploitation. It assumes that whatever wages people are willing to accept is just. However, most of the jobs in question are among the best paying in these less-developed countries, so the case for exploitation is weak. Moreover, the "living wage" position seems to entail that no job at all is preferable to one below the living-wage standard. Although developing countries are forced to keep wages low in their competition with each other to attract foreign investment, they still seem to prefer all the low-wage jobs they can get, regardless of whether they pay a "living wage."

Toward a Solution

In contrast to the issue of wages, which remains controversial, there is general agreement on standards for working conditions. When the television personality Kathie Lee Gifford was confronted in 1996 with evidence that the line of clothes she endorsed was made in Honduras by young girls 13 and 14 years old, working 20-hour days for 31 cents an hour, she resolved to correct these abuses. The same year, *Life* magazine published a photograph of a 12-year-old boy in Pakistan stitching a Nike soccer ball. Phil Knight replied that "Nike has zero tolerance for under-age labor." Reports on contractors for other American companies described women who were confined to factory compounds, berated and beaten for violating rules or failing to meet quotas, forbidden to use toilets, and fired for protesting or attempting to organize. In some instances, young women have been forced to take contraceptive pills or undergo pregnancy tests, and they have been dismissed for becoming pregnant. Many factories lack adequate ventilation, sanitation facilities, medical supplies, and fire safety provisions, and workers often have little protection from dangerous machines and toxic chemicals.

For many companies, the first step has been to adopt codes of conduct for their own operations and those of contractors. In 1992, Nike adopted a "Code of Conduct" and a "Memorandum of Understanding" which are included with all contracts. The Nike code forbids hiring anyone under 18 in shoe manufacture and under 16 for producing clothing (unless higher ages are mandated by law). It stipulates that workers be paid the higher of the legal minimum wage or the prevailing wage, with a clear, written accounting of all hours and deductions. Although forced overtime is permitted, provided employees are informed and fully compensated according to local law, the code requires one day off in seven and no more than 60 hours a week. Nike also developed a comprehensive Management of Environment, Safety and Health (MESH) that provides for safety standards, a safety committee in each factory, and free personal protective equipment for at-risk employees.

Although these actions addressed the major areas of concern, critics charged that Nike had not gone far enough in setting high standards. In 1990, Reebok, a Nike competitor, adopted a far-reaching human rights policy and inserted human rights language in its contracts. Reebok also committed itself to auditing its contractors for compliance with the human rights policy. Nike, too, agreed to auditing by hiring the firm Ernst & Young to conduct site visits of its contractors. In 1996, Nike also hired the civil rights leader Andrew Young to investigate factories in Asia and to report his findings. Both efforts were denigrated by critics, who challenged the competence of these parties to conduct thorough audits and questioned their independence inasmuch as Nike was footing the bill. Nike's commitment was further undermined when an internal Ernst & Young report, leaked to the press in 1997, revealed serious health and safety issues in a Vietnamese factory.

The challenges of managing foreign contractors are beyond the capability of any single company. First, any firm that invests resources when its competitors do not is put at a competitive disadvantage. Second, each firm deals with thousands of contractors, which in turn manufacture for many brands. The only solution, therefore, is an industry-wide effort. The first initiative occurred in 1997 with the launch of the Apparel Industry Partnership (AIP), which Nike immediately joined. Convened by the White House, a group of industry, labor, consumer, and human rights leaders committed themselves to develop a strong workplace code of ethics with internal monitoring and an independent, external monitoring system. The AIP was succeeded the next year by the Fair Labor Association (FLA), which has preserved the same goals. In response to the concern of college students, the Worker Rights Consortium (WRC) was organized to address specifically the conditions under which collegiate apparel with a school's logo is manufactured.

The experiences of the FLA and the WRC reveal substantial agreement on principles and standards, although the issue of a "living wage" has been divisive. The main stumbling block has been monitoring. The practical difficulties of monitoring tens of thousands of contractors around the globe—not to mention the cost of $3,000 to $6,000 for each factory visit—is daunting enough, but the participants have sharply disagreed on issues of principle. For starters, who should do the monitoring? Accounting firms often lack expertise in local situations, whereas activist groups may not be wholly objective. What qualifications should monitors have? How should audits be conducted? Should audits be unannounced or scheduled in advance? Should all of a firm's contractors be audited or only a sample? Should the reports be made public? What actions should be taken when violations are discovered?

As these questions suggest, the solution to the problem of sweatshops requires a sustained, committed effort by all concerned parties. Considerable progress has been made on working conditions—but not on wages. A *New York Times* article profiled a woman who was fired in 1995 for protesting conditions at a factory in El Salvador. Six year later, the woman returned to work at the factory where workers now enjoy coffee breaks in a terrace cafeteria and work in clean, breezy surroundings, but she earns only 60 cents an hour, 5 cents more than before.[35]

Child labor presents an especially thorny issue. Although an estimated 150 million children under the age of 14 work worldwide, less than 5 percent of these make goods for export. The vast majority are employed in the informal economy which contains the most dangerous jobs. Virtually every country bans child labor, but enforcement is often ineffective. Although multinationals should abide by the law and refrain from employing children, the main challenge is how to deal with existing factories that employ children. A *New York Times* editorial observes, "American consumers are right to insist that the goods we buy are not made with child labor. But these efforts will backfire if children kicked out of these factories drift to more hazardous occupations."[36]

In response to this problem, the International Labour Organization has worked with governments and businesses to establish special schools for approximately 10,000 children who worked in garment factories and to pay their parents for the lost wages. Ultimately, the solution to the problem of child labor is not merely to prohibit the employment of underage workers but also to provide schooling for children and jobs for parents so that child labor is no longer an economic necessity.

FOREIGN BRIBERY

Bribery is one of the most common and controversial issues that multinational corporations face. Bribery is universally condemned, and no government in the world legally permits the bribery of its own officials. However, bribery exists to some extent in every country and is endemic to more than a few. The main ethical question about bribery is whether companies are justified in making corrupt payments when they believe them to be necessary for doing business in a corrupt environment. Although the demand for a bribe may be unethical, is it unethical to give in to a demand? Those who pay bribes often appeal to the slogan, "We don't agree with the Romans, but find it necessary to do things their way." Others may defend their actions by citing the fine line between outright bribery and other kinds of more innocent payments. Some even argue that bribery, under certain conditions, is a beneficial practice. The United States has legally prohibited certain kinds of payments since the passage of the Foreign Corrupt Practices Act (FCPA) in 1977, and more recently other developed countries have agreed to make payments to foreign officials illegal. Such laws require some justification, though, since they put the companies of these countries at a disadvantage in competing with less scrupulous rivals.

The issue of bribery is far from simple. First, the term "bribe" is vague. It applies to many different kinds of payments with varying interpretations, ranging from gift giving and influence peddling to kickbacks and extortion. There is need, therefore, to develop a definition and make some distinctions, as well as to understand the factors that foster bribery and allow it to flourish. An understanding of these causes enables us not only to explain where bribery is more likely to occur but also to develop means to reduce it. Second, this section addresses the question of what is wrong with bribery and the arguments, advanced by some, that question the harm. Finally, the means for combating bribery, including the U.S. Foreign Corrupt Practices Act, and its justification are discussed.

What is Bribery?

The FCPA forbids American corporations to offer or make any payment to a foreign official for the purpose of "influencing any act or decision of such foreign official in his official capacity or of inducing such foreign official to do or omit to do any act in violation of the lawful duty of such official" in order to obtain or retain business.[37] This legal prohibition accords with standard philosophical definitions of bribery.[38] The key point is that a bribe is a payment made with an intention to corrupt and accepted in a way that is corrupting. More specifically, a public official has a duty to make all decisions in the interest of a country's people, and a briber makes a payment with the intention of inducing an official to violate that duty. This violation of duty is a form of corruption. A corrupt official, the bribee, is one who willingly accepts a payment—often after a request or a demand—that would lead him or her to act in a way that violates a duty. A bribe occurs once an offered payment has been accepted, regardless of whether the bribee acts as the briber intends. Indeed, such a failure to achieve the desired result is one of the risks of offering a bribe to a corrupt official since such a dishonest person is not easily trusted.

In a common scenario, bribes are made in cash payments either directly in "under-the-table" transactions or indirectly through deposit in a bank account. However, the forms of payment, which are numerous, can include seemingly legitimate arrangements in which a relative or confederate is hired, usually for little or no work; goods or services are purchased from a favored supplier, usually at inflated prices; the official or another party becomes a partner in a joint venture, usually sharing in the profit but making no investment; or a contribution is made to some philanthropy that is usually a front for personal gain. Typically, bribes are not paid directly by employees of a bribing company but funneled indirectly through locally hired consultants or joint-venture partners, and funds for the bribes may be disguised as consulting fees or joint-venture expenses. The purposes for which bribes are paid are similarly diverse. In addition to the approvals of bids or sales, which are commonly sought by bribery, bribers may be seeking licenses to operate, access to scarce or subsidized resources, favorable legal rulings, avoidance of investigations or political pressures, and the like. The only common factor is that what is sought is something within the decision-making authority of a public official who has the discretion to grant or withhold it.

Like other kinds of misconduct, the incidence of bribery is a function of the opportunity presented, the amount to be gained, and the likelihood of success—or alternatively the risk of prosecution. Consequently, bribery is more likely to occur in countries in which the approval of government officials is required for doing business. In a country with well-developed laws and regulations that allow little discretion for public officials, and with a small public sector that leaves most business to be conducted in markets by private individuals and corporations, there is little opportunity for bribes to be demanded or offered. On the other hand, in a state-dominated economy in which much business is conducted with the national or local government, where public officials make key decisions about the purchase of goods, the approval of projects, and the like, great opportunities are created for bribes to be demanded and/or offered.

For example, a bribe might be paid not only to gain approval of a bid for the operation of, say, a large construction project, but also to gain advance information about the bid requirements or to shape the terms of the bid requests to favor one bidder. Economies in which multiple licenses are needed to operate a business, or in which the state controls access to scarce or subsidized resources, are also fertile conditions for bribery to occur. Bribes may also be paid to avoid costs, such as those associated with paying taxes or complying with regulations. Bribes are more likely to occur when the risk of discovery and apprehension are low because of lax or erratic enforcement. Even a high risk for accepting bribes may be offset by the size of the bribe offered, which leads to the dilemma that more vigilant enforcement of antibribery laws may reduce small payments but increase the amount that other officials demand in order to make bribery worth the risk.

What's Wrong with Bribery?

The immorality of demanding or accepting bribes is implicit in the definition of bribery: A government official is violating a duty, which in itself is a wrong. In addition, inducing such a violation by offering a bribe is commonly recognized as wrong as well. Corrupting others is as wrong as being corrupt oneself. Beyond these obvious points, however, lies the more relevant question of whether the wrongfulness of bribery is of sufficient gravity to make it an object of concern. That is, how serious is the problem of bribery? If bribery is relatively harmless or even somewhat beneficial, then there is no reason to make it illegal by such means as the FCPA and to expend great resources combating it.

Some economists have argued that bribery has the capacity to aid development by introducing an element of efficiency by "greasing the wheels" in an otherwise inefficient economy.[39] These defenders of bribery begin with the observation that in many developing economies, the government officials and other elites tend to dominate the economy for their own benefit, and they are often indifferent or hostile to foreign investors and local entrepreneurs, who may upset the cozy status quo. When outsiders are able to overcome this bureaucratic inertia by paying bribes—which they can afford to do because of their greater efficiency in conducting business—they aid development by putting resources to their most productive use. Indeed, competition among potential bribers itself is a factor in promoting efficiency since the party that is able to afford the highest bribe is likely to be the most efficient producer. Combating bribery, on this view, may impede development by maintaining an inefficient status quo. Thus, the political scientist Samuel P. Huntington observes, "In terms of economic growth, the only thing worse than a society with a rigid, over-centralized, dishonest bureaucracy is one with a rigid, over-centralized and honest bureaucracy."[40]

The "greasing the wheels" argument does not give sufficient weight to the full costs of bribery in a less-developed country.[41] First, bribery reduces the resources available in an economy when elites transfer money out of the country into secret foreign bank accounts. In the case of some African countries, this loss has amounted to billions of dollars. Second, money for bribes need not come from the greater efficiency of the bribe payer but from overcharging or delivering substandard products or services. In this way, the ultimate purchasers, the citizens of a country, lose by getting less for what they pay. Ordinary citizens may suffer in other ways when taxes are raised or spending is cut to cover the loss when the government overpays for goods and services, or when the bribes lead to lax enforcement of regulations concerning tax collection, working conditions, or environmental protection. Third, the spending priorities of a country may be distorted when government officials choose large, complex projects from which bribes can be extracted instead of more urgently needed goods and services that do not offer the same opportunities for demanding bribes. Thus, developing countries often end up with an abundance of dams and power plants to the neglect of education and medical care. Fourth, the sheer amount of time that business people in corrupt countries must spend dealing with government officials and complying with needless regulation detracts from productive activity. Finally, the potential for demanding bribes leads government officials to create even more efficiency-impeding laws and regulations that confer ever more discretion on them. One expert on corruption writes, "Thus, instead of corruption being the grease for the squeaky wheels of a rigid administration, it becomes the fuel for excessive and discretionary regulations. This is one mechanism whereby corruption feeds on itself."[42]

In addition, bribery has many adverse noneconomic consequences. For one, it enriches elites in a country, which leads to greater inequality and also to loss of public confidence in government. Susan Rose Ackerman writes, "Systematic corruption undermines the legitimacy of governments, especially in democracies, where it can even lead to coups by undemocratic leaders. By contrast, nondemocratic governments can use corruption to maintain power by spreading benefits."[43] These factors may also result in greater political instability, which, in turn, discourages foreign direct investment. Furthermore, in a culture of bribery, the most unscrupulous prosper, and others must emulate them if they are to succeed. Such a corrupt culture is corrosive for the development of personal character and a healthy social order. Thus, the evidence is that bribery imposes a great cost, both economic and noneconomic, on developing countries. Although estimates are difficult to formulate across so many diverse countries, one calculation is that bribery constitutes an additional tax of 20 percent on investment.[44] Thus, each investment dollar could bring, on average, one-fifth more development if the country could eliminate the damaging effects of bribery.

What Should Be Done about Bribery?

If bribery is morally wrong as well as economically and socially undesirable, then corporations and governments should take reasonable steps to reduce the incidence of bribery around the world. Unfortunately, bribery is difficult to combat due to its secretive nature and deep penetration. It occurs, of necessity, out of the public eye, and it often involves networks of individuals and institutions that thwart efforts to prosecute wrongdoers and to bring about reform. For example, when the proceeds from bribery are widely shared by government officials, including bureaucrats, legislators, and judges, then everyone who might act constructively has an interest in maintaining a corrupt system. Moreover, bribery is a classic collective choice problem in that no single honest company or official can singlehandedly make any difference: Any company that refuses to offer bribe or any official who declines to accept one will have no effect as long as others are willing to engage in the practice. Any solution to the problem must involve action that affects everyone. Finally, any effective action must address the root causes of bribery, which are the conditions that create numerous opportunities for bribes in substantial amounts without significant risk.

STRATEGIES FOR COMBATING BRIBERY. It has already been observed that the opportunities for bribery are created in the area of overlap between business and government where public officials have discretionary authority to make decisions that affect economic activity. One strategy to combat bribery, then, is to alter the role of government in the economy. Limiting government involvement and increasing the prominence of free markets is one possibility. However, merely limiting the involvement of government may not be an improvement if corruption is replaced only by oligopoly, in which elites can still make exorbitant profits. Genuine progress can be made only by reforms that promote healthy competition and proper regulation. Such progress may occur with extensive government involvement in the economy as long as there are well-designed rules, known by all and impartially applied, that leave little room for discretion. The efficacy of such rules is increased by openness and accountability in the decision-making process. For example, the incidence of bribery might be reduced if fewer licenses were required for operating a business and the licensing process was made simpler and more routine. Similarly, the fewer government contracts that are let, the less opportunity there is for bribery, but the same result can be achieved if bidding on contracts is conducted openly and in accord with fair, consistently applied rules.

Since much bribery involves civil servants in government bureaucracies, a second strategy consists of civil service reform, in which pay is increased in order to reduce the temptation among low-paid officials to demand or accept bribes. In some countries, the pay of civil servants is extremely low on the assumption that they will supplement their meager wages with bribes, which becomes a self-fulfilling expectation. Reform might also include more selective recruitment and better training in order to build a more professional civil service. Higher pay for civil servants, accompanied by good pension, may reduce the incidence of bribery not only by removing the need for the income but also by making the jobs so attractive that the risk of losing them will deter bribe taking.

A third strategy for reducing the opportunities for bribery consists of more careful selection of government projects, eliminating those that are most vulnerable to bribery and closely monitoring the ones that go forward. This check can be imposed most effectively on developing countries by funding agencies, such as the World Bank and the International Monetary Fund, as well as the investment banks that provide loans. These agencies and banks, most of which have adopted formal antibribery policies and procedures, combat bribery by evaluating the integrity of individual projects and the ability of the countries in question to control bribery, as well as by providing expertise and other kinds of support for well-intentioned governments seeking to reduce bribery.[45] The motive for funding agencies and banks to consider bribery in their loan practices stems not only from an economic concern that their funds not be wasted through bribery but also from the recognition that the political conditions that foster bribery strongly impact economic development. In other words, they recognize that the economic function of lending cannot be separated from the politics of a country.

In addition to reducing the opportunities for bribery, the problem can be addressed by more vigorous enforcement of antibribery laws and the activity of international organizations. For example, the Hong Kong Independent Commission Against Corruption and the Corrupt Practices Investigation Bureau in Singapore are government-created units that have proven to be highly effective at uncovering and prosecuting instances of bribery. A private NGO, Transparency International, consists of more than 90 chapters in countries around the world which seek, according to its website, "to promote transparency in elections, in public administration, in procurement and in business. . . . [and] to use advocacy campaigns to lobby governments to implement anti-corruption reforms." Highly visible tools of Transparency International are the annual "Corruption Perception Index," which ranks countries on the perceived level of corruption, and the "Bribe Payers Index," which ranks countries according to their willingness to restrict bribery by domestic companies. In 2003, the United Nations General Assembly adopted the "Convention Against Corruption," which focuses on the prevention and criminalization of bribery and on international cooperation to combat it and recover plundered assets.

The most prominent examples of antibribery initiatives are the U.S. Foreign Corrupt Practices Act of 1977 (amended in 1988) and the "Convention on Combating Bribery of Foreign Public Officials in International Business Transactions," adopted by the countries of the Organization for Economic Cooperation and Development (OECD) in 1997. The OECD convention commits each member country to change its laws to accord roughly with the FCPA. Specifically, OECD members, which include the world's richest nations, have agreed to prohibit bribery of foreign officials, impose criminal penalties on those found guilty, and allow for the seizure of profits gained by bribery. Both initiatives concentrate on the "supply" side by changing the conduct of corporations that have been paying bribes. Many observers are optimistic that the FCPA and the OECD convention will significantly reduce the incidence of foreign bribery and produce a more level playing field for all multinational corporations.

THE FOREIGN CORRUPT PRACTICES ACT.   Since 1997, it has been against U.S. law for an individual or a company to bribe a foreign official for the purpose of obtaining or retaining business. The FCPA was enacted by Congress in part to protect American interests. The widespread use of slush funds to make payments during the 1970s raised fears that U.S. corporations were engaging in false financial reporting that compromised the integrity of securities markets. When the Securities and Exchange Commission encouraged the voluntary disclosure of foreign payments without fear of prosecution, more than 400 companies admitted to paying a total of $300 million that was not fully accounted for in their books. In addition, Congress was concerned that foreign payments by American corporations were undermining the governments of friendly countries around the world and interfering in the conduct of U.S. foreign policy.

The FCPA applies not only to American citizens and companies but also to certain foreign entities that conduct business in the United States. In addition to the prohibition of bribery, the act contains an accounting section that requires companies to maintain financial records that accurately and fairly represent transactions in reasonable detail, including the amount and the purpose of all payments, and to develop a system of internal accounting controls sufficient to ensure that these records are accurately and fairly stated. A foreign official is defined broadly to include not only government employees but also any person acting in an "official capacity," and the act also covers payments to political parties and candidates for office in foreign countries. The payment must be intended to induce a foreign official to violate a duty by misusing his or her official position in a way that confers some benefit to the bribing party. The law does not require that the payment be accepted or achieve its purpose; the mere offer or promise of a payment constitutes a violation of the act.

The FCPA also prohibits payments through intermediaries or third-parties while knowing or having reason to know that any portion will be used to bribe foreign officials. Much business in foreign countries is conducted through intermediaries, who may pay bribes without the knowledge of the American firm. When American firms enter into joint ventures with foreign companies, they may have a similar lack of control over the conduct of their business partners and the maintenance of their books. Deliberately avoiding knowledge of an agent's activities is not an adequate defense, and so companies should take precautions to "know their agents." Among the advised precautions are checking out the reputation of the agent and being sure that the agent has some genuine service to provide; paying the agent only an amount commensurate with the services provided and seeking an accounting of all expenses incurred; avoiding suspicious requests, such as depositing the money in a certain bank account; and obtaining a detailed agreement that includes a pledge not to violate the FCPA and the right to terminate the contract for any violation.

Certain kinds of payments are legally permitted and do not constitute bribes under the FCPA. These include "facilitating payments," which are made to expedite the performance of "routine governmental action." Also called "grease payments," these are small sums paid to lower-level officials to lubricate the rusty machinery that provides government services. Facilitating payments do not induce anyone to violate a duty. Still, they are generally prohibited by the same governments that create the need for them, although the laws on such matters are rarely enforced. Also excluded from the category of bribes by the FCPA are reasonable expenditures for legitimate expenses, such as entertaining a foreign official in the course of doing business. Finally, any payments that are permitted or required by the written laws of the country in question are legal under the FCPA. Although such payments might still be considered bribes, the drafters of the FCPA did not believe that individuals or corporations should be prosecuted in the United States for abiding by local laws elsewhere. The stipulation that the laws be written is designed to ensure that the payments are really legal and not merely customary. For violations of the FCPA, corporations may be fined up to $2 million and individuals may be fined up to $100,000 and imprisoned for up to five years (and the fine for an individual may not be paid by the corporation).

The justification for a legal prohibition on foreign bribery is rather straightforward. A double standard is employed if a country permits its companies to do abroad what they are forbidden to do at home. It has already been demonstrated that bribery is not only a moral wrong but also severely harms economic development. The main arguments to the contrary are that bribery is necessary for doing business in some countries and that a country that prohibits its own companies from bribing places them at an unfair competitive advantage. Some have argued that the FCPA is a form of "ethical imperialism" that imposes our values on other countries.

These contrary arguments are not very persuasive. First, if foreign bribery is wrong, then the fact that America's competitors around the globe practice it does not provide a justification. Second, American firms have been able to compete in many instances without bribing, in part by developing better products and services and marketing them aggressively. Anecdotal evidence suggests that bribery is involved in many contracts that U.S. firms fail to attain, but it is difficult to determine who would have obtained the award had there been a level playing field. No academic studies to date have documented substantial loss of business due to the FCPA.[46] Even if some loss of business has occurred, it must be weighed against the other benefits that led Congress to enact the FCPA. That is, is the United States as a nation better off for the passage of this act? Third, the FCPA is scarcely an instance of "ethical imperialism" because it applies only to the conduct of American firms. In addition, the immorality of bribery comes close to being a universal norm.

HUMAN RIGHTS ABUSES

As part of an aggressive effort to combat the unlicensed use of its popular software programs, Microsoft employs lawyers and cooperates with government agencies worldwide in systematic enforcement campaigns. In September 2010, the *New York Times* broke a story about how the police in Russia were using illegal, pirated software as a pretext for raiding advocacy groups and opposition newspapers and for carting off computers filled with critical documents.[47] In some cases, the targets of these raids had proper licenses for the software installed, and often charges of software piracy were never filed; but the disruption of activities and the cost of fighting the charges were enough to cripple their operations. Although software piracy is rampant in Russia, the *Times* article reported that the police "rarely if ever carry out raids against advocacy groups or news organizations that back the government." Microsoft lawyers were reported to work closely with the police, sometimes initiating investigations and defending the company as a victim of the criminal conduct, and some were accused of helping corrupt police to extort money from the targets of piracy investigations.[48] Although Microsoft executives denied that company lawyers initiated any investigations, they admitted that they had participated in them but only because their involvement was required by Russian law. The victims appealed to Microsoft for protection, and the Moscow Helsinki Group, an influential human rights watch organization, accused Microsoft of being complicit in "the persecution of civil society activists."[49]

Initially, Microsoft responded to these charges and the damaging publicity by stressing its right to protect the company's products from piracy and explaining how the company carefully selects, trains, and monitors its local lawyers and how it seeks to prevent individuals and organizations from falsely claiming to represent Microsoft.[50] Within a few days, Microsoft reversed course and announced new policies. A spokesperson declared, "We want to be clear that we unequivocally abhor any attempt to leverage intellectual property rights to stifle political advocacy or pursue improper personal gain. We are moving swiftly to seek to remove any incentive or ability to engage in such behavior."[51] Specifically, Microsoft announced that it had barred its lawyers from taking part in piracy investigations, was granting blanket software licenses to all advocacy groups and newspapers, and was providing legal aid to all victims of the piracy crackdown. These actions effectively undercut the legal basis for police action against groups opposed to the Russian government. However, Microsoft has yet to condemn the raids or criticize the Russian government for violations of human rights for fear of jeopardizing its ability to do business in the country.

The experience of Microsoft in Russia exemplifies the challenges faced by multinational corporations as they operate in countries with repressive governments that engage in massive violations of human rights. A few countries, one being Burma (also called Myanmar), are so repressive that many companies avoid them entirely, and the ones that operate there face international censure. No company can operate in such a country without giving substantial support to an utterly corrupt and brutal regime, and Burma earns Freedom House's "absolute worst rating for political rights and civil liberties."[52] In other countries, such as Russia, China, Nigeria, Indonesia, and Venezuela, it is possible for multinational corporations to conduct business ethically, albeit with some challenges.

For example, Chrysler, which operates a Jeep plant in a joint venture with the Chinese government, was pressured in 1994 by the government to dismiss an employee, Gao Feng, a devout Christian, who had been arrested for planning a worship service and candlelight vigil on the fifth anniversary of the Tiananmen Square massacre.[53] After firing him for being absent during his interrogation in jail, Chrysler relented in the face of international criticism and reinstated his employment, following which he was arrested again and sent to a reeducation camp. In 1995, Royal Dutch/Shell, which produced oil in the Ogoniland region of Nigeria, became embroiled in controversy when the company was called upon to intervene to prevent the execution of Ogoni activist Ken Saro-Wiwa, who had criticized Shell's environmental record and was convicted for murder in what was perceived as a kangaroo trial.

Multinational corporations must decide, first, whether to enter certain countries by making direct investments, selling products, or sourcing materials. Then, they must consider how to operate ethically and respond to situations once they do enter. The second kind of decision can generally be made in accord with the guidelines for multinationals discussed prior in this chapter. Accordingly, this section addresses the first question of country selection. Is it ethical to operate in a country with a repressive government that engages in systemic human rights abuses? Furthermore, if a company engages, can it separate itself from any human rights abuses committed by the government or should it be held morally and legally liable for these abuses?

Engagement versus Nonengagement

Companies that operate in Burma and other "ethically challenging environments"[54] commonly defend themselves by describing their strategy as "constructive engagement." The argument is that although human rights abuses do occur, the company, on the whole, is making a positive contribution that would not occur in its absence. Such a defense rests on utilitarian grounds of benefit or welfare, which may be strong, but it does not address the possible charge that a company may do some good but still be complicit in human rights abuses. The success of this strategy depends, first, on the receptiveness of the government in a country to change and, second, on the commitment and effectiveness of a company with regard to such change. Constructive engagement is a high-minded approach, filled with good intentions, but it is difficult to implement effectively. Progress is not easily documented, and the approach may serve as a convenient rationalization for "business as usual," especially when there is no realistic hope for change or the company is insincere or ineffectual in seeking it. However, some effort may be preferable to unrestricted engagement, in which no attempt is made to be constructive.

Guidelines for constructive engagement are difficult to formulate since so much depends on the local context. For example, the original Sullivan Principles, drafted in 1977 to guide companies choosing to do business in apartheid-era South Africa, were focused mainly on equal treatment and improved conditions for black and colored employees. Later, a different set of Global Sullivan Principles was developed to provide more general guidance under all conditions. John R. Schermerhorn suggests that companies doing business in a country such as Burma ought to adhere to the following basic principles.[55]

- Management control over all aspects of local operations, including labor practices, conditions of employment, and subcontracting.
- Management commitment to inviolable respect for human dignity, basic rights, and good citizenship in all aspects of local operations.

- Management control over local use of the corporate identity and brand names, including government-sponsored public relations and advertising.
- Management commitment to make control revenue set-asides to improve conditions of life for local employees and broader citizenry, including housing, public services, education, and healthcare.
- Management confidence in basic right of local citizens to personal safety, freedom of movement, political participation, and economic advancement.
- Management commitment to annual and objective external audits of all aspects of local operations and to the public release of audit results.

Nonengagement occurs when a company chooses not to enter a certain country. Such a decision may be based solely on sound business considerations. Among these considerations are threats to a company's brand image and intellectual property; exposure of employees to risks of health and safety or human rights violations; and subjection of the company to risks from corruption and social and political instability that would impede normal operations. Alternatively, a company may decide for explicitly moral reasons not to engage. These reasons may include an incompatibility of particular environments with a company's mission or values or a commitment to support certain social causes, including organized boycotts such as the boycott in the 1970s designed to end apartheid in South Africa. For example, Robert Haas, the CEO of Levi Strauss, made the decision in 1993 to discontinue relations with suppliers in China and to defer any direct investment because of "pervasive violations of basic human rights." A company document declares, "Levi-Strauss & Co. has a heritage of conducting business in a manner that reflects its values. As we expand our sourcing base to more diverse cultures and countries, we must take special care in selecting business partners and countries whose practices are not incompatible with our values."[56] However, five years later, in 1998, Levi Strauss decided to resume sourcing in China and to sell clothing there.

Liability for Abuses

Although multinational corporations may rightly claim that they do not commit human rights abuses in countries where they operate, they may still have knowledge of and provide some resources for actions by a government that violates people's rights, and they may also be the intended beneficiary of the government's repression. For example, Unocal, a U.S.-based oil company, committed to build a 256-mile pipeline to deliver natural gas from the Yadana field in Burma to a terminal in Thailand. During the construction, which occurred between 1993 and 1998, several human rights groups, including Greenpeace, Amnesty International, and Human Rights Watch, charged that the Burmese army was conscripting forced labor, relocating people without compensation, and brutally suppressing dissent. A consultant hired by Unocal in 1995 confirmed these charges. Also in the 1990s, Mobil Oil Company (now ExxonMobil) operated gas wells in the Aceh region of Indonesia, where the government was fighting local separatist rebels. It is alleged that Mobil provided buildings where villagers were tortured, raped, and executed; loaned heavy equipment such as excavators to dig mass graves; and paid the wages of soldiers who burned and pillaged homes in the surrounding area. In each of these cases, the companies did not themselves actively commit these crimes, but they had some knowledge of the events (how much is disputed), provided not insignificant support (perhaps unwittingly), and received substantial benefits (willingly or not).

If the allegations against Unocal and Mobil are true, then the companies are morally culpable of complicity in human rights abuses in accord with standard conditions for responsibility, which are the actions performed (what is done) and one's state of mind (knowledge and intent). Each company denies the allegations, but the guiding principles are clear. Less clear is the legal right of victims of human rights abuses to seek remedy in court. Should foreign nationals have the right to bring suit against U.S. companies in American courts for human rights violations? Some victims from Burma and Aceh have sought to do so by means of a law, the Alien Tort Claims Act (ATCA), which was enacted by Congress in 1789 for reasons that remain murky. The ACTA states, "The district courts shall have original jurisdiction of any civil action by an alien for a tort only, committed in violation of the law of nations or a treaty of the United States." The "law of nations" apparently refers to any wrongs that are generally prohibited in different legal systems, such as torture. Indeed, the law remained unused for 200 years before it was invoked to allow a suit against military officers from Paraguay, now living in the United States, by the family of a man they tortured to death.

Both the legal interpretation and the justification of the ATCA are in dispute. Many cases are now winding their way through the courts with conflicting and inconclusive rulings, and debate is raging over the wisdom of allowing such suits in U.S. courts.[57] Legal questions concern who has standing to sue and whether corporations, or only individuals, can be sued. Questions of justification tend to pit considerations of justice—whether victims of human rights abuses should not have some legal remedy in U.S. courts when American corporations are complicit—against practical concerns about how extensive liability might impact the ability of corporations to operate abroad.

Conclusion

Operating abroad, especially in less-developed countries, creates dilemmas that lead to charges of serious ethical failings. Multinational corporations generally recognize a social responsibility and attempt to fulfill their responsibilities everywhere they are located. The major causes of occasional failures to act responsibly are not inattention and lack of effort but the diversity of political and legal systems around the world and differences in economic development. Foreign operations give rise to challenges—and also create opportunities for misconduct—that simply do not exist for purely domestic enterprises.

The main quandary facing all MNCs is deciding which standards to follow. We have seen that neither of the two extreme positions is satisfactory. The familiar adage "When in Rome, do as the Romans do" and the opposite, "When in Rome or anywhere else, do as you would at home," are both inadequate guides. Instead, this chapter offers guidelines for developing special standards for the conduct of international business that can be applied to such matters as so-called sweatshops, foreign bribery, and human rights abuses. Ultimately, the solution to many of the ethical problems of international business lies in the development of international agreements and codes of ethics. As the guidelines for multinational corporations become more detailed and comprehensive, the need for special standards of international business may diminish, and business conduct may eventually be the same worldwide.

CASE 14.2 ●─ Explore the Concept on mythinkinglab.com

H. B. Fuller in Honduras

In 1985, journalists began writing about a new social problem in Honduras that created an acute dilemma for H. B. Fuller Company, based in St. Paul, Minnesota.[58] The news stories described the ravaging effects of glue sniffing among the street children of Tegucigalpa, the capital of Honduras, and other Central American cities. The drug of choice for these addicts was Resistol, a glue produced by a Honduran subsidiary of H. B. Fuller, and the victims of this debilitating habit were known, in Spanish, as *resistoleros*. The negative publicity was sullying the company's stellar reputation for corporate social responsibility, and company executives came under great pressure to address the problem quickly.

Poverty in Honduras had forced many families to send their children into the streets to beg or do odd jobs. The earnings of these children were critical to the support of many families, especially those headed by a single mother. Some children lived in the streets in order to avoid abusive homes; others were abandoned or orphaned. Many children, some as young as five or six, sought relief from their misery by sniffing glue containing volatile solvents which produces a temporary elation and sense of power. These chemicals are addictive and lead to irreversible damage to the brain and liver. The victims of solvent abuse generally stagger as they walk and exhibit tense, aggressive behavior.

Resistol is a brand name for a line of adhesives manufactured by a wholly owned subsidiary of H. B. Fuller and marketed throughout Latin America. The solvent-based adhesives favored by glue sniffers were widely used in shoemaking and shoe repair and were readily available on the street. H. B. Fuller had urged the press not to use the term "resistoleros" because other brands of adhesives were used as well and the problem was with the abuse of Resistol, not the product itself. Nevertheless, the name was commonly used in Honduras to describe the street children addicted to solvents. One of H. B. Fuller's most successful brands had thus become synonymous with a major social problem.

Criticism of H. B. Fuller for its involvement in this problem came not only from activists and public health officials in Honduras but also from customers and shareholders in the United States. One shareholder asked, "How can a company like H. B. Fuller claim to have a social conscience and continue to sell Resistol, which is 'literally burning out the brains' of children in Latin America?" The company's mission statement placed its commitment to customers first, followed by its responsibilities to employees and shareholders. And the statement affirms: "H. B. Fuller will conduct business legally and ethically . . . and be a responsible corporate citizen." When the company acquired its subsidiary in Honduras, the CEO at the time said,

> We were convinced that we had something to offer Latin America that the region did not have locally. In our own small way, we also wanted to be of help to that part of the world. We believed that by producing adhesives in Latin America and by employing only local people, we would create new jobs and help elevate the standard of living. We were convinced that the way to aid world peace was to help Latin America become more prosperous.

Company executives faced the dilemma of whether these expressions of H. B. Fuller's aspirations could be reconciled with the continued production of Resistol in Honduras.

Community activists in Honduras proposed the addition of oil of mustard to all solvent-based adhesives. This chemical, allyl isothiocyanate, produces a reaction that has been compared to getting an overdose of horseradish. Adding it to Resistol would effectively deter anyone attempting to inhale the fumes. However, research revealed that oil of mustard has many side effects, including severe irritation of the eyes, nose, throat, and lungs, and it can even be fatal if inhaled, swallowed, or absorbed through the skin. In addition, adhesives with oil of mustard have a shelf life of only six months. H. B. Fuller executives were convinced that the addition of oil of mustard was not an acceptable solution. However, in 1989, the Honduran legislature passed a law requiring oil of mustard, despite the lobbying efforts of H. B. Fuller.

Another alternative was a community relations effort to alert people about the dangers of glue sniffing and to address the underlying social causes. By working with community groups and the government, the company could spread the responsibility and expand its resources. On the other hand, the community groups in Honduras and elsewhere in the region were not well organized, and the government was unstable and unreliable. In 1982, the Gillette Company had faced a similar problem with its solvent-based typewriter correction fluid, Liquid Paper, which was being abused by youngsters in the United States. Gillette also rejected the possibility of adding oil of mustard, but the company's community relations effort was facilitated by the existing network of private and government-sponsored drug education programs. In Honduras, H. B. Fuller did not have the same base of community and government support. A community relations effort would be much more difficult in a less-developed country.

H. B. Fuller executives also considered withdrawing all solvent-based adhesives from the market and perhaps substituting water-based products, but these alternatives were not very attractive from a business point of view. Furthermore, they would have no impact on the critical social problem of glue sniffing by street children. The waste of young lives would continue unless conditions were changed. But what could a modest-sized company located in St. Paul, Minnesota, do to address a problem caused by deep cultural, social, political, and economic forces? A failure to act, however, would seriously damage H. B. Fuller's carefully built reputation for corporate social responsibility.

CASE 14.3   ✳ Explore the Concept on mythinkinglab.com

Bribery at Siemens

In the early morning hours of November 15, 2007, 200 German police arrested six employees of Siemens AG and seized documents from their homes and the company's headquarters in Munich.[59] These coordinated raids followed a multiyear investigation by several European countries into Siemens's international operations, which led eventually to charges that the company paid a total of $1.4 billion in bribes since 1999 in Asia, Africa, Europe, the Middle East, and Latin America. Prior to 1999, bribing foreign officials was not illegal under German law, and payments necessary for obtaining business could even be deducted as a legitimate expense. However, in that year, Germany joined the United States and other major industrial countries in outlawing the bribery of foreign officials, and the next year, the tax deductibility of bribes was removed from the German tax code. Although Siemens's management was aware of changes in the law on bribery, little attention had been given to ensuring compliance and especially to countering the acceptance of bribery in the company's culture. After these raids, though, the leadership of Siemens faced the challenges of understanding how such widespread, deliberate, and carefully organized illegal activity had been allowed to flourish, of responding to the unfolding investigation, and of dismantling the deeply entrenched culture of bribery in the company.

Based in Berlin, Munich, and Erlangen, Germany, Siemens AG was Europe's largest electronics and electrical engineering company by revenues, developing, manufacturing, and marketing a wide range of industrial, energy, and healthcare products. The company was founded in 1847 to enter the telegraph business. By 2007, the company was widely diversified in its products and employed approximately 425,000 people in 190 countries. In every market, but especially telecommunication and electric generation (where the bribes were concentrated), Siemens had intense competition, and its global presence meant that it operated in many countries with state-controlled economies, where public officials often demand corrupt payments. As the company rebuilt after the damage inflicted on Germany in World War II, it found its greatest opportunities in less-developed countries where corruption is often endemic.

The evidence gathered by investigators indicates that bribery was not an occasional occurrence at Siemens, driven only by the necessity of doing business in corrupt environments, but was a deliberately chosen mode of operation, which was widely acknowledged and condoned among certain employees and also encouraged or, at least, tolerated by their superiors. According to one investigator, "Their actions were not an anomaly. . . . They were standard operating procedures for corporate executives who viewed bribery as a business strategy."[60] One of the six executives arrested on November 15 was Reinhard Siekaczek, a former manager in the fixed-line telephone division. He testified in his trial that after German law was changed in 1999 to prohibit bribery, he was ordered by his superiors to develop a new system for the now-illegal payments to disguise their purpose. The system adopted involved sham payments for nonexistent consulting services, with the proceeds funneled to bank accounts for a network of shell companies that served solely as conduits for the funds. Between 2002 and 2006, 40 to 50 million dollars annually were diverted in this manner. Typically, bribes were not paid by Siemens employees but by "consultants" who had close contacts with local elites. During this period, an estimated 2,700 "consultants" were used for the payment of bribes.

Mr. Siekaczek was apparently selected for this critical role due to his reputation for personal honesty and loyalty, since a trustworthy person was required to ensure that the money was properly diverted, deposited, and distributed. He explained that he never benefited personally and said, "It was about keeping the business unit alive and not jeopardizing thousands of jobs overnight. . . . We thought we had to do it. Otherwise we'd ruin the company."[61] Among the bribes paid during this period in various divisions of the company were $5 million for mobile phone contracts in Bangladesh; $12.7 million for government contracts in Nigeria; $40 million to create a system of national identity cards in Argentina; $20 million for government officials in Israel to supply equipment for power plants; $16 million in Venezuela for urban rail lines; $14 million in China for medical equipment; and $1.7 million in Iraq to Saddam Hussein and his cronies as part of the controversial United Nations food-for-oil program. The largest bribes were paid in China, Russian, Argentina, Israel, and Venezuela. Some bribes were for amounts as high as 40 percent of the contract value, but most of them were around 5 to 6 percent.

The first bribery case involving Siemens to be prosecuted concerned payments between 1999 and 2002 to two managers of Enel, an Italian energy producer, in the sale of gas turbines. Prosecutors charged that two Siemens employees paid 6 million euros in bribes to secure contracts worth 450 million euros through banks in Liechtenstein and Switzerland. The two Siemens employees claimed that the demand for bribes came from the Enel managers during the bidding process and that the payments were legal at the time inasmuch as the law prohibited payments only to *government* officials and Enel was in the process of becoming a private company. Although the formerly state-owned company was being privatized at the time, 65 percent was still owned by the Italian government. (In 2002, the German law was amended to prohibit bribes to private as well as public officials.) Siemens forfeited the 38 million euros profit that it made on the sales, and the two Siemens managers were convicted and given suspended sentences. One of those convicted offered the defense, "The alternative would have been to turn down the project, which would have denied Siemens not only that business but also a foot in the door in the Italian market."[62]

Siemens also faced prosecution in the United States, where the bribery of foreign officials had been illegal since the passage of the Foreign Corrupt Practices Act in 1977. Siemens was bound by that law since it had operations and employees in the United States and its stock had been registered since 2001 on the New York Stock Exchange. The company paid $800 million to settle charges by American regulators. The fines could have been as much as $2.7 billion, but federal authorities were impressed with Siemens cooperation in investigating their own wrongdoing, aiding the government prosecution, and taking corrective action to create a corruption-free culture. In the end, Siemens paid $1.6 billion in fines and forfeited profits to authorities in Europe and the United States, and the company estimated that it spent $1 billion to investigate itself and take corrective action, so that the total cost of the bribery scandal for Siemens was $2.6 billion.

The task of responding to the bribery scandal at Siemens fell to its chief executive officer Klaus Kleinfeld, CEO since 2005, who claimed to have no knowledge of the illegal actions of the company's employees. One of Mr. Kleinfeld's first actions was to engage an American accounting firm, Debevoise & Plimpton, to conduct a thorough investigation of bribery activities and to hire a prominent consultant on corruption, who had advised many governments and was a cofounder of Transparency International, to develop a program for preventing bribes in the future. Mr. Kleinfeld also implemented a whistle-blowing amnesty program that encouraged employees to bring forth information about illegal payments. Although employees were ordered to cease all bribery activity immediately, this proved difficult since many authorized payments had been scheduled over long periods of time. The Debevoise & Plimpton report also faulted the company's auditor, KPMG Germany, for not bringing information about suspicious payments to board members. In addition to changing policies, it was essential to reform the culture of Siemens and, in particular, to expunge the thinking that bribes were "not really wrong" and were "necessary to do business" in some parts of the world. According to Mr. Kleinfeld, "If you, in your mind, get it wrong and think, 'I just have to beat the competition', you are fundamentally doing something wrong."[63] Mr. Kleinfeld vowed to make Siemens a model of corporate ethics within five years and said that his efforts might even be "a Harvard Business case on how you do it right."[64] A Harvard Business School case was indeed written. Regardless of whether Mr. Kleinfeld "did it right," the board decided on April 25, 2007, not to renew his contract. He subsequently became CEO of U.S.-based Alcoa.

CASE 14.4   ✳ Explore the Concept on mythinkinglab.com

Google in China

At a congressional hearing on February 15, 2006, a Google executive sat with representatives from Microsoft and Cisco as their companies were charged with violating human rights in China. One member of Congress declared, "It is astounding that Google, whose corporate philosophy is 'don't be evil', would enable evil by cooperating with China's censorship policies just to make a buck." He continued, "Many Chinese have suffered imprisonment and torture in the service of truth—and now Google is collaborating with their persecutors."[65] Another congressman complained, "Instead of using their power and creativity to bring openness and free speech to China, they have caved in to Beijing's outrageous but predictable demands, simply for the sake of profits. . . . They enthusiastically volunteered for the Chinese censorship brigade."[66] What had Google done to receive such criticism?

Google, which was founded in 1998, quickly became a leading provider of Web-based services on the strength of its popular search engine Google.com. With a mission "to organize the world's information and make it universally accessible and useful," the founders deliberately set about to build an unconventional company. In the Registration Statement filed when the company went public in 2004, the founders, Larry Page and Sergey Brin, said that their goal was "to develop services that significantly improve the lives of as many people as possible," and they explained that the slogan "Don't be evil" was intended to convey the belief that in the long term, Google employees and its shareholders will be better served "by a company that does good things for the world even if we forgo some short-term gains."[67]

In an effort to bring the benefits of its search engine to China, a land of 1.3 billion people with an estimated 110 million Internet users, Google created in 2002 a Chinese-language home page, similar to the home pages in other languages that appear when the location of a computer is recognized by the website. Because Google's servers were located outside China, the website was not subject to any Chinese legal restrictions. Google searches were completed just as they would be if the site were accessed in any other country. However, the Internet entered China through fiber optic cables that ran through nine licensed international Internet service providers. This control of the physical pathways of the Internet enabled the Chinese government to filter signal transmissions in and out of the country. When Chinese users requested searches on sensitive topics, such as the Tiananmen Square protests of 1989, Tibet, or the banned group Falun Gong, screens would go blank, error messages would appear, or else the connection would be diverted to government-approved websites free of any objectionable content. Because of the filtering—known as the "Great Firewall of China"—access to Google in China was slow and unreliable, but a great deal of information was still available.

On September 3, 2002, Google vanished entirely from computer screens across China. The Chinese government had blocked all access. Although service was restored two weeks later, the intensity of filtering appeared to have increased. Google executives eventually realized that the company could not fulfill its mission without a presence in China. Other American companies, including Yahoo! and Microsoft already had operations in the country, and Google was losing market share not only to these domestic competitors but also to Chinese start-ups. The local company Baidu increased its market share from less than 3 percent in 2003 to 46 percent in 2005, while Google's share was 30 percent and falling.[68] In late 2004, Google undertook an assessment of its strategy in the Chinese market by consulting with Chinese Internet experts and users, human rights activists, government officials, and business leaders. According to a Google executive,

> From these discussions, we reached the conclusion that perhaps we had been taking the wrong path. Our search results were being filtered; our service was being crippled; our users were flocking to local Chinese competitors; and, ultimately, Chinese Internet users had less access to information than they would have had.[69]

On January 27, 2006, Google launched Google.cn, a China-based website. In order to operate in China, the company had to obtain a license that committed it to observe Chinese laws and regulations, which required that a licensed Internet company censor its own content. Google explained its decision as a matter of balancing its commitment to its users and its own mission:

> The requirements of doing business in China include self-censorship—something that runs counter to Google's most basic values and commitments as a company. Despite that, we made a decision to launch a new product for China—Google.cn—that respects the content restrictions imposed by Chinese laws and regulations . . . . [O]ur decision was based on a judgment that Google.cn will make a meaningful—though imperfect–contribution to the overall expansion of access to information in China.[70]

Abiding by Chinese laws and regulations was not an easy matter, though. Censorship in China did not operate by clear and specific guidelines about what is and is not permitted. Instead, a climate of intimidation was created by vague rules that were enforced in an unpredictable but harsh manner. Prohibited content included material that "damages the honor or interests of the state" or "disturbs the public order or destroys public stability" or "infringes upon national customs and habits."[71] Moreover, censorship was enforced by numerous state agencies with overlapping authority, and the material considered objectionable changed frequently. The intended effect was to make Internet services use their own judgment about what content to allow. In order to know the permissible limits, Google developed its own list of forbidden words and topics by testing the Chinese filtering system and noting what content was blocked.

In developing Google.cn, the company followed three key principles. First, Google resolved to notify users when search results had been removed. In this way, the act of filtering was made transparent. Second, the private information about users was not collected so that the company could not be compelled to disclose it to the government. As a result, Google made the decision not to offer e-mail or blog sites in China, which had led to difficulties for other American companies. Yahoo!, for example, had been criticized for acceding to government demands that it disclose e-mail records, which enabled authorities to learn the identity of two dissidents, who were subsequently tried and sentenced to prison terms. Third, the Chinese version of Google.com continued to be available in addition to Google.cn, so that Google.cn would only expand the information available to Chinese users and not reduce it in any way.

Some critics complained that these measures were not enough. In particular, the notification to users that content had been blocked did not disclose the nature of the content. One dissident complained that the user could no longer tell what was being blocked: "It was one thing when you hit on links that did not work. You could see what was blocked. The new Google hides the hand of the censor."[72] On the other hand, many Chinese users were becoming more savvy about hiding their tracks by using proxy servers and anonymizer programs and getting around the Great Firewall of China to access foreign material. Information and software for using the Internet were spread by "hactivists" working outside China.[73] So Google's self-censorship would have less effect on the ability of users to benefit from the Internet.

Moreover, Google was not alone in enabling the censorship of the Internet in China. Cisco and Microsoft had provided the hardware and software that sat atop the fiber optic cables at the border that conducted the filtering. And Google is not the only Web information source faced with the question of whether to enter China. The operators of Wikipedia.com have been urged by Chinese users to create a version of the online encyclopedia that would be acceptable to Chinese authorities.[74] All of Wikopedia.com has been blocked in China. The activists argue that 99.9 percent of the encyclopedia would remain intact after self-censoring and that access to all of this information would be of great benefit to the Chinese people. However, Wikipedia, like Google, is founded on the principle of uncensored information.

Google's leaders believed that given the choice of staying out of China and going in under the conditions imposed by the Chinese government, they made the right decision, one in keeping with the company's own mission and principles. As one executive explained, "Don't be evil" is "an admonition that reminds us to consider the moral and ethical implications of every single business decision we make. We believe that our current approach to China is consistent with this mantra."[75]

Notes

1. Information for this case is taken largely from David Barboza and Louise Story, "Toymaking in China, Mattel's Way," *New York Times,* 26 July 2007; Louise Storey, "After Stumbling, Mattel Cracks Down in China," *New York Times,* 29 August 2007; Louise Story, "Mattel Official Delivers an Apology in China," *New York Times,* 22 September 2007; Jonathan Dee, "A Toy Maker's Conscience," *New York Times,* 23 December 2007; and "Testimony of Robert A. Eckert, Chairman and Chief Executive Officer, Mattel, Inc.," Subcommittee on Commerce, Trade, and Consumer Protection of the Committee on Energy and Commerce, Washington, DC, 19 September 2007.

2. Barboza and Story, "Toymaking in China, "Mattel's Way."

3. Mattel Media Statement, 14 August 2007.

4. Story, "Mattel Official Delivers an Apology in China."

5. Paul Beamish and Hari Bapuji, "Toy Recalls and China: Emotion vs. Evidence," *Management and Organization,* 4 (2008), 197–209.

6. Dee, "A Toy Maker's Conscience."

7. Ibid.

8. Story, "Mattel Official Delivers an Apology in China."

9. Mattel Media Statement, 21 September 2007.

10. Norman E. Bowie, "The Moral Obligations of Multinational Corporations," in *Problems of International Justice,* ed. Steven Luper-Foy (Boulder, CO: Westview Press, 1987), 97.

11. Ralph J. Ledogar, *Hungry for Profits: U.S. and Drug Multinationals in Latin American* (New York: IDOC/North America, 1975), 46–47.

12. Dan Kurtzman, *A Killing Wind: Inside Union Carbide and the Bhopal Catastrophe* (New York: McGraw-Hill, 1987); and Paul Shrivastava, *Bhopal: Anatomy of a Crisis* (Cambridge, MA: Ballinger, 1987).

13. The test is this: "The practice is permissible if and only if the members of the home country would, under conditions of economic development relevantly similar to those of the host country, regard the practice as permissible." Thomas Donaldson, *The Ethics of International Business* (New York: Oxford University Press, 1989).

14. See Paul Steidlmeier, "Gift Giving, Bribery and Corruption: Management of Business Relationships in China," *Journal of Business Ethics,* 12 (1993), 157–64.

15. Sheila M. Puffer and Daniel J. McCarthy, "Finding Common Ground in Russian and American Business Ethics," *California Management Review,* 37 (Winter 1995), 29–46. The points in this paragraph are drawn from this article.

16. Ernest Gundling, "Ethics and Working with the Japanese: The Entrepreneur and the 'Elite Course,'" *California Management Review,* 33 (Spring 1991), 27.

17. Donaldson, *The Ethics of International Business.*

18. Ibid., 62.

19. Ibid., 81.

20. Ibid., 124.

21. Richard T. De George, *Competing with Integrity in International Business* (New York: Oxford University Press, 1993), 45–56.

22. Manuel Velasquez, "International Business Ethics: The Aluminum Companies in Jamaica," *Business Ethics Quarterly,* 5 (1995), 878.

23. Messaoud Mehafdi, "The Ethics of International Transfer Pricing," *Journal of Business Ethics,* 28 (2000), 365–81.

24. Bowie, "The Moral Obligations of Multinational Corporations," 529.

25. Hans Küng, "A Global Ethics in an Age of Globalization," *Business Ethics Quarterly,* 7 (1997), 18.

26. Simon Webley, "The Interfaith Declaration: Constructing a Code of Ethics for International Business," *Business Ethics: A European Review,* 5 (1996), 52–57.

27. Duane Windsor, "Toward a Transnational Code of Business Conduct," in *Emerging Global Business Ethics,* ed. W. Michael Hoffman et al. (Westport, CT: Quorum Books, 1994), 173.

28. William C. Frederick, "The Moral Authority of Transnational Corporate Codes," *Journal of Business Ethics*, 10 (1991), 165–77.

29. John H. Cushman, Jr., "Nike to Step Forward on Plant Conditions," *San Diego Union-Tribune*, 13 May 1998, A1.

30. Richard J. Barnet and John Cavanagh, *Global Dreams: Imperial Corporations and the New World Order* (New York: Simon & Schuster, 1994), 326.

31. Adam Schwarz, "Running a Business," *Far Eastern Economic Review*, 20 June 1991, 16.

32. Barnet and Cavanagh, *Global Dreams*, 326.

33. Jagdish Bhagwati and Robert E. Hudec, eds., *Fair Trade and Harmonization*, vol. 1 (Cambridge, MA: MIT Press, 1996), 2.

34. World Bank, *Workers in an Integrating World Economy* (1995), 75.

35. Leslie Kaufman and David Gonzalez, "Labor Standards Clash with Global Reality," *New York Times*, 24 April 2001, A1.

36. "The Invisible Children," *New York Times*, 20 February 2000, sec. 4, p. 12.

37. U.S.C. §78dd-1 (a)(1).

38. Michael Phillips, "Bribery," *Ethics*, 94 (1984), 621–36; Thomas L. Carson, "Bribery, Extortion, and the 'Foreign Corrupt Practices Act'," *Philosophy and Public Affairs*, 14 (1985) 66–90; John Danley, "Toward a Theory of Bribery," *Business and Professional Ethics Journal*, 2 (1983), 19–39; and Kendall D'Andrade, Jr., "Bribery," *Journal of Business Ethics*, 4 (1985), 239–48.

39. Most notably, Nathaniel H. Leff, "Economic Development Through Bureaucratic Corruption," *American Behavioral Scientist*, 8 (1964), 8–14.

40. Samuel P. Huntington, *Political Order in Changing Societies* (New Haven, CT: Yale University Press, 1968), 386.

41. For discussions of the effect of bribery on development, see Susan Rose Ackerman, *Corruption: A Study in Political Economy* (New York: Academic Press, 1978); Andrei Schleifer and Robert Vishny, "Corruption," *Quarterly Journal of Economics*, 109 (1993), 599–617; and Paolo Mauro, "Corruption and Growth," *Quarterly Journal of Economics*, 110 (1995), 681–712.

42. Daniel Kaufman, "Corruption: The Facts," *Foreign Policy*, Summer 1997, 116–17.

43. Susan Rose Ackerman, "The Political Economy of Corruption—Causes and Consequences," The World Bank, Public Policy for the Private Sector, Note No. 74, April 1996.

44. Kaufman, "Corruption: The Facts," 120.

45. See, for example, Susan Rose Ackerman, "The Role of the World Bank in Controlling Corruption," *Law and Policy in International Business*, 29 (1997), 93–114.

46. See Kate Gillispie, "Middle East Response to the U.S. Foreign Corrupt Policies Act," *California Management Review*, 29 (1987), 9–30; and Paul J. Beck, Michael W. Maher, and Adrian E. Tschoegl, "The Impact of the Foreign Corrupt Policies Act on U.S. Exports," *Managerial and Decision Economics*, 12 (1991), 295–303.

47. Clifford J. Levy, "Russia Uses Microsoft to Suppress Dissent," *New York Times*, 11 September 2010.

48. Clifford J. Levy, "Microsoft Under Fire Over Lawyers' Actions," *New York Times*, 11 September 2010.

49. Levy, "Russia Uses Microsoft to Suppress Dissent."

50. "Statement by Microsoft," *New York Times*, 11 September 2010.

51. Clifford J. Levy, "Microsoft Changes Policy Over Russian Crackdown," *New York Times*, 13 September 2010.

52. http://www.freedomhouse.org/template.cfm?page=70&release=705

53. Michael H. Santoro, *Profits and Principles: Global Capitalism and Human Rights in China* (Ithaca, NY: Cornell University Press, 2000), 103.

54. John R. Schermerhorn, Jr., "Terms of Global Business Engagement in Ethically Challenging Environments: Applications to Burma," *Business Ethics Quarterly*, 9 (1999), 485–505. Much of the present discussion of engagement is taken from this article.

55. Ibid., 497.

56. Levi-Strauss & Co., Business Partner Terms of Engagement and Guidelines for Country Selection.

57. See, for example, Courtney Shaw, "Uncertain Justice: Liability of Multinationals under the Alien Tort Claims Act," *Stanford Law Review*, 54 (2002), 1359–86; Kerrie M. Taylor, "Thicker than Blood: Holding Exxon Mobil Liable for Human Rights Abuses Committed Abroad," *Syracuse Journal of International Law and Commerce*, 31 (2004), 273–97; and Gary Clyde Hufbauer and Nicholas K. Mitrokostas, *Awakening the Monster: The Alien Tort Statute of 1789* (Washington, DC: Institute for International Economics, 2003).

58. This case was adapted from "H. B. Fuller in Honduras: Street Children and Substance Abuse," prepared by Norman E. Bowie and Stefanie Ann Lenway.

59. Information on this case is taken from Mark Landler and Carter Dougherty, "Scandal at Siemens Tarnishes Promising Results," *New York Times*, 28 February 2007; Carter Dougherty, "Ex-Siemens Executives on Trial for Bribery," *New York Times*, 14 March 2007; G. Thomas Sims, "2 Former Siemens Officials Convicted for Bribery," *New York Times*, 15 May 2007; Carter Dougherty, "Siemens's Prosperity Doesn't Obscure Bribery Scandal," *New York Times*, 22 January 2008; Carter Dougherty, "Ex-Manager Tells of Bribery at Siemens," *New York Times*, 27 May 2008; Carter Dougherty, "The Sheriff at Siemens, at Work under Justice Dept.'s Watchful Eye," *New York Times*, 8 October 2008; Eric Lichtblau and Carter Dougherty, "Siemens to Pay $1.34 Billion Fine," *New York Times*, 16 December 2008; Siri Schubert and T. Christian Miller, "At Siemens, Bribery Was Just a Line Item," *New York Times*, 21 December 2008; Chris V. Nicholson, "Siemens to Collect Damages from Former Chiefs in Bribery Scandal," *New York Times*, 3 December 2009.

60. Lichtblau and Dougherty, "Siemens to Pay $1.34 Billion Fine."

61. Schubert and Miller, "At Siemens, Bribery Was Just a Line Item."

62. Dougherty, "Ex-Siemens Executives on Trial for Bribery."

63. Landler and Dougherty, "Scandal at Siemens Tarnishes Promising Results."

64. Ibid.

65. "News from Congressman Chris Smith," U.S, House of Representatives, press release, 26 January 2006.

66. Elliot Schrage, Testimony of Google Inc. before the Subcommittee on Asia and the Pacific, and the Subcommittee on Africa, Global Human Rights, and International Operations, Committee on International Relations, United States House of Representatives, 15 February 2006 [hereinafter "Schrage Testimony"].

67. "Letter from the Founders: 'An Owner's Manual' for Google Shareholders," company document.

68. "China Online Search Market Survey Report," China Network Information Center, August 2005.

69. "Schrage Testimony."

70. Ibid.

71. Clive Thompson, "Google's China Problem (and China's Google Problem)," *New York Times Magazine*, 23 April 2006, 64.

72. Joseph Kahn, "So Long, Dalai Lama: Google Adapts to China," *New York Times*, 12 February 2006, sec. 5, p. 5.

73. Clay Chandler, Dan Zhang, Eugenia Levinson, and Joan L. Levinstein, "Inside the Great Firewall of China," *Fortune* 6 March 2006, 148–58.

74. Thompson, "Google's China Problem (and China's Google Problem)."

75. "Schrage Testimony."

INDEX